GENDER AND HEALTH

GENDER AND HEALTH

An International Perspective

Edited by

Carolyn F. Sargent
Caroline B. Brettell

PRENTICE HALL, *Upper Saddle River, New Jersey 07458*

Library of Congress Cataloging-in-Publication Data

Gender and health : an international perspective / edited by Carolyn
 F. Sargent and Caroline B. Brettell.
    p. cm.
   Includes bibliographical references.
   ISBN 0–13–079427–9
    1. Women—Health and hygiene—Sociological aspects.   2. Sexism in
medicine.   3. Women's health services—Social aspects.   4. Social
medicine.   5. Medical anthropology.   I. Sargent, Carolyn Fishel,
1947–   . II. Brettell, Caroline, 1950–
RA564.85.G46   1996
610'.82—dc20   95-37457
                                                           CIP

Acquisitions editor: Sharon Chambliss
Editorial/production supervision: Joseph Barron/P. M. Gordon Associates
Interior design: Peggy Gordon
Copy editor: Pamela T. Price
Cover design: Bruce Kenselaar
Buyer: Mary Ann Gloriande

© 1996 by Prentice-Hall, Inc.
Simon & Schuster/A Viacom Company
Upper Saddle River, New Jersey 07458

Printed in the United States of America
10 9 8 7 6 5 4 3 2 1

ISBN 0-13-079427-9

Prentice-Hall International (UK) Limited, *London*
Prentice-Hall of Australia Pty. Limited, *Sydney*
Prentice-Hall Canada Inc., *Toronto*
Prentice-Hall Hispanoamericana, S.A., *Mexico*
Prentice-Hall of India Private Limited, *New Delhi*
Prentice-Hall of Japan, Inc., *Tokyo*
Simon & Schuster Asia Pte. Ltd., *Singapore*
Editora Prentice-Hall do Brasil, Ltda., *Rio de Janeiro*

Contents

About the Contributors

Caroline Brettell is Professor and Chair of Anthropology at Southern Methodist University. She is the author of *We Have Already Cried Many Tears: The Stories of Three Portuguese Migrant Women* and *Men Who Migrate, Women Who Wait: Population and History in a Portuguese Parish.* She is co-editor of *International Migration: The Female Experience* and *Gender in Cross-Cultural Perspective,* and the editor of *When They Read What We Write: The Politics of Ethnography.*

Carole H. Browner is a professor in the Department of Psychiatry and Biobehavioral Sciences and the Department of Anthropology at the University of California at Los Angeles. She is a medical anthropologist with nearly twenty years of research experience in Colombia, Mexico, and the United States on the politics of reproduction. Her current work focuses on the considerations Mexican-origin couples residing in the United States take into account when they decide whether or not to agree to prenatal diagnostic testing, and specifically how power differences between women and men influence women's decisions about prenatal diagnosis.

Naomi R. Cahn is an associate professor at the George Washington University National Law Center, specializing in family law and feminist jurisprudence. She is the author of numerous articles on domestic violence, legal ethics, and law and narrative.

Maria G. Cattell is a research associate at Bryn Mawr College and the Field Museum. She has been doing ethnographic research among the Abaluyia of Kenya since 1982. She has also done field work with the elderly in Philadelphia and among the Zulus in South Africa, the latter while a research fellow at the University of Natal. In addition to articles and book chapters, she is co-author of *Old Age in Global Perspective: Cross-Cultural and Cross-National Views.*

Thomas J. Csordas is Associate Professor of Anthropology at Case Western Reserve University. He is the author of *The Sacred Self: A Cultural Phenomenology of Charismatic Healing* and the editor of *Embodiment and Experience: The Existential Ground of Culture and Self.* His research interests include embodiment, healing, and cultural phenomenology. He has conducted ethnographic field work among Navajo Indians and Charismatic Catholics.

Dona Davis is a professor in the Department of Social Behavior at the University of South Dakota. She is the author of *Blood and Nerves: An Ethnographic Focus on Menopause,* and co-editor of *Gender, Health and Illness: The Case of Nerves* and *To Work and to Weep: Women in Fishing Economies*. Her areas of research interest are medical anthropology, psychological anthropology, anthropology and aging, gender studies, Canadian studies, and Scandinavian culture and society.

Robbie Davis-Floyd received her Ph.D. from University of Texas at Austin, where she is currently a research fellow in the Department of Anthropology. She is a cultural anthropologist specializing in the anthropology of gender and reproduction and in futures research. She lectures widely on ritual, technology, and childbirth in the United States and is the author of *Birth as an American Rite of Passage* and *The Technocratic Body and the Organic Body*. She revised and updated Brigitte Jordan's classic *Birth in Four Cultures* and co-edited *Childbirth and Authoritative Knowledge*.

Maryland Grier, MSW/MPH candidate, is Associate Director of the Institute for Community Research in Hartford, Connecticut. She assists in the coordination of several AIDS prevention programs for substance abusers, including coordinating data collection and staff development. Her research interests include women and AIDS, substance abuse, and related health issues in the inner city. She is currently conducting a study of teenage girls who are gang members. She is the author of several social science and AIDS publications.

Jean A. Hamilton, M.D. is Betty A. Cohen Professor of Women's Health and Director of the Institute for Women's Health at the Medical College of Pennsylvania and Hahnemann University in Philadelphia. She is currently on leave from Duke University, where she is a professor of health and social psychology, women's studies, and psychiatry. She has served as the head of the Biology of Depression Research Unit at the National Institute of Mental Health and co-founded the Institute for Research on Women's Health (IRWH), a nonprofit organization in Washington, DC.

Janis H. Jenkins is Associate Professor of Anthropology and Psychiatry and Director of the Women's Studies Program at Case Western Reserve University. She is an anthropologist who has conducted NIMH-sponsored studies of culture, gender, and mental health among Latino and Latin American populations and published articles and book chapters on related issues.

Patricia A. Kaufert earned a Ph.D. in sociology from the University of Birmingham in 1976 and is currently a professor in the Department of Community Health Sciences at the University of Manitoba, Canada. A former National Health Research Scholar, she has published extensively on the topics of women's reproductive health, health policy relating to women's health, childbirth, and menopause. She is currently doing research on screening for breast cancer.

Joanne Leslie, a public health nutritionist, is an adjunct assistant professor in the Community Health Sciences Department at the School of Public Health of the University of

California, Los Angeles, and Co-Director of the Pacific Institute of Women's Health. She worked for many years in Washington, DC, first at the World Bank, and then at the International Center for Research on Women, where she directed a major small grants research program on maternal nutrition and health care. She is the co-editor of *Women, Work and Child Welfare in the Third World,* and the author of numerous publications on the relationship between nutrition and education, and on the health and nutrition of women and children in developing countries.

Carol MacCormack is Professor of Anthropology at Bryn Mawr College and previously taught at the London School of Hygiene and Tropical Medicine (University of London) and at Cambridge University. She has done anthropological field work intermittently in West Africa since the 1960s and has also worked in East Africa, Asia, and the Caribbean. Her publications cover a wide range of anthropological and public health topics. She edited *Ethnography of Fertility and Birth* and co-edited *Nature, Culture and Gender.*

Patricia A. Marshall is Associate Director of the Medical Humanities Program and Associate Professor in the Department of Medicine at Loyola University Stritch School of Medicine in Maywood, Illinois. As a member of the Clinical Ethics Consultation Service at Loyola Medical Center, she works closely with health care staff, patients, and families in resolving moral dilemmas that arise in patient care. Her publications address a range of topics including cultural diversity and bioethics, research ethics in medical anthropology, problems surrounding fear of AIDS in health care settings, and ethical decision making in organ procurement and transplantation.

Emily Martin is Professor of Anthropology at Princeton University. Her work on ideology and power in Chinese society was published in *The Cult of the Dead in a Chinese Village* and *Chinese Ritual and Politics.* Beginning with *The Woman in the Body: A Cultural Analysis of Reproduction,* she has been working on the anthropology of science and reproduction in the United States. Her latest research is described in *Flexible Bodies: Tracking Immunity in America from the Days of Polio to the Age of AIDS.*

Helena Michie is a professor of English and Acting Director of the Program for the Study of Women and Gender at Rice University. She is the author of two books, *The Flesh Made Word: Female Figures, Women's Bodies* and *Sorophobia: Differences among Women in Literature and Culture.* She and Naomi Cahn are completing a book on the policing of the reproductive body in contemporary culture.

Carolyn F. Sargent is Professor of Anthropology and Director of Women's Studies at Southern Methodist University. She has a doctorate from Michigan State University and a master's degree in social anthropology from the University of Manchester, England. Her interests include reproductive health, child survival, and medical ethics. She has done field work in Africa and the Caribbean. She is the author of *The Cultural Context of Therapeutic Choice, Maternity, Medicine and Power* and co-editor of *Medical Anthropology: Contemporary Theory and Method* and *Gender in Cross-Cultural Perspective.*

Jean Schensul is the Executive Director of the Institute for Community Research in Hartford, Connecticut. She is a medical and educational anthropologist with expertise in basic and applied research in health-related issues of Latino, African-American, and low-income communities, with a special emphasis on the management of chronic health problems and the development and testing of culturally appropriate services in AIDS, substance abuse, and maternal and child care. In addition to work among low-income communities in the United States, Dr. Schensul has conducted field work in Mexico, Peru, Sri Lanka, and Mauritius.

Susan Sherwin is Professor of Philosophy and Women's Studies at Dalhousie University in Halifax, Nova Scotia. Her teaching and research activities focus on questions in feminist health care ethics. She is the author of *No Longer Patient: Feminist Ethics and Health Care* and a co-editor of two textbooks in health care ethics. She is currently involved in a multidisciplinary research project exploring the role and interpretation of the autonomy ideal in health care for patients subject to systemic oppression.

Merrill Singer is Director of Research at the Hispanic Health Council in Hartford and Assistant Clinical Professor at the University of Connecticut Medical School. His major interests are substance abuse and AIDS issues among inner city populations (especially Puerto Ricans), applied anthropology, and critical medical anthropology. He is a member of the American Anthropological Association Commission on AIDS and the Governing Council of the National Association for the Practice of Anthropology. He also directs several AIDS prevention and AIDS research programs at the Hispanic Health Council. His publications include *Critical Medical Anthropology, African American Religion in the Twentieth Century,* and *Rethinking AIDS Prevention: Cultural Approaches.*

Margaret R. Weeks is Associate Director of the Institute for Community Research in Hartford, Connecticut. She is Co-Principal Investigator of Project COPE, a National Institute on Drug Abuse–funded study of AIDS risk, drug use patterns, and culturally targeted prevention among injection drug users and non-injection users. In addition, she co-directs the Hartford Needle Exchange Evaluation Project and Project CONNECT, an AIDS outreach prevention program aimed at individuals involved in high risk behavior. Her research interests include gender relations as they affect the health, social status, and power of women in the United States and China.

Linda M. Whiteford is Professor of Anthropology and Director of Graduate Programs at the University of South Florida in Tampa. A medical anthropologist, she has a doctorate in anthropology from the University of Wisconsin and a master's degree in public health from the University of Texas. In addition to her academic responsibilities, she does consulting in international health, concentrating on maternal-child health, and women and the environment in Latin America and the Caribbean. She is the co-editor of *New Approaches to Human Reproduction* and the author of numerous book chapters and journal articles on gender, health, and political economy.

GENDER AND HEALTH

Introduction: Gender, Medicine, and Health

◧ *Carolyn Sargent*
Caroline Brettell

A growing anthropological literature addresses the articulation of gender roles and ideology with health status, the organization of health care, and health policy. This book presents an interdisciplinary focus on these issues viewed in cross-cultural perspective. We envision that the book will be relevant to advanced undergraduates, graduate students in the fields of women's studies, anthropology, and the health sciences, and to clinicians and others interested in public health policy.

Most of the contributors to the book are anthropologists engaged in cross-cultural research. Others include a literary theorist, a physician, and an ethicist, all of whom are primarily concerned with medical discourse, medical research, and the delivery of health care within North America. The premise of all these authors is that women and men seeking medical care should be conceptualized as gendered persons functioning in particular socioeconomic contexts. In addition, all the authors share the assumption that analysis of the production of health, as well as the provision of health care, must consider gender, ethnicity, and class as relevant factors (Lewin and Olesen 1985; Ginsburg and Rapp 1991). Those chapters drawing on cross-cultural research also shed light on multicultural issues pertaining to gender and health in the United States.

Following emergent lines of inquiry in medical anthropology, the chapters trace the linkages between gender roles, ideology, and 1) the language of science and medicine; 2) the cultural construction and medicalization of the life cycle; 3) the impact of new reproductive technologies on concepts of childbearing and parenting; 4) ethical dilemmas arising in the provision of medical care; 5) the social production of health; and 6) health policy.

THE LANGUAGE OF SCIENCE AND MEDICINE

Within anthropological thought, it is commonly accepted that language constructs and shapes our perceptions of reality. The language we speak influences the way that we react to the world and behave in it. It mediates our values and carries our ideological concerns. It is with this realization that a number of scholars engaged in a feminist reexamination of science have pointed to the gendered rhetoric and masculine metaphors that are characteristic of the language of science (Haraway 1981; Jacobus, Keller, and Shuttleworth 1990; Keller 1985; Merchant 1980). "Scientific enterprise, since at least the 16th century, has repeatedly been described and discussed in the language of sexuality and gender; science and medicine have been associated with sexual metaphors clearly designating nature as a woman to be unveiled, unclothed, and penetrated by masculine science" (Fee 1991:44–45). In these scientific texts, women, as body and emotion, are not only equated with nature, they are also defined as inferior to male as culture, mind, and reason. Hence, women's bodies are justifiably subject to masculine or scientific control (Berman 1989; Jacobus et. al 1990; Jordanova 1980; Russett 1989; Tuana 1989).

The major contribution of this feminist rethinking of the scientific enterprise in general, and of medical research in particular, has been to increase our awareness of the extent to which seemingly value-free descriptions of physiological processes are layered with cultural meaning. As Ruth Bleier has so aptly argued, scientists "do not recognize or acknowledge the degree to which their scientific writing itself participates in producing the reality they wish to present nor would scientists acknowledge the multiplicity of meanings of their texts" (1991:160). In Bleier's view, literary criticism has been brought to bear on scientific writing precisely to debunk the "myth of neutrality" of the scientific text.

It is within this perspective that both Emily Martin and Helena Michie frame their contributions to the analysis of the epistemology and language of biomedicine as it pertains to issues of gender. In her book *The Woman in the Body: A Cultural Analysis of Reproduction* (1987), Martin suggests that images of women's bodies in medical textbooks employ metaphors drawn from the language of capitalism and emphasize production, control, and hierarchy. Female reproductive processes are discussed in terms of efficiency and organizational function; menopause becomes a deficiency disorder rather than a life cycle phase (Kaufert and Lock 1992).

In her essay in this volume Martin focuses on language that represents menstruation as failed production. This negative and bemoanful rhetoric has no parallel in the descriptions of male spermatogenesis, a process that is described, Martin suggests, with intense enthusiasm. Martin illustrates her argument about the gendered discourse of conception with a detailed discussion of the textbook imagery of the egg and the sperm, the former a sleeping beauty patiently awaiting the arrival of her charming prince/hero who must endure a perilous journey to achieve his mission. The power of rhetoric is apparent in the fact that, even when new research has demonstrated a more aggressive role for the egg and a more mutually interactive process of conception, scientific writing adheres to the notion of the sperm as the active penetrator, albeit performing these actions more weakly than originally thought.

The new research on conception continues to employ the kind of masculine military metaphors—"kamikaze-sperm" or "vanguard" sperm that "seek and destroy"—that Berman (1989:227) has identified in other arenas of medical discourse—the "battle" or "war" against cancer or AIDS; the "magic bullet," for drugs; and the "mobilization of the troops" referring to white blood cell activity. At the close of her essay, Martin offers a more egalitarian set of metaphors drawing on cybernetic models, but cautions that these, too, may be influenced by their own set of cultural biases. In short, Martin's essay forces us to consider the powerful links between the metaphors we use to describe the body "scientifically" and the gender dynamics of our society. If such links exist they should be made explicit in medical education.

In the area of reproduction, masculinized metaphors of domination and success are not restricted to representations of conception. They are equally prevalent in the medical discourse of childbirth. Treichler (1990) draws on a passage from Margaret Atwood's *Surfacing* to engage this issue. Using a language that deliberately evokes the power and control with which natural processes are co-opted by the culture of science, Atwood describes technicians, mechanics, butchers, and clumsy and sniggering students who practice on your body, and take the baby out "with a fork like a pickle out of a pickle jar." "Most medical discourse," Treichler comments, "focuses on the act of the fetus alone, and further represents it as an act in which the physician's presence is crucial. Indeed, in some obstetrics and gynecology textbooks the woman is erased altogether" (1990:122). The medical view of childbirth is of a "potentially diseased condition that routinely requires arts of medicine to overcome the processes of nature" (Treichler 1990:119).

In her contribution to this volume, Michie also explores the way in which "natural" childbirth has been appropriated by institutional medicine. However, her provocative perspective asks us to question whether the movement to regain control of childbirth should operate within the rhetorical idiom of "the natural." Focusing on the Cesarean as a mechanism by which birth is separated from the female body, Michie, like Martin, notes the ways in which language denies woman agency in reproduction. Language such as this implies that the cesarean mother, in some sense, is not a mother at all. Vaginal birth equals success; cesarean birth equals failure. The natural way and the cultural way are opposed and, in constructing this opposition, we set limits on what it means to be female.

Michie is drawing attention to women's own use of language and how, through it, they "buy in" to a particular conception of the world. In an article focusing on nineteenth-century medical discourse on mental illness in the United States, Theriot (1993) argues that women, as physicians and as patients, were "active participants in the process of medicalizing woman" (1993:2). Women patients' illness narratives indicate that in many cases they "came to physicians asking to be committed or to be given medication for behavior the patients themselves described as insane or nervous, including lack of interest in husband and family, violent feelings toward their children, and continual sadness or suicidal urges in spite of being well taken care of by husband or family" (Theriot 1993:17). It was not at all unusual for mothers to bring in daughters who were not conforming to behavioral norms. Whether as patient or family member, women commonly linked their symptoms of mental illness to physical problems with their reproductive organs.

The twentieth century counterpart to Theriot's analysis is to be found in the language with which patients speak of their health and ill-health and the differences that can be noted according to gender, class, ethnicity, and cultural context. For example, in a study of white middle-class, middle-aged men and women in the United States, Saltonstall (1993) demonstrates that men speak of themselves as having power over their bodies, while women generally do not use the language of ownership in talking about their bodies. Rather, they view their bodies as having a momentum of their own (1993:9). Concepts of self, which are shaped by gender ideology and embedded in the language people use to represent their state of well-being or ill-health, differ between men and women and must be considered in the process of treatment. Similarly, the decisions that men and women make "about what actions to take to be healthy [are] colored by ideas about appropriate masculine and feminine behavior" (1993:12).

Rapp's (1988) study of amniocentesis patients demonstrates class and ethnic differences that are pertinent to the discourse of genetic counseling. While middle-class and scientifically educated pregnant women respond to a question about why they are talking to the genetic counselor with a quick "we're planning to have amniocentesis," an Hispanic patient might claim it is because of "the fault of my age." Medical language, Rapp argues, must be "adjusted to the language and assumptions of the pregnant patient" (1988:146), something that is easier said than done when the communication involves translation. For example, there is no word in Haitian Creole for mongolism or Down's Syndrome.

Rapp concludes that "the language of biomedicine limits communication by locking counselors into a discourse in which technical language dominates, despite a sincere desire on their part to reach out to patients. Counselors are caught between the need to sound authoritative and the desire to glide on the patient's wavelength" (Rapp 1988:151).

The research on the reporting and experience of illness or disease by Rapp, Saltonstall, and others (see, for example, Celentano, Linet, and Stewart 1990; Macintyre 1993) illustrates that the perception of one's own body is culturally constituted. This perception is to some extent shaped by language, particularly by the fact of whether or not there is a vocabulary with which to talk about symptoms and disease.

This is perhaps most apparent in the literature dealing with the Premenstrual Syndrome. By talking about it, many women have been able to codify a set of symptoms. And yet, Zita (1989) has noted that the observation language used to describe PMS has the same negative effect as that used to describe menstruation and menopause. Very quickly the subjective meanings voiced by women are replaced by a language of objectivity. "All too quickly women's cyclicity is turned into adversity and reconstrued within the labeling process of 'symptom,' 'syndrome' and 'disease.' This linguistic tour de force is preconditioned by hidden research assumptions which presume the negativity of premenstrual changes, leave unclear the baseline against which deviation is measured, and expand the list of symptoms so that the syndrome seems to become a fact about women or women's nature" (Zita 1989:197). Clearly, much of the research on the epistemology and language of biomedicine is directed to drawing our attention to the bias of nature inherent in the understanding of women's bodies. To medicalize is to "biologize."

Similarly, Warshaw (1993) argues that subjective information is devalued in medical discourse, while objective information is considered to be that observed by the clinician. She shows that in domestic abuse cases, physicians focus on physical trauma, subordinating the meaning of the woman's symptoms. The ways in which medicine is taught and practiced validate and institutionalize socially sanctioned hierarchies of domination and control that constrain the possibility of effective communication regarding domestic abuse (1993:75). Her research suggests that the language of medicine structures interactions so that battered women are unable to voice their concerns. One emergency room chart illustrates how a woman's experience is translated by medical staff: the nurse's note remarks "Hit by a fist to Rt eye . . ." while the physician writes "blunt trauma face." The trauma, rather than the woman, becomes the focus of the medical record, thus obscuring the cause and meaning of the woman's symptoms (Warshaw 1993:75). Thus gender-based trauma, a serious public health problem facing women, and one that has only recently been acknowledged by the medical community, is biologized and reduced to isolated body symptoms manageable within the context of medicine.

GENDER, HEALTH, AND THE LIFE CYCLE

Gloria Steinem (1978) once asked what would happen if men could menstruate. "Men would brag about how long and how much. Boys would mark the onset of menses . . . with religious ritual and stag parties. Congress would fund a National Institute of Dysmenorrhea to help stamp out monthly discomforts. Sanitary supplies would be federally funded and free . . . Military men, right-wing politicians, and religious fundamentalists would cite menstruation as proof that only men could serve in the Army, . . . occupy political office, . . . be priests and ministers, . . . or rabbis." In this provocative thought exercise, Steinem draws attention to the way in which women's biological processes throughout the life cycle are constructed within a cultural context.

Following in Steinem's footsteps, numerous other feminists have repeatedly pointed to the social and cultural factors that shape the way in which women experience their bodies and the normal changes that are part of the life cycle (Flint 1982; Martin 1988; Sargent 1992). As Margaret Lock (1993:xx) has recently phrased it with respect to menopause, the "endocrinological changes associated with female midlife are universal facts on which culture weaves its tapestry." If culture shapes the experience of reproductive processes such as menstruation and menopause, so too does the medical profession. "Biomedical researchers," writes Carol Tavris (1992:133), "have taken a set of bodily changes that are normal to women over the menstrual cycle, packaged them into a 'Premenstrual Syndrome,' and sold them back to women as a disorder, a problem that needs treatment and attention."

Increasingly, women's reproductive processes have become pathologized and subject to the management and control of a medical community that can "create a market for its services by redefining certain events, behaviors, and problems as diseases" (Lock 1993:257). This is precisely what has happened to PMS, a phenomenon that did not exist as a medically defined category prior to the 1930s but that has become the focus of research, diagnosis, and therapy in recent years (Bell 1987). Although the recognition of PMS as "real" is gratifying to some women whose monthly discomfort had for years been tossed aside as "all in the head," more recently feminists have warned of the implications of the medicalization of PMS, which has occurred not only through the use of biomedical language to define symptoms, as noted above, but also through its categorization as a debilitating disease.

Both Martin (1987) and Johnson (1987) have noted the association between PMS and women's productivity. According to Martin, the emphasis on PMS grew with women's participation in the labor force—when this is seen as a threat to the social order, menstruation becomes a liability. Muller (1990) argues that PMS has been used as a mechanism of social control that excludes women from participation in sports, education, and public office. Most recently, the National Organization of Women has suggested that the creation of PMS as a depressive disorder in the new diagnostic manual of mental illness put out by the American Psychiatric Association can only lead to further discrimination against women in jobs, custody hearings, and insurance. "So far," NOW argues, "the psychiatric association hasn't paid equal attention to the effects of testosterone on male behavior and mental health" (Chase 1993:B1).

Others have noted the lucrative market for PMS cures in the form of books, tapes, seminars, drugs, and support groups established throughout the United States to help women deal with their debilitating disease. Finally, some researchers have simply chosen to highlight the serious flaws in the very definition of the syndrome with its vague, numerous, and frequently contradictory set of symptoms (Fausto-Sterling 1985).

If PMS is extensively medicalized in North American culture, so, too, is menopause. Physicians will tell a woman "that the continuation of sexual activity is normal, but that to lose the desire for sex is an expression of a disease state, the menopause, which is to be managed by hormone therapy. Just as obstetricians and pediatricians would define how women should feel and behave when becoming mothers, gynecologists and psychiatrists tell women what it is to be menopausal" (Kaufert and Lock 1992:203).

Several authors have observed that menopause, like PMS, is big business, whether it is surgically induced by means of a hysterectomy (Corea 1985) or treated through a regime of estrogen therapy. During 1990 over 200 articles dealt with hormone replacement and, in the same year, estrogen sales in the United States were estimated at $460 million (Lock 1993:xxxi). Tavris (1992:158) predicts that, despite the attempts of some writers to reconceptualize menopause as "post-menstrual freedom" or "post-menopausal zest," the aging baby-boom generation is simply too large to leave menopause undiagnosed and untreated. According to Lock (1993:345), research that shows no difficulties for the majority of women going through menopause is uninteresting to most physicians. This parallels the observation made by biologists such as Anne Fausto-Sterling (1985) and Ruth Bleier (1988) about sex-differences research—that those studies showing little or no difference between males and females in such phenomena as mental abilities or aggressivity are virtually ignored—buried in the back pages of the newspaper rather than featured on the front page.

In her contribution to this volume, Dona Davis explores the literature on premenstrual and menopausal syndromes within a cross-cultural framework. This framework allows her to challenge a number of commonly held assumptions: that biomedical constructions of premenstrual and menopausal syndromes are universal; that they are based on female reproductive and hormonal biology; and that they are manifest in negative elaborations of biological, psychosomatic, psychological, and psychosocial symptomatologies.

As Davis points out, in a range of cultures around the world menstruation and menopause are experienced differently and are by no means automatically defined as a source of stigma, depression, or emotional stress. While menstrual blood is frequently viewed as a source of pollution (Buckley and Gottlieb 1988; Delaney, Lupton, and Toth 1988), in some cultures it is associated with the creative spirituality of women (Buckley 1988; Gottlieb 1988; Powers 1980). In many cultures, menopause is not even emphasized biologically or socially. Maya women, for example, do not view it as a life crisis characterized by specific psychological or physiological problems. Nor do they expect hot flashes or make salient other kinds of aging complaints, such as osteoporosis, that are a common focus of attention in the Western industrialized world (Beyene 1989).

Lock (1993:32) observes that the Japanese have no single and unequivocal word that describes the hot flash, the core symptom that defines menopause in the West. Furthermore, although Japanese physicians read the same medical literature about menopause that is read by North American doctors, they are less likely to prescribe hormones. Instead, they recommend herbal teas (Kaufert and Lock 1992). In Japan, menopausal syndrome is considered by many to be a luxury disease, characteristic of women who are selfish and have too much time on their hands (Lock 1986). This social class dimension is important to consider in any cultural context. Recently, the Women's Health Network has noted that the bulk of research into menopause has used Caucasian middle-class women as subjects. "Extrapolations to all middle-aged women then occur, although we know there are, for example, very different rates of osteoporosis, heart disease, and breast cancer among Black and Asian women than among Caucasian women (Lock 1993:357).

If Western women seek treatment for the decline in sexuality that they have learned is associated with menopause, Bengali women, according to Vatuk (1992), simply believe that sexual activity is inappropriate for postmenopausal women. By contrast, among the Lusi of Papua New Guinea, "menopause brings no radical changes. A woman no longer produces menstrual blood, but a postreproductive woman is not perceived as being less feminine than a fertile one. As long as she is sexually active, she continues to produce odors and substances that are contaminating and dangerous to vulnerable people" (Counts 1992:71). While Lusi women experience little change in status after menopause, for !Kung San women of northwestern Botswana, menopause is a time of blossoming. This is associated with a greater respect for the elderly among the !Kung than exists in many Western societies (Lee 1992). The improvement of life after menopause is characteristic of a number of societies around the world (Brown 1982; Kerns 1992; Vatuk 1992). Indeed some studies show that menopausal women can assume high status roles, as healers (Kerns and Brown 1985) or as midwives (Sargent 1989).

From a somewhat different perspective, Boddy (1992:147) argues that to define middle age universally for women as the time of life that surrounds menopause is to "succumb . . . to a Western biological model." Drawing on her research among the Hofriyat of northern Sudan, Boddy suggests that middle age can be defined in social terms as the "deactivation of procreative ability. . . . Menopause is but one event among several that might usher [a woman] into midlife, a status variously intermediate between bridehood and senescence, heralded either by legal or by physical cessation of reproduction and bringing with it increased personal autonomy and enhanced opportunity to manipulate the social environment for her own ends. However, if midlife is not coincidental with menopause, the status might also bring a loss of prestige" (1992:147).

What much of the cross-cultural literature on menopause demonstrates is that there is a close association between the conceptualization of menopause and that of aging, especially the aging of women. These conceptualizations have important implications for health care and medical treatment. Certainly many women "buy in" to Hormone Replacement Therapy because their culture has told them that menopause is ovarian failure, estrogen deficiency, and the onset of aging. Less frequently are women told that removal of the ovaries or the uterus can increase the risk of breast cancer or heart disease or that HRT can increase the risk of uterine cancer. The problem, as Tavris (1992) notes, is that HRT is being recommended for ALL women. "It is as foolhardy to argue that no women should take estrogen as to argue that all women should. The point is that these hormones are not a panacea or a cure for aging" (1992:1650). And yet, the negativism associated with aging, especially for North American women, makes HRT, together with a range of other surgical or medical treatments, highly sought after.

Margaret Lock (1993:367) suggests that it is the "potent fear of aging, coupled with a quest for immortal youthfulness and sexual desire, [that seems] to be driving the medicalization of menopause." She goes on to point out that there is much less research on the decline in male reproductive functions precisely because there is less stigma attached to the male aging process. Gullette (1993:36) calls this the great taboo subject—"that men age, have mid-life problems, and have fears about aging." Clearly, age, like gender, is more than a biological category; it, too, is a cultural construct.

Maria Cattell's contribution to this volume begins with this premise. She explores the relationship between gender, health, and aging using a life-course model. Throughout the life course, females experience discrimination, which directly affects their health status, whether it is in the form of the neglect and malnutrition of disfavored infant daughters (Miller 1987); surgical procedures to modify the genitalia, which place young girls at risk (Gordon 1991); domestic violence, including such phenomena as bride burnings in India (Willigen and Channa 1991), and wife beating in societies throughout the world (Smyke 1993). Also significant is the outright neglect of widows, who may have no place in society apart from their ties to a husband or son and who often possess few economic resources of their own. Aging adds additional health burdens to those consequences of gender discrimination that women have already experienced throughout the life course.

Cattell notes that the health implications of widowhood, extreme poverty and, in some cases, filial neglect are not well understood. If this is true in a cross-cultural context, it is equally true in the United States where the elderly and women are often excluded from medical research. Studies of biological senescence, as is the case with medical research in general (Hamilton 1993; Muller 1990), are often conducted on males and extrapolated to females. And yet, in the United States, and around the world, it is the population of female elderly that is expanding significantly.

In the small number of studies that have included gender and age as variables, significant differences in male and female health are demonstrated. For example, based on an analysis of data drawn from the British General Household Survey, Arber and Ginn (1993) demonstrate that elderly women assess their health less positively than men and are seriously disadvantaged compared to men in terms of functional disability (measured by such things as the ability to climb stairs, cut one's own toenails, wash one's entire body, get in and out of bed, etc.). In addition, such studies show that elderly men and women who are materially advantaged enjoy better health than those who are economically disadvantaged.

Similar results come from Popay, Bartley, and Owen's (1993) analysis of data from a national cross-sectional survey of the British population from age 18 to 59. Women and men in the most disadvantaged socioeconomic positions reported higher rates of affective disorders and minor physical illness than did those in more advantaged situations.

Class, and the attendant wealth disparities with which it is associated, is clearly an important factor to consider in any assessment of health differentials among the elderly. But it is often ignored. "Aging within the amoral realm of science," writes Margaret Lock (1993:367), "screens us from reflection on the consequences for their health of economic differences among women and above all from the politics of aging while we dwell ad nauseam on ovaries, flashes, vaginas, libido, fragile bones, and risk-benefit analyses." In short, we would be better served by considering the relationship between the feminization of poverty world-wide and women's health.

Although it has been subject to controversy in recent years, anthropologist Margaret Mead's classic work on adolescence in Samoa was expressly designed to draw our attention to the fact that life-cycle changes must be understood in a cross-cultural context. It is culture that marks and gives meaning to certain biological changes. It is culture that defines both health and ill health. It is culture that defines different gender roles for men and women and hence different evaluations of the biological processes associated with aging. "Women and men both need to acknowledge that mid-life crisis is a disease created in European cultures. Learning this should make us angry, and learning its effects should make us resistant. We know we'll all age by the rule of nature. Should we let ourselves be aged by the tyranny of our culture too?" (Gullette 1993:37).

TECHNOLOGY, GENDER, AND HEALTH

As is evident in the preceding discussions of language and the life cycle, during the past two decades, sociologists and anthropologists have examined the process and consequences of the medicalization of society, the extension of medical jurisdiction to a range of human experiences and social problems (Zola 1972; Fox 1977). Critiques of medicalization are especially prevalent in studies of reproduction (Browner and Sargent 1990; Jordan 1993; Michaelson 1988; Muller 1990; Oakley 1980; Rapp 1991; Romalis 1981; Rothman 1988). Medicalization in the domain of reproduction encompasses the routinization of technocratic birth (Davis-Floyd 1993), infertility interventions (Whiteford and Poland 1989), as well as technologies for prenatal diagnosis, such as amniocentesis and ultrasound imaging, which have attained legitimacy in societies as diverse as the United States, China, India, and Greece (Davis-Floyd and Sargent, in press; Georges, in press; Miller 1993; Rapp 1993).

The routinization of prenatal diagnosis not only illustrates the widespread legitimation of technological intervention in reproductive processes but also illuminates the linkages between reproductive technology, cultural constructs of parenthood, and the political economy within which particular pregnancies acquire meanings (Browner and Press, in press; Browner and Sargent 1990; Rapp 1993). Rapp, building on the research discussed above, considers gender, class, and ethnic differences in maternalist and medical discourses surrounding the use of amniocentesis by low-income African-American and Hispanic women in New York (1990, 1993). Her work traces the "multilayered forces at work" in the process of decisions regarding prenatal diagnosis. She shows that women's choices are not only individual and psychological, but are ultimately informed by religious, ethnic, and communal identities generated in an advanced capitalist society.

Correspondingly, Miller (1992:429) describes the growing popularity of amniocentesis as a means for sex selection in India, which she relates to broader structural principles. The disadvantaged position of women and the cultural disfavor for daughters is reflected in the market in India for sex-selective abortion, following determination of the sex of the fetus through amniocentesis. This application of amniocentesis occurs in the social context of female infanticide and daughter neglect in rural North India, which Miller links to the importance of sons as economic assets and as strategists in local power struggles.

Rapp has argued that the study of power relations is at the core of the investigation of medicine (1993:71), an assertion that Georges (in press) documents in her recent study of the increasing medicalization of birth in Greece. Over the past decade, fetal ultrasound imaging has been adopted as a routine feature of Greek prenatal care, with women undergoing several sessions per pregnancy. Women enthusiastically endorse ultrasound for its visual enhancement of the experience of pregnancy. Georges argues that ultrasound technology contributes to the production of obstetricians' authoritative knowledge, and reinforces hierarchical power relations between physicians and the women who consult them. Ultrasound thus reinforces Greek physicians' medical authority and diminishes the importance of women's body experience as a source of information.

As Davis-Floyd has observed, the highly technocratic model of birth dominates American biomedicine, and, increasingly, has been exported to preindustrial societies. Globally, the growing cultural valuation of technical expertise and the reliance on biomedical specialists as the source of authoritative knowledge concerning birth (Davis-Floyd and Sargent, in press) reflect the widespread subordination of low-technology birthing systems.

In this book, Davis-Floyd describes the hegemony of "technobirth" in the United States, where 98 percent of American women give birth in hospitals, most with some form of intervention. Her research addresses the contrast between the technocratic ideology accepted by the majority of women, and the holistic and organic model of birth characterizing a minority population of homebirthers. Those women favoring the technocratic model of birth share a Cartesian understanding of mind and body, in which, ideally, "the self should control the body"; technology plays an important role in birth, and medical knowledge is seen as authoritative. Home-birthers view self and body as one, the body as uncontrollable, and giving up control as desirable; intuition is more highly valued than scientific expertise. For Davis-Floyd, although the home-birthers' organic and holistic model represents a minority perspective, it serves a crucial function in counterbalancing the dominant technocratic paradigm with an alternative vision of birth as an embodied process.

In contrast to the extensive research on reproduction, breast cancer has rarely received attention from medical anthropologists, perhaps because the feminist model critiquing medicalization and portraying science as malignant is less applicable to the study of cancer. In this volume, Kaufert explores the campaign to promote mammography in the United States, situating mammography screening in the moral discourse and political economy of breast cancer in North America. Her unsettling conclusions illustrate that confidence in technology as well as its profitability are central to the success of the mammography campaign. Efforts to routinize mammography screening have established breast cancer as a social issue, in part by generating widespread fear surrounding the topic. Kaufert's chapter thus directs our attention to the ways in which technology may be used to generate or increase the demand for its existence. With regard to technology as well as medical research, we need to ask not only who benefits but who may suffer from its use.

GENDER AND MEDICAL ETHICS

The field of bioethics is dominated by tenets of Western philosophical thought and structured by a discourse of principles and rights that has generated a reductionist and ethnocentric approach to moral dilemmas (Marshall 1992:49). Bioethics has emerged from the persistent moral questions that surround the application of technologies in biomedicine. Primary among the issues drawing concern are confidentiality in patient-practitioner relationships, informed consent in treatment and medical experimentation, transplantation of body parts and genetic materials, withholding or withdrawing of treatment, and allocation of scarce medical resources. Bioethical debate reflects not only the problematic aspects of medical technology, but powerful and conflicting societal values regarding individual rights to privacy and autonomy, definitions of personhood, and meanings of life and death.

In spite of intensified public and academic interest, ethical issues have not attracted much concern within anthropology (Lieban 1990). In a recent article, Marshall (1992) urged that more attention be directed to social, cultural, and historical determinants that shape moral questioning. She argues that anthropologists bring an important perspective to the analysis of ethical dilemmas by viewing ethical problems as culturally constituted and situationally contextualized. Correspondingly, we argue that such analysis needs to explore how gender plays into ethical negotiations in biomedicine and in other medical traditions. Little research has examined variation among men and women in medical issues perceived as morally relevant, gender as a factor in the disclosure of information to patients, or gender as an issue in decisions regarding life-sustaining treatment.

In a provocative study of gender as a factor in appellate-level, civil, state "right-to-die" cases involving incompetent adults, Miles and August (1990) argue that judicial reasoning "belies a premise of a universal, purportedly gender-neutral, right to refuse treatment" (1990:85). Rather, judicial reasoning about men receiving life-sustaining treatment is more likely to accept evidence of mens' treatment preferences, while judicial decisions about women in similar circumstances tend to either reject or to not consider evidence of womens' preferences. The authors contend that the major differences in court rulings reflect broadly held cultural views that men's opinions are rational while women's are unreflective, emotional, or immature (1990:87).

   Similarly, research on assisted and "acquiescent" suicide (Osgood and Eisenhandler 1994) suggests that gender issues are paramount in understanding individual decisions to end life. Most victims of assisted suicide in the United States are older women, leading Osgood and Eisenhandler to state "in view of the sexism and ageism experienced by older women in our society, it is not surprising that older women are so often the victims of assisted suicide" (1994:35). Women faced with physical or mental decline, inadequate resources, and the prospect of burdening family members may choose the culturally appropriate strategy of self-sacrifice and choose to end their lives, by means of either assisted or acquiescent suicide. The authors describe acquiescent suicide as a "silent struggle against confinement," in which older women in nursing homes reject medication, refuse food and interaction, ultimately leading to death (1994:37). They conclude that the institutional settings in which many older women find themselves is a social and ecological context that is especially conducive to acquiescent suicide, raising many issues regarding the vulnerability of older women in the United States.

   Implicit or explicit considerations of gender in the allocation of medical resources also merit attention. Selection of transplant recipients, for instance, includes an assessment of who is deserving, based on life stories illustrating moral worth. Gender may well figure into such decisions, as when a single mother of several children was selected for a transplant after consideration of her responsibilities and life situation (Marshall 1992:61). Lieban notes important unanswered questions regarding differential resource allocation for sons and daughters in South Asia. He observes that Western medical ethics defines distribution of resources affecting health as a moral issue, but cross-cultural research has not addressed the extent to which differential treatment of children by sex is perceived to involve moral dilemmas and choices for the families involved (Lieban 1990:227–8).

   Sherwin argues that biomedical ethicists have generally ignored the roles of health-care practices and research in perpetuating oppressive systems. For example, medical education has used male experience as the norm and clinical studies have long focused on male subjects and disorders most commonly affecting Caucasian men, except in reproduction—where the emphasis has been on manipulating women's bodies to control fertility. She suggests that ethicists would benefit from a feminist perspective that asserts the immorality of oppression. Thus feminist ethics can help to make explicit the ways in which gender bias in research and teaching has worked to the detriment of women's health.

   Sherwin applies these feminist ethical concerns to women diagnosed with cancer. Like Kaufert, she notes the political dimensions of fear: fear of experiencing cancer, fear of alienating health professionals, fear of losing control over one's own health care. She contends that cancer is a feminist issue and that feminist ethics may contribute to the creation of more promising health policies and to developing alternative models of medical decision making. We need to take into account underlying features that shape options for medical choice such as the distribution of wealth and power in society, the allocation of health care resources, and the dominance of biomedicine. Examining cancer in particular, she suggests that certain oppressed groups are particularly at risk for cancer and directs our attention to environmental, social, and political conditions related to cancer risks, rather than to cancer as an individual problem and responsibility.

Patricia Marshall explores the interactional dynamics surrounding clinical ethics consultations, which she argues are infused with issues of gender, class, and power. Gender ideology may influence a patient's experience of sickness, sense of empowerment, and relationship with family, physicians, and other health care providers. Moreover, expressions of gender and power inform the interpretation and resolution of moral dilemmas in medical care. Gender also may play a role in provider decisions concerning appropriate treatment. These themes are assessed through the analysis of a case concerning a woman confronted with deciding whether or not to pursue a third lung transplant. Based on Marshall's participation in a clinical ethics consultation service, on interviews, and on diary information offered to her by the patient, Marshall examines how ethics consultants mediate power in clinical contexts. She explores how beliefs and values concerning gender affect the role of the ethics consultant as well as patient-provider relations and the phenomenology of end-of-life decisions.

In her detailed description of a patient narrative that involves a critically ill woman searching for personal power and identity, Marshall directs our attention to the negotiation of personhood in relation to biomedical, community, and family culture. The ethical implications of the cultural construction of the person is also explored in this book by Csordas, who discusses the definition of fetal personhood in two cultural contexts. Among American Catholic Charismatics, the experience of abortion is defined as intrinsically traumatic, not only for the woman involved, who suffers grief and guilt, but also for the traumatized fetus. Ritual healing of memories provides a potential source of relief from the suffering of both woman and fetus, as the fetus is given gender, name, and baptism and is thus granted the cultural status of a person. Csordas contrasts the definition of personhood held by Charismatic Catholics with that of Japanese Buddhists, who also hold rituals to propitiate the spirits of aborted fetuses. His discussion of these rituals shows how female gender identity is constructed in the context of the abortion debate, enhances our understanding of cultural variation in concepts of the person, and explicates the creation of guilt and its absolution in this facet of moral debate in the United States.

GENDER, HEALING, AND THE SOCIAL PRODUCTION OF HEALTH

Addressing the determinants of morbidity and mortality in the United States, Salk et al. argue that "poverty is the most basic cause of ill health and early death in our society. The poor, who are mostly women and children and disproportionately people of color, have more illnesses and die in greater numbers and earlier than people with more income and education. Many of their health problems are diseases that result from malnutrition, workplace dangers, inadequate housing, environmental pollution or excessive stress" (Salk et al. 1992:655). In recent years a political economy perspective that takes into account class-based poverty, as well as the impact of global forces and global power relations on the lives of individuals and the functioning of local communities, has influenced medical anthropological research in international health as well as research based in the United States and Europe (Morsy 1990).

Scholars adopting this perspective are interested in how a range of national and international social, political, and economic conditions shape sickness and healing. Turshen (1977), for example, has argued that a system of labor migration encouraged by the colonial government in Tanzania resulted in the neglect of local food production and, ultimately, the malnutrition of women and children who remained in village communities.

The political economy perspective also encompasses research that explores how social class and other aspects of the social environment affect access to medical services (Frankenberg 1980). Gish (1979:209) suggests that the delivery of just and efficent health care to populations in the developing world is not obstructed by poor communication, the lack of technological knowledge, or limited resources, but rather by "social systems that place a low value on the health care needs of the poor." In the United States, Chavez (1986:348) argues, certain racial and ethnic groups are limited in the health care they receive by the precariousness of their political and economic position. In nonemergency situations, "medical care . . . has become dependent upon the ability to pay, which in turn is dependent upon large personal resources or, more commonly, the guarantee of third party payment. . . . In addition to the financial factor, a number of intangible factors—i.e., knowledge of available resources, ease of communication—affect a population's access to health services."

It is these issues of the social production of illness and the class-based control of access to health care that Whiteford addresses in her case study of a poor African American woman named Deidre, who confronted a Florida statute making it possible to imprison women who delivered babies with positive postpartum drug screens. This statute, Whiteford argues, targets women unfairly based on class, ethnicity, and a lack of power. In Florida, women who deliver their babies in nonpublicly funded hospitals are not screened routinely for drugs and hence are less likely to lose custody of their babies or be sent to jail than those women who seek care in public institutions. A law that is supposedly designed to encourage women to take advantage of prenatal care instead frightens them off. The health of their babies is hence placed at further risk by a regulation that opposes maternal rights to fetal rights. Paradoxically, however, it is the women rather than the system who receive the blame. Health administrators claim that they "just won't come" (Salk et al. 1992:656) instead of trying to understand the reasons for their reluctance to use the services that are available to them.

In the process of discussing Deidre's case, Whiteford makes a theoretical argument for the inclusion of gender in the political economy perspective in medical anthropology. "Instead of simply asking how women are treated in various health care systems, a political economy orientation seeks to understand the history of social relations that give rise to particular gender roles and to relations between groups and the State, and among social classes." She argues that, while there is a large literature on political economy and health, and on gender and health, little research focuses on the intersection of political economy, health, and gender.

Similarly, in their comparative analysis of populations in rural Mexico and Jamaica, Browner and Leslie argue that health policy makers must focus more on gender issues, and particularly on the implications of changes in women's economic activities for their own and their children's health. Women in developing countries assume major labor responsibilities, many of which increase the risk of ill-health. These may include exposure to pesticides in an economy that is changing from subsistence-based to cash-crop production; exposure to waterborne diseases resulting from household activities; exposure to industrial hazards or the stress of long working hours resulting from employment in multinational industrial production, or nutritional deficits resulting from the demands of multiple roles in the household and in market production.

The research on the impact of expanded maternal employment on children's health shows mixed effects. What is most apparent is that the impact of development and of women's productive activities on child and maternal health is by no means uniform. For example, Browner and Leslie show, based on research in Jamaica, that the impact of women's employment on breastfeeding is not clearcut. Maternal employment *per se* does not necessarily negatively affect infant nutritional status. Thus any analysis of women's work, fertility, and health must take into account local social, cultural, political and economic conditions. Similarly, health policy, including policy that deals with family planning and reproductive behavior, must be formulated on the basis of these differences.

One result of development, urbanization, and the other changes that have accompanied the evolution of an increasingly interdependent global economy is international labor migration. Women now comprise a significant proportion of immigrants in the developed world (Donato 1992; Houstoun et al. 1984; Pedraza 1991). The health status of immigrant women has therefore become an important area of research and can be divided into three broad areas of inquiry: studies of the relationship between ethnomedical and biomedical orientations toward sickness and healing; studies of mental health and stress; and studies of the use of the health care system (Brettell and de Berjeois 1992). For example, DeSantis (1989), based on a comparison of Cuban and Haitian immigrant women, shows that the former have a biomedical orientation to illness and health care that is similar to that of Western health care professionals, while Haitian women apply a folk interpretation. Kirby (1989), in her study of Cuban immigrant women, found use of both prescription tranquilizers and herbal teas and other home remedies to cure *nervios.*

Nervios is a common stress condition manifested among immigrant women in the United States (Dunk 1989; Kay and Portillo 1989). Jenkins indicates in her contribution to this volume that it is equally manifested among refugee women from El Salvador who show symptoms of depression and post-traumatic stress disorder that can be directly related to their experience of *la situacion*—the political violence that has rocked El Salvador. Her research on the consequences of traumatic events associated with political violence for women's emotional and mental well-being shows that Salvadoran women refugees display a gender-specific response to the extreme events they have experienced. These women reported suffering from *nervios* and also fit diagnostic criteria for major depressive illness. However, the women varied in whether they represented the violence they had experienced as mundane or extreme. Jenkins contends that cultural proscriptions regarding the expression of negative emotion by women influence the varying responses these women display to political violence.

As Jenkins notes, research shows that there is a higher percentage of women than men among those suffering from chronic conditions such as depression (see also Mowbray et al. 1992). However, research on immigrant and refugee populations shows that both men and women suffer from mental distress, some of it resulting from the gender role conflicts that emerge in a cross-cultural context (Chai 1987). In a study of Hmong refugees in Minnesota, Westermeyer et al. (1984:241) have shown that men experience greater stress in the initial phase of migration while women experience less than men because they continue their traditional domestic roles and do not have to deal with the financial support issues that men do. Exceptions are the women who become employed who report more "phobic anxiety symptoms . . . due to the new and relatively non-traditional roles as wage workers outside the Hmong community."

Vega et al. (1986, 1987) show that depression symptom levels are higher among Mexican immigrants who have been in the United States for less than five years. "The effort to maintain traditional cultural role expectations within the context of a highly urbanized and affluent social system could be expected to increase stress and economic marginality" (1986:650). Whether immigrant and refugee women, like the female population in general (Mowbray et al. 1992:109), have a more positive therapeutic response to treatment and a better prognosis than do men, is open to further investigation. Such an investigation should take into account the diversity of experiences of these women, experiences that may include the traumatic political events that have shaped their lives as well as rigid gender hierarchies that affect how illness and distress are expressed.

GENDER AND HEALTH POLICY

The engendering of health policy in the United States has marked federal government health initiatives in the 1990s, in response to increasing awareness of longstanding inattention to women as subjects of medical research (JAMA 1992:469). Concerns over risks to fetuses and the confounding effects of the menstrual cycle among women of childbearing age have resulted in research protocols that exclude women in their childbearing years, although research results are often generalized to this same population without reliable data. Accordingly, congressional and community activists have pressured the National Institutes of Health to enforce its ruling that research funded by NIH must include women and minorities or provide a clear rationale for their exclusion.

In her contribution to this volume, Jean Hamilton takes up this issue of the exclusion or underinclusion of women in clinical research in the United States. She describes a highly politicized debate that has moved from denial and rationalization to the legislation of research design that includes data analyzed by sex. In addition to the risk factors cited above, the tendency to exclude women has also been influenced by matters of cost, and by the fear caused by highly visible historical examples—the use of thalidomide or of DES. Hamilton's discussion of Tuskegee, a forty-year-old study of untreated syphilis among rural black men in Alabama, demonstrates that biases in clinical trials are racist as well as sexist. Although Hamilton concludes that the 1990 congressional mandate for blanket inclusion of women and minorities may have gone too far in the opposite direction, she does see a positive outcome in moving away from the male norm in health care, education, research, and practice. Her own solution is a more targeted approach that identifies selected areas that require sex-specific research.

While efforts to address these issues are encouraging, bias central to medical education and the practice of medicine remains problematic. Biomedical training rests on a model of the white, middle-class male as normative, and medical texts often present deprecating views of women (Altekruse and Rosser 1992:28; Muller 1990:33; Stone 1992:90). An important underlying issue is the premise in biomedicine that the individual can be effectively detached from social, cultural, and familial context for purposes of diagnosis and treatment (Hamilton 1993; Warshaw 1993). This premise has led to the failure of medical education to address the importance of the contextualization of health, including the implications of gender for access to care and health status.

A broad review of research on the utilization of health care services (Muller 1990) shows how gender directly and indirectly affects treatment decisions, financing of care, communication between physicians and patients, and women's and men's health status. In addition to the inclusion of women in medical research and attention to gender-based health needs, access to appropriate treatment emerges as a focus for health policy. For example, there appears to be a possible sex bias in decisions to refer men and women for coronary bypass surgery (Muller 1990:37–38). Women are too often subject to certain forms of unnecessary surgery (for instance, Cesarean section, hysterectomy, or radical mastectomy) and overprescription of psychotropic drugs (Davis-Floyd 1992; Kaufert and McKinlay 1985; Muller 1990; Lewin and Olesen 1985:2–3). Muller astutely observes that "sex stereotypes that result in overtreatment, undertreatment, or misdirected treatment for women waste resources of the system or compromise the patient's health" (1990:99). Correspondingly, male social roles and cultural expectations may lead to denial of illness—a culturally approved behavior for men. Similarly, the negative effects of chronic illness labeling for men may lead to a delay in seeking needed care and benefiting from it. Thus definition of, and access to, appropriate treatment remain gender issues central to the creation of more equitable and responsive health policy.

The feminization of poverty has affected both health status and the provision of health care in the United States, as poor women may lack access to fertility services and to more general care for chronic and acute conditions. As Cattell has shown, elderly women with a history of low labor-force participation, low wages, and limited insurance benefits, are particularly likely to lack necessary health care, while both elderly men and women face problems financing adequate long-term care.

The chapters in Part VI explore the implications of gender roles and ideology, as well as other cultural, social, political, and economic dynamics for health policy in the United States and elsewhere in the world. In their discussion of gender relations, sexuality, and AIDS risk among African American and Latina women, Weeks et al. assess the macrostructural power relations that shape gender interactions and inform sexual behavior among groups at risk for HIV. They observe that changes in sexual practices to reduce the risk of HIV transmission are constrained by the necessity of overcoming powerful cultural definitions of sex and sexuality, as well as the structure of gender relations. Issues such as condom use are not merely intimate and private concerns; cultural models of heterosexual and homosexual relations are shaped by political and economic relations across class, ethnic, religious, and gender lines. Thus, policy directed at AIDS prevention must focus not only on individual behavior, but must consider the broader cultural and structural contexts in which individuals engage in sexual interaction.

An important theme in this chapter is the differences in the discourse on gender and sex among inner-city African Americans and Latinos. For African Americans, the dominant factor shaping gender and sexual relations is the impact of racial oppression, while for Latinos, cultural ideologies defining female and male roles and relationships play a primary role. Significantly, research on gender and sexual relations in both populations suggests that individuals hold contradictory and conflicting beliefs, generated by broader social forces, which affect their relationships. However, the ways in which women interpret these contradictory images is unclear. Effective AIDS-prevention efforts for African American and Latina women at risk of heterosexually transmitted HIV must address their notions of gender roles and sexual relations, and explicate the links between expectations, ideals, and actual behavior with male partners. Organizing women in communities of color around HIV/AIDS research and prevention will assume critical importance in the construction of effective health policy.

The growing literature on HIV/AIDS elsewhere in the world, where heterosexual transmission predominates, equally addresses the relationship between macrostructural power relations shaping gender interactions, sexual behavior, and disease risk (Caldwell et al. 1992). For example, research on Baganda women in Uganda (McGrath et al. 1993) shows that the norms that allow men to have multiple sexual partners limit the ability of women to control their exposure to the risk of AIDS. For women in Lesotho, the exchange of sexual favors for money or basic necessities that occurs in economically disadvantaged communities may generate particular risks for the transmission of STDs, including AIDS (Romero-Daza 1994:201). Similarly, Standing (1992), in a survey of studies on sexual behavior and AIDS in Africa, suggests that such patterns of sexual exchange are critical to urban women's survival strategies. Other research indicates that women may be blamed for disseminating sexually transmitted diseases in general, and AIDS in particular, and may become scapegoats in the social crisis surrounding AIDS (De Bruin 1992; Caldwell et al. 1992:1173; Schoepf 1991:756). This is especially true for sex workers, who are viewed in a critical and accusatory light, suspected of infecting their unborn infants, their clients, and their clients' other female sex partners. In several countries (Rwanda, Mexico, and Zimbabwe), fear of AIDS-carrying female prostitutes has led to the general harassment and imprisonment of unaccompanied women in capital cities (de Zalduondo 1991:225). In India, women who had sex with foreigners were blamed for spreading AIDS in that country (Nataraj 1990:195). Focusing on sex workers to the exclusion of the men who use their services is clearly an inadequate AIDS-prevention strategy. Furthermore, emphasizing prostitution as an occupational choice deflects our attention from the structural conditions that may make it the only possibility for many impoverished women and girls.

In general, many of the factors that placed women at risk from ill health prior to the AIDS epidemic increase their vulnerability to AIDS, including malnutrition, high fertility, complications of childbirth, labor migration, and economic scarcity (Ulin 1992). In addition to understanding macrolevel factors placing women at risk for ill health in the developing world, successful health policy needs to take into account women's positive and health-enhancing roles in production, reproduction, and in the provision of health care at the community level. In the domain of international health, scholars, and policymakers have tended to underestimate the significant implications of women's activities for their health and that of their families (see Browner and Leslie in this volume). Thus MacCormack, in her chapter on risk, prevention, and international health policy, argues that global health care policy, epidemiology, and economics must be balanced against careful local-level studies. We need to understand the sexual division of labor in particular societies, as well as the health risks associated with daily activities. Women's and men's activities may carry differing degrees of direct and indirect health risks (for example, women who spend more time than men in standing water experience greater risks for schistosomiasis haematobium). MacCormack describes the numerous risks to women from gendered food taboos, unequal access to food, complications of pregnancy, childbirth, and abortion, a heavy workload, hazardous working conditions, and economic and cultural barriers to health care.

This chapter clearly illustrates the discrepancies in risk of maternal mortality between rich and poor populations, and suggests prevention strategies that might lower health risks to women in developing countries. Like Weeks et al., MacCormack suggests that local women be central to planning, evaluating, and sustaining appropriate health care. Browner and Leslie also acknowledge the important existing role of women in the production of household and community health. Drawing on the resources of local women, traditional practitioners such as midwives and community health workers to provide more equitable distribution of health care is more likely to result in sustainable, long-term improvements in health than is a top-down, targeted, and disease-specific strategy.

SUMMARY

All of the chapters in this book emphasize the importance of a gendered perspective on both national and international health issues. Such a perspective acknowledges the diversity of women's and men's experiences, attitudes, and behaviors in the pursuit of health. The authors share an orientation clearly demonstrating that biology, medicine, health, and ethical dilemmas are most effectively understood as culturally informed and shaped by broad social, political, and economic forces. Taken as a whole, the chapters offer powerful examples of the pervasiveness of medicalization in the late twentieth century. This medicalization occurs through such phenomena as language, the technological domination of the body, the subordination of alternative sources of knowledge and experience that are not derived from biomedicine, and the influence of market forces on medical practice. The outcome of widespread medicalization and the narrow biologizing of health is the increasing loss of personhood, appropriation of individual decision making by medical experts, and the decontextualizing of sickness. The critiques of this process, as presented in this book, have implications not only for our intellectual understanding of the relationship between gender, ethnicity, class, and health, but also for clinical practice, medical education, and health policy. True transformations in these domains require multifaceted approaches that address gender-related cultural, social, and economic issues, as well as those that are narrowly defined as medical.

REFERENCES

Altekruse, Joan, and Sue Rosser
  1992   Feminism and Medicine: Co-optation or Cooperation. *In* The Knowledge
          Explosion. Generations of Feminist Scholarship. Cheris Kramarae and Dale
          Spender, eds. Pp. 27–41. New York: Teachers College Press.
Arber, Sara, and Jay Ginn
  1993   Gender and Inequalities in Health in Later Life. Social Science and Medicine
          36(1):33–46.
Bell, Susan E.
  1987   Premenstrual Syndrome and the Medicalization of Menopause: A Sociological
          Perspective. *In* Premenstrual Syndrome. Benson E. Ginsburg and Bonnie
          Frank Carter, eds. Pp. 151–187. New York: Plenum Press.
Berman, Ruth
  1989   From Aristotle's Dualism to Materialist Dialectics: Feminist Transformation of
          Science and Society. *In* Gender/Body/Knowledge: Feminist Reconstructions of
          Being and Knowing. Alison M. Jaggar and Susan R. Bordo, eds. Pp. 224–255.
          New Brunswick, NJ: Rutgers University Press.

Beyene, Yewoubdar
    1989   From Menarche to Menopause: Reproductive Lives of Peasant Women in Two Cultures. Albany: State University of New York Press.

Bleier, Ruth
    1991   Sex Differences Research: Science or Belief? *In* Feminist Approaches to Science. Ruth Bleier, ed. Pp. 147–164. New York: Teachers College Press.

Boddy, Janice
    1992   Bucking the Agnatic System: Status and Strategies in Rural Northern Sudan. *In* In Her Prime: A New View of Middle-Aged Women. Virginia Kerns and Judith K. Brown, eds. Pp. 141–153. South Hadley, MA: Bergin and Garvey.

Brettell, Caroline B., and Patricia A. deBerjeois
    1991   Anthropology and the Study of Immigrant Women. *In* Seeking Common Ground: Multidisciplinary Studies of Immigrant Women in the United States. Donna Gabaccia, ed. Pp. 41–63. Westport CT: Greenwood Press.

Brown, Judith K.
    1982   Cross-Cultural Perspectives on Middle-Aged Women. Current Anthropology 23(2):143–156.

Browner, C. H., and Nancy Anne Press
    In press The Production of Authoritative Knowledge in Prenatal Care. *In* Childbirth across Cultures: The Social Display of Authoritative Knowledge. Robbie Davis-Floyd and Carolyn Sargent, eds. Berkeley: University of California Press.

Browner, Carole, and Carolyn Sargent
    1990   Anthropology and Studies of Human Reproduction. *In* Medical Anthropology: Contemporary Theory and Method. Thomas Johnson and Carolyn Sargent, eds. Pp. 215–230. New York: Praeger.

Buckley, Thomas
    1988   Menstruation and the Power of Yurok Women. *In* Blood Magic: The Anthropology of Menstruation. Thomas Buckley and Alma Gottlieb, eds. Pp. 187–210. Berkeley: University of California Press.

Buckley, Thomas, and Alma Gottlieb, eds.
    1988   Blood Magic: The Anthropology of Menstruation. Berkeley: University of California Press.

Caldwell, John C., I. O. Orubuloye, and Pat Caldwell
    1992   Underreaction to AIDS in Sub-Saharan Africa. Social Science and Medicine 34(11f):1169–1183.

Celentano, David D., Martha S. Linet, and Walter F. Stewart
    1990   Gender Differences in the Experience of Headache. Social Science and Medicine 20(12):1289–1295.

Chai, Alice Yun
    1987   Adaptive Strategies of Recent Korean Immigrant Women in Hawaii. *In* Beyond the Public/Domestic Dichotomy: Contemporary Perspectives on Women's Public Lives. Janet Sharistanian, ed. Pp. 65–100. New York: Greenwood Press.

Chase, Marilyn
    1993   Psychiatrists Declare Severe PMS a Depressive Disorder. The Wall Street Journal, May 28, p. B1.

Chavez, Leo R.
    1986   Mexican Immigration and Health Care: A Political Economy Perspective. Human Organization 45(4):344–352.

Corea, Gena
    1985   The Hidden Malpractice. New York: Harper and Row.

Counts, Dorothy Ayers
1992 Tamparonga: The Big Women of Kaliai (Papua New Guinea). *In* In Her Prime: A New View of Middle-Aged Women. Virginia Kerns and Judith K. Brown, eds. Pp. 61–74. South Hadley, MA: Bergin and Garvey.

Davis-Floyd, Robbie
1992 Birth as an American Rite of Passage. Berkeley: University of California Press.

Davis-Floyd, Robbie, and Carolyn Sargent, eds.
In press Childbirth across Cultures: The Social Display of Authoritative Knowledge. Berkeley: University of California Press.

De Bruin, Maria
1992 Women and AIDS in Developing Countries. Social Science and Medicine 34(3):249–262.

Delaney, Janice, Mary Jane Lupton, and Emily Toth
1988 The Curse: A Cultural History of Menstruation. Urbana: University of Illinois Press.

DeSantis, Lydia
1989 Health Care Orientations of Cuban and Haitian Immigrant Mothers: Implications for Health Care Professionals. Medical Anthropology 12:69–89.

de Zalduondo, Barbara O.
1991 Prostitution Viewed Cross-Culturally: Toward Recontextualizing Sex Work in AIDS Intervention Research. The Journal of Sex Research 28(2):223–248.

Donato, Katherine
1992 Understanding U.S. Immigration: Why Some Countries Send Women and Others Send Men. *In* Seeking Common Ground: Multidisciplinary Studies of Immigrant Women in the United States. Donna Gabaccia, ed. Pp. 159–184. Westport, CT: Greenwood Press.

Dunk, Pamela
1989 Greek Women and Broken Nerves in Montreal. Medical Anthropology 11:29–45

Fausto-Sterling, Anne
1985 Myths of Gender: Biological Theories about Women and Men. New York: Basic Books.

Fee, Elizabeth
1991 Critiques of Modern Science: The Relationship of Feminism to Other Radical Epistemologies. *In* Feminist Approaches to Science, Ruth Bleier, ed. Pp. 42–56. New York: Teachers College Press.

Flint, Marsha
1982 Male and Female Menopause: A Cultural Put-On. *In* Changing Perspectives on Menopause. A. Voda, M. Dinnerstein, and S. O'Donnell, eds. Pp. 363–378. Austin: University of Texas Press.

Fox, Renee C.
1977 The Medicalization and Demedicalization of American Society. Daedalus (Winter).

Frankenberg, Ronald
1980 Medical Anthropology and Development: A Theoretical Perspective. Social Science and Medicine 14B:197–207.

Georges, Eugenia
In press Fetal Ultrasound Imaging and the Production of Authoritative Knowledge in Greece. *In* Childbirth across Cultures: The Social Display of Authoritative Knowledge. Robbie Davis-Floyd and Carolyn Sargent, eds. Berkeley: University of California Press.

Ginsburg, Faye and Rayna Rapp
  1991   The Politics of Reproduction. Annual Reviews in Anthropology 20:311–343.
Gish, Oscar
  1979   The Political Economy of Primary Care and "Health by the People": An His-
          torical Exploration. Social Science and Medicine 13C:203–211.
Gordon, Daniel
  1991   Female Circumcision and Genital Operations in Egypt and the Sudan: A
          Dilemma for Medical Anthropology. Medical Anthropology Quarterly 5:3–14.
Gottlieb, Alma
  1988   Menstrual Cosmology among the Beng of Ivory Coast. *In* Blood Magic: The
          Anthropology of Menstruation. Thomas Buckley and Alma Gottlieb, eds.
          Pp. 55–74. Berkeley: University of California Press.
Gullette, Margaret M.
  1993   What, Menopause Again? MS, July/August, pp. 34–37.
Hamilton, Jean
  1993   Feminist Theory and Health Psychology: Tools for an Egalitarian, Woman-Cen-
          tered Approach to Women's Health. Journal of Women's Health 2(1):49–54.
Haraway, Donna J.
  1981   In the Beginning Was the Word: The Genesis of Biological Theory. Signs
          6(3):469–481.
Houstoun, Marion F., Roger G. Kramer, and Joan M. Barrett
  1984   Female Predominance of Immigration to the United States Since 1930: A First
          Look. International Migration Review 18:908–963.
Jacobus, Mary, Evelyn Fox Keller, and Sally Shuttleworth
  1990   Body/Politics: Women and the Discourses of Science. New York: Routledge.
Johnson, Thomas M.
  1987   Premenstrual Syndrome as a Western Culture-Specific Disorder. Culture, Med-
          icine and Psychiatry 11:337–356.
Jordan, Brigitte
  1978   Birth in Four Cultures. Montreal: Eden Press.
  1993   Birth in Four Cultures. Revised Edition. Prospect Heights, IL: Waveland Press.
Jordanova, Lila
  1980   Natural Facts: A Historical Perspective on Science and Sexuality. *In* Nature,
          Culture and Gender. Carol MacCormack and Marilyn Strathern, eds.
          Pp. 42–69. Cambridge: Cambridge University Press.
Journal of the American Medical Association
  1992   Women's Health Initiative Leads Way as Research Begins to Fill Gender Gaps.
          JAMA 267(4):469–473.
Kaufert, Patricia A.
  1985   Midlife in the Midwest: Canadian Women in Manitoba. *In* In Her Prime: A
          New View of Middle-Aged Women. Virginia Kerns and Judith K. Brown, eds.
          Pp. 181–197. South Hadley, MA: Bergin and Garvey.
Kaufert, Patricia A., and Margaret Lock
  1992   What Are Women For? Cultural Constructions of Menopausal Women in Japan
          and Canada. *In* In Her Prime: A New View of Middle-Aged Women. Virginia
          Kerns and Judith K. Brown, eds. Pp. 201–220. South Hadley, MA: Bergin and
          Garvey.
Kaufert, Patricia A., and Sonja M. McKinlay
  1985   Estrogen-replacement Therapy: The Production of Medical Knowledge and
          the Emergence of Policy. *In* Women, Health and Healing. Ellen Lewin and Vir-
          ginia Olesen, eds. Pp. 113–139. London: Tavistock.

Kay, Margarita, and Carmen Portillo
    1989   *Nervios* and Dysphoria in Mexican American Widows. *In* Gender, Health and Illness: The Case of *Nervios*. Dona L. Davis and Setha M. Low, eds. Pp. 181–201. New York: Praeger.

Keller, Evelyn Fox
    1985   Reflections on Gender and Science. New Haven, CT: Yale University Press.

Kerns, Virginia
    1992   Female Control of Sexuality: Garifuna Women at Middle Age. *In* In Her Prime: A New View of Middle-Aged Women. Virginia Kerns and Judith K. Brown, eds. Pp. 95–112. South Hadley, MA: Bergin and Garvey.

Kerns, Virginia, and Judith K. Brown, eds.
    1985   In Her Prime: A New View of Middle-Aged Women. South Hadley, MA: Bergin and Garvey.

Kirby, Diana G.
    1989   Immigrants, Stress and Prescription Drug Use among Cuban Women in South Florida. Medical Anthropology 10:287–295.

Lee, Richard B.
    1992   Work, Sexuality, and Aging among !Kung Women. *In* In Her Prime: A New View of Middle-Aged Women. Virginia Kerns and Judith K. Brown, eds. Pp. 35–46. South Hadley, MA: Bergin and Garvey.

Lewin, Ellen, and Virginia Olesen
    1985   Women, Health and Healing. London: Tavistock.

Lieban, Richard
    1990   Medical Anthropology and the Comparative Study of Medical Ethics. Social Science Perspectives on Medical Ethics. G. Weisz, ed. Pp. 221–239. Netherlands: Kluwer Academic Publishers.

Lock, Margaret
    1986   Ambiguities of Aging: Japanese Experience and Perceptions of Menopause. Culture, Medicine and Psychiatry 10:23–47.
    1993   Encounters with Aging: Mythologies of Menopause in Japan and North America. Berkeley: University of California Press.

Macintyre, Sally
    1993   Gender Differences in the Perceptions of Common Cold Symptoms. Social Science and Medicine 36(1):15 20.

Marshall, Patricia
    1992   Anthropology and Bioethics. Medical Anthropology Quarterly. 6(1):49–73.

Martin, Emily
    1987   The Woman in the Body. A Cultural Analysis of Reproduction. Boston: Beacon Press.
    1988   Premenstrual Syndrome: Discipline, Work, and Anger in Late Industrial Societies. *In* Blood Magic: The Anthropology of Menstruation. Thomas Buckley and Alma Gottlieb, eds. Pp. 161–181. Berkeley: University of California Press.
    1990   Science and Women's Bodies: Forms of Anthropological Knowledge. *In* Body/Politics: Women and the Discourses of Science. Mary Jacobus, Evelyn Fox Keller, and Sally Shuttleworth, eds. Pp. 69–82. New York: Routledge.

McGrath, Janet W. et al.
    1993   Anthropology and AIDS: The Cultural Context of Sexual Risk Behavior among Urban Baganda Women in Kampala, Uganda. Social Science and Medicine 36(4):429–439.

Merchant, Carolyn
    1980   The Death of Nature: Women, Ecology, and the Scientific Revolution. San Francisco: Harper & Row.

Miles, Steven H., and Allison August
  1990   Courts, Gender and "The Right to Die." Law, Medicine and Health Care 13(1–2):85–95.

Miller, Barbara
  1987   Female Infanticide and Child Neglect in Rural India. *In* Child Survival. Nancy Scheper-Hughes, ed. Pp. 95–112. Dordrect: D. Reidel Publishing Co.

Miller, Barbara D.
  1992   Female Infanticide and Child Neglect in Rural North India. *In* Gender in Cross-Cultural Perspective. Caroline Brettell and Carolyn Sargent, eds. Pp. 423–435. Englewood Cliffs, NJ: Prentice Hall.

Morsy, Soheir
  1990   Political Economy in Medical Anthropology. *In* Medical Anthropology: A Handbook of Theory and Method. Thomas M. Johnson and Carolyn F. Sargent, eds. Pp. 26–46. Westport, CT: Greenwood.

Mowbray, Carol T., Sandra E. Herman, and Kelly L. Hazel
  1992   Gender and Serious Mental Illness: A Feminist Perspective. Psychology of Women Quarterly 16:107–126.

Muller, Charlotte F.
  1990   Health Care and Gender. New York: Russell Sage Foundation.

Nataraj, Shyamala
  1990   Madras, India: Locking Up Prostitutes. *In* The 3rd Epidemic: Repercussions of the Fear of AIDS. Pp. 194–199. London: Panos Publications Ltd.

Oakley, Ann
  1980   Women Confined: Towards a Sociology of Childbirth. New York: Schocken Books.

Osgood, Nancy J., and Susan A. Eisenhandler
  1994   Gender and Assisted and Acquiescent Suicide: A Suicidologist's Perspective. Issues in Law and Medicine 4:33–43.

Pedraza, Silvia
  1991   Women and Migration: The Social Consequences of Gender. Annual Review of Sociology 17:303–325.

Popay, Jennie, Mel Bartley, and Charlie Owen
  1993   Gender Inequalities in Health: Social Position, Affective Disorders and Minor Physical Morbidity. Social Science and Medicine 36(1):21–32.

Powers, Marla
  1980   Menstruation and Reproduction: An Oglala Case. Signs 6(1):54–65.

Rapp, Rayna
  1988   Chromosomes and Communication: The Discourse of Genetic Counseling. Medical Anthropology Quarterly 2(2):143–157.
  1991   Moral Pioneers: Women, Men, and Fetuses on a Frontier of Reproductive Technology. *In* Gender at the Crossroads of Knowledge: Feminist Anthropology in the Postmodern Era. Micaela di Leonardo, ed. Pp. 383–395. Berkeley: University of California Press.
  1993   Accounting for Amniocentesis. In Knowledge, Power and Practice: The Anthropology of Medicine and Everyday Life. Shirley Lindenbaum and Margaret Lock, eds. Pp. 55–79. Berkeley: University of California Press.

Romalis, Shelly
  1981   Childbirth: Alternatives to Medical Control. Austin: University of Texas Press.

Romero-Daza, Nancy
  1994   Multiple Sexual Partners, Migrant Labor, and the Makings for an Epidemic: Knowledge and Beliefs about AIDS among Women in Highland Lesotho. Human Organization 53(2):192–205.

Rothman, Barbara K.
  1988   The Decision To Have or Not To Have Amniocentesis. *In* Childbirth in Amer-
          ica: Anthropological Perspectives. Karen Michaelson, ed. Pp. 90–102. South
          Hadley, MA: Bergin and Garvey.
Russett, Cynthia Eagle
  1989   Sexual Science: The Victorian Construction of Womanhood. Cambridge, MA:
          Harvard University Press.
Salk, Hilary, Wendy Sanford, Norma Swenson, and Judith Dickson Luce
  1992   The Politics of Women and Medical Care. *In* The New Our Bodies, Ourselves.
          The Boston Women's Health Book Collective. Pp. 651–698. New York: Touch-
          stone.
Sargent, Carolyn F.
  1989   Maternity, Medicine, and Power: Reproductive Decisions in Urban Benin.
          Berkeley: University of California Press.
  1992   Gender, Reproduction, and Health Care: Comparative Perspectives. Reviews in
          Anthropology 21:263–273.
Saltonstall, Robin
  1993   Healthy Bodies, Social Bodies: Men's and Women's Concepts and Practices of
          Health in Everyday Life. Social Science 36(1):7–15.
Schoepf, Brooke Grundfest
  1991   Ethical, Methodological and Political Issues of AIDS Research in Central
          Africa. Social Science and Medicine 33(7):749–763.
Smyke, Patricia
  1993   Women and Health. London: Zed Books.
Standing, Hilary
  1992   AIDS: Conceptual and Methodological Issues in Researching Sexual Behaviour
          in Sub-Saharan Africa. Social Science and Medicine 34(5):475–485.
Steinem, Gloria
  1978   If Men Could Menstruate. MS, October, p. 101.
Stone, Deborah
  1992   Women, Men, and Health Care. Issues in Science and Technology, Spring:
          89–90.
Tavris, Carol
  1992   The Mismeasure of Woman. New York: Simon and Schuster.
Theriot, Nancy M.
  1993   Women's Voices in Nineteenth-Century Medical Discourse: A Step toward
          Deconstructing Science. Signs 19 (1):1–31.
Treichler, Paula A.
  1990   Feminism, Medicine, and the Meaning of Childbirth. *In* Body/Politics: Women
          and the Discourses of Science. Mary Jacobus, Evelyn Fox Keller, and Sally Shut-
          tleworth eds. Pp. 113–138. New York: Routledge.
Tuana, Nancy
  1989   The Weaker Seed: The Sexist Bias of Reproductive Theory. *In* Feminism and
          Science. Nancy Tuana, ed. Pp. 147–171. Indiana: Indiana University Press.
  1993   Forum: Feminism and Science. National Women's Studies Association Journal
          (NWSA Journal) 5(1):56–64.
Turshen, Meredith
  1977   The Impact of Colonialism on Health and Health Services in Tanzania. Inter-
          national Journal of Health Services 7(1):7–35.
  1986   Health and Human Rights in a South African Bantustan. Social Science and
          Medicine 22(9):887–892.

Ulin, Priscilla R.
  1992   Africa women and AIDS: Negotiating Behavioral Change. Social Science and Medicine 34(1):63–75.

Vatuk, Sylvia
  1992   Sexuality and the Middle-Aged Woman in South Asia. *In* In Her Prime: A New View of Middle-Aged Women. Virginia Kerns and Judith K. Brown, eds. Pp. 155–172. South Hadley, MA; Bergin and Garvey.

Vega, William A., Bohdan Kolody, and Juan Ramon Valle.
  1987   Migration and Mental Health: An Empirical Test of Depression Risk Factors among Immigrant Mexican Women. International Migration Review 21:512–529.

Vega, William A., Bohdan Kolody, Juan Ramon Valle, and Richard Hough
  1986   Depressive Symptoms and Their Correlates among Immigrant Mexican Women in the United States. Social Science and Medicine 22:645–652.

Warshaw, Carole
  1993   Domestic Violence: Challenges to Medical Practice. Journal of Women's Health 2(1):73–80.

Westermeyer, Joseph, John Neider, and Tou fu Vang
  1984   Acculturation and Mental Health: A Study of Hmong Refugees at 1.5 and 3.5 Years Postmigration. Social Science and Medicine 18:87–941.

Whiteford, Linda M. and Marily L. Poland
  1989   New Approaches to Human Reproduction. Social and Ethical Dimensions. Boulder: Westview Press.

Willigen, John Van and V. c. Channa
  1991   Law, Custom, and Crimes against Women: The Problem of Dowry Death in India. Human Organization 50(4):369–377.

Zita, Jacquelyn N.
  1989   The Premenstrual Syndrome: Dis-easing the Female Cycle. In Feminism and Science. Nancy Tuana, ed. Pp. 188–210. Bloomington; Indiana University Press.

Zola, Irving Kenneth
  1972   Medicine as an Institution of Social Control. Sociological Review 20:487–504.

The Egg and the Sperm: How Science Has Constructed a Romance Based on Stereotypical Male-Female Roles[1]

◨ *Emily Martin*

As an anthropologist, I am intrigued by the possibility that culture might shape how biological scientists describe what they discover about the natural world. If this were so, we would be learning about more than the natural world in places like high school biology class; we would be learning about cultural beliefs and practices as if they were part of nature. In the course of my research I realized that the picture of egg and sperm drawn in popular as well as scientific accounts of reproductive biology relies on stereotypes central to our cultural definitions of male and female. The implication of the stereotypes is not only that female biological processes are less worthy than male, but also that women are less worthy than men. Part of my goal in writing about this subject is to shine a bright light on the ways gender stereotypes are hidden within the scientific language of biology: exposed in such a light I hope they will lose much of their power to harm us.

To begin with some 17th-century fantasies that men saw when they looked at sperm through the microscope, Anthony van Leeuwenhoek observed animalcules in fresh ejaculate, which were "composed of such a multitude of parts as compose our bodies."[2] Hartsoeker claimed that the sperm contained a homunculus, a tiny but fully formed man supposed to be embodied in the male sperm.[3]

Contemporary accounts of gametes are perhaps more complex than these early views, but nonetheless they contain some elements of a scientific fairy tale. At a fundamental level, all major scientific textbooks depict male and female

Reprinted with the permission of the University of Chicago Press from *Signs: Journal of Women in Society*, 1991, Vol. 16, no. 3, © 1991 by the University of Chicago: all rights reserved; and of Pharmaceutical Marketing Services, Inc. from *Orgyn*, 1994, no. 4.

reproductive organs as systems for the production of valuable substances, such as eggs and sperm.[4] In the case of women, the monthly cycle is described as being designed to produce eggs and prepare a suitable place for them to be fertilized and grown—all to the end of making babies. But the enthusiasm ends there. By extolling the female cycle as a productive enterprise, menstruation must necessarily be viewed as a failure. Medical texts describe menstruation as the "debris" of the uterine lining, the result of necrosis or death of tissue. The descriptions imply that a system has gone awry, making products of no use, not to specification, unsalable, wasted, scrap. An illustration in a widely used medical text shows menstruation as a chaotic disintegration of form, complementing the many texts that describe it as "ceasing," "dying," "losing," "denuding," "expelling."[5]

Male reproductive physiology is evaluated quite differently. One of the texts that sees menstruation as failed production employs a sort of breathless prose in its description of the maturation of sperm: "The mechanisms which guide the remarkable cellular transformation from spermatid to mature sperm remain uncertain.... Perhaps the most amazing characteristic of spermatogenesis is its sheer magnitude: the normal human male may manufacture several hundred million sperm per day."[6]

In the classic text *Medical Physiology*, edited by Vernon Mountcastle, the male/female, productive/destructive comparison is more explicit: "Whereas the female *sheds* only a single gamete each month, the seminiferous tubules *produce* hundreds of millions of sperm each day" (emphasis mine).[7] The female author of another text marvels at the length of the microscopic seminiferous tubules, which, if uncoiled and placed end to end, "would span almost one-third of a mile!" She writes, "In an adult male these structures produce millions of sperm cells each day." Later she asks, "How is this feat accomplished?"[8] None of these texts expresses such intense enthusiasm for any female processes. It is surely no accident that the "remarkable" process of making sperm involves precisely what, in the medical view, menstruation does not: production of something deemed valuable.[9]

One could argue that menstruation and spermatogenesis are not analogous processes and, therefore, should not be expected to elicit the same kind of response. The proper female analogy to spermatogenesis, biologically, is ovulation. Yet ovulation does not merit enthusiasm in these texts either. Textbook descriptions stress that all of the ovarian follicles containing ova are already present at birth. Far from being *produced*, as sperm are, they merely sit on the shelf, slowly degenerating and aging like overstocked inventory:

> At birth, normal human ovaries contain an estimated one million follicles [each], and no new ones appear after birth. Thus, in marked contrast to the male, the newborn female already has all the germ cells she will ever have. Only a few, perhaps 400, are destined to reach full maturity during her active productive life. All the others degenerate at some point in their development so that few, if any, remain by the time she reaches menopause at approximately 50 years of age.[10]

Note the "marked contrast" that this description sets up between male and female: the male, who continuously produces fresh germ cells, and the female, who has stockpiled germ cells by birth and is faced with their degeneration. Nor are the female organs spared such vivid descriptions. One scientist writes in a newspaper article that a woman's ovaries become old and worn out from ripening eggs every month, even though the woman herself is still relatively young: "When you look through a laparoscope . . . at an ovary that has been through hundreds of cycles, even in a superbly healthy American female, you see a scarred, battered organ."[11] To avoid the negative connotations that some people associate with the female reproductive system, scientists could begin to describe male and female processes as homologous. They might credit females with "producing" mature ova one at a time, as they're needed each month, and describe males as having to face problems of degenerating germ cells. This degeneration would occur throughout life among spermatogonia, the undifferentiated germ cells in the testis that are the long-lived, dormant precursors of sperm.

But the texts have an almost dogged insistence on casting female processes in a negative light. On the one hand, the texts celebrate sperm production because it is continuous from puberty to senescence, while they portray egg production as inferior because it is finished at birth. This makes the female seem unproductive, but some texts will also insist that it is she who is wasteful.[12] In a section heading for *Molecular Biology of the Cell*, a best-selling text, we are told that "Oogenesis is wasteful." The text goes on to emphasize that of the 7 million oogonia, or egg germ cells, in the female embryo, most degenerate in the ovary. Of those that do go on to become oocytes, or eggs, many also degenerate, so that at birth only 2 million eggs remain in the ovaries. Degeneration continues throughout a woman's life: By puberty 300,000 eggs remain, and only a few are present by menopause. "During the 40 or so years of a woman's reproductive life, only 400 to 500 eggs will have been released," the authors write. "All the rest will have degenerated. It is still a mystery why so many eggs are formed only to die in the ovaries."[13]

The real mystery is why the male's vast production of sperm is not seen as wasteful.[14] Assuming that a man "produces" 10^8 sperm per day (a conservative estimate) during an average reproductive life of 60 years, he would produce well over two trillion sperm in his lifetime. Assuming that a woman "ripens" one egg per lunar month, or 13 per year, over the course of her 40-year reproductive life, she would total 500 eggs in her lifetime. But the word "waste" implies an excess, too much produced. Assuming two or three offspring, for every baby a woman produces, she wastes only around 200 eggs. For every baby a man produces, he wastes MORE THAN ONE TRILLION (10^{12}) sperm.

How is it that positive images are denied to the bodies of women? A look at language—in this case, scientific language—provides the first clue. Take the egg and the sperm.[15] It is remarkable how "femininely" the egg behaves and how "masculinely" the sperm.[16] The egg is seen as large and passive.[17] It does not *move* or *journey*, but passively "is transported," "is swept,"[18] or even, in a popular account, "drifts"[19] along the fallopian tube. In utter contrast, sperm are small, "streamlined,"[20] and invariably active. They go on a "journey" . . . They "deliver" their genes to the egg, "activate the developmental program of the egg,"[21] and have a "velocity" that is often remarked upon.[22] Their tails are "strong" and efficiently powered.[23] Together with the forces of ejaculation, they can "propel the semen into the deepest recesses of the vagina."[24] For this they need "energy," "fuel,"[25] so that with a "whiplashlike motion and strong lurches"[26] they can "burrow through the egg coat"[27] and "penetrate" it.[28]

The relative strength of sperm is such a preoccupation that there is a substantial literature based on efforts to measure how it differs among different species, measurements that are sometimes taken to the second decimal place.[29] At its extreme, the age-old relationship of the egg and the sperm takes on a royal or religious patina. The egg coat, its protective barrier, is sometimes called its "vestments," a term usually reserved for sacred, religious dress. The egg is said to have a "corona," a crown,[30] and to be accompanied by "attendant cells."[31] It is holy, set apart and above, the queen to the sperm's king. The egg is also passive, which means it must depend on sperm for rescue. Gerald Schatten and Helen Schatten liken the egg's role to that of Sleeping Beauty: "a dormant bride awaiting her mate's magic kiss, which instills the spirit that brings her to life."[32] Egg as sleeping beauty is also graphically depicted on the cover of the journal *Cell Differentiation and Development.*[33]

Sperm, by contrast, have a "mission,"[34] which is to "move through the female genital tract in quest of the ovum."[35] A popular book, Jonathan Miller's *The Facts of Life,* has it that the sperm carry out a "perilous journey" into the "warm darkness," where some fall away "exhausted." "Survivors" "assault" the egg, the successful candidates "surrounding the prize."[36]

Part of the urgency of this journey, in more scientific terms, is that "once released from the supportive environment of the ovary, an egg will die within hours unless rescued by a sperm."[37] The wording stresses the fragility and dependency of the egg, even though the same text acknowledges elsewhere that sperm also live for only a few hours.[38]

All of the poses bestowed upon egg and sperm are multivalent, amenable to more than one interpretation. So sperm as heroic rescuer exerting all his strength to save the egg can shift to become sperm the dangerous projectile weapon. A correspondent of Ann Landers writes to warn young women how easy it is to get pregnant: "How would you like to stand in a narrow hall and have someone shoot 200 million machine gun bullets at you? With odds like this, is it any wonder a million and a half teen-agers get pregnant every year?"[39] *Discover* Magazine takes this side of the sperm's persona to an extreme in its cover article "Sperm Wars: The Battle for Conception." For example, the article states "the sperm cell is a formidable .00024-inch weapon, tipped with a chemical warhead."[40]

In 1948, in a book remarkable for its early insights into these matters, Ruth Herschberger argued that female reproductive organs are seen as biologically interdependent, while male organs are viewed as autonomous, operating independently and in isolation:

At present the functional is stressed only in connection with women: it is in them that ovaries, tubes, uterus, and vagina have endless interdependence. In the male, reproduction would seem to involve "organs" only.

Yet the sperm, just as much as the egg, is dependent on a great many related processes. There are secretions which mitigate the urine in the urethra before ejaculation, to protect the sperm. There is the reflex shutting off of the bladder connection, the provision of prostatic secretions, and various types of muscular propulsion. The sperm is no more independent of its milieu than the egg, and yet from a wish that it were, biologists have lent their support to the notion that the human female, beginning with the egg, is congenitally more dependent than the male.[41]

Bringing out another aspect of the sperm's autonomy, an article from the journal *Cell* has the sperm making an "existential decision" to penetrate the egg: "Sperm are cells with a limited behavioral repertoire, one that is directed toward fertilizing eggs. To execute the decision to abandon the haploid state, sperm swim to an egg and there acquire the ability to effect membrane fusion."[42] Is this a corporate manager's version of the sperm's activities—"executing decisions" while fraught with dismay over difficult options that bring with them very high risk?

In one photograph from the *National Geographic*, sperm are "masters of subversion." In another *National Geographic* article, "human sperm cells seek to penetrate an ovum. Foreigners in a hostile body, they employ several strategies to survive their mission . . ."[43] Even in the face of all this, sometimes the egg has her own defenses. In a Farside cartoon, the egg is seen as a housewife besieged by clever sperm who try to get a foot inside the door. Sperm as postman says "Package for you to sign for Ma'am." Sperm as phone repairman says "Need to check your lines, Ma'am" and sperm as insurance salesman says "Mind if I step inside?" *Science News* presents a more brutal effort to break into the egg's interior: "Sperm at Work" are attacking "her" with a jack hammer, sledge hammer and pick.[44]

There is another way sperm can be made to loom in importance over the egg, despite their small size. In a collection of scientific papers, an electron micrograph appeared titled "A Portrait of the Sperm."[45] Because of the enormous size of the egg in the micrograph, surrounded by tiny sperm, this is a little like showing a photo of a dog and saying it is a picture of the fleas. Of course, it is harder to photograph microscopic sperm than eggs, which are just large enough to see with the naked eye. But surely the use of the term "portrait," a term associated with the powerful and the wealthy is significant. Eggs have only micrographs or pictures, not portraits.

And the same goes for popular publications that purport to represent the latest scientific knowledge. In a recent issue of *Life* magazine, the dynamic activities of sperm and the passive response of the egg are presented yet again.[46] In "The First Days of Creation," we read, "Although few will finish, about 250 million sperm start the 5–7 inch journey from the vagina to the uterus and then on the fallopian tubes where an egg may be waiting." At "two hours" we read, "like an eerie planet floating through space, a woman's egg or ovum . . . has been ejected by one of her ovaries into the fallopian tube. Over the next several hours sperm will begin beating their tails vigorously as they rotate like drill bits into the outer wall of the egg."

Other popular materials also do their part: the popular film, "Look Who's Talking," begins with a simulation of a hugely magnified egg floating, drifting, gently bouncing along the fallopian tube of a woman who is in the midst of making love with a man. The sound track is "I Love You So" by the Chantals. Then we see, also hugely magnified, the man's sperm barreling down the tunnel of her vagina to the tune of "I Get Around" by the Beach Boys. The sperm are shouting and calling to each other like a gang of boys: "Come on, follow me, I know where I am, keep up, come on you kids, I've got the map." Then, as the egg hoves into view, they shout, "This is it, yeah, this is definitely it, this is the place, Jackpot, right here, come on, dig in you kids." And when one sperm finally pushes hard enough to open a vulvalike slit in the egg, that sperm (as his whole self is swallowed up!) cries out as if he were having intercourse: "Oh, oh, oh, I'm in!"

One portrait of sperm as weak and timid, instead of strong and powerful— so far as I know, the only such representation in Western civilization—occurs in Woody Allen's movie *Everything You Always Wanted To Know About Sex* *But Were Afraid to Ask*. Allen, playing the part of an apprehensive sperm inside a man's testicles, is scared of the man's approaching orgasm. He is reluctant to launch himself into the darkness, afraid of contraceptive devices, afraid of winding up on the ceiling if the man masturbates.

The more common picture—egg as damsel in distress, shielded only by her sacred garments; sperm as heroic warrior to the rescue—cannot be proved to be dictated by the biology of these events. While the "facts" of biology may not *always* be constructed in cultural terms, I would argue that in this case they are. The degree of metaphorical content in these descriptions, the extent to which differences between egg and sperm are emphasized, and the parallels between cultural stereotypes of male and female behavior and the character of egg and sperm all point to this conclusion.

NEW RESEARCH, OLD IMAGES

As new understandings of egg and sperm emerge, textbook gender imagery is being revised. But the new research—far from escaping the stereotypical representations of egg and sperm—simply replicates elements of textbook gender imagery in a different form. The persistence of this imagery calls to mind what Ludwik Fleck termed "the self-contained" nature of scientific thought. As he described it, "the interaction between what is already known, what remains to be learned, and those who are to apprehend it, go to ensure harmony within the system. But at the same time they also preserve the harmony of illusions, which is quite secure within the confines of a given thought style."[47] We need to understand the way in which the cultural content in scientific descriptions changes as biological discoveries unfold, and whether that cultural content is solidly entrenched or easily changed.

In all of the texts quoted above, sperm are described as penetrating the egg, and specific substances on a sperm's head are described as binding to the egg. Recently, this description of events was rewritten in a biophysics lab at The Johns Hopkins University—transforming the egg from the passive to the active party.[48]

Prior to this research, it was thought that the zona, the inner vestments of the egg, formed an impenetrable barrier. Sperm overcame the barrier by mechanically burrowing through, thrashing their tails and slowly working their way along. Later research showed that the sperm released digestive enzymes that chemically broke down the zona. Scientists presumed that the sperm used mechanical *and* chemical means to get through to the egg.

In this recent investigation, the researchers began to ask questions about the mechanical force of the sperm's tail. (The lab's goal was to develop a contraceptive that worked topically on sperm.) They discovered, to their great surprise, that the forward thrust of sperm is extremely weak, which contradicts the assumption that sperm are forceful penetrators.[49] Rather than thrusting forward, the sperm's head was now seen to move mostly back and forth. The sideways motion of the sperm's tail makes the head move sideways with a force that is 10 times stronger than its forward movement. So even if the overall force of the sperm were strong enough to mechanically break the zona, most of its force would be directed sideways rather than forward. In fact, its strongest tendency, by tenfold, is to escape by attempting to pry itself off the egg. Sperm, then, must be exceptionally efficient at *escaping* from any cell surface they contact. And the surface of the egg must be designed to trap the sperm and prevent their escape. Otherwise, few if any sperm would reach the egg.

The researchers at Johns Hopkins concluded that the sperm and egg stick together because of adhesive molecules on the surfaces of each. The egg traps the sperm and adheres to it so tightly that the sperm's head is forced to lie flat against the surface of the zona, a little bit, they told me, "like Br'er Rabbit getting more and more stuck to tar baby the more he wriggles." The trapped sperm continues to wiggle ineffectually side to side. The mechanical force of its tail is so weak that a sperm cannot break even one chemical bond. This is where the digestive enzymes released by the sperm come in. If they start to soften the zona just at the tip of the sperm and the sides remain stuck, then the weak, flailing sperm can get oriented in the right direction and make it through the zona—provided that its bonds to the zona dissolve as it moves in.

Although this new version of the saga of the egg and the sperm broke through cultural expectations, the researchers who made the discovery continued to write papers and abstracts as if the sperm were the active party who attacks, binds, penetrates, and enters the egg. The only difference was that sperm were now seen as performing these actions weakly.[50] Not until August 1987, more than three years after the findings described above, did these researchers reconceptualize the process to give the egg a more active role. They began to describe the zona as an aggressive sperm catcher, covered with adhesive molecules that can capture a sperm with a single bond and clasp it to the zona's surface.[51] In the words of their published account,

> The innermost vestment, the *zona pellucida*, is a glycoprotein shell, which captures and tethers the sperm before they penetrate it. . . . The sperm is captured at the initial contact between the sperm tip and the *zona*. . . . Since the thrust [of the sperm] is much smaller than the force needed to break a single affinity bond, the first bond made upon the tip-first meeting of the sperm and *zona* can result in the capture of the sperm.[52]

Experiments in another lab reveal similar patterns of data interpretation. Gerald and Helen Schatten set out to show that, contrary to conventional wisdom, the "egg is not merely a large, yolk-filled sphere into which the sperm burrows to endow new life. Rather, recent research suggests the almost heretical view that sperm and egg are mutually active partners."[53] This sounds like a departure from the stereotypical textbook view, but further reading reveals Schatten and Schatten's conformity to the aggressive-sperm metaphor. They describe how "the sperm and egg first touch when, from the tip of the sperm's triangular head, a long, thin filament shoots out and harpoons the egg." Then we learn that "remarkably, the harpoon is not so much fired as assembled at great speed, molecule by molecule, from a pool of protein stored in a specialized region called the acrosome. The filament may grow as much as twenty times longer than the sperm head itself before its tip reaches the egg and sticks."[54] Why not call this "making a bridge" or "throwing out a line" rather than firing a harpoon? Harpoons pierce prey and injure or kill them, while this filament only sticks. And why not focus, as the Hopkins lab did, on the stickiness of the egg, rather than the stickiness of the sperm?[55] Later in the article, the Schattens replicate the common view of the sperm's perilous journey into the warm darkness of the vagina, this time for the purpose of explaining its journey into the egg itself:

> [The sperm] still has an arduous journey ahead. It must penetrate farther into the egg's huge sphere of cytoplasm and somehow locate the nucleus, so that the two cells' chromosomes can fuse. The sperm dives down into the cytoplasm, its tail beating. But it is soon interrupted by the sudden and swift migration of the egg nucleus, which rushes toward the sperm with a velocity triple that of the movement of chromosomes during cell division, crossing the entire egg in about a minute.[56]

Like Schatten and Schatten and the biophysicists at Johns Hopkins, another researcher has recently made discoveries that seem to point to a more interactive view of the relationship of egg and sperm. This work, which Paul Wassarman conducted on the sperm and eggs of mice, focuses on identifying the specific molecules in the egg coat (the zona pellucida) that are involved in egg-sperm interaction. At first glance, the descriptions fit the model of an egalitarian relationship. Male and female gametes "recognize one another," and "interactions . . . take place between sperm and egg."[57]

But an article in *Scientific American* summarizing Wassarman's work begins with a vignette that presages the dominant motif of their presentation: "It has been more than a century since Hermann Fol, a Swiss zoologist, peered into his microscope and became the first person to see a sperm penetrate an egg, fertilize it and form the first cell of a new embryo."[58] This portrayal of the sperm as the active party—the one that *penetrates* and *fertilizes* the egg and *produces* the embryo—is not cited as an example of an earlier, now outmoded view. In fact, the author reiterates the point later in the article: "Many sperm can bind to and penetrate the zona pellucida, or outer coat, of an unfertilized mouse egg, but only one sperm will eventually fuse with the thin plasma membrane surrounding the egg proper (*inner sphere*), fertilizing the egg and giving rise to a new embryo."[59]

The imagery of sperm as aggressor is particularly startling in this case: The main discovery being reported is isolation of a particular molecule *on the egg coat* that plays an important role in fertilization! Wassarman's choice of language sustains the picture. He calls the molecule that has been isolated, ZP3, a "sperm receptor." By allocating the passive, waiting role to the egg, Wassarman can continue to describe the sperm as the one who takes action, who makes it all happen:

> The basic process begins when many sperm first attach loosely and then bind tenaciously to receptors on the surface of the egg's thick outer coat, the zona pellucida. Each sperm, which has a large number of egg-binding proteins on its surface, binds to many sperm receptors on the egg. More specifically, a site on each of the egg-binding proteins fits a complementary site on a sperm receptor, much as a key fits a lock.[60]

With the sperm designated as the "key" and the egg the "lock," it is obvious which one acts, and which one waits for something to act upon it. Could this imagery not be reversed, letting the sperm (the lock) wait until the egg produces the key? Or could we speak of two halves of a locket matching, and regard the matching itself as the action that initiates the fertilization?

SOCIAL IMPLICATIONS: THINKING BEYOND

All three of these revisionist accounts of egg and sperm can't seem to escape the hierarchical imagery of older accounts. Even though each new account gives the egg a larger and more active role, taken together they bring into play another cultural stereotype: woman as a dangerous and aggressive threat. In the Hopkins lab's revised model, the egg ends up as the female aggressor who "captures and tethers" the sperm with her sticky zona, rather like a spider lying in wait in her web.[61] The Schatten lab has her nucleus "interrupt" the sperm's dive with a "sudden and swift" rush by which she "clasps the sperm and guides its nucleus to the center."[62] Wassarman's description of the surface of the egg "covered with thousands of plasma membrane-bound projections, called microvilli" that reach out and clasp the sperm adds to the spiderlike imagery.[63]

These images grant the egg an active role but at the cost of appearing disturbingly aggressive. Images of woman as dangerous and aggressive, the *femme fatale*, victimizing men, are widespread in Western literature and culture.[64] More specifically, there is a widespread theme connecting the spider as an image with the idea of an engulfing and devouring mother.[65] Some examples are the logo of the TV series "Charlie's Angels," in which these strong women combine to form the silhouette of a spider; the aggressive figure of a female spider in many comics and films; and the ad for the London Zoo featuring Daphne, the spider who gives fatal bites to all her male mates. New data did not lead scientists to eliminate gender stereotypes in their descriptions of egg and sperm. Instead, they simply described egg and sperm in different, but no less damagingly stereotypical terms.

The lability of the imagery that can be attached to egg and sperm, standing in as they do for women and men, is illustrated by a cartoonist's response to the new scientific finding that the egg plays an active role in conception. Oliphant depicts the egg as a fickle coquette, even a cock-tease. And in his second generation egg and sperm cartoon, Gary Larson reflects the latest scientific news about the way sperm may cooperate to enable the fittest to reach the egg. These scientific findings, widely reported in the popular press, provide room simultaneously for male bonding and male aggression. Based on research in rats, it was reported that some sperm cells "seem to play an almost altruistic role, giving up their own chances of reproductive success to help the top-seeded sperm in an ejaculation." As in football, "some cells carry the ball while others block the opposition."[66] Interestingly, the general press coverage of this scientific research was far more low key and less laden with metaphor than the actual scientific paper in which it was reported. In that paper, we get a taste of the more vivid language used among researchers: one type of sperm are "kamikaze-sperm" who are not "egg-get-ers." Another type, called "vanguard," have as their function to "seek and destroy" sperm deposited by other males.[67] The commercial appeal of different sperm-(men) having different abilities has already been put to use in a Black Label beer ad campaign in Canada. Ads featured "thousands of sperm cells swimming around with music from the 'Mission Impossible' television series. Then one Black Label sperm cell breaks away from the pack. 'The idea being that when it comes to conception, all it takes is one sperm cell to impregnate the egg and that Black Label is the lone beer to drink,' explained D'Amico [from the firm that handles the Black Label advertising account]."[68]

Can we envision a less stereotypical view? Biology itself provides another model that could be applied to egg and sperm. The cybernetic model—with its feedback loops, flexible adaptation to change, coordination of the parts within a whole, evolution over time, and changing response to the environment—is common in genetics, endocrinology, and ecology and has a growing influence in medicine generally.[69] This model shifts our imagery from the negative, in which the female reproductive system is castigated both for not producing eggs after birth and for producing (and thus wasting) too many eggs overall, to more positive imagery. The female reproductive system could be seen as responding to the environment (pregnancy or menopause), adjusting to monthly changes (menstruation), and flexibly changing from reproductivity after puberty to nonreproductivity later in life.

The sperm and egg's interaction could also be described in cybernetic terms. J.F. Hartman's research in reproductive biology showed 15 years ago that if an egg is killed by being pricked with a needle, live sperm cannot get through the zona.[70] Clearly, this evidence demonstrates that the egg and sperm *do* interact on more mutual terms, making biology's refusal to portray them that way all the more disturbing.

If we used cybernetic imagery, we would do well to be aware that this imagery is hardly neutral. In some cases cybernetic models have been an important part of the imposition of social control. These models inherently provide a way of thinking about a "field" containing interacting components. Once the field can be seen, it can become the object of new forms of knowledge. This knowledge then can allow new forms of social control to be exerted over the components of the field. For example, during the 1950s, a new medical field was recognized, in the form of the psychosocial *environment* of the patient: the patient's family and its psychodynamics. This new environment came to be the focus of study by professions such as social work and the resulting knowledge became one means of further control of the patient. Patients began to be seen not as isolated bodies, but as psychosocial entities located in an "ecological" system: management of "the patient's psychology was a new entré to patient control."[71]

We have every reason to think the models biologists use to describe their data can have important social effects. In the 19th century, the social and natural sciences strongly influenced each other: the social ideas of Malthus about how to avoid the natural increase of the poor inspired Darwin's *Origin of Species*.[72] Once the *Origin* stood as a description of the natural world, complete with competition and market struggles, then it could be reimported into social science as social darwinism, to justify the social order of the time. What we are seeing now is similar: the importation of cultural ideas about passive females and heroic males into the "personalities" of gametes. This amounts to the "implanting of social imagery on representations of nature so as to lay a firm basis for reimporting exactly that same imagery as natural explanations of social phenomena."[73]

Further research would be able to show us what kind of social effects the biological imagery of egg and sperm is having today. At the very least the imagery provides one context in which some of the hoariest old stereotypes about weak female damsels in distress and strong male rescuers are kept alive. That these stereotypes are now being written in at the level of the *cell* constitutes a powerful move to make them seem so natural as to be beyond reach of alteration.

The imagery might also encourage us to imagine that what results from the interaction of egg and sperm—a fertilized egg—is the result of intentional "human" action *at the cellular level*. In other words, whatever the intentions of the human couple, in this microscopic "culture," a cellular "bride" (or "*femme fatale*") and a cellular "groom" (or her victim) make a cellular baby. Rosalind Petchesky makes the point that through visual representations such as sonograms, we are given "*images* of younger and younger, and tinier and tinier, fetuses being 'saved'."

This leads to "the point of viability being 'pushed back' *indefinitely.*"[74] Endowing egg and sperm with intentional action, a key aspect of personhood in our culture, lays the foundation for the point of viability being pushed back to the moment of fertilization. This in turn seems likely to add to our willingness to accept new technological developments and new forms of scrutiny and manipulation, for the benefit of these inner "persons": court-ordered restrictions on a pregnant woman's activities to protect her fetus, the rescinding of abortion rights, fetal surgery, and amniocentesis, to name but a few examples.[75]

Soberingly, even if we succeed in substituting more egalitarian, interactive metaphors to describe the activities of egg and sperm, and manage to avoid the pitfalls of cybernetic models, we would still be participating in the endowing of cellular entities with life and personhood. This process, rather than the details of what kind of personalities cells are given, may turn out to be most crucial for enhancing the social effects of biological imagery.

One clear feminist challenge is continually to "wake up" "sleeping" metaphors in science, such as those involved in descriptions of the egg and the sperm. Although the literary convention is to call such metaphors "dead," they are not so much "dead" as sleeping, hidden within the scientific content of texts, and the more powerful for it.[76] Waking such metaphors up, by making ourselves more aware of when we are projecting cultural imagery onto what we study, will improve our ability to investigate and understand nature. Waking such metaphors up, by making ourselves more aware of their implications, is one way of robbing them of their power to naturalize our social conventions about gender.

NOTES

1. Portions of this essay were published in *Signs*, 16 (1991):485–501. I am grateful for permission to use these materials here. I am also grateful to the many people in the United States, England, and Canada who have been sending me ads, cartoons, newspaper articles, and observations in the years since this paper was first published.
2. John Farley, *Gametes and Spores: Ideas about Sexual Reproduction 1750–1914* (Baltimore: Johns Hopkins University Press, 1982), 18–19.
3. Farley, 20.
4. The textbooks I consulted are the main ones used in classes for undergraduate premedical students or medical students (or those held on reserve in the library for these classes) during the past few years at The Johns Hopkins University. These texts are widely used at other universities in the country as well.
5. Arthur C. Guyton, *Physiology of the Human Body*, 6th ed. (Philadelphia: Saunders College Publishing, 1984), 624.
6. Arthur J. Vander, James H. Sherman, and Dorothy S. Luciano, *Human Physiology: The Mechanisms of Body Function*, 3rd ed. (New York: McGraw-Hill, 1980), 483–84.
7. Vernon B. Mountcastle, *Medical Physiology*, Vol. 2, 14th ed. (London: The C.V. Mosby Co., 1980), 1624.
8. Eldra Pearl Solomon, *Human Anatomy and Physiology* (New York: CBS College Publishing, 1983), 678.
9. For elaboration, see Emily Martin, *The Woman in the Body: A Cultural Analysis of Reproduction* (Boston: Beacon Press, 1987), pp. 27–53.

10. Vander, et al., 568.

11. Melvin Konner, "Childbearing and Age," *The New York Times Magazine* (Dec. 27, 1987), 22–23 esp. 22.

12. I have found but one exception to the opinion that the female is wasteful: "Smallpox being the nasty disease it is, one might expect nature to have designed antibody molecules with combining sites that specifically recognize the epitopes on smallpox virus. Nature differs from technology, however: it thinks nothing of wastefulness. (For example, rather than improving the chance that a spermatozoon will meet an egg cell, nature finds it easier to produce millions of spermatozoa.)" Niels Kaj Jerne, "The Immune System," *Scientific American*, vol. 229, no. 1, p. 53. Thanks to a *Signs* reviewer for bringing this reference to my attention.

13. Bruce Alberts, et al., *Molecular Biology of the Cell* (New York: Garland Publishing, Inc., 1983), 795.

14. In her essay "Have Only Men Evolved?," *Women Looking at Biology Looking at Women: A Collection of Feminist Critiques*, eds. Ruth Hubbard, Mary Sue Henifen, and Barbara Fried (Boston: G.K. Hall, 1979), 7–36, esp. 24–25, Ruth Hubbard points out that sociobiologists have said the female invests more energy than the male in the production of her large gametes. This explains why the female provides parental care. Hubbard questions whether it "really takes more 'energy' to generate the one or relatively few eggs than the large excess of sperms required to achieve fertilization." For further critique of how the greater size of eggs is interpreted in sociobiology, see Donna Haraway, "Investment Strategies for the Evolving Portfolio of Primate Females," in *Body/Politics*, eds. Mary Jacobus, Evelyn Fox Keller, and Sally Shuttleworth (New York: Routledge), 155–56.

15. The sources I used for this article provide compelling information on interactions among sperm. Lack of space prevents me from taking up this theme here, but the elements include competition, hierarchy, and sacrifice. For a newspaper report, see Malcolm W. Browne, "Some Thoughts on Self Sacrifice," *The New York Times* (1988), C6. For a literary rendition, see John Barth, "Night-Sea Journey," *Lost in the Funhouse* (Garden City, NY: Doubleday, 1968), 3–13.

16. Carol Delaney, "The Meaning of Paternity and the Virgin Birth Debate," *Man* 21 (1986): 234–48, discusses the difference between this scientific view that women contribute genetic material to the fetus and long-standing Western folk theories that the origin and identity of the fetus comes from the male, as in the metaphor of planting a seed in soil.

17. For a suggested direct link between purportedly passive eggs and active sperm and human behavior, see Erik H. Erikson, "Inner and Outer Space: Reflections on Womanhood," *Daedalus* 93 no. 2 (1964): 582–606, esp. 591.

18. Guyton, 619, and Mountcastle, 1609.

19. Jonathan Miller and David Pelham, *The Facts of Life* (New York: Viking Penguin Inc., 1984).

20. Alberts, et al., 796.

21. Alberts, et al., 796.

22. William F. Ganong, *Review of Medical Physiology*, 7th ed. (Los Altos, CA: Lange Medical Publications, 1975), 322.

23. Alberts, et al., 796.

24. Guyton, 615.

25. Solomon, 683.

26. Vander, et al. (1985), 580.

27. Alberts, et al., 796.

28. All biology texts quoted above.

29. D. P. L. Green, "Sperm Thrusts and the Problem of Penetration," *Biological Review*, Vol. 63 (1988): 79–105.

30. Solomon, 700.

31. A. Beldecos, et al., "The Importance of Feminist Critique for Contemporary Cell Biology," *Hypatia*, (1988).

32. Gerald Schatten and Helen Schatten, "The Energetic Egg," *Medical World News*, 23 (1984): 51–53, esp. 51.

33. Vol. 29, no. 1 (1990).

34. Alberts, et al., 796.

35. Guyton, 613.

36. Miller and Pelham, 7.

37. Alberts, et al., 804.

38. Alberts, et al., 801.

39. Ann Landers, *Des Moines Register*, Sept. 16, 1990.

40. Meredith F. Small, "Sperm Wars," *Discover*, 12 (1991):48–53, esp. 51.

41. Ruth Herschberger, *Adam's Rib* (New York: Pelligrini and Cudaby, 1948, esp. 84). I am indebted to Ruth Hubbard for telling me about Herschberger's work, at a point when this paper was already in draft form.

42. Bennett M. Shapiro, "The Existential Decision of a Sperm," *Cell*, 49 (1987): 293–4, esp. 293.

43. Peter Jaret, "Our Immune System: The Wars Within," *National Geographic*, 169 (1986):702–35, esp. 731.

44. *Science News*, vol. 138 (1990).

45. Lennart Nilsson, "A Portrait of the Sperm," in *The Functional Anatomy of the Spermatozoan*, ed. Bjorn A. Afzelius (New York: Pergamon Press, 1975), pp. 79–82.

46. "The First Days of Creation," *Life*, Vol. 14, no. 10 (1990): 26–43. Photographs by Lennart Nilsson.

47. Ludwik Fleck, *Genesis and Development of a Scientific Fact*, ed. Thaddeus J. Trenn, Robert K. Merton (Chicago: University of Chicago Press, 1979), 38.

48. Jay M. Baltz carried out the research I describe when he was a graduate student in the Thomas C. Jenkins Department of Biophysics at Johns Hopkins University.

49. Far less is known about the physiology of sperm than comparable female substances, which some feminists claim is no accident. Greater scientific scrutiny of female reproduction has long enabled the burden of birth control to be placed on women. The researchers' discovery, for instance, did not depend on development of any new technology. The experiments made use of glass pipettes, a manometer, and a simple microscope, all of which have been available for more than 100 years.

50. Jay Baltz and Richard A. Cone, "What Force Is Needed to Tether a Sperm?" abstract for Society for the Study of Reproduction, 1985; Jay Baltz and Richard A. Cone, "Flagellar Torque on the Head Determines the Force Needed to Tether a Sperm," abstract for Biophysical Society, 1986.

51. Jay M. Baltz, David F. Katz, and Richard A. Cone, "The Mechanics of the Sperm-Egg Interaction at the Zona Pellucida," *Biophysical Journal* 54 (1988):643–654. Lab members were all somewhat familiar with work on metaphors in the biology of female reproduction. Richard Cone, who runs the lab, is my husband and he talked with them about my earlier research on the subject from time to time. Even though my current research focusses on biological imagery and I heard about the lab's work from my husband every day, I myself did not recognize the role of imagery in the sperm research

until many weeks after the entire period of research and writing I describe. Therefore I assume any awareness the lab may have had about how underlying metaphor might be guiding this particular research in certain directions must have been fairly inchoate.

52. Baltz, et al., 643, 650.
53. Schatten and Schatten, 51.
54. Schatten and Schatten, 52.
55. Surprisingly, in an article intended for a general audience, the authors do not point out that these are sea-urchin sperm and note that human sperm don't shoot out filaments at all.
56. Schatten and Schatten, 53.
57. Paul M. Wassarman, "Fertilization in Mammals," *Scientific American,* December (1988):78–84, esp. 78, 84.
58. Wassarman, 78.
59. Wassarman, 79.
60. Wassarman, 78.
61. Baltz, et al., 643, 650.
62. Schatten and Schatten, 53.
63. Wassarman (1987), 557.
64. Mary Ellman, *Thinking About Women* (New York: Harcourt Brace Jovanovich, 1968), 140; Nina Auerbach, *Woman and the Demon* (Cambridge: Harvard University Press, 1982), esp. 186.
65. Kenneth Alan Adams, "Arachnophobia: Love American Style," *Journal of Psychoanalytic Anthropology,* 4, no. 2 (1981):157–197.
66. Malcolm Brown, "Cooperation on a Small Scale," *San Francisco Chronicle,* July 17, 1988; Malcolm Brown, "Some Thoughts on Self Sacrifice," *New York Times,* July 5, 1988, C6.
67. Mark A. Bellis, R. Robin Baker, and Matthew J. G. Gage, "Variation in Rat Ejaculates Consistent with the Kamikaze-Sperm Hypothesis," *Journal of Mammalogy,* 71, no. 3 (1990):479–80.
68. Brian Dunn, "Adventurous Advertising," *The Gazette,* Montreal, July 12, (1993) F8–9.
69. William Ray Arney and Bernard Bergen, *Medicine and the Management of Living* (Chicago: University of Chicago Press, 1984).
70. J. F. Hartman, R. B. Gwatkin, and C. F. Hutchison, "Early Contact Interactions Between Mammalian Gametes *In Vitro,*" *Proc. Nat. Acad. Sci. (U.S.),* 69, no. 10 (1972):2767–2769.
71. Arney and Bergen, 68.
72. Ruth Hubbard, "Have Only Men Evolved?" in *Discovering Reality: Feminist Perspectives on Epistemology, Metaphysics, Methodology, and Philosophy of Science,* eds. Sandra Harding and Merrill B. Hintikka (Dordrecht: D. Reidel Publishing Company, 1983), 51–52.
73. David Harvey, personal communication.
74. Rosalind Petchesky, "Fetal Images: The Power of Visual Culture in the Politics of Reproduction," *Feminist Studies,* 13, no. 2 (Summer 1987):263–92, esp. 272.
75. Rita Arditti, Renate Klein, and Shelley Minden, *Test-tube Women* (London: Pandora Press, 1984). Ellen Goodman, "Whose Right to Life?" *The Sun,* (Nov. 17, 1987). Tamar Lewin, "Courts Acting to Force Care of the Unborn," *New York Times,* (Nov. 23, 1987): A1 and B10. Susan Irwin and Brigitte Jordan, "Knowledge, Practice, and Power: Court-Ordered Cesarean Sections," *Medical Anthropology Quarterly,* 1, no. 3 (Sept. 1987):319–34.
76. Thanks to Elizabeth Fee and David Spain, who made points related to this on separate occasions.

Unnatural Births: Cesarean Sections in the Discourse of the "Natural Childbirth" Movement

Helena Michie
Naomi R. Cahn

The natural childbirth movement in the United States and Britain has done much over the past twenty years to change women's relations to institutionalized medicine, to labor and childbirth, and, even more fundamentally, to how women understand and live within their bodies. The movement has also made significant changes within medical institutions themselves. Hospitals across the United States, for instance, now routinely offer some version of childbirth education that often includes some aspect of natural childbirth. Proponents of natural childbirth have also produced innumerable books and articles, from academic analyses of birthing practices to how-to-manuals for expectant parents. Although, as I will discuss in some detail below, there is some confusion about what constitutes natural childbirth, self-identified proponents and practitioners tend to locate the origin of the movement and of their own positions in the paradigm-breaking work of Lamaze and Grantly Dick-Read at the beginning of this century. All have attempted systematically to intervene in what they see as the increased (and increasing) medicalization of birthing practices in this and other countries and to offer as an alternative some account and experience of birth less dependent on medical intervention and technology.

Despite the successes of the movement, the term "natural childbirth" and the series of practices to which that term refers is a complex and contested one. A number of writers and practitioners from within the natural childbirth movement bemoan what they see as the impoverishment or appropriation of the term. As sociologist Barbara Katz Rothman puts it, " 'Natural childbirth' is a slippery concept: it may mean anything from there being no surgical incision at the time of birth (episiotomy), whether or not the woman was conscious, to consciousness alone, even with an epidural or spinal anaesthetic" (Rothman 1982:79). Cohen and Estner echo this uneasy sense of the increasing capaciousness of the term in their popular book on cesarean prevention, *Silent Knife.* "Suzanne Arms remarks that 'natural childbirth in America today may mean anything short of a cesarian section.' We fear that natural childbirth may soon include cesarian section!" (Cohen and Estner 1983:117). Rothman cites the example of a 1974 television show celebrating the labor of a woman who was using Lamaze breathing techniques associated with the natural childbirth movement, but was also numbed by an epidural and "strapped to the delivery table." "How did this come to be the 1970s resolution of the natural-childbirth movement?" Rothman asks (Rothman 1982:79).

Rothman's not-quite-rhetorical question exhibits an underlying structure common to much discourse about natural childbirth. I call this structure a dysphoric narrative, a story that begins with a relatively positive situation and describes how that situation deteriorates over time. This structuring of the dysphoric narrative characterizes language about natural childbirth on at least three levels: first, on the level of a macrohistory in which childbirth moves from the realm of nature into the realm of culture as the medical profession begins to take over the process of birthing in the mid-nineteenth century; second, on the level of a more limited or microhistory of the last two decades in the United States in which feminist gains in the natural childbirth movement are vitiated as natural childbirth is appropriated and deformed by institutional medicine; and third, on the level of individual birth narratives with which many books on childbirth begin. Typically, in these stories, a woman prepares for or expects a natural childbirth only to have her labor interfered with by a sequential array of medical interventions. Rothman's critique of the "slipperiness" of the term obviously enters the debate at the second level, where a specifically feminist *movement* gives way to classes held in hospitals staffed by hospital employees. Finally, Rothman argues, the more appropriate—although still problematic—term is "prepared childbirth" (Rothman 1982:79).

The meaning of the term "natural childbirth" is not, however, the only arena of contestation. The political allegiances of those who practice and/or advocate natural childbirth are extremely diverse, especially as they pertain to the role of women. Many authors of books advocating natural childbirth point out that the founders of the movement, especially Lamaze and Dick-Read, were hardly feminists. Dick-Read's methods depended on an equation of women and maternity and a passive acceptance by women of medical expertise (Michaelson and Contributors 1988:5). Perhaps more relevant to the evolution of natural childbirth today is the unlikely alliance between, as Rothman calls them, "feminists" and "traditionalists." The home-birth movement, perhaps the most committed wing of the natural childbirth movement, draws from several very different groups.

> Some of the women come from the feminist health movement, women who have been fighting for abortion rights and see birth as another issue in reproductive freedom. A very different group sees the husband/father as having a right to be with his

wife, and birth as belonging to his territory. And still others, such as a home-birth group in Kansas see birth as bringing genuine fulfillment to husband and wife, concluding that birth belongs in the bedroom. Feminists, traditionalists, spiritualists, and sensualists: a puzzlement. . . . (Rothman 1982:32)

This "puzzlement" derives, I think, from a paradox at the heart of the natural childbirth movement whose rhetorical location is the charged and resonant term "nature" itself. Over the last twenty years, of course, feminist theorists have been deeply divided over the relation of women to nature, with liberal and materialist feminists seeking to interrupt the equation of women and nature so central to hegemonic culture, and matriarchal and cultural feminists reappropriating and celebrating that connection. The very existence of the debate indicates the degree to which nature cannot be used unproblematically with reference to feminist concerns; in a culture that has traditionally chastised women in the name of the natural, it is hard to see how the term can be completely unanchored from its prescriptive and proscriptive cultural functions, especially as it applies to discussions about women's bodies.

While I share with other feminists an abiding concern with the institutionalization and medicalization of childbirth, as well as an urgent sense of the necessity for resistance to a wide range of pregnancy management and childbirth practices including the thoughtless introduction of technology into routine labor, the routinizing of cesarean sections, and the more general cultural policing of the female reproductive body, I question whether this resistance should take place from within the idiom of the natural. This paper is an exploration of that idiom in feminist and protofeminist[1] discourse about childbirth. Throughout my discussion I try to show how the natural is embedded in other discursive and cultural systems historically oppressive to women. While feminist scholars have done important and productive work untangling hegemonic medical discourse, no one, to my knowledge, has looked at the implications of feminist counter-discourse of birthing (Rothman 1986; see also Summey 1986). While feminist scholars have appropriately seen hegemonic birthing methods in the United States as an initiation into cultural formations, no one has looked at how natural childbirth discourse itself serves as a cultural initiation (Davis-Floyd 1988). The larger project of which this is a part performs what some feminist literary scholars have called "symptomatic readings" of feminist and protofeminist birthing discourse. Such readings typically look for textual "symptoms"—clumsy or revealing metaphors, mistakes, or odd phrasings—as evidence for underlying assumptions that may or may not be part of the author's conscious intention. My work focuses on the appearance of metaphors of "home," "autonomy," and "rights" in the discourse of natural childbirth. Identifying and following out metaphors of nature and the natural seem especially fundamental to any understanding of women's relations to their bodies.

In this reading, I will focus on the idiom of the natural as it appears in discussions of cesarean sections written by natural childbirth proponents. The first part of this paper explores the special status of the cesarean in the feminist discourse of natural childbirth, while subsequent sections explore the implication of the lexicon of the natural for assumptions about femininity, sexuality, and self-hood. Throughout the paper I draw from a variety of sources which I loosely bring together with the somewhat clumsy locutions "feminist and protofeminist discourse" and "natural childbirth discourse." Most of my sources announce their allegiance to the natural childbirth movement; many but not all of the authors identify themselves and/or their projects as feminist. In preparing to write this essay, I read academic and popular sources—from articles on medical anthropology to popular how-to books—in an attempt to unravel their multiple and conflicted relations to the natural. My goal is neither to prescribe nor to proscribe any particular set of birthing practices for women; this reading attempts instead to intervene in the *rhetorical* practices of the natural childbirth movement in order that women who make individual decisions about pregnancy and birthing not be limited to a prescriptive notion of the "natural."

UNNATURAL BIRTHS

Many accounts of the impoverishment of natural childbirth, on all three narrative levels, end with a cesarean. As Rothman points out in her introduction to the revised edition of her 1982 *In Labor*, by 1991 the "cesarian epidemic (had grown) so rapidly that even the most mainstream caregivers became concerned" (Rothman 1982:5). Most statistical accounts show the national cesarean rate in the United States at about one-quarter to one-third of all births, while many advocates of natural childbirth think that the appropriate figure should be somewhere from 3–5 percent. Natural childbirth advocates point out that the cesarean rate has increased steadily over the last twenty years, although some think it might have peaked in the late 1980s. If feminist macro- and microhistories of childbirth typically end with the present "epidemic" of cesareans in the United States, many personal stories of natural birth gone wrong end with the birthing woman undergoing a C-section. If cesareans function as the ending to a dysphoric narrative of childbirth, they also register as signs or symptoms in those narratives. As Cohen and Estner put it, the cesarean is "the ultimate unnatural birth" (Cohen and Estner 1983:xv). Anthropologist Shelly Romalis goes even further; in her complaint about "the cultural acceptance of the Cesarian (sic) 'birth' (as it is being referred to by childbirth educators and enlightened physicians)," (Romalis 1981:24) the "sic," the quotation marks around "birth," the parentheses, and the ironic use of "enlightened," drive an orthographic and political wedge between the terms "cesarian" and "birth," reframing "cesarian birth" as an oxymoron. Stripped of its status as a birth, the cesarean loses its connection to the female body, which acts rhetorically as a guarantor of the natural. The formulation "cesarian 'birth,' " then, repeats the presumed violence of the cesarean, stripping the experience of its connection to the female body.

This stripping, of course, dehumanizes the woman giving birth (I choose to use this formulation instead of "having the operation" for my own rhetorical purposes) and denies her any agency in an attempt to drive home the agency the cesarean apparently denies her. For example, Summey argues that a cesarean "involves little or no participation of the birthing woman or her family" (Eakins 1986:182). While it certainly is true that cesareans take the place of active labor, the definition of "participation" seems unnecessarily narrow. Perhaps more telling in the dehumanization of the woman undergoing a cesarean is the repeated alignment of her operation with her identity. Many writers refer to women who give birth via cesarean as "cesarian women" or "cesarian mothers." An example from Cohen and Estner should give the flavor of this construction of identity: "A cesarian mother grieves for her healthy body. ... Bampton explains that cesarian mothers see other new mothers caring for their babies while they cannot, and they may feel inadequate and helpless" (Cohen and Estner 1983:63).[2] Although "cesarian mothers" are agents in this sentence they are agents only insofar as they "grieve"; for some reason they "cannot care," cannot, according to cultural norms, be mothers at all. Cesarean mother, then, like cesarean birth, collapses into an oxymoron: the cesarean mother is not, in some sense, a mother at all.

It is not only the woman who is denied agency and humanity by anti-cesarean rhetoric, but also the baby who is born via the operation. In the most remarkable instance of dehumanizing rhetoric, Estner tells the story of giving birth to her second child vaginally after her first child was cesarean: "Had we not been so determined (to prevent a repeat cesaerean) before, had we not stuck to our unpopular decision, our second child would have *been another unnecessary surgical insult*" (Cohen and Estner 1983:xvii; italics mine). The formulation of the baby as "surgical insult" should alert us to the presence of a metonymic chain in which the surgery comes first to stand for the mother and then for the baby. Again, we can see an uneasy parallel between the supposed effects of the operation—in this case the possible rejection of the baby—and the rhetoric about cesareans. The rhetorical process that turns baby into "surgical insult" uncannily mimics the surgical process that intervenes in mother-infant bonding.

Up to this point in this reading, "nature" in the context of the cesarean has been postulated in opposition to something like "surgery" or "the medicalization of childbirth." The cesarean is unnatural because it is linked with technology and with the technologization of the body. The opposition between natural childbirth on the one hand and medical technology on the other distracts from the content of the term "nature" and from the complicated, problematic, and explicitly *cultural* work that term performs. While it is easy for feminists to be "against" the control of the female body by medical technology, the situation becomes more complex when nature is explicitly opposed to other constructs, such as, "unnatural femininity" or "unnatural sexuality," or when it is examined for its own political assumptions. Anti-cesarean literature remains a useful place for unraveling the series of assumptions about women, their bodies, and their sexuality that are embedded in the idiom of the natural.

If anti-cesarean discourse asserts the rights of women to control what is done to their bodies, also at stake are definitions of those bodies and of the relations of those bodies to culture. Almost universally, women are represented *as* bodies in anti-cesarean discourse. The problem, in these accounts, occurs when culture—seen almost exclusively as problematic—drives women away from a natural and unproblematic relation to their bodies. The female body, in these discussions, tends to be seen as a constant, while culture is seen as artificially shaping the needs and perceptions of that body, making for variations over time and place. As Carl Jones, in the popular *The Expectant Parent's Guide to Preventing a Cesarean Section*, succinctly puts it, "The human body has not changed, but American childbirth has" (Jones 1991:2). *Silent Knife* begins with the female body securely in place; it is a body which has not changed in "eons":

> Nature has designed a system in which a baby travels through its mother's body in order to be born: from the safety and comfort of her womb to the reassurance and comfort of her arms. It is a process that has worked for eons, one in which each step has a distinct purpose and a specific goal. . . . The design is beautiful, intricate, unique, delicately balanced, and not easily duplicated. Birth's design was patented years and years ago; the original blueprints are not accessible, nor will they ever be. (Cohen and Estner 1983:1)

As the baby travels from the mother's womb to her arms, so this passage travels from nature to culture. The "reassurance" of the baby once born is as assured as the process of gestation and labor itself. This double passage—on the level of both rhetoric and biology—is guaranteed by the agency of "nature," which serves as the first word in *Silent Knife*; it is Nature, perhaps herself a mother, who has "designed" the system. By the end of the passage, nature's designs become even more mystical as the final sentence emphasizes the inaccessibility of the "blueprint." The passive construction, "birth's design was patented," does not so much undermine as mystify the concept of agency. Nature absorbs culture as it takes on the cultural ability to "patent." The authority of nature is equated with the authority of an emphatically ahistorical and anticultural notion of time: nature has done its job "for eons," the blueprints will not "ever" be accessible.

Sometimes culture is seen in terms of its geographical rather than its historical and temporal dimensions. As Romalis notes, much American writing on the history of reproduction tends to "romanticize" childbirth in other cultures, framing it as "more natural than our own" (Romalis 1981:9). These repeated assertions of the unchangeable nature of the female body make rhetorical moves in two directions: first, they assert a historical moment and/or a place in which the body existed prior to culture, and second, they suggest that rhetorical recourse to that natural body is not in itself cultural. Both moves converge to suggest that there *is no culture of the natural*, that, in more explicitly Marxist terms, nature exists outside of ideology. Although cultural anthropologists have worked to make careful distinctions between the universal and the culture-specific aspects of childbirth, much of the material on natural childbirth does not take advantage of such work (Michaelson 1988:8–10).

GRIEVING FOR FEMININITY

The unproblematically natural female body asserted as the ground for anti-cesarean discourse is also, by and large, an unproblematically gendered one. The ideal relationship between the body and nature both depends on and constructs a notion of ideal femininity. The informing tautology of much of this discourse goes something like this: women have a natural relation to their body; the intimate connection of the body to nature is a sign of appropriate femininity. Femininity resides then in both the body itself and in the relation of that body to nature. A cesarean interrupts the relation of the body to nature at the cost of the feminine. In a long and evocative passage about the experience of disappointment following a cesarean, Cohen and Estner structure their analysis as a series of cumulative losses:

> A cesarian mother grieves for her healthy body.... She grieves about the separations from spouse, newborn, and other children. She grieves about the loss of control that Willmuth spoke about. She grieves for her self-esteem.... A cesarean woman grieves for her energy, stamina, and strength. She grieves for her femininity and for a feeling of trust and confidence in her body. (Cohen and Estner 1983:63)

The climactic loss, the last in the series, is the loss of "femininity," which becomes rhetorically equated with the other losses: the "healthy body," the closeness to spouse and children, the "control" and "energy." The discourse of loss, with the empathy it generates and the negative syntax on which it depends, obscures the fact that what is being asserted is a normative femininity that is associated with control, energy, family, and health. The generally positive and powerful associations with the feminine (more on that reference to the "spouse" later) in turn obscure the coercive dynamics of this equation: if these things are feminine, one must be feminine to have these things.

The disciplinary aspect of that femininity is hinted at in a sentence that follows closely on the end of the quoted passage: "Some women had little trust and confidence in the first place, and this may have been a factor leading to the cesarian" (Cohen and Estner 1983:62). The "cesarean woman," then, is caught in a familiar double bind of femininity; she loses her femininity as a result of the operation, but it was an incomplete or absent "trust and confidence" in her body associated with femininity that might have caused the operation in the first place. Cesareans, as I will discuss in detail below, become then both the sign of a problematic femininity and a punishment for it. The punishment, cruelly but perhaps predictably, takes the form of a further distancing of the woman from feminine norms. As one of Cohen and Estner's informants puts it: " 'I know I'm not a man, but I certainly don't feel like a woman. Is there a third sex?' " (Cohen and Estner 1983: 64). The answer, at least for Cohen and Estner in *Silent Knife*, seems to be yes. To paraphrase Betty Friedan, there are men, there are women, and there are cesarean mothers.

NATURAL SEXUALITY

Many feminist and protofeminist texts about childbirth helpfully stress the eroticism of the birthing process. For example, in her guide for pregnant women, *Your Baby, Your Way: Making Pregnancy Decisions and Birth Plans*, Sheila Kitzinger accounts in a variety of different ways for what might be called an erotics of birth. Sex serves, in her analysis, as a possible distraction from pain, and childbirth itself is explicitly seen as a potentially erotic experience.

> Sexual arousal in childbirth also releases estrogen into your circulation. This helps the uterus to contract effectively, speeds up labor, and if uterine action has been uncoordinated, can get your uterus working better and enable the cervix to open more easily. . . . For many women, the whole of childbirth is a psychosexual experience. The energy produced by the uterus, the feeling of the baby's head pressing down and all the tissues fanning out and opening up—these sensations are in themselves felt as sexual, and produce the same joyous feelings that might come from being held and caressed by a lover. (Kitzinger 1987:247)

Kitzinger, an extremely well-known British natural childbirth activist, is one of the few people to write about sexuality during childbirth without immediately translating it into heterosexual terms; she is also one of a very few writers to use the word "lover" rather than "husband" or "father" in describing any stage in the birth process. Jones combines the discourse of heterosexuality with assumptions about normative femininity in his account of the problems associated with the recovery from cesarean birth.

> After a cesarian, the father shoulders a far greater burden than would *normally* be the case [italics added]. He must (or at least he should) take off an additional week from work to be with his partner and baby in the hospital, and later on at home. He must take on a greater share of the parenting role, the housekeeping, and so forth. (Jones 1991:9)

One possible reaction to this scenario is that the father's forced participation in child care and housekeeping might be one of the few benefits of a cesarean. The passage, however, reflects an anxiety not only about the obvious difficulties attending recovery from major abdominal surgery, but about their effect on hegemonic domestic arrangements.

Heterosexuality is only one aspect of a normative sexuality that gets entangled in debates over cesarean sections. The equation of vaginal birth with femininity produces a series of cultural resonances. In an uncanny parallel to Freud's opposition of the vaginal and clitoral orgasm, vaginal birth is almost universally seen as more mature, more feminine and, of course, more intimately tied to the proper relation to reproduction. If the link between clitoral orgasm and cesarean birth seems ridiculously and dangerously celebratory, it is nonetheless true that both the cesarean and the clitoral orgasm are scandalous for their location outside of a strictly reproductive economy. The link between the privileging of the vagina in both vaginal birth and vaginal orgasm might seem, however, more productive. Both vaginal events serve rhetorically as the climax of a reproductive teleology that structures discussion about sexuality and birth. This teleology becomes clear as a structuring principle of anti-cesarean and natural childbirth discourse in its repeated conflation of female sexuality with reproduction.

Jones's *Guide* persistently makes the equation between sexuality and reproduction at the service of vaginal birth. "Like lovemaking," he says, "vaginal birth is normal. Major abdominal surgery, on the other hand, is anything but normal" (Jones 1991:4). Underlying the liberationist rhetoric of phrases like "lovemaking is normal," is a far less liberatory ideology of sexual normalcy. Jones's book can be said to be structured around an analogy between sexuality and birthing which allows the concept of normalcy to enter under the guise of liberation. In a typical warning about how modern birthing practices lead too often to cesareans he explains:

> The highly sensitive laboring woman is not likely to labor normally if she feels upset by interference, any more than lovemaking would function normally under similar conditions. Her hormonal balance is thrown off. Her uterine contractions may slow down or stop altogether. Her anxiety may be severe enough to cause fetal distress, necessitating more intervention. And all too often, the final scene is cesarian surgery. (Jones 1991:41)

The "highly sensitive" hypothetical woman is trapped here in what can only be described as the idiom of failed orgasm. The failure of labor becomes a failed sexual experience. This passage is relatively unusual—although no less problematic—because it suggests that the blame for this sexual and reproductive failure lies with some outside (male?) agency responsible for bringing the woman's physical responses to a euphoric conclusion.

UNNATURAL SELVES

It is not, finally, only sexuality that is at issue, but female subjectivity itself. Jones moves fluidly from sexuality to identity in an asserted truism: "Giving birth is part of a woman's sexuality, her self-image" (Jones 1991:8). The repeated recourse of the psychosexual, even in works as careful as Kitzinger's, suggests that labor—failed or successful—is a working out of a previous psychic state. In the suggestively titled *Birthing Normally: A Personal Growth Approach to Childbirth*, Gayle Peterson explains her holistic approach to pregnancy and labor:

> Pregnancy, labor, and birth is [*sic*] a process existing within a greater life process of each individual woman. Psychological factors, existing within the woman herself, in addition to the interaction of environment and human relationship, are apparent in the labor. Recognizing psychological beliefs and attitudes affecting labor can render greater opportunity for uncomplicated labor and birth. (Peterson 1984:8)

Embedded in the notion of the holistic is a sense that labor is not so much a process as a symptom. Preparing for labor by doing psychological work during, and perhaps even before, pregnancy can help to make easier labors, but a long or difficult labor suggests—too late?—a series of psychological problems.

The problems that surface and become legible in labor are, not surprisingly, often related to gender. In her list of problematic attitudes potentially affecting labor, Peterson names "the ability to be uninhibited," "activity vs. passivity," "victimization," "low self-esteem and body image," and "beliefs about womanhood." Nowhere is there an account of material conditions that might lead, say, to a woman's feelings of "victimization" or poor body image. In one of the few moments in the book where women's oppression is mentioned as a reality, it surfaces as one side of an almost impossibly paradoxical position a laboring woman is supposed to maintain. "If a woman's definition of womanhood is weak, fragile, or passive, or, in contrast, if identity as a female is denied in order to deny acculturation of women as weak and inferior, she suffers an identity crisis in pregnancy which, if not resolved, can be brought to a crisis situation in labor" (Peterson 1984:29). Normative femininity becomes a matter of gingerly negotiating a paradox of oppression and power. It is no wonder that, in *Birthing Normally*, even the eventual success stories involve women with inappropriate relations to femininity. In this book, as in so many others, the cesarean looms as a threat for women who have not made accommodations to normative gender ideals. Peterson offers the example of "Lana," who, late in pregnancy, had a baby in transverse position:

> Throughout pregnancy and childbirth classes, Lana remained tense and quiet. . . . As we began discussing the coming birth, it became very clear that Lana was not confronting herself with the reality of her situation. She knew she would have to go into the hospital if the baby did not turn head down, however she was not confronting herself with the inevitability of Cesarean section should the baby not turn either head down or breech by the time labor ensued. As she became aware of the physical reality of her situation, Lana put both hands on her *pregnant uterus* and wondered aloud if she was not *letting the baby turn down* due to her fear of labor and becoming a mother. (Peterson 1984:21; italics mine)

The result of this revelation is, of course, that the baby "turns" and Lana is rewarded with a six-hour labor and a healthy baby. This kind of story is repeated, with variations, throughout *Birthing Normally*. For Peterson, the issue is explicitly a matter of women taking power and gaining agency. She makes the matriarchal argument that women have reacted to oppression by becoming too much "like men" and denying their special powers in relation to labor, birth, and motherhood. Lana and others in the book are empowered by taking onto themselves the responsibility for babies in transverse or breech positions, for long labors, and for cesarean sections. While this clearly worked for the women featured in *Birthing Normally*, one might ask what happens on the other side of the "inevitable cesarean," to women who do not make the realization of their special and natural powers in time?

The psychologizing of the problematic labor experience—especially as that labor climaxes in a cesarean section—ironically embeds the idiom of the natural in the idiom of performance. Women are then caught in the double bind of natural femininity: What does it mean to fail to be natural? What does it mean to learn to be natural?

One problem with the performative, of course, is that it implies the possibility of failure. Indeed, much of the counter-discourse to natural childbirth focuses on the problem of women who "fail" to labor naturally and in how natural childbirth advocates lapse into tropes of failure or success. In describing how unlikely it is in the context of United States hospitals that a woman will have a completely unmedicated and unsurgical birth, Romalis contends that "unless a woman's labor is extremely short, . . . she is very motivated, has a physician who is a real advocate of Lamaze, and is supported by an energetic partner, her chances of *making it* are slim" (Romalis 1981:72; italics mine). In this warning the discourse of failure and emergency come together to produce a woman in personal and institutional crisis, a female birthing subject who must battle all odds to "make it." "Making it," or, perhaps more to the point, "not making it" (since this is the likely outcome) suggests, oddly enough, the lexicon of a medical emergency, an emergency which the discourse of natural childbirth claims to deemphasize.

Both proponents and critics of the natural childbirth movement must negotiate another paradox of performance: that expectations of a natural birth can contribute to a sense of failure in the event of a cesarean. As Jones puts it, "Those who have planned for a natural childbirth almost always feel the most guilt" (Jones 1991:7). Margaret Blackstone, whose *Recovering from a C Section* is aimed at consoling women who have had a cesarean through a critique of the excesses of the natural childbirth movement, states the case more colloquially:

> Postpartum is hard enough, but when you've Bradleyed or Lamazed or otherwise primed yourself for a vaginal birth only to end up on the operating table for a C section, postpartum may feel impossible. And a sense of not having done the job well enough well may ensue, taking away some of the joy of this long awaited and precious moment. When it's vaginal delivery or bust, some of us may find ourselves apologizing for a surgery that may have saved the baby's life and ours as well. (Blackstone and Homayun 1991:2)

The idiom of success is a seductive one given the teleology of natural birth. Anticesarean writer and doctor Bruce Flamm struggles with its implications, but finally succumbs:

> The discussion of "success" brings up a topic that deserves a little clarification. It is certainly true that many women have feelings of inadequacy or failure when labor ends with a cesarean section. I do not mean to perpetuate this concept, so let me clearly define what I mean by "success". . . . By "success" I mean only that the cesarean section has been avoided. . . . Essentially every medical report ever written about VBAC uses the term "success" when referring to vaginal birth. For logistical purposes this makes sense. If I were to go through every chapter and change "success" to

"labor after cesarean section culminating in a vaginal birth," this book would be much harder to read and about ten pages longer! (Flamm 1990:65)

This passage is not so much a definition as it is a restatement that vaginal birth equals success. Interestingly, Flamm's argument depends on the very notions of efficiency, routine, and precedent that are featured so frequently in the defense of cesareans: women are threatened with a labor that will be ten hours longer, his readers with an extra ten pages and more difficult reading.

Critiques of the notion of failure often fall into the same structuring assumptions about femininity as do arguments in support of natural childbirth. Blackstone finally resists what she thinks of as the hegemony of natural childbirth by the assertion that "real moms aren't macho" (Blackstone 1991:12, 43). This hardly moves beyond the discourse of natural femininity.

The fact that arguments both for and against accepting cesareans as a more or less routine intervention in the birthing process are caught up in the idiom of a normative and natural femininity should alert us to the possibility that the ground of both these arguments is shaky at best. In asserting a "nature" to which women giving birth must conform, advocates of natural childbirth run the risk of activating a series of deeply problematic ties between women and nature that are, themselves, ironically implicated in what feminists might otherwise recognize as specifically *cultural* norms of femininity and heterosexuality. Just as in other contexts some feminists have seen the idiom of "choice" as limiting to a truly liberatory discourse of reproduction, the idiom of nature sets limits on how we can conceive motherhood, parenthood, and the daily practice of living within a body culturally designated as "female."

NOTES

1. I use the term "protofeminist," not to make distinctions between something I see as "real" feminism and something else, but because I do not want to make assumptions about the politics of many of the authors I cite here, many of whom use language familiar to feminism without in any way identifying themselves as feminists or indeed as part of any political project. I am also interested, of course, in the extent to which feminist insights can be articulated in the service of specifically antifeminist positions. (See Rothman's discussion of "feminists" vs. "traditionalists," above.
2. Interestingly, not all women who have actually given birth via cesarean seem to share in the assumptions behind this dysphoric narrative. See Carolyn Sargent and Nancy Stark, "Childbirth Education and Childbirth Models: Parental Perspectives on Control, Anesthesia, and Technological Intervention in the Birth Process," *Medical Anthropology Quarterly* 3:1, March 1989. The authors found a surprisingly high level of reported satisfaction with their birth experiences among women who had undergone C-sections and had taken in-hospital birthing classes. The authors speculate that, despite disclaimers by their informants, these women may have been unduly influenced by accomodationist attitudes on the part of hospital childbirth educators. This question of true choice, of "real" as opposed to socially constructed affect reverberates through feminist discussions of reproduction.

REFERENCES

Blackstone, Margaret, with Tahira Homayun, M.D.
  1991   Recovering from a C Section. Stamford, CT: Longmeadow Press.
Cohen, Nancy Wainer, and Lois J. Estner
  1983   Silent Knife: Cesarean Prevention and Vaginal Birth after Cesarean (VBAC).
          South Hadley, MA: Bergin and Garvey Publishers.
Davis-Floyd, Robbie E.
  1988   Birth as an American Rite of Passage. *In* Childbirth in America: Anthropolog-
          ical Perspectives. South Hadley, MA: Bergin and Garvey Publishers.
          Pp. 153–172.
Flamm, Bruce L., M.D.
  1990   Birth after Cesarean: The Medical Facts. Englewood Cliffs, NY: Prentice Hall.
Jones, Carl
  1991   The Expectant Parent's Guide to Preventing a Cesarean Section. Westport, CT:
          Bergin and Garvey Publishers.
Kitzinger, Sheila
  1987   Your Baby, Your Way: Making Pregnancy Decisions and Birth Plans. New York:
          Pantheon Books.
Michaelson, Karen L. and Contributors
  1988   Childbirth in America: Anthropological Perspectives. South Hadley, MA:
          Bergin and Garvey Publishers.
Peterson, Gayle
  1984   Birthing Normally: A Personal Growth Approach to Childbirth. Berkeley:
          Shadow and Light.
Romalis, Shelly, ed.
  1981   Childbirth: Alternatives to Medical Control. Austin: University of Texas Press.
Rothman, Barbara Katz
  1982   In Labor: Women and Power in the Birthplace. New York: Norton.
  1986   The Social Construction of Birth. *In* The American Way of Birth. Pamela S.
          Eakins, ed. Pp. 104–118. Philadelphia: Temple University.
Summey, Pamela S.
  1986   Cesarean Birth. *In* The American Way of Birth. Pamela S. Eakins, ed.
          Pp. 75–195. Philadelphia: Temple University Press.
Williams, Joan
  1991   Gender Wars: Selfless Women in the Republic of Choice. *In* New York Uni-
          versity Law Review (66[December]): 1559–1619.

The Cultural Constructions of the Premenstrual and Menopause Syndromes

◻ *Dona Davis*

Like the nineteenth-century constructions of the female maladies hysteria and neurasthenia (King 1990), today's constructions of premenstrual and menopausal syndromes reflect acceptance of the increasing medicalization of women's behavior and physiological processes. Consisting of protean manifestations, comprised by ever expanding symptom lists, and existing in a nosological limbo with no specific diagnosis or confirmed etiology, each syndrome has its own history of treatment with unproven therapies and potentially adverse effects. In this chapter, anthropological data, perspectives, methods, and theories, combined with a feminist critique, will be drawn upon to challenge popular Western and biomedical constructions of the premenstrual and menopausal syndromes as a) universal, b) based in female reproductive and hormonal biology, and c) manifest in negative elaborations of biological, psychosomatic, psychological, and psychosocial symptomatologies. An alternative, culturally informed view of menstrual cycling and the cessation of menses at midlife as essentially normal, nonpathological experiences for the majority of the world's women will be presented.[1]

Seen as embedded in Western conceptualizations of women in relationship to the moral-social and natural order, the biomedical construction of the premenstrual and menopausal syndromes has emerged as a popular topic of feminist and anthropological critique. The anthropological or cross-cultural critique, however, has been more fully developed for the menopause syndrome. This has resulted in distinct themes of analysis in the two bodies of literature that have important implications for the development of social or cultural constructivist critique. The discussion that follows highlights this distinction and illustrates the important contribution cross-cultural perspectives and data can make in the assessment of what is universal or variable and what is normal or abnormal in women's experience of reproductive cycling.

THE PREMENSTRUAL SYNDROME

The Premenstrual Syndrome (PMS)[2] emerged in the medical literature in the 1980s as a psychoneuroendocrine disorder[3] whose adverse effects have far-reaching implications for individual and society. The term PMS refers to the cyclic reoccurrence in the later luteal phase of the menstrual cycle of a combination of distressing physical, psychological, and behavioral changes of sufficient severity to result in recurrent but temporary deterioration of interpersonal relationships and interference with normal activities. All symptoms are held to remit at onset of menses. Over 150 symptoms have been linked to the hormonal biology of PMS but the defining symptoms are usually identified as mood swings and feelings of being out of control. Up to 90 percent of women are said to experience symptoms; of these, 20–40 percent report mild to moderate symptoms, and 10 percent report severe symptoms (Reid 1987). Five percent of the total population are said be afflicted with PMS's latest reincarnation as a major psychiatric disorder (Suh 1993). PMS is characterized as a factor contributing to marital discord, social isolation, work inefficiency or absenteeism, accidents requiring admission to hospital, and criminal activities including child battering, theft, and murder (Reid 1987). Although originating in medical discourse, PMS has emerged as a part of popular culture. The media, adopting the medical model, has tended to portray PMS as a scientifically valid disorder for which there is effective treatment. To the extent that these beliefs are absorbed by women, they may actually come to affect their experience of PMS (Klebanov and Ruble 1994; Parlee 1987).

Conceptual and Definitional Issues and PMS

The scientific or positivist claims of PMS research have been challenged by a number of scholars who argue that the medical construction of PMS is poorly conceived and lacks definition (e.g., Abplanalp 1988; Brooks-Gunn 1986; Fausto-Sterling 1985; Gannon 1985; Golub 1988; Koeske 1983; Lander 1988; McFarlane and Williams 1990; Parlee 1982; Rodin 1992; and Zita 1989). As Fausto-Sterling (1985:101) so aptly states, "never have so many, for so long, done such poor research." A number of flaws in PMS research are noted. First, symptoms associated with PMS include physical/somatic symptoms (abdominal bloating, soreness of breasts, headache, backache), mood changes (irritability, depression, tension, anxiety and hostility) and behavioral symptoms (crying spells, feeling out of control, change in work habits, picking fights and social withdrawal), but there is a lack of agreement on which set of symptoms should be considered the defining criteria (Brooks-Gunn 1986). Second, although symptoms are supposed to coincide with the hormonal changes of the premenstrum, there is no agreement on what that time frame should be. Third, although PMS is associated with only negative features, severity of symptoms are rarely taken into account. Since there is no consensus on when normal psychological or physical stress associated with normal menstrual cycles becomes a pathological, clinical entity, prevalence rates for PMS are often overestimated. Fourth, although a large number of biological hypotheses have been proposed to explain the etiology of PMS, not one has yet received scientific confirmation (Fausto-Sterling 1985; McFarlane and Williams 1990; Parry and Rausch 1988; Schmidt et al. 1991). And fifth, despite the proliferation of profit-making PMS clinics and the continuing support of pharmaceutical companies, no claims to successful treatments have survived rigorous controlled clinical trials (Chakmakjian 1983; Green 1982; Lander 1988; Steiner and Haskett 1987). Even the efficacy of the much touted progesterone therapy has yet to be established (Freeman et al. 1990; Maxson 1988). All that has been established in numerous treatment-efficacy studies is that there is a high placebo effect.[4]

Although PMS is supposed to be a distinct clinical entity, it is often confounded with dysmenorrhea. Dysmenorrhea is primarily associated with the onset of menses and the somatic symptoms (abdominal pain or cramps, backache, and bloating), which are attributed to elevated levels of prostaglandins and respond well to newly developed treatment (Fuchs 1982). As we shall see, there is good evidence that these symptoms are universally experienced or recognized by the world's women. PMS, on the other hand, although it does include somatic symptoms that overlap with those of dysmenorrhea, is characterized primarily by premenstrual mood swings and alterations in behavior. These mental disruptions are supposedly due to reduced progesterone or high estrogen levels. Unlike the cramps of dysmenorrhea, which are clearly associated with the onset of menses, there has been a failure actually to document the mood fluctuations attributed to PMS over the menstrual cycle (Parry and Rausch 1988). The belief that moods fluctuate is, however, well documented (Parlee 1976). Confusion of the two syndromes, stemming from a failure to differentiate between women who experience bloating and cramps and women who experience mood swings, inflates reports of the number of women said to suffer from PMS. Finally, the PMS time frame that spans from two weeks before onset of menses to one week after also obscures the distinction between the two disorders (Reid 1991).

Those who question PMS as a biophysical entity do so in two ways. While some maintain that the wide range of symptoms associated with the premenstrual syndrome actually constitute a number of yet to be identified or differentiated, etiologically distinct syndromes rather than just one (Brooks-Gunn 1986; Endicott and Halbreich 1988), others would argue that the lack of a concise definition is related to the fact that PMS does not really exist as a biophysical entity, but is merely an artifact of research interests and design into which has been added a good dose of Euro-American misogyny (Caplan 1991; Fausto-Sterling 1985; Gannon 1985; Martin 1992). Three versions of the latter argument dominate the social constructivist critique of the PMS literature. These include the critical evaluation of PMS research constructs, designs, and methods; the medicalization of female reproductive functions; and the nature of PMS as a culture-bound syndrome. Each of these is described in the following section.

Methodological Issues in the Cultural Construction of PMS

Studies of PMS are criticized for poor research design and measurement problems. The first and most prominent critique is that studies only measure the degree to which women reflect the negative cultural stereotypes of menstrual experience shared by researchers who design the studies. This is especially true for a large number of quantitative studies that depend on a very narrow range of standardized attitude indices and symptom checklists (Parlee 1974). Not only do these instruments reflect stereotypes, but they actually may serve to perpetuate them among the women sampled. Second is the issue of symptom perception. The relationship between cultural stereotypes and perceptual bias has been demonstrated in a number of studies (Gannon 1985; Ruble and Brooks-Gunn 1979). Reliance on self-reports, whether retrospective (by recall) or prospective (daily diaries), is problematic since cultural beliefs have been shown to confound the data. If women are not kept blind to the purposes of the study (if they know this is a PMS study) or if they are told that they arc premenstrual (Abplanalp 1988; Ruble and Brooks-Gun 1979) they will report more mood variation than if they are blind to study purpose or believe themselves to be at midcycle. A third problem involves sampling procedures. Since the incidence of women reporting PMS is low, a very large segment of the general population must be screened to find enough women with PMS. Yet, even when clinical and nonclinical samples are compared, significant differences in symptom experience fail to emerge. Although women in their 30s and 40s are considered to be most at risk for PMS, most studies are done with samples of college women (Abplanalp 1988). Sampling also involves the problem of control or comparison groups; for example, who or what is the norm? Is it to be men, intermenstrual women, or perhaps some form of a supposedly "nonpathological" cycle like days of the week (McFarlane and Williams 1990)? Fourth, methods for determining time of ovulation are problematic. If the research design assumes the mythic 28-day cycle, then there is only a 50 percent chance of correctly determining the actual timing of ovulation for each individual woman in the sample. Also, most studies trace symptoms through only one or two cycles (Gannon 1985). Finally, problems of validity and reliability abound. Studies tend to be inferentially weak, one-shot studies, where correlation is mistaken for cause (Koeske 1983) and where categories of experience are defined through statistical analysis of easily quantifiable data. Little attention is paid to the relevance of variables being tested. For example, do attitudes reflect actual experience? Competing beliefs (Fitzgerald 1990; Laws 1990), especially those of sociocultural causation (e.g., changing expectations of female behavior, the inherent sexism of menstruation beliefs, or the social construction of emotions), are dismissed on methodological grounds as being too hard to measure.

The Feminist Critique

Western feminists raise a number of issues to challenge the biomedical conceptualizations of PMS and the authority that goes with it (Fausto-Sterling 1985).

First, they question popular and medical portrayals of premenstrual distress as an inevitable and universal consequence of normal hormonal fluctuations. Instead of being accepted as a product of biology, PMS is viewed as a reflection of the myths and stereotypes about the nature of women as naturally abnormal and maladjusted in our own society (Chrisler and Levy 1990; Fausto-Sterling 1985; Gannon 1985; Kupers 1991; Zita 1989). Alternative, more positive conceptualizations of menstruation are offered. These include menstrual joy questionnaires as well as constructions of PMS as a window of sensitivity, a time for self-reflection and insight, or a period of heightened awareness and creativity (Endicott and Halbreich 1988; Martin 1992; McFarlane and Williams 1990; Zita 1989). Second, given the potentially iatrogenic effects of treatments for PMS, (Ashton 1991; Heneson 1984; Rome 1986), feminists are concerned with exposing the muddy thinking that characterizes PMS studies. They question why PMS is seen as inherently, rather than contextually, disadvantageous (Zita 1989). Current theoretical views about the reproductive cycle are held to be inadequate to the tasks of understanding the emotional ups and downs of people functioning in a complex world (Fausto-Sterling 1985; Martin 1992).

Criticism is also targeted at Dalton's (1972) portrayal of women who suffer from PMS as victims who victimize, who, if they fail to seek treatment get what they deserve from men (Lander 1988; Zita 1989). Assumptions that the normative woman should be continually placid (Zita 1989) and that males are the standard of emotional stability are also called into question. Third, the feminist critique points to the political implications of PMS. For example, if women buy into the PMS construct then women's failure to maintain domestic harmony becomes a symptom of PMS, and PMS self-help books become manuals on how to accommodate to a man's world rather than how to change it (McFarlane and Williams 1990). PMS is criticized as a sickness label that splits women into categories of good women and bad women (Laws 1983). It trivializes and ridicules female behaviors by robbing them of their social context and by invalidating the source of their anger; and it reduces women's feelings of impotence and frustration to markers of pathology (Zita 1989). Anger is good if it groups women together to fight against oppression; it is bad if it sends them to the doctor (Martin 1992). Other politically oriented critics (Martin 1992; Kupers 1991; Fausto-Sterling 1985; and Rittenhouse 1991) view PMS and its concern with absenteeism as a backlash against women's entrance into, and demands for, equality in the labor force.

PMS as a Culture-Bound Syndrome

PMS as a social construction rather than an individual reality has been the focus of two recent anthropological portrayals of PMS as a Western culture-bound syndrome (CBS). A CBS consists of a constellation of symptoms categorized as a disease where the etiology symbolizes core meanings and reflects the preoccupations of a culture and where diagnosis and treatment are dependent on a culturally specific technology and ideology. Johnson (1987) traces the origins of PMS as a popular and medical concept to the conflict between productive/career and reproductive/family roles and expectations that accompanied women's entry into the labor force during the 1970s. PMS, as a culture-bound syndrome, Johnson argues, encodes ambiguities between and within both sets of roles. In terms of women's reproductive roles, menstruation marks women as potentially fertile but not pregnant. And in terms of women's productive roles, incapacitating symptoms at menstruation threaten to limit womens' recently realized potential for productive work. Gottleib (1988) focuses on the mood changes associated with PMS and emphasizes ideologies of ambivalence in the female personality, which are deeply embedded in, and intrinsic to, the Western understanding of women. In American culture, there are two ranges of female personality, which may be scripted on a Jekyll (the pure and selfless woman who makes a house a home) and Hyde (the out-of-control, angry, and hostile woman who makes her family suffer) continuum. Culturally legitimated PMS becomes the time a woman can express her other side. Yet, since the good is supposed to subsume the bad, PMS does not legitimate protest and women are made to feel guilty.

Neither Gottleib (1988) nor Johnson (1987) deny that women's suffering is real, but both view PMS as first and foremost a medical construction based in a specific cultural context that has far-reaching implications for our understanding of biobehavioral differences between the sexes. Although the symptoms attributed to PMS are neither unique to Western industrial cultures nor to the last twenty-five years, their configuration into a specific, medically formalized syndrome or disease category involving bizarre symptoms is unique. According to Johnson (1987) and Gottleib (1988), Western women have learned their behavior from medical scripts and PMS as a medical, legal entity has become a part of popular, lay culture. PMS as a CBS thus expresses key elements of a society's social structure and the central cultural meanings and norms that legitimize them. Similarly, Klebanov and Ruble (1994) conclude that, although there are no established hormonal factors for PMS, there are well-established psychological factors. These are the product of sociocultural learning and reflect a Western, culture-bound shaping of women's experience that facilitates attribution of stress to the menstrual cycle.

The dynamic quality of PMS as a culturally constructed or culture-specific syndrome that continues to be negotiated, is well illustrated by the recent controversy over attempts to formalize PMS into a major psychiatric syndrome—first as Late Luteal Phase Dysphoric Disorder (LLPDD) and most recently as Premenstrual Dysphoric Disorder (PMDD)—to be included in the latest edition of the American Psychiatric's Association's Diagnostic and Statistical Manual (DSM IV).[5] The present controversy over the latest incarnations of PMS involves three sets of players, all of which represent different preoccupations of Western culture. First, there are the mental health professionals who treat PMS. Second, there are the women who suffer from PMS and organized PMS action groups (Cassara 1988), who advocate the development of PMS clinics, and who lobby physicians for progesterone therapy and want the wider public to see them as genuine sufferers from a treatable biochemical disorder. The third group consists of critical feminists, who do not want to deny that some women do suffer,[6] but continue to question the reputed relationship between women's hormones and definitions of illness, as well as the recent emergence of PMS as a psychiatric rather than a gynecological issue (Tarvis 1993). This debate echoes many of the concerns already raised in this chapter and has come to dominate the literature on the medicalization or cultural construction of PMS.

PMS debuted as Late Luteal Phase Dysphoric Disorder (LLPDD) in the American Psychiatric Association's *Diagnostic and Statistical Manual of Mental Disorders III-R* in 1987.[7] It was listed in the Appendix under "Other Major Disorders Not Otherwise Specified" and proposed as a disorder in need of further research before inclusion in DSM IV could be considered. Mood swings, anger and anxiety, and feeling out of control were proposed as key symptoms of LLPDD.[8] In 1993 a controversial decision was made to include PMS, this time as Premenstrual Depressive Disorder (PMDD) in DSM IV. This time it is listed under "Depressive Disorders Not Otherwise Specified," but its criteria will remain in the Appendix as a still-to-be studied diagnosis (DeAngelis 1993). The criteria of PMDD are somewhat different from those for LLPDD. Emphasis is on the depressed and hopeless, rather than angry and anxious, feelings. The sense of being out of control has been dropped, but the notion of marked affective lability remains (Task Force on DSM-IV 1993). It is estimated that 14–45 percent of women with severe PMS (5 percent of all women) will meet the criteria for PMDD (Suh 1993). Despite the new name, the same methodological, definitional, and diagnosis-related critiques detailed above continue to characterize the research and conceptualization of these newly named disorders.[9]

Encouragement and support of research, recognition of the seriousness of women's complaints about their bodies, need for the development of treatments, and the necessity for coverage by health insurance policies are cited by those who support the inclusion of PMDD in DSM IV. Supporters contend that there is scientific evidence for PMDD and say that not including it can hurt a woman with a legitimate disorder who needs special attention and treatment (DeAngelis 1993; Rodin 1992). They suggest that PMDD may serve as a model to help us understand pathophysiology and changes in mood and behavior (Endicott and Halbreich 1988). Yet, it is of interest that the American Psychiatric Association Committee on Women (the APA is 86 percent male) has unanimously opposed including PMDD in the DSM text (see Caplan [1991] for political assessment of the in-house APA debate) and recommended that it stay entirely in the Appendix until more is learned about it (DeAngelis 1993).

The old problem of whether PMS creates or reflects women's experience characterizes the arguments of those who object to PMDD as a psychiatric diagnosis. Arguments against PMDD point to the continually flawed nature of the support studies and the tendency to keep slapping new labels on an already discredited PMS (Caplan 1991; DeAngelis 1993; Tarvis 1993). Critics ask why PMDD, with its supposed biological etiology, is listed in a manual on mental disorders while other biological disorders (e.g., thyroid abnormalities) that can also cause mood changes are not (Tarvis 1993). The link with depression is also questioned. Why should PMDD be categorized as a major form of depression while menopausal and postpartum depression are not? (DeAngelis 1993; Endicott and Halbreich 1988)[10] Most damaging, as a criticism, is the fact that despite its recent incarnation, there is no evidence for a biological marker supporting the association of PMDD with menstrual cycling. Women who complain of PMS do not differ in any biologically determined way from women who do not have PMS (Abplanalp 1988; Gannon 1985). Still others cite the small number of women who will be affected by the diagnosis (Suh 1993). There are those who maintain that the components of the syndrome may actually be a number of distinct syndromes that are yet to be determined (Brooks-Gunn 1986; Endicott and Halbreich 1988; Vander Ploeg 1990; Monagle et al. 1986). A final series of criticisms concerns the potential for misdiagnosis of more serious physical or mental problems, the reinforcement of traditional stereotypes of menstruation, and the potential for misuse of diagnosis in legal cases (e.g., child custody).

As in the case of the hysterias and neurasthenias of the nineteenth century, research results that consistently question the very existence and nature of PMS have made few inroads into the popular imagination or into clinical practice and diagnosis (Bullough and Voght 1973; King 1990). Although the methodological critiques have resulted in somewhat reconfigured symptomatologies, they have failed to bring about any substantive refinement of research method or design. Despite the most current medical characterization of PMS as primarily a depressive disorder, it is PMS and not LLPDD or PMDD that continues to capture the popular imagination. Women who seek treatment for PMS continue to seek treatment for hostility and mood swings, which they associate with the premenstrual or menstrual period. They identify themselves as suffering from PMS because of their tendency to become irritable and to exhibit a low threshold of anger. A common presenting complaint is "I have a tendency to nag and complain" (Endicott and Halbreich 1988; McFarlane and Williams 1990). Although the status of PMS as a mental disorder has focused the discourse over the social and cultural constructions of PMS, the cross-cultural literature also provides some interesting insights into the construction of PMS as a culture-bound syndrome. For, indeed, if PMS is based in biology, as the raging-hormone hypotheses of biomedicine continue to assume, there ought to be cross-cultural evidence for mood swings, be they anger, anxiety, or depression, for all women.

Cross-cultural Studies of PMS

It is ironic that the two cross-cultural studies most frequently cited as proof of the universality of PMS actually demonstrate quite the opposite. Janiger, Riffenburgh, and Kersch (1972) base their claim that PMS is a universal phenomenon, and not a disease of comfort and industrialization, on preliminary analysis of quantitative data from menstrual-cycle symptom checklists obtained in five different cultural settings.[11] Despite their claims, the researchers actually made no attempt to assess the occurrence of PMS because, as the authors put it, that would have required an arbitrary definition as to what incidence or patterns of symptoms were necessary for diagnosis of the syndrome. As in the case of so many other studies, there was no attempt to distinguish symptoms of dysmenorrhea (cramps) from the mood symptoms of PMS. Actually, data from this study show that number, type, and severity of complaints are subject to considerable variation across cultural groups. The most frequently reported symptom was that of lower-back pain (indicative of dysmenorrhea) and the least frequently reported symptom was that the woman described herself as being easily upset (indicative of PMS). Finally the authors conclude that their data do not support an etiological hypothesis based on female biology.

The same critique applies to the commonly cited World Health Organization's (WHO) survey of menstrual-cycle symptom reports among 5,322 parous women in 14 different cultural groups. Originally designed to survey attitudes towards perceived changes in menstrual bleeding patterns in relation to use of fertility regulation methods (Snowdon and Christian 1983; WHO 1981), data from this study have been cited both to support (Golub 1988) and to refute (Paige 1987, Gottlieb 1988) the universal occurrence of PMS. The WHO study found physical discomfort rates were held to be comparable across cultures and reported by 50–70 percent of women (symptom severity was not assessed). The most commonly reported physical symptoms were backache and abdominal pain. As in the Janiger et al. study (1972), no attempt was made to distinguish symptoms of dysmenorrhea from those attributed to PMS. Results, however, argue against a universal occurrence of PMS since, when compared with the sample from the United Kingdom, Third-World women reported substantially lower rates of premenstrual mood shifts. If mood shifts did occur, they did not follow the Western pattern in that these changes were observed during, not before, menstrual bleeding and were related to having longer and heavier menses (Paige 1987).[12] Data from the WHO study also show that the majority of women in most cultures see menstruation in a positive light as a sign of good health, youth, fertility, and femininity. Where negative attitudes existed they showed no correlation with negative experience.

In sum, the cross-cultural data indicate that the expressions of physical symptoms are not Western phenomena—although testing for them is (Paige 1987). If not universal, the ethnographic data shows that symptoms such as abdominal cramps and back pain may be widespread (Gottlieb 1988). However, what has not been demonstrated is the cross-cultural existence (or recognition) of any syndromic equivalent to the supposedly biologically based PMS mood shifts or mental disruptions. As cultural constructions, PMS, LLPDD, or PMDD only exist as syndromes that have been formalized in the last 2½ decades and involve bizarre behavior, which is recognized and defined and redefined, and is treated as a specific syndrome only by biomedical healers in Western industrial cultures. This becomes especially clear when ethnographic studies of modernization and culture change are taken into account.

Although cross-cultural surveys indicate that the body may be mediated by social factors, the sociocultural dynamics that can shape a woman's perception and experience of menstrual symptoms remain relatively unexamined. However, anthropologists such as Maureen Fitzgerald (1990) are beginning to take a new approach by looking at how subjective experiences of the body may be communicated, expressed, and shaped by cultural understandings of subliminal sensations, ignored in one culture and patterned into evidence for disease in another. Asserting that the experience of symptoms is the same, Fitzgerald (1990) argues that culture intervenes in terms of how people are socialized to recognize and express these symptoms. Culture, as an interactive system, thus, affects the kinds of symptoms reported, what symptoms are attributed to menstruation, as well as whether or not menstrual symptoms will be recognized, given attention, and/or seen as distressful.

Fitzgerald (1990) uses structured and semistructured interviews to collect data from male and female Samoans in traditional-to-modern communities (Western Samoa, American Samoa, Samoans in Honolulu) to demonstrate how exposure to modernization results in changes in menstrual experience toward that which approximates the Western model. Traditional Samoans have not heard of PMS, report the fewest symptoms, and offer the fewest kinds of symptoms, mentioning only somatic ones. In contrast, the most modern Samoans could converse at length about PMS and offer the most number and kinds of symptoms (affective as well as somatic) in symptomatologies that are far more elaborated than those of the traditional Samoans.

Fitzgerald (1990) argues that symptoms are culturally constructed and therefore differently experienced. An example of the differential experience of physical symptoms lies in the fact that bloating is perceived by more modern Samoans as uncomfortable because modern women wear fixed-waist clothes while traditional women do not. In addition, traditional women are more stoic and their experience of symptoms is compounded by backaches from hard labor and weaving mats as well as a higher incidence of parasites, diarrhea, and skin lesions. Yet, Fitzgerald also relates experience of symptoms to more abstract entities such as Samoan cultural constructions of emotions and self. Samoans exist on the somatic end of the somatic-affective continuum, meaning that they do not psychologize experience. Rather than focus on self or internal situations, traditional Samoans are more context-, situation-, and relationship-oriented people.

According to Fitzgerald (1990), symptoms do not increase with modernization. However, the options for dealing with symptoms as well as the tendency to give them notice, do increase. Among the modern Samoans, there appears to be a breakdown of restraints about talking about self; the development of a vocabulary of internal states; and the ability, adapted from Western culture, to psychologize experience. Modern Samoans thus have new models for expressing and dissecting their feelings. Yet, even as Samoans develop modern ideas, they keep older ones, such as positive attitudes and association of sex with puberty, as well as the attitude that menstrual cycles may be simultaneously normal and distressing.

Given the foregoing, it is remarkable that in various guises the concept of PMS remains sufficiently viable to gain entry into Western psychiatric nosology. Therefore, it is interesting to compare the literature on PMS to that on menopause, where the case for a universal menopausal syndrome is much more suspect, thanks in part to a strong multifaceted contribution from anthropologists.

THE MENOPAUSE SYNDROME

As is the case with PMS and the nineteenth century's neurasthenias and hysterias, the menopause syndrome has also evolved in the medical and popular literature as a disease constructed around expanding lists of somatic, psychosomatic, psychological symptoms (Davis and Hatle 1986). It equally exists in a nosological limbo and has problematic diagnosis, etiology, and treatment. Like PMS, the medicalization of menopause and it development as a syndrome is based in hormonal biology of the female reproductive system; is depicted as an estrogen deficiency disease; and has its origins as a disease in the scientific discovery and development of treatments (Bell 1986, 1987).[13] As with PMS, methodological flaws, such as dependence on symptom checklists and attitude scales, and culture-bound *a priori* assumptions about the nature of menopause, greatly impair research validity. Although the biochemistry of menopause and the menopause syndrome has received more scientific attention than the biochemistry of PMS, it remains poorly understood (Gannon 1985; Voda 1993). Unlike the case for PMS, menopause as a depressive psychosis involutional syndrome was included in earlier editions of the DSM but was dropped from later editions for lack of sufficient evidence. Most importantly, unlike PMS, the sociocultural and biocultural dimensions of the menopausal syndrome have been the topic of research by a series of social science studies that not only seriously challenged the biomedical reductionists to retreat from the association of psychological or psychosomatic symptoms with the menopause, but also call into question the most basic biological constructions of the few remaining symptoms.

It is important to note, however, that, despite the challenge from anthropology, a biomedical construction and promotion of Hormone Replacement Therapy (HRT) continues to dominate popular thinking and the literature on menopause. Between 1966 and 1975, the popular and medical literature on HRT promised eternal beauty and femininity. From 1975 to 1980, a symptom-free menopause was promised (MacPherson 1993), but the range of symptoms amenable to treatment became progressively more narrowly defined. The latest reincarnation of menopause as a deficiency disease reconceptualizes menopause as a risk factor for the chronic diseases of old age, such as osteoporosis and cardiovascular disease (Worcester and Whatley 1992). Middle age, no longer viewed as an inherently illness-prone stage of the life cycle, has instead become the age of choice between a healthy or debilitated old age (Kaufert and Lock 1992). Today, menopause has been fully medicalized to the extent that it is a recognized clinical speciality. There are menopause clinics in Europe and the U.S. and some medical practitioners still voice the opinion that every woman past age 35 be put on HRT for the rest of her life (Ettinger 1989; see also Flint, Kronenberg and Utian 1990:192; Worcester and Whatley 1992; Wren 1987). The disease of menopause is big business (Fausto-Sterling 1985). The potential markets from aging baby-boomers and non-Western women are so huge that the medicalization of menopause is unlikely to show abatement.

The medicalization of menopause and the politics of gender have been the topic of feminist[14] scrutiny: the negativity of menopause has been challenged; the empty-nest syndrome has been exposed as a myth, and menopause is no longer equated with the onset of old age or loss of youth and sexuality. The cover of a recent edited collection of feminist articles on menopause (Callahan 1993) shows women holding a banner that says "They are not hot flashes. They are power surges." Yet, in the case of menopause, questioning negative medicalized stereotypes has been more than a simple issue of alternativist rhetoric. However, before addressing this issue it is useful to consider some questions of definition.

Menopause: Medical Definitions

The human female ceases to menstruate around age fifty, which is a midpoint on the human life-span (Pavelka and Fedigan 1991).[15] The term menopause refers to the last menses, which can only be known retrospectively, since twelve months with no menses defines a women as having gone through menopause (Kaufert et al. 1986). Hormonal changes at menopause are attributed to the cessation of ovulation, which results in an increase in circulating levels of gonadotrophins (particularly FSH) and a decrease in circulating estrogens. (See Gannon [1990] and Voda [1993] for good reviews of the physiology of menopause and Martin [1992] for a critique of the medical discourse on menopause.) But medicine is not interested in the cessation of menses *per se*, but in that phase of the aging process during which a woman passes from a reproductive to a nonreproductive stage (Van Keep 1991). This is distinguished from menopause and medically termed the climacteric. The climacteric is then subdivided into three stages: the premenopause, the perimenopause, and postmenopause. The perimenopause is the period which is supposed to be accompanied by irregular or heavy periods and which can last for a few months or for years.

Women in the perimenopause are said to experience a combination of vasomotor and psychosomatic symptoms characterized as the climacteric or menopause syndrome. In the current, medically enlightened view, although the perception of these symptoms may differ, vasomotor symptoms, such as the hot flash, cold sweats, and vaginal atrophy are considered to be biologically caused and universal. Psychosomatic symptoms such as irritability, nervousness, depression, sleeplessness, headaches, and fatigue are more variably experienced and have come to be increasingly recognized as related to the psychological, social, and cultural characteristics of women, rather than to biology (Van Keep 1991).

The latter part of the current, enlightened view is largely the result of a series of large-scale, sophisticated, quantitative studies that show, more clearly than ever before, that menopause is most remarkable for being unremarkable. These studies[16] demonstrate commonalities in women's experience of menopause in a variety of North American and European settings (Holte and Mikkelsen 1991; Hunter 1993; Kaufert and Gilbert 1986; McKinlay and McKinlay 1985; Matthews, Wing, Kuller, Meilahn, and Kelsey 1990). Data from these studies demonstrate that for the general population, menopause does not have a negative impact on sense of well being or mental health among the majority of women; that the experience of physical symptoms apart from vasomotor ones is insignificant; that hot flashes and sweats were experienced by 56–60 percent of women (earlier estimates were higher); that vaginal dryness is not a complaint specific to the perimenopause; and that menopause does not affect ratings of general health or health-related behaviors or visits to a physician (Hunter 1993). Those women who do report considerable distress at the menopause tend to be women who have poor health status throughout their lives. Taken together, these studies challenge the assumption of an estrogen-related climacteric syndrome and suggest that the evaluation of the middle-aged patient should be based on specific life circumstances and risk factors rather than menopausal status *per se.*[17]

These findings gain significance in light of the fact that the biochemical etiology of the ever narrowing range of symptoms now attributed to menopause has yet to be determined and effectiveness of treatments has yet to be conclusively established. The exact etiology of the perimenopause's key symptom, hot flash, is as yet still unknown (Voda 1993). Although HRT is recognized as most effective for treating hot flashes and atrophic vaginitis, some studies show that only 50 percent of women report improvement in HRT treatment of vasomotor symptoms and that most learn to live with them and some even welcome them.[18] Vaginal dryness, which may result in painful intercourse (dyspareunia) is estimated to occur only in a small number of women (5 percent) and is not exclusive to the perimenopause (Gallagher 1993, Hunter 1993). Relaxation and stress reduction have been shown to significantly reduce hot flashes and sex at menopause is associated with the same factors that lead to self satisfaction at other times of life. The association of cardiovascular disease and osteoporosis with the hormonal changes of menopause are also problematic and it is unclear if these should be viewed as diseases of menopause or diseases of chronological aging. If the latter is true, then the association of these diseases with menopause is premature (Kaufert and Lock 1992). Cross-cultural data reveals that osteoporosis is not an inevitable outcome of aging (Brown 1988) but is related to the diet and lifestyles (physical inactivity and obsession with thinness) of Western industrialized culture. Studies of the long-term effectiveness of the various types of hormone therapy are plagued by methodological difficulties and exaggerated claims.[19] Critics have voiced the concern that disease prevention may be expanded to include the concept of disease substitution since estrogen and hormone replacement therapies have been shown to have an iatrogenic effect including endometrial cancer, 30-to-40 percent rise in risk levels for breast cancer, gall bladder disease, and abnormal bleeding (Gannon 1985; Worcester and Whatley 1992).

The list of symptoms attributed to menopause may be shrinking as is the number of symptoms seen as amenable to hormone therapy. However, the medicalization of menopause, as has already been noted, continues. In view of the potential negative effects of HRT, one would expect that the major goal of researchers would be to establish minimum doses for relieving flashes, but this is not the case. Instead, research has been designed from the perspective that hot flashes are not the problem. They are only a symptom of the problem, which is menopause itself. Consequently, studies are designed to assess the higher doses required to restore a premenopausal hormone balance, e.g., the "cure" is not to be found in the relief of symptoms but in the blood level of estrogens (Gannon 1985). In the case of osteoporosis and heart disease, it is appropriate to ask if it is ethical to give potentially dangerous drugs to healthy women as a preventative public health matter (MacPherson 1993; Worcester and Whatley 1992).

Yet, as is the case with PMS, there are women who do suffer at menopause. The problem aptly defined by Kaufert (1990:64) is one of seeking to balance potential "real" need for health care and the risks of medicalizing a normal process. She grants that menopause is not life threatening and treatments may be iatrogenic but many of the symptoms of menopause, such as pain, spotting, and heavy bleeding, have dual meaning and should receive medical attention.

Anthropology and the Menopause

As noted previously, anthropology has played a far more important role in the development of research on menopause than is the case for PMS. National and International Menopause Research Societies have recognized the importance of anthropological research as well as the necessity for a cross-cultural perspective (Kaufert 1990; Flint 1982). While psychologists[20] continue to worry about survey design (Kaufert 1990), through a recent series of full-length ethnographies on menopause (e.g., Beyene 1989; Davis 1983; duToit 1990; and Lock 1993), anthropologists have turned to social construction theory to look at the links between science, women's experience, and the wider societies in which women live (Kaufert 1990). During the 1980s, qualitative, ethnographically oriented studies of menopause tended to be dismissed by the champions of quantitative analysis (i.e., Greene 1984) for their idiosyncrasy and a cultural particularism that defied generalization. Studies with a strong cultural constructivist orientation were critiqued for their failure to fit the major positivist, biologically reductionist medical and established sociopsychological paradigms of menopause. However, today, the current generation of more qualitative, constructivist ethnographic studies are challenging both a) the very foundations of medical reasoning (Koeske 1983), and b) the feminist argument that if biology is not destiny than biology is not relevant.

Since the positivist biologicalism and reliance on self report and questionnaire data have failed to show any relationship between biology and symptoms, there is certainly room for a more interpretive approach. This approach would recognize the complexity of menopause as a biocultural phenomenon, as the product of a dialectical rather than a linear relationship between biology and culture, and would assume that the conceptualization of phenomena begins with the subjectively and socially meaningful actions and experience of women at middle age (Parlee 1990). The set of studies that follow are based on long-term, participant-observation research, where researchers have day-to-day, first-hand, intimate knowledge of women's individually and collectively lived experience. Thus, research focuses on the experiences and interpretations of women themselves.

Noted for their "qualitative depth" (duToit 1990:260) or described as "ethnographic road maps" (Goodman 1990:146), these studies are designed to capture the totality of women's lives.

The Biocultural Approach

Beyene's (1989) comparative analysis of women's experience of menopause among rural Greeks and rural Mayan Indians (Yucatan Mexico) illustrates the biocultural approach. Based on long-term participant observation fieldwork in the two sites and on data from interviews with local physicians, midwives, traditional healers, and the native women themselves, Beyene (1989) notes that the only symptom of menopause recognized by Mayan women was cessation of menses (and even that may be compounded by the fact that middle-aged mothers may never experience the return of menses after the birth and nursing of their last child). The hot flash or sweat or any equivalents Beyene asked about, such as "like fever," were neither reported nor known by healers, midwives or the Mayan informants. Although Mayan women did report discomfort and pain (dysmenorrhea, not PMS) at menstruation, they looked forward to a symptomless menopause, which they associated with youth and freedom. Greek women, however, did report vasomotor symptoms. Seventy three percent reported hot flashes and 30 percent reported cold sweats, but flashes and sweats were considered to be normal and no medical treatment was sought. Less than 2 percent reported irritability or melancholy. Beyene hypothesizes that the differences found between the Greek and Mayan women are due to physiological phenomena, which both affect, and are affected by, sociocultural factors.

According to Beyene (1989), diet and fertility patterns are two categories of cultural factors that could influence the production of hormones (such as estrogen), thereby affecting ovarian function and adrenal activity. The two populations show a striking difference in both of these. The Mayans have a high incidence of vitamin deficiency and anemia. They have little protein in their diet and drink no milk. Greeks, on the other hand, have a wide variety of nutrients in their diet. Mayan women have early and repeated pregnancies and spend their reproductive careers in pregnancy and lactation (i.e., they experience fewer menstrual cycles), while Greek women marry later in life, practice birth control, and have shorter periods of lactation (neither group suffers from osteoporosis). Beyene also identifies the poor overall health and disease history of the Mayans, who suffer from malnutrition, anemia, TB, parasites, diarrhea, and pneumonia, as a potentially important biocultural factor.[21]

Lock (1991b) also questions the assumption of biological universality in women's experience of menopause with data from Japan, which shows that hot flashes are uncommon. While only 19.6 percent of Japanese women reported hot flashes, 64.6 percent of women in a large Manitoba survey did. According to Lock, this finding questions the assumption that the hot flash is the most usual symptom of menopause and challenges scientists to seriously consider that there are real and meaningful biological differences between populations. Although Lock

(1991b) raises the issue of the potential for basic genetic differences among populations, she seriously questions the idea that menopause is universal at any level—biological, psychological, or social—and calls for a more interpretive and less linear examination of the relation between the physical sensation, subjective perception, and social construction of symptoms. This is a dialectical approach to the study of the interaction of biology and culture (Lock, Kaufert, and Gilbert 1989).

The Social Construction of Menopause Symptoms

A recent trend in the social construction approach to menopause embraces the complexities of women's experience of menopause and focuses on the perception, formation, and expression of symptoms and their relationship to the wider sociocultural environment. Lock's (1986, 1989, 1991a, 1991b, 1991c, 1993) Japan study and my own in Newfoundland (Davis 1982, 1983, 1986a, 1986b, 1986c, 1989b, 1993a, 1994) illustrate this approach in that we are both interested in the cultural development of symptomatologies that show variance from the Western, and/or medical models, as well as in the relationships of the perception and expression of symptoms to the wider changing social order.

Basing her analysis on interview and questionnaire data from menopausal-aged women and physicians in Japan, Lock (1986, 1991a, 1991b, 1991c)[22] demonstrates that the relationship among physical symptomatology, subjective experience, and social and environmental variables is neither simple nor linear. According to Lock, symptom reports should not be viewed as straightforward reflections of biological reality since different physical processes may be associated with the same symptoms and socialization into a particular culture can exert a strong influence on the recognition and labeling of somatic sensations. Lock (1991b) argues, instead, that physical symptoms are culturally constructed and diagnosis is a social process. For example, in order to tap the Japanese experience, Lock had to design a symptom checklist that included far more symptoms than appear on standardized checklists used with Western populations. This is because the Japanese are highly conscious of a wide variety of somatic states that are neither recognized nor named in English.

The social construction of symptoms, as in the studies of Fitzgerald (1990) and Beyene (1989), is also illustrated by the problems Lock (1986, 1991b) encountered in attempting to translate the term, "hot flash." There is no equivalent word in Japanese. Instead, Lock had to rely on words roughly translating as "glow or heat," "a hot fit," "sudden feeling of heat," or "to become hot" to assess the presence or absence of flashes. None of these expressions, however, was the equivalent of the English term. Lock speculates that either bodily sensations we label as a flash are experienced but not noted (which is unlikely since Japanese women tend to somatize symptoms and are very finely attuned to their bodies) or that flashes are not experienced. In addition, according to Lock (1991b), Japanese women judge themselves to be in menopause based on their experience of symptoms such as stiff shoulders, lumbago, and chilliness. Because Japanese women focus on symptoms associated with aging, not menopause, their experience bears little resemblance to Western clinical markers of menopause.

From Lock's perspective, symptoms may be culturally constructed in the sense that they may be a) biologically experienced but not recognized or culturally elaborated; b) not recognized and therefore not experienced, or c) simply not physically present in the population. My work (Davis 1982, 1983, 1986a, 1986c, 1989b 1993b, 1994), on the other hand, is less concerned with the cultural construction of perception or sensory experience than with explaining how the sociocultural dynamics of interpersonal relations influence the conceptualizations and strategies governing the active expression and communication of menopausal symptoms in the day-to-day lived experience of women in a Newfoundland fishing village.

Although I used them in my study, I found that standardized questionnaires and symptom checklists did little to tap the experience of Newfoundland women (1986b, 1986c, 1993b).[23] Instead, the best way to understand menopause as a dynamic, culturally constructed phenomena was to observe women in their daily interactions as they relied on discourse (i.e., conversation capital) about their bodies to negotiate their individual and collective agendas and self-images in terms of the social relations, role expectations, and shared values and dramas of life in a small community.

The Newfoundland women I lived with in the late 1970s described their experiences of menopause, as they described all female health experiences, in terms of nerves and blood. These complex idioms interlinked the depiction of and expression of somatic and psychological states with expressions of character, personal history, and occupational and collective community identity (Davis 1983). Thus, women's talk about menopause was embedded in the wider circumstances and multiple meanings of folk biology/psychology and of their lives as member of fisher families who lived in a cold and cruel environment, and who had endured life histories of exploitation, poverty, deprivation, and tragedy. To talk of menopause was to talk about everything else. The language of menopause, encapsulated in metaphors of blood and nerves, was used to dramatize or "heroinize" one's self. To focus on the complex discourse of nerves and blood and the complex, mutually understood rules for talking about them is to capture what Early (1993:217) calls "culture in action." These were the idioms a woman relied on to publicly and privately actively negotiate an impression of herself as a good woman (e.g., hard working, long suffering, stoic, and emotionally strong) in the private and public spheres of village life. The nature or character of one's blood and nerves was public knowledge, and one's body and its processes were subject to critical public evaluation and moral judgment. Although menopause was embedded in negative metaphors of suffering and endurance, women used the language of nerves and blood to express high self-esteem. In the local rationale it was a good woman's duty to worry about her menfolk who made a dangerous living as fishers. Coping with the demands and hardships of Newfoundland fisher life required a great deal of physical and emotional strength. A lifetime of hardship, worry, self sacrifice, and stoic endurance wore out or used up one's nerves. Worn out nerves caused problems on "the change." Therefore, women with nerves on the change, who had sacrificed their own health for the benefit of others, were and are good women. Following this reasoning, all middle-aged women at that time held a high and valued status in their community and this was reflected (albeit in what appears to be a convoluted fashion) in their discourse about blood and nerves—a discourse that could be both abstract and concrete, and that shaped both self-reflection and social action.

Social Constructions in Wider Society

Lock (1989) puts this kind of negotiation of the meaning of menopause into the wider context of social change in Japan, where, borrowed at face value by Japanese gynecologists, the negative, Western, biomedical model of menopause is applied to a totally different clinical context where it does not fit with empirical reality and fits even less well with the experience of Japanese women. Yet, despite lack of symptoms, Japanese women are acquiring a negative view of menopause. They are influenced by current images of Japanese women in the mass media, where menopause has emerged as a metaphor for internal debates over changing roles of women in Japan. Perceived as a luxury disease, menopause is used to decry the laziness of contemporary Japanese women, who are portrayed as turning in on themselves; just playing around all day; or who are over-socialized, over-controlled, too tidy, and too controlling. Changing constructions of menopause in Japan are, Lock argues, related to changing notions of self and of the relationship of the individual to the family and the State. The popular literature describes breakdowns in morality and social control. Rhetoric about menopause draws from this debate where supposed personality deficits and behavioral faults of individuals are exposed to national scrutiny as a displacement of political concerns about modernization, growth, and national identity.

My most recent experiences with Newfoundland women, in the 1990s (Davis 1993b, 1994), also point to dramatic changes in their lives, which have had a profound impact on women's perceptions of their bodies. What was once a relatively isolated community with a viable fishery and a strong tradition-oriented, collective identity, dominated by a moral order that enforced sameness, consensus, and equality, has become (due to a failed fishery) a welfare unemployment community. Numerous social factions and marked forms of stratification by income, occupation, and education have come to pervade the local social order. The extended family has been undermined and today's middle-aged and older women are seen as examples of life's failures rather than successes. It is only in retrospect that I have come to realize the extent to which nerves and blood was a language of women's personal and collective empowerment, actively employed in a small community whose public life was governed by face-to-face relations, to negotiate individual and collective goals and to gain the compliance of others.

Those who voice nerves-and-blood complaints are now ridiculed as old-fashioned and ignorant. Most importantly for the issue at hand, talk about the body has become just that: talk about the body. Nerves and blood have lost their utility as metaphors that condense multiple levels of meaning and experience. Like the local houses that now have locks on their doors, the Newfoundland woman's body has become privatized. Robbed of the expressive, supportive, and esteem-enhancing functions of traditional talk about nerves and blood, contemporary women seek help and advice from medical practitioners. They have bought into the medical model and psychologize what they are coming to see as personal failures and bad life choices. The strength of women's networks and collective culture has been undermined. Today, women learn about their bodies in school or through television and magazines, rather than from the shared experiences of other women. Material possessions, education and income, physical attractiveness, rather than inner strength or shared hardships provide women with self-esteem today. Unlike the language of blood and nerves, which encoded social power and action, the medical language of menopause (and menstruation) is neither empowering nor conducive to social action. Unlike the language of blood and nerves, medical language cannot be manipulated to condemn others or to enhance self-esteem. Like the Samoans and Japanese women, I see that Newfoundland women have "bought into" the Western biomedical rhetoric of menopause and the negative gender ideology that goes with it.

CONCLUSION

The contention that the premenstrual and the menopausal syndromes are not universally occurring, biologically based phenomena, but instead are cultural constructions, is supported through two complementary lines of argument. The first lies in the critique of research design and methods and in the exposure of the Western, culture-bound, and biased assumptions that underlie the conceptualization of the two disorders. Critical reassessments of the social construction of gender in Euro-American cultural traditions and of the biological reductionism of Western biomedicine characterize the highly politicized discourse on PMS and its emergence as a major mental disorder. Cross-cultural evidence provides little support for the contention that PMS, including mood swings or mental disruptions, is a universally occurring phenomenon. The evidence does, however, support the notion that women's experience and behavior may be shaped by exposure to the concept of PMS through medical scripts and popular literature.

The second line of critique is more characteristic of the menopause literature. It views menopause as a biocultural event where perception, experience, and the private and public relevance and meaning of symptoms are negotiated and constructed in the daily, lived experiences of women and where the dialectical rather than linear interaction of biology and culture underlies the cultural specificity that characterizes women's experiences of menopause. Taken together, these two critiques challenge the medical models of the premenstrual and menopause syndromes and make an important contribution to our understanding of gender and health.

Acknowledgement. I would like to thank my research assistant, Evelyn Johnson, a sociology graduate student, for her valuable contribution to this chapter.

NOTES

1. Constraints on article length and my focus on medicalization do not allow me to address a number of issues that have received considerable attention in the anthropological literature on PMS and menopause. This includes the literature on menstrual pollution/taboos and menarche as a rite of passage as well as more emically oriented ethnographies of menstrual-related sociocultural phenomena (Buckley and Gottleib 1988); the evolution of menstruation (Lander 1988, Profet 1993) and menopause (Pavelka and Fedigan 1991); menstruation, fertility and fertility regulation (Harrell 1991, Maynard-Tucker 1989); the relationships of menstrual beliefs and practices to health-care decision making (Davis 1988a 1988b, 1992; Skultans 1970); and the history of the medicalization of menopause and menstruation in Western biomedicine (Bell 1986, 1987; Davis 1989a; King 1990; Lander 1987; Weideger 1976).

2. Generally, Americans have used the term Premenstrual Syndrome. In England the term is Premenstrual Tension. I use PMS throughout this chapter because, despite the attempts to develop more sophisticated medical terms, LLPDD and PMDD are still popularly identified as PMS.

3. Robert Frank (1939:1054) is generally recognized as the physician who first delineated PMS as a clinical entity in his depiction of 15 patients suffering from "indescribable tension" or feelings of unrest, irritability, and desire to find relief through "ill considered actions" 10–7 days before menstruation. Although onset of menstruation brought complete relief, Frank noted that the husbands and families of these women were to be pitied and patients were treated with blood aspiration, radiation of ovaries, and saline laxatives. PMS, however, was brought into its current limelight by Katharina Dalton (1979), a British physician, self-diagnosed PMS sufferer, and advocate of progesterone therapy. Dalton has become a "full time evangelist" (Lander 1988:87) of PMS. She has written books and numerous articles, opened a PMS clinic in London, and successfully developed the PMS defense in the trials of two British women charged with manslaughter in the early 1980s.

4. This represents a dilemma for clinicians since treatments may be iatrogenic. Progesterone may increase the risk of cancer and can result in bleeding or amenorrhea, spotting, weight gain or loss, cramps, yeast infections, diarrhea, and changes in sex drive (Landers 1988). The antidepressant Prozac is becoming a more popularly prescribed treatment for the depressive symptoms of PMS. Prozac is known to have negative side effects in 5 percent of women. Xanax, an anti-anxiety drug recently promoted for treating PMS irritability, is known to be addictive (Rapkin and Tonessen 1993). Although diet and exercise are often advocated as the first line of defense against PMS (Murray 1994), vitamin B-6 in large doses can lead to nerve damage (Fausto-Sterling 1985).

5. All categories of DSM should be subjected to this level of scrutiny. Diagnostic and definitional problems are not unique to PMS. Similar cases could be made for Chronic Fatigue Syndrome, Attention Deficit Disorder, and Traumatic Stress Syndrome (see Mezzich et al. 1994).

6. Here we enter into an interesting conceptual bind. One of the complaints of the women's health movements of the 1960s and 1970s was that physicians did not take

women's health complaints seriously. Instead women were seen as neurotic and told it was "all in their heads."

7. For research purposes by NIMH, PMS was initially defined by the following: documentation over two cycles of a 30 percent change in intensity of symptoms (unspecified) measured intermenstrually as compared to those measured within six days prior to menstruation (Gise 1988; McFarlane and Williams 1990). In ICD-9 (International Classification of Disease) Premenstrual Tension (PMT) was recognized but classified on Axis III as a physical disorder. No mention of PMT occurs in ICD-10.

8. More specifically, these were marked affective lability (sad, irritable, or angry), persistent anger or irritability, feeling extremely tense, keyed up, or on the edge; and depressed mood, marked pessimism, or self-depreciating thought. Although "other physical symptoms" constituted a tenth criterion and included the traditional symptoms of headache, breast tenderness, the experience of physical symptoms in this set of criteria was not considered necessary for diagnosis of the syndrome.

9. LLPDD has been criticized for vagueness of the symptoms (no other disorder has as many symptoms) and the assumption of remission at onset of menses (studies have failed to show this). No guidelines for determining what constitutes a significant change in premenstrual moods are offered and assessment of the severity of impairment is left to clinical judgment. Dependence on prospective diaries is faulted since two months is considered an insufficient time period for tracking symptoms and studies of the use of prospective ratings show that over 80 percent of women who report symptoms of PMS fail to have them confirmed. The relationship between mood swings and other disorders (for example, anemia, thyroid deficiency, chronic fatigue syndrome, depression, anxiety, and panic disorders) remains unexamined (Gise 1988; Murray 1994).

10. Actually, DSM IV will include a new subtype of depression called Major Depressive Episode with Postpartum Onset (Task force on DSM-IV 1994). The reasons for privileging depression (as the defining feature PMDD) over hostility and mood lability (defining features of LLPDD) remain unclear. Since most of the data on which the constructs of LLPDD and PMDD are based come from PMS research (Caplan 1991), the privileging of "depression" over "hostility" and "out of control" may have more to do with concessions to the feminist critique than it does with evidence accumulated from research.

11. This study is based on data on menstrual symptoms collected from student and clinical samples of women from the U.S. (including a sample of Apache women), Japan, Turkey, Greece, and Nigeria. Zoo reports were also solicited and findings describe female gorillas, chimps, and rhesus monkeys as prone to becoming restless and irritable premenstrually.

12. It is interesting that, although heavy menses may be related to anemia and under- or malnourished women may be at risk for iron deficiency, no cross-cultural effort has focussed on how diet, genetics, overall health, parity lactations, etc., affect symptoms experienced as PMS.

13. The Dalton (1979) equivalent for menopause (medical specialist feminists love to hate) is R. A. Wilson who, in his book *Feminine Forever* (1966), described menopausal women as living decay and advocated estrogen treatment from puberty to grave (McCrea 1983).

14. Many of the medicalization-of-PMS critics have extended their critiques to include menopause (Fausto-Sterling 1985; Gannon 1988; Koeske 1983; Lander 1988; Parlee 1990; and MacPherson 1993) noting the same conceptual and methodological traps.

Also see Dickson's (1993) analysis of the paradigmatic shifts that have occurred in the menopause literature.

15. Pavelka and Fedigan (1991) do not correlate menopause with the end of the reproductive period in women. They argue that this occurs well before menopause in the late 30s.

16. All of these studies have large nonclinical samples, differentiate among pre-, peri-, and postmenopausal states, are longitudinal, and use prospective symptom reports. This group of researchers has been extremely prolific; I cite only one publication for each of them.

17. There are some interesting relationships between HRT and experience of menopause. The data reported in Matthews et al. (1990) show that women who report difficulty (have a hard time) at menopause are women who have two things in common: low self-esteem and taking HRT. Moreover, women with low self-esteem who are not on HRT do not report a "hard time." In this study, women who used HRT tended to be better educated, less obese, and have lower blood pressure than women who did not. But the HRT users were more introspective. Thus Matthews et al. argue that women who do or do not have HRT may report different symptoms because they are different types of women to begin with. Hunter (1993) reports that women who are depressed at menopause are those who have been depressed in the past. Holte and Mikkelsen's (1991) Study of 2,349 women ages 45–55 in Norway indicated that, aside from hot flashes, excessive bleeding, and vaginal dryness, most climacteric complaints described in the literature were not associated with menopause and could be explained by a mixture of biological (chronological age, current smoking); psychological (negative attitudes, styles of reacting); and social (traditional sex-role identity) factors.

18. Skultan's (1970) study of Welsh women shows that they welcome heavy bleeding and hot flashes at menopause. The former is thought to set the body right for old age and the latter to carry one swiftly and safely through menopause. Women worry if they are not flashing enough.

19. See Gannon (1985), MacPherson (1993), National Women's Health Network (1989) and Worcester and Whatley (1992) for comprehensive critical reviews of the effectiveness of various forms of HRT. For a more positive view of HRT see Ferguson et al. (1989) and Utian (1987). For modern-day equivalents of R.A. Wilson, see Wren (1987) and Ettinger (1989).

20. Early cross-cultural studies of women's experience of menopause tended to focus on adapting the highly structured, quantitative, attitude-and-symptom surveys (which had been developed for use in middle-class, Western populations) for use in diverse cultural or ethnic groups. The major purpose was to collect data that would be comparable across cultural groups, using Western women as the standard of comparison (Datan, Antonovsky, and Maoz 1981; duToit 1990; Flint 1975; Flint and Garcia 1979; Goodman, Stewart, and Gilbert 1977; Kearns 1982; and Wright 1982).

21. Davis (1989b) also describes women's experience of menopause as being compounded by the diseases of poverty. These included untreated complications from pregnancy and childbirth, chronic vaginal infections, prolapsed uteri, hemorrhoids, bad teeth, scabies, chilblains, untreated cancers, worms, lice, fleas, chronic malnutrition, tuberculosis, diptheria, and scarlet fever.

22. Lock's work in Japan is of special interest because it has challenged the medical establishment by playing by their own rules. In her research, she utilized large samples, standardized questionnaires, symptoms checklists, and sophisticated statistical tech-

niques, as well as in-depth interviews, life histories, and ethnographically sensitive analysis.

23. In the 1970s, two women in Newfoundland who were administered a questionnaires on symptoms during menstruation did report that they could become moody at some point during their menstrual cycles. They were, however, totally unapologetic about doing so.

REFERENCES

Abplanalp, Judith
  1983a   Psychological Components of the Premenstrual Syndrome. Journal of Reproductive Medicine 28(8):517–524.
  1983b   Premenstrual Syndrome: A Selective Review. Women and Health 8(2/3): 107–123.
  1988   Psychosocial Theories. *In* The Premenstrual Syndrome. William R. Keye, ed. Pp. 95–112. Philadelphia: W.B. Saunders Co.

American Psychiatric Association
  1987   Diagnostic and Statistical Manual of Mental Disorders. Third Edition, Revised. Washington, DC: American Psychiatric Association.

Ashton, Heather
  1991   Psychotropic Drug Prescribing for Women. British Journal of Psychiatry 158(Supp 10):30–35.

Bell, Susan
  1986   A New Model of Medical Technology Development: A Case Study of DES. Research in the Sociology of Health Care 4:1–32.
  1987   Changing Ideas: The Medicalization of Menopause. Social Science and Medicine 24(6):535–542.

Beyene, Yewoubdar
  1989   From Menarche to Menopause: Reproductive Lives of Peasant Women in Two Cultures. Albany: SUNY Press.

Brooks-Gunn, Jeanne
  1987   Differentiating Premenstrual Symptoms and Syndromes. Psychosomatic Medicine 48:385–387.

Brown, Susan
  1988   Osteoporosis: An Anthropologist Sorts Fact from Fallacy. National Women's Health Network's Network News July/August 1,5–6.

Buckley, Thomas, and Alma Gottlieb
  1988   A Critical Appraisal of Theories of Menstrual Symbolism. *In* Blood Magic. Thomas Buckley and Alma Gottlieb, eds. Pp. 1–50. Berkeley: University of California Press.

Bullough, Vern, and Martha Voght
  1973   Women, Menstruation and 19th Century Medicine. Bulletin of the History of Medicine 47:66–82.

Callahan, Joan (ed.)
  1993   Menopause: A Midlife Passage. Bloomington: University of Indiana Press.

Caplan, Paula
  1991   Professional Issues. How Do They Decide Who Is Normal? The Bizarre, but True, Tale of the DSM Process. Canadian Psychology 32(2):162–170.

Cassara, Virginia
1988   A Consumer Organization's Perspective. *In* The Premenstrual Syndromes. Leslie Gise, ed. Pp. 145–149. New York: Churchill Livingstone.

Chakmakjian, Zaven
1983   A Critical Assessment of Therapy for the Premenstrual Tension Syndrome. Journal of Reproductive Medicine 28(8):532–538.

Chrisler, Joan, and Karen Levy
1990   The Media Construct as Menstrual Monster: A Content Analysis of PMS Articles in the Popular Press. Women and Health 16(2):89–105.

Dalton, Katharina
1979   Once a Month. Pomona CA: Hunter House.

Datan, Nancy, Aaron Antonovsky, and Benjamin Maoz
1981   A Time to Reap: The Middle-Age of Women in Five Israeli Subcultures. Baltimore: Johns Hopkins University Press.

Davis, Dona L.
1982   Women's Experience of Menopause in a Newfoundland Fishing Village. Maturitas 3(4):207–216.

1983   Blood and Nerves: An Ethnographic Focus on Menopause. St. John's: Memorial University of Newfoundland Institute of Social and Economic Research.

1986a   The Climacteric in a Newfoundland Fishing Village. *In* The Climacteric in Perspective. M. Notelovitz and P. Van Keep, eds. Pp. 149–159. Lancaster, U.K.: MTP Press Limited.

1986b   Changing Self-Image: Studying Menopausal Women in a Newfoundland Fishing Village. *In* Self, Sex and Gender in Cross-Cultural Fieldwork. Tony Whitehead and Mary-Ellen Conaway, eds. Pp. 240–262. Urbana: University of Illinois Press.

1986c   The Meaning of Menopause in a Newfoundland Fishing Village. Culture, Medicine and Psychiatry 10(1):73–94.

1988a   Folk Images of Health Care and Menstrual Patterns Among Newfoundland Women. Health Care for Women International 9(3):65–77.

1988b   Bad Blood and the Cultural Management of Health in a Newfoundland Outport Community. *In* Anthropology of Women's Health. Pat Whelehan, ed. Pp. 5–20. New York: J. F. Bergin and Garvey.

1989a   George Beard and Lydia Pinkham: Gender, Class and Late 19th Century Nerves. Health Care for Women International 8(2):93–114.

1989b   The Newfoundland Change of Life: Insights Into the Medicalization of Menopause. Journal of Cross-Cultural Gerontology 3(4):1–24.

1992   Gender and Elective Surgery in a Newfoundland Fishing Village. *In* Gender Constructs and Social Issues. Tony Whitehead and Barbara Reid, eds. Pp. 183–208. Urbana: University of Illinois Press.

1993a   "You Best Read It To Me My Dear": Methodological Issues with Marginally Literate Subjects. The Great Plains Sociologist 6(1):1–24.

1993b   When Men Become Women: The Changing Geography of Work in Newfoundland. Sex Roles 29(7/8):1–18.

1994   Blood and Nerves Revisited: Menopause and the Body Private in a Post Industrial Fishery. Paper presented at American Anthropological Association Meetings. Atlanta, GA.

Davis, Dona L., and Harlowe Hatle
1986   Climacteric Word Games: A Critique of Psychosomatic and Somatic Semantics. Northern Social Science Review 11:47–69.

DeAngelis, Tori
1993   Controversial Diagnosis Is Voted into Latest DSM. Monitor (September): 30–33.

Dickson, Geri
    1993   Metaphors of Menopause. *In* Menopause: A Midlife Passage. Joan Callahan, ed. Pp. 36–58. Bloomington: University of Indiana Press.

duToit, Brian
    1990   Aging and Menopause Among Indian South African Women. Albany: SUNY Press.

Early, Evelyn
    1993   Baladi Women of Cairo. Boulder, CO: Lynne Rienner.

Endicott, Jean, and Uriel Halbreich
    1988   Practical Problems and Evaluation. *In* The Premenstrual Syndromes. Leslie Gise, ed. Pp. 1–6. New York: Churchill Livingstone.

Ettinger, Bruce
    1989   Update: Estrogen and Postmenopausal Osteoporosis 1976–1986. Health Values 11(4):31–36.

Fausto-Sterling, Anne
    1985   Myth of Gender. New York: Basic Books.

Ferguson, Kristi, C. Hoegh, and S. Johnson
    1989   Estrogen Replacement Therapy: A Survey of Women's Knowledge and Attitudes. Archives of Internal Medicine 149:133–136.

Fitzgerald, Maureen H.
    1990   The Interplay of Culture and Symptoms: Menstrual Symptoms Among Samoans. Medical Anthropology 12:145–167.

Flint, Marcha
    1975   The Menopause: Reward or Punishment. Psychosomatics 16:161–163.
    1982   Anthropological Perspectives of the Menopause and Middle Age. Maturitas 4:173–180.

Flint, Marcha, and M. Garcia
    1979   Culture and the Climacteric. Journal of Biosocial Science Supplement 6, 197–215.

Flint, Marcha, Fred Kronenberg, and Wulf Utian
    1990   Multidisciplinary Perspectives on Menopause. Annals of the New York Academy of Sciences 52.

Frank, Robert
    1939   The Hormonal Causes of Premenstrual Tension. Archives of Neurology and Psychiatry 26:1052–1057.

Freeman, Ellen, Karl Rickels, Steven Sondheimer, and Marcia Polansky
    1990   Ineffectiveness of Progesterone Suppository Treatment for Premenstrual Syndrome. Journal of the American Medical Association 264(3):349–353.

Fuchs, Fritz
    1982   Dysmenorrhea and Dyspareunia. *In* Behavior and the Menstrual Cycle. R.C. Freidman, ed. Pp. 199–215. New York: Marcel Dekker.

Gallagher, Winifred
    1993   Midlife Myths. Atlantic Monthly (May):51–68.

Gannon, Linda R.
    1985   Menstrual Disorders and Menopause: Biological Psychological and Cultural Research. New York: Praeger Special Studies.
    1990   Endocrinology of Menopause. *In* The Meanings of Menopause. Ruth Formanek, ed. Pp. 179–238. Hillsdale, NJ: The Analytic Press.

Gise Leslie
    1988   Introduction. *In* The Premenstrual Syndromes. Leslie Gise, ed. Pp. xv–xx. New York: Churchill Livingstone.

Golub, Sharon
  1988   A Developmental Perspective. *In* The Premenstrual Syndromes. Leslie Gise, ed.
            Pp. 7–19. New York: Churchill Livingstone.

Goodman, Madeleine
  1990   The Biomedical Study of Menopause. *In* The Meanings of Menopause. Ruth
            Formanek, ed. Pp. 133–156. Hillsdale, NJ: The Analytic Press.

Goodman, Madeleine, Cynthia Stewart, and Fred Gilbert
  1977   Patterns of Menopause. Journal of Gerontology 32(3):291–98.

Gottleib, Alma
  1988   American Premenstrual Syndrome. Anthropology Today 4(6):10–13.

Green, Judith
  1982   Recent Trends in the Treatment of PMS: A Critical Review. *In* Behavior and
            the Menstrual Cycle. R. C. Freidman, ed. Pp. 367–384. New York: Marcel
            Dekker.

Greene, John
  1984   The Social and Psychological Origins of the Climacteric Syndrome. Brookfield,
            VT: Gower Publishing Company.

Harrell, Barbara B.
  1991   Lactation and Menstruation in Cultural Perspective. American Anthropologist
            83:796–823.

Heneson, Nancy
  1984   The Selling of PMS. Science 84(May):66–71.

Holte, Arne, and Karen Mikkelsen
  1991   Psychosocial Determinants of Climacteric Complaints. Maturitas 13:205–215.

Hunter, Myra
  1993   Predictors of Menopausal Symptoms: Psychosocial Aspects. Balliere's Clinical
            Endrocrinology and Metabolism 7(1):33–45.

Janiger, Oscar, Ralph Riffenburgh, and Ronald Kersch
  1972   Cross-Cultural Study of Premenstrual Syndrome. Psychosomatics 13:226–35.

Johnson, Thomas A.
  1987   Premenstrual Syndrome: A Western Culture-Specific Disorder. Culture, Medi-
            cine and Psychiatry 11:337–356.

Kaufert, Patricia
  1990   Methodological Issues in Menopause Research. *In* Multidisciplinary Perspec-
            tives on Menopause. Marcha Flint, Fred Kronenberg, and Wulf Utian, eds.
            Annals of the New York Academy of Sciences 52:114–123.

Kaufert, Patricia, and Penny Gilbert
  1986   Women, Menopause and Medicalization. Culture, Medicine and Psychiatry
            10:7–21.

Kaufert, Patricia, and Margaret Lock
  1992   "What Are Women For?": Cultural Constructions of Menopausal Women in
            Japan and Canada. *In* In Her Prime: New Views of Middle-Aged Women. Vir-
            ginia Kerns and Judith K. Brown, eds. Pp. 201–202. South Hadley, MA: Bergin
            and Garvey.

Kaufert, Patricia, Margaret Lock, Sonja McKinlay, Yewoubdar Beyenne, Dona Davis, Jean
Coope, Mona Eliasson, Maryvonne Gognalons-Nicloet, Madeleine Goodman, and Arne
Holte
  1986   Menopause Research: The Korpilampi Workshop. Social Science and Medicine
            22(11):1285–1289.

Kearns, Bessie
   1982   Perceptions of Menopause by Papago Women. *In* Changing Perspectives on Menopause. Ann Voda, Myra Dinnerstein, and Sheryl O'Donnel, eds. Pp. 70–83. Austin: University of Texas Press.

King, Charles R.
   1990   Parallels Between Neurasthenia and Premenstrual Syndrome. Women and Health 15(4):1–23.

Klebanov, Pamela, and Diane Ruble
   1994   Mind and Pain: Toward an Understanding of Women's Experience of Menstrual Cycle Symptoms. *In* Psychological Perspectives on Women's Health. V. Adesso, D. Reddy and R. Flemming, eds. Pp. 183–215. Madison: University of Wisconsin Press.

Koeske, Randi
   1983   Lifting the Curse of Menstruation. Women and Health 8(2/3):1–16.

Koeske, Randi K., and Gary F. Koeske
   1975   An Attributional Approach to Moods and the Menstrual Cycle. Journal of Personality and Social Psychology 31(3):473–478.

Kupers, Terry
   1991   Pathological Arrythmicity in Men. Tikkun 6(2):35–85.

Lander, Louise
   1988   Images of Bleeding. New York: Orlando Press.

Laws, Sophie
   1983   The Sexual Politics of Pre-menstrual Tension. Women's Studies International Forum 6(1):19–31.
   1990   Issues of Blood: The Politics of Menstruation. London: MacMillan.

Lock, Margaret
   1986   Ambiguities of Aging: Japanese Experience and Perception of Menopause. Culture, Medicine and Psychiatry 10:23–46.
   1989   Castigations of a Selfish Housewife: National Identity and Menopausal Rhetoric in Japan. Kroeber Anthropology Society Papers 69/70:1–13.
   1991a   Contested Meanings of Menopause. The Lancet 337:1270–1272.
   1991b   Hot Flushing in Cultural Context: The Japanese Case as a Cautionary Tale of the West. *In* The Climacteric Hot Flash. E. Schonbaum, ed. Pp. 40–60. Basel: Karger.
   1991c   Life-Cycle Transactions. Encyclopedia of Human Biology 4:697–710.
   1993   Encounters with Aging: Mythologies of Menopause in Japan and North America. Berkeley: University of California Press.

Lock, Margaret, Patricia Kaufert, and Penny Gilbert
   1989   Cultural Construction of the Menopausal Syndrome: The Japanese Case. Maturitas 10:317–32.

MacPherson, Kathleen
   1993   The False Promises of Hormone Replacement Therapy and Current Dilemmas. *In* Menopause: A Midlife Passage. Joan Callahan, ed. Pp. 145–159. Bloomington: University of Indiana Press.

Martin, Emily
   1992   The Women in the Body: A Cultural Analysis of Reproduction. Boston: Beacon Press.

Matthews, Karen, Rena R. Wing, Lewis Kuller, Elaine Meilahn, and Sheryl Kelsey
   1990   Influences of Natural Menopause on Psychological Characteristics and Symptoms of Middle-aged Healthy Women. Journal of Consulting and Clinical Psychology 58(3):345–51.

Maxson, Wayne
  1988   Progesterone: Biologic Effects and Evaluation of Therapy for PMS. *In* The Premenstrual Syndromes. Leslie Gise, ed. Pp. 119–135. New York: Churchill Livingstone.

Maynard-Tucker, Gisele
  1989   Knowledge of Reproductive Physiology and Modern Contraceptives in Peru. Studies in Family Planning 20(4):215–24.

McCrea, Frances
  1983   The Politics of Menopause. Social Problems 31(1):111–123.

McFarlane, Jessica, and Tannis MacBeth Williams
  1990   The Enigma of Premenstrual Syndrome. Canadian Psychology 31(2):95–108.

McKinlay, Sonia, and John McKinlay
  1985   Health Status and Health Utilization by Menopausal Women. *In* Aging, Reproduction and the Climacteric. L. Mastrionni and C. Paulson, eds. New York: Plenum Press.

Mezzich, Juan; Arthur Kleinman, Horagio Faberga and Delores Parron
  1994   Cultural Issues for DSM IV: A Source Book. Washington, DC: American Psychiatric Association.

Monagle, L., A. Dan, R. Chatterton, F. DeLeon-Jones, and G. Hudgens
  1986   Toward Delineating Menstrual Symptom Groupings. *In* Culture, Menstruation and Society. V. Olesen and N. Woods, eds. Pp. 131–143. Washington, DC: Hemisphere Press.

Murray, Marry
  1994   Relieved from PMS. Glamour (May):74, 78, 80.

National Women's Health Network
  1989   Taking Hormones and Women's Heatlh. Washington, DC: NWHN.

Paige, Karen
  1987   Menstrual Symptoms and Menstrual Beliefs: National and Cross-National Patterns. *In* Premenstrual Syndrome: Ethical and Legal Implications in a Biomedical Perspective. Bensen Ginsberg and Bonnie Carter, eds. Pp. 175–187. New York: Plenum Press.

Parlee, Mary Brown
  1974   Stereotypic Beliefs About Menstruation: A Methodological Note on the Moos Menstrual Distress Questionnaire and Some New Data. Psychosomatic Medicine 36(3):229–240.
  1976   Social Factors in the Psychology of Menstruation, Birth and Menopause. Health Care for Women International 3(3):477–490.
  1982   The Psychology of the Menstrual Cycle. *In* Behavior and the Menstrual Cycle. R. C. Freidman, ed. Pp. 77–99. New York: Marcel Dekker.
  1987   Media Treatment of Premenstrual Syndrome. *In* Premenstrual Syndrome. Bensen Ginsberg and Bonnie Carter, eds. Pp. 189–205. New York: Plenum Press.
  1990   Integrating Biological and Social Scientific Research on Menopause. *In* Multidisciplinary Perspectives on Menopause. Marcha Flint, Fred Kronenberg and Wulf Utian, eds. Annals of the New York Academy of Sciences 52:379–89.

Parry, Barbara, and Jeffrey Rausch
  1988   Evaluation of Biologic Research. *In* The Premenstrual Syndromes. Leslie Gise, ed. Pp. 47–58. New York: Churchill Livingstone.

Pavelka, Mary, and Linda Fedigan
    1991   Menopause: A Comparative Life History Perspective. Yearbook of Physical Anthropology 34:13–38.

Profet, Margie
    1993   Menstruation as a Defense Against Pathogens Transported by Sperm. Quarterly Review of Biology 68(3):335–381.

Randall, Sara C.
    1993   Blood is Hotter than Water: Popular Uses of Hot and Cold in Kel Tamashaq Illness Management. Social Science and Medicine 36(5):673–668.

Rapkin, Andrea, and Diane Tonnessen
    1993   A Woman Doctor's Guide to PMS: Essential Facts and Up-to-the-Minute Information. New York: Hyperion.

Reid, Robert L.
    1987   Pathophysiology and Treatment of the Premenstrual Syndrome. *In* Premenstrual Syndrome. Bensen Ginsberg and Bonnie Carter, eds. New York: Plenum.
    1991   Premenstrual Syndrome (editorial). The New England Journal of Medicine 324(17):1208–1210.

Rittenhouse, C. Amanda
    1991   The Emergence of Premenstrual Syndrome as a Social Problem. Social Problems 38(3):412–426.

Rodin, Mari
    1992   The Social Construction of Premenstrual Syndrome. Social Science and Medicine 35(1):49–56.

Rome, Esther
    1986   PMS Examined through a Feminist Lens. *In* Culture, Menstruation and Society. V. Oleson and N. Woods, eds. Washington, DC: Hemisphere Press.

Ruble, Diane N., and Jeanne Brooks-Gunn
    1979   Menstrual Symptoms: A Social Cognition Analysis. Journal of Behavioral Medicine 2(2):171–194.

Schmidt, Peter, Lynnette Nieman, Gay Grover, Kari Muller, George Merriam, and David Rubinow
    1991   Lack of Effect of Induced Menses in Women with Premenstrual Syndrome. New England Journal Medicine 324:1174–1179.

Skultans, Veida
    1970   The Symbolic Significance of Menstruation and the Menopause. Man 5:639–51.

Snowdon, Robert, and Barbara Christian eds.
    1983   Patterns and Perceptions of Menstruation: A World Health Organization International Collaborative Study. London and Canberra; Croon Helm and New York: St. Martin's Press.

Steiner, Meir, and Roger Haskett
    1987   The Psychobiology of Premenstrual Syndromes: The Michigan Studies. *In* Premenstrual Syndromes. Bensen Ginsberg and Bonnie Carter, eds. New York: Plenum Press.

Suh, Mary
    1993   Severe PMS: Is It Mental Illness or Just Normal Behavior. MS. (May–June) 3(6):90.

Task Force on DSM-IV
    1993   DSM-IV Draft Criteria (March 1). Washington, DC: American Psychiatric Association.
    1994   DSM-IV Update. March 1994. Washington, DC: American Psychiatric Association.

Tavris, Carol
  1993   Do You Menstruate? If So, Psychiatrists Think You May Be Nuts. Glamour (November):172.

Utian, Wulf
  1987   Overview on Menopause. American Journal of Obstetrics and Gynecology 156(5):1280–1283.

Van Keep, P. A.
  1991   The Menopause, the Climacteric and Hot Flushes. *In* The Climacteric Hot Flash. E. Schonbaum, ed. Pp. 1–5. Basel: Karger.

Vander Ploeg, Henk M.
  1990   The Factor Structure of the Menstrual Distress Questionnaire. Dutch Psychological Reports 66:707–714.

Voda, Ann
  1993   A Journey to the Center of the Cell: Understanding the Physiology and Endocrinology of Menopause. *In* Menopause: A Midlife Passage. Joan Callahan, ed. Bloomington: University of Indiana Press.

Weideger, Paula
  1976   Female Cycles: Menstruation and Menopause. London: Women's Press.

Wilson, Robert
  1966   Feminine Forever. London: W. H. Allen.

Worcester, Nancy and Mariamme Whatley
  1992   The Selling of PMS: Playing on the Fear Factor. Feminist Review 41:1–26.

World Health Organization Task Force on Psychosocial Research in Family Planning
  1981   A Cross-Cultural Study of Menstruation: Implications for Contraceptive Development and Use. Studies in Family Planning 12(1):3–16.

Wren, Barry
  1987   Cost-Effectiveness of Hormone Replacement Therapy. *In* The Climateric and Beyond. L. Zichella, M. I. Whitehead and P. A. Van Keep, eds. Pp. 55–62. Park Ridge, NJ: Parthenon Publishing Group.

Wright, Ann L.
  1982   Variation in Navajo Menopause: Toward An Explanation. *In* Changing Perspectives on Menopause. Ann Voda, Myra Dinnerstein and Sheryl O'Donnel, eds. Pp. 84–99. Austin: Unviersity of Texas Press.

Zita, Jacquelyn
  1989   The Premenstrual Syndrome "Dis-easing" the Female Cycle. *In* Feminism and Science. Nancy Tuana, ed. Bloomington: Indiana University Press. Pp. 188–210.

Gender, Aging, and Health:
A Comparative Approach

◧ *Maria G. Cattell*

GENDER, AGING, AND HEALTH

Gender . . . aging . . . health . . . each has biological referents and is at the same time a sociocultural construct with variable meanings in different societies. With the development of feminist scholarship and medical anthropology we have learned to think beyond physiology to the social and cultural constructions of gender and health. Gerontology, however, has yet to advance much beyond the view of aging as physical and mental decline and old age as a condition requiring "treatment" and "care." To understand gender, aging, and health, we must consider their nonbiological (social, cultural, political, economic) as well as biological aspects and the interactions among them (Koblinsky, Campbell, and Harlow 1993; Minkler and Estes 1991; Rossi 1985).

As anthropological research has made abundantly clear, gender may have little to do with biological sex. Women and men are socially created (Ortner and Whitehead 1981). It is now widely accepted that every culture makes its own interpretations of biological sex through the sexual division of labor, the allocation of resources, beliefs in the value of persons, and other phenomena.

By contrast, in the United States, aging is widely regarded by professionals and the general public alike as a physiological condition requiring medical intervention (Estes and Binney 1989; Sankar 1984). Under this "biomedicalization-of-aging" paradigm (Estes and Binney 1989), social, cultural, and economic influences on the aging process and experiences of old age are often neglected. But aging is far more than the accumulation of years and the physiological changes of maturity and senescence. For example, the dementia labeled Alzheimer's is commonly treated as a brain disease, though research suggests that social and cultural forces (cultural definitions, care settings, caregiving relationships) are significant in the construction of Alzheimer's disease (Lyman 1989). Similarly, life stages, including old age (Cohen 1984), are culturally constructed and vary in different societies. Many other nonbiological influences affect individuals' experiences of old age (Albert and Cattell 1994; Fry 1985; Keith 1990; Keith et al. 1994).

Again, the Euroamerican view of health as primarily physiological persists, despite the efforts of medical anthropologists and the World Health Organization's definition of health as complete physical, mental, and social well-being. The result is the medicalization of the human body, including menopause (Lock 1993) and frailty (Kaufman 1994). In many cultures, however, conceptions of health encompass social well-being, with sick individuals treated in the context of family and community, beliefs and values (e.g., Masamba 1984; Rosenmayr 1991).

There is much to be learned about the interactions of gender, aging, and health. Gender, aging, and health are rarely combined in scientific research, though each is a significant research arena. For example, in the two decades since the publication of *Woman, Culture and Society* (Rosaldo and Lamphere 1974) awakened anthropologists to their neglect of women, there has been an explosion of research and publications on women and gender and the development of the new field of women's studies encompassing a wide range of gender-related issues. However, in all this there has been little attention to gender issues in aging (Rubinstein 1990; Udvardy and Cattell 1992).

The multidisciplinary field of gerontology developed largely as a post–World War II phenomenon in conjunction with the dramatic aging of the American population. Serious anthropological attention to age, aging, and old people dates from the appearance of Clark and Anderson's *Culture and Aging* (1967) and Cowgill and Holmes' *Aging and Modernization* (1972). However, gerontologists often deal with "the elderly" with little regard for gender except in relation to certain issues that have come to be seen as women's aging issues: caregiving, widowhood, and, increasingly, poverty.[1]

Adding health to the equation only reduces the availability of relevant data, though biological and health variations over the lifecourse have recently come into scrutiny (Crews and Garruto 1994; Feachem, Kjellstrom, et al. 1992; Verbrugge 1987). However, gender differences and attention to women's health (Koblinsky, Timyan, and Gay 1993) have yet to be brought fully into the picture. In the United States, medical research has often excluded both women (Healy 1992)—especially in clinical trials (LaRosa and Pinn 1993)—and the elderly (Dickey 1994; Paltiel 1993).[2]

This chapter is organized into two sections. The first discusses biological, demographic, and sociocultural aging and some gender differences in each. The second utilizes a life-course perspective as the framework for a consideration of three broad life stages: infancy and childhood, reproductive years, and old age. The conclusion briefly presents some research and practical implications. Throughout, data are presented from both more developed nations (especially the

United States) and less developed nations.[3] The reason for this is that health environments (including demographic and epidemiologic trends and approaches to health care) differ significantly between these two broad categories of nations. Specific examples from different societies are also given to illustrate the importance of social and cultural factors in health issues. This comparative approach is taken in the belief that worldwide comparison will enrich our understanding of gender, aging, and health by suggesting at the very least the range of variation and some practical solutions to the health needs of individuals (cf. Albert and Cattell 1994).

GENDER AND AGING

Human Biological Aging: Senescence

The aim of research on normal human aging is to depict the inevitable—the biological baseline of health and aging processes—in contrast to those aspects that are shaped by cultural, social, and economic forces.

Biological aging involves predictable physiological changes that occur over time; it consists of "all time-dependent structural and functional changes, both maturational and senescent, that normally occur in the postpubertal period among males and females of a species" (Crews 1990). What "normally" occurs in biological aging is not yet fully known. But it is known that senescent changes occur in body composition, skeletal mass, the brain and nervous system, the skin and lungs, and body biochemistry (Crews 1990; Crews and Garruto 1993; Spence 1989). These changes involve reduced functional capacity but do not include diseases, although some diseases (e.g., arthritis, diabetes, heart disease, malignant neoplasms) are more common in old age.

Although senescence occurs over time, chronological age is only moderately correlated with biological age; individuals differ greatly from each other in the rate at which they age (Hochschild 1989; Shock et al. 1984). Thus there may be 60-year-olds who are more like 40-year-olds in their physiological characteristics, and vice versa. Nor does aging occur at the same rate in all parts of one person (Spence 1989); an individual might, for example, have "old" skin and a "young" heart.

All the above statements are implicitly gender-biased, because they are based largely on research conducted on males and extrapolated to females. Two major exceptions are osteoporosis and menopause—inescapably female issues. Osteoporosis, or progressive loss of bone-mineral density, happens at younger ages and to a greater extent among women—and puts them more at risk for fractures. In this particular area, men are virtually ignored in research, although they also suffer bone loss with aging. Menopause, or the loss of ovarian function, and other changes associated with the aging female reproductive system have perhaps a modest counterpart in males in prostate cancer, the incidence of which rises sharply with age.[4] All need further research.

Population Aging: A Graying World

The processes of individual aging and population aging are intertwined. The aging of many individuals shifts population structures into an "aging" mode, the current world trend. The aging of a population profoundly affects many aspects of private and public life; for example, the likelihood of family support for vulnerable members, including children and elderly, as well as many public policy and budget issues. As more people live longer, patterns of work, leisure, and retirement change (Riley 1992), along with the nature of family relationships. For example, in the 20th century, greater longevity has extended grandparent-grandchild relationships in the United States into the adulthood of grandchildren (Riley 1985).

As a result of declining fertility and mortality, the world is becoming "gray." Every nation in the world has increasing *numbers* of old people (age 60+ or 65+) and in many cases, increasing *proportions* of elderly. All developed countries have high proportions of persons age 65 and over (65+), for example: Sweden, 18 percent; United Kingdom, 15 percent; United States, 12 percent; Japan, 11 percent; and Canada, 11 percent (Albert and Cattell 1994:39). Many less developed countries have similar trends. The major exception is sub-Saharan Africa, which has growing numbers but will continue to have small proportions of old people (under 4 percent in most African nations) until well into the 21st century (Okojie 1988).

The less developed countries, which generally have "young" populations, will experience the greatest increases in absolute numbers of old people. In developing countries overall, the population aged 65+ is expected to jump from 156 million in 1985 to 289 million by the year 2005, and to 569 million by 2025 (Myers 1992). In addition, in many countries the oldest old (age 80+) is the fastest growing age segment, with 92 million projected by the year 2025, two-thirds of them in developing countries, particularly Asia (Myers 1992). By the year 2050 the number of elderly in China alone will exceed the total population of the United States (Grigsby and Olshansky 1989).

In many countries, because of differences in female and male longevity and mortality, the majority of elders are female; in particular, women constitute large proportions of the oldest old and frail elderly, and also widows and those living alone (Kinsella 1988, 1990; Myers 1990). Countries where older women do not outnumber men (among those aged 75+) include Bangladesh, India, and Pakistan and a number of African nations—though in every case this situation is expected to reverse by the year 2020 (U.S. Bureau of the Census 1991).

Gender Gaps: Longevity, Morbidity, and Mortality

In the twentieth century, women have been living longer than men. This gender gap in longevity is the male-female difference in life expectancy at birth. It is wider in the more developed nations but is also found in many less developed nations. In the latter, the differences between male and female longevity are smaller. In a relatively few developing countries, the gender gap is negligible or reversed. In India, often thought to be a country where female mortality greatly exceeds that of males, female mortality is indeed higher, 3.4 percent higher. However, this holds only until about age 30 or 35, when there is a "mortality crossover" and later-life male-mortality rates exceed those of females, with the age at which crossover occurs apparently declining (Murray, Yang, and Qiao 1992).

Why do women live longer than men? One possibility is that women are better able to achieve their longevity potential when they are no longer in a "physiological setting of multiple births and nearly constant lactation" (Crews and Fitzsimons, in press). But the issues are complex, and the gender gap is affected by biological factors, behavioral and environmental influences, and sociocultural conditions (Nathanson 1990). Among these are chromosomal and hormonal advantages of females, such as the female body's handling of cholesterol and incidence of ischemic heart disease (women lag behind men by 5-to-10 years in the United States) (Smith 1992, 1993; Smith and Warner 1990). Behavioral and environmental differences, such as greater male mortality from accidents (including exposure to occupational hazards), homicide, suicide, war, smoking, and alcohol abuse are a worldwide pattern (Feachem, Kjellstrom et al. 1992). Sociocultural factors—conceptions of gender, the locations and opportunities of women and men in work and family, marital status, and role dissatisfaction—are also major influences (Crews and Fitzsimons, in press; Hess 1992; Verbrugge 1988, 1989, 1990).

Riley (1990) calls it a "gender paradox" that in the United States women of all ages report greater morbidity (illness) and more therapeutic care than men—but women also live longer.[5] Even among similarly disabled elderly, women at all ages have lower mortality rates than men (Manton 1988, 1990).[6] In fact, these gender differences are not so paradoxical. American women have a higher prevalence of chronic nonfatal conditions, leading them to report many symptoms and disabilities and to seek medical care more frequently, while men have a higher prevalence of fatal or "killer" conditions and receive less frequent medical and dental care (Verbrugge 1987). These patterns, persisting into old age, may provide long-term health benefits, which continue to enhance women's survival until old age, when their rates for killer conditions, especially cardiovascular disease, increase rapidly (Verbrugge 1985). Nevertheless, why female and male patterns of morbidity differ remains a question.

To speak of women's longevity (even if it exceeds that of men) may seem a bitter irony in developing countries. It may seem more reflective of reality, in Africa, Asia and elsewhere, to speak of women's mortality and the risks to mortality that they encounter throughout their lives (Freedman and Maine 1993). In many cultures, parental preference for sons leads to preferential treatment of sons in nutrition and healthcare, with girls being relatively more malnourished and sickly and receiving less frequent medical care than their brothers. Sons are also more likely to be sent to school, while girls miss out on the education that is critical in many aspects of life, including access to material resources and income, reproductive choice, and their own and their families' health. Women are also at risk for maternal death in numerous pregnancies and deliveries with little or no access to medical care (Freedman and Maine 1993; Timyan et al. 1993). For these hundreds of millions of women, the causes of poor health, illness, and premature death are tied to lifelong social and economic discrimination and subordination (Koblinsky, Timyan and Gay 1993; Turshen 1991). And they are linked to poverty—poverty at macro levels, and at the level of individual women for whom poverty is one effect of their low status and limited opportunities (Jacobson 1993; World Bank 1993).

But, in spite of everything, many women do survive. Their longevity leads them through the difficulties of childhood, youth, and midlife to the difficulties of old age. Living longer does not mean living better. Indeed, living longer may mean suffering longer with the health consequences of a lifetime of overwork, undernutrition, multiple childbirths, and emotional stress.

Socioeconomic Aspects of Aging: Lifelong Inequities

If being born female is a physiological advantage (at least in regard to longevity), growing up female is "a psychosocial challenge" (Weg 1985:206), and growing old female brings with it even more challenges. As Hess (1992:16) notes: "Inequalities between the sexes in old age are not unique to that life stage but are continuous, with patterned inequities throughout the life course." She was speaking of women in the United States, but could have been speaking of women anywhere. Everywhere, women suffer from inequities such as low status, devaluation of women's work, lesser opportunities to acquire valued resources, and other socioeconomic disadvantages. Everywhere, women are overworked and underpaid: "women's labor accounts for two-thirds of the world's work hours yet they receive only 10% of the income and own less than 1% of the property" (United Nations data, cited in Tiano 1987:216). Their very real contributions to their household economies through subsistence production, domestic labor, and activities in the informal economy are marginal and invisible in the capitalist mode of production (Tiano 1987).

In the United States, over half of older women live at or below the poverty line—almost double the poverty rate of older men. Women of color are significantly worse off than white women. The impoverishment of so many older American women is the outcome of lifelong gender, racial, and class stratification and discrimination and economic deprivation (Arendell and Estes 1991; Davis, Grant, and Rowland 1992; Dressel 1991; McLanahan, Sorensen, and Watson 1989). Hence, old-age poverty among women is partially the outcome of the cumulative effects of unpaid and generally unrecognized and devalued domestic work, less lifetime labor force participation, wage and hiring discrimination, and lower Social Security and other pension benefits. Later-life factors include marital status, with widows being worse off than married women and older women likely to experience lengthy widowhood. Further, mortality differences—which favor women even in poverty—increase the relative proportion of poor women to men even at the oldest ages.

What is the case in the world's wealthiest nation is even more true for the majority of the world's women who live in much poorer nations (Jacobson 1993; Sennott-Miller 1989). Of course, men also live in conditions of poverty. The World Bank estimates that 1.2 billion of the world's 5.5 billion men, women, and children live in "absolute poverty . . . beneath any reasonable definition of human decency" (cited in Jacobson 1993). In developing countries the "diseases of the poor"—tuberculosis (the leading killer of adults) and diarrheal and respiratory diseases—are major killers of children and adults, males and females, plus, for women, maternal mortality (Kjellstrom, Koplan, and Rothenberg 1992). Adequate health care and nutrition may be relatively unattainable for nearly an entire continent, as in the case of Africa (Falola and Ityavyar 1992).

Even where poverty is general, as in much of the developing world, women are likely to have poorer access to education, employment, and other valued resources, lower status, and less power than men. Women have lower participation in the formal economy and, even when they participate, have lower earnings than men. These economic disadvantages continue into old age. While elderly persons in developing nations are, as a category, more at risk for poverty than younger adults (Neysmith 1991; Neysmith and Edwardh 1984), older women are more at risk than older men—even where greater age may bring women greater power and control of resources (Kerns and Brown 1992; Udvardy and Cattell 1992). For older women in developing countries, their greater risk of poverty, poor health, and lack of family support in old age is but the last round in a lifetime of inequities (Cattell 1992a).

GENDER AND HEALTH THROUGH THE LIFE COURSE

Female Health Stages of Life: An Exploratory Model

A life-course approach to aging and health is a useful framework for examining the interactions of aging, a lifelong process for everyone, and health, a lifetime concern for everyone, since events from conception through death have cumulative effects. The life-course perspective has been widely used in gerontology, especially by anthropologists and sociologists, but its value is just being recognized in health studies (Feachem, Kjellstrom et al. 1992; Harris and Feldman 1991; Koblinsky, Timyan, and Gay 1993).

Every culture divides the life course into at least the minimal categories, or stages, of infant, child, adult and old person; some societies have many more categories, and in some cultures the spirits of ancestors are included in the continuum of existence.[7] In many cultures—including the culture of social science—the "old" category is divided into "old" and "very old" (Glascock and Feinman 1981). The old and very old are referred to in the gerontological literature by various terms; for example, intact and decrepit, young-old and old-old, or healthy/functional and frail.

For analytic or heuristic purposes, there is no right conceptualization of the life course but biological development underlies all models. For example, Merchant and Kurz (1993), dealing with female nutrition over the life course, use the following life/health stages: infancy and childhood; adolescence/early reproductive years; reproductive years; later years. Discussing female mortality, Freedman and Maine (1993) divide life into three stages: infancy and childhood; reproductive years; midlife and older age. The National Institutes of Health women's health initiatives (NIH 1992) utilize another scheme: birth to young adulthood (to age 15); young adult to perimenopausal years (ages 15–44); perimenopausal to mature years (ages 45–64); mature years (age 65+).

While such models make each life stage or health stage seem distinct, in real life, shifts in age and health status are often gradual, taking place over several or even many years. Whether gradual or sudden, health changes may result not only from single causes (trauma, infection) but from the interaction of physiological and sociocultural events, along with individual differences. Variation is the name of the game, within one society and between societies. Nevertheless, some patterns are emerging. More and better data may alter the picture, but for now let us consider female health status over the life course in relation to both the normal human biological sequence and the sociocultural and economic conditions of girls' and women's lives.

Table 1 is a life-course model for exploring connections between female health, biological aging, and the sociocultural and economic conditions of girls' and women's lives. Life stages and the passage of time are implicit, though I have not used chronological or life-stage designations. The model is based on the biological progression from infancy and childhood through the reproductive years into older and old age. These stages are explicit in the discussion that follows, though the categories are gross and the borders between them (in terms of age and life events such as genital surgery, marriage, and menopause) are intentionally undefined. The main purpose of the model is to suggest some interactions of social, cultural, and economic factors with human biology over the life course, not to present local details.[8] I have not attempted to balance the model by fully incorporating males, but there are both direct and implicit comparisons with males.

Degenerative diseases are major problems in more developed regions; other factors are more prominent in less developed regions. However, social and cultural practices, economic discrimination and other conditions that expose women to greater health risks throughout their lives are found everywhere in the world.

What follows is a discussion of the three female health stages of life illustrated by a case study based on my long-term anthropological research among the Samia in rural western Kenya. This research has focused on older persons in their families and communities.[9] As is likely to be true of any one culture, the Samia illustrate many, but not all, of the elements in the model.

Infancy and Childhood

In many cultures, an overwhelming influence on the lives of female infants and children is parental preference for sons, perceived as greater net assets to their

TABLE 1 Female Health Stages of Life: An Exploratory Model

Biological Sequence	Health Status	Sociocultural and Economic Conditions
Conception Birth Physical growth and development	{ Malnutrition * { Untreated disease { Early mortality	*Cultural/parental preference for sons, undervaluation of females; greater allocation of resources (food, health care, education) to males
Menarche Reproductive maturity	*Early mortality, lifelong } health problems	*Genital surgeries: clitoridectomy, excision of labia, infibulation
From c. age 30: loss of muscle mass	*Continued undernutrition } *Chronic anemia	*Eating customs and food taboos favoring males
From c. age 40: osteoarthritis		Female powerlessness, subordination to males
Menopause	Injury and death	*Early/forced marriage Male violence against women
	Chronic fatigue, emotional stress	Multiple roles/chronic overwork: Production Reproduction (*repeated pregnancy and lactation) Domestic work Caregiving
	*Maternal morbidity and mortality	
Increasing physical and mental frailty: Osteoporosis Organic brain disorders Cataracts Weight loss †Degenerative disease (heart, cancer, etc.)	Back problems, fractures Dementias Poor vision Increasing functional disability in self-care and daily activities	Discrimination in property ownership, employment, and business opportunities; female poverty exceeds male poverty through life
Death		Widowhood and social marginalization

*Greater in less developed world regions
†Greater in more developed world regions

families and the best source of support in old age. Parental motivations are not entirely materialistic. They may include cultural mystiques derived from kinship systems—inheritance practices and ideas about immortality beliefs in which women count for relatively little. Indeed, the worldwide undervaluation of females is at the heart of many practices favoring males—for example, the *machismo* culture of Latin America (Sennott-Miller 1989).

When preference for males/sons occurs in a context of material poverty, families may significantly favor sons over daughters when allocating food, health care, and education. The consequences for many girls as infants and children are greater malnutrition; untreated disease; greater susceptibility to, and prolongation of, illness; and early mortality as compared with their brothers (Freedman and Maine 1993; Merchant and Kurz 1993). This is not to suggest that male health, morbidity, and mortality are not also a source of concern. In much of the developing world, boys and girls alike get off to a bad start in regard to health, setting the stage for lifelong problems, but girls' exposure to risk—in these environments of high risks for everyone—is increased by sociocultural beliefs and practices favoring males.

In addition, millions of females in Asia and Africa undergo various forms of genital surgeries, often referred to as female circumcision or female genital mutilation (FGM).[10] Unknown numbers of girls die from these surgeries. For the survivors, especially those who were infibulated, there are lifelong health problems including painful urination, menstruation, intercourse, and childbirth, as well as chronic infections, cysts, and psychic trauma (Lightfoot-Klein 1989).

These customs are woven into cultural constructions of womanhood and marital relations (Boddy 1989; Kratz 1994), making it impossible for individual women to oppose them. As an African woman, Berhane Ras Work (quoted in Heise 1993) said: "Female circumcision is a clear example of social violence which women have to bear in silence as a price for marriage and social identity." Women themselves often support the practices. For example, among the strongest proponents of infibulation in Sudan are "the grandmothers" who do the surgeries and benefit financially and in terms of social status (Lightfoot-Klein 1989), though Sudanese women in general also support the practice as essential in their own political agendas (Boddy 1989).

Ultimately these issues must be resolved at local levels, because only that way will the cultural issues of identity, personhood, and social relations be successfully transformed (Kratz 1994). There are also issues of political autonomy: "The work of eliminating FGM [among Africans] belongs to African women and African men in their communities and abroad" (Dawitt 1994). Footbinding was similarly positioned in Chinese culture for a thousand years. It caused women lifelong, often excruciating pain and disability—but the Chinese eliminated footbinding without destroying Chinese culture or Chinese women (Chang 1991). In Africa, changes giving women greater economic independence and empowering self-concepts—through social and economic reforms and women's military service—have already enabled women in Egypt and Eritrea to resist genital surgeries (Gunning 1991–92).[11]

Case Study: The Samia of Kenya

A century ago, the Samia were fairly isolated farmers and cattle herders, self-sufficient in terms of food and other necessities except for some trading with neighbors. They were just at the beginning of forced incorporation into the world political economy and the process of what we often, rather loosely, call "modernization." Since then the Samia have experienced profound changes. Today most Samia, women and men, are peasant farmers. They grow much of their food plus cash crops, go to urban areas for employment, send their children to school, seek both indigenous healers and medical care when sick. Since people are tied to rural land rights, there is a continual flow of family members between rural and urban areas. Thus many Samia spend periods of time in Nairobi and other cities. But "upcountry" work and lifestyles are rural. There are markets and small trading centers in Samia but no urban areas. Samia has churches, schools, police, government administrators, telephone and electric lines, roads, and public transportation. But most work is by hand labor, all roads are dirt, and "footing it" is the most common mode of transportation. Most people are poor, and many are uneducated. The health environment includes endemic malaria and other parasitic and infectious diseases, unsafe water, poor hygiene, and a steadily increasing incidence of AIDS. There are annual preharvest food shortages and frequent droughts, which reduce the availability of food in households.

Year after year, malaria and associated anemia and enlarged spleen plus infectious diseases are leading causes of morbidity and mortality among children and adults at Nangina Hospital and its Maternal and Child Health (MCH) clinics, as well as among inpatients.[12] Malaria and its complications (anemia, enlarged spleen) have been steadily increasing in recent years, presumably resulting from chloroquine resistance in *Plasmodium falciparum* parasites. In 1990 AIDS joined the top ten inpatient diagnoses, though it was only 2 percent of the cases; malaria (47 percent) and anemia (22 percent) dominated (n = 5880).[13] AIDS cases have continued to increase since 1990.

The Samia: Infancy and Childhood.   Samia society is patriarchal and males are favored in many respects (land inheritance, for example). To have no sons is a tragedy—but to have only sons is undesirable. Older Samia without a living son lament their situation.[14] A man will say, "I have no son to inherit my land." His generations, his line of patrilineal descent, will end with him; he will not become the founding ancestor of a patrilineage. Women, who expect sons to support them in later life, express their concern differently: "Who will care for me now that I am old?" Daughters are also valued, especially for their labor and as sources of bridewealth for the family and support for elderly parents.

In the early years of the 20th century, sons were given preferential treatment in education and consequently, better opportunities in the modern economy—a possible cultural preference, definitely colonial policy. Almost no women elderly today (age 50+) had any formal education or were ever in wage employment. Today, however, primary education is nearly universal in Kenya, and Samia families struggle to educate daughters as well as sons: "You never know which child will get a job and help you."

Another indicator of preference given sons can be children's nutritional status. K'Okul (1991) estimates that roughly half of Samia children under the age of five suffer from malnutrition. Since 1984 until the present, MCH clinics of Nangina Holy Family Hospital have had an annual mean of 3,261 child visits involving mild-to-severe protein energy malnutrition.[15] Thus child malnutrition is an ongoing concern. However, it affects boys equally with girls. Throughout Kenya, very slightly higher proportions of boys under age five exhibit nutritional stunting and wasting (national data in K'Okul 1991). Poverty leading to lack of food is the main cause of malnutrition, though mothers' lack of knowledge about diet, early weaning because of pregnancy, and social problems are also implicated. Social problems include children born in premarital pregnancies, divorce, and families where the father is away. In addition, infants whose mothers are away from home for petty trading or other work may leave their infants to be bottlefed by others.[16]

The Samia eat, as they say, "from one pot," though not always at one table. Food served from the one pot (that is, from one kitchen) may be eaten in different spaces: in the house by men, their older sons, and formal visitors (in-laws, priests, anthropologists) and in the kitchen (a separate building) by women, daughters, and younger children. Men's and boys' servings may be larger but uneaten portions are returned to the kitchen where women, girls, and young children finish them off. Eggs, once forbidden to women, probably were always eaten by children, since eggs were and are a favorite gift from grandmothers to grandchildren. Young children of both sexes get added nutrition from snacks—such as fresh fruit or just-harvested peanuts being shelled for storage—which are served informally in the home. Older children freely eat fruit such as mangos, guavas, and *emjobola* (*Syzygium cumini*), which they pull from trees on their way to or from school or when they are running errands.

Samia children begin working when they are only a few years old. While they are young, they help their mothers. Their chores may include: going for water, collecting firewood, cooking, washing dishes and clothes, sweeping the house and compound, rubbing kernels off corncobs, peeling cassava, grinding flour. Boys, especially older boys and adolescents, escape such female chores, but for girls, this is their apprenticeship for a lifetime of hard work. Most children of both sexes spend time caring for younger siblings. Adults often speak fondly of the sibling who was their *ayah* or child caretaker. For boys, being an *ayah* goes no further than caring for a sibling, but girls—especially school dropouts—are often forced to work as *ayahs* for women employed or engaged in entrepreneurial activities outside the home. These *ayahs* do more than childcare, however; most household burdens fall on them. They work long hours for little pay and some are abused by others in the home, including sexual abuse from their employer's husband.

The Samia have never circumcised either males or females but they did practice "tooth removal," extraction of the four lower incisors in late childhood or early adolescence. This had some coming-of-age significance. Tooth removal was done privately by local experts under unhygienic conditions, including packing mud around the gums to stop the bleeding. There were health hazards from septicemia and severe, even fatal bleeding, but the risks were democratic: both boys and girls suffered from the practice, which was abandoned about 30 or 40 years ago.

The Samia: Reproductive Years. In less developed regions, reaching the reproductive years adds maternal morbidity and mortality to women's continuing health risks from the "diseases of the poor," such as tuberculosis, the number-one killer, plus respiratory and diarrheal diseases (Kjellstrom et al. 1992).

The risks of pregnancy and childbirth are much greater in developing countries because of much higher fertility rates, hence greater exposure to risk, and poor access to prenatal care and emergency medical service during obstetric complications. Maternal mortality accounts for about 10 percent of all adult female deaths in less developed regions (Kjellstrom et al. 1992). For example, in Africa, 1 in every 21 women dies of complications of pregnancy or delivery, compared to only 1 in about 10,000 women in northern Europe (Freedman and Maine 1993). The lifetime risk of maternal death is at least 300 times greater in sub-Saharan Africa than in North America (Smith 1993).

Male violence against females, commonly that of sexual partners, occurs everywhere in the world (Counts 1987; Counts, Brown, and Campbell 1991; Levinson 1989). From 20 percent to over 50 percent of women in many developed and developing countries report beatings by their partners (World Bank 1993). A classic example is the "dowry deaths" of young Hindu wives in India, accounting for about half the female deaths by burning in India (Kjellstrom et al. 1992).[17] High proportions of female injuries and violent deaths result from male violence (Heise 1993), though the true extent of male violence is unknown (Sheffield 1987) and largely invisible (Ofei-Aboagye 1994). Male physical aggression against females leads to other health problems such as depression, suicide attempts, and alcohol and drug abuse.

A third important aspect of female health during the reproductive years is the multiple roles of women leading to long hours of work, chronic fatigue, and emotional stress (Merchant and Kurz 1993). In developing countries, in addition to the burdens of reproduction and childcare, women do much of the productive labor—though without, at the same time, achieving equity with men in economic, political, and social terms (Boserup 1970; Hay and Stichter 1984; Leacock and Safa 1986). If production, reproduction, childcare, and domestic labor are not enough overwork, it is primarily women—as wives, daughters, and daughters-in-law—who give hands-on care to the elderly everywhere in the world (Cattell 1992a, 1993).

Marriage patterns among the Samia are changing, with girls marrying later, men earlier. Formerly marriages were arranged by parents; many older women told of being forced to marry when they were still children. Now young people are making their own choices and forced marriage has become rare. However, premarital pregnancies have become common. Such pregnancies seem to have been rare in the past, when girls' early marriage, prohibitions against premarital intercourse, and a virginity test on the wedding night were effective deterrents in a society with much tighter control over individual behavior than is the case in the modern situation. In many instances, premarital pregnancies result from rape, with schoolboys and teachers and other older men cajoling or forcing adolescent girls into sexual activity. It is the girls and their families, especially the girls' mothers, who bear the consequences of stigma and added financial and childcare burdens; sometimes the children are neglected, abused, or killed (Kilbride 1992; Kilbride and Kilbride 1990, in press).

Male violence against women is rife in Kenyan society and in Samia. Teachers, and sometimes parents, beat children, husbands beat wives—all with cultural approval. "I have to discipline my wife," men say; "We just have to accept what our husbands do," women say. In one survey I conducted, schoolgirls expressed fear of beatings, boys did not. Girls are expected to behave with *esoni* (shame, modesty) before adults; boys are expected to respect their elders but not to lower their eyes, hang their heads, and speak softly or remain silent in the face of adult questioning or abuse. Girls are socialized to accept a husband's beatings, to put up with his drunken behavior, to feed him and have sex with him at his wish and at any time he chooses. Young wives—strangers living in their husband's home, often far from their own kin, and socially inferior to nearly everyone in the home—are extremely vulnerable. While Samia women grow stronger and more powerful in later life and may successfully resist male domination on many fronts, girls and young wives are easy targets for male violence and abuse.[18]

Historically, customary food taboos in Samia favored males; today these restrictions have nearly vanished, the major exception being rules involving pregnant women. Apparently, in the past, women did not eat eggs, chicken, or mudfish. Nowadays, younger women do not observe these taboos, except that they avoid chicken gizzards (still regarded as a male prerogative). Everyone eats chicken, although some older women refuse eggs. Pregnant women may observe dietary restrictions and prescriptions, which may either reduce or increase their protein and vegetable intake. In the 1960s Ojiambo (1967) found pregnant women avoiding taboo vegetables and proteins. Makuto (1979), in a sample of 202 mothers attending Nangina's MCH clinics in 1978, found nearly half the women observing food taboos during pregnancy though others were increasing their protein intake on the advice of Community Health Workers.[19] Olenja (1986) in 1984 found pregnant women in Samia eating local or wild vegetable and protein foods believed to benefit mother and fetus and avoiding a few foods believed to bring problems to the fetus or make delivery more difficult.

Like most women throughout the world, and certainly throughout sub-Saharan Africa, Samia women work long, hard hours at many different tasks. Their work is labor intensive and unremitting. Indeed, all Samia work, young and old, males and females, but women spend most of their time in work activities while men spend more time in social activities and beer drinking.

The most time-consuming daily work tasks are, for everyone, going to the *shamba* or field to cultivate or harvest crops. In addition, women and girls fetch firewood and water collected from sources outside the home. For many, this means walking long distances with heavy loads on their heads. Twenty-liter jerrycans of water, weighing 20 kilograms (44 pounds), are common; bundles of firewood weigh up to 45 kilograms (99 pounds) (Aloo 1993). Women are completely responsible for food preparation, from "going to the *shamba* to look for vegetables" and/or grinding flour for the cooking, done over open wood fires or on small charcoal burners. Women spend many hours each day in smoky kitchens.[20] Childcare is the responsibility of women, though the actual caretaking may be done by a mother's older children or by a hired *ayah*. Women's work goes on regardless of pregnancies, which tend to be frequent, and often regardless of ill health, including widespread malaria and anemia.

In most public talk and action Samia women appear to be subordinate to men, but in most of their daily activities they are independent. Women work in their own spaces, especially the kitchen, which men seldom enter. They control their own work activities and completely control food, deciding which foods to prepare and when to serve them. A hungry man can only "sit around waiting for food" because it is shameful for a man to cook when there is a woman or girl in the home. This female control of food gives women the opportunity to engage in acts of "everyday resistance" to male domination (Abu-Lughod 1990:41) as well as to snack. As one man told K'Okul (1991:90), "you never know what a woman eats in her kitchen if the food is there!" One might add: one does not know what food a woman reserves for her children and others eating in the kitchen before sending her husband's food to him.

Old Age

When is a person old? Old age is differently defined by various people and for various purposes. Chronological criteria are useful for comparison but less precise than they seem, less predictive than one might hope of a person's health or other characteristics. This is because the onset of old age varies among individuals and tends to be a gradual process.

Governments and researchers almost always use chronological criteria to define old age, as the most practical (if imperfect) means to keep records and make comparisons. The United Nations (1983) has defined "old age" as beginning at 60; but ages ranging from 50 to 75 have been used in ethnographic, cross-national, and demographic research. For political and economic reasons related to pension and other entitlement issues, legal and chronological definitions vary widely from nation to nation. However defined, for a sizable proportion of a national population to be old is a modern phenomenon in more developed countries, and a rapidly increasing phenomenon in the rest of the world, as discussed earlier.

Cultural definitions of old age (and other life stages) often have little or nothing to do with chronology, partly because they developed among people without calendars, dates of birth, or the concept of age in years—though even in societies with calendars, clocks, and vital registration systems (the United States, for example) there are nonchronological concepts of old age. Cultural constructions of old age derive from physical and/or social markers. For example, among the Samia, the majority of older people (especially women, few of whom have had any formal education) do not know their age in years. Most Samia consider a woman to be old (*omukofu,* "old person") when she stops menstruating and/or giving birth. A man is said to be old when he loses strength, a rather vague standard, that allows men to put off becoming old and leads many to say, "Women grow old quickly, [or] . . . faster than men." All this translates roughly into age 50 and up, although many Samia in their 50s and even into their 60s (mostly men) do not regard themselves as old. Those who can no longer work, but only sit and wait to be fed, are *omukofu muno,* "very old person." In gerontological lingo, they are the frail elderly.

Using the UN criterion of age 60+, older women numbered about 271 million worldwide in 1990; 54 percent of them were in less developed nations. By the year 2015, older women are projected to number 482 million, with approximately half in less developed areas (from UN data, cited in Rix 1991). There will be a smaller but substantial number of older men, many of whom will also be living in poverty.

What is different about health in old age? Is it just more of the same? Yes—but there are also health issues and socioeconomic difficulties that are more common and/or more problematic for old people. Physiologically, old age means reduced capacity to deal with infections and trauma. In developed regions, where more people live to very old age, degenerative conditions and diseases become prominent. In the United States, for example, among elders one finds increased arthritis (the single greatest cause of disability in the United States); osteoporosis and loss of muscle mass, which contribute to physical weakness; sensory impairments—especially cataracts and hearing loss; organic brain disorders and dementias (George 1992); and other diseases of old age, especially cardiovascular disease and cancers.[21] In her Detroit study Verbrugge (1987) found that the five major health problems of women and men aged 65+ were the same, with some gender differences in rates: more women suffered from arthritis, hypertensive conditions, and chronic sinusitis; more men, from hearing impairments. Both had similar rates of heart conditions. Many gender differences in psychiatric disorders narrow or disappear in old age (George 1992).

Some health problems related to old age may be more serious for females than for males because of their different histories in regard to infectious diseases and chronic overwork and undernutrition, in addition to the exclusively female problems of genital surgeries and numerous pregnancies. Osteoporosis is primarily a problem of postmenopausal women in industrialized countries (little is known about it elsewhere [Merchant and Kurz 1992]). In addition, because of their greater longevity, many women have greater lifetime exposure to health risks and greater exposure to the diseases and disabilities of old age than do men. For men and women, living to a very old age (roughly 75 or 80 and above) greatly increases the likelihood of frailty, functional disabilities (physical and mental), and dependence (Foner 1985).[22] In the United States women live more years free of disability, but they also live more years with disability and are more likely to be institutionalized (Markides 1992). Little is known about disability in less developed regions because of a lack of research—and perhaps because the frail elderly simply do not survive for long (Dorjahn 1989).

Physical frailty and disability have serious outcomes for the elderly everywhere. In Europe and North America, frailty threatens independent living, which is highly valued, and may frustrate the desire to "age in place," to continue living in one's own home (Cattell 1991; Rubinstein, Kilbride, and Nagy 1992). In developing countries, where most work is labor-intensive and requires the ability to walk, carry heavy loads (such as wood, water, harvested foods), and engage in productive labor, frailty threatens the entire fabric of an individual's life. Thus caregiving becomes a serious health issue in old age. Caregiving is also a women's issue, since women predominate as both caregivers and care receivers throughout the world (Cattell 1992a), including Africa (Cattell 1993) and the United States. For example, in the United States, the greater part of caregiving for elders (including nursing-home care) is from wives and daughters to husbands and mothers (Stone, Cafferata, and Sangl 1987).

The lack of availability of culturally appropriate caregivers is a growing problem throughout the world (Albert and Cattell 1994; Cattell 1992a, 1993; Cattell and Albert 1994). Shortages of caregivers exist for many reasons. One cause is complex social structural changes involving extensive labor migration and the development of multilocal or multihousehold extended families (Weisner, in press). Caregiver shortages also result from fertility decline, not only in Europe and America, but also in countries like Kenya, long the world's leader in population growth (Bradley and Ndege, in press) and China, the world's most populous nation (Banister 1988). A growing problem, especially in parts of sub-Saharan Africa, is the decimation of the caregiving generation of young and middle-aged adults by AIDS and the resultant increased caregiving burdens being placed upon grandparents.

The lifetime cumulative effects of economic inequities result in older women's lack of ownership and/or control over material assets compared to men, including their ineligibility for pensions or their receipt of very low pensions. In addition, older people often experience economic discrimination simply because they are older (Logue 1990; Treas and Logue 1986). The result is a poverty of old age, a poverty that affects older women more seriously than older men. At the same time, women's work roles may change little. In sub-Saharan Africa, for instance, older women continue to farm (the majority live in rural areas), do domestic work, care for children (especially grandchildren), and participate in the informal economy.

Older women's primary social roles are likely to shift from "wife" to "retired wife" or "widow" (Cattell 1992a, in press; Potash 1986). Widowhood, while not exclusively an experience of the elder years, nor of women, is much more common among older women than among men, worldwide (Lopata 1987). This is partly due to spousal age differences and greater female longevity. In many societies, polygyny (marriage of one man to two or more women simultaneously) improves the likelihood that men will remain married till death. If a man's wife dies or divorces him, he is likely to remarry. Older women who are widowed or abandoned are unlikely to remarry. Many widows suffer loss of status, social marginalization, and even greater poverty than they experienced as wives. The health implications of widowhood—extreme poverty and, in some cases, filial neglect—are undoubtedly enormous but scarcely understood.

Widows in India are a classic case because of the well-known ritual of *sati* (widow immolation). *Sati* is much less common nowadays, but it was not universal in the past: the practice of *sati* never meant there were no widows in India. Dreze (1990) reports that in 1981 India had more than 25 million widows, and that a large majority of Indian women age 60+ were widows. In her research in villages in three North Indian states, Dreze found regional differences in the old-age security of widows. She found greater filial neglect in Gujerat, possibly due to increasing poverty in that state. In Bengal, widows had greater security through rights to land and official encouragement to remarry, thanks to recent reforms. In general, however, Indian widows rarely own or have secure rights in land or other property. They are also subject to employment and other economic constraints, which make it difficult for them to acquire cash, and they are stigmatized if they remarry (Dreze 1990; Vatuk 1982). Overall, in India, widows—nearly synonymous with older women—are markedly worse off than married women.

Research on widowhood in the United States suggests that the widow/widower has greater morbidity and mortality risks for a period of several months to several years after the spouse's death. Men are more at risk than women, perhaps because they are less likely to be involved in supportive social networks (Ferraro 1989). However, other research indicating that women with more income and education cope better with the stresses of widowhood raises the possibility that many problems of old age are determined by a complex of factors including race and socioeconomic status, and not by gender alone (Dressel 1991). In any case, elderly widows in the United States, like widows around the world, are more likely to suffer from poverty and its consequences than elderly men or elderly married women (Burkhauser 1990).

As we have seen repeatedly, many of the health problems of women throughout life are associated with poverty and social and economic discrimination. Though older women may command more resources—both material and human—than younger women, they are also likely to continue to be relatively deprived compared to men. And frail older women are also more likely to be widowed, poor, and socially marginalized than frail older men. Old age is not just a women's issue, nor is poverty just a women's issue, but older women are both more numerous than older men and more likely to face serious difficulties with socioeconomic issues and issues of nutrition, health, and frailty.

The Samia: Old Age

For Samia women, daily life changes little as they age. They continue to struggle with poverty and do the same kinds of work, perhaps with the added burden of caring for grandchildren from their daughters' premarital pregnancies. However, they are likely to have developed strong, forceful personalities. They look others right in the eye when speaking to them, and their voices resound with the self-assurance of age and experience. *Esoni* (shame, modesty) is for girls, not for mature women. As senior women in their natal patrilineages, they have important decision-making and ritual roles in lineage affairs such as marriages and funerals. As older women who command others' labor, they may have more time than ever before in their lives for religious or social activities such as participating in prayer groups, visiting the sick, serving as community health workers, and working on school committees.

As widows (this category makes up the majority of Samia women over age 60), women are freed from the demands of a husband while retaining the essential marital rights to cultivate, and be buried on, their husband's land. Though widows are "in the hands" of their sons, they are unlikely to be under their sons' thumbs. "A son will bring you tea and sugar, but a husband will drink it up," as Anjelina, a widow in her 60s, said in the public forum of a funeral speech. She was advocating the radical idea that a widow should not accept leviratic marriage (as she had not, some years earlier) because it is against God's law: "God has made it that old women like us can control our own homes." Clearly Anjelina saw controlling her own home as the means to more food for herself. No doubt other advantages were also in her mind.[23]

Health is a major concern among Samia elders. Queried about their specific health problems, 416 older women and men (in my 1985 survey) mentioned (in order of frequency of responses) back pains, aching bones, chest pains, weakness, malaria, stomach discomforts, problems walking, poor vision, frequent illness, poor hearing, diarrhea, skin infections, and dental problems. These responses reflect health concerns that are likely to increase with age, along with problems (such as malaria) that are endemic and affect all ages. A major problem is difficulty walking, which is essential to many activities, both economic and social. This was mentioned by about one quarter of both women and men, most of them age 70+.

Among the Samia, elders' responses to illness may include consulting local healers, a government dispensary, or Holy Family Hospital at Nangina Hospital. Sometimes no treatment is sought, as is the same with cataracts, which are almost never treated.[24] Sometimes, treatment is sought too late. One man in his 60s who broke his leg refused treatment at Nangina Hospital, where the leg could have been properly set, and went instead to a local bonehealer. Now he can barely walk, although he has young children to support. In another case, my friend Consolata, a woman in her 50s who had painful sores on her breast, refused her family's urging to go to the hospital until it was too late to treat the cancer. Until her death she was cared for in her home by a devoted daughter-in-law.

Some old people refuse treatment as useless since death is inevitable. In his 80s, Opiyo spent his last few years sitting on a stool outside his house or lying on his bed, cared for by his wife and daughter-in-law. Advised by local hospital personnel to have a blood transfusion, Opiyo refused: "Let me just be this way. Will

I put off death?" Other elders, questioned whether they feared death, echoed Opiyo's sentiments with responses such as: "Do I fear death? Why should I fear death? I am old, my blood is cool. I am just waiting to die."

As everywhere, physical and mental frailty leads to self-care problems, reduced productive activities, and lessened participation in kinship exchange and social networks. When frailty forces Samia elders to retire from their usual activities they become economically and socially marginalized. For example, in my 1985 survey, 66 men and women said they had given up an income-producing craft activity or the job of being village headman (a few men) because of "sickness" or "old age." The very frail may—like Opiyo—just sit in their homes, often alone, doing little or nothing, waiting to be fed, waiting for death.

Though the cultural ideal is that children should care for elderly parents, some of the aged may not receive needed assistance. This is especially true for those with no children or no sons, although even some with children are neglected or abandoned. About 10 percent of older Samia have no son, with women about twice as likely as men to be sonless. Sonless women's risk is even higher than men's in another sense, however, in that women are more dependent on sons than men. Most men remain married until death and receive personal care and food from wives. But husbands do not give personal care or prepare food even if they are available. However, not all women feel as did Anjelina, that they are better off without a husband. An old Samia mother named Manyuru was a widow with no son and only one daughter who lived far away. Manyuru was frail, blind, nearing her 90s. Every meal was a struggle. One day when I gave her a few shillings she smiled and said: "Now I can be sure [of eating], like a woman with a husband."

Though Manyuru lived with two of her co-wives (each with her own house), nearly all older Samia women (and most men) live in multigenerational households with other family members, often the daughters-in-law who provide much of the hands-on care required by frail older women. Daughters and grandchildren are also providers of assistance. If the elders' relationships with these family members are good, then assistance is likely, though it may be limited by a family's material resources and available labor.

RESEARCH AND PRACTICAL IMPLICATIONS: POLITICAL AND MORAL CHALLENGES

If gender is "the public meaning, the politicalization . . . of one's chromosomes" (Hendricks 1992:1), the same could also be said of health and aging. Health for all and successful aging for as many as possible will become realities only through meeting the political and moral challenges of achieving gender, race, class, and economic justice at all levels of human organization, from families and local communities to national governments and international agencies. This means ending poverty, poor nutrition, lack of access to health care, social and economic discrimination, and political oppression.

We must change our ideas about health. To begin, we must accept fully the broader conception of health advocated by the World Health Organization, and found in many of the world's cultures as well, as involving mental, physical, and social well-being. We must go beyond a view of health as the result of individual physiology and behavior to a conception of health, including health in old age, as a consequence of broad cultural, social, political, and economic forces (Estes and Rundall 1991; Falola and Ityavyar 1992; Koblinsky, Timyan, and Gay 1993). Such a perspective will move us away from mere "treatment" of "problems" to changing the underlying conditions of life, which deny to so many the possibility of good health even in the most limited sense of physical status.

In the United States, the biomedicalization of aging has produced a narrow focus on physical health, medical interventions, and an enormous geriatric "medical-industrial complex" (Estes and Binney 1989; Relman 1980). Gerontologists are only beginning to realize the significance of issues such as gender, race, ethnicity and culture, class, and rural-urban differences in aging processes. Further steps should lead to nonmedical approaches to the elderly, such as social support assistance and improved living environments of both community-dwelling (the great majority) and institutionalized elderly—especially taking into account older persons' own perceptions of their needs and their preferences in meeting these needs.

Worldwide, meeting the health needs of aging women begins with meeting the health needs of females from conception through the reproductive years. Ideally, the health needs of older women should be addressed directly. The likelihood of this is slim in underdeveloped regions where the goal of achieving good health for children and women in their reproductive years is still a long way from realization. Improved health for younger women would benefit them into their own old age. It would also help their children, along with males and older women in their families, because these are the women "holding up the world" through their roles in production, family nutrition, caregiving, and in other critical arenas.

The necessary changes will not happen overnight, nor even by the year 2000. Some will devolve from macrolevel policy and program adjustments and democratic economic and social development, but many improvements will come about only through local grassroots initiatives. Both thrusts are needed if we are to meet the health challenges of the 21st century and improve health not simply by medical interventions and lengthening life, but by improving the quality of life from birth to death.

Certainly, part of the solution involves filling the data gaps in knowledge about gender, aging, and health. This will require multidisciplinary research, listening carefully to women (of all ages), and recognizing the significance to human health of the interaction of biological, social, cultural, and economic processes. It will also require recognition that old people are not homogeneous and that they have differing needs. Among these considerations are the special vulnerabilities of older women and the special needs of frail elders.

Another element in the process is the empowerment of women, including older women, whose health and lives are at stake but who have been silenced.

Empowering women will have direct benefits for their health and overall quality of life, but it will also enable them to choose their own directions and work toward meeting the needs to which the women themselves give priority. Basic ingredients in the process of empowering women include education, access to resources including credit and information, income generation, collective action, reduced work burden, and improved nutrition and physical health.

The first principle may well be to listen—and listen well—to what women have to say (Brems and Griffiths 1993). Women's priorities may differ from those of donors; for example, women in India said vaginal white discharge was their top health problem; an expatriate expert dismissed the idea and learned little from them, but other researchers, willing to listen to the women, learned a great deal. Women may rate "nonhealth" over "health" programs. In research in Zambia, India, Bangladesh, Nepal, and Haiti, women preferred action on hunger, land, water, political persecution, literacy, day care, credit, and income generation above family planning, reduction of maternal morbidity, or AIDS prevention. In several of these cases, women whose incomes were increased were then more likely to seek contraceptive and health services.

Even in the United States, if we listen well to older persons (men as well as women), as I did in research in a Philadelphia neighborhood, we might find that better medical care or access to a retirement or lifecare community is not at the top of their list. Rather, for many, remaining in their own homes, in their familiar community, and participating in their existing social networks is what they most want (Cattell 1991).[25]

But listening is not enough, as seen in the long-term difficulties of establishing sustained condom use by Zairean women without support from other levels of society, especially high-status men (Schoepf et al. 1991). In this AIDS reduction program, the majority of men refused condoms, leaving women with no choice. Thus, "socioeconomic constraints . . . limit the possibilities of even highly motivated individuals to alter their behavior" (p. 203). A lesson to be learned from this experience seems to be that the desired effect might better be achieved through educating Zairean men to understand the hazards of AIDS and encouraging men to insist that their sexual partners accept condoms, rather than trying to effect the change through powerless sex workers and subordinate wives. While this would do nothing for gender equity, it would reduce exposure to AIDS, which is an urgent health need in Zaire and much of Africa.

Powerless, low-status women who organize can do much to empower themselves and bring about change even in the face of opposition from powerful males and other impediments (Jacobson 1993). At the national level in India, the Self-Employed Women's Organization (SEWA), a registered trade union, has made progress on Indian women's health and health-related working conditions and income security through collective action and the self-assurance gained by it. But women can also organize on local levels to form mutual aid savings and work groups, for example, which were common among the Samia in Kenya. Sometimes women can turn the unexpected to advantage, as when elderly Samia widows refuse customary leviratic marriage and renewed male domination in their homes with the support of men as well as women in their saved (born-again Christian) prayer groups (Cattell 1992b).

From the top-down perspective, women and elders should be included in international donor and development programs. At national levels, framing and enforcing property, marriage, and family laws to protect the rights of women and children are another possibility—though easier said than done, of course. The United States has yet to pass an equal rights amendment to its constitution! In Kenya, a marriage law to require financial support for the children of unwed fathers (among other provisions) has stumbled time and again in a parliament composed almost entirely of male MPs. Nevertheless, the effort continues, and perhaps some day the law will become reality—and then the struggle will shift to enforcing the law.

Looking for successful developing-country programs targeted to benefit older women, one finds practically none. However, programs intended to benefit "women" or "old people" may benefit older women in particular. Tout (1989) describes a wide range of small-scale, locally financed and operated projects to benefit the "elderly" (including women) in developing countries. These schemes, under the aegis of HelpAge International and local HelpAge organizations, emphasize local participation, immediate benefits, and sustainability. They include food assistance, house building, medical clinics, and income-generating projects, some of which utilize nearly forgotten indigenous technology such as a pottery-making scheme in rural Kenya. In a more ambitious undertaking, Help-Age worked with local elders in Colombia. With five years' support from international expertise and funding, HelpAge developed a viable national voluntary program to benefit elderly Colombians. The program, Pro Vida, began as a commercial bakery operated by and for old people but quickly expanded to include a laundry, handicraft workshops, and retail outlet, along with home-visit, intergenerational, and school programs. While only a few of these are directed at physical health as such, all benefit health in the wider sense.

To sum up, then, health cannot be separated from other issues such as poverty and political powerlessness, nor can health in one stage of life be divorced from lifetime health. Health involves many gender issues in which girls and women are disadvantaged compared to boys and men, but in the long run what benefits the health of females will also benefit male health. We cannot expect men to forego or share their privileges on the basis of this logic, however. So the challenges remain, and the struggle for health equity will continue.

NOTES

1. For example, the Baltimore Longitudinal Study on Aging, which aims to define normal aging, did not include women until twenty years into its program (Shock et al. 1984).
2. This should change rapidly with the establishment in 1990 of the Office of Research on Women's Health and the Women's Health Initiative of the National Institutes of Health, especially as these and other NIH initiatives emphasize a life-course approach

and the importance of doing research on older as well as younger women (NIH 1992; Pinn 1992a,b).

3. Following the United Nations, I use the terms more developed and less developed nations, or developed and developing, which reflect differences in technological capacity, wealth, and economic development.

4. Women are not always the ones who are shortchanged. It is estimated that in the United States 35,000 men will die of prostate cancer and 46,000 women will die of breast cancer in 1994. In the same year, the National Institutes of Health will spend $51 million on prostate cancer research and $299 million on breast cancer research. ("To Test or Not to Test," Newsweek 12/27/93:42–43).

5. This gender difference in self-assessed health (women reporting more illness/poorer health than men) is not universal, but it does occur in other countries, as among elderly in ten European countries and Kuwait interviewed during a World Health Organization cross-national survey (Heikkinen, Waters, and Brzezinski 1983). However, this pattern was not observed in the four nations covered in the Western Pacific version of the survey (Andrews et al. 1986).

6. In this research, Manton also found sex differences in the patterns of the causes of disability.

7. For discussions of the life course and life stages, see, for example, Albert and Cattell (1994); Elder (1985); Fry (1990); Fry and Keith (1982); Hagestad (1990); and the extensive literature on age-set systems—see Stewart's (1977) bibliography.

8. Many details in this model are not attributable to any single or several sources. Inspiration came largely from Crews (1990) and Spence (1989) on the biological sequence; George (1992) and Paltiel (1989, 1993) on mental health; and the following on various other aspects of health and society: Albert and Cattell (1994); Cattell (1992a); Freedman and Maine (1993); Heise (1993); Jacobson (1993); McLanahan, Sorensen, and Watson (1989); and Merchant and Kurz (1993).

9. This research was done in Samia Location, Busia District. I lived in Samia for two years in 1984–85 and made shorter visits in 1982, 1987, 1990, 1992, and 1993. Research methods included participant observation, informal and structured interviews, and a survey of 416 Samia women and men age 50+. I thank especially John Barasa "JB" Owiti for his invaluable research assistance over the past decade; my other Samia field assistants; Medical Mission Sisters and Holy Family Hospital at Nangina; and, as always, my husband Bob Moss, who has contributed so much over the years. Above all, *mutio muno* to the many people of Samia who have allowed me to share their lives in various ways. The research was partially funded by the National Science Foundation (grant BNS8306802), the Wenner-Gren Foundation (grant 4506), and Bryn Mawr College (Frederica de Laguna Fund grant). I was a Research Associate at the Institute of African Studies, University of Nairobi, in 1984–85. I have written extensively about both gender and old age among the Samia (Cattell 1989a,b; 1990; 1992b,c; 1993; 1994a,b,c; 1995a,b; n.d.).

10. Procedures range from minor alteration of the clitoris to its complete removal to infibulation, or excision, of most external genitalia and sewing up (infibulating) the remaining tissue, leaving a tiny opening through which it is barely possible to urinate or pass menstrual fluids. Husbands enlarge the opening for intercourse by force; for childbirth, a woman is cut open, then reinfibulated (Lightfoot-Klein 1989). Clearly women suffer enormously from these practices. An estimated 85 to 114 million women now living have experienced genital surgeries and 2 million girls undergo it each year (World Bank 1993).

11. Another twist on the issue occurs among immigrants to nations that prohibit excision and infibulation (Winter 1994).

12. The 106-bed Holy Family Hospital at Nangina, under the Roman Catholic Diocese of Bungoma, serves a 400-square-mile area with a population of about 75,000. It is the only hospital in the area, which is also served by two government health centers and four dispensaries.

13. Health statistics are from Holy Family Hospital, Nangina, annual reports covering a number of years from 1979 to 1993; crop and livestock data are from a household survey the hospital carried out in 1985 (unpublished data).

14. In my survey of 416 older Samia, 11 women and 8 men had no living children; 28 women and 17 men had no living son. Women were about twice as likely as men to be sonless.

15. Kwashiorkor and marasmus constitute from 9 to 28 percent of the malnutrition attendances. Total child attendances during this period have varied, from a high of 75,879 in 1984 to around 25,000 annually since 1990. Data are from Nangina Holy Family Hospital's annual reports for the years from 1984 through 1993 except 1987 and 1991 (the latter not in my possession).

16. Much of this material comes from Nangina Hospital annual reports from 1980 to 1993, particularly their discussions of the Nutrition Rehabilitation Unit operated by the hospital from 1973 through 1985; some is from K'Okul (1991) and Olenja (1986).

17. The other half of burning deaths result from accidents during cooking. Burns are a major cause of injuries among women in developing countries (Kjellstrom et al. 1992).

18. Issues concerning male violence against women are hot topics today in Kenya (e.g. Mutuli 1992). Ideas such as marital rape (incomprehensible to many) or rejecting the acceptability of beating girls and women are encountering tremendous resistance from men, although Kenya's Attorney-General Amos Wako is not only listening to women, he has proposed a law on rape within marriage (Ngugi 1993; *Weekly Review* 1994a, 1994b). The *Weekly Review*, Kenya's news magazine, which is usually overladen with stories about male politicians, recently instituted a feature titled "Gender Issues." The battle is joined; it will no doubt be a long and bitter war.

19. The Community Health Worker program was established by Nangina Holy Family Hospital in October 1976; the CHWs are local people who receive a course of training and then work in their home communities.

20. This kind of smoke exposure is damaging to adults' respiratory systems and contributes to acute respiratory infections, especially pneumonia, in young children (World Bank 1993). Cigarette smoking is not common in Samia; most smokers I have seen were old women. In 1993 an old woman I will call "Namenya wa Sigara" (Namenya, a clan name, "of the Cigarette") told me she smoked four cigarettes each day, buying them at 70 cents each. Thus Namenya wa Sigara spent 2.80 Kenya shillings (Kshs) a day, or about 80 Kshs a month, for smoke inhalation—probably a major expenditure, as many older women have little cash income. The neighbor selling cigarettes one by one made 2 Kshs per pack and is an example of the effort people make to get very small sums of money. At that time (July 1993) the 2 Kshs would not have bought even one soda; a kilo of sugar was 22 Kshs, a kilo of meat, 50.

21. While the so-called degenerative diseases are today's leading causes of death in the developed regions, this is a recent development. The causes of death in the United States a century ago were similar to those in developing countries today, that is, primarily infectious communicable diseases. The epidemiologic or health transition is a 20th-century phenomenon. It refers to the shift in age-specific causes of death from

predominantly communicable diseases and reproductive causes to noncommunicable causes (including cancers, cardiovascular, and senile and ill-defined conditions) (Borgatta et al. 1990; Feachem, Phillips, and Bulatao 1992; Kjellstrom et al. 1992; Murray et al. 1992). These changes are associated with diminished risk exposure through interventions such as vaccination and environmental sanitation, and through urbanization, industrialization, and lifestyle changes, along with increased access to, utilization of, and effectiveness of, curative health services (Feachem, Phillips, and Bulatao 1992).

22. Functional disability is the inability to carry out the everyday tasks of self-care and independent living. Functionality is commonly measured by two scales standardized for use in industrial nations: the Activities of Daily Living (ADL) and Instrumental Activities of Daily Living (IADL). At present there are no adequate instruments for measuring physical or cognitive functionality across all cultures/societies (Albert and Cattell 1994). Gender- and culture-sensitive mental health research is even less advanced (Paltiel 1993).

23. Anjelina and other women have become leaders in Samia women's struggle for greater autonomy in their lives (Cattell 1992b).

24. Formal health care in Samia is directed mostly to primary health-care concerns such as immunizations, antenatal care, treating infectious diseases and other acute conditions, and improving hygiene.

25. This research was funded by The Retirement Research Foundation in a grant made to the Philadelphia Geriatric Center.

REFERENCES

Abu-Lughod, Leila
  1990   The Romance of Resistance: Tracing Transformations of Power through Bedouin Women. American Ethnologist 17:41–55.
Albert, Steven M., and Maria G. Cattell
  1994   Old Age in Global Perspective: Cross-Cultural and Cross-National Views. New York: G. K. Hall/MacMillan.
Aloo, Theresa C.
  1993   Fuelwood and Tree Planting: A Case Study from Funyula Division in Western Kenya. Ph.D. Dissertation: Department of Forest Resources Management, University of British Columbia. Ottawa: National Library of Canada.
Andrews, Gary R., Adrian J. Esterman, Annette J. Braunack-Mayer, and Cam M. Rungie
  1986   Aging in the Western Pacific: A Four-Country Study. Manila: World Health Organization.
Arendell, Terry, and Carroll L. Estes
  1991   Older Women in the Post-Reagan Era. *In* Critical Perspectives on Aging: The Political and Moral Economy of Growing Old. Meredith Minkler and Carroll L. Estes, eds. Pp. 209–226. Amityville, NY: Baywood.
Banister, J.
  1988   Implications of the Aging of China's Population. Staff Paper No. 4. Washington, DC: U.S. Bureau of the Census, Center for International Research.
Boddy, Janice
  1989   Wombs and Alien Spirits: Women, Men and the Zar Cult in Northern Sudan. Madison: University of Wisconsin Press.

Borgatta, Edgar F., Kris Bulcroft, Rhonda J. V. Montgomery, and Richard Bulcroft
   1990   Health Promotion Over the Life Course. Research on Aging 12:373–388.

Boserup, Ester
   1970   Woman's Role in Economic Development. New York: St. Martin's Press.

Bradley, Candice, and James Onyango Ndege
   In press Fertility Decline in a Maragoli Sublocation. *In* African Families and the Crisis
             of Social Change. Thomas S. Weisner, Candice Bradley, and Philip L. Kilbride,
             eds. Westport, CT: Greenwood.

Brems, Susan, and Marcia Griffiths
   1993   Health Women's Way: Learning to Listen. *In* The Health of Women: A Glob-
             al Perspective. Marge Koblinsky, Judith Timyan, and Jill Gay, eds. Pp. 255–273.
             Boulder/San Francisco/Oxford: Westview.

Burkhauser, R. V.
   1990   How Public Policy Increases the Vulnerability of Older Widows. Journal of
             Aging and Social Policy 2(3/4):117–130.

Cattell, Maria G.
   1989a   Old Age in Rural Kenya: Gender, the Life Course and Social Change. Ph.D.
             Dissertation, Department of Anthropology, Bryn Mawr College. Ann Arbor:
             University Microfilms.
   1989b   Knowledge and Social Change in Samia, Western Kenya. Journal of Cross-Cul-
             tural Gerontology 4:225–244.
   1990   Models of Old Age among the Samia of Kenya: Family Support of the Elderly.
             Journal of Cross-Cultural Gerontology 5:375–394.
   1991   Aging in Place: Older Persons' Assessment of Urban Neighborhood Resources.
             Final Report to The Retirement Research Foundation (unpublished).
   1992a   Informal Systems of Old Age Support in Developing Countries: Anthropolog-
             ical Perspectives. World Bank Seminar Discussion Paper (unpublished).
   1992b   Praise the Lord and Say No to Men: Older Samia Women Empowering Them-
             selves. Journal of Cross-Cultural Gerontology 7:307–330.
   1992c   Burying Mary Omundu: The Politics of Death and Gender in Samia, Kenya.
             Paper presented at the annual meeting of the African Studies Association,
             Seattle.
   1993   Caring for the Elderly in Sub-Saharan Africa. Ageing International
             XX(2):13–19.
   1994a   Gender and Old Age among the Samia of Kenya. Southern African Journal of
             Gerontology 3(1):1–7.
   1994b   "Nowadays It Isn't Easy to Advise the Young": Grandmothers and Grand-
             daughters among Abaluyia of Kenya. Journal of Cross-Cultural Gerontology
             9:157–178.
   1994c   Intergenerational Relations among the Samia of Kenya: Culture and Experi-
             ence. Southern African Journal of Gerontology 3(2):30–36.
   1995a   Gender, Age and Power among Abaluyia Women of Kenya. Women in Inter-
             national Development Working Papers (under review).
   1995b   Between the Generations: Exchange, Intergenerational Contracts and Elder
             Care in Samia, Kenya. *In* African Families and the Crisis of Social Change.
             Thomas S. Weisner, Candice Bradley, and Philip L. Kilbride, eds. Westport, CT:
             Greenwood (in press).
   In press. African Widows: Case Studies from Kenya. *In* The Cultural Context of Aging.
             Revised edition. Jay Sokolovsky, ed. South Hadley, MA: Bergin & Garvey.

Cattell, Maria G., and Steven M. Albert
   1994   Caring for the Elderly. *In* Research Frontiers in Anthropology. Carol R. Ember
             and Melvin Ember, eds. Pp. 101–119. Englewood Cliffs, NJ: Prentice Hall.

Chang, Jung
    1991   Wild Swans: Three Daughters of China. New York: Simon & Schuster.

Clark, Margaret, and Barbara G. Anderson
    1967   Culture and Aging: An Anthropological Study of Older Americans. Springfield, IL: Thomas.

Cohen, Ronald
    1984   Age and Culture as Theory. *In* Age and Anthropological Theory. David I. Kertzer and Jennie Keith, eds. Pp. 234–239. Ithaca, NY: Cornell University Press.

Counts, Dorothy
    1987   Female Suicide and Wife Abuse: A Cross-Cultural Perspective. Suicide and Life-Threatening Behavior 17(3):194–205.

Counts, Dorothy Ayers, Judith K. Brown, and Jacquelyn C. Campbell
    1992   Sanctions and Sanctuary: Cultural Perspectives on the Beating of Wives. Boulder, CO: Westview.

Cowgill, Donald O., and Lowell D. Holmes, eds.
    1972   Aging and Modernization. New York: Appleton-Century-Crofts.

Crews, Douglas E.
    1990   Anthropological Issues in Biological Gerontology. *In* Anthropology and Aging: Comprehensive Reviews. Robert L. Rubinstein, ed. Pp. 11–38. Dordrecht: Kluwer Academic Publishers.

Crews, Douglas E., and Sharon Fitzsimons
    In press   Reciprocal Relationships between Family and Health. *In* Handbook of Marriage and the Family. 2nd edition. Marvin B. Sussman and Suzanne K. Steinmetz, eds. New York: Plenum.

Crews, Douglas E., and Ralph M. Garruto, eds.
    1994   Biological Anthropology and Aging: Perspectives on Human Variation over the Life Span. New York: Oxford.

Davis, Karen, Paula Grant, and Diane Rowland
    1992   Alone and Poor: The Plight of Elderly Women. *In* Gender and Aging. Lou Glasse and Jon Hendricks, eds. Pp. 79–90. Amityville, NY: Baywood.

Dawitt, Seble
    1994   African Women in the Diaspora and the Problem of Female Genital Mutilation. Paper presented at the annual meeting of the African Studies Association, Toronto.

Dickey, Marilyn
    1994   Drugs Fighting Drugs Pose Growing Threat. AARP Bulletin 35(1):2, 16–17.

Dorjahn, Vernon
    1989   Where Do the Old Folks Live? The Residence of the Elderly among the Temne of Sierra Leone. Journal of Cross-Cultural Gerontology 4:257–278.

Dressel, Paula L.
    1991   Gender, Race, and Class: Beyond the Feminization of Poverty in Later Life. *In* Critical Perspectives on Aging: The Political and Moral Economy of Growing Old. Meredith Minkler and Carroll L. Estes, eds. Pp. 245–252. Amityville, NY: Baywood.

Dreze, Jean
    1990   Widows in Rural India. London: Development Economics Research Programme.

Elder, Glen H., Jr.
    1985   Perspectives on the Life Course. *In* Life Course Dynamics: Trajectories and Transitions, 1968–1980. G. H. Elder, Jr., ed. Pp. 23–49. Ithaca: Cornell University Press.

Estes, Carroll L., and Elizabeth A. Binney
    1989   The Biomedicalization of Aging: Dangers and Dilemmas. The Gerontologist 29:587–596.

Estes, Carroll L., and Thomas G. Rundall
    1991   Social Characteristics, Social Structure, and Health in the Aging Population. *In* Aging, Health, and Behavior. Marcia G. Ory, Ronald P. Abeles, and Paul Darby Lipman, eds. Pp. 299–326. Newbury Park, CA: Sage.

Falola, Toyin, and Dennis Ityavyar
    1992   The Political Economy of Health in Africa. Athens, OH: Ohio University Center for International Studies.

Feachem, Richard G. A., Tord Kjellstrom, Christopher J. L. Murray, Mead Over, and Margaret A. Phillips, eds.
    1992   The Health of Adults in the Developing World. New York: Oxford University Press/The World Bank.

Feachem, Richard G. A., Margaret A. Phillips, and Rodolfo A. Bulatao
    1992   Introducing Adult Health. *In* The Health of Adults in the Developing World. Richard G. A. Feachem, Tord Kjellstrom, Christopher J. L. Murray, Mead Over, and Margaret A. Phillips, eds. Pp. 1–22. New York: Oxford University Press/The World Bank.

Ferraro, Kenneth F.
    1989   Widowhood and Health. *In* Aging, Stress and Health. Kyriakos S. Markides and Cary L. Cooper, eds. Pp. 69–83. Chichester, NY: John Wiley & Sons.

Foner, Nancy
    1985   Old and Frail and Everywhere Unequal. The Hastings Center Report 15(2):27–31.

Freedman, Lynn P., and Deborah Maine
    1993   Women's Mortality: A Legacy of Neglect. *In* The Health of Women: A Global Perspective. Marge Koblinsky, Judith Timyan, and Jill Gay, eds. Pp. 147–170. Boulder/San Francisco/Oxford: Westview.

Fry, Christine L.
    1985   Culture, Behavior, and Aging in the Comparative Perspective. *In* Handbook of The Psychology of Aging. 2nd edition. James E. Birren and K. Warner Schaie, eds. Pp. 216–244. New York: Van Nostrand Reinhold Company.
    1990   The Life Course in Context: Implications of Research. *In* Anthropology and Aging: Comprehensive Reviews. Robert L. Rubinstein, ed. Pp. 129–149. Norwell, MA: Kluwer.

Fry, Christine L., and Jennie Keith
    1982   The Life Course as a Cultural Unit. *In* Aging and Society, Volume 3: A Sociology of Age Stratification. Matilda White Riley, Marilyn Johnson, and Anne Foner, eds. Pp. 51–70. New York: Russell Sage Foundation.

George, Linda K.
    1992   Gender, Age, and Psychiatric Disorders. *In* Gender and Aging. Lou Glasse and Jon Hendricks, eds. Pp. 33–43. Amityville, NY: Baywood.

Glascock, Anthony P., and Susan L. Feinman
    1981   Social Asset or Social Burden: Treatment of the Aged in Non-Industrial Societies. *In* Dimensions: Aging, Culture, and Health. Christine L. Fry, ed. Pp. 13–31. New York: J. F. Bergin.

Grigsby, Jill S., and S. Jay Olshansky
    1989   The Demographic Components of Population Aging in China. Journal of Cross-Cultural Gerontology 4:307–335.

Gunning, Isabelle R.
  1991–92   Arrogant Perception, World-Travelling and Multicultural Feminism: The Case
            of Female Genital Surgeries. Columbia Human Rights Law Review 23:189–248.

Hagestad, G. O.
  1990   Social Perspectives on the Life Course. *In* Handbook of Aging and the Social
            Sciences. 3d edition. Robert H. Binstock and Linda K. George, eds. Pp.
            151–168. New York: Academic.

Harris, Tamara B., and Jacob J. Feldman
  1991   Implications of Health Status in Analysis of Risk in Older Persons. Journal of
            Aging and Health 3:262–284.

Hay, Margaret Jean and Sharon Stichter, eds.
  1984   African Women South of the Sahara. London and New York: Longman.

Healy, Bernadine
  1992   Foreword. *In* National Institutes of Health: Opportunities for Research on
            Women's Health. Summary Report of Conference, September 4–6, 1991, Hunt
            Valley MD. U.S. Department of Health and Human Services.

Heikkinen, E., W. E. Waters, and Z. J. Brzezinski
  1983   The Elderly in Eleven Countries: A Sociomedical Survey. Copenhagen: World
            Health Organization.

Heise, Lori
  1993   Violence Against Women: The Missing Agenda. *In* The Health of Women: A
            Global Perspective. Marge Koblinsky, Judith Timyan, and Jill Gay, eds. Pp.
            171–195. Boulder/San Francisco/Oxford: Westview.

Hendricks, Jon
  1992   Introduction: Making Something of Our Chromosomes. *In* Gender and Aging.
            Lou Glasse and Jon Hendricks, eds. Pp. 1–4. Amityville, NY: Baywood.

Hess, Beth B.
  1992   Gender and Aging: The Demographic Parameters. *In* Gender and Aging. Lou
            Glasse and Jon Hendricks, eds. Pp. 15–23. Amityville, NY: Baywood.

Hochschild, R.
  1989   Improving the Precision of Biological Age Determinations. Part 2: Automatic
            Human Tests, Age Norms and Variability. Experimental Gerontology
            24:301–316.

Jacobson, Jodi L.
  1993   Women's Health: The Price of Poverty. *In* The Health of Women: A Global
            Perspective. Marge Koblinsky, Judith Timyan, and Jill Gay, eds. Pp. 3–31. Boul-
            der/San Francisco/Oxford: Westview.

Kaufman, Sharon R.
  1994   The Social Construction of Frailty: An Anthropological Perspective. Journal of
            Aging Studies 8:45–58.

Keith, Jennie
  1990   Age in Social and Cultural Context: Anthropological Perspectives. *In* Hand-
            book of Aging and the Social Sciences. 3d edition. Robert H. Binstock and
            Linda K. George, eds. Pp. 91–111. New York: Academic Press.

Keith, Jennie, Christine L. Fry, Anthony P. Glascock, Charlotte Ikels, Jeanette Dickerson-
Putman, Henry C. Harpending, Patricia Draper
  1994   The Aging Experience: Diversity and Commonality Across Cultures. Thousand
            Oaks, CA: Sage.

Kerns, Virginia, and Judith K. Brown, eds.
  1992   In Her Prime: New Views of Middle-Aged Women. 2nd edition. Urbana: Uni-
            versity of Illinois Press.

Kilbride, Philip L.
  1992   Unwanted Children as a Consequence of Delocalization in Modern Kenya. *In* Anthropological Research: Process and Application. John J. Poggie, Jr., Billie R. DeWalt, and William W. Dressler, eds. Pp. 185–315. Albany: SUNY Press.

Kilbride, Philip L., and Janet C. Kilbride
  1990   Changing Family Life in East Africa: Women and Children at Risk. University Park: Pennsylvania State University Press.
  In press. Stigma, Role Overload, and the Delocalization of Family Tradition: Problems Facing the Contemporary Kenyan Woman. *In* African Families and the Crisis of Social Change. Thomas S. Weisner, Candice Bradley, and Philip L. Kilbride, eds. Westport, CT: Greenwood.

Kinsella, Kevin
  1988   Aging in the Third World. Staff Paper No. 35. Washington, DC: U.S. Bureau of the Census, Center for International Research.
  1990   Living Arrangements of the Elderly and Social Policy: A Cross-National Perspective. Staff Paper No. 52. Washington, DC: U.S. Bureau of the Census, Center for International Research.

Kjellstrom, Tord, Jeffrey P. Koplan, and Richard B. Rothenberg
  1992   Current and Future Determinants of Adult Ill-Health. *In* The Health of Adults in the Developing World. Richard G. A. Feachem, Tord Kjellstrom, Christopher J. L. Murray, Mead Over, and Margaret A. Phillips, eds. Pp. 209–259. New York: Oxford University Press/The World Bank.

Koblinsky, Marge, Oona M. R. Campbell, and Sioban D. Harlow
  1993   Mother and More: A Broader Perspective on Women's Health. *In* The Health of Women: A Global Perspective. Marge Koblinksky, Judith Timyan, and Jill Gay, eds. Pp. 33–62. Boulder/San Francisco/Oxford: Westview.

Koblinsky, Marge, Judith Timyan, and Jill Gay, eds.
  1993   The Health of Women: A Global Perspective. Boulder/San Francisco/Oxford: Westview.

K'Okul, Richard N. O.
  1991   Maternal and Child Health in Kenya: A Study of Poverty, Disease and Malnutrition in Samia. Monograph of the Finnish Society for Development Studies No. 4. Uppsala: The Scandinavian Institute of African Studies.

Kratz, Corinne A.
  1994   Affecting Performance: Meaning, Movement, and Experience in Okiek Women's Initiation. Washington, DC: Smithsonian.

LaRosa, Judith H., and Vivian W. Pinn
  1993   Gender Bias in Biomedical Research. Journal of the American Medical Women's Association 48:145–151.

Leacock, Eleanor, Helen I. Safa, and Contributors
  1986   Women's Work: Development and the Division of Labor by Gender. South Hadley, MA: Bergin & Garvey.

Levinson, David
  1989   Violence in Cross-Cultural Perspective. Newbury Park, CA: Sage.

Lightfoot-Klein, Hanny
  1989   Prisoners of Ritual: An Odyssey into Female Genital Circumcision in Africa. Binghamton, NY: Harrington Park Press.

Lock, Margaret
  1993   The Politics of Mid-Life and Menopause: Ideologies for the Second Sex in North America and Japan. *In* Knowledge, Power, and Practice: The Anthropology of Medicine and Everyday Life. Pp. 330–363. Berkeley: University of California Press.

Logue, Barbara J.
1990   Modernization and the Status of the Frail Elderly: Perspectives on Continuity and Change. Journal of Cross-Cultural Gerontology 5:345–375.

Lopata, Helena Z.
1987   Widowhood: World Perspectives on Support Systems. *In* Widows, Volume 1: The Middle East, Asia, and the Pacific. Helena Z. Lopata, ed. Pp. 1–23. Durham: Duke University Press.

Lyman, Karen A.
1989   Bringing the Social Back In: A Critique of the Biomedicalization of Dementia. The Gerontologist 29:597–605.

Makuto, Daniel G.
1979   Evaluation of the Nangina Hospital Community Health Worker Programme and Its Effects in Promoting Maternal and Child Health. M.Sc. Dissertation: University of London.

Manton, Kenneth G.
1988   A Longitudinal Study of Functional Change and Mortality in the United States. Journal of Gerontology 43:153–161.
1990   Population Models of Gender Differences in Mortality, Morbidity, and Disability Risks. *In* Gender, Health, and Longevity: Multidisciplinary Perspectives. Marcia G. Ory and Huber R. Warner, eds. Pp. 201–253. New York: Springer.

Markides, Kyriakos S.
1992   Risk Factors, Gender and Health. *In* Gender and Aging. Lou Glasse and Jon Hendricks, eds. Pp. 25–42. Amityville, NY: Baywood.

Masamba ma Mpolo
1984   Older Persons and Their Families in a Changing Village Society: A Perspective from Zaire. Washington, DC: The International Federation on Ageing and The World Council of Churches.

McLanahan, Sara S., Annemette Sorensen, and Dorothy Watson
1989   Sex Differences in Poverty, 1950–1980. Signs: Journal of Women in Culture and Society 15:102–122.

Merchant, Kathleen M., and Kathleen M. Kurz
1992   Women's Nutrition through the Life Cycle: Social and Biological Vulnerabilities. *In* The Health of Women: A Global Perspective. Marge Koblinsky, Judith Timyan, and Jill Gay, eds. Pp. 63–90. Boulder/San Francisco/Oxford: Westview.

Minkler, Meredith, and Carroll L. Estes, eds.
1991   Critical Perspectives on Aging: The Political and Moral Economy of Growing Old. Amityville, NY: Baywood.

Murray, Christopher J. L., Goghuan Yang, and Xinjian Qiao
1992   Adult Mortality: Levels, Patterns, and Causes. *In* The Health of Adults in the Developing World. Richard G. A. Feachem, Tord Kjellstrom, Christopher J. L. Murray, Mead Over, and Margaret A. Phillips, eds. Pp. 23–111. New York: Oxford University Press for The World Bank.

Mutuli, Millicent
1992   A Crusader Against Rape. Nairobi: The Standard on Sunday "Now" Magazine, August 23 (Issue 082):2–4.

Myers, George C.
1990   Demography and Aging. *In* Handbook of Aging and the Social Sciences. 3d edition. Robert H. Binstock and Linda K. George, eds. Pp. 19–44. New York: Academic.
1992   Demographic Aging and Family Support for Older Persons. *In* Family Support for the Elderly: The International Experience. Hal L. Kendig, Akiko Hashimo-

to, and Larry C. Coppard, eds. Pp. 31–68. Oxford/New York/Tokyo: Oxford University Press for the World Health Organization.

Nangina Hospital (Holy Family Hospital)
Annual Reports for 1980, 1981, 1985, 1986, 1988, 1989, 1990, 1992–1993. Nangina, Kenya.

Nathanson, Constance A.
1990   The Gender-Mortality Differential in Developed Countries: Demographic and Sociocultural Dimensions. *In* Gender, Health, and Longevity: Multidisciplinary Perspectives. Marcia G. Ory and Huber R. Warner, eds. Pp. 3–23. New York: Springer.

National Institutes of Health (NIH)
1992   Opportunities for Research on Women's Health. Summary Report of Conference, U.S. Department of Health and Human Services, September 4–6, 1991, Hunt Valley, MD.

Neysmith, Sheila M.
1991   Dependency among Third World Elderly: A Need for New Direction in the Nineties. *In* Critical Perspectives on Aging: The Political and Moral Economy of Growing Old. Meredith Minkler and Carroll L. Estes, eds. Pp. 311–321. Amityville, NY: Baywood.

Neysmith, Sheila M., and Joey Edwardh
1984   Economic Dependency in the 1980s: Its Impact on Third World Elderly. Ageing and Society 4:21–44.

Ngugi, Patrick
1993   Women in Plea to A-G over Violence. Nairobi: Daily Nation, June 4:3.

Ofei-Aboagye, Rosemary Ofeibea
1994   Altering the Strands of the Fabric: A Preliminary Look at Domestic Violence in Ghana. Signs 19:924–938.

Ojiambo, Julia A.
1967   Maternal and Infant Dietary Practices of the Abasamia of Busia District, Western Province, Kenya: A Preliminary Study 1966–67. East African Medical Journal 44(12):518–523.

Okojie, Felix
1988   Aging in Sub-Saharan Africa: Toward a Redefinition of Needs Research and Policy Direction. Journal of Cross-Cultural Gerontology 3:3–20.

Olenja, Joyce
1986   Traditional Diet. *In* Kenya Socio-Cultural Profiles: Busia District. Robert Soper, ed. Pp. 52–66. Nairobi: Ministry of Planning and National Development and Institute of African Studies, University of Nairobi.

Ortner, Sherry B., and Harriet Whitehead, eds.
1981   Sexual Meanings: The Cultural Construction of Gender and Sexuality. Cambridge: Cambridge University Press.

Paltiel, Freda L.
1989   Occupational Health of Midlife and Older Women in Latin America and the Caribbean. *In* Midlife and Older Women in Latin America and the Caribbean. Pp. 142–158. Washington, DC: AARP & PAHO.
1993   Women's Mental Health: A Global Perspective. *In* The Health of Women: A Global Perspective. Marge Koblinsky, Judith Timyan, and Jill Gay, eds. Pp. 197–216. Boulder/San Francisco/Oxford: Westview.

Pinn, Vivian W.
1992a   Commentary: Women, Research, and the National Institutes of Health. Journal of Preventive Medicine 8:324–327.

1992b   Women's Health Research: Prescribing Change and Addressing the Issues. Journal of the American Medical Association 268:1921–1922.

Potash, Betty, ed.
1986   Widows in African Societies: Choices and Constraints. Stanford, CA: Stanford University Press.

Relman, A. S.
1980   The New Medical-Industrial Complex. New England Journal of Medicine 303(17):963–970.

Riley, Matilda White
1985   Women, Men and the Lengthening Life Course. *In* Gender and the Life Course. Alice S. Rossi, ed. Pp. 333–347. New York: Aldine.
1990   Foreword: The Gender Paradox. *In* Gender, Health, and Longevity. Marcia G. Ory and Huber R. Warner, eds. Pp. xxiii–xxix. New York: Springer.
1992   Aging in the Twenty-first Century. *In* Aging, Money, and Life Satisfaction: Aspects of Financial Gerontology. Neal E. Cutler, Davis W. Gregg and M. Powell Lawton, eds. Pp. 23–36. New York: Springer.

Rix, Sara E.
1991   Older Women and Development. Paper presented at the Expert Group Meeting, Integration of Ageing and Elderly Women into Development, Vienna.

Rosaldo, Michelle Zimbalist, and Louise Lamphere
1974   Woman, Culture and Society. Stanford: Stanford University Press.

Rosenmayr, Leopold
1991   Improving the Health Status of the Rural Elderly in Mali. Journal of Cross-Cultural Gerontology 6:301–318.

Rossi, Alice S., ed.
1985   Gender and the Life Course. New York: Aldine.

Rubinstein, Robert L.
1990   Nature, Culture, Gender, Age: A Critical Review. In Anthropology and Aging. Robert L. Rubinstein, ed. Pp. 109–128. Dordrecht: Kluwer Academic.

Rubinstein, Robert L., Janet C. Kilbride, and Sharon Nagy
1992   Elders Living Alone: Frailty and the Perception of Choice. Hawthorne NY: Aldine de Gruyter.

Sankar, Andrea
1984   "It's Just Old Age": Old Age as a Diagnosis in American and Chinese Medicine. *In* Age and Anthropological Theory. David Kertzer and Jennie Keith, eds. Pp. 250–280. Ithaca: Cornell University Press.

Schoepf, Brooke Grundfest, Walu Engundu, Rukarangira wa Nkera, Payanzo Ntsomo, and Claude Schoepf
1991   Gender, Power, and Risk of AIDS in Zaire. *In* Women and Health in Africa. Meredeth Turshen, ed. Pp. 187–203. Trenton: Africa World Press.

Sennott-Miller, Lee
1989   The Health and Socioeconomic Situation of Midlife and Older Women in Latin America and the Caribbean. *In* Midlife and Older Women in Latin America and the Caribbean. Pp. 1–120. Washington DC: AARP & PAHO.

Sheffield, Carole
1987   Sexual Terrorism: The Social Control of Women. *In* Analyzing Gender: A Handbook of Social Science Research. Beth B. Hess and Myra Marx Ferree, eds. Pp. 171–189. Newbury Park, CA: Sage.

Shock, Nathan, R. C. Greulich, R. Andres, D. Arenberg, P. T. Costa, E. G. Lakatta, and J. D. Tobin
1984   Normal Human Aging: The Baltimore Study of Aging. NIH Publication No. 84–2450. Washington, DC: U.S. Government Printing Office.

Smith, David W. E.
1992   The Biology of Gender and Aging. *In* Gender and Aging. Lou Glasse and Jon Hendricks, eds. Pp. 5–13. Amityville, NY: Baywood.
1993   Human Longevity. New York/Oxford: Oxford University Press.

Smith, David W. E., and Huber R. Warner
1990   Overview of Biomedical Perspectives: Possible Relationships between Genes on the Sex Chromosomes and Longevity. *In* Gender, Health, and Longevity: Multidisciplinary Perspectives. Marcia G. Ory and Huber R. Warner, eds. Pp. 41–55. New York: Springer.

Spence, Alexander P.
1989   Biology of Human Aging. Englewood Cliffs, NJ: Prentice Hall.

Stewart, Frank H.
1977   Fundamentals of Age-Group Systems. New York: Academic.

Stone, Robyn, Gail Lee Cafferata, and Judith Sangl
1987   Caregivers of the Frail Elderly: A National Profile. The Gerontologist 27:616–626.

Tiano, Susan
1987   Gender, Work, and World Capitalism: Third World Women's Role in Development. *In* Analyzing Gender: A Handbook of Social Science Research. Beth B. Hess and Myra Marx Ferree, eds. Pp. 216–243. Newbury Park, CA: Sage.

Timyan, Judith, Susan J. Griffey Brechin, Diana M. Measham, and Bisi Ogunleye
1993   Access to Care: More Than a Problem of Distance. *In* The Health of Women: A Global Perspective. Marge Koblinsky, Judith Timyan, and Jill Gay, eds. Pp. 217–234. Boulder/San Francisco/Oxford: Westview.

Tout, Ken
1989   Ageing in Developing Countries. New York: Oxford University Press.

Treas, Judith and Barbara Logue
1986   Economic Development and the Older Population. Population and Development Review 12:645–673.

Turshen, Meredeth
1991   Gender and Health in Africa. *In* Women and Health in Africa. Meredeth Turshen, ed. Pp. 107–123. Trenton, NJ: Africa World Press.

Udvardy, Monica, and Maria G. Cattell
1992   Gender, Aging and Power in Sub-Saharan Africa: Challenges and Puzzles. Journal of Cross-Cultural Gerontology 7:275–288.

United Nations
1983   Vienna International Plan of Action on Aging. New York: United Nations.

U.S. Bureau of the Census
1991   Global Aging. Washington, DC: U.S. Department of Commerce.

Vatuk, Sylvia
1982   Old Age in India. *In* Old Age in Preindustrial Society. Peter N. Stearns, ed. Pp. 70–103. New York/London: Holmes & Meier.

Verbrugge, Lois M.
1985   Women and Men: Mortality and Health of Older People. *In* Growing Old in America: New Perspectives on Old Age. 3d edition. Beth B. Hess and Elizabeth W. Markson, eds. Pp. 181–205. New Brunswick/Oxford: Transaction.
1987   From Sneezes to Adieux: Stages of Health for American Men and Women. *In* Health in Aging: Sociological Issues and Policy Directions. Russell A. Ward and Sheldon S. Tobin, eds. Pp. 17–57. New York: Springer.
1988   Unveiling Higher Morbidity for Men. *In* Social Structures and Human Lives, Vol. 1, Social Change and the Life Course. Matilda White Riley, ed. American Sociological Association Presidential Series. Pp. 138–160. Newbury Park, CA: Sage.

1989   Pathways to Health and Death. *In* The History of Women, Health, and Medicine in America. R. D. Apple, ed. Pp. 41–79. New York: Garland.

1990   The Twain Meet: Empirical Explanations of Sex Differences in Health and Mortality. *In* Gender, Health, and Longevity: Multidisciplinary Perspectives. Marcia G. Ory and Huber R. Warner, eds. Pp. 159–199. New York: Springer.

Weekly Review

1994a   A-G Stirs Up a Hornet's Nest. Nairobi: The Weekly Review, April 29:18–19.

1994b   Pursuing Justice for Women. Nairobi: The Weekly Review, May 6:15–16.

Weg, Ruth B.

1985   Beyond Babies and Orgasm. *In* Growing Old in America: New Perspectives on Old Age. 3d edition. Beth B. Hess and Elizabeth W. Markson, eds. Pp. 206–222. New Brunswick/Oxford: Transaction.

Weisner, Thomas S.

In press Shared Social Support for Children and the African Family Crisis. *In* African Families and the Crisis of Social Change. Thomas S. Weisner, Candice Bradley, and Philip L. Kilbride, eds. Westport, CT: Greenwood.

Winter, Bronwyn

1994   Women, the Law, and Cultural Relativism in France: The Case of Excision. Signs 19:939–974.

World Bank

1993   World Development Report 1993: Investing in Health. Published for The World Bank by Oxford University Press.

The Technocratic Body and the Organic Body: Hegemony and Heresy in Women's Birth Choices

◘   *Robbie E. Davis-Floyd*

INTRODUCTION: THE ANTHROPOLOGY OF CHILDBIRTH

> The human drama is first and foremost a somatic one.
> —Morris Berman, *Coming to Our Senses: Body and Spirit in the Hidden History of the West*, 1989:108

Cross-cultural Approaches to the Study of Childbirth

The birth process is a universal part of human female physiology and biology, but in recent decades anthropologists have come to understand that birth is almost never simply a biological act; on the contrary, as Brigitte Jordan has said, "birth is everywhere socially marked and shaped" (1993:1). During anthropology's first century, most anthropological fieldwork was carried out by males, who in general either were not interested in or were denied access to the birth experience in the various cultures they studied. Those who did write about parturition tended toward providing long lists of seemingly irrational food taboos and folk beliefs (see for example Ford 1964) or toward examining childbirth not for its own sake but as a means for studying native practitioners and ritual (Levi-Strauss 1967; Paul 1975; Paul and Paul 1975; Schulze Jena 1933). As early as 1950 it was pointed out that "there are practically no good, direct, personal observations of childbirth among primitives by competent observers" (Freedman and Ferguson 1950:365)— a statement which remained largely true[1] into the 1970s, when women entering the field began to explore indigenous birth customs from the inside, and to understand them as integrated systems of knowledge and praxis.

In my initial attempts at writing the history of the field, I tried to sort out who was first, second, and so on—in other words, I sought to establish a hierarchy of primacy. But I quickly became aware that this sort of top-down schema was inappropriate to describe what has emerged as a sometimes individualistic but often profoundly cooperative endeavor undertaken almost simultaneously during the 1970s by a number of pioneering women who can be said to be the mothers and grandmothers of the field. These include Niles Newton (1955, 1972; Newton and Newton 1972); Sheila Kitzinger (1962, 1977, 1979); Lucile Newman (1965, 1976); Margaret Mead (Mead and Newton 1967); Nancy Stoller Shaw (1974); Dana Raphael (1975); Sheila Cosminsky (1977), and Brigitte Jordan (1978). Indeed, it was the 1978 publication of Jordan's *Birth in Four Cultures* that most saliently served to focus anthropological attention on childbirth as a subject worthy of in-depth ethnographic fieldwork and cross-cultural comparison, and inspired many others to enter the field (Ginsburg and Rapp 1991:320–321).

Jordan provided detailed ethnographic accounts of childbirth in a Mayan community in Yucatan, contrasting this woman-centered communal style of birthing with the highly technologized birthways of the U.S. and the midwife-attended births of Holland and Sweden. Her biosocial perspective gave her a comparative framework for integrating "the local view and meaning of the event, its associated biobehaviors, and its relevance to cross-system issues regarding the conduct of birth" (1993:11). In other words, she analyzed each culture's birthways as a system that made internal sense and could be compared with all other systems—a holistic conceptualization that enabled her to avoid reifying any one system, including American biomedicine. Recognizing the need for strong policy recommendations, Jordan made it clear that the wholesale exportation of the American model of birth to the Third World was having an extremely detrimental effect on indigenous birthways, a theme which she further clarified in her subsequent study of the training workshops given for Yucatecan midwives by physicians and nurses (Jordan 1989). These medical personnel sent to the rural areas from Mexico City so devalued the indigenous system that they did not recognize the existence of the many hands-on skills of the experienced midwives they were "training." Much birth ethnography now points to the disservice done to such community midwives by the application of the label "TBA"—traditional birth attendant. This acronym diverts attention from the wide range of services provided by indigenous midwives—their embeddedness in their communities, and their importance to those communities as wise women, healers, and respected authority figures (Cosminsky 1977; Paul 1978; Hunte 1981; Sukkary 1981; Laderman 1983; O'Neil and Kaufert 1990; Pigg 1996).

The first two edited collections to focus on pregnancy and birth from an ethnographic perspective were Margarita Kay's *Anthropology of Human Birth* (1982) and Carol MacCormack's *Ethnography of Fertility and Birth* (1982). Subsequently, the 1980s saw an explosion of anthropological interest in childbirth, as more and more women entered the field. In-depth ethnographic studies of birth were conducted in Guatemala by Sheila Cosminsky (1977, 1982); in Jamaica and Great Britain by Sheila Kitzinger (1978); among the Bariba of Benin by Carolyn Sargent (1982, 1989, 1990); among Egyptian villagers by Soheir Morsy (1982); in Sierra Leone by Carol MacCormack (1982); in Malaysia by Carol Laderman (1983); in Colombia and Mexico by Carole Browner (1983, 1985, 1986, 1989); among the !Kung of the Kalahari by Melvin Konner and Marjorie Shostak (1987); among the Efe by Tronick, Winn, and Morelli (1985, 1987); among the Inuit by John O'Neil and Patricia Kaufert (1990); and among Greek women (Lefkarites 1992; Georges 1995).[2] In general, such studies paint a picture of viable, healthy, and culturally embedded indigenous systems that have been or are in danger of being severely disrupted by the importation of a technomedical system that grants them no validity, and seeks to replace them with a type of birth "management" that relies heavily on machines that are poorly understood, difficult or impossible to fix in rural areas, too costly to be widely offered, and that, even in the West, have not been shown to improve birth outcome in a variety of large-scale studies.[3] Because of biomedical practitioners' general disregard for and lack of knowledge of the specifics of indigenous systems, the areas in which biomedical information might be useful to those systems are usually not identified. Thus, countless potentially fruitful opportunities for complementarity and cooperation between the indigenous health care system and biomedicine are too often lost. It is incumbent on anthropologists interested in the study of childbirth to actively seek ways to enhance this potential for complementarity (see for example Jordan 1993:Ch. 5, 8).

The Anthropology of Childbirth in America

Although Jordan's work has long been a focal point, it is the work of anthropologist and childbirth educator Sheila Kitzinger that has done the most to bring anthropological awareness of the cultural relativity of birth practices into the popular consciousness. Her 1978 publication of *Women as Mothers: How They See Themselves in Different Cultures* gave new legitimacy to the natural childbirth movement then gaining adherents in Europe and the U.S. by demonstrating the arbitrary and culture-bound aspects of Western technological birth. During the 1980s, Kitzinger was joined in this endeavor by a number of anthropologists who focused their critical gaze on Western birthways. They included Shelly Romalis (1981); Robbie Davis-Floyd (1983, 1987a,b); Pamela Eakins (1986); Emily Martin (1987); Robert Hahn (1987); and Karen Michaelson (1988); as well as noted sociologists Ann Oakley (1977, 1980, 1984) and Barbara Katz Rothman (1981, 1982, 1983, 1985, 1989). Such researchers unanimously agree on the narrow and intensely ethnocentric bias in Western, and especially American, technomedicine—a system of health care that objectifies the patient, mechanizes the body, and exalts practitioner over patient in a status hierarchy that attributes "authoritative knowledge" (Jordan 1993:152–154) only to those who know how to manipulate the technology and decode the information it provides. The early and provocative in-hospital fieldwork of Nancy Stoller Shaw (1974), in combination with Diana Scully's ethnographic observations of obstetricians-in-training, shed new light on what Scully termed *The Mis-Education of Obstetrician/Gynecologists* (1981), a process that

Davis-Floyd later analyzed as ritual initiation into the medical technocracy (1987, 1992 Ch. 7; see also Konner 1987).

Nancy Shaw's seminal book, *Forced Labor*, was also the first anthropological work to note the assembly-line aspects of American childbirth, a theme that Emily Martin (1987) expanded into a full-fledged analysis of the medical application of mechanistic metaphors of production and dysfunction to menstruation, childbirth, and menopause. Martin and her research team conducted 165 interviews with middle- and working-class women. Martin found that their responses to the medicalization of their body functions varied according to race and social class: working class women tended to resist this medicalization, while middle-class women more or less accepted it. Complementing Martin's analysis, my own study of the responses of 100 white middle-class women to their pregnancy and birth experiences showed a high degree of acceptance of, and satisfaction with, what I termed "the technocratic model of birth" (Davis-Floyd 1992), as did similar studies by Carol McClain (1983; 1985; 1987a, b); Margaret Nelson (1983); and Carolyn Sargent and Nancy Stark (1989). In contrast, Ellen Lazarus's rich ethnographic studies of the medical treatment of poor and working-class Puerto Rican and black women in clinics reveal universal resentment of their rushed, impersonal, and often indifferent treatment (1988, 1990; see also Johnson and Snow 1982; McClann 1987b; Boone 1988; Poland 1988, 1989). The systematic discrediting and elimination of black midwives in the American South has been well-documented by M. Dougherty (1982); Deborah Susie (1988); and Gertrude Fraser (1988, 1992). Fraser's work also reveals the often tragically cruel treatment of poor black women by hospital personnel. To date, there have been no studies at all of the experiences of middle-class minority women.

HEGEMONY AND HERESY IN WOMEN'S BIRTH CHOICES

> Heresy says, "you can do it yourself," whereas orthodoxy says, "We'll do it for you" (for a political and economic price). This is no small difference, and it accounts, in part, for the bitter war between heresy and orthodoxy that has characterized so much of Western history, in various forms. One is about direct somatic experience, the other is about fear of the same and finding substitutes for it.
>
> —Morris Berman, *Coming to Our Senses*, 1989:139

This chapter addresses middle-class women's agency in childbirth and the politics of birth as cultural representation and expression. It describes the technocratic ideology that women's culturally mediated desires and choices have helped to hegemonize over the course of this century, and contrasts that hegemonic ideology with the heretical holistic mode of birth and the organic view of the body it charters.

In *Coming to Our Senses: Body and Spirit in the Hidden History of the West*, historian Morris Berman points out that dominant hegemonies, religious or secular, need heretical movements to oppose them so that they can co-opt them and steal their energy. When the natural childbirth movement first came to popular attention in the 1960s, *it* was the heretical model, as it sought to empower women to educate themselves about pregnancy and birth, to reject total domination by physicians, to give birth consciously, awake and aware, with their husbands present. All these were radical ideas at the time. Today, with a cesarean rate of 24 percent, an epidural rate of 80 percent, an episiotomy rate of 90 percent for first-time births, and near-universal use of electronic fetal monitoring in hospitals, it has become clear that the idea of "natural childbirth" has been co-opted into plants on the IV pole, designer sheets on the birthing bed, Jacuzzis for labor that look wonderful in ads but are seldom used, and lobster-and-champagne dinners for the happy couple. In other words, the heretical energy of the natural childbirth campaign has been re-directed into making technocratic birth more humanistic, more appealing, more palatable to the increasing numbers of women who are choosing it.

Why do so many women choose to give birth under epidural anesthesia? Why do they elect to be monitored, when they could reject the imprisoning and uncomfortable monitor and walk during labor—a more physiologically sound option? Why do we find a 24 percent cesarean rate culturally and medically acceptable? I address these and similar questions, through presenting the results of a study of the pregnancy and birth experiences of 32 professional, career-oriented women in positions of power and prestige in the wider society, all of whom chose to give birth in the hospital. The study focuses on the correlations between their self- and body images and world-views, contrasting these correlations with the widely divergent body images and world-views of eight women (four professionals, four stay-at-home mothers) who chose to give birth at home. During in-depth interviews with these women, I tried to get at their body images especially as they dealt with the physical changes of pregnancy and the symbolic aspects of motherhood in relation to their conceptions of self.[4] Later, as I sought to make sense of the pile of transcriptions before me, I began to see that certain fundamental notions about the nature of reality were mirrored in the words these women used to describe their thoughts and feelings about their physiological experiences of pregnancy and motherhood. In short, I came to understand that body image can serve as a microcosmic mirror of world-view.

In recent works, Emily Martin (1987, 1991) focuses her anthropological lens on revealing differences in the images of body and birth held by middle- and working-class American women—differences that center around the issue of control. In their efforts to wrest control of birth away from the medical establishment, the middle-class women in Martin's study strove not only for control of their birth settings and attendants, but also, and most fundamentally, for control of themselves as they labored and gave birth. Meanwhile, their working-class sisters rejected this middle-class emphasis on self-control during birth, saying "They were talking about breathing and panting and—what are you talking about? It hurts!"

The differences between the two groups in my study are equally compelling. The women in both groups are all relatively affluent members of the white middle-class between the ages of 28 and 42: the fact that they hold so many other things in common makes all the more noteworthy the dramatic contrasts in their images of body and birth, and in the world-views I could glimpse through their expressions of those images. Just as Martin seeks not only to present the differences between middle- and working-class women's ideologies of the body and birth but also to discover the meanings of those differences, so in this chapter I will seek both to delineate the ideological differences between these two groups of middle-class home- and hospital-birthers, and to discover what these differences reveal about American culture and its engendered and embodied—or disengendered and disembodied—future.

CULTURAL MODELS OF THE BODY: TECHNOCRATIC AND HOLISTIC

Birth. This is the complete expulsion or extraction from the mother of a fetus irrespective of whether the umbilical cord has been cut or the placenta is attached.
—Cunningham, MacDonald, and Gant,
Williams Obstetrics, 17th edition, 1989:1

It is in technological societies that we find the greatest terror of the organic, in fact, the deepest hatred and fear of life that this planet has ever known.
—Morris Berman, *Coming to Our Senses,* 1989:82

When I first began research on American birth in 1981, most women I spoke with said they wanted some form of "natural childbirth in the hospital," in resistance to the consciousness obliterations their mothers experienced as they gave birth from the 1930s to the 1960s. Given this desire for natural childbirth, I expected to find that most women would resent and resist the increasing number of impersonal intrusions of technology into birth, and what I and others (Arms 1975; Hazzell 1976; Haire 1979; Romalis 1981; Rothman 1982; Shaw 1974) perceived as women's concomitant loss of their power as birth-givers. But when that initial study was completed several years later, I found instead that 70 of my 100 interviewees, if not exactly thrilled, were at least comfortable with their highly technologized obstetrical experiences, and were not much interested in resistance.[5]

Of these seventy women, nine seemed especially to have actively sought and been personally empowered by the technological interventions in their births (they stood in sharp contrast to nine other women in my sample who had sought natural childbirth but were in the end utterly devastated by their hospital experiences, and who expressed long-lasting feelings of disempowerment, alienation, and rage). Although this earlier study did not specifically focus on occupation, I noticed that these nine women were all high-powered professionals in positions of prestige, power, and authority. When they hired an obstetrician, they were hiring another professional to perform a service. From him or her they expected the same sort of professionalism and competence in matters of the body as they expected from themselves in their own areas of expertise. They seemed to see technology as integral and central to all areas of American life, and they fully expected that the very best in the modern technology of the body would be brought to bear on their pregnant bodies and the babies within in order to ensure that their births were competently managed and controlled, and therefore safe. I was both surprised and intrigued by the attitudes and desires these professional women expressed, and by their ability to manipulate medical ideology and procedures to their advantage. On the other hand, I was equally intrigued by the near-total resistance to such ideology of the women I came across who had chosen to give birth at home. I was fascinated to see that the women in both these categories actively defined themselves, in myriad ways, as future-shapers. It seemed to me that these two groups represented fruitful ground for further study.

In the book in which I describe that earlier study, *Birth as an American Rite of Passage* (1992), I utilized medical texts, childbirth literature, the analyses of other social scientists, and my own data obtained from interviews not only with women, but also with obstetricians, nurses, childbirth educators, and midwives to formulate descriptions of two fundamentally opposed models of birth that define the ends of a spectrum of beliefs about birth in the U.S. I labelled these the "technocratic"[6] and "holistic" models. The middle range of this spectrum is defined by the various "natural childbirth" models such as those of Dick-Read, Lamaze, and Bradley; these were given considerable attention in the book, but will not be discussed here, as my focus in this article is on the conceptual extremes, which provide baselines for understanding the experiences and attitudes of the two groups of women in this study.

The technocratic extreme is dominant in most American hospitals and hegemonically defines the American way of birth. This technocratic paradigm metaphorizes the female body as a defective machine unable to produce a healthy baby without technological assistance. In contrast, the holistic paradigm interprets the female body as an organic system, and birth as an ecological process that can only be harmed by dissection and intervention. This article investigates the interplay between these paradigms and women's lived experiences of body and self. The basic tenets of these two opposing paradigms will be presented in italics throughout the article as they emerge from the words and experiences of these two groups of white middle-class women, and then will be summarized in a chart near the end.

THE TECHNOCRATIC BODY AND THE PROFESSIONAL WOMAN

> When it came time for Susan Blume to deliver her baby, she was blessedly calm. No sweat soaked her brow, no pain lined her face. She uttered not a sound. As the baby squeezed down the birth canal, Blume [anesthetized by an epidural] lay placidly on her side, reading *People* magazine and robbing the gods of one more woman bringing forth children in sorrow.
>
> —Elaine Herscher, *San Francisco Chronicle*, 1990

> Orthodoxy, in other words, opts for the map instead of the territory, the travelogue instead of the trip.
>
> —Morris Berman, *Coming to Our Senses*, 1989:147

The thirty-two professionals who chose hospital-birth hold a wide range of occupations: four are midlevel managers for banks, and three for insurance companies, two head up fund-raising for political campaigns, one is a museum curator, two are realtors, two are physicians, three college professors, two regional sales managers, six managers or directors of large government agencies, one is a CPA, one a high-level manager for a major airline, and five own their own companies. Most of them make as much or more money than their husbands.

The Professional/Personal Split

During the interviews, it quickly became apparent that these women live their lives in terms of a fundamental and clear-cut distinction between the personal and professional realms. How these women primarily define themselves in relation to society at any given moment is usually a function of what realm they are in. In the professional realm they *are* their role: professor, division manager, CEO. Secure in their professional identities, in the personal realm many of these women seem actually to be amused to define themselves as "John's wife," or "Suzie's mother," almost as if being John's wife or Suzie's mother was a sort of game that they played sometimes. Some perspective on this security of identity was provided by an older woman I spoke with recently, who had been Mrs. James Bowen since she was 20. She said, "I have always been defined by who my husband was. Now that he is dead, I am forced to confront the fact that I am 65 years old and have no identity of my own." In dramatic contrast stands Lina's description of why she defines herself so strongly in terms of her career, while many of her friends do not:

> I find that some of my friends that I was in college or graduate school with have given up too much.... They have compromised their careers in really significant fashion. Either they don't work or they will work part time, and they just haven't really made a go of it professionally but ... have put their energies into the relationship and into the family. [That] is very dangerous. [Q. Why?] Men leave.... They are relying on their husbands to such a degree that if they leave they are really in trouble. They have totally compromised their careers. They have great potential and they let it go.... They in essence capitulated to the family.

Presence in either the personal or professional realm is expressed through bodily adornment: suits and tailored dresses at work, shorts or jogging suits at home. Leah explained:

> I see [the body] as a way to have people respond to you.... The way I dress reflects the level of professionalism that I have and the type of response I get from other people. I don't dress in flounces and frills, I dress very tailored and that is reflected even in the glasses I wear. They are pretty much straightforward and businesslike.... I like to give a straightforward presentation so that people can deal with me straight.

I found it noteworthy that when I interviewed these women in their homes, they almost invariably would glance down at their casual sweats and tennis shoes and laughingly comment, "You are seeing my other self, my home self"; but when I went to their offices, they never said, "You are seeing my professional self." For most, the professional self was the primary self.

In general, any overlap between the personal and professional realms went one way: personal aspects, such as children, relationships, emotional display, did not belong at work, while professional aspects, like paperwork, faxing, and phone calling, often were taken home. (The specific and notable exceptions to this rule will be discussed later on.) Enforcing the boundaries of this one-way street did not present much of a problem for most of these women at first; even those who dated and/or married male colleagues were usually able to keep these relationships separate from their everyday professional activities.

Pregnancy as a Violation of the Professional/Personal Split

Pregnancy perforce entails a violation of the conceptual boundary separating these personal and professional realms of life. Sexuality and children are plainly part of the personal domain; they do not belong at work. But pregnant women visibly and obviously take their children not only into the workplace, but also to even the most important meetings! Predictably, many of these women worried about how this boundary violation would affect their work relationships with their colleagues and superiors:

> [Q. Were you worried about how your colleagues might react to your pregnancy?] Yes, that's an unqualified yes. . . . They look at me as the president, and I . . . was worried that they might start thinking about me not as much as a professional, but as a woman, and that shouldn't necessarily be bad, but I was worried that it might affect the respect level . . . it's kind of more obvious that you're a woman, I think, if you're pregnant, I mean it's just constantly reminding people of that rather than just thinking of you as a professional. It gave them another thing to think about, and it wasn't something I wanted them to think about, because I wanted them to think about me as a business kind of guy. . . . [Kay]

However, in contrast to what I had originally expected to find, very few of these women found their fears to be justified. Only three reported that they suffered any sort of job discrimination as a result of their pregnancy, while most others reported the joyful discovery of unexpected benefits from their physical blurring of the personal/professional distinction:

> When I was pregnant for the first time, I was working in a large corporation, and always it was to dress for success, and you were very much on guard as a woman. And as soon as I revealed I was pregnant, people who were not friends of mine, executives many levels up on the corporate ladder, just opened up their personal lives. They identified so strongly with being a father or having a wife who was pregnant. I mean, they would go into 10- or 15-minute conversations. I was stunned at how open

and personal everything became when they were around a woman who was bearing a child. [Joanne]

As it evolved for most of these women, the conflict between work and pregnancy was not between their pregnant bodies and their male colleagues, as most had expected, but between their own expectations for their work performance and the biological realities of those pregnant bodies. Catherine said:

> I hated it that people were always wanting to have personal conversations with me about how I was feeling. I was not interested in that at all, and so I made it very plain right at the start that I didn't want to deal with any of that stuff. When I'm at work I am strictly business. I think the reason I didn't have any problems with how I was treated when I was pregnant was that I made it so clear that there was no difference. [Q. Did pregnancy pose any problems at all for you at work?] I would sometimes get so tired that I would tell my secretary to hold my calls, and put my head down on my desk and just sleep for an hour. But I never let anyone know about it, and I made sure that I always got just as much work done anyway, even if that meant I had to stay there longer.

The Centrality of Control

This tension between the professional and personal domains is often heightened by the woman's own perception of herself in relation to her body. Just as with the middle-class women in Martin's study (1990), an overriding concern of these professional women is *control.* They hold the strong belief that *life is controllable, and that to be strong and powerful in the world, one must be in control.* As long as these women feel in control, they are "happy," "everything is fine." They achieve control over their lives through careful planning and organization of their time and activities. (I asked all of them what they thought about the notion of applying corporate management techniques to family life, such as scheduling family summit meetings, etc. A few thought the notion detracted from the unstructured flow that they saw as the essence of the personal, as opposed to the professional domain, but most heartily approved of the idea.) They achieve control over their *bodies* through regularly scheduled exercise (most were very athletic in school) and over their own *destinies* through reaching positions of independence and importance in the wider society. Interestingly, those who admitted to wanting and enjoying power insisted that it was not power over others that appealed to them, but power to make things happen in the world. Lina said:

> I didn't want to be like my mother . . . I didn't want to be picked on by my husband all the time, and be powerless. You know, she was powerless. [Q. What did you do to be powerful?] I got a Ph.D. and a job.

The Self/Body Split: Pregnancy and Birth as Out-of-Control

These professional women seem to judge every situation by the degree of control they feel they can maintain over it. Even their pregnancies are usually carefully controlled, planned to occur at just the chosen time in their careers. But once those processes were set into motion, they became uncontrollable, and thus presented these women with a division within their most treasured notions of self: between the cultural, professional parts within their control, and the personal, biological processes outside of it. Lina experienced this division so intensely that she could hardly believe it when she became pregnant:

> Deep down inside of me I believed that I had desexed myself by being the successful professional and I would have to pay for that. . . . I thought I would have a hard time getting pregnant because I thought I would have to pay for what I had gotten away with. . . . I have succeeded at a man's game. . . . A couple of my male faculty colleagues, when they would see me on the campus with the baby, would constantly say, "I can't believe you are a mother, I can't believe you are such a good mother—you are like my mother. I can't believe it." What they were really saying to me is, "I thought you were a guy."

This separation of self from biology is clearly reflected in the body concepts held by many of these women. I asked each one, "How do you think about your body? What is your body?" I was interested to notice that most, instead of giving me a definition, immediately began to talk about how they judged their bodies—as too fat, not in good enough shape, or healthy, in good shape. Such statements reflect their shared belief that *the body is imperfect*:

- I think it's pretty functional [but] . . . it's fat around the middle, and my boobs are too small. [Lou]
- Women, unless we've had it greatly enhanced by plastic surgery, I don't think we like it. I don't know anybody who *likes* their body. [Louise]

The words of most of those who did provide definitions expressed the additional and equally fundamental belief that *the body is separate from the self*:

- You know, I think there is me and then there is what I'm like physically which can be changed or modified—clothes, makeup, exercise, hairstyles, food. [Georgia]
- My body is mine. It's only mine. I think it was something that was given to me for a reason, you know, to get around in this particular life, because I think it's a place for my soul to be. [Lou]
- A vehicle. Something that moves me from place to place. A repository for thought, for creation, for beliefs, philosophies. [Leah]
- My body is a vehicle that allows me to move around, a tool for my success in the world. [Joanne]
- My body is the recipient of the abuse from the lifestyle that I choose. . . . It's my weakest link—it's like you have to pay the price somewhere—I'm out of shape, overweight, and not eating right—my body to me is what has paid the price for this career. [Q. Can you describe your relationship with your body?] Abusive. [Beth]

Predictably, then, the physical state of pregnancy was problematic at best for some of these women. For intrinsic to the notion of the *body as a vehicle,* a *tool for the self,* are the corollary ideas that *the body is worth less than the self it houses, which, being worth more, should control the body,* should be "in charge." Concomitantly, most of these hospital birthers experienced the bodily condition of *pregnancy as unpleasant because it is beyond the control of the self,* or, as they put it, "out of control." Here is how they expressed that feeling. Linda said:

> I think there are a lot of women who love being pregnant and they would say that. My sister, the Earth Mother, did. Especially before I got pregnant, I thought, "Maybe I'll get into it." But I didn't get into it. I felt bad and large and awkward and nauseated. And oh, I love having the baby, but I wish there were an easier way.

To the question, "How did you feel about your body while you were pregnant?" Lina responded, "I didn't like it. It just overwhelmed me, the kinds and the variety of sensations, and the things that happen to your body because of the pregnancy. I didn't like it at all. I felt totally alienated from my body." Even Leah's positive experience of pregnancy is expressed in terms of separation and a feeling of lack of control:

> I really did feel very healthy. It was different being so focused in my body. That's what was so curious. I was watching all this happening. It was something taking control all over me and it was all good. To a certain extent I try to live outside my body so it doesn't control me. Only in this case it was very much controlling me. And that's ok—it was guiding me.

Joanne added:

> I was real apprehensive about going into labor. It kind of terrified me, mostly because I like to be in control . . . and you don't have any control when that happens. I used to have nightmares about standing in front of the president and making a presentation and having my water break.

And here is how Beth experienced birth:

> I mean, it's like a demon to me. There's another being in your body that has to get out and it's looking for a way to get out. And all of a sudden, it's like my center of control left my brain and went to this, this thing in my body. And I had no control. I'm very much an in-control person. I like to think that I'm in control of what's going on here, that I can control whatever happens. It was like the control center moved from me to this other being. And you know, all I was doing was lying there— I had to do whatever this other being said was going to happen. And it was my body that it was happening to. That was the thing I liked the least.

As they viewed the body as a vehicle for the mind or soul, so these women tended to see *the pregnant body as a vessel, a container for the fetus (who is a being separate from the mother) and to interpret its growth and birth as occurring through a mechan-*

ical process in which the mother is not actively involved. (Sarah flatly stated, "You're just a vessel. That's all you are, just this vessel.") These beliefs were behaviorally expressed in myriad ways during pregnancy. For example, the evidence these women relied on for proof of the baby's health and growth was objective, coming primarily from ultrasound photographs and electronic amplification of the fetal heart rate. They understood the importance of nutrition and knew that they had to eat well so the baby would be well-nourished. But, unlike the home-birthers, they saw this in terms of a simple, mechanical cause-effect relationship. If they ingested good foods, the necessary nourishment would travel to the baby through the placenta, enhancing overall development and especially brain growth. Excessive ingestion of alchohol or junk food, however, might result in a child with less-than-optimal brain capacity. Thus, eating well was a mother's duty to her unborn child and one of the most important things, along with ultrasound and amniocentesis, that she could do to ensure optimal growth conditions. Although most of these women experienced giving up alchohol and junk food as something of a burden, to them it was also a logical necessity, something they did as a matter of course. But it did not, conceptually speaking, entail their active participation in growing the child. It merely made them into the best possible "vessels."

In keeping with these attitudes, most of these women did not view the processes of labor and birth as intrinsic to their feminine natures. Said Linda, "If my husband could do it the next time instead of me, that would be just fine." Added Joanne:

> Even though I'm a woman, I'm unsuited for delivering . . . and I couldn't nurse. . . . I've told my mother—I just look like a woman, but none of the other parts function like a mother. I don't have the need or the desire to be biological. . . . I've never really been able to understand women who want to watch the birthing process in a mirror—just you know, I'm not, that's not—I'd rather see the finished product than the manufacturing process.

The Mind/Body Split: Mind Over Biology

Emergent in Joanne's words we see the technocratic notions that *birth is a mechanical process* and that *there is no intrinsic value in giving birth "naturally," because technology is better than nature anyway.* Thus we can understand when Joanne says that she enjoyed her cesarean birth because her anesthesiologist explained what was happening step by step, and because, since she felt no pain, she was able to be so *intellectually* present to the birth that she could watch the time to see which of her many friends who had placed bets on the time of the birth would win the $18 in the pot. She stated:

> [I liked that because] I didn't feel like I had dropped into a biological being. . . . I'm not real fond of things that remind me I'm a biological creature—I prefer to think and be an intellectual, emotional person. So you know, it was sort of my giving in to biology to go through all this.

Here Joanne expresses a view held by most of the women in this group: *The ideal, whole woman is intellectual and emotional, but not necessarily biological.* (Some behavioral ramifications of this notion will be discussed later on.)

Like Joanne, Katie preferred the sense of control provided by a cesarean, and in no way saw this as a disempowering loss, but only as an empowering gain because it was something *she* had caused to happen (see also Sargent and Stark 1987). When her baby was two weeks overdue and labor had not begun, she told her doctor, who was urging restraint, "I am really getting sick of this. Please schedule [the cesarean]." In response to the question, "How did you feel about yourself after the birth?" she responded, "I felt pretty special. Proud. . . . I felt as if I had accomplished quite a bit."

Kathy, who also described her cesarean as personally empowering, said:

> I don't feel like I missed out on anything. With my first two I was put to sleep. With my third, Bryan, I was given an epidural. Heaven! I would never do it any other way. A cesarean with an epidural. I was awake, everything. Ah, it was just wonderful. . . . I would have to say, hey, I participated in it. I was awake and I felt the pulling and the tugging. I did not push or anything. But I was definitely a part of what was going on.

Elaine summarized:

> Well they induced labor and I wasn't very good at my relaxation techniques and my breathing and after about four hours of labor I decided I would prefer to have a cesarean and so that's what we did. . . . I know some women get all uptight about that, that it wasn't a normal delivery, but I didn't feel the least bit cheated and I feel my birth experience was just as happy as it would have been. I was very happy when I heard them cry, and it was a very pleasant experience.

In their words we hear again the belief these women strongly hold, that *the mind is more important than the body, that as long as their minds are aware, they are active participants in the birth process.* We hear this expressed even in Clara's recounting of her rapid and unmedicated vaginal delivery:

> Travis came in a little over an hour and that was just not enough time to get mentally prepared. I felt . . . my body was pushing me into having this baby. My mind was not there to work with it. I needed more time to be able to get on top of it and be there.

As a corollary of the idea that technology is better than nature, most of the hospital-birthers in this study felt rather strongly that *labor is naturally painful, that pain is bad, and that not to have to feel pain during labor is good and is their intrinsic right as modern women* (see also Sargent and Stark 1989). To the question, "What did you want out of the birth experience?" Joanne responded, "Out of the birth experience itself I wanted no pain. I wanted it to be as simple and easy and uncomplicated as most everything else has been for me. Said Leah, "I made the decision: I had two hits of Demerol in the IV. I controlled the pain through that." Beth, who "had planned for but did not end up with natural childbirth," was nevertheless very pleased to feel that she also was in control of the decisions that were made. She had expected a long labor with little pain. When the pain became severe, she asked for relief, "and you know, even though I hadn't planned on an epidural, they were very responsive when I said I wanted one." The next time around, Beth planned for an epidural:

> When I got there, I was probably about five centimeters and they said, "Uh, I'm not sure we have time," and I said, "I want the epidural. We must go ahead and do it right now!" So, we had an epidural.

And Elaine stressed:

> Ultimately the decision to have a cesarean while I was in labor was mine. I told my doctor I'd had enough of this labor business and I'd like to have a cesarean and get it over with. So he whisked me off to the delivery room and we did it.

In keeping with this *high value on making their own decisions*, the major discontents these women expressed with the medical handling of their labors and deliveries resulted not from the administration of anesthesia, but from its withholding. Kay reported:

> I [asked] for an epidural at one point, but they said they didn't have time to do it. [Q. Was that okay with you?] Not really! I was awfully uncomfortable and I had remembered how wonderful it was [with my first birth] and that I had instantly felt terrific. . . . I was mad that I was in so much pain, and then they would tell me something like "we don't have time," you know—that just drove me wild. I didn't like that at all—I wanted to have it when *I* wanted to have it.

Another woman expressed outrage that a friend of hers in advanced labor had been denied anesthesia for the same reason as Kay, saying earnestly, "No one has the right to tell you that you have to go through that kind of pain." Although a good bit of evidence exists on the depressive effects of analgesia and anesthesia on the baby during labor and birth, most of these women felt very strongly that they had an absolute right to the mind-body separation offered by such drugs, especially the epidural.[7] Lina spoke for the majority:

> I read all this stuff that told me I would be a complete asshole to have an epidural and I revolted. [The books said that] I would be able to see that it's much better for the baby and it's a natural experience, and there's just all this pressure. . . . I quit smoking, ate meat, drank milk for months and months—I had been such a good girl. A couple of hours of whatever an epidural was going to do to me, tough. You can put up with it, kid.

Later on Lina insisted that her physician would be the one to know if the drugs used in labor posed any dangers. She and many others stated firmly that they did not believe that their doctors would let any harm come to their babies. In this belief is illustrated yet another technocratic precept: *Medical knowledge is authoritative* (Jordan 1989, 1990). In contrast to the home-birthers, as we shall see in a moment, none of the 32 hospital-birthers reported much respect for, or reliance on, their own intuition or "inner knowing."

For their 1989 study of the influence of childbirth education classes on parents' birth choices, Carolyn Sargent and Nancy Stark interviewed 84 couples, most of whom were educated and middle-class. Their findings indicate that most such women in the U.S. may share the attitudes toward birth expressed by the high-powered professionals in my study:

> To our informants, the crucial concern during delivery was to be awake rather than asleep. Yet these women also expressed anxiety regarding their capacity to cope with pain. Epidural anesthesia thus emerged as the resolution to these dual concerns. The majority of parents perceived epidurals to be free of complications and side effects for mother or child and thus the ideal form of pain relief. With two exceptions (husbands, in both cases), parents showed little desire to experience the physiological process of birth. One woman articulated this perspective most clearly, saying that it would have been fine with her if she could have just picked her baby up at the nursery, without giving birth. She didn't need to "feel" anything. To these informants, being awake represented participation in the delivery, regardless of the degree of technological intervention that was needed to permit this to happen painlessly. (1989:45–46)

Mediation and Integration through Nurturance—at Home and in the Workplace

Hand-in-hand with their intense desire for control, for not dropping down into biology, goes, at least for some of the professionals in my study, a lack of interest in breast-feeding for any extended length of time. To breast-feed is to be out of control—the milk comes unbidden and runs down your blouse; you must drop what you are doing and attend to the child's hunger; this is a job that cannot be delegated. Bottle-feeding, on the other hand, enables someone else to do that for you, and frees you from enslavement to biology as surely as does an epidural. With good reason, a woman in a novel of the 1930s tells her daughter, "The bottle was the war cry of my generation!" (McCarthy 1954:247). That cry is echoed in 1990:

> I really thought I wanted to breast-feed, but I didn't. I wanted my body back. [Lina]

> Yes, it's good for the baby, but if you're uncomfortable with it, for any reason, don't do it. It just isn't worth the trauma. This time I'm not going to do it at all, uh-uh. Part of it goes back to not having the need or the desire to be biological. The other is the confinement of nursing. You know, I wanted to be able to get up and go, and let somebody else feed the baby, and the idea of expressing just nauseated me. [Joanne]

Linda did want to nurse, but ran right up against the boundary between the personal and professional realms:

> I don't have my own office, so I've been trying to think where I'm going to pump when I'm at the hospital. The best I've come up with is the examining room, you know, because that has a lock on the door and I hope it'll work out, because it's not optimal, it's not optimal at all.

Yet, in spite of the difficulties, she was willing to find a way because, as she expresses it,

> A lot of my friends who have worked and have nursed say they feel a little better about working if they're nursing. You know, you still have that connection. I was talking to one of my friends yesterday and she said, "That's one thing the babysitter can't do, you know. That's mine." And I sort of feel that way too. That makes it a little better, a little easier about going back to work. Plus the immunological aspect about putting him in daycare—I feel a little better about that, giving him a little better chance of fighting all the germs out there.

Nursing for Linda, as well as for several others, provided a much-valued mediation/integration of the personal and professional realms. Another seeker of integration was Kay, president of her own company, who nursed and kept both her babies in her office until they were a year old. (When I went in to interview her, her two-month old was sleeping on a chair.) Joanne expressed her difficulties with the personal/professional dichotomy:

> I think there is that split, and that's one of the toughest transitions that professional women have to deal with, and that is: I want to be the soft mommy, and then I have to strip my gears and get back into being the tough businesswoman. And I think that's a tough transition to make.

She goes on to describe two women who serve as role models for her who are "very tough businesswomen," yet will bring their children to the office and will even get down on the floor in full corporate attire in the middle of a busy day to play with someone else's children. She continues:

> It's very encouraging to see people break out of the corporate mold because the corporate personality is so hard and cold and really kind of distasteful . . . I think having families makes people kinder. . . . If people would just step back from corporate greed and get back into relating to people in terms of their interdependence and their affection for each other, it would be a better world.

Louise, when asked what she thought about applying corporate strategies to family life, replied that for her, it was more a question of applying family strategies to the business world:

> I treat my clients as if they were as important to me as my family, and it pays off. They really respond, and I have turned this business around from losing to making money in less than a year because of it.

As is evident in Louise's statement, these women place *high value on their emotional and nurturing abilities*, abilities which they feel spill over from the personal to the benefit of the professional realm. For example, when Janis was head of the customer-service office of an electric utility, she often worked intensively one-on-one with delinquent bill payers to help them develop an overall economic plan that would work for them. She said,

> And I still get visits from people who tell me that I turned their lives around for good, because instead of being their adversary, I nurtured them, and I'm proud of that. I think being a mommy makes me a better professional.

Likewise, Kay specifically designs her presidential style to be "participative, democratic, understanding, and kind." Thus caring for her children in her office can be viewed as an extension of her presidential self rather than a contradiction to it; their presence in her office simply represents further integration of the personal and professional spheres that she, as president, has tried to bring together since the beginning of her company.

These women in general, even as they devalued feminine biological processes, consistently placed high value on what they saw as the feminine qualities of nurturance and emotionality, and sought to bring these qualities into the workplace in a very conscious effort to "humanize" the office environment. Their efforts toward such integration included both more personalized relationships with clients and employees (such as implementing client-education programs, flex-time, etc.), and creating friendlier environments. Wherever these women had enough control, they redecorated sterile office buildings with softer colors, warmer lighting, conversational areas, artwork, and potted plants, finding that such efforts repeatedly paid off in enhanced intraoffice relationships and increased productivity.

Such integration of the personal and professional realms, however, is usually minimal compared to the degree of separation between these realms. For example, about leaving her six-week-old baby at a day care center, Linda, a pediatrician, had this to say:

> [Q. Do you feel that it would be better for your baby to be with you?] Possibly. On the other hand, I also feel like I probably wouldn't be very happy. I'd probably start climbing the walls, and in a way that would be a bad thing to do to him, to say well alright, I'm going to throw away twenty years of education to stay home with you so that you can be the perfect child.

Thus, we arrive at a central question for most of these women, one that I hope to address in more detail in a future work: where are they going to put their bodies, carriers of their selves, in relation to their children, the products of those bodies? The answer in general is that as the children were thought of as separate in the womb, so this separation achieves near-immediate geographical reality after birth. The majority of these women work ten-hour days, and so they see their children only for a maximum of one-and-a-half to two hours per day. I suggest that this situation is a logical extension of their own body images. Their perceptions and experiences of this parent/child separation are varied and cannot be addressed here. This is an area in which little anthropological investigation has been done (but see Nelson 1983; Sandelowski 1990); much more research is needed.

The Dichotomies of Technocratic Life

The similarities in the desires, experiences, and perceptions of pregnancy and birth of these professional women raise many questions. For example, what happens when you can't control everything? Janis had fibroids in her uterus that made her pregnancy very difficult and dangerous. Carolyn, after not exercising for one very busy year, woke up one morning with such a severe pre-arthritic condition in her legs that she could not walk for days. Susan experienced a hormone shift towards the end of her pregnancy that resulted in intense and long-lasting anxiety attacks from which she did not recover until the proper medication was found five years later. Bewildered and angered by their out-of-control bodies, rather than surrendering, these women intensified their commitments to control: Janis was determined to keep working until time for birth, and she did; Carla embarked on a rigorous exercise program and is doing much better; and Susan fought her near-paralyzing anxiety so successfully that no one at work ever knew of her problem.

When the body works right, it is a vehicle for success. When it does not, it is an impediment to be overcome. As professional and personal are separate domains, so are mind and body, so are mother and baby (even when contained in one body), and so are parents and child:

professional/personal
self/body
mind/body
mother/baby
parent/child

These dichotomies seem to encapsulate and express the separations and divisions of technocratic life as most of these women experience it. To some degree, they appear to be mediated by the emotional and nurturant qualities through which these women see themselves as enriching both the workplace and the home.

HOME-BIRTHERS AND THE ORGANIC BODY

The contractions kept coming. Each one of them pushed. . . . I tried joining in, very carefully. I pushed with my stomach muscles, just a little . . . but whoa, my uterus grabbed me and drove me along with itself. I couldn't push just a little. It had to be a lot. . . . It was so powerful and uncontrollable. I might push myself inside out if I went too far. But who cares? I didn't try to hold back any more. I pushed hard. I grabbed onto Vic, onto the folds of his clothes. I held my breath and pushed as hard as I could and it felt good. It felt better. The contractions didn't hurt as much any more. It was exciting. I'm pushing!

—Janet Isaacs Ashford, "Doing It Myself"

History is finally an activity of the flesh. . . . I seek now to apply the techniques of somatic analysis to one particular problem in the history of Western civilization: the presence of a heretical or countercultural tradition that is rooted in bodily experience and that rejects the cerebral, or formulistic, way of life of the dominant culture (orthodoxy). This tradition, despite relentless persecution, has refused to go away; and despite (or perhaps because of) its somatic and subterranean quality, it has managed to influence, and in an important sense, shape the dominant culture over the last two thousand years.

—Morris Berman, *Coming to Our Senses*, 1989:136

We will turn now to consideration of the body images and world-views of the eight home-birthers in my study. Four of these—Kristin, Ryla, Karen, and Liza—were the most extreme proponents of what I have called the holistic model of birth. These four, like Linda's sister, were the sort of women that Linda would call "Earth Mothers." They did not have professional careers in the business or academic worlds; they worked out of their houses as "New Age" counselors and rebirthers, and devoted a large proportion of their walking hours to motherhood. The other four—Tara, Susan, Elizabeth, and Sandra—are professionals of the same ilk as the hospital-birthers. (Tara and Susan run political campaigns, Elizabeth teaches at a university, and Sandra manages a store.)

Self/Body Integration

Interesting differences emerge between the body images of these two subsets of home-birthers. The women in the first group (the home-workers) place no distance between self and body, saying "I *am* my body," or "My body is the physical expression of me." In so saying, they are expressing a basic tenet of the holistic model (which emphasizes connection instead of separation)—the very un-Cartesian notion that *self and body are One.*

Differing in many ways from these "Earth Mothers," the four professionals in this study who gave birth at home share much with their hospital-birth sisters, most notably including their desire to be in control and their feelings that body and self are separate. Yet somehow they sense that these notions are inconsistent with their choice of birthplace and the philosophy that accompanies it, as well as with their lived experiences of pregnancy and birth. You can hear them struggling with this inconsistency in the way they discuss their relationship with their bodies. Tara gets herself halfway toward wholeness, saying, "I think that probably 50 percent of who I am is my body." And Susan shows us how her lived experience of pregnancy contradicted and changed her former notions. She stated:

I used to see my body as the vehicle in which I can run around and project myself to the world. . . . I never thought about my body as being me until I did get pregnant. And then you feel very much in tune because you can feel everything that is going on . . . and now I am so much more comfortable with my body, and more and more I see it as part of my Self.

These home-birthers, like Martin's working-class women, tended to reject medical definitions and value judgments in favor of their own lived experience. Experiencing the body as the self, or as part of the self, they came to stress in belief and behavior the body's *organic interconnectedness*, as opposed to its mechanicity, and to view *the female body as normal, attractive, and healthy*. Susan said:

> Before, I was very uncomfortable with my body—the way I looked, the way I felt, just everything. Since I gave birth, it's just not a problem. I'm not all that modest any more. We went to Canada, stripped off all our clothes, and jumped in the ocean, and it didn't bother me that somebody might look at me and say "she could lose ten pounds". . . . I kind of like the way I look.

These home-birthers felt deeply and strongly that *female physiological processes, including birth, are healthy and safe*:

> [She] . . . said, "Sandra, are you still thinking about having this baby at home?" . . . I think you're absolutely insane. What if something happened?" I said, "Are you not going to drive your car because you could have a wreck? You've got a higher risk doing that than having a baby at home." My friends think I'm crazy. But I think they are. I mean really, *they* are—they're the ones that have missed the whole birth experience, not me.

Letting Go of Control

In dramatic contrast to the high value placed on control by the hospital-birthers, the nonprofessional, spiritually oriented Earth Mothers in my study felt that *giving up control was far more valuable in birth and in life than trying to maintain it*—a philosophical position again arrived at through lived experience. Said Liza:

> I was brought up in the mainstream, and I used to knock myself out trying to control everything. Then I got sick, and I realized that I actually can't control anything or anyone. As soon as I let go of trying, and just began to surrender to what is, everything in my life started to work. I got well, I got married, I had a baby. And if the lesson needed reinforcing, labor did it. That is a force beyond control, a powerful wave that will drown you if you fight it. Better then to dive into it, to relax, let it carry you. Whenever I tried to control my labor or myself during labor, I was in agony. But when I let go and surrendered to the waves, they carried me.

Again, we see Tara and Susan moving in that philosophical direction through their lived experience. To the question, "How important is it to you to be in control?" Susan responded:

> You know the answer to that! It's more important than it should be. Because I get very carried away with it sometimes, and [I need to learn to let it go sometimes]. I've been a lot happier since I started practicing that.

Tara put it this way:

> I always had in my mind that morning sickness was psychological and that basic-ally I could control all these things. If I did things right, ate the right things, and treated my body the right way, then I wouldn't have to worry about kinds of morn-ing sickness that people have, and I could have a quick and easy labor. I exercised a lot, you know, I paid attention to my diet and everything, and I realized, finally, after nine months and a birth, that there are a lot of things you just don't have con-trol over. But it took me that long to admit it.

Tara's kinship with the professional women discussed in the prior section is reflected in her early desire for control over the birth process, and her belief that she could achieve such control by doing all the "right" things in preparation for the birth. Her holistic view of birth kept her from wishing to utilize the techno-cratic forms of control so important to her professional sisters. Unlike them, she was willing to give up her desire for control to the experience; she realized that such control was not, and had never been, hers.

Pregnancy as Integration

As we might expect, Tara and Susan, like Linda's "Earth Mother" sister, enjoyed pregnancy's constant changes, and came to value their lack of control over these changes. Tara declared, "I loved being pregnant. I just loved all of it. I liked look-ing at my body in the mirror. I couldn't wait to see what would happen next." Susan said, "I was in awe. . . . Being pregnant was fascinating. . . . It isn't when you're barfing in the toilet bowl every morning, but when that part is over, you feel good. You feel better than you ever had in your life."

To the direct question, "Other women I have interviewed experienced their body changes during pregnancy as being out of control, meaning that they didn't have control. Why didn't you?" Susan responded:

> Whenever anything like that happened to me, I had already read up or talked to midwives and I knew it was coming. I knew that that was going to happen next and it was all part of this wonderful experience of getting pregnant. It felt like it was nat-ural. It was what your body was supposed to do. One step closer to having that baby there.

This response and others like it show that these home-birth women place just as much importance on their minds as do the hospital-birthers in this study, but in a rather more integrated way that sees the body and its changes as equally impor-tant, and holds body and mind to be equally important parts of the whole.

According to the holistic model espoused by these home-birthers, like self and body, *mother and baby are essentially One—that is, they form part of an integrated system that can only be harmed by dissection into its individual parts.* Much more than a passive host, or "vessel," *the mother sees herself as actively growing the baby.* Susan said:

Especially when you're actually actively doing all the exercises you're supposed to be doing and you're actively eating and drinking what you're supposed to be eating and drinking, then you really feel like you are feeding and nourishing and growing the baby. . . .

For Kristin, this feeling of active involvement in pregnancy combined in an unusual way with psychic experiences that generated in her sensations of, and then belief in, the reality of *active communication, unity, and partnership with her unborn baby*:

When I was about two months pregnant I was lying on my waterbed one night in the dark, not sleeping, but also not really thinking, just drifting along, when suddenly, from somewhere inside of the front of my head I heard these words, "I'm here, I'm a girl, and my name is Joy Elizabeth" . . . One night [much later on], I had a Braxton Hicks contraction and I heard a voice inside say "I'm scared." I told her I was scared, too, and that everything would be okay because we were partners and we would do this thing together.

Elizabeth experienced this sort of active communication and sense of partnership with her unborn in a rather dramatic way:

Two weeks before he was born, he was still breech. My midwives felt confident about a breech delivery, but I . . . very much wanted him to turn. I went to a therapist who, several people had told me, was really good at visualization, and asked her to help me get in touch with him. She helped me see myself as tiny, and to travel through my nose down to my stomach, and then to see a little window opening into my uterus, which got bigger until I could step through. I swam over his body, past his genitals, which I could clearly see were male, and up to his face. I told him I loved him, and couldn't wait to hold him in my arms, and then I asked him please to turn. I told him it was really important to me. He looked right at me and I suddenly felt that if I would show him what to do, he would do it. So I started swimming down, towards my cervix, motioning for him to follow me. . . . By the time I woke up the next morning, he had completely turned, and he stayed that way until he was born!

Mind/Body Integration: Active Agency and Inner Knowing During Birth

For these home-birthers (as, in their very different way, for the hospital-birthers) this active, agentic role was key. Near the beginning of her first pregnancy, during her very first interview with an obstetrician, Susan became angry because his response to her questions was, "You don't need to worry about that. I'll take care of that." She said, "He thought he knew more about it than I did!" When I asked her, "Why didn't you assume that he did know more than you?" she replied:

Well, I didn't consider having a baby something I wasn't supposed to take part in. That I was just there to grow this baby and he was going to take it out of me, but I couldn't do that on my own. I knew better than that. I knew enough about the way a body functions and the way people have babies to know that it was me 100 percent that was going to get this baby through the birth canal and out into the world. And once it's out there, you know, you do need people to take care and make sure the baby is okay and to make sure that I'm okay and that everything went well, but as far as bringing that baby through, that was my job. And I needed to know something about it. I needed to know exactly how that was going to work and I wanted somebody who would work with me to do the best job I could.

Just as these home-birthers see themselves as actively growing their babies, so they also see *labor and birth as hard work that a woman does*. This holistic view that does not separate the woman from the process of labor accepts *pain as an integral part of that process*. To eliminate that one part would interfere with the systemic whole, and would begin a cycle of interference that might have unforeseen results. When I asked, "Did it mean anything to you that you went through the pain?" Tara responded:

> Oh yes. It's part of the whole experience. In this society, we try not to experience pain. We take lots of drugs, I mean legal things. And I feel that's why a lot of people get into other forms of drug abuse. . . . Even though during labor I remember feeling it was almost unbearable, it never entered my mind to wish I had "something for the pain". . . . I wanted the pain to stop, but not because somebody gave me something. I guess part of it is . . . the wonderful physical and emotional stuff that is going on at the same time as the pain. If you took drugs for the pain, you would change all the rest of it, too.

Brigitte Jordan defines authoritative knowledge as "legitimate, consequential, official, worthy of discussion, and useful for justifying actions by people engaged in accomplishing a certain task or objective" (1987:319). Under the technocratic model, only technologically obtained medical knowledge is said to be authoritative. But home-birthers operating under the holistic model often regard *a woman's intuition or "inner knowing" more highly than the objectively obtained information of tests*.

For example, one of the hospital-birthers, Sarah, felt from very early on in labor that her baby was "stuck," as she put it, and would not come down. She tried over and over during the course of a 32-hour labor to convey this inner knowing to her obstetricians and obtain a cesarean, but was repeatedly ignored. When the baby was finally pulled out with forceps, her own diagnosis of "stuckness" was confirmed by the delivering physician. Elizabeth's home-birth experience will provide a useful contrast. Her midwife became concerned because the baby's heart tones were dropping, and muttered under her breath about possibly going to the hospital. Elizabeth heard her, and was "flooded with the total certainty that her baby was fine." She leaned forward between pushing contractions, and whispered this inner knowing to the midwife, who immediately and visibly relaxed. Later Elizabeth asked the midwife about her response. The midwife replied, "Over the course of my years of doing home-birth, if I have learned anything, it is to trust what mothers know."[8]

On the subject of whose knowledge to trust, home-birth professional Susan expressed herself very strongly. She said:

> I went to an OB when I found out I was pregnant. And I told him, son of a bitch, that I was pregnant, and he said, "Let's test you and see." And I said, "No, I am pregnant and I'm trying to pick an OB." And he said, "Let's pee in the little cup and let me see." And that infuriated me . . . . [And then someone suggested that I call a lay midwife,] and we just hit it off like that. Instantly I knew that this was what you were supposed to do. This was the way to have a baby.

In technocratic reality, not only are mother and baby viewed as separate, but the best interests of each are often perceived as conflicting. In such circumstances, the mother's emotional needs and desires are almost always subordinated to the medical interpretation of the best interests of the baby as the all-important product of this "manufacturing process." Thus, individuals operating under this paradigm often criticize home-birthers as "selfish" and "irresponsible" for putting their own desires above their baby's needs. But under the holistic paradigm held by these home-birthers, just as mother and baby form part of one integral and indivisible unit until birth, so *the safety of the baby and the emotional needs of the mother are also one. The safest birth for the baby will be the one that provides the most nurturing environment for the mother.*[9] Said Tara, "The bottom line was that I felt safer [at home] and I think that's what it boils down to for most people. . . . It seemed strange to me that people feel safer with the drugs and all that." Elizabeth said, "My safest place is my bed. That's where I feel the most protected and the most nurtured. And so I knew that was where I had to give birth." And Ryla said:

> I got criticized for choosing a home-birth, for not considering the safety of the baby. But that's exactly what I *was* considering! How could it possibly serve my baby for me to give birth in a place that causes my whole body to tense up in anxiety as soon as I walk in the door?

According to the technocratic model, the uterus is an involuntary muscle, and labor proceeds mechanically in response to hormonal signals. Both Susan and Tara were attended at home by midwives who see *the uterus as a responsive part of the whole*, and who therefore believe that *the best labor care will involve attention to the mother's emotional and spiritual desires, as well as her physical needs.* The difference between these two approaches is clearly illustrated by the responses of a physician and a lay midwife to the stopped labor of a client. The physician said, "It was obvious that she needed some pitocin, so I ordered it," and the midwife said, "It was obvious that she needed some rest, so she went to sleep, and we went home." Here is Susan's story:

> Nikki [the midwife] kind of got worried towards the afternoon, because it just kept going on and nothing was changing. And she took me to the shower and said, "Just stay in there till the hot water goes away." And then Nikki asked my friend Diane, "What's the deal with Susan? Is she stressed out about work?" And Diane said, "Well, yeah, I think she's afraid to have the baby . . . that she's not going to be able to go back to her job." So when I came back out Nikki said, "Right now your job is not

important. What you have to do right now is have this baby. This baby is important."
And I just burst into tears and was screaming at her and crying and I could feel
everything just relax. It all went out of me and then my water broke and we had a
baby in thirty minutes. Just like that.

It is important to understand that the holistic ideology held by these women both
potentiates and explains these dramatic experiences of mind-body and mother-
child connectedness. Such experiences are common in the narratives of home-
birthers (Star 1986; Davis-Floyd 1992, 1995; Ashford 1984), as are experiences of
birth as enhancing that integration. Kristin said:

Pregnancy and birth changed my whole view of myself. I had never valued myself as
a woman. I valued the masculine aspects of my personality, but I considered my wom-
anly traits weak and counterproductive. [Birth was] an incredible discovery of the
power of my intuition, and of the value of trusting myself.

Integration as a Life Principle

Just as the principle of separation governs so many domains of life for the hospital-birthers in this study, so the principles of integration and interconnectedness
that the home-birthers internalize through pregnancy and birth spill over into
many other areas of their lives. For example, Susan reports that she is learning
to put the principle of giving up control to use in the office, and is finding that
the results include lowered stress levels and improved relationships with subordi-
nates, who feel freer to innovate and take on more responsibility as she becomes
less controlling. Elizabeth began experimenting with the same principle in her
teaching, and finds that when she gives up trying to control her students by making them see things her way, potentially tense confrontations and disagreements
transform into mutually productive discussions. Likewise, when her children
become ill, Elizabeth rarely takes them to a doctor:

Since I learned so much about mind-body integration from giving birth, I know that
most of the time, they can heal themselves, if I can just listen well enough to help
them figure out what's really wrong emotionally. Once we handle that, usually their
bodies can quickly take care of the rest.

Susan uses her experience of birth to conceptualize more concretely her link to
all of life:

I would prefer that birth remain as natural as possible. . . . Birth is what ties us to
other forms of life, creates a bond between human women that goes back hundreds
of generations, and bonds us to other species as well. The more technological birth
becomes, the more it differentiates us, and the more unlike other species—and
other members of our own species—we become.

SOME COMMONALITIES

A caveat: in my efforts to make clear the profound differences in body image and world-view between these two groups of women, I have no doubt overemphasized the polarities. Although these are evident and real, there are important commonalities that need to be acknowledged. Most important, I think, and most reflective of recent events in American society is the fact that all these women are far from resembling the passive victims of technocracy that many of their mothers may have been. All were active agents in their birth-giving, although in radically different ways, as we have seen. For both groups, curiously enough, that agency took the form of control. We have seen the importance of control to the hospital-birthers; we might also note its importance to the home-birthers. For, although they gave up trying to control their bodies, they very actively sought to retain control of other sorts of things, most particularly of their birth-space. "Nosy neighbors," "nervous parents," and "medical types" were to be kept out; besides partners and children, only carefully selected midwives and certain friends were allowed in. As Elizabeth put it, "I had to control my birth environment, so that nobody would control my birth."

I find another important commonality in the fact that the integrative principles so important to the home-birthers were also much in evidence in the lives of some of the professionals. Their techniques of integration, as we saw earlier, included breast-feeding and bringing their children to the office both before and after birth. Most, even if they devalued feminine biological processes, did place high value on what they saw as the feminine qualities of nurturance and emotionality, and sought to bring these qualities into the workplace in order to "humanize" the office environment.

Concomitantly, the separation so pervasive in the lives of the professionals was also an issue for the home-birthers, some of whom had to deal with the same issues of separation from their children during working hours, even when they were working at home. Ryla said:

> It's happened lots of times—I'll be seeing a client, and trying to come across like a professional, and then my two-year-old, who is supposed to be getting watched by his sister, will bang on the door and say, "Mommy, I pooped in the hall!" And I know it's because he wants my attention, and I feel just as guilty as if I had gone to the office—maybe more so because he's right there in front of me, and I'm telling him to go away.

BODY IMAGE AS A TEMPLATE FOR THE FUTURE?

> Nothing will have more of an impact on the future than medical science, with advances posing a series of ethical questions. Anyone thinking of starting a family will begin with a Sears catalogue of options: A woman wishing to postpone child-bearing for career development may want to freeze a few eggs for later use; a woman

TABLE 1   The Technocratic and Holistic Models of Birth Compared

> The possibility that form and essence, orthodoxy and heterodoxy, are bipolar, are actually necessary for each other's existence, is one that continues to elude us.
> —Morris Berman, *Coming to Our Senses,* 1989:148

This table presents a comparison of the basic tenets of the hegemonic-technocratic model and the alternative-holistic model as they have emerged from the words and behaviors of the women in the study.

The Technocratic Model of Birth	*The Holistic Model of Birth*
The body is imperfect, and separate from the self.	Self and body are One.
The body is mechanical—a vehicle, a tool for the self.	The body is an organism, intimately interconnected with mind and environment.
Life is controllable.	Life is not controllable.
The self should control the body.	The body cannot be controlled.
Pregnancy is out-of-control, and therefore unpleasant.	Pregnancy is uncontrollable and pleasurable.
The pregnant body is a vessel for the fetus, who is a separate being.	Mother and baby are essentially One—they form part of an integrated system that can only be harmed by dissection into parts.
Fetal growth is a mechanical process in which the mother is not actively involved.	The mother actively grows the baby.
The desires of the mother and the needs of the baby can and often do conflict during labor and birth.	The safety of the baby and the emotional needs of the mother are the same. The safest birth for the baby will be the one that provides the most nurturing environment for the mother.
Birth is a mechanical process.	Birth is hard work a woman does.
Technology is better than untrustworthy nature.	Nature is best, and can be trusted. Technology should support but not interfere.
The mind is more important than the body.	Mind and body are one—organically interconnected.
Active participation and control in life are good.	The most active participation can involve giving up control.
As long as a woman's mind is aware, she is an active participant in birth.	A woman gives birth with her whole being.
Pain is bad. Not to have to feel pain in labor is a modern woman's intrinsic right.	Pain is an integral part of the labor process. To eliminate that part interferes with the systemic whole.
Medical knowledge is authoritative.	Intuition/inner knowing are authoritative.
To be strong and powerful, one must be in control.	Strength and power come from letting go of control.

who is unable to conceive may want to "adopt" an embryo deposited by an anonymous donor at a frozen embryo bank, then carry it in her own body.

—*Life* Magazine, February 1989:54

Fear of organic life . . . is so central and pervasive a feature of modern technological societies that it is, paradoxically, almost invisible. Like . . . the mind/body split, it is virtually everywhere, so it seems to be nowhere. . . . It runs much of our lives, and determines much of our relationships and our social and cultural history. Modern technological society rests on the repression of these fears, and may even be an expression of them. But this means that it rests on a shaky foundation, and it is getting visibly shakier every year.

—Morris Berman, *Coming to Our Senses*, 1989:97

Emily Martin sees the efforts of the middle-class women's health movement to regain control of birth as resulting in

middle-class women's becoming controlled themselves, being the agents of exerting control over themselves, as silent, except for certain controlled forms of breathing they perform in the public arena of the hospital. In so doing they may be ignoring other aspects of their experiences, which are less easily articulated because they are (as our culture sees them) more physical and less controllable. Working-class women more readily articulate precisely these kinds of experiences: I am in pain, this hurts, it is enough to make me scream; I am not really in control of this situation, and no one could be. (1991:310–11)

Martin suggests that this situation mirrors social structures in the workplace, where

middle-class women more than working-class women advocate and practice "mind over matter" and seek mental concentration that does not allow the body to dictate events. . . . While resisting the medical ideology of reproduction, some middle-class women may be reproducing the ideology and practice of control, in this case exerting control over themselves. By enacting out-of-control behavior, some working-class women may be resisting both the treatment they expect from medical managers and middle-class ideology about the desirability of always being in control. That middle-class women find the idea of going out-of-control in labor repellent and even grotesque is evidence of an opposition among women that does not serve our common interests. (1991:310–11)

The opposition between home- and hospital-birthers of the middle class over this same issue of control is equally dramatic, and we may equally well question whether it serves our common interest as women.

The professionals in my study insist on control, and they, like Martin's middle-class women, tend to be silent in the hospital: they do not scream out their pain; rather, they anesthetize it away. However, it does not look to them like they are being controlled by the medical establishment, but rather that they are manipulating the technocratic resources of the medical establishment to control their own bodily experiences. Martin suggests that such feelings of being "empowered and in control" are illusory, and that "losing control" in birth "can mean having one's body physically penetrated [by] Cesarean" (1991:309). But for these professional women (one of whom scheduled her cesarean to take place between conference calls), having a cesarean is not losing control but gaining it—given the models of reality they individually hold. Regardless of how they came to believe in the value of technocratic control, the fact that they do believe in and value such control is not an illusion, and their feelings of empowerment when they achieve such control through the agencies of the professionals they have hired for that purpose—their physicians—are not illusions either. Although I may personally perceive unnecessary cesareans as disempowering for birthing women, as an anthropologist I know that those who participate most fully in a society's hegemonic core value system, as these women do, are most likely to be empowered by and to succeed within that system, as these women have.

In "Society and Sex Roles," Ernestine Friedl postulates that

> in any society, status goes to those who control the distribution of valued goods and resources outside the family. . . . Only as managers, executives, and professionals are women in a position to trade goods and services, to do others favors, and therefore to obligate others to them. Only as controllers of valued resources can women achieve prestige, power, and equality. Within the household, women who bring in income from jobs are able to function on a more nearly equal basis with their husbands. . . . (1990:218)

Certainly, these professional women confirm Friedl's hypotheses—they are highly successful in the wider society as controllers of valued goods and resources, and at home all but one reported that their marriages were extremely egalitarian. While the "Earth Mothers" in my study certainly do not see themselves as unsuccessful, the criteria of the technocracy would judge them less so than the professionals, as they are not in general controllers of valued goods and resources (although they do enjoy egalitarian marriages with husbands who share their alternative world-view).

Proponents of a paradigm tend to create the world in its image. Childbirth educators and midwives today often speak of the 1990s as the age of the "epidural epidemic." The deeper we probe into the world-views of these professional women as they emerge in their descriptions of their beliefs about birth and their female bodies, the more we can understand why this is so. As the epidural numbs the birthing woman, eliminating the pain of childbirth, it also graphically demonstrates to her through her lived experience the truth of the Cartesian maxim that mind and body are separate, that the biological realm can be completely cut off from the realm of the intellect and the emotions. This microcosmic mirror of our technocratic society casts its reflection in ever-widening ripples in the pond of social life. As the drugged baby so mechanically birthed is carried off to the nursery to be separate from the mother, and spends much of infancy in cribs and plastic seats and carriers, so that same infant in later years will be carried off to day care and to school. Ours is a nation founded on principles of separation, and we enact and transmit those principles to each other in the spatial and interactional relational patterns we have developed between mind and body, mother and baby, and parents and child.

Proponents of a paradigm tend also to envision the future in its image. When asked about her vision for the future of American birth, Joanne, the professional who did not want to "drop into biology," spoke of the benefits of genetic engineering, saying, "I think people in the future are going to expect medicine and science to have more answers." And Katie said, "I cannot envision how birth could be any different, except perhaps the drugs will be better and they will be able to measure the amounts more exactly."

The technocratic model's emphasis on separation potentiates various sorts of futuristic behavioral extremes in the cultural arena of birth. These technocratic extremes include, among many others: court-ordered cesareans—cases in which the mother refuses to have a cesarean, but is forced to do so by the courts against her will (Jordan and Irwin 1990; Shearer 1989); the new reproductive technologies (see Introduction); genetic engineering—altering genes to select for certain desired traits or eliminate undesirable ones; and the development of artificial wombs that could grow a baby to term outside a woman's body. (It is worth remembering that such futuristic reproductive technologies are envisioned, invented, and "chosen" in a sociocultural context that values them more than the female bodies they act upon.) In contrast to such futuristic scenarios of separation, Tara's vision for the future makes an explicit connection between the ecological principles of the environmental movement and home-birth:

> How do we change this trend toward more drugs for birth, more machines? . . . If we get back to caring about the Earth, being caretakers, it would be difficult not to translate that into other parts of our lives. Sooner or later people will ask themselves how they can give birth drugged and hooked up to machines, when they are trying to stop treating their own Mother Earth that way.

One of the home-birthers in my study, Ryla, is engaged in research on water-birth, and on birthing in the ocean with dolphins in order to tap the potential of interspecies communication—two futuristic extremes made possible by the holistic model's emphasis on interconnectedness. Other such extremes of interconnectedness include attempting to conceive babies consciously (Parvati-Baker 1986a; Huxley and Ferucci 1992) and working to enhance psychic communication between mother and child (Peterson 1984; Marnie 1988; Jones 1989; Schwartz 1991; Verny and Weintraub 1991). Such holistically oriented researchers are consciously attempting to counterbalance the disembodied future towards which the technocratic model seems inexorably to be leading us.

Extremes, on both ends of the spectrum, play an important role in defining the outer edges of the possible and the imagined. Most especially, those at the extreme of conceptual opposition to a society's hegemonic paradigm—the radical fringe—create much more room for growth and change within that society than would exist without them. How much more technocratic might hospital-birth look, if no one in this country believed that mother and baby are One, that there is an inner knowing that can be tapped, that fulfilling the emotional needs of the mother is the best approach to the health of the child?

Let us consider for a moment the nature of hegemony. In small-scale societies in which people generally share in the same overall worldview—one emergent from the interaction of people with their environment—there are no hegemonies. Hegemonies only happen in larger societies in which groups in power hold certain world-views and are able to make them culturally dominant, to impose them on everyone else:

> ... the power of a ruling class, exercised through the state, does not merely dominate but ultimately comes to merge with civil society. The ruling class dominates by force but directs through the ... consensual commonsense of culture. The combination of apparently merely instrumental force with apparently merely expressive ideas is what constitutes hegemony. (Frankenberg 1988:328)

Hegemonies, whether religious, political, ideological—or biomedical—are frequently contested by one or another social group. As Berman has shown, such contestations are essential to the continued vitality of the hegemonic form:

> All orthodoxies need heresies, all political regimes need dissenters, not only to jail or burn them, but also to coopt them. For as marginal figures, they hold the secret of creative transformations. If anomalies can be plowed back into the system—composted, as Mary Douglas puts it—the system becomes stronger; if you eat your enemy, you absorb his power. If, on the other hand, you insist on purity, you become like a body without orifices, which means you die very quickly. (1989:82)

Because the technocratic paradigm *is* hegemonic, pervading medical practice and guiding almost all reproductive research, no middle-class woman who gives birth at home can fail to be aware that she is battling almost overwhelming social forces that would drive her to the hospital. The home-birthers in my study who espouse the holistic model do so in direct and very conscious opposition to the dominant technocratic model. They represent the one percent of American women who choose to give birth at home. I suggest that the importance to American society of this tiny percentage of alternative model women is tremendous, for they are holding open a giant conceptual space in which mothers and babies can find room to be jointly embodied and spiritually linked. Home-birthers I have interviewed use rich metaphors to describe pregnancy, labor, and birth that work to naturalize, personalize, feminize, and spiritualize the processes of procreation. They speak of mothers and babies as unified energy fields, coparticipants in the creative mysteries, entrained and joyous dancers in the rhythms and harmonies of life. They talk of labor as a river, as the ebb and flow of ocean waves, as ripened fruit falling in its own good time.

Jeanine Parvati-Baker, author of *Hygeia: A Woman's Herbal* (1978), *Conscious Conception* (1986a), and *Prenatal Yoga* (1986b), and self-acknowledged "Earth

Mother," has this to say about being a cultural heretic, "hanging out on the radical fringe" (personal communication):

> Some years ago, I wrote a visualization . . . which led the participants in gradual steps to a door, and encouraged them to open it without giving any hints as to what might be on the other side. Experimenting, I tried it out on myself, and found that when I opened the door, I stepped out into the starry night sky, which began to swirl and swirl. . . . The next time someone told me that I "hang out on the fringe," something I've been hearing for most of my life, I suddenly saw that yes, I am on the fringe—on the fringe of the skirt of the goddess as she dances around the universe. That starry sky, that's the fringe of her skirt, and it swirls and swirls as she dances. And that's my place, and it's a wonderful place to be, full of movement and excitement and joy.

Home-birthers in the United States are an endangered species. (As part of a fund-raising effort, a group of local lay midwives is selling T-shirts with whales painted on the front; the caption underneath reads "*SAVE THE MIDWIVES!*") Should midwives cease to exist, the options available in American society for thinking about and treating pregnancy, birth, and the female body would sharply decrease, and our society would be enormously impoverished. Should they thrive, we will continue to be enriched by their alternative visions.

As feminists, we fight for the right to make our bodies our own, to metaphorize, adorn, and technologize as we please. We are just beginning to guess at the cultural and individual impact of the symbolic messages today's professional women are sending through their symbolic placement of their bodies in relation to their families, and through their mental attitudes to the physical changes brought about by the biological processes of pregnancy, birth, and motherhood. The intensifying quest of many of these women for distance from these processes leads inevitably to the question: as women increasingly break out of the confines of the biological domain of motherhood, will/should our culture still define that domain as primarily belonging to women? What do we want? As we move into the twenty-first century, will the options opened to us by our technology leave equal conceptual room for the women who want to *be* their bodies, as well as for the women for whom the body is only a tool? To what extent do we desire to give up those processes that since the beginning of the species have defined us as women, in order to compete with men on their terms and succeed? In the new society we are making, will the home-birthers and the home-schoolers, the goddesses and the Earth Mothers, have equal opportunity to live out their choices alongside those who want to schedule their cesareans, and those who want their babies incubated in a test tube? If it is true, as Berman says, that hegemonies cannot survive without the revitalization heresies bring, then our technocratic society's chances for survival may be greatly enhanced by the "secret of creative transformations" emergent in the visceral, organic body cognition of women who celebrate the full connectedness of pregnancy, mothering, and birth.

Acknowledgments.   I wish to thank Carolyn Sargent for her patience and her editorial skills, Courtney Hollyfield for her invaluable assistance with interviewing and tape transcription, Adela Popp for her outstanding transcriptions, and the women in this study for their willingness to share their lives with me, and for their time.

NOTES

1. A notable exception is physician George Engelmann, who traveled widely observing childbirth, and in 1882 wrote *Labor among Primitive Peoples* (1977). For a valuable summary of his work, including excellent reproductions of his drawings of the positions women adopted for birth, see Ashford 1988.
2. For an outstanding review of all available literature relevant to the broader field of the anthropology of reproduction, see Ginsburg and Rapp 1991.
3. The medical literature on these subjects is too vast to cite here. For recent summaries of much of this literature, see Enkin et al. 1989; Davis-Floyd 1992, Ch. 3; and Goer 1995.
4. Fifteen of these interviews were conducted and transcribed by the following students: Kim Durham, Michelle Gomez, Melody Hatfield, Courtney Hollyfield, Lori Pressley, Erin Rogers, and Mark Thompson. I wish to express my appreciation to these students for their hard work, their enthusiasm, and their continuing inspiration.
5. The results of this study can be summarized as follows: 70 percent were comfortable with their technological births to varying degrees (42 of them had started out with the expressed intention of "doing natural childbirth," but ended up with highly technological births instead, while the other 28 wanted technological births to begin with, and were generally satisfied with the ones they got); 15 percent desired and achieved natural childbirth in the hospital; 9 percent desired natural childbirth but did not achieve it and were seriously disturbed as a result; and 6 percent gave birth at home (Davis-Floyd 1992, Ch. 5).
6. Birth practitioners and social scientists usually refer to this paradigm as the "medical model" (e.g. Rothman 1982). In previous works (Davis-Floyd 1987a,b, 1988, 1990a,b), I have called it the "technological model" in order to stress its connections to the technologically oriented core-value system of American society. But I find that the term "technocratic" is a more precise representation of what I mean that the broader term, "technological." "Technocratic" connotes a society that places a high value on, and organizes itself in terms of, its technology, as well as one that is bureaucratic, autocratic, and hierarchically organized. The label "the technocratic model" indicates that the model is hegemonic, as I suggest in *Birth as an American Rite of Passage* (1992).
7. It is worth noting that most of these women had amniocentesis in an effort to ensure that they would have perfect babies, and that all expected their babies to, in fact, be perfect. All believed themselves to be well educated for birth, but that education did not include research into the effects of anesthesia. Not one who had anesthesia expressed any sort of concern about what it might do to their children, in spite of mounting evidence of the possibility of long- and short-term damage (Brackbill et al. 1984; Brackbill et al. 1988:23; Golding et al. 1990.) For example, most American women believe that epidurals are risk-free. Yet a recent British study of 11,701 women found a link between epidural anesthesia during labor and chronic back pain (McArthur et al. 1992). A still more recent study shows that epidurals often prolong

both the first and second stages of labor, resulting in a need for further interventions and dramatically increasing the cesarean section rate (Thorp et al. 1989, 1993). Epidural anesthesia, like all drugs, crosses the placenta and is absorbed by the baby. In a recent study using Brazelton's "neonatal behavioral assessment scale" on babies during the first month after birth, a significant dose effect was found (Sepkoski et al. 1992). Long-term effects on babies are unknown, but some researchers, like Sweden's Dr. Bertil Jacobson, are beginning to suspect that babies drugged at birth may be more prone to drug addiction in later life (Jacobson et al. 1987, 1988, 1990). While I do not question women's right to choose the mind-body separation such drugs provide, I would suggest that the popularity of such choices, given the possibility that they may prove harmful, provides fruitful ground for further study, and that as more information emerges, medical social scientists have a responsibility to make it as widely available as possible.

8. A recent study of mine examines the use of intuition as authoritative knowledge by home-birth midwives (Davis-Floyd 1995). Their trust in intuition, which they understand as body cognition, reflects their holistic philosophy.

9. Planned, midwife-attended home-birth does not increase risk. For a discussion of the relative safety of home- vs. hospital-birth, and for summaries of midwifery statistics, see Davis-Floyd 1992:Ch. 4; Goer 1995.

REFERENCES

Arms, Suzanne
  1981 (orig. pub. 1975)   Immaculate Deception. New York: Bantam Books.
Ashford, Janet Isaacs, ed.
  1984   Birth Stories: The Experience Remembered. Trumansburg, NY: The Crossing Press.
  1988   George Engelmann and "Primitive" Birth. Solana Beach, CA: Janet Isaacs Ashford.
Berman, Morris
  1989   Coming to Our Senses: Body and Spirit in the Hidden History of the West. New York: Simon and Schuster.
Boone, Margaret
  1988   Social Support for Pregnancy and Childbearing among Disadvantaged Blacks in an American Inner City. *In* Childbirth in America: Anthropological Perspectives. Karen Michaelson, ed. Pp. 66–79. South Hadley, MA: Bergin and Garvey.
Brackbill, Yvonne, Karen McManus, and Lynn Woodward
  1988   Medication in Maternity: Infant Exposure and Maternal Information. Ann Arbor: University of Michigan Press.
Brackbill, Yvonne, June Rice, and Diony Young
  1984   Birth Trap: The Legal Low-Down on High-Tech Obstetrics. St. Louis, MO: C. V. Mosby.
Browner, Carole
  1983   Male Pregnancy Symptoms in Urban Colombia. American Ethnologist 13(3):494–510.
  1985   Traditional Techniques for Diagnosis, Treatment, and Control of Pregnancy in Cali, Colombia. *In* Women's Medicine: A Cross-Cultural Study of Fertility Reg-

ulation. Lucile F. Newman, ed. Pp. 99–124. New Brunswick, NJ: Rutgers University Press.

1986   The Politics of Reproduction in a Mexican Village. Signs 11:710–724.

1989   The Management of Reproduction in an Egalitarian Society. *In* Women as Healers: Cross-Cultural Perspectives. Carol S. McClain, ed. Pp. 58–71. New Brunswick, NJ: Rutgers University Press.

Cosminsky, Sheila

1977   Childbirth and Midwifery on a Guatemalan Finca. Medical Anthropology 6(3):69–104.

1982   Childbirth and Change: A Guatemalan Study. *In* Ethnography of Fertility and Birth. Carol MacCormack, ed. Pp. 205–230. New York: Academic Press.

Cunningham, F. Gary, Paul C. MacDonald, and Norman F. Gant

1989   Williams Obstetrics, 18th edition. Norwalk, CT: Appleton & Lange.

Davis-Floyd, Robbie E.

1983   Pregnancy and Cultural Confusion: Contradictions in Socialization. *In* Cultural Constructions of Woman. Pauline Kolenda, ed. Prospect Heights, OH: Waveland Press.

1987   Obstetric Training as a Rite of Passage. Medical Anthropology Quarterly 1(3):288–318.

1987b   The Technological Model of Birth. Journal of American Folklore 100(398):93–109.

1988   Birth as an American Rite of Passage. *In* Childbirth in America: Anthropological Perspectives. Karen Michaelson and Contributors. Beacon Hill, MA: Bergin and Garvey.

1989   Knowing: A Story of Two Births. Unpublished ms.

1990   The Role of American Obstetrics in the Resolution of Cultural Anomaly. Social Science and Medicine 31(2):175–189.

1992   Birth as an American Rite of Passage. Berkeley and London: University of California Press.

1994   Mind Over Body: The Pregnant Professional. *In* Many Mirrors: Body Image and Social Relations in Anthropological Perspective. Nicole Sault, ed. New Brunswick, NJ: Rutgers University Press.

1996   Intuition as Authoritative Knowledge. *In* Childbirth and Authoritative Knowledge: Crosscultural Perspectives. Robbie Davis-Floyd and Carolyn Sargent, eds. Berkeley: University of California Press.

Dougherty, Molly C.

1978   Southern Lay Midwives as Ritual Specialists. *In* Women in Ritual and Symbolic Roles. Judith Hoch-Smith and Anita Spring, eds. Pp. 151–164. New York: Plenum.

Eakins, Pamela, ed.

1986   The American Way of Birth. Philadelphia: University of Pennsylvania Press.

Ehrenreich, Barbara, and Deirdre English

1973a   Complaints and Disorders: The Sexual Politics of Sickness. Old Westbury, NY: The Feminist Press.

1973b   Witches, Midwives, and Nurses: A History of Women Healers. Old Westbury, NY: The Feminist Press.

Engelmann, George

1977   (orig. pub. 1882) Labor among Primitive Peoples. New York: AMS Press.

Enkin, Murray, Marc Kierse, and Iaian Chalmers

1989   Effective Cure in Pregnancy and Childbirth. Oxford: Oxford University Press.

Faust, Betty B.
  1988   When Is a Midwife a Witch? A Case Study from a Modernizing Maya Village. *In* Women and Health: Cross-Cultural Perspectives. Patricia Whelehan, ed. Pp. 21–39. South Hadley, MA: Bergin and Garvey.

Ford, Clellan Stearns
  1964 (1945)   A Comparative Study of Human Reproduction. Reissue. New Haven, CT: Human Relations Area Files Press.

Frankenberg, Ronald
  1988   Gramsci, Culture, and Medical Anthropology: Kundry and Parsifal? or Rat's Tail to Sea Serpent? Medical Anthropology Quarterly 2(4):324–337.

Fraser, Gertrude
  1988   Afro-American Midwives, Biomedicine, and the State: An Ethnohistorical Account of Birth and Its Transformation in Rural Virginia. Ph.D. dissertation, Department of Anthropology, Baltimore, MD: Johns Hopkins University.
  1992   Afro-American Midwives, Biomedicine, and the State. Cambridge, MA: Harvard University Press.

Freedman, Lawrence Z., and Verna Masius Ferguson
  1950   The Question of Painless Childbirth in Primitive Cultures. American Journal of Orthopsychiatry 20(2):363–372.

Friedl, Ernestine
  1990   Society and Sex Roles. *In* Anthropology: Contemporary Perspectives. Phillip Whitten and David Hunter, eds. Pp. 215–219. Glenview, IL: Scott Foresman.

Fuller, Nancy, and Brigitte Jordan
  1981   Maya Women and the End of the Birthing Period: Postpartum Massage and Binding in Yucatan, Mexico. Medical Anthropology 5(1):35–50.

Georges, Eugenia
  1996   Fetal Ultrasound Imaging and the Production of Authoritative Knowledge. *In* Childbirth and Authoritative Knowledge: Cross-Cultural Perspectives. Robbie Davis-Floyd and Carolyn Sargent, eds. Berkeley: University of California Press.

Ginsburg, Faye, and Rayna Rapp
  1991   The Politics of Reproduction. Annual Reviews in Anthropology 20:311–343.

Gocr, Henci
  1995   Obstetric Myths Versus Research Realities. New Haven, CT: Bergin and Garvey.

Golding, J., M. Paterson, and L. J. Kimlen
  1990   Factors Associated with Childhood Cancer in a National Cohort Study. British Journal of Cancer 62:304–308.

Gray, Brenda
  1982   Enga Birth, Maturation, and Survival. *In* Ethnography of Fertility and Birth. Carol MacCormack, ed. Pp. 75–113. New York: Academic Press.

Hahn, Robert A.
  1987   Divisions of Labor: Obstetrician, Woman and Society. *In* Williams Obstetrics, 1903–1985. Medical Anthropology Quarterly 1(3):256–282.

Handwerker, W. Penn
  1990   Births and Power: Social Change and the Politics of Reproduction. Boulder, CO: Westview Press.
  1990   Politics and Reproduction: A Window on Social Change. *In* Births and Power: Social Change and the Politics of Reproduction. W. Penn Handwerker, ed. Pp. 1–38. Boulder, CO: Westview Press.

Hazzell, Lester Dessez
  1976   Commonsense Childbirth. New York: Berkely Medallion Books.

Hunte, Pamela A.
 1981   The Role of the *Dai* in Urban Afghanistan. Medical Anthropology 5(1):
          17–26.

Huxley, Laura, and Pierro Ferrucci
 1992   The Child of Your Dreams: Approaching Conception and Pregnancy with
          Inner Peace. Rochester, VT: Destiny Books.

Jacobson, B., G. Eklund, L. Hamberger, D. Linarsson, G. Sedvall, and M. Valvereius
 1987   Perinatal Origin of Adult Self-Destructive Behavior. Acta Psychiatrica Scandi-
          navica 76:364–371.

Jacobson, B., Karin Nyberg, Gunnar Eklund, Marc Bygdeman, and Ulf Rydberg
 1988   Obstetric Pain Medication and Eventual Adult Amphetamine Addiction in Off-
          spring. Acta Obstetrica Gynecoliga 67:677–682.

Jacobson, B., K. Nyberg, L. Grondlabh, et al.
 1990   Opiate Addiction in Adult Offspring through Possible Imprinting after Obstet-
          ric Treatment. British Medical Journal 301:1067–1070.

Johnson, Shirley M., and Loudell F. Snow
 1982   Assessment of Reproductive Knowledge in an Inner City Clinic. Social Science
          and Medicine 16:1657–1662.

Jones, Carl
 1987   From Parent to Child: The Psychic Link. New York: Warner Books.

Jordan, Brigitte
 1977   The Self-Diagnosis of Early Pregnancy: An Investigation of Lay Competence.
          Medical Anthropology 1(2):1–38.
 1984   External Cephalic Version as an Alternative to Breech Delivery and Cesarean
          Section. Social Science and Medicine 18(8):637–651.
 1986   The Hut and the Hospital: Information, Power and Symbolism in the Artifacts
          of Birth. Birth 13(2).
 1989   Cosmopolitical Obstetrics: Some Insights from the Training of Traditional Mid-
          wives. Social Science and Medicine 28(9):925–944.
 1990   Technology and the Social Distribution of Knowledge. *In* Anthropology and
          Primary Health Care. J. Coreil and D. Mull, eds. Boulder, CO: Westview Press.
 1993   (original publication 1977) Birth in Four Cultures: A Cross-Cultural Investiga-
          tion of Childbirth in Yucatan, Holland, Sweden and the United States.
          Prospect Heights, OH: Waveland Press.

Jordan, Brigitte, and Susan Irwin
 1989   The Ultimate Failure: Court-Ordered Cesarean Section. *In* New Approaches to
          Human Reproduction. Linda Whiteford and Marilyn Poland, eds. Boulder,
          CO: Westview Press.

Kaminski, H. M., A. Stafl., and J. Aiman
 1987   The Effect of Epidural Analgesia on the Frequency of Instrumental Obstetric
          Delivery. Obstetrics and Gynecology 69:770.

Kay, Margarita, ed.
 1982   Anthropology and Human Birth. Philadelphia: F. A. Davis.

Kitzinger, Sheila
 1972   (orig. pub. 1962) The Experience of Childbirth. 3rd edition. Baltimore: Pen-
          guin Books.
 1979   Birth at Home. New York: Penguin Books.
 1980   Women as Mothers: How They See Themselves in Different Cultures. New
          York: Vintage Books.
 1985   The Sexuality of Birth. *In* Women's Experience of Sex. Pp. 209–218. New York:
          Penguin Books.

Kitzinger, Sheila, ed.
1991   The Midwife Challenge. London: Pandora Press.
Konner, Melvin
1987   Becoming a Doctor: A Journey of Initiation in Medical School. New York: Viking.
Konner, Melvin, and Marjorie Shostak
1987   Timing and Management of Birth among the !Kung: Biocultural Interaction in Reproductive Adaptation. Cultural Anthropology 2(1):11–28.
Kopytoff, Igor
1990   Women's Roles and Existential Identities. *In* Beyond the Second Sex: New Directions in the Anthropology of Gender. Peggy Reeves Sanday and Ruth Gallagher Goodenough, eds. Philadelphia: University of Pennsylvania Press.
Laderman, Carol
1983   Wives and Midwives: Childbirth and Nutrition in Rural Malaysia. Berkeley: University of California Press.
Layne, Linda
1990   Motherhood Lost: Cultural Dimensions of Miscarriage and Stillbirth in America. Women and Health 16(3):69–98.
Lazarus, Ellen
1988   Poor Women, Poor Outcomes: Social Class and Reproductive Health. *In* Childbirth in America: Anthropological Perspectives. Karen Michaelson, ed. South Hadley, MA: Bergin and Garvey Publishers.
1990   Falling through the Cracks: Contradictions and Barriers to Care in a Prenatal Clinic. Medical Anthropology 12(3):269–288.
Lazarus, Ellen, and Elliott H. Phillipson
1990   A Longitudinal Study Comparing the Prenatal Care of Puerto Rican and White Women. Birth 17(1):6–11.
Lefkarites, Mary P.
1992   The Sociocultural Implications of Modernizing Childbirth among Greek Women on the Island of Rhodes. Medical Anthropology 13(4):385–412.
Levi-Strauss, Claude
1967   The Effectiveness of Symbols. *In* Structural Anthropology. Garden City, NY: Doubleday.
Life Magazine
1989   Birth Without Women. February, p. 54.
Litoff, Judy Barrett
1978   American Midwives: 1860 to the Present. Westport, CT: Greenwood Press.
1986   The American Midwife Debate: A Sourcebook on Its Modern Origins. New York: Greenwood Press.
MacCormack, Carol P.
1982   Health, Fertility, and Birth in Moyamba District, Sierra Leone. *In* Ethnography of Fertility and Birth. Carol P. MacCormack, ed. New York: Academic Press.
MacCormack, Carol P., ed.
1982   Ethnography of Fertility and Birth. New York: Academic Press.
Marnie, Eve
1988   LoveStart: Prenatal Bonding. Santa Monica, CA: Hay House.
Martin, Emily
1987   The Woman in the Body. Boston: Beacon Press.
1991   The Ideology of Reproduction: The Reproduction of Ideology. *In* Uncertain Terms: Negotiating Gender in American Society. Faye Ginsburg and Anna Lowenhaupt Tsing, eds. Pp. 300–314. Boston: Beacon Press.

1991   The Egg and the Sperm. Signs 16(3):485–501.

Mathews, Holly
    1990   Killing the Medical Self-Help Tradition among Afro-Americans: The Case of Midwifery in North Carolina, 1917–1983. Unpublished manuscript.

McArthur, C., M. Lewis, and E. G. Know
    1992   Investigation of Long-term Problems after Obstetric Epidural Anesthesia. British Medical Journal 304:1279–1282.

McCarthy, Mary
    1954   The Group. New York: Harcourt, Brace and World, Inc. Quoted in Richard W. Wertz and Dorothy C. Wertz, Lying-In: A History of Childbirth in America, 2nd edition. New Haven: Yale University Press, 1989. p. 150.

McClain, Carol
    1983   Perceived Risk and Choice of Childbirth Service. Social Science and Medicine 17(23):1857–1865.
    1985   Why Women Choose Trial of Labor or Repeat Cesarean Section. Journal of Family Practice 21(3):210–216.
    1987a   Some Social Network Differences between Women Choosing Home and Hospital Birth. Human Organization 46(2):146–152.
    1987b   Patient Decision-Making: The Case of Delivery Method After a Previous Cesarean Section. Culture, Medicine, and Psychiatry 11:495–508.

McClain, Carol, ed.
    1989   Women as Healers: Cross-Cultural Perspectives. New Brunswick, NJ: Rutgers University Press.

Mead, Margaret, and Niles Newton
    1967   Cultural Patterning of Perinatal Behavior. In Childbearing: Its Social and Psychological Aspects. S. Richardson and A. F. Guttmacher, eds. Pp. 142–244. Baltimore: Williams and Wilkins.

Michaelson, Karen
    1988   Childbirth in America: Anthropological Perspectives. South Hadley, MA: Bergin and Garvey.

Morse, Janice M., and Carolyn Park
    1988   Differences in Cultural Expectations of the Perceived Painfulness of Childbirth. In Childbirth in America: Anthropological Perspectives. Karen L. Michaelson, ed. Pp. 121–129. South Hadley, MA: Bergin and Garvey.

Morsy, Soheir
    1982   Childbirth in an Egyptian Village. In Anthropology and Human Birth. Margarita Kay, ed. Pp. 147–174. Philadephia: F. A. Davis.

Munroe, R. L., R. H. Munroe, and J. W. M. Whiting
    1973   The Couvade: A Psychological Analysis. Ethos 1:30–74.

Nelson, Margaret K.
    1982   The Effect of Childbirth Preparation on Women of Different Social Classes. Journal of Health and Social Behavior 23(4):339–352.
    1983   Working-Class Women, Middle-Class Women, and Models of Childbirth. Social Problems 30(3):284–297.

Newman, Lucille F.
    1965   Culture and Perinatal Environment in American Society. PhD. dissertation. Berkeley: University of California.
    1976   Unwanted Pregnancy in California: Some Cultural Considerations. In Culture, Natality, and Family Planning. J. F. Marshall and S. Polgar, eds. Pp. 156–166. Chapel Hill: University of North Carolina Press.

1980 Parents' Perceptions of their Low Birth Weight Infants. Pediatrician 9:182–190.

1981 Midwives and Modernization. Medical Anthropology 5(1):1–12.

1986 Premature Infant Behavior: An Ethological Study in a Special Care Nursery. Human Organization 45(4):327–333.

1988 The Artificial Womb: Social and Sensory Environments of Low Birthweight Infants. *In* Childbirth in America: Anthropological Perspectives. Karen Michaelson, ed. Pp. 204–210. South Hadley, MA: Bergin and Garvey.

Newton, Niles

1972 Childbearing in Broad Perspective. *In* Pregnancy, Birth, and the Newborn Baby. Boston: Delacorte Press.

1973 The Interrelationships between Sexual Responsiveness, Birth, and Breast-feeding. *In* Contemporary Sexual Behavior: Critical Issues in the 1970s. Joseph Zubin and John Money, eds. Baltimore: Johns Hopkins University Press.

1977 (orig. pub. 1955) Maternal Emotions: A Study of Women's Feelings toward Menstruation, Pregnancy, Childbirth, Breastfeeding, Infant Care, and Other Aspects of their Femininity. Pp. 77–98. Paul B. Hoeber, Inc.

Newton, Niles, and Michael Newton

1972 Childbirth in Crosscultural Perspective. In Modern Perspectives in Psycho-Obstetrics. J. Howells, ed. Edinburgh: Oliver and Boyd.

Newton, Niles, Michael Newton, and Jeanine Broach

1988 Psychologic, Physical, Nutritional, and Technologic Aspects of Intravenous Infusion During Labor. Birth 15(2):67–72.

Newton, Niles, D. Peeler, and Michael Newton

1968 Effect of Disturbance on Labor: An Experiment Using 100 Mice with Dated Pregnancies. American Journal of Obstetrics and Gynecology 101:1096–1102.

Oakley, Ann

1977 Becoming a Mother. New York: Schocken Books.

1980 Women Confined: Towards a Sociology of Childbirth. New York: Schocken Books.

1984 The Captured Womb: A History of the Medical Care of Pregnant Women. New York and Oxford: Basil Blackwell.

O'Neil, John, and Patricia A. Kaufert

1990 The Politics of Obstetric Care: The Inuit Experience. *In* Births and Power: Social Change and the Politics of Reproduction. W. Penn Handwerker, ed. Pp. 53–68. Boulder, CO: Westview Press.

Parvati-Baker, Jeannine

1978 Hygeia: A Woman's Herbal. Monroe, UT: Freestone Publishing.

1986a Conscious Conception: Elemental Journey through the Labyrinth of Sexuality. Monroe, UT: Freestone Publishing.

1986b (orig. publ. 1974) Prenatal Yoga and Natural Birth (revised edition). Monroe, UT: Freestone Publishing.

1991 The Deep Ecology of Birth: Healing Birth Is Healing Our Earth. Monroe, UT: Freestone Publishing.

1992 The Shamanic Dimension of Childbirth. Pre- and Perinatal Psychology Journal 7(1):5–20.

Paul, Lois

1975 Recruitment to a Ritual Role: The Midwife in a Maya Community. Ethos 3:449–467.

1978 Careers of Midwives in a Mayan community. In Women in Ritual and Symbolic Roles. Judith HochSmith and Anita Spring, eds. Pp. 129–150. New York: Plenum.

Paul, Lois, and Benjamin D. Paul
  1975   The Maya Midwife as Sacred Specialist: A Guatemalan Case. American Ethnologist 2(4):707–725.
Peterson, Gayle
  1981   Birthing Normally: A Personal Growth Approach to Childbirth. Berkeley: Mindbody Press.
Peterson, Gayle, and Lewis Mehl
  1984   Pregnancy as Healing: A Holistic Philosophy for Pre-Natal Care. Vols. 1 and 2. Berkeley: Mindbody Press.
Pigg, Stacey Lee
  1996   Authority in Translation: Finding, Knowing, Naming and Training "Traditional Birth Attendants" in Nepal. *In* Childbirth and Authoritative Knowledge: Crosscultural Perspectives. Robbie Davis-Floyd and Carolyn Sargent, eds. Berkeley: University of California Press.
Poland, Marilyn L.
  1988   Adequate Prenatal Care and Reproductive Outcome. *In* Childbirth in America: Anthropological Perspectives. Karen Michaelson, ed. Pp. 55–65. South Hadley, MA: Bergin and Garvey.
  1989   Ethical Issues in the Delivery of Quality Care to Pregnant Indigent Women. *In* New Approaches to Human Reproduction: Social and Ethical Dimensions. Linda M. Whiteford and M. L. Poland, eds. Boulder, CO: Westview Press.
Raphael, Dana
  1973   The Role of Breastfeeding in a Bottle-Oriented World. Ecology and Food Nutrition 2:121–126.
Raphael, Dana, ed.
  1975   Women and Reproduction. The Hague: Mouton.
Riviere, P. G.
  1974   The Couvade: A Problem Reborn. Man 9:423–435.
Romalis, Coleman
  1981   Taking Care of the Little Woman: Father-Physician Relations during Pregnancy and Childbirth. *In* Childbirth: Alternatives to Medical Control. Shelly Romalis, ed. Pp. 92–121. Austin: University of Texas Press.
Romalis, Shelly, ed.
  1981   Childbirth: Alternatives to Medical Control. Austin: University of Texas Press.
Rothman, Barbara Katz
  1981   Awake and Aware, or False Consciousness?: The Cooption of Childbirth Reform in America. *In* Childbirth: Alternatives to Medical Control. Shelly Romalis, ed. Pp. 150–180. Austin: University of Texas Press.
  1982   In Labor: Women and Power in the Birthplace. New York: W. W. Norton and Co. (Reprinted in paperback under the title Giving Birth: Alternatives in Childbirth. New York: Penguin Books, 1985.)
  1989   Recreating Motherhood: Ideology and Technology in Patriarchal Society. New York: W. W. Norton.
Sandelowski, M.
  1990   Fault Lines: Infertility and Imperiled Sisterhood. Feminist Studies 16(1):33–52.
Sargent, Carolyn
  1982   The Cultural Context for Therapeutic Choice. Dordrecht: D. Reidel.
  1985   Witches, Merchants, and Midwives: Domains of Power among Bariba Women. *In* African Healing Strategies. Brian du Toit and Ismail H. Abdallas, eds. New York: Trado-Medic Books.

1989a   Women's Roles and Women Healers in Contemporary Rural and Urban Benin. *In* Women as Healers: Cross-Cultural Perspectives. Carol S. McClain, ed. New Brunswick, NJ: Rutgers University Press.

1989b   Maternity, Medicine, and Power: Reproductive Decisions in Urban Benin. Berkeley: University of California Press.

1990   The Politics of Birth: Cultural Dimensions of Pain, Virtue, and Control among the Bariba of Benin. *In* Births and Power: Social Change and the Politics of Reproduction. W. Penn Handwerker, ed. Pp. 69–80. Boulder, CO: Westview Press.

Sargent, Carolyn, and Nancy Stark
1987   Surgical Birth: Interpretations of Cesarean Deliveries among Private Hospital Patients and Nursing Staff. Social Science and Medicine 25(12): 1269–1276.

1989   Childbirth Education and Childbirth Models: Parental Perspectives on Control, Anesthesia, and Technological Intervention in the Birth Process. Medical Anthropology Quarterly 3(1):36–51.

Sault, Nicole
1994   Surrogate Mothers and Godmothers: Defining Parenthood and the Body in the U.S. and Mexico. *In* Many Mirrors: Body Image and Social Relations in Anthropological Perspective. Nicole Sault, ed. New Brunswick, NJ: Rutgers University Press.

Schultze Jena, Leonhard
1933   Indiana 1: Leben, Glaube, and Sprache der Quiche von Guatemala. Jena: Verlag von Gustav Fischer.

Scully, Diana
1980   Men Who Control Women's Health: The Miseducation of Obstetrician-Gynecologists. Boston: Houghton-Mifflin.

Sepkoski, C., T. B. Brazelton et al.
1992   The Effects of Maternal Epidural Anesthesia on Neonatal Behavior During the First Month. Developmental Medicine and Child Neurology 34: 1072–1080.

Shaw, Nancy Stoller
1974   Forced Labor: Maternity Care in the United States. New York: Pergamon Press.

Shearer, Beth
1989   Forced Cesareans: The Case of the Disappearing Mother. International Journal of Childbirth Education 4(1):7–10.

Star, Rima Beth
1986   The Healing Power of Birth. Austin, TX: Star Publishing.

Stolcke, V.
1986   New Reproductive Technologies: Same Old Fatherhood. Critical Anthropology 6(3):5–31.

Sukkary, Soheir
1981   She Is No Stranger: The Traditional Midwife in Egypt. Medical Anthropology 5(1):27–34.

Sullivan, Deborah, and Rose Weitz
1988   Labor Pains: Modern Midwives and Home Birth. New Haven: Yale University Press.

Susie, Debra Ann
1988   In the Way of Our Grandmothers: A Cultural View of Twentieth-Century Midwifery in Florida. Athens, GA: University of Georgia Press.

Thorp, James A., V. M. Parisi, P. C. Boylan, and D. A. Johnston
    1989   The Effect of Continuous Epidural Analgesia on Cesarean Section for Dysto-cia in Nulliparous Women. American Journal of Obstetrics and Gynecology 161(3):670–675.
    1993   The Effect of Intrapartum Epidural Analgesia on Nulliparous Labor. American Journal of Obstetrics and Gynecology 169(4):851–858.
Tronick, E. Z., G. A. Morelli, and S. Winn
    1987   Multiple Caretaking of Efe (Pygmy) Infants. American Anthropologist 89:96–106.
Tronick, E. Z., S. Winn, and G. A. Morelli
    1985   Multiple Caretaking in the Context of Human Evolution: Why Don't the Efe Know the Western Prescription for Child Care? In The Psychobiology of Attachment and Separation. M. Reite and T. Field, eds. New York: Academic Press.
Verny, Thomas, and Pamela Weintraub
    1991   Nurturing the Unborn Child: A Nine Month Program for Soothing, Stimulat-ing, and Communicating with Your Baby. New York: Delacorte.
Woodward, L., et al.
    1982   Exposure to Drugs with Possible Adverse Effects During Pregnancy and Child-birth. Birth 9:165.

Women and the Debate over Mammography: An Economic, Political, and Moral History

■ *Patricia A. Kaufert*

This reading uses the debate over mammography to discuss the political, economic, and moral dimensions of a discourse centered on the mass screening of women for breast cancer. The experience of being a woman with breast cancer has been explored by artists (such as Matuschka 1993) and poets (such as Audre Lorde 1980), but has been largely ignored in the feminist health literature. Relative to the volumes of work on childbirth, only a handful of medical anthropologists have taken breast cancer as their subject (Good et al. 1990; Gordon 1990; Gifford 1986). There are no references to breast cancer in Ruth Hubbard's (1990) discussion of the politics of women's biology and very few in Susan Sherwin's (1992) book on feminist ethics and health care. Emily Martin (1987) builds her paradigm of women's relationships to medical science drawing her examples from childbirth, menses, and menopause, but not cancer. In a way, this neglect is understandable. The feminist model of nature as beneficent and science as malignant is attractive and powerful, but difficult to sustain once the subject becomes breast cancer rather than birth. The result, however, is that the woman with breast cancer is left out of the feminist health discourse and her experience silenced.

Screening is a part of the feminist discourse, but has become synonymous with prenatal screening for genetic disease (Stanworth 1987; Strathern 1992; Hubbard 1990; Rapp 1990). The meaning and experiential reality of having a pap smear, or going for a mammogram, have received scant attention. Yet, these are an annual ritual in the lives of a majority of North American women. We need an ethnography of the screening process, but we need also to understand the fear of their own bodies that propels women into being screened.

The roots of women's fear lie partly in the experience of hearing that some-

167

one known has died from breast cancer. Fear in this form has always existed, engendered by identification with the other woman and the awareness that the cause of her death may become the cause of one's own. Yet, the fear that leads to the increasing prominence of screening in the lives of women cannot be understood simply through an analysis of the individual experience. Fear of breast cancer is also the product of a careful campaign designed not only to convince women of their danger from cancer, but also to persuade them that the best defense is in mammography.

I am concerned in this essay with the sources of this other form of fear. More particularly, I want to use the history and framing of the campaign to promote mammography in the United States to explore how this fear was engendered and why. As my starting point, I have taken the current debate over the age at which mammography should begin. My questions include, "Who has been involved in putting this campaign together?," "Who has benefited and in what ways?," "What were the scientific and moral bases of this campaign?"

AGE AND MAMMOGRAPHY

The age at which women should start having regular mammograms became the subject of public controversy with the publication of results from the Canadian National Breast Screening Study (CNBSS) in November 1992. The CNBSS had recruited its first volunteer in 1980 and by its end in 1987 had enrolled just over 90,000 Canadian women at 15 centers across the country. Designed as a randomized trial, its results showed that among women aged 40–49 when they entered the study, there was a nonsignificant, but higher number of deaths from breast cancer among those having an annual mammogram (38 deaths relative to 28). Among women aged 50–59, there was a nonsignificant but lower number of deaths among women randomly assigned to an annual mammogram plus physical examination relative to physical examination alone (38 deaths relative to 39) (Miller et al. 1992).

Rumors about these results had been circulating for at least the previous three years, but once published, the debate over the CNBSS spilled out of medical circles to be played out before television cameras, on radio talk shows, and in the pages of national and local newspapers. Claims and counterclaims about problems in the implementation of the CNBSS ranged from the scientific to the slightly scurrilous, and enlivened the equivalent in scientific journals to the gossip column in the popular press. Debates between researchers over the methodological merits or demerits of a particular study are commonplace elements in scientific culture. The difference between this dispute and others was partly in the degree of publicity and partly in the level of anger.

The American practice of recommending screening for women aged 40–49 was at the center of the debate. Epidemiologists, cancer surgeons, policymakers, and administrators of screening programs rallied to one side or another, but the main attack on the CNBSS was lead by the radiologists and focused less on its design than its implementation. Critics assailed the age of the mammography equipment used in the CNBSS, the quality of the mammograms, and the expertise of the radiologists (Kopans 1990). In reply, the Canadian investigators defended every element in the execution of the study—from their equipment to their clinicians. In the view of the director of the study, Anthony Miller, the CNBSS was pilloried partly because he had been more open in his description of the research process, more consultative with outside experts, more frank about any problems of implementation (Miller 1993).

The methodological arguments for and against the CNBSS are not the subject of this essay; they can be read in a series of papers, editorials, and letters to the editor in the major medical and oncology journals. The extent of the controversy is illustrated, however, in the different conclusions reached in two workshops. The first was summoned by the American Cancer Society (ACS) in January 1993 and the other was convened the following month by the National Cancer Institute (NCI). Both were held to discuss the results of the Canadian study and their implications for screening policy in the United States. Both were attended by the key protagonists in the debate. Each workshop had essentially the same information; however, the first one recommended that the ACS should continue its support for screening women aged 40–49. By contrast, the recommendations made from the second workshop resulted in the NCI withdrawing support from the use of mammography to screen these younger women.

The different conclusions reached by these two workshops were phrased in the language of science. The superficial impression is of a disagreement between experts over the merits of a particular study. Yet, a full explanation of why these two workshops came to different conclusions has to start further back than the publication of the CNBSS results. It is necessary to take a closer look at the history of mammography in the United States. For it was this history, and the place that mammography screening had come to assume in the complex politics and economics of breast cancer in North America, which made acceptance of the results of the Canadian Trial so problematic for many of the participants at these two workshops.

THE HISTORY OF MAMMOGRAPHY

Mammography was used initially as an aid to diagnosis in women with symptoms, but a report in the early 1960s demonstrated its ability to detect nonpalpable carcinomas (Gershon-Cohen et al. 1961). Interest grew in its possible uses as a method of screening the woman without symptoms—the apparently healthy woman—for cancer. A large and expensive—relative to the standards of the time—randomized trial was launched in New York in 1963 with funding provided by NCI. Known as the Health Insurance Plan (HIP) study, the intention was to test whether or not a combination of mammography and physical examination would reduce breast-cancer related mortality. The early results were favorable, but inconclusive (Shapiro et al. 1971).

The NCI and the ACS responded to the reports coming in from the HIP by funding a project in the early 1970s to "disseminate the techniques of early detection of breast cancer to both the public and the medical profession" (Baker 1982). This project, the Breast Cancer Detection Demonstration Project (BCDDP), grew into a remarkably large enterprise; 280,000 women were screened using a combination of mammography and physical examination at centers across the United States between 1973 and 1981. Radiologists taking part in the project reported the detection of much smaller tumors than those found in the HIP study and finding them more easily in the breasts of younger women.

Support for mammography declined in the mid-1970s following the suggestion that mammograms might be a potential cause of cancer (Bailar 1976). In Bailar's view, the resulting fear of radiation among women had beneficial results:

> The first rush of uninhibited, uninformed enthusiasm for breast cancer screening had passed, permitting more sober evaluation of the pros and cons of various screening programs and modalities. (Bailar 1977:2783)

Yet Bailar was to be proved wrong; "enthusiasm for breast cancer screening" not only returned, but grew in strength. By 1979, Strax, a radiologist who had been instrumental in setting up the HIP study, was talking about mammography in the following terms:

> We physicians should emphasize its benefits rather than the risks—which have become negligible—and get on with the real task that faces us: the development of a more cost-effective, efficient and practical method of mass screening for breast cancer. (Strax 1979:52)

One reason for Strax's call for a renewal of confidence in mammography was that the manufacturers had redesigned their equipment, reducing the radiation dose. By 1982, the American Cancer Society was referring to "unwarranted fears about the danger of radiation" (American Cancer Society's National Task Force on Breast Cancer Control 1982:226). Reports from the BCDDP were the main factor, being seen as an impressive demonstration of how much mammography had improved since the HIP study (Strax 1979).

Many radiologists were convinced that the BCDDP had shown conclusively that mammography could save lives, but it was only a demonstration project; by the standards of scientific evidence, its results had less ranking than those from a randomized trial. The only trial data available in the early 1980s came from the HIP study, which rapidly acquired a pivotal role in the new and official discourse on screening. According to Moskowitz, a strong champion of mammography, "the results of the HIP mammography study bar any argument about the medical effectiveness of screening" (quoted in Skrabanek 1989:425). A more recent assessment of the historical role of the HIP study concluded that, "The HIP program not only confirmed the clinical efficacy of mammography, it established an unassailable foundation for the concept of mass screening" (Dodd 1990:110).

Convinced that the value of mammography was already proven by the combination of the BCDDP and the HIP results, the American "Cancer Establishment"[1] decided to put its money into screening rather than research. Further study of the impact of mammography on mortality rates was left to the Canadians and the Europeans—the Dutch (Verbeek et al. 1985; Collette et al. 1984), the Italians (Palli et al. 1986), the British (UK Trial of Early Detection of Breast Cancer 1988), and particularly the Scandinavians (Tabar et al. 1988; Andersson et al. 1988).

The Medical and Scientific Committee of the ACS approved a statement in 1982 recommending a baseline mammogram for women between the ages of 35 and 40 and an annual mammogram for all women over 50. Women aged 40–49 were advised to consult their physician (American Cancer Society 1982), but a year later the ACS decided to advise regular mammograms for women in this age group (Dodd 1992). This decision was based not on the HIP results, but on the report that one-third of cancers in the BCDDP had been found in women between 35 and 49 years of age. Commenting on its decision, the ACS noted that:

> When considered in conjunction with the interim improvements in the quality and accuracy of mammography and a significant decrease in the amount of radiation delivered to the patients, it was concluded that a favorable benefit risk ratio could be anticipated in women 40 years of age and older. (Dodd 1992:178)

The American practice of screening women below the age of 50 was vested from its beginning in a belief in the technology, rather than evidence of a reduced risk of mortality.

Based on this lack of evidence, dissenting groups wanted 50 set as the lower age limit for mammography, but their impact on medical discourse was relatively minimal compared with the proponents of screening. The skeptics were eventually to include the American College of Surgeons, the U.S. Preventive Services Task Force, and the American College of Physicians (the latter only since 1989). Aside from these groups, support within the medical community for mammography grew steadily. In 1988, twelve medical organizations signed an agreement on guidelines for screening which included a recommendation that women aged 40–49 should be screened. The organizations included the American Medical Association, the American Society of Internal Medicine, the National Cancer Institute, the National Medical Association, the American College of Radiology, and the American Cancer Society (Dodd 1992). If the few dissenting groups and individuals are excepted, this agreement represented a virtual medical consensus on the value of mammography. It was still in place when the CNBSS results were published in 1992.

The consensus on the value of mammography screening for women in their forties extended beyond the medical world and into the wider community. Going for a mammogram is not a pleasant experience, either physically or psychologically; it also requires of a woman that she admit to herself that she is at risk. If screening was to be developed, women had to be convinced into becoming collaborators in the search for breast cancer. It was the ACS which took on this responsibility. From the early 1980s onwards, the society focused most of its efforts "around breast cancer detection programs and not on research and prevention" (Horsch and Wilson 1993).

CAMPAIGNING FOR MAMMOGRAPHY

The ACS launched the first in a series of campaigns in support of mammography in 1983. Over the next several years, messages promoting mammography appeared on television, in newspapers, in women's magazines, and on billboards along American highways. The majority were paid for by the ACS. One advertisement for mammography carried the message: "Smart woman; she spends $50.00 for a bargain that saved her life" (Fink 1989:2677). Another ran: "If you are over 35 and have not had a mammogram, you need your head examined"; a third read: "You may not know yourself as well as you think. If you're 40 or over, take a good look ... Get a Mammogram." The overt message was that women should have mammograms; the underlying message was that women should fear and mistrust their bodies and their own sense of good health. The promise was that mammography would save a woman's life.

In 1986, the ACS started to reenforce its advertising messages by organizing Breast Cancer Awareness Programs in communities throughout the United States (Fink 1989). Reading the published reports on these programs suggested that their format was based on principles of community mobilization from the 1960s, shrewd marketing strategies, and elements of evangelical revivalism. Promoted in terms of lives to be saved, program success was measured, rather, by the number of women having mammograms for the first time (Fink 1989).

Mammography lent itself particularly well to packaging as a communitywide issue, capable of uniting groups with widely different interests. Describing how a Breast Cancer Awareness Program should be organized, Sienko et al. (1992) provided a list of those who should be contacted and involved:

> At the local level these groups would include hospitals, mammography facilities, county medical societies, physicians, nurses, local health departments, churches, businesses, community extension offices, rural social groups, associations for retired persons, and offices on aging. (Sienko et al. 1992:173)

Local social and corporate elites were solicited for their support. Donating money, or making screening easily available to one's staff, became a very public sign of good citizenship. Having a mammogram, if one was a woman, became almost a matter of civic duty.

The ACS made extensive use of the media in its campaign for mammography. Journalistic taboos against writing about cancer had already been broken with the wide publicity given to stories about breast cancer in the wives of President Gerald Ford and Vice-President Nelson Rockefeller. By virtue of their marriages, their personal experience made cancer public news and a form of recruiting device for the BCDDP project (American Cancer Society 1982).

Relationships between the ACS and the press were not always cordial. In the mid-1970s, a newspaper columnist was blamed for spreading information on the risks of radiation to the general public (Holleb 1976). More recently, the ACS responded angrily to a report in the *New York Times* which implied that the society's presentation of cancer statistics had been deliberately manipulative of women's fears (Blakeslee 1992). For the most part, however, the media was a supportive player in the campaign for mammography; for example, Fink described how "getting information to the public through the media (radio, television, newspapers, magazines, etc.)" was a cornerstone of the Breast Cancer Awareness Programs (Fink 1989:2676).

Yet, the role played by the media is rarely confined to the dissemination of information.

> By selecting events to report, by interviewing and quoting experts who interpret those events, and by assembling and distributing news products, news organizations create an important component of public discourse. (Stallings 1990:80)

In the case of breast cancer, media stories about mammography had powerful public appeal, combining the miracles of medical science and the power of technology with images of the breast, death, and sexuality, particularly if the victim was young and beautiful. It was in this way, therefore, that journalists presented the woman with cancer, despite the reality that the majority of women dying from breast cancer are postmenopausal. The effect of this image-making within the wider community was that younger women flocked to screening at a much higher rate than older women (Allison 1992).

Lead by the ACS but with the involvement of other groups, mammography advocates turned into political lobbyists. The American College of Radiology, for example, "mounted a vigorous advocacy campaign that has been active at the state level since about 1987" (Moore 1991:105). Political action was partly in response to research reports showing that cost was a barrier to utilization; the aim of the lobbying effort was to get coverage for mammography screening by government programs and private health insurance. At the federal level, a long and ultimately successful campaign was waged to have mammography screening included in Medicare (Health Technology Trends 1990). At the state level, lobby groups concentrated on the passage of legislation requiring insurance companies to pay for screening. By the end of 1992, mandatory coverage had been established in 42 states plus the District of Columbia.

Insurance companies lobbied unsuccessfully against this legislation (Moore 1991), foiled largely by the climate of community support for mammography created by the media and the ACS campaigns. Politicians also saw advantages to supporting mammography, reaping such rewards as media exposure, press coverage, and an occasion to show concern for women without getting into anything controversial (such as poverty or abortion). Marshall (1993) suggests that U.S. senators were particularly anxious to show support for women's issues in 1992 because of the embarrassment over the Clarence Thomas–Anita Hill hearings.

As the result of the campaign to promote mammography, the results of the CNBSS were published in the context of a public climate marked by high enthusiasm for mammography coupled with a deep fear of breast cancer. The fact that this fear had been deliberately engendered in women makes it nonetheless real. Seen from the perspective of the health professionals and others who had worked on the campaign, men as well as women, the CNBSS results were a threat to their reputations and credibility. For some of them, however, more was involved than loss of face; they also risked losing money. Understanding the economics of screening is essential to understanding the history of mammography in the United States.

THE ECONOMICS OF MAMMOGRAPHY SCREENING

Twelve years of effort have gone not only into community mobilization, but also into the creation of an elaborate infrastructure capable of delivering screening mammography to age-eligible women across the United States. As a direct result, some groups and individuals found themselves in a classic "win, win" situation; mammography screening offered them the opportunity of doing good while making profits.

Defenders of the CNBSS were quick to point out the economic interests of its attackers:

> What we are going to see here is a massive attempt to discredit this study. And the attack is going to come from the huge multi-billion dollar industry that has developed around screening, which includes the manufacturers, the radiologists, and the technicians. (Charles Wright, quoted in Demarco 1993:21)

The manufacturers of mammography equipment were simply the most obvious in a line of beneficiaries.

The number of mammography machines expanded exponentially during the 1980s, due partly to the aggressive marketing techniques used by the industry and partly to its successful promotion of mammography:

> General Electric, maker of mammography machines and Dupont, purveyor of films, support screening with powerful advertisements on television, most often addressed to young women. (Baines 1993:2)

Only 134 new units were installed in 1982 in the United States, but approximately 8,000 machines were in operation by 1988 (Brown et al. 1990). The end result was an over-supply of equipment, particularly in metropolitan areas (McLelland 1990), where according to one estimate "the densities of mammography machines can meet and in most cases vastly exceed current demand" (Brown et al. 1990:550).

The market for mammography screening was of economic concern for actors other than equipment manufacturers. While many U.S. physicians were taught during the 1980s that lives were to be saved by screening, some also learned that money was to be made. Physicians bought their own equipment, or had shares in the units to which they referred patients. Surgeons benefited from the increased demand for biopsies, but it was the radiologists who gained the most in economic terms. The demand for mammography screening occurred at a critical time for this specialty. According to the Medical Education Advisory Committee, the profession faced an estimated surplus of 6,450 diagnostic radiologists by 1990. Economic motives were not the main reason why radiologists supported mammography and attacked the CNBSS, but many defenders of the Canadian study were convinced that money was a factor (Goldman 1993; Gray 1993).

Health facilities also had an economic interest in mammography, particularly those that had established clinics specializing in "Well-woman Care" (Looker 1993). A phenomenon of the 1980s, these clinics offered a total-care package in which mammography often figured as a key item. The prime target was the woman who was basically fit, but slightly worried about her health as she entered early middle age. Screening mammography, which had become a symbol of responsible health behavior, made an ideal marketing tool.

Mammography screening could also generate profits for health facilities. An article with the self-explicit title, "Mammography Screening: How to Operate Successfully at Low Cost" includes the following advice:

> The income lost from asymptomatic patients, who will pay lower fees compared with the traditional mammography fees they now pay, is more than offset by the income generated by additional problem-solving mammograms needed to characterize screen-detected abnormalities fully and by the increased use of needle localization procedures to guide biopsy. (Sickles 1991:93)

Put in economic terms, mammography was a demand generator.

While the amounts of money involved in mammography were not as high as in other areas of medical technology, the costs to the medical establishment were quite low.[2] The potential market was also temptingly large, particularly if estimated in the form of regular screening for all women over the age of forty rather than fifty. Costs (therefore, profitability) were highly dependent, however, on volume. According to one report:

> Many mammography facilities with a low patient volume operate inefficiently and must overcharge for a screening mammogram to cover their operating costs. (Health Technology Trends 1990:6)

The same report quotes an administrator as he pondered the impact of the $50 fee to be paid for mammography by Medicare: "My hope is that the volume increase is enough to offset any lost revenue from charging below what we normally charge." (His facility was charging between $95 and $135 per scan at that time.)

The classic economic response to an oversupply situation is to increase demand, while at the same time defending the existing market. If seen with the skepticism of a health economist, many of the community actions described in the previous section take on a different interpretation; for example, the Breast Cancer Awareness Programs turn into demand-generating devices. Mandating coverage for mammography by health insurance companies, or the inclusion of mammography under the provisions of Medicare or Medicaid, become successful ploys to increase the size of the market.

The economic interests involved in the campaign for mammography included the ACS itself and the research community to which it provided funds. Fund-raising charities and research foundations are just as much in the business of making money as equipment manufacturers and insurance companies. It is simply that charitable organizations and the individuals working for them measure their achievement by donations, rather than profits. Seen from a fund-raising perspective, breast cancer had far more public appeal as a fund-raiser than colon or lung cancer, particularly when the image used is that of the younger woman dying in her prime. Community campaigns and public lobbying helped raise the funding available for research and for other ACS activities.

The CNBSS results threatened each of these different economic interests. Interviewed by the *New York Times*, Dr. Larry Kessler, chief of applied research at NCI, commented:

> Telling all those 40-something women that a mammogram is not going to affect their chances of dying of breast cancer, despite endless glossy magazine articles urging them to be screened, would shrink the mammography market dramatically. (quoted in Gray 1993:622)

By one means or another, mammography screening had become a multimillion dollar industry, generating income and increasing profits. The resulting combination of "doing good" with financial and other gains helps explain some part of the bitterness and intensity of the reaction against the CNBSS results. But the profitability of mammography was not the only reason for the attack on the CNBSS. The situation was further complicated by the changing politics of breast cancer, particularly the role and commitment of women.

WOMEN, MAMMOGRAPHY, AND COMMITMENT

Many of the individuals who worked on the campaign for mammography did so from a deep emotional commitment; some were women with breast cancer and others were their family members. Kay Dickerson, a member of the Breast Cancer Coalition, had cancer herself (Marshall 1993). Senator Harkin, one of the strongest political allies of the breast cancer movement in the United States, had two sisters with breast cancer (Marshall 1993). From the wives of presidents to small-town journalists, individuals were drawn into the campaign, often because they had personally gone through the experience of wishing that a tumor had been found earlier, treated sooner.

Women were the objects of the campaign for mammography, but they were also the actors in that campaign. Occasionally they were the researchers; sometimes they were the clinicians and radiologists (although more often they were the nurses, technicians, health educators, and community organizers. Most importantly of all, from the perspective of the ACS, women were the volunteers and fund-raisers (Horsch and Wilson 1993). The Society's Breast Cancer Awareness Programs depended on the women who raised the money and did much of the work of community organization (Fink 1989). It was also women who lobbied local politicians, held rallies on the steps of local legislative buildings, and wrote senators to get legislation of mammography coverage.

The mobilization of women in the campaign for mammography created a wider consciousness of breast cancer as a women's issue. New groups emerged, formed and run by women with breast cancer, which were far less medically dominated than the ACS. These groups included "Y-ME," an association primarily concerned with education and support, and "Breast Cancer Action," a group that brought radical politics into the breast cancer movement, consciously modelling some of its tactics on those used by AIDS activists.

These new groups helped form the National Breast Cancer Coalition, a loose affiliation of 150 organizations, ranging in ideological perspective from the radical activism of Breast Cancer Action to the conservatism of the ACS. The coalition gave women a sense of their own power to bring change, although admittedly, the alliance was often somewhat uneasy. The new groups had emerged partly out of frustration with the ACS and NCI, whom they accused of neglecting research on the prevention and treatment of breast cancer (Langer 1992). For its part, members of the ACS sometimes sound resentful at being displaced as the main spokesperson for women with breast cancer. Writing about the future role of ACS, two members of the Society's Public Issues Committee commented:

> We must reassert our leadership role in breast cancer control. We have the advocacy track record and community-based programs to support this claim, but we have become complacent in recent years, and legislators are fickle friends. All too often, policy decisions are based on the most insistent or strident voices, rather than those that speak with quiet authority. (Horsch and Wilson 1993:1485)

The new groups were not only critical of the past record of the ACS and the research community; they also introduced new goals and objectives into the discourse on breast cancer. The Breast Cancer Coalition, for example, was concerned about access to treatment for poor women rather than access to mammography (Langer 1992).

The strength of the Coalition undoubtedly lay in its power to organize at the grass roots, mobilizing public opinion through letter-writing campaigns, rallies, and fund-raising events. Early after its formation, the Coalition was able to deliver more than 600,000 letters to Congress. The Coalition soon boasted that:

(it has) become familiar to Washington lawmakers, commenting on and attempting to shape and influence breast cancer research appropriations and public policy relating to our goals. (Langer 1992:207)

One result of this campaigning was that funding for breast cancer research at NCI increased from $133 million to $197 million in 1992; another $210 million for breast cancer research was added to the defense budget (Love 1993). Having worked hard and successfully to get money for research, the Coalition then wanted a say in how these monies were spent (Marshall 1993), demanding a seat on the National Cancer Advisory Board and active participation on NCI peer-review committees (Fintor 1993).

The CNBSS results were published, then debated in the same year in which the Coalition was so successful in increasing the research budget for breast cancer. Unlike the ACS, the Coalition had not promoted screening; nevertheless, the unavoidable flip side of the activities of the Coalition was a heightened awareness among women of the dangers of breast cancer. Groups such as Breast Cancer Action were working hard to publicize the lack of information on the causes of breast cancer and the very limited improvements in its treatment but women were left feeling more, rather than less, vulnerable. The only form of protection being offered was mammography, but that hope was challenged by the CNBSS results, or at least it was for the women most afraid, the women in their forties.

FEAR, HOPE, AND SCIENTIFIC MORALITY

The debate over the CNBSS was about different models of cancer, different views on the nature of scientific proof, and different moral and ideological perspectives on the responsibility of the scientist-clinician. Researchers certainly accused each other of acting from economic or political motives, but it was the strong feelings of moral and ideological commitment that explain the depth of their anger. One side felt that statistics were being misused and women's lives were being set at risk. The other side was outraged that women should have been promised protection on the basis of what they saw as insufficient evidence.

The rationale for mammography screening depends on a series of propositions connecting survival with the timing of diagnosis. If delayed diagnosis guarantees metastases and imminent death, then logic would seem to require that early diagnosis would improve a woman's chances of avoiding both death and metastases. Mammography is the technological "fixer" in this equation; the cancer is found earlier, the diagnosis is made sooner; treatment begins before growth is visible or even tangible. This is the model promoted to women in all the advertisements for mammography screening, but it is also a model that makes strong emotional and intuitive sense to women. It accords with our sense of how breast cancer works.

Once this model is accepted, it then becomes almost inconceivable that screening would not save lives. Faced with a contradiction between what they believed and the results of the CNBSS, radiologists concluded that something must be wrong with the trial rather than the technology. Kopans, a radiologist and critic of the CNBSS commented:

> It is likely that the Canadian data may ultimately confirm the fact that poor quality mammography, performed and interpreted by technologists and radiologists learn-ing as they go along, may not have a significant impact on cancer mortality. . . . (Kopans 1990:749)

The implication is that, had the study been executed with the equipment avail-able in 1992, using the mammography techniques now in use, and radiologists trained to present-day standards, then the results would be quite different. Belief in the technology is preserved; the error lies in poor equipment and unskilled workers. It also becomes a duty on the part of radiologists to convince others— such as NCI—that the CNBSS is wrong; otherwise, women will die.

Despite being members in the same medico-scientific culture as radiologists, epidemiologists brought a different set of assumptions concerning the nature of scientific evidence to their evaluations of the CNBSS results. Epidemiologists accepted the criticisms of technology and technique, but almost as a strength of the study. Their point is that the CNBSS was not intended as a demonstration of a technology at its best (like the BCDDP project) but as a test of screening as it would be practised, (Nancy Lee quoted by Smigel 1993):

> The reason for doing these trials is to see if they work, but the real world does not have state of the art mammography and state of the art clinical exams. . . . The Cana-dian trial is going to give us some idea of what we can expect in the real world.

Yet, epidemiologists tend to be unconvinced by references to clinical experience; the history of their discipline contains too many examples of physicians using clinical experience to justify practices that were later proved by epidemiologists to be unwise or overused. The examples with which women are most familiar include the prescription of DES to women during pregnancy and overly high rates of hysterectomy and C-section.

The preferred pathway to knowledge for epidemiologists is the randomized controlled trial in which proof is a matter of good research design and the appro-priate use of the appropriate statistical test. The CNBSS was a major trial in terms of its size, its budget, and the impeccability of its design. From their particular perspective, it was inconceivable to epidemiologists that its results could be jetti-soned on the grounds that technology in 1990 was better then technology in 1980. Indeed, if this argument were accepted, it would destroy the basis for most long-term prospective studies and most epidemiologically based evaluations of health-care practices. One defender of the CNBSS results asked rhetorically:

> Are potentially flawed results from a large, prospective, randomized, controlled trial better or worse than inherently biased results from a small, retrospective, hospital case-based study? (Hahn 1992:1538)

The response from the radiologists was quite different; as Kopans writes:

> Merely because a study is randomized with controls does not guarantee its validity. One cannot put women into the front end of a trial and expect that since it is "scientific", what comes out at the end is "truth". (Kopans and Stacey-Clear 1992:1539)

For Kopans, "truth" lay in the records of his own career as a radiologist.

Radiologists, like Kopans, "know" that mammography works. Their evidence for screening lies in the very personal experience of looking at a mammogram, detecting a tumor, and knowing that it could not be found by palpation alone. For radiologists, the "truth" of screening lies in the technology and what technology allows them to see within the hidden spaces of the body. Whatever their other political or economic motivations, their faith in screening had been absolute. By questioning this faith, the CNBSS and its defenders had committed the equivalent of heresy.

> You can play the professor and that's all fine, but we have to deal with reality. We favor the public and the patient and our concern is not involving ourselves in dialectic discussions. (Murphy quoted by Darby 1993:3)

The anger is palpable and is not to be explained simply as loss of face or loss of profits. Many radiologists were genuinely convinced that young women would die if the CNBSS results dissuaded them from having mammography.

Supporters of the CNBSS also saw the debate in moral terms. In their view, screening without benefit represented not only an unnecessary expenditure of scarce resources, but also a diversion away from the hunt for the causes of cancer. For Bailar, the ethical response to the CNBSS results was clear:

> In fact, screening mammography is not the answer. After 40 years and countless billions of dollars, we have made progress, but not much. We must stop, re-examine and start in a new direction. It's time to get serious about cancer prevention. (quoted in Demarco 1993:24)

Fletcher and Fletcher, reviewing the results of the CNBSS, wrote:

> Regardless of the reasons for the findings in all these studies, the simple fact is that universal hope has not stood up to scientific scrutiny. Medical scientists and physicians do not do modern women a service by promulgating a screening practice that medical science has not been able to substantiate after so many tries. (Fletcher and Fletcher 1992:970)

This view of screening has been most movingly expressed by Maureen Roberts, the former director of a mammography screening study in Edinburgh. She was herself dying of breast cancer when she wrote the following piece about mammography:

> I am in a reflective mood as I lie here in the sunshine at the end of my life. . . . What can screening actually achieve? Two randomized trials, the Health Insurance Plan

and the Swedish two county trial showed a reduction in mortality of 30 percent. Other trials, such as the Malmo, United Kingdom and Edinburgh trials, found a non-significant reduction in mortality. We cannot ignore them, and it is not enough to say that our techniques weren't good enough a few years ago but are adequate now. . . . We can no longer ignore the possibility that screening may not reduce mortality in women of any age, however disappointing this may be. . . . Are we brain-washing ourselves into thinking that we are making a dramatic impact on a serious disease before we brainwash the public? I believe that a rethink is required before the programme goes much further. I feel sad to be writing this: sad because naturally after so many years I am sorry that breast screening may not be of any benefit. I am also sad to be critical of so many dear and valued colleagues I've worked with over the years. But they will recognize that I am telling the truth. I ask them to bring breast cancer screening into its proper perspective and ask again what we really wish to achieve in terms of benefit for women. (Roberts 1989)

CONCLUSION

Power and patriarchy, rather than costs and profitability, have been the key concepts in much of feminist analysis of women's relationship to the health-care system. Yet, women's bodies are a major source of income, not only for the individual clinician, but for the whole corporate structure of modern medicine. As I have tried to show in this analysis of the history of mammography, women also need information on the economic forces that drive the delivery of their health care.

Medical anthropologists, particularly feminist medical anthropologists, have also tended to focus on the experience of the individual woman and her relationship to her physician, ignoring the wider context in which this relationship is set. Yet, the woman going for a mammogram on the advice of her gynecologist is only the final act in a complex process involving the American Cancer Society, the National Cancer Institute, an assortment of medical associations, the research community, community groups, politicians and media, and women themselves. Part of the responsibility of the anthropologist is to understand women's own experience, but it is also to make the context of this experience visible to women.

Exploring the context of care requires an analysis of the medical profession, not as some monolithic structure, but as a composite of different groups with different perspectives and different interests. The debate over the CNBSS, for example, reflects not only the interests of the radiological community in the continued promotion of screening to younger women, but also their very different perspective on the nature of scientific inquiry and the benefits of medical technology. By contrast, epidemiologists are far more skeptical of technology, but passionately committed to the scientific method as interpreted within their own discipline.

Feminist criticism quite often misses the impact of emotion and belief on medical decision making. This is partly the fault of the medical profession and its compulsion to present all its actions as if based on scientific fact. Yet, neither the promotion of mammography nor the attacks on the CNBSS can be understood unless allowance is made for the emotional component in this equation. Many clinicians were convinced that mammography screening could save the lives of young women, who would otherwise die of cancer. The clinicians' critics were equally passionate in their reaction, seeing this claim as a form of false promise to women.

Finally, I have tried to use this history of mammography to show that women are not simply the passive objects of medical care. The community of women is itself diverse; for example, individual women have played many different roles in the creation of this history of mammography; they have defended mammography in their roles as radiologists or administrators of screening programs; they have defended the CNBSS as epidemiologists and researchers; they have worked as politicians, journalists, and health activists. Thousands of women volunteered to take part in the CNBSS; thousands of women worked in the United States in the campaigns for mammography organized by the ACS; thousands of women have taken part in vigils and demonstrations organized by Breast Cancer Action. Individually and collectively, these examples reflect the growing fear of breast cancer, but also the determination of some women to change their own fate or the fate of other women. I would see them all as political acts, expressions of women's resistance against death and cancer, and demanding their own ethnographer.

NOTES

1. The term "Cancer Establishment" is borrowed from Samuel Epstein (1992) and provides a convenient designation for a loose conglomerate of the major charitable and research foundations, government agencies, researchers, and clinicians.
2. A recent survey reported that 70 percent of participating women under 50 had regular mammograms relative to only 34 percent of women over age 50.

REFERENCES

Allison, Malorye
    1992   Mammography Trial Comes under Fire. Science 256:1128–1130.
American Cancer Society's National Task Force on Breast Cancer Control
    1982   Mammography 1982: A Statement of the American Cancer Society. CA-A Cancer Journal for Clinicians 32(4):226–230.
Andersson, I., et al.
    1988   Mammographic Screening and Mortality from Breast Cancer: The Malmo Mammographic Screening Trial. British Medical Journal 297:943–948.
Bailar, John G.
    1976   Mammography: A Contrary View. Annals of Internal Medicine 84:77–84.
    1977   Screening for Early Breast Cancer: Pros and Cons. Cancer 39(6):2783–2795.

Baines, Cornelia
  1993   Critiquing the National Breast Screening Study: Creative Misinformation
          Builds Barriers to the Dissemination of Research Findings. British Columbia
          Office Health Technology Assessment Newsletter (BCOHTA): 2–4.

Baker, L. H.
  1982   Breast Cancer Detection Demonstration Project: Five-Year Summary Report.
          CA-A Cancer Journal for Clinicians 32(4):194–227.

Blakeslee, Sandra
  1992   Faulty Math Heightens Fears of Breast Cancer. New York Times, Section 4,
          Sunday, March 15.

Brown, M. L., L. G. Kessler, and F. G. Rueter
  1990   Is the Supply of Mammography Machines Outstripping Need and Demand?
          An Economic Analysis. Annals of Internal Medicine 113(7):547–552.

Collette, H. J. A., J. J. Rombach, N. E. Day, and F. de Waard
  1984   Evaluation of Screening for Breast Cancer in a Non-Randomized Study (The
          Dom Project) by Means of a Case-Control Study. The Lancet 1(8338):
          1224–1226.

Darby, M.
  1993   Disagreement on Screening Mammography Left Unresolved. Report on Med-
          ical Guidelines and Outcomes Research 4(5):1–5.

Demarco, Carolyn
  1993   The Great Mammogram Debate. Wellness MD 3(1):19–24.

Dodd, Gerald D.
  1990   Classics in Oncology: Introduction to "Evaluation of Periodic Breast Cancer
          Screening with Mammography: Methodology and Early Observations" by
          Shapiro, Strax and Venet. CA-A Cancer Journal for Clinicians, 40(2):109–111.
  1992   American Cancer Society Guidelines on Screening for Breast Cancer: An
          Overview. CA-A Cancer Journal for Clinicians 42:177–180.

Epstein, Samuel S.
  1992   Losing the "War Against Cancer": A Need for Public Policy Reforms. Interna-
          tional Journal of Health Services 22(3):455–469.

Fink, Diane J.
  1989   Community Programs: Breast Cancer Detection Awareness. Cancer Supple-
          ment, December 15, 64(12):2674–2681.

Fintor, L.
  1993   Advocacy Group Update: Setting the Cancer Agenda. Journal of the National
          Cancer Institute 85(8):608.

Fletcher, Suzanne W., and Robert H. Fletcher
  1992   The Breast Is Close to the Heart. Annals of Internal Medicine 117(11):
          969–971.

Gershon-Cohen, J., M. B. Hermel, and S. M. Berger
  1961   Detection of Breast Cancer by Periodic X-ray Examinations: A Five-Year Survey.
          Journal of the American Medical Association 176:1114–1116.

Gifford, Sandra M.
  1986   The Meaning of Lumps: A Case Study of the Ambiguities of Risk. *In* Anthro-
          pology and Epidemiology. Craig R. Janes, Ron Stall, and Sandra M. Gifford,
          eds. Pp. 213–246. Dordrecht: D. Reidel Publishing Company.

Goldman, Brian
  1993   When Considering Attacks against the National Breast Screening Study, Con-
          sider the Sources. Canadian Medical Association Journal 148(3):427–428.

Good, Mary-Jo DelVecchio, Byron J. Good, Cynthia Schaffer, and Stuart E. Lind
 1990   American Oncology and the Discourse on Hope. Culture, Medicine and Psychiatry 14(1):59–79.

Gordon, Deborah R.
 1990   Embodying Illness, Embodying Cancer. Culture, Medicine and Psychiatry 14(2):275–297.

Gray, Charlotte
 1993   US Resistance to Canadian Mammogram Study not Only about Data. Canadian Medical Association Journal 148(4):622–623.

Hahn, D. L.
 1992   Letters. Mammography. The Lancet 340:1538.

Health Technology Trends
 1990   Congress Enacts New Medicare Benefit, December, 2(12):2,6.

Holleb, A. I.
 1976   Risks vs. Benefits in Breast Cancer Diagnosis. CA-A Cancer Journal for Clinicians 26(1):63–64.

Horsch, Kathleen, and Kerrie Wilson
 1993   Legislative Issues Related to Breast Cancer. Cancer Supplement, August 15, 72(4):1483–1485.

Hubbard, Ruth
 1990   The Politics of Women's Biology. New Brunswick, NJ and London: Rutgers University Press.

Kopans, Daniel B.
 1990   The Canadian Screening Program: A Different Perspective. American Journal of Roentgenology 155:748–749.

Kopans, Daniel B., and A. Stacey-Clear
 1992   Letters. Mammography. The Lancet 340:1539.

Langer, Amy S.
 1992   The Politics of Breast Cancer. JAMWA 47(5):207–209.

Looker, Patty
 1993   Women's Health Centers: History and Evolution. Women's Health Issues 3(2):95–100.

Lorde, Audre
 1980   The Cancer Journals. San Francisco: spinsters\aunt lute.

Love, S. M.
 1993   Breast Cancer. What the Department of Defense Should Do with Its $210 Million. Journal of the American Medical Association 269(18):2417.

Marshall, E.
 1993   The Politics of Breast Cancer. Science 259:616–617.

Martin, Emily
 1987   The Woman in the Body: A Cultural Analysis of Reproduction. Boston: Beacon Press.

Matuschka
 1993   Beauty Out of Damage: A Self-portrait. The New York Times Magazine, August 15, Section 6.

McLelland, R.
 1990   Supply and Quality of Screening Mammography: A Radiologist's View. Annals of Internal Medicine 113(7):490–491.

Miller, Anthony B.
 1993   Commentary: Response from Author. Canadian Journal of Public Health 84(1):21–22.

Miller, Anthony B., Cornelia Baines, Teresa To, and Claus Wall
  1992   Canadian National Breast Screening Study: 1. Breast Cancer Detection and
          Death Rates among Women Aged 40-to-49 Years. 2. Breast Cancer Detection
          and Death Rates Among Women Aged 50-to-59 Years. Canadian Medical Asso-
          ciation Journal 147(10):1459–1488.

Moore, K. G.
  1991   States Enact Mammography Coverage Laws. Women's Health Issues 1(2):
          102–108.

National Cancer Institute
  1993   Report of the International Workshop on Screening for Breast Cancer, Bethes-
          da, Maryland, February 24–25.

Palli, Domenico, Marco Rosselli Del Turco, Eva Buiatti, Simona Carli, Stefano Ciatto, Lucia
Toscani, and Giancarlo Maltoni
  1986   A Case-Control Study of the Efficiency of a Non-Randomized Breast Cancer
          Screening Program in Florence (Italy). International Journal of Cancer
          38:501–504.

Rapp, Rayna
  1990   Constructing Amniocentesis: Maternal and Medical Discourses. *In* Uncertain
          Terms: Negotiating Gender in American Culture. Faye Ginsburg and Anna
          Lowenhaupt Tsing, eds. Pp. 28–42. Boston: Beacon Press.

Roberts, Maureen M.
  1989   Breast Screening: Time for a Rethink? British Medical Journal 299:1153–1155.

Shapiro, Sam, Philip Strax, and Louis Venet
  1971   Periodic Breast Cancer Screening in Reducing Mortality from Breast Cancer.
          Journal of the American Medical Association 215(11):1777–1785.

Sherwin, Susan
  1992   No Longer Patient: Feminist Ethics and Health Care. Philadelphia: Temple
          University Press.

Sickles, E. A.
  1991   Mammographic Screening: How to Operate Successfully at Low Cost. Women's
          Health Issues 1(2):95.

Sienko, Dean G., Janet R. Osuch, Carol Garlinghouse, Vicki Rakowski, and Barbara Given
  1992   The Design and Implementation of a Community Breast Cancer Screening
          Project. CA-A Cancer Journal for Clinicians 42(3):163–175.

Skrabanek, P.
  1989   Mass Mammography: The Time for Reappraisal. International Journal of Tech-
          nology Assessment in Health Care 5:423–430.

Smigel, Kara
  1993   International Workshop Assesses Evidence for Breast Screening. Journal of the
          National Cancer Institute 85(6):438.

Stallings, Robert A.
  1990   Media Discourse and the Social Construction of Risk. Social Problems
          37(1):80–95.

Stanworth, Michelle, ed.
  1987   Reproductive Technologies and the Deconstruction of Motherhood. *In* Repro-
          ductive Technologies: Gender, Motherhood and Medicine. Michelle Stan-
          worth, ed. Pp. 10–35. Minneapolis: University of Minnesota Press.

Strathern, Marilyn
  1992   Reproducing the Future: Essays on Anthropology, Kinship and the New Repro-
          ductive Technologies. New York: Routledge.

Strax, P.
  1979   Mammography: A Radiologist's View. CA-A Cancer Journal for Clinicians 29:46–52.
Tabar, L., C. S. G. Fagerberg, and N. E. Day
  1988   The Results of Periodic One-View Mammography Screening in a Randomized Controlled Trial in Sweden. Part 2: Evaluation of the Results. *In* Screening for Breast Cancer. N. E. Day and A. B. Miller, eds. Pp. 39–44. Toronto: Huber.
UK Trial of Early Detection of Breast Cancer Group
  1988   First Results on Mortality Reduction in the UK Trial of Early Detection of Breast Cancer. The Lancet 2:411–416.
Verbeek, A. L. M., J. H. C. L. Hendriks, R. Holland, M. Mravunac, and F. Sturmans
  1985   Mammographic Screening and Breast Cancer Mortality: Age-Specific Effects in Nijmegen Project, 1975–82. The Lancet 1(8433):865–866.

Cancer and Women:
Some Feminist Ethics Concerns

◨   *Susan Sherwin*

This essay emerged from a talk I was invited to deliver at the Ontario Cancer Institute, in March of 1993.[1] As I was reflecting on what I might say to an audience composed largely of researchers and clinicians specializing in cancer treatments, I realized that I was feeling unusually intimidated. It took me some time to understand why this particular talk seemed especially frightening to me, and I finally figured out that the problem was that I would be speaking to a group of cancer specialists. Like most other adults (and a good many children), I am familiar with many of the horrors that can accompany cancer treatment, and I carry around with me the barely suppressed fear that cancer could strike at any time. Hence, I was all too aware that if I do become one of the one in three North American women to be diagnosed with cancer (Brady 1991), I will be dependent on some of these very experts, or at least on their Nova Scotia counterparts, to guide me through the myriad of choices I will face and to care for me whatever the outcome of my treatment. No wonder, then, that I felt so conscious of the need to tread carefully in this talk, to try to be heard despite the anger my perspective might generate, and to maintain my convictions despite my fears of alienating the health professionals I addressed.

Moreover, I believe that this sort of fear is quite common. Feminism has taught me how fear functions to silence the oppressed and, in so doing, helps to perpetuate oppression; it has revealed the political dimensions of widespread fear and has shown that it is usually better to fight such fears than to submit to them. Hence, I share these feelings not to try to elicit sympathy, but because I think that they are indicative of the double bind that many patients and potential patients find themselves in when trying to assert their own priorities around cancer treat-

187

ment, research, and policy. Double binds are situations in which one feels torn between unacceptable options—in this case, asserting my views and risking alienating specialists my life may someday depend upon or remaining silent about matters I consider important. Feminists encourage us to be very attentive to double binds and to recognize their role in oppression (Frye 1983). I decided, therefore, to explore some of the ways in which women can become caught up in double binds where our fear of offending the experts responsible for caring for us if we are diagnosed with cancer may leave us with no sense of control over the course of our own health care. I will elaborate on what I take to be the significance of the complex feelings cancer provokes while explaining some of the ways in which cancer is, among other things, a feminist issue, and I shall concentrate on the specifically ethical dimensions of these matters.

I shall begin by explaining the theoretical perspective I adopt in the area of health-care ethics. Since my general perspective is feminist, I will first state briefly what I mean by feminism, and then I will clarify what feminism implies for the field of health-care ethics. Finally, I shall turn to some examples of how feminist ethics may contribute to discussions about specific policies and practices relating to cancer.

FEMINISM, OPPRESSION, AND HEALTH CARE

Because there are so many different and competing definitions and theories of "feminism," it is not possible to offer a single definition that is both comprehensive and uncontested; in fact, it has become common to speak of feminisms—in the plural—to acknowledge the diversity of understandings and commitments pursued in the name of feminism. It is necessary, then, to specify my own understanding of feminism, which I take to be a social and political theory that involves both a recognition that women are oppressed by sexism and a commitment to ending that sort of oppression. I understand oppression to be a systematic pattern of discrimination that is practiced against a social group that has been defined around some shared characteristic, such as gender, race, class, or religion (Frye 1983; Young 1990). Members of an oppressed group generally have significantly less power, privilege, and opportunity than comparable individuals who do not share in the relevant defining characteristic.

Following Iris Young (1990), I take oppression to involve some combination of five different (though often interrelated) conditions: exploitation, marginalization, powerlessness, cultural imperialism, and being subject to certain forms of violence. Any one of these conditions can be sufficient evidence of oppression, though it is common to find several in combination with one another. These criteria provide clear measures by which to establish that women are oppressed. I shall briefly review these five categories of oppression, concentrating primarily on the realm of health care in North America. It should be kept in mind, however, that comparable data is available for other societies and for other aspects of public and private life. There is overwhelming evidence that women are also disadvantaged in economic, political, legal, religious, academic, and cultural contexts.

First, women are systematically exploited in the marketplace: on average, they earn less than two-thirds of what men earn in North America. Worldwide, according to Kurt Waldheim, the former Secretary-General of the United Nations, "while women represent half the global population, and one-third of the labor force, they receive only one-tenth of the world income and own less than one percent of world property. They also are responsible for two-thirds of all working hours" (quoted in Morgan 1984, 1). Women health professionals are concentrated in the ranks of nurses, while men retain a significant majority of higher paid, higher prestige positions as physicians.

Second, women are also marginalized, in that their labor is often devalued and rendered invisible (e.g., contrast the recognition afforded nursing versus medicine in the realm of health care); they are the "last hired, first fired" contingent of dispensable workers, subject to a disproportional share of lay-offs whenever finances become tight. Further, in virtually every discipline, male experience is treated as the norm, and women, if addressed at all, are discussed in terms of being the "same as" or "deviant" from males; their experiences are not considered interesting or important in their own right. This tendency is quite pronounced in the realm of medical research, where clinical studies concentrate on male subjects, and fail to collect the data necessary to provide good medical care for women (Dresser 1992; Tavris 1992). The only notable exception to this focus is in the realm of reproduction, where research tends to concentrate on ways of manipulating women's (not men's) bodies in efforts to control conception.

The third criterion, powerlessness, is a relative measure. Thus, although some women have significantly more personal power than some men, and women have recently learned how to acquire and exercise collective power with increasing effectiveness, women as a group still have relatively less public power than men do collectively, and individual women, whatever their personal power is relative to the rest of society, tend to have less power than comparable men (i.e., men of their particular class, race, and educational status). Hence, while women are increasingly found in middle-management positions of health-care institutions, final decision-making authority tends still to rest with men, and the policies and practices of those institutions frequently favor men's interests over women's (McMurray 1990).

The fourth measure, cultural imperialism, has to do with the ways the dominant culture ignores or distorts the experiences of a group; the usual representations of women found in the mass media provide clear examples of such stereotyping and exclusion. Stereotypes of women as excessively anxious, devious, and unintelligent are commonly found within medical education (Corea 1985; Martin 1987), and the promotion and tolerance of such attitudes result in medical care for women that is often inferior (Fisher 1986; Todd 1989).

Finally, in terms of violence, women are subject to a very high rate of sexual assault and domestic violence. While it is true that men are also subject to violence at the hands of other men, women are far more often the victims than the aggressors of violence; also, the violence women experience at the hands of men is typically associated with their sexuality and, hence, is explicitly gender-related. Indeed, the violence perpetrated by men on women constitutes a major source of health problems for women, but relatively little health research money is directed at finding ways of reducing its occurrence or lessening its impact. This neglect is all part of a larger pattern in which, in virtually every sphere of contemporary life, women have less power and privilege, their interests are less highly valued, and their opportunities are restricted relative to men of comparable race, class, and educational backgrounds.

Clearly though, gender is not the only basis of oppression in our society. Race, class, disability status, sexual orientation, ethnicity, religion, and age are among the other features that serve as the basis of systematic patterns of discrimination and oppression. Moreover, the various forms of oppression overlap and intersect, so particular individuals may well be subject to multiple forms of oppression, and, as a result, the ways in which different individuals within the same social group experience oppression can vary greatly. Moreover, it is possible for those who are oppressed in some respects (e.g., on the basis of gender), to be agents of oppression in other areas (e.g., with respect to race). Native women, women of African descent, elderly women, poor women, lesbians, etc. (and all the permutations among these categories) are all at significant disadvantage relative to other women with respect to each of the forms of oppression reviewed. Given the wide range of difference that exists in the degrees, forms, and harms of gender oppression, feminists need to be wary about concentrating only on the varieties that are most personally familiar to us as individuals.

In my view, then, feminism is concerned with identifying and understanding the many forms and faces of oppression. It condemns all types of oppression as moral and political wrongs and works towards their eradication. Ending oppression is a particularly complicated task, however, since one of the most troublesome features of oppression is the degree to which its patterns are integrated into the very fabric of our society. Well-established forms of oppression have long histories; the patterns and beliefs that support them are habitual and may not even be made explicit. The often unconscious attitudes that sustain oppressive practices tend to be deeply entrenched in the consciousness of both the beneficiaries and the victims of oppression. In fact, internalized oppression, in which members of an oppressed group accept the conventional view that they are inferior and appropriately subordinate, is a common element of some forms of oppression, notably gender oppression (Bartky 1990). Thus, oppressive systems perpetuate themselves even without the deliberate malicious direction of some malevolent oppressor; they remain in force so long as people carry on in accustomed patterns without questioning the foundation or implications of familiar habits. To dismantle gender oppression (commonly known as sexism) and other forms of oppression, then, it is first necessary to uncover it. That requires careful and deliberate exploration of the significance of many of the practices that constitute our culture to see what role each plays in the structures of existing patterns of oppression. For example, we need to ask of familiar practices, whose interests do they serve and whose do they harm?

FEMINIST ETHICS

Ethics in general, and health-care ethics in particular, are disciplines concerned with identifying criteria by which to judge the moral legitimacy of practices. Their task is to identify the considerations that are morally relevant in determining the acceptability and justification of a practice. Elsewhere, I have argued that ethics requires a feminist perspective in that it requires us to appreciate the fact that oppression is a moral wrong (Sherwin 1992). That is, when we are trying to decide upon an ethically acceptable course of action we need to take into account the effect that action, or the practice of which it is a part, will have on existing patterns of oppression. This is not the only ethical criterion to consider, of course, but it is an important and long-neglected one. While ethicists and bio-medical ethicists have directed us to pay attention to such criteria as the protection of individual rights, the well-being of patients, and justice in the distribution of scarce resources when evaluating the ethics of practices in health care, they have, for the most part, been quite insensitive to the roles that health-care practices play in the perpetuation of oppressive systems. The position of feminist ethics is that oppression is a moral matter and hence questions about oppression must be added to any evaluation of the ethics of particular practices in health care. I have proposed that we ask of each practice reviewed what role it plays in the existing patterns of oppression: does it promote, reduce, or leave untouched the existing forms of oppression? I have found that such a perspective not only enriches and sometimes transforms current debates in health-care ethics, it also helps us to see ethical problems in areas that were previously ignored by bioethicists and expands our understanding of the ethics landscape in health care.

For example, I have argued (Sherwin 1992) that feminist ethics provides reasons to resist the traditional construction of biomedical ethics that views its subject matter as a contest between two opposed models of patient care: (1) paternalism (where doctors act according to their own judgments of their patients' best interests but without the patients' explicit consent) and (2) autonomy (where patients are informed of relevant facts and allowed to make their own decisions on treatment) (e.g., Beauchamp and McCullough 1984). Each of these familiar models tends to exaggerate and thereby distort patients' capacities and interests in decision making. Each focuses discussion on the single issue of control of medical decision making at the moment of treatment as the most prominent ethical crisis facing practitioners and patients. But feminists have reason to distrust both the options offered in this dichotomous mapping: paternalism because it assumes that doctors are better at knowing their patients' interests than patients are, and this is an especially dangerous and unreliable assumption when doctors are predominately male, affluent, and white and the majority of their patients are female, and often poor and nonwhite; autonomy because it assumes that patients are free, independent agents who are in control of other major decisions in their lives, and this, too, is likely to be a dangerous and false assumption when applied to many female patients. Hence, I believe feminism provides us with a reason to seek other ways of conceiving of the relationship between patients and health professionals that are less oppressive and more supporting of patients' actual needs and interests than are either of these alternatives.

Moreover, we need to challenge the model of decision making that is implicit in both of the traditional models where each specific treatment decision is approached as if it is simply an individual matter between patients and physicians, carried out at the precise moment of individual treatment. The traditional models tend to obscure the fact that by the time particular treatment decisions have to be made, the range of options available to both parties has usually already been narrowed significantly by political and policy decisions that have been taken within the larger structures of institutional health care. The treatments available to patients are a product of such features as earlier choices made in setting research agendas, the allocation and accessibility of economic and health-care resources, and the power of the dominant medical tradition. The explicitly political orientation of feminism, focused as it is on matters of oppression and domination, demands that this prior layer of decision making, which is hidden in the standard autonomy and paternalism debates, also be exposed and evaluated.

As another example of the role feminist ethics can play in analyses of health-care practices, we can consider how it helps us to redefine the terrain surrounding the widely discussed subject of justice and health care. The traditional biomedical ethics literature defines this issue either as one of rights and responsibility, or of accessibility and payment. In most nonfeminist discussions, one side insists that everyone should have a right to needed health care and the other insists people have a right not to be taxed to pay for the health needs of others. Feminist ethics, in contrast, suggests that we redefine both terms of the debate: "justice" and "health care." Its concern for matters of oppression and privilege help us to see that "health care" is a term that has been reserved for the services that happen to be offered within the existing health-care system, where diagnosis and treatment are given priority and both of these activities are increasingly understood as activities best pursued through costly, highly technological interventions. In the heat of largely ideological debates about justice and health care, it has proven easy to forget that most of the dramatic improvements in the mortality and morbidity rates of developed countries must be attributed to progressive improvements in basic services such as sewage, water, and nutrition, not to expensive medical interventions. Moreover, many of the continuing health problems in every society can be more effectively alleviated by making changes in the prevailing social, economic, or political conditions, than by specifically medical means. Proper nutrition, clean water, warm housing, good prenatal care, safety from physical violence, and protection from toxins in the environment are at least as important to good health as is high-tech health care, yet the health-care systems in most developed countries concentrate their resources mostly on the latter services.

From the perspective of feminist ethics, it is significant that illness is not randomly distributed throughout the population. Those who are most oppressed tend to suffer from a disproportionate share of preventable illnesses, so it is important that health services be understood as including the full set of measures that can be taken to improve the health status of particularly vulnerable members of the population.

In addition, feminist ethics demands that we rethink the philosophical concept of justice that underlies debates about health care. Most theories of justice tend to focus only on its distributive aspects, seeking a fair distribution of defined benefits (such as allocation of health services) and burdens (e.g., taxes) among members of society. Feminists, too, are concerned with such traditional distributive concerns, since members of oppressed groups generally receive less than their fair share of health care resources (McMurray 1990; White 1990). But their ethical concerns extend beyond this traditional agenda to raise questions about matters of domination and oppression as also falling within the realm of justice (Young 1990). Under this broader conception, we are encouraged to explore not only the widely cited dilemma of who should get the last bed in the Intensive Care Unit, but also to ask about the ethical significance of the hierarchical organization of health-care institutions in which women constitute over 80 percent of paid workers, and men retain a firm hold over positions of authority through their dominant roles as physicians, researchers, senior administrators, and policy makers (Sherwin 1992). Feminist ethics encourages us to be very careful in our interpretation of the ethical concepts we adopt and in the uses to which we put these concepts in our deliberations.

FEMINISM AND CANCER POLICIES AND PRACTICES

We are now ready to apply this perspective of feminism and feminist ethics to some problems that arise in the specific realm of cancer care. There are a number of ethical concerns feminists have raised about cancer and the medical responses to it, which I shall review from the framework of feminist ethics. I will begin by returning to my own, presumably typical, fears about speaking to caregivers at a major cancer treatment and research center. In light of the high incidence of cancer in women and the still discouraging morbidity and mortality statistics associated with many forms of cancer, both my fear of contracting cancer and my worries about alienating myself from the very experts on whom my cancer care would then depend seem both rational and appropriate, perhaps even inevitable. Even though I have not concentrated on cancer in my research, I have encountered countless discussions of different dimensions of the illness in my ordinary reading (both popular and academic). Common to almost all of these accounts are two specific themes: (1) the activities that an individual can undertake to reduce her risk of contracting cancer (e.g., stopping smoking), and (2) the technological medical responses that are available to patients who contract cancer or are believed to be at especially high risk of contracting it. In other words, cancer is usually addressed as a disease of individuals, where individuals are expected to take responsibility for reducing their personal risks, and, if they do end up contracting the illness, they must turn to technological experts for help. The burden of both prevention and treatment rests with the individual, and each person learns to be personally afraid of cancer. But there are ethical as well as practical reasons to challenge this familiar understanding and response to cancer and to question some of the decisions that underlie current cancer policy.

Feminist ethics begins each investigation with the assumption that women and other social groups are systematically oppressed in our society and it directs us to ask whether particular practices and policies deepen or help to reduce that oppression. In considering the role of current cancer policies, we might begin by asking what relation each has to existing patterns of oppression. At first glance, these matters might seem unconnected to questions about oppression; after all, cancer seems to be "an equal-opportunity" disease, in that no one, no matter how socially privileged, is immune from risk. Yet, in many cases, specific oppressed groups are at a striking disadvantage with respect to cancer: e.g., breast cancer, which now afflicts at least one in every nine women in North America, is a disease that affects relatively few men. Further, in Canada, native women contract cervical cancer at many times the rates of white women (Gaudette 1991; Gaudette 1993), and in the U.S., African American women die of cancer at a far higher rate than white women (Clayton 1993).

Across the population as a whole, we see rapidly escalating rates of cancer diagnoses for both women and men. Although cancer accounted for only 4 percent of deaths in the United States in 1900, that number has increased more than five-fold today (Brady 1991); in Canada, cancer now accounts for 24 percent of deaths, and the death rate has risen 50 percent just since 1971 (Globe and Mail 1993). The incidence of breast cancer among women in North America continues to increase; the Canadian Standing Committee on the Status of Women (1992) investigating issues associated with breast cancer in Canada cites statistics that indicate that "the incidence of breast cancer in Ontario has increased at a rate of approximately 1 percent per year between 1964 and the late 1980s" (p. 3). While survival rates for many cancers have not improved and cancer rates are exploding, women seem to be especially vulnerable in that cancers of women's reproductive tissues—breast, uterus, and ovary—are accelerating at an especially rapid rate. Such increasing rates are cause for both feminist and medical concern. Clearly, there are ethical and political questions to be raised here.

What is most distressing about these figures is that it appears that most forms of cancer are preventable—that it is within human power to reverse these trends and eliminate the vast majority of cancers (Brady 1991). Yet much of the research emphasis continues to be on treatment of individuals, not on prevention. Studies that do explore issues of prevention mostly focus on the sorts of conditions patients are thought to have some degree of personal control over, e.g., smoking, fat consumption, and participation in screening programs; that is, they are programs that treat cancer as an individual problem and responsibility. It seems that relatively little attention is afforded to environmental factors, such as toxic chemicals, exposure to radiation, synthetic hormones fed to farm animals, ozone depletion, and the iatrogenic (medically induced) effects of earlier radiation, drugs, or medical devices. The preventive focus is overwhelmingly concentrated on individual lifestyle issues and not on the sort of prevention that can only be achieved by instituting broad social and political action (e.g., rigid pollution controls). To the degree that cancer is tied to large-scale economic priorities and special interests, its incidence must be seen as a political issue. It is not sufficient to treat it and investigate it as if it were entirely a problem of distinct and unrelated individuals, each caught up in her own private tragedy. Yet, the social and political activism required to investigate and challenge the role of large corporate and social institutions in this epidemic is generally seen as lying outside of the proper sphere of medical research.

We are now entering a more extreme version of this mind-set that sees cancer prevention in terms of changing or restricting the activities of individuals, but not corporations: governments worldwide have committed huge sums of money to the human genome project with the hope that, among other achievements, it will succeed in identifying the specific genes that place individuals at high risk of contracting various cancers. The idea, presumably, is that identified individuals can then take special precautions to avoid exposure to the triggering mechanisms, e.g., by avoiding certain work places, foods, etc. The implicit expectation is that this research will give specialists better guidance as to who can most safely assume defined risks and avoid the necessity of spending the money to clean up toxic carcinogenic environments. It is surely obvious, though, that the freedom to choose safe work environments is very closely linked with an individual's class and social privilege; those who are especially oppressed in society are far less likely than more powerful members to be able to afford to make these sorts of healthy environmental choices. The decision to pour resources into genetic and other individual-based prevention strategies is a political decision about health policy that will have potentially enormous social and health consequences, but this decision has been taken with virtually no public discussion. Policy options must be evaluated in terms of what alternatives they replace, and, from the perspective of feminist ethics it seems clear that a cancer prevention policy that concentrates on individual responsibility in the absence of efforts to restrict corporate sources of pollution is more a product of power and influence than of careful ethical deliberation.

Nevertheless, genetic cancer strategies are already with us. A recent issue of *Science* reports with enthusiasm that researchers are within a year of identifying the "gene that predisposes women to cancer," though they acknowledge that this gene is likely responsible for only 5 percent of breast cancer (Roberts 1993). In breathless journalistic fashion, the article reports: "A slew of big-name gene hunters, attracted by this major prize, are now in hot pursuit of the gene" (p. 622). Although the gene has not yet been precisely identified, the journal reports that screening programs around it have already begun. According to this report, once a woman is identified as having the suspect gene, the best medical advice available to her is that she undergo bilateral mastectomy and removal of her ovaries as prophylactic measures. I do not want to dispute this medical advice: in the current climate, such radical surgery may indeed be the best medical option for a woman with a genetic predisposition to breast cancer. My point is to stress that genes do not work in isolation; rather, their effect is a product of their DNA programming operating within particular environmental conditions, and, under different conditions, their effects may well be different. This is one more example of the ways in which the research emphasis is set on finding the disease in the individual so we can change the individual to eradicate or contain the gene's predicted effects. There is, however, another research option available: we could explore ways of preventing the gene from ever triggering the development of cancer by ensuring that the person who carries the offending gene is able to avoid the conditions in which breast cancer most easily flourishes. A feminist research agenda would insist that we remember that all our evidence to date suggests that most disease is, to put it conservatively, at least as much a matter of environmental and social conditions as it is of genetic ones; indeed, even in this case, 95 percent of breast cancers are not clearly associated with the gene in question. And since even environmental conditions can be modified by social changes, identifying and changing relevant social conditions should be seen as the most urgent cancer-related task. From the social and political perspective of feminism it seems clear, then, that we must place a priority on exploring ways to improve the environment we inhabit and the conditions people are forced to live under, rather than concentrating on identifying and surgically altering individuals who may become ill within a hazardous environment.

Another dimension of the traditional focus on the individual is the tendency of many health-care practitioners and researchers to direct their public, political energies to promoting the view that individuals can reduce their risk by accepting personal responsibility for their health-related behaviors. We are told we can avoid cancer by improving our lifestyles, being vigilant about monitoring our bodies for the most minimal of changes, and, in still too many cases, maintaining an appropriate attitude of calm and cheerfulness (Sontag 1989). The message is unmistakable: those who do contract cancer are somehow responsible for their fate; they must have failed to take proper care of their bodies or their minds, and the rest of us can reassure ourselves that it is within our power to avoid their fate if we are only conscientious enough. Thus, while fearful, we can try to lure ourselves into the complacency of believing that full compliance with expert advice will protect us from developing incurable forms of cancer.

These public morality tales are usually offered with the best of intentions and they may make good sense in the face of current understandings (though there is room to contest particular suggestions). Nonetheless, there is something disturbing about this sort of advice. My uneasiness can best be explained by observing the ways in which this pattern of advice is reminiscent of the messages women receive about the dangers that sexism poses for them. From childhood, we are all trained to be aware of the terrible violence women may be subject to; television, movies, and newspapers feed us terrifying stories of rape and brutality as cautionary tales (Griffin 1971). The moral, at least for white, middle-class women, is that if we behave properly, that is, if we make sure to have a (reliable) male companion on hand, make him feel good about himself and us, and avoid provocative activities, we can probably avoid such fates. Lest we be uncertain of the mechanics of "keeping a man happy," women's magazines, novels, and films are filled with specific advice. In this way, we are taught to read other women's experiences of assault as evidence of their personal failings, and we learn to look to see what they did to provoke the violence so we can avoid similar repercussions in our own lives. These scare tactics were effective, for quite a long time, at keeping us from recognizing rape, battering, and sexual harassment as political issues, by persuading us that each case was personal and unique, involving some mistake on the part of the victim (she dressed inappropriately, walked alone in a dangerous neighborhood, dated a disreputable man, nagged her husband excessively, or was insufficiently cheerful). But feminism has helped many of us to understand that such ways of presenting and interpreting experience are a means of keeping women isolated from one another, submissive, and under control.

It is not necessary to assume that anyone set out deliberately to deceive or manipulate women in this fashion; gender oppression does not require any mastermind or conspiracy to account for it. It is sufficient to understand the deep historical roots of certain culturally accepted attitudes and to recognize that these conventional habits of thought about female victims of violence have the effect of privatizing the experience and hiding its social dimensions. Feminism has helped many women learn to see that the widespread incidence of violence against women in society is not a series of disconnected actions directed against reckless or pitiable women who are different from ourselves, but is evidence of the objectifying and devaluing attitudes in which our culture views women. We have learned that the women who are victims of sexual or domestic violence are not "different" or "other" from us; they are not to blame for their misfortune, since all women are vulnerable to such attacks so long as our society tolerates and glorifies sexualized violence. Only when we learned to see violence against women as a political issue, as a matter of dominance and power and not an example of individual failure, were we able to get beyond our personal struggles to try to avoid it and start work on finding ways to end it.

For similar reasons, it seems likely that the action required to develop effective campaigns for cancer prevention will also require widespread recognition of the fact that cancer is a political issue. Again, it is not necessary to seek out the responsible perpetrators or presume some elaborate social conspiracy behind the individualist approach, since it may just be the product of deeply ingrained habits of thought. Nonetheless, establishing acceptable levels of risk exposure will involve clear cases of conflicts of interest in which those whose interests are at stake have different and unequal access to power. Certain powerful segments of society benefit financially by actions that poison our collective environment and they can be expected to resist efforts to curtail their dangerous activities. Others have careers built on pursuing the traditional medical agenda of focusing on disease as (solely) a problem of individuals. Social action is necessary to change the basic assumptions of society that encourage and subsidize carcinogenic-producing industries and that support the funneling of research money almost entirely towards expensive, technological interventions on individuals. The first step in this campaign is that we each understand that acting merely as individuals we are least able to prevent cancer or even protect ourselves. Feminist ethics reveals the importance of addressing cancer prevention and cancer treatment on a political as well as individual level and raises questions about the neglect of the social aspects of this issue as a matter of public policy and concern.

Thus, feminists have, for example, challenged the forces that silence women from speaking out about the politics of cancer. They have observed the ways that certain varieties of cancer are still often regarded with shame and embarrassment and they have noted the ways in which conventional medical expectations, however inadvertently, help to support the status quo on these matters. In her very moving book, *The Cancer Journals*, Audre Lorde (1980), speaks of her experience with breast cancer and mastectomy. In describing the strong pressure health-care workers applied to persuade her always to wear a prosthesis in public on the grounds that failure to wear it was bad for the morale of other patients, Lorde comments:

> Here we were, in the offices of one of the top breast cancer surgeons in New York City. Every woman there either had a breast removed, might have to have a breast removed, or was afraid of having a breast removed. And every woman there could have used a reminder that having one breast did not mean her life was over, nor that she was less a woman, nor that she was condemned to the use of a placebo in order to feel good about herself and how she looked. (p. 59)

While Lorde acknowledged the importance of each woman making her own decision on such matters and was careful to make clear that she did not condemn women who choose a prosthesis or even breast reconstruction, she did object to the rationale offered for such strategies, which insisted that a prosthesis would allow them to appear "no different than before." She worried that such approaches encourage women to focus on mastectomy as a cosmetic problem and they interfere with patients' ability to come to terms with their loss by insisting that appearance is all that matters. More urgently, she perceived that this approach encourages women to remain silent about their experience with breast cancer, to keep it secret and private and hence outside the realm of political activism:

> If we are to translate the silence surrounding breast cancer into language and action against this scourge, then the first step is that women with mastectomies must become visible to each other, for silence and invisibility go hand in hand with powerlessness. . . . We reinforce our own isolation and invisibility from each other, as well as the false complacency of a society which would rather not face the results of its own insanities. In addition, we withhold that visibility and support from one another which is such an aid to perspective and self-acceptance. . . . Yet once I face death as a life process, what is there possibly left for me to fear? Who can ever really have power over me again? (p. 61)

In other words, Lorde identifies the political power of women acknowledging their experiences with cancer, and condemns the ways in which our society and so many of its agents in the medical institutions that treat cancer actively discourage women from forming political alliances around breast cancer. She speaks of the need to raise "a female outcry against all preventable cancers, as well as against the secret fears that allow those cancers to flourish" (Lorde 1980:10). She saw that standard breast cancer treatment depoliticizes the disease, just as other feminists have seen standard legal treatment as having depoliticized violence against women by isolating and silencing its victims. A feminist consciousness, in contrast, demands recognition of the incidence and meaning of the disease and it encourages collective action towards the political changes necessary to eliminate it. A politicized feminist stance urges women who have contracted cancer not to settle only for passive dependence on medical authority and not to accept the isolating interpretation of disease as an individual phenomenon, but to identify themselves as a social group in search of collective changes and action. It seeks to transform some of the energy that is associated with fear of cancer, disease, and death into positive political action for needed changes in the social conditions that now support the spread of this disease. Feminist ethics helps us to recognize that there are moral reasons to contest the conventional assumptions that address only the medical dimensions of the disease.

It is clearly not sufficient to focus only on prevention strategies, however; we must also explore ethical questions about the treatment patients receive when confronted with a diagnosis of cancer. Here, too, feminists have objected to the limited range of treatment options usually available to those diagnosed with cancer—i.e., surgery, radiation, and chemotherapy (or as some patients wryly put it: slash, burn, and poison)—since all have serious costs and risks associated and they are of questionable efficacy in many cancers. Most patients find it difficult to receive any medical support for pursuit of other sorts of modalities, even when the orthodox treatments have not proven themselves effective. As in the area of prevention, the available medical treatments must be understood to be the product of a research and policy agenda that has concentrated on certain sorts of interventions and neglected others, so there are ethical questions to be raised about why certain choices have been made and who has been able to influence those priorities.

Specifically, Kathryn Strother Ratcliff argues, "[our] health care system is characterized by a strong 'technological favoritism' " (Ratcliff 1989:173). In documenting the factors responsible for this tendency towards invasive technology, she observes that each one "includes strong gender forces that make the 'technological favoritism' of the system a particular problem for women" (p. 175). For example, she notes that there are clear financial incentives for cost-conscious hospitals, individual clinicians, and those who invest in medical research to promote the use of technologies that promise to provide good economic returns if they are widely utilized. Ratcliff fears that women are at particular risk in such systems: the decisions about investment in technology are generally made by men who seem, often, to be indifferent towards, or at least ignorant about, women's particular interests. By extension, those who are most removed from the decision-making authorities, i.e., those who are most oppressed, are likely to be least well served by technology. Moreover, Ratcliff observes, basic medical training does not often educate students to be critical consumers of technology. As a result, without training in the research methods that might help them evaluate a new technology, and reliant upon sales agents as their major source of information about it, doctors are primed to accept uncritically promising reports of new technological solutions.

The considerations supporting the introduction of technology have to do with questions of profit or cost, prestige, and, ideally, scientific acceptability on the basis of quantifiable measures. Social factors, especially those having to do with the effect of any particular technology on oppressed groups, are not made part of the calculations behind decisions to use it; if addressed at all, such factors are reduced to cost-benefit analyses in which the well-being of members of oppressed groups is typically valued less highly than that of more highly placed individuals. Neither Ratcliff nor I want to discount or reject the use of technologies altogether; clearly, they can be of great benefit in health care. The point is that they cannot be supported purely on the basis of their manufacturer's data; they must also be evaluated by the standards of feminist ethics. Far too often technology has been used to create or increase inequity: for example, many cases of infertility result from preventable forms of pelvic inflammatory disease, but rather than directing resources at far-reaching educational programs that would help to prevent the spread of the offending infectious agents throughout the population, expensive forms of reproductive technologies designed to circumvent such problems are marketed to those who can afford them. "Technology has everything to do with who benefits and who suffers, whose opportunities increase and whose decrease, who creates and who accommodates" (Bush 1983:163). Feminists seek appropriate technology that meets the needs of patients, especially those who belong to oppressed groups, and does not expose them to unjustifiable risk.

Another area in the field of cancer research that requires more attention than it has received to date is investigation into ways of helping patients live with cancer when it cannot be cured. With so many resources being poured into the ongoing search for the elusive "cure(s)," relatively few resources are allocated to exploring ways of improving quality of life with the illness when cure is not possible. This choice of priorities should, once again, be seen as a political matter. We should understand that it represents the sacrifice of the needs and interests of patients with incurable diseases for the quest for "the big prize." Here, too, we need to ask whose interests are served by these choices and whose are harmed.

As an example of the sort of research and training that may be helpful here, I shall turn to the writings of a physician, Arthur Kleinman. Although he does not speak from a specifically feminist perspective, Kleinman does offer some proposals that are responsive to this area of feminist concern. In his book, *The Illness Narratives* (1988), he distinguishes between disease and illness, such that illness is "how the sick person and the members of the family or wider social network perceive, live with, and respond to symptoms and disability" and has to do with "the innately human experience of symptoms and suffering" (p. 3). Disease, in contrast, "is what the practitioner creates in the recasting of illness in terms of theories of disorder," such that a theoretically trained practitioner "reconfigures the patient's and family's illness problems as narrow technical issues, disease problems. . . . In the narrow biological terms of the biomedical model, this means that the disease is reconfigured *only* as an alteration in biological structure" (p. 5). In the process of this medical translation, the experience of illness becomes lost; it is not granted legitimacy or even recognition. But illness does have meaning, for both patients and physicians, and it is necessary for physicians to develop the skills, such as "empathic witnessing of the existential experience of suffering" (p. 10), which will help them interpret these meanings and respond to them appropriately. He argues that people with chronic illness have important things to teach the rest of us, and health workers would do well to understand their relationships with patients as reciprocal and recognize that they can learn valuable lessons from the patients they help. Kleinman laments the fact that medical training concentrates on eliminating or reducing suffering and provides physicians with few resources for responding to patients whose suffering cannot be erased. He envisions and describes new, more mutually supportive models of patient-physician relationships that are possible within the long-term health-care relationships associated with incurable illness.

The need for such alternative visions of the patient-physician relationship is clear if we attend to the voices of the feminists who have spoken of their personal experiences with cancer and described the difficulties they confront when they seek to establish nontraditional relationships with the health-care professionals they deal with. Again, I will appeal to the wise words of Audre Lorde, who speaks so eloquently of her own cancer experience and its meaning for her, writing out of "the need to give voice to living with cancer outside of that numbing acceptance of death as a resignation waiting after fury and before despair" (Lorde 1988:111). The strength of Kleinman's proposal can be appreciated if we contrast it with the alternative approach of the specialist who, when he diagnosed that Lorde's breast cancer had metasticized to her liver, wanted to treat the disease, and not the illness, by insisting on an immediate operation. When she explained her desire to wait a bit so she could absorb the shock, reach her own decision, and not act out of panic, he responded: " 'If you do not do exactly what I tell you to do right now without questions you are going to die a horrible death.' In exactly those words" (p. 111). Lorde rejected his "disease-oriented" approach since it was out of touch with her own understanding of her illness and her ways of responding to it. In speaking of the meaning she found in her illness, she said: "As warriors, our job is to actively and consciously survive it for as long as possible, remembering that in order to win, the aggressor must conquer, but the resisters need only survive. Our battle is to define survival in ways that are acceptable and nourishing to us" (p. 98). Moreover, she helps make the political significance of this effort clear, by explaining, "Battling racism and battling heterosexism and battling apartheid share the same urgency inside me as battling cancer. None of these struggles are ever easy, and even the smallest victory is never to be taken for granted. Each victory must be applauded, because it is so easy not to battle at all, to just accept and call that acceptance inevitable" (pp. 116–17).

Feminists seek new models of patient-physician interactions. We also understand that the realm of health-care ethics does not end with improvements in the personal dynamics of this two-party relationship, but extends far beyond it. Therefore, we focus, as well, on process and we seek innovative, egalitarian ways of deciding on the policies that ultimately shape health-care priorities, options, and practices. To transform current patterns and processes in health care, it will be necessary to change not only the attitudes of individual practitioners and individual patients, but also the structures that set and determine our society's approach to cancer and the sorts of care made available to its victims. Such social change will require the active cooperation of patients, health professionals, theorists, and those whose lives have been touched by cancer.

Fortunately, these sorts of changes are proving to be both possible and promising. A National Forum on Breast Cancer was held in Montreal, Canada in November of 1993, in which patients, family members, clinicians, researchers, and government bureaucrats associated with health-care research and practice came together in working groups to share information and concerns and to develop recommendations on priorities and policies to be pursued in the national campaign against breast cancer. The Forum proceeded on the assumption that breast cancer was a problem of concern to all participants and all had something important to contribute to the development of a strategy for responding to it; researchers, clinicians, and those who fund medical research and treatment are accountable to the public, and the group of patients and their supporters had much to share with those responsible for the medical agenda. While the communication that occurred at this event was often difficult, it was effective, and all parties emerged with a better sense of the possibilities of collective action on this disease. The success of this event helped confirm the feminist assumption that it is only when we all learn to communicate widely about both the broad social and political issues and the deeply personal treatment decisions, that society and its institutions will be able to meet the demands of feminist ethics in cancer care.

NOTE

1. The talk was the 1993 Philippa Harris lecture at the Ontario Cancer Institute, Toronto, Canada, March 26, 1993.

REFERENCES

Bartky, S.
   1990   *Femininity and Domination: Studies in the Phenomenology of Oppression.* New York: Routledge.

Beauchamp, T. L., and L. B. McCullough
    1984   Medical Ethics: The Moral Responsibilities of Physicians. Englewood Cliffs, NJ: Prentice Hall.

Brady, J., ed.
    1991   1 in 3: Women with Cancer Confront an Epidemic. Pittsburgh, PA: Cleis Press.

Bush, C. G.
    1983   Women and the Assessment of Technology: To Think, To Be; To Unthink, To Free. *In* Machina ex Dea: Feminist Perspectives on Technology. Joan Rothschild, ed. New York: Pergammon Press.

Clayton, L. A., and W. M. Byrd
    1993   American Cancer Crisis, Part I: The Problem. Journal of Health Care for the Poor and Underserved 4(2):83–101.

Corea, Gena
    1985   The Hidden Malpractice: How American Medicine Mistreats Women. rev. ed. New York: Harper Colophon Books.

Dresser, R.
    1992   Wanted: Single, White Male for Medical Research. Hastings Center Report, 22(1):24–29.

Fisher, S.
    1986   In the Patient's Best Interests: Women and the Politics of Medical Decisions. New Brunswick, NJ: Rutgers University Press.

Frye, M.
    1983   The Politics of Reality. Trumansburg, NY: Crossing Press.

Gaudette, L. A., E. M. Illing, and G. B. Hill
    1991   Canadian Cancer Statistics 1991. Health Reports 3(2):107–135.

Gaudette, L. A., R-N Gao, S. Freitag, and M. Wideman
    1993   Cancer Incidence by Ethnic Group in the Northwest Territories (NWT) 1969–1988. Health Reports 5(1):23–32.

The Globe and Mail
    1993   The War against Cancer. Toronto, Feb. 20, D3–D4.

Griffin, S.
    1971   Rape: The All-American Crime. Ramparts, Sept.: 26–35.

Kleinman, A.
    1988   The Illness Narratives: Suffering, Healing, and the Human Condition. New York: Basic.

Lorde, A.
    1980   The Cancer Journals. San Francisco: Spinsters/Aunt Lute.
    1988   A Burst of Light. Ithaca, NY: Firebrand.

Martin, E.
    1987   The Woman in the Body: A Cultural Analysis of Reproduction. Boston: Beacon Press.

McMurray, R. J.
    1990   Gender Disparities in Clinical Decision-making. Report to the American Medical Association Council on Ethical and Judicial Affairs.

Morgan, Robin
    1984   Sisterhood Is Global: The International Women's Movement Anthology. Middlesex: Penguin Books.

Ratcliff, Kathryn S.
    1989   Healing Technologies for Women: Whose Health? Whose Technology? *In* Healing Technology: Feminist Perspectives. Kathryn Strother Ratcliff et al., eds. Ann Arbor: University of Michigan Press.

Roberts, L.
   1993   Zeroing In on a Breast Cancer Susceptibility Gene. Science 259:622–625.
Sherwin, S.
   1992   No Longer Patient: Feminist Ethics and Health Care. Philadelphia: Temple
           University Press.
Sontag, S.
   1989   Illness as Metaphor and AIDS and Its Metaphors. New York: Anchor.
Standing Committee on the Status of Women
   1992   Breast Cancer: Unanswered Questions. Ottawa, Canada: Report of the Stand-
           ing Committee on Health and Welfare, Social Affairs, Seniors, and the Status
           of Women.
Tavris, Carol
   1992   The Mismeasure of Woman. New York: Simon and Schuster.
Todd, A. D.
   1989   Intimate Adversaries: Cultural Conflict between Doctors and Women Patients.
           Philadelphia: University of Pennsylvania Press.
White, E., ed.
   1990   The Black Women's Health Book: Speaking for Ourselves. Seattle: Seal Press.
Young, I. M.
   1990   Justice and the Politics of Difference. Princeton: Princeton University Press.

Boundary Crossings:
Gender and Power
in Clinical Ethics Consultations

■ *Patricia A. Marshall*

> I hope I have a future. I'm getting so scared now. I guess I'm not ready to die. Some-
> times I think I am. I think of all I've gone through and all I won't be able to go
> through and all that seems inevitable and I figure it must be over, but I dream of so
> many things that I could have done. I want to laugh and be outside before I ever
> die. One more time. I want every second to count. I want everyone to know I was
> here. I want to know why I was here! (Faith, May 30, 1994)

In the last decade, clinical ethics consultation services have become increasingly available in hospital, outpatient, and long-term care settings. A primary
objective of ethics consultation is to assist patients, family members, and health
professionals facing moral dilemmas in medical care. Bioethicists and others
working in the field emphasize the importance of reaching a negotiated resolution of ethical conflicts. Although considerable weight is attached to respect for
patient and family values and their goals for medical treatment, the experiential
reality of ethics consultations is complicated and often bewildering.

Clinical ethics consultations occur within a biomedical context at particular
historical moments in time. Individuals involved in a consultation bring to the
case unique social and cultural backgrounds and varying degrees of medical
knowledge. The interactional dynamics surrounding ethics consultations are
infused with issues of power, status, class, and gender. The conflicted nature and
contested territory of ethics consultation generate a number of questions: What
are the underlying assumptions about the patient-physician relationship? How do
these assumptions influence the resolution of moral dilemmas in medical care?
In the scientific and rational world of biomedicine, how does a patient identify

power, hold power, and express it—with family and with health-care providers? What impact does gender have in relation to a patient's experience of empowerment? Do expressions of gender or power affect the way in which the ethical problem is defined, interpreted, and analyzed? What role does the ethics consultant have in mediating power? How do normative beliefs about gender position the ethics consultant in relation to patients, physicians, and other members of the health-care team?

In this chapter, the historical development of ethics consultation within the context of biomedicine is briefly reviewed. An ethics consultation involving a woman who must decide whether or not to pursue a third lung transplant is presented and explored. The morally difficult and confusing aspects of the lived experience of making an end-of-life decision is examined.

I argue that the implicit and explicit articulation of gender and power in the negotiation of treatment interventions perpetuates and sustains the ideology of biomedicine. I contend that the moral discourse of clinical ethics consultation is both engendered and contextualized rather than abstract, neutral, or objective. In my analysis of the patient narrative, I establish that local knowledge of human suffering is expressed, constructed, and reconstructed through the multivocal experience of the patient, her family, the health-care providers, and the bioethicist. I maintain that the negotiation of medical and ethical decision making occurs within, and cannot be separated from, the broader politicized agenda of scientific biomedicine. The patient narrative presented provides rich material for an in-depth and critical analysis of individuals grappling for power and identity as they cross the boundaries of biomedical, organizational, and family culture.

CLINICAL ETHICS CONSULTATION

The early development of the field of bioethics relied heavily on the ideological orientation of philosophers and theologians (Fletcher 1954; Ramsey 1970). Thus, moral problems in health care have been evaluated historically from the philosophical basis of principles and rights. The principles approach, or the "Georgetown mantra" as it is sometimes called, remains strong. In this tradition, medical ethical dilemmas are framed in terms of the Western philosophical principles of respect for individual autonomy, beneficence, nonmalevolence, and distributive justice (see e.g., Beauchamp and Childress 1989; Engelhardt 1986; Pellegrino and Thomasma 1981, 1989; Ramsey 1978; Veatch 1981).

Throughout the decade of the 1980s, and continuing into the 1990s, hospital ethics committees and clinical ethics consultation services have become increasingly available for patients, families, and health-care providers (see e.g., Fletcher, Quist, and Jonsen 1989; Culver 1990; Siegler, Pellegrino, Singer 1990; Fry-Revere 1992; Ross, Glaser, Rasinski-Gregory, et al. 1993; La Puma and Schiedermayer 1994[1]). The development and expansion of these services have been reinforced by the passage of the Patient Self Determination Act (McCloskey 1991) and new governmental regulations that require every health-care institution receiving federal funds to identify a means of resolving ethical dilemmas (Heitman 1993).

There is considerable variability among ethics consultation services. This is due in part to the wide range of professional backgrounds represented by individuals involved in clinical ethics (e.g., medicine, nursing, philosophy, or religious studies, law, social work, and the social or behavioral sciences). The issue of certification has begun to surface and it is likely that in the future there will be efforts to standardize training (Fry-Revere 1992; Fletcher 1993; Fletcher and Hoffmann 1994).

In addition to the diverse professional backgrounds of ethics consultants, the local culture of organizations and their special requirements influence the practice of clinical ethics in particular settings. In spite of the variability, an overriding concern in ethics consultation is the collaborative experience of medical decision making between patients, families, and health-care staff. Ideally, patients' values and beliefs and their goals for medical treatment are accorded singular importance in reaching a consensus. Achieving this objective is problematic, however, because it rests on a number of assumptions about the patient-physician relationship. A critical assumption, for example, is that the patient has the ability to act autonomously regarding her or his health care.

Until recently, clinical ethics consultation has been dominated by the principles approach to resolving moral problems. There is a comfortable fit between the Cartesian duality associated with the biomedical model of disease and the application of philosophical principles to an ethical dilemma in health care. The disease model and the principles paradigm are both mechanistic, rationalistic, and analytical. Each model attempts to identify a problem, isolate it, detach it from its environment, and ultimately, "fix" it. These paradigms, however, are constrained and restricted, providing only a limited assessment of contextual issues. The principles approach to ethics consultation can be dissatisfying because it represents, at best, an incomplete picture and, at worst, a distorted view of both the patient's and the providers' story.

Dissatisfaction with the positivist and reductionist orientation of conventional bioethics that stresses normative rules, universal maxims, and rational arguments (Hoffmaster 1990; Callahan 1984; Pellegrino and Thomasma 1989; Fox and Swazey 1984; Fox 1990; Jennings 1990) has led in recent years to the development of several innovative approaches to ethics in clinical care. These new theoretical frameworks and methodologies have been promulgated under the guise of casuistry (Jonsen and Toulmin 1988; Tomlinson 1994; Kopelman 1994), of virtue ethics (Drane 1988; Pellegrino and Thomasma 1993), of narrative ethics (Hunter 1989, 1991; Brody 1988, 1994a; Reich 1987), and of feminist ethics (Sherwin 1992; Benhabib 1992; Gilligan, Ward, and Taylor 1988; Holmes and Purdy 1992; Kittay and Meyers 1987). Each of these approaches offer a unique view of issues surrounding ethical problems in medical treatment. Nevertheless, they all emphasize the importance of contextual features and human relationships. Moreover, in different ways, these approaches give particular attention to the hermeneutical nature of clinical medicine and the significance of moral phenomenology (e.g., Carson 1990; Churchill 1990; Leder 1990; J. Lock 1990).

The development of new frameworks for discerning moral dimensions of patient care will continue to flourish. Their methodologies are somewhat more difficult to apply in clinical settings steeped in biomedical traditions. However, these approaches offer greater sensitivity to the perplexing reality of moral conflicts.

Because I will be exploring a patient's narrative in my discussion of clinical ethics consultation—and because the patient is a woman—I will outline briefly several features of narrative ethics and feminist ethics. A full discussion of these approaches is beyond the scope of this essay.

In recent years, scholars in the medical humanities, the social sciences, and other fields have considered the relevance of narrative for medicine. Anthropological explorations of narrative and healing, for example, have demonstrated the importance of patients' stories for discerning the social construction of illness and the lived reality of pain and suffering (Early 1982; Kleinman 1988; Good 1994; Good and Good 1994; Mattingly 1991; Garro 1994; Hunt 1994; Marshall and O'Keefe 1994).

In bioethics, investigators have focused attention on the story as a means of exploring specific moral dimensions of health-care delivery and medical treatment. Brody (1988, 1992), for example, explores the life-altering capability of illness, noting the compelling nature of power and how it is expressed in the patient-physician relationship. Reich (1987) demonstrates how parables and narrative might be applied to ethical dilemmas in neonatology. Hunter (1989, 1991, 1992) argues that the informative power of a patient's story is made explicit in the use of the case method among physicians. Indeed, Hunter (1989:209) observes that narrative construction is "the principle way of knowing in medicine." Other scholars (Donnelly 1988; Poirier, Ayres, Brauner, et al. 1992; Charon 1992) have examined the medical record as an interpretative and multivocal "text" that tells the story of both the patient and the health-care team.

The strength of narrative for clinical ethics consultation is that it calls attention to moral dilemmas within a biographical and developmental framework. Thus, the situational context, individual character, and the social, cultural, and political determinants that influence behavior all play a role in defining and resolving the ethical dilemma. In his discussion of narrative ethics, Brody (1994:209) suggests that, ". . . one tries to decide what to do in a given case by telling a very detailed story about that case; and one tries to decide on issues of moral character and integrity by telling a detailed story of a person's life." According to Brody (1994:209), the "right" course of action does not necessarily conform to an abstract principle, but instead, it allows the patient and the physician to navigate "all the contextual factors" in a direction that best serves their interests and life plans.

Narrative ethics offers a more expansive view of the problems encountered by individuals involved in a clinical ethics consultation. Despite the promise of narrative to provide a robust exploration of issues, questions persist concerning our use of the stories we are told. Is it enough simply to "listen" to an illness narrative? As "authors of the text," do we have a responsibility to be instruments of change regarding organizational rules or national health policy?

Feminist ethics, like narrative ethics, is concerned with the contextual and relational dimensions of an individual's problem. However, there are additional features that distinguish feminist approaches to ethical challenges in medical care. It is important to note that there is not one monolithic orientation in feminist ethics; rather, there exists a range of approaches distinguished by their political and philosophical emphases. Feminists are identified with labels such as liberal, cultural, radical, socialist, lesbian, ecological, and postmodern (Sherwin 1992; Cook 1994; Benhabib 1992; Harding 1986; Addelson 1987; Hooks 1984; Hoagland 1988; Gilligan 1982; Friedman 1987). Liberal feminists, for example, focus attention on social and political reforms to ensure equality for women; liberal feminism is decidedly rights-based in its orientation. Radical feminists and socialist feminists might argue that liberal feminism does not go far enough in identifying the oppressive and hegemonic nature of power structures to maintain social order through subjugation of those without "rights." In contrast, cultural feminists are committed to the view that men and women are, by nature, inherently different in their moral outlook and in their approach to solving moral problems. The "different voice" (Gilligan 1982) of women emphasizes caring and relational aspects of moral problems; instead of solving a crisis by appealing to an abstract rule, women will consider the needs and desires of all of the individuals involved. Clearly, the particular focus of the feminist approach influences the way in which a morally problematic situation in health care is described and explained.

Sherwin (1992:34–57) differentiates between what she calls "feminine ethics" and "feminist ethics." According to Sherwin (1992) feminine ethics represents the "cultural" view described above; that is, women are, by disposition, more intuitive concerning the needs of others and more caring in their behavior towards others. Scholars such as Noddings (1984) suggest that both men and women ought to pursue a feminine ethic of caring rather than rely on abstract and depersonalized moral rules.

What sets feminist ethics apart from feminine ethics is its concern with deeply entrenched and historically reinforced patterns of oppression. An important goal is the empowerment of subordinate individuals through the creation of new relationships and nonoppressive social structures (Sherwin 1992:56). Noting that feminist ethics is, to a certain extent, aligned with communitarianism, Sherwin (1992:53) observes that, "In place of the isolated, independent, rational agent of traditional moral theory, feminist ethics appeals to a more realistic and politically accurate notion of a self as socially constructed and complex, defined in the context of relationships with others." Sherwin points to the need for moral analysis to consider individual behavior in the context of political relations and experiences; she is critical of conventional moral theory for being silent on these issues.

Narrative ethics and feminist ethics pursue a course of analysis that requires careful attention to the individual within a particular social and psychological environment. Thus, medical discourse, and the "text" it reflects, occur within a cultural and political world that is experientially both subjective and relational.

THE ETHICS CONSULTATION: A CASE NARRATIVE

The initial telephone call for this ethics consult occurred on June 1, 1994.[2] A social worker from the lung-transplant team expressed concern about one of their patients. A woman, 28 years old, with cystic fibrosis, had undergone a lung transplant in 1992. At that time, she was hospitalized for forty-six days. After several months of relatively good health, she began to experience problems with her new lung. Her condition worsened, requiring a second transplantation. A heart-lung transplant was performed in October 1993. She spent several weeks in the hospital but was able to return home for the month of December. By January, 1994, she was back in the hospital; the transplant was unsuccessful.

The lung-transplant team decided that it would be medically futile to pursue a third lung transplant. They offered to treat the patient's medical problems, to provide her with palliative care when it became appropriate, and they encouraged her to consider a hospice program.

Lung transplantations for the third time in the same individual are extremely rare. The judgement of the lung transplant team concerning the futility of attempting another transplant was based on the patient's medical condition and the unlikelihood of a successful operation. However, one of the physicians on the transplant team believed that the patient might have a chance of surviving a third lung transplant. He expressed his opinion to the patient. This physician was planning to join the staff at another hospital to develop their lung-transplant center. The patient would be required to move to this hospital if she agreed to be considered for another lung transplant.

The patient was faced with a very difficult decision—to stay where she was, knowing that she would die soon—or to try for a third lung transplant at a different medical center. If she remained where she was, the patient would be with staff who had become her "surrogate" family throughout the last few years. At the new hospital, the patient would be unfamiliar with everyone except for the physician and one nurse.

The patient and the lung-transplant team decided to allow two weeks for a final decision to be made. During this time, the team agreed to treat her medical problems aggressively and to provide her with supplemental nutrition (e.g., hyperalimentation through a central line—an intravenous tube placed in the chest) to encourage weight gain. Their goal was to do everything possible to reinforce her strength in case she decided to attempt the third lung transplant.

The ethics consult was called because members of the staff were concerned that the patient was experiencing tremendous conflict because of pressure from individuals, at home and in the hospital, to decide one way or another. The lung-transplant team wanted the ethics consultation because they thought it would be helpful to have "an outsider," someone "unbiased," to talk with the patient about her decision.

Between June 1 and June 10, 1994, I spoke with the social worker and attending physician several times. I met with the patient on five occasions. In addition, at the request of the health-care team, I met with eleven members of the transplant service to discuss their concerns about the patient's decision.

At our second meeting, I asked the patient if she would allow me to tell her story in a book chapter I was writing; she agreed. I explained to her that I changed individuals' names when I wrote about them and asked her if she wanted to choose a pseudonym for herself. She chose the name "Faith."[3]

Faith and I spoke in depth about the many issues confronting her. Our meetings lasted between one and two hours. Each time, I took extensive notes.

Faith was in the Intensive Care Unit. Because her immune system was compromised, it was necessary for visitors to wear a face mask. In addition, Faith was on a ventilator during all but one of our meetings. While she was on the ventilator, she was unable to speak out loud. Thus, during our conversations, I wore a paper mask that covered my nose and mouth; Faith moved her lips and wrote on a pad.

Faith was very thin; she weighed approximately 88 pounds. She had long brown hair, pulled back with a band. Her eyes were dark and large; her focus was direct and attentive. Faith had placed posters on the walls of her hospital room. The window ledge held art supplies and several photo albums. Her journal was always at the bedside table. Each time I visited, she was sitting in a chair by the bed, a mobile tray placed in front of her. The tray held water, juice, leftover food from breakfast or lunch, a pad of paper on which to write notes to visitors, and several pens. A commode was positioned by her chair. Periodically during our visits, the intravenous lines would sound an alarm. Faith or I would reach up and flip the switch to turn the alarm off.

Faith gave me written permission to tell her story. She also let me copy parts of her journal entries. All names have been changed to protect confidentiality. In my discussion of this case, as much as possible, I have tried to let Faith tell her own story through her journal accounts.

FAITH'S STORY

A Search for Meaning.   In her book *Reconstructing Illness: Studies in Pathography,* Hawkins (1993:1) observes that, "Life becomes filled with risk and danger as the ill person is transported out of the familiar everyday world into the realm of a body that no longer functions and an institution as bizarre as only a hospital can be; life in all its myriad dimensions is reduced to a series of battles against death; and there is the inescapable sense, both for the sick person and his or her family, of being suddenly plunged into 'essential' experience—the deeper realities of life."

The other-worldliness of the hospital as it is portrayed by Hawkins throws into sharp relief the need to establish meaning and purpose for one's life. It is within this context that Faith grappled with the decision to pursue a third lung transplant. The existential confusion experienced by Faith, and her sense of identity and expectations for the future, influenced significantly her ability to make a decision.

Faith's persistent search for answers to questions such as "Why me?," and "Why now?" were evident at our first encounter. At one point in our conversation, Faith expressed frustration with her condition, saying, "I want to know why I am here!" I asked her if she was referring to being in the hospital; she said, "No . . . no." Her reference point for "here" was being "on earth"; a journal entry of May 30th expresses the same theme, "I want everyone to know I was here. I want to know why I was here!" She was persistent in her search for meaning:

> June 6: I want to live without machines that breathe for me or one that pumps in calories for nutrition. Maybe that's asking too much. Maybe I already had my good time after the first transplant. But why am I still here? There has to be a reason and I have to figure it out.

Faith called upon the ultimate reasoning of God to achieve some sense of understanding, "June 9: Dear Lord, I'd like to say a prayer to thank you for all the good years you've put in my life. I know you must have a reason for the painful parts."

"Giving it up to God" did not relieve Faith of questions about her own identity—an identity both constrained by the immediacy of the hospital room and its mechanical reminders of dysfunction and an imagined identity of gendered possibilities and dreams. At our first conversation, Faith described herself as pervasively dependent on others to take care of her: "People are always there for me, but I want to be there for them; I want to help them for a change." She said, "I have accomplished nothing in my life . . . I don't even have children!" In achieving her normative expectations about what it means to be a woman, Faith imagined a life posttransplant in which she and her boyfriend were married with children, a life in which she reclaimed a physical body and an emotional state that allowed her to be effectual in her environment and self-fulfilled in her relationships:

> June 4: There are lots of things to do if I get better—drive a car, shop for clothes, get rid of old clothes, learn art, keep in touch with new friends I've made, clean my own house! (if [I am] ok), redecorate, *exercise*!

As Bruner (1986, 1990) has observed, life experiences are organized primarily in narrative form that is culturally defined *and* culturally transmitted. In her account of her illness, the substantive and symbolic language used by Faith signifies a cultural landscape of personal meaning and underlying social ideology that is both transformative and fluid. Thus, Faith's narrative suggests a world infused with values about what it means to be culturally "normal"—shopping for clothes, keeping a clean house, cleaning it herself, and staying in touch with friends. The metaphor of buying new clothes insinuates the transformative potential of surviving a third lung transplantation. The life Faith imagines is empowering in relation to making a decision about transplantation in part because it implies a continuity of existence and simultaneously an alteration of her fractured identity both as a patient and as a woman. Moreover, the existential questions of meaning may be partially answered in the life she envisions. Why is she here? Not to suffer and experience pain, but to marry, have children, and manage her house and the everyday aspects of her life.

Experiencing Time. In the phenomenological world of sickness, time becomes distorted. Objectively, days and hours might be marked by the routine schedule of meals, therapeutic interventions, and visitors. Subjectively, however, the lived reality of time is incommensurable with objective measures. Faith makes frequent references in her journal to the temporal quality of her experience:

> May 30: Memorial Day Weekend. The weather was supposedly gorgeous. I can't believe I've been here so long. I have to make every day count somehow.
> June 3: It seems like every day at sometime or another I get my doubts coming in. I think of all I'm missing and how things just keep going on without me, like I'm getting further behind.
> June 4: It seems I've been here so long I don't know what life is really like anymore.
> June 6: I've got to go one day at a time. No rituals. . . . All this time that I've been here, and it's going on 5 months, will seem like a very short time someday and while I'm here I want to make the most of it.
> June 7: Something has to change soon. I don't know what but something does. Please let it be for good. It's only 9:15 but I think I'll close my eyes and try to forget everything for a while.

Faith's appraisal of time may be both empowering and disempowering in relation to her need to make a decision about transplantation. Her journal notes suggest that, on one hand, she feels suspended from the temporal world of everyday life, as if she is embodied in a timeless place without referents to an "outside" life. From this perspective, a decision can be projected into a future that may never end, if her past referent for time's progression is any indication. On the other hand, Faith seems to have a sense of urgency about time, believing that she is falling "further behind," yet knowing that "something has to change soon." In this context, she is compelled to decide, despite her inclination to "close" her eyes and "forget everything" for a while.

Faith's experience of a distorted sense of time stands in sharp contrast to the biomedical reality in which temporal existence is treated categorically and rationally, as if time exists outside of oneself, outside of one's body and soul. Yet, affectively, Faith seems to be in a progressive state of limbo. Hours pass, days become months, and her time is measured by intervals of monitoring, medicine, baths, and a continual stream of visitors who cajole her to accept, to understand, to try harder, to rest easy, to not worry, to be still, or to be active.

Family Issues. In recent bioethics literature, several scholars (Hardwig 1990; Nelson 1992; Blustein 1993) have called for greater attention to the moral significance of family members for medical decision making (significant others are included in their definitions of what constitutes a family). In their arguments for greater sensitivity to family values, these scholars suggest that a decision affecting one family member has implications for other members. Their concern reflects dissatisfaction with the notion that patients are capable of making medical decisions autonomously and independently. While, in some cases, the locus of decisional capacity may be individually centered, in most circumstances, health-care decisions are made after consultation with family, friends, and medical staff.

Family dynamics are often complicated, enmeshed in idiosyncratic biographies that exist apart from the world of the medical center or physician's office where decisions about treatment interventions occur (Marshall 1994:137). Additionally, relationships with family and friends are enduring, and usually, in the course of a patient's life, of more significance than associations with health-care providers. Beliefs and values about relationships with family and friends and the interactional quality of these relationships influence profoundly decisions that patients or their families make about medical interventions.

There were many problems surrounding Faith's relationship with her boyfriend, Joe, his family, and her own family. Faith had been living with Joe since 1987. During this time, she had developed a close relationship with his family. The closeness to them was perhaps influenced by her alienation from her own parents. Her mother and father were alcoholics; Faith had been out of touch with them for a number of years. However, she maintained a good relationship with her sister during this time, and in the last two years, she had begun to renew her contact with her parents.

Historically, the relationship between Joe and his family and Faith's parents and her sister had been difficult.[4] In regard to the present crisis, there were disagreements about what Faith ought to decide. Joe and his family believed that Faith should attempt a third lung transplant. Joe was upset with Faith's doctor for refusing to consider Faith for transplantation. Initially, Faith's family agreed with the decision of the lung-transplant team to avoid surgery; they were ready to accept that Faith was terminally ill and to support her during her final days.

In her journal, Faith alludes to the antagonistic relationship between her family and Joe's family and the pressure she felt from all of them concerning the decision about transplantation. "June 5: This morning [Joe's parents] came to visit early. I was really glad to see them. . . . Then [my sister] came and waited outside cause she doesn't get along with them. I hate that. I love them both, and neither one of them is perfect. I guess I could pray for them to get through the problem, but I know it has a lot to do with me. They both want me to make my own decision but they can't help but push a little."

During one of our conversations, Faith acknowledged the guilt that she experienced in relation to Joe and her family. A chief concern was that she would alienate those closest to her. She felt she was in a no-win situation: if she decided to go for the transplant, she was doing exactly what Joe wanted her to do, if she decided not to, he would be angry.

Faith's concern about caring for others reflects the engendered moral posture described by feminist ethicists, who view it with ambivalence. At its best, it reflects a commitment to consider and respect the needs of others; alternatively, it suggests a gender stereotype that perpetuates the subordination and oppression of women.

Faith's journal entries indicate the extent to which she had internalized the normative expectation to "care" for others, to please them and accommodate their needs. The resulting uncertainty and conflict she experienced, particularly in her relationship with Joe, is clearly evident:

> May 30: The nights with Joe are so fast. . . . I know I don't look very well, that's got to be very hard to keep happy with someone as weepy as me. We shared a (beer) . . . today and toasted me, us, and the future.
> June 3: Joe . . . seemed in a preoccupied mood. I know this whole thing is getting to him. He wants to be here every day and have his life and take care of everything. He needs help and I don't know how to help. I guess I can just be in the best possible mood when he comes. Hopefully tomorrow is a better day between us.
> June 4: [Lord] Please give Joe the patience to deal with all he faces and the ability to focus his anger on something useful. Thank you so much for the support he's been for me. . . . Let him understand and accept my decisions and know that I never mean to hurt him.
> June 6: Now I'm sitting here wondering where Joe is. He said he'd be here by 3:00 and its almost 4:00. I think he's probably golfing. . . . Joe's got so much he wants to do though and there's not enough time for everything. He just called and said he'd be here in 40 minutes and not to be sleeping. Nice command! Sometimes I get so mad at the way he controls me. But it is I who choose the way I act. I could get all paranoid or I could talk things out. Lately, I've been an emotional wreck and he ends up getting frustrated or angry with me for always dumping on myself instead of being and thinking positive.

Faith's compelling need to think positively, to "fight" literally for her life, was mentioned repeatedly during our conversations and in her journal: "June 4: I want to do well so bad but I'm so tired. There's a lot of people pulling for me I know. I've got to fight for them and myself."

The Hospital Domain.   Faith navigated the contested terrain of her emotional life in the relational world of her partner and family and in the cultural domain of the hospital. Faith was familiar with the lung-transplant team; she had been "their" patient over the course of several years and during this time she had formed on-going relationships with a number of staff members. Indeed, the hospital had been "home" and the providers a "surrogate" family for the last five months. The devotion of the staff to Faith was evident in their expressions of concern during our conversations and also in their treatment of her when she required help. According to Faith, the feelings were mutual.

Despite this closeness, as Toombs (1992) observes in her critical account of the phenomenological experience of illness, patients, physicians, and other health-care providers have a biomedical agenda to administer. Thus, relationships with patients will always be influenced by two facts: first, the relationship exists because the patient is ill; and second, the patient is vulnerable because she is sick.

In the hierarchical and bureaucratic context of biomedicine, the patient does not have the same power as her health-care providers. She is on their territory and subject to their organizational needs and timetables.

Faith alludes to her underlying expectations and beliefs about the health-care team in the following passages from her journal:

> June 3: I hope I see Dr. Smith again soon. [Dr. Smith is the physician who promised to consider her for transplantation at a different medical center.] He seems to always pop in when I least expect but I definitely need to know he's there.
> June 4: The nurses are here but they can't come and sit by you just 'cause you're lonely. I've got to be able to occupy myself. I've been praying a lot and that helps. I wish I could laugh again. All these feelings are dying to get out: Anger, Frustration, Despair, Hope, Anxiety, Fear, Loneliness.
> June 4: I don't understand a lot of this disease but I hope the doctors can somehow learn from me to save others.
> June 9: I woke up in a horrible mood. Sick of being here in the same place, no patience for anything, being a whiner. All it does is make things harder. Jim is my nurse. I know I must piss him off. Then I got a big dose of Morphine and that just about knocked me out—so now I'm laying dizzy and paying for it. I bring this on myself I think. . . .
> June 9: [Dr. Jones] said he would talk to Dr. Smith and get back to me. Of course something must have happened 'cause he never came back but he wrote in the chart that Dr. Smith would be in to talk this weekend. So now I get to worry till then. But I'm not. I'm gonna give it up to you Lord.

Faith's account reveals the degree to which she is dependent on the staff to be with her at their convenience. Her journal notes also indicate her concern with not upsetting the staff. Sherwin (1992:92) observes that a feminist ethics of health care demonstrates how, "Patients are required to submit to medical authority and respond with gratitude for attention offered. Most recognize their vulnerability to medical power and learn the value of offering a cheerful disposition in the face of extraordinary suffering, because complaints are often met with hostility and impatience."

A concern expressed by Faith during several conversations was that the staff would be angry if she decided to try for the third lung transplant. Members of the staff were eager to dispel her fears and told her directly that whatever decision she made would be fine with them. However, indicative of her vulnerability with her family and the staff, Faith's feelings were not so easily dismissed. The guilt that Faith experienced towards Joe and her family is "mirrored" in the guilt she felt towards the staff, knowing that she might disappoint them with the decision she makes. Who is in control here? Faith? Joe? Her family? The hospital staff?

Faith is both at the center of the "story" and yet experiences herself as marginalized in relation to her boyfriend, her family, and the health-care team. Faith's comments revealed her sense of being positioned at the periphery of her life both at home and in the hospital setting. Faith is continually negotiating her position, her requests, her beliefs, and her dreams in the contested terrain of biomedical and family power.

Faith's Decision. In his analysis of perception and phenomenology, Merleau-Ponty (1962), argues that the body is the primary medium of experience and understanding. Thus, an individual experiences illness through an embodied awareness of environmental stimuli; in this way, the body acts as a conduit for knowledge and meaning. During the two-week period in which Faith had to make a decision concerning transplantation, she was acutely aware of her physiological being and what it signified for her future. Faith expressed a desire for certainty about the outcome of a third lung transplant both in our conversations and in her journal, "June 4: I wish I had some solid guarantee. I've got to get back on my positive track." A positive disposition was an important measure in Faith's assessment of her progress and it was, to a certain extent, dependent upon her phenomenological experience of her body and her ability to "make" it perform in a way that suggested wellness, normalcy, and strength:

> June 3: Good thought for the day. I weigh 88 lbs.! So it's working.
> June 8: Time is moving faster now. I've been having a rough time this morning. I'd like to wash my hair. I think that's a good goal today. I did my legs and pretty well am right on my new schedule. . . . [later] It's night time now. I was off the vent for 4 hours today. I did wash my hair too and did all I wanted to. I'm much stronger, I believe.

Faith's narrative account of her illness reveals considerable ambivalence and doubt about seeking a third lung transplant.[5] Her journal could have had several possible "endings." The indeterminacy of stories and their openness to multiple readings and outcomes expresses what Bruner (1986) has called the "subjunctivizing" feature of narrative: "To be in the subjunctive mode is . . . to be trafficking in human possibilities rather than in settled certainties" (Bruner 1986:26; cf, Good and Del Vecchio Good 1994:838).

In their examination of subjunctivizing elements in epilepsy narratives in a Turkish village, Good and Del Vecchio-Good (1994) suggest that the story tellers were absorbed in an ongoing process of making sense of their illness. Moreover, Good and Del Vecchio Good (1994) argue that the narrators were actively involved in creating possible worlds in which healing remained a conceivable outcome. Similarly, Faith's narrative signifies an openness to the life saving possibility of a third lung transplantation and a recognition that ultimately, the outcome—her life or death—is not in her hands:

> June 3: I think I've only got about a week left before there's gonna be another meeting on what to do.
> June 4: Lord, I ask for strength to get through each day and the knowledge to know what's right. I only want to do right.
> June 4: . . . and Lord, if I am to die at 28 please forgive all the time spent uselessly and thank you for all the times I was somehow protected.
> June 7: Dear Lord, I have faith in you that I'm doing the right things . . . I'm going for another try for a transplant with Dr. Smith. Thursday I'll tell them [the staff]. Please continue to give me strength to get through this scary time. It's becoming easier the more I lean on you. Thank you for sobering up my parents' thinking and for

their stated confidence in Dr. Smith and support for me. I finally feel I'm doing something that matters a lot to them. I think I'm finally seeing a light. Whatever happens, happens. I'm at peace with myself as much as I can be right now. Maybe just for today, but it's a start. [Everyone] wants me to go for it. They will all support me too, I can feel it. I will support as much as I can also. Joe as always is there as is his/our family. Even the nurses here support me either way. Emmy [nurse] sat with me yesterday during a very tough time. I know Mary [nurse] doesn't think I'm strong enough but that's only opinions. You know the truth. I have faith that you will make something happen to lead me where to go, and so far it seems the signs all point for "go ahead."

June 7: I went to a meeting tonight [family/staff conference]. I got so emotional there and scared. Joe's very comfortable but I feel guilty for some reason like I did something wrong. That's why I'm not doing well. But it's wrong. It's just life and the way things work out. They all support me whatever happens. It's so scary Lord. Please somehow help me. Forgive me for being selfish. I know they are hurting too.

June 8: Well, tomorrow I'll see what Dr. Jones [attending] says. I wrote him a letter so I wouldn't forget anything.

June 9: Today is the day, the end of the two weeks. . . . I talked to Dr. Jones and gave him my letter, he said my weight's gone up around 3 and some lbs. and my nutrition has gotten some better. They still won't do it [consider lung transplantation] but I didn't really expect that.

When Faith discussed with me her decision to try for a third lung transplant she looked around her hospital room, gesturing to the monitors and tubes, and said, "What is my choice? To live like this for the rest of my life? Or to try it again and see what happens? Is there a choice?" Faith had spent a lifetime with cystic fibrosis and the last two years undergoing one lung transplant and one lung/heart transplant. Her will to live was strong.

Faith was transferred to another local medical center on June 10, 1994. She died on July 3, 1994. July 1, 1994, was the first day that she might have been placed on the list to receive a donated lung; but by then she was too sick to be considered a candidate for transplantation. When she was still physically able, Faith wrote several letters to the staff at Loyola, saying that she "missed" them. Many members of the lung-transplant team went to her funeral.

In many respects, Faith's decision to try for the third lung transplant articulates a traditional response to the miraculous and life-sustaining promise of biotechnology. Faith embraced wholeheartedly the profound commitment of biomedicine to "not give up" on patients in need. Even if she viewed her decision as relatively futile, Faith's act illustrates a sacrificial gesture to the advancement of science and medical technology. Given her orientation to the world of biomedicine and her personal experience as a beneficiary of what it can offer, Faith had little choice but to try again.

Despite the reluctance of the transplant team to consider Faith for a third lung transplantation, the "never give up mentality" had certainly been promulgated by them repeatedly in the past. Moreover, the staff's ambivalence about the hope of a third lung transplant was evident in their willingness to provide Faith with nutritional supplements to increase her physical strength should she decide to try for the lung transplant. The staff gave Faith a mixed message. On one hand, their behavior suggested that the lung transplant would be a futile intervention, but on the other hand, their provision of nutritional support indicates they were "hedging their bets" just in case Faith would live for the third transplantation.

The Role of the Ethicist.   As the ethics consultant for Faith and the lung-transplant team, my role was to facilitate the decision-making process. As I have suggested elsewhere (Marshall 1992:55), the status differentials between the health practitioners, the patient and family, and the clinical ethicist influence profoundly the process of negotiation in medical and ethical decision making. When a moral dilemma occurs, the ethics consultant runs the risk of serving as a power-broker between opposing parties, mediating and translating the value and belief constructs of the individuals involved.

The specific activities performed by a clinical ethicist vary considerably depending upon the particular case (La Puma and Schiedermayer 1991; Pellegrino 1988; Thomasma 1991; Weeks and Nelson 1993; West and Gibson 1992). In this situation, my charge was to help Faith reconcile her ambivalence about the third lung transplant. This was Faith's understanding also, according to her journal note of June 3, "I met with a woman from an ethics committee. . . . She's trying to help me make a decision from an outsider's point of view."

Being an "outsider," as Faith calls it, has the advantage of separating me from the health-care team she normally encountered. Yet, my status as an "outsider" is diluted because I am paid by the medical center, I am on the faculty, and I am, in my own way, a member of the "team." As Barnard (1992:15) observes, the integration of the ethicist into the clinical milieu has the potential to diminish "critical distance" and therefore the ethicist's ability to question seriously the assumptions and values of biomedicine (Gordon 1988).

However, the marginal position of ethics consultation in biomedicine may reduce significantly the potential to effect change in circumstances that call for a strong critique of the status quo. Moreover, gender and professional background further empower or disempower the clinical ethicist. For example, a physician ethicist may have more credibility with a patient's physician than an ethicist without clinical training, especially when recommendations are made that disagree with the attending physician's views. Additionally, the believability quotient of male clinical ethicists might be greater than their female counterparts. In fact, according to Taylor (1993), ethics consultation can never be gender neutral.

CONCLUSION

The enterprise of organ transplantation is steeped with ethical problems. The allocation of scarce medical resources, an individual's right to pursue multiple organ transplants, beliefs about the nature and ownership of human body parts, and concerns about medical futility are all important considerations.

Faith's story is uniquely her own. However, there are certain elements that transcend her story. All patients who have experienced organ transplantation understand the fears associated with waiting for a donor, and then waiting to see if the body "rejects" or "accepts" the organ. The promise of a "gift of life" exists for some individuals; death remains a certainty for others.

As a woman, Faith is counted among the population of women represented in statistical information on organ recipients; and the evidence suggests that the industry of organ transplantation has been accessed differentially by various populations (e.g., Kasiske et al. 1991; Kjellstrant 1988). Anglo males are the most likely to receive organ transplants, followed by Anglo females; people of color and the poor are less likely to be referred for organ transplantation. In the area of heart transplantation, for example, 81 percent of the recipients of 2,700 transplants performed worldwide in 1992 were men (Randall 1993). There is some indication that women may be less willing to undergo transplantation, but other factors are also involved, including their advanced age when cardiomyopathy develops, biases of referring physicians, and their insurance status (Randall 1993:2718).

As her narrative account suggests, Faith's decision to consider a third lung transplant was not made easily. Her individual character, past experience with transplantation, and current relationships with her family and the health-care team influenced her final decision. The degree to which Faith experienced power, as a woman and as a patient, reflects the social production of knowledge and behavior—and the political constraints engendered—within the cultures of biomedicine and family.

In arguing for a "joint construction" of a medical narrative, Brody (1994b) contends that healing is most effective when it is approached in a way that encourages a sharing of power between the physician and patient. This can only happen when those involved in the healing process listen carefully to the stories being told. Faith's attentiveness to the voices around her, combined with the staff's capacity to hear her story, created a paradoxical situation. Faith experienced heightened anxiety and discomfort precisely because she was empowered and supported to make her own choice regarding further medical intervention.

Contextual and relational features of the lived and embodied experience of illness are significant in the identification and resolution of ethical dilemmas in clinical care. Indeed, Hoffmaster (1992), Jennings (1990), and others contend that an ethnographic approach in ethical analysis would challenge ethicists to consider more carefully the embedded nature of moral phenomenology in ongoing forms of social practice. As new approaches to bioethics continue to evolve and develop, it is likely that greater attention will be given to the cultural and political reality claimed by all participants in an ethics consultation.

Acknowledgments.   I want to express my deep appreciation to all the members of the lung-transplant team at Loyola University of Chicago for their candor in expressing their concerns and their profound commitment to caring. I am grateful to Dr. Edward Garrity for taking time to discuss Faith's condition with me and for his help in identifying important background information concerning lung transplantation. I am especially thankful to Nancy Jarecki, who spoke at length with me about Faith's story. Finally, I am honored to have had the opportunity to spend time with Faith during the last few weeks of her life. Faith was courageous, persistent, and vulnerable. She will not be forgotten. Faith has made a difference in all of our lives.

NOTES

1. La Puma and Schiedermayer (1994:203–225) include an annotated bibliography of ethics case consultation, ethics consultants and committees, and training and skills at the end of their book.
2. Loyola University of Chicago Medical Center has both a Hospital Ethics Committee and an Ethics Consult Service. The Ethics Consult Service responds to requests from family members, patients, physicians, nurses, social workers, pastoral care counselors, and other members of the health-care team who are concerned about a moral problem in medical treatment. Four individuals from different backgrounds (philosophy, anthropology, nursing, and medicine) rotate a monthly "on-call" schedule. We support a team approach to health care. Thus, we work with the patient, family, and various members of the health-care team throughout a consult. In some cases, a family/staff conference is called. In other cases, a conference would not be appropriate. Recommendations are written in the patient's chart. Ethics consultations are reviewed at the quarterly meetings of the Hospital Ethics Committee. Approximately fifty ethics consultations take place each year.
3. In choosing her name, Faith may have reflected her strong inclination to trust in God when knowing the "right" thing to do seemed overwhelming and confusing. On June 9, she wrote in her journal, "[Lord] I have faith in you that everything will turn out."
4. Other problems arose in regard to Faith's relationships with her partner and family. For example, members of the staff were concerned about Joe's disruptive behavior at the hospital. One day, the staff had to intervene in an argument taking place in Faith's room. Joe was on one side of the bed and Faith's parents were on the other side; they were yelling at each other over the issue of who would be the beneficiaries of Faith's estate after she died.
5. Parts of a longer poem, written by Faith on May 30th, reflect her fears and hopes about her future:

> Riding on a bike, pushing with all your might,
> you can see the top of the hill
> so far away from sight
> push a little harder, just a bit more time
> if you can make the top, the ride down
> will be just fine
> you could stop right now
> put on your brakes, rest, or turn around and go
> down easy; haven't you done your best?
> Listen to the people as they
> encourage you to try and push on . . .
> but your bike is starting to fall apart,
> the gears stripped,

leaving you with the exact one you don't need.
you hit a couple ruts and fall down hard,
so hard you need help just to get back on.
They fix the gears and tell you go on . . . keep going
it's gonna get easier,
something's wrong though cause you fall again, hard
and this time the gears can't be fixed . . .
Every turn is harder now. Take a good look around you
and look how far you've come.
You did a good job . . .
A lot of people say never give up. Others tell
you to do as . . . best as you can.
How do you learn to accept?
Or do you fight till the absolute end.

REFERENCES

Addelson, Kathryn Pyne
  1987   Moral Passages. *In* Women and Moral Theory. Eva Feder Kittay and Diana
            T. Meyers, eds. Totowa, NJ: Rowman & Littlefield.
Barnard, David
  1992   Reflections of a Reluctant Clinical Ethicist: Ethics Consultation and the Col-
            lapse of Critical Distance. Theoretical Medicine 13:15–22.
Beauchamp, Tom L., and John Childress
  1989   Principles of Biomedical Ethics. 3rd edition. New York: Oxford Press.
Benhabib, Seyla
  1992   Situating the Self: Gender, Community and Postmodernism in Contemporary
            Ethics. New York: Routledge.
Blustein, Jeffrey
  1993   The Family in Medical Decisionmaking. Hastings Center Report 23(3):6–13.
Brody, Howard
  1988   Stories of Sickness. New Haven: Yale University Press:
  1992   The Healer's Power. New Haven: Yale University Press.
  1994a   The Four Principles and Narrative Ethics. *In* Principles of Health Care Ethics.
            Raanan Gillon, ed. Pp. 208–215. New York: John Wiley & Sons.
  1994b   "My Story Is Broken; Can You Help Me Fix It?" Medical Ethics and the Joint
            Construction of Narrative. Literature and Medicine 13(1):79–92.
Bruner, J. S.
  1986   Actual Minds, Possible Worlds. Cambridge: Harvard University Press.
  1990   Acts of Meaning: Four Lectures on Mind and Culture. Cambridge: Harvard
            University Press.
Callahan, Daniel
  1984   Autonomy: A Moral Good, Not a Moral Obsession. Hastings Center Report
            14(5):40–42.
Carson, Ronald A.
  1990   Interpretive Bioethics: The Way of Discernment. Theoretical Medicine
            11(1):51–60.
Charon, Rita
  1992   To Build a Case: Medical Histories as Traditions in Conflict. Literature and
            Medicine 11:115.

Churchill, Larry R.
  1990   Hermeneutics in Science and Medicine: A Thesis Understated. Theoretical
            Medicine 11(2):141–144.
Cook, Rebecca J.
  1994   Feminism and the Four Principles. *In* Principles of Health Care Ethics. Raanan
            Gillon, ed. Pp. 194–206. New York: John Wiley & Sons.
Culver, Charles, ed.
  1990   Ethics at the Bedside. Hanover, NH, and London: Dartmouth University Press
            of England.
Donnelly, William
  1988   Righting the Medical Record: Transforming Story into Chronicle. Journal of
            the American Medical Association 260:823–825.
Drane, James
  1988   Becoming a Good Doctor. Kansas City, MO: Sheed and Ward.
Early, E.A.
  1982   The Logic of Well-Being: Therapeutic Narratives in Cairo, Egypt. Social Sci-
            ence and Medicine 16:1498–1499.
Engelhardt, Jr., H. Tristam
  1986   The Foundations of Bioethics. New York: Oxford University Press.
Fletcher, Joseph
  1954   Morals and Medicine. Princeton, NJ: Princeton University Press.
Fletcher, John C.
  1993   Commentary: Constructiveness Where It Counts. Cambridge Quarterly of
            Healthcare Ethics 2(4):426–434.
Fletcher, John C., and Diane E. Hoffman
  1994   Ethics Committees: Time to Experiment with Standards. Annals of Internal
            Medicine 120(4):335–337.
Fletcher, John C., Norman Quist, and Albert R. Jonsen, eds.
  1989   Ethics Consultation in Health Care. Ann Arbor, MI: Health Administration.
Fox, Renee C.
  1990   The Evolution of American Bioethics: A Sociological Perspective. *In* Social Sci-
            ence Perspectives on Medical Ethics. George Weisz, ed. Pp. 201–220. Philadel-
            phia: University of Pennsylvania Press.
Fox, Renee C., and Judith P. Swazey
  1984   Medical Morality Is Not Bioethics: Medical Ethics in China and the United
            States. Perspectives in Biology and Medicine 27:336–360.
Friedman, Marilyn
  1987   Care and Context in Moral Reasoning. *In* Women and Moral Theory. Eva
            Feder Kittay and Diana T. Meyers, eds. Totowa, NJ: Rowman & Littlefield.
Fry-Revere, Sigrid
  1992   The Accountability of Bioethics Committees and Consultants. Frederick, MD:
            University Publishing Group, Inc.
Garro, Linda
  1994   Narrative Representations of Chronic Illness Experiences: Cultural Models of
            Illness, Mind, and Body in Stories Concerning Temporomandibular Joint
            (TMJ). Social Science and Medicine 38(6):775–788.
Gilligan, Carol
  1982   In a Different Voice: Psychological Theory and Women's Moral Development.
            Cambridge: Harvard University Press.
Gilligan, Carol, Janie Victoria Ward, and Jill McLean Taylor, eds.
  1988   Mapping the Moral Domain. Cambridge, MA: Harvard University Press.

Good, Byron
  1994   Medicine, Rationality and Experience. New York: Cambridge University Press.
Good, Byron, and Mary-Jo Del Vecchio Good
  1993   In the Subjunctive Mode: Epilepsy Narratives in Turkey. Social Science and
            Medicine 38(6):835–842.
Gordon, Deborah R.
  1988   Tenacious Assumptions in Western Medicine. *In* Biomedicine Examined. Mar-
            garet Lock and Deborah R. Gordon, eds. Pp. 19–57. Boston: Kluwer Academ-
            ic Publishers.
Harding, Sandra
  1986   The Science Question in Feminism. Ithaca, NY: Cornell University Press.
Hardwig, John
  1990   What About the Family? Hastings Center Report 10(2):5–10.
Hawkins, Anne Hunsaker
  1993   Reconstructing Illness: Studies in Pathography. West Lafayette, IN: Purdue
            University Press.
Heitman, Elizabeth
  1993   A Pro-Active Role for the Ethics Committee or Ethics Consultant. Health Care,
            Law & Ethics 8(4):11–16.
Held, Virginia
  1987   Feminism and Moral Theory. *In* Women and Moral Theory. Eva Feder Kittay
            and Diana T. Meyers. Totowa, NJ: Rowman & Littlefield.
Hoagland, Sara Lucia
  1988   Lesbian Ethics: Toward New Value. Palo Alto, CA: Institute of Lesbian Studies.
Hoffmaster, Barry
  1990   Morality and the Social Sciences. *In* Social Science Perspectives on Medical
            Ethics. George Weisz, ed. Pp. 241–260. Philadelphia: University of Pennsylva-
            nia Press.
  1992   Can Ethnography Save the Life of Medical Ethics? Social Science and Medi-
            cine 35:1421.
Holmes, Helen Bequaert, and Laura M. Purdy
  1992   Feminist Perspectives in Medical Ethics. Bloomington: Indiana University Press.
Hunter, Kathryn Montgomery
  1989   A Science of Individuals: Medicine and Casuistry. Journal of Medicine and
            Philosphy 14:193–212.
  1991   Doctor Stories: The Narrative Structure of Medical Knowledge. Princeton, NJ:
            Princeton University Press.
  1992   Remaking the case. Literature and Medicine. 11:163.
Irwin Susan, and Brigette Jordan
  1987   Knowledge, Practice, and Power: Court-Ordered Cesarean Sections. Medical
            Anthropology Quarterly (n.s.) 1(3):319–334.
Jennings, Bruce
  1990   Ethics and Ethnography in Neonatal Intensive Care. *In* Social Science Per-
            spectives on Medical Ethics. George Weisz, ed. Pp. 261–272. Philadelphia: Uni-
            versity of Pennsylvania Press.
Jonsen, Albert, and Stephen Toulmin
  1988   The Abuse of Casuistry. Berkeley: University of California Press.
Kasiske, Bertram, John Neylan, Robert Riggio, et al.
  1991   The Effect of Race on Access and Outcome in Transplantation. New England
            Journal of Medicine 324(3):302–307.

Kittay, Eva Fader, and Diana T. Meyers, eds.
   1987   Women and Moral Theory. Savage, MD: Rowman and Littlefield Publishers, Inc.
Kjellstrant, C. M.
   1988   Age, Sex, and Race Inequality in Renal Transplantation. Archives of Internal Medicine 148:1305–1309.
Kleinman, Arthur
   1988   Illness Narratives: Suffering, Healing, and the Human Condition. New York: Basic Books.
Kopelman, Loretta M.
   1994   Case Method and Casuistry: The Problem of Bias. Theoretical Medicine 15(1):21–38.
La Puma, John, and David L. Schiedermayer
   1991   Ethics Consultation: Skills, Roles, and Training. Annals of Internal Medicine 114(2):155–160.
   1994   Ethics Consultation: A Practical Guide. Boston: Jones and Bartlett Publishers.
Leder, Drew
   1990   Clinical Interpretation: The Hermeneutics of Medicine. Theoretical Medicine 11(1):9–24.
Lieban, Richard
   1990   Medical Anthropology and the Comparative Study of Medical Ethics. *In* Social Science Perspectives on Medical Ethics. George Weisz, ed. Pp. 221–240. Philadelphia: University of Pennsylvania Press.
Lock, James D.
   1990   Some Aspects of Medical Hermeneutics: The Role of Dialectic and Narrative. Theoretical Medicine 11(1):41–50.
Marshall, Patricia
   1992   Anthropology and Bioethics. Medical Anthropology Quarterly 6(1):49–73.
   1994   Commentary on the Case of "The Coercive Family." Cambridge Quarterly of Healthcare Ethics 3(1):136–138.
Marshall, Patricia and Paul O'Keefe
   1994   Medical Students' First Person Narratives of a Patient's Story of AIDS. Social Science Medicine 40(1):67–76.
Mattingly, Cheryl
   1991   The Narrative Structure of Clinical Reasoning. American Journal of Occupational Therapy 54:972.
McClosky, Elizabeth L.
   1991   The Patient Self-Determination Act. Kennedy Institute of Ethics Journal 1:163–169.
Nelson, James Lindermann
   1992   Taking Families Seriously. Hastings Center Report 22(4):6–12.
Noddings, Nel
   1984   Caring: A Feminine Approach to Ethics and Moral Education. Berkeley: University of California Press.
Pellegrino, Edmund D.
   1988   Clinical Ethics: Biomedical Ethics at the Bedside. Journal of the American Medical Association 260:837–839.
Pellegrino, Edmund D., and David C. Thomasma
   1981   A Philosophical Basis of Medical Practice: Toward a Philosophy and Ethic of the Healing Professions. New York: Oxford University Press.

1989   For the Patient's Good: The Restoration of Beneficence in Health Care. New York: Oxford University Press.

1993   Virtue Ethics in Medical Practice. New York: Oxford University Press.

Poirier, S., L. Rosenblum, et al.
1992   Charting the Chart—an Exercise in Interpretation(s). Literature and Medicine 11:1.

Ramsey, Paul
1970   The Patient as Person. New Haven: Yale University Press.
1978   Ethics at the Edges of Life. New Haven: Yale University Press.

Randall, Teri
1993   The Gender Gap in Selection of Cardiac Transplantation Candidates: Bogus or Bias? Journal of the American Medical Association 269(21):1718–1720.

Reich, Warren
1987   Caring for Life in the First of It: Moral Dilemmas for Perinatal and Neonatal Ethics. Seminars in Perinatology 11(3):279–287.

Ross, Judith Wilson, J. Glaser, D. Rasinski-Gregory, et al.
1993   Health Care Committees: The Next Generation. American Hospital Publishing, Inc.

Sherwin, Susan
1992   No Longer Patient: Feminist Ethics and Health Care. Philadelphia: Temple University Press.

Siegler, Mark, Edmund D. Pellegrino, and Peter A. Singer
1990   Clinical Medical Ethics. Journal of Clinical Ethics 1(1):5–9.

Taylor, Sandra J.
1993   Can Ethics Consultation Be Gender Neutral? Health Care, Law and Ethics 8(4)25–27.

Thomasma, David C.
1991   Why Philosophers Should Offer Ethics Consultations. Theoretical Medicine 12(2):129–140.

Tomlinson, Tom
1994   Casuistry in Medical Ethics: Rehabilitated, or Repeat Offender? Theoretical Medicine 15(1):5–20.

Toombs, S. Kay
1992   The Meaning of Illness: A Phenomenological Account of the Different Perspectives of Physician and Patient. Dordrecht: Kluwer Academic Publishers.

Veatch, Robert M.
1981   A Theory of Medical Ethics. New York: Basic Books.
1984   Autonomy's Temporary Triumph. Hastings Center Report 14(5):38–40.

Waitzkin, H.
1991   The Politics of Medical Encounters. New Haven: Yale University Press.

Weeks, William, and William Nelson
1993   The Ethical role of the Consultant. Cambridge Quarterly of Healthcare Ethics 2(4):477–484.

West, Mary Beth, and Joan McIver Gibson
1992   Facilitating Medical Ethics Case Review: What Ethics Committees Can Learn from Mediation and Facilitation Techniques. Cambridge Quarterly of Healthcare Ethics 1:63–74.

A Handmaid's Tale: The Rhetoric of Personhood in American and Japanese Healing of Abortions

☐ *Thomas J. Csordas*

This chapter has to do with religious rituals directed at the experience of women in North America and Japan who have undergone abortions. In each case, they are rituals aimed at the healing of a particular cultural construction of grief and guilt predicated upon a particular ethnopsychology of the person. I will first present the North American ritual, and then contrast it with a parallel ritual in contemporary Japan.

The North American ritual, or more precisely the ritual technique, is disturbing in the way it taps into one of the most emotionally, ethically, and politically provocative issues in contemporary society. It is disturbing in the same sense as is Margaret Atwood's powerful novel, *A Handmaid's Tale*, from which I've borrowed my title. Atwood describes a North American society in the very near and almost-present future in which fundamentalist Christianity has acceded to political power and created a totalitarian state. In this society, the act of performing abortion is punishable by death and the public exhibition of one's humiliated corpse. Because environmental pollution has decreased the population's fertility to a dangerously low level, the Commanders who constitute a ruling elite are assigned Handmaids. These fertile young women complement the Commanders' privileged Wives as reproductive servants within their sanctified households.

When I first encountered Atwood's work, I was frankly jolted by the similarity of terminology to that prevalent in some of the Catholic Charismatic "covenant communities" I had been studying. "Household" was indeed a specialized term for a Christian living arrangement that included more members than a nuclear family. There was an office of "handmaid," admittedly without reproductive function, but understood as a role in which some women had additional responsibilities for community service, particularly regarding the well-being of other women, but always under direct male "headship" or authority. Somewhat ominously, in the leading covenant community, the office of handmaid was itself suspended for a period of several years, presumably because those who held it were arrogating more authority than was regarded as biblically warranted by the male ruling elite. The ruling elite of these communities, which considered themselves vanguard outposts of a coming kingdom of God (the logical extension of which seemed to me to be Atwood's Republic of Gilead), styled themselves not as Commanders within a religious police state, but in a slightly more bureaucratic vein, as "Coordinators."

The possibility of seeing the Charismatics as "proto-Gileadean" was enhanced during my study of their system of ritual healing when I discovered the rite I will describe below. Let me note from the outset that some Catholic Charismatics are quite active in the political opposition to abortion, prompted by the double influence of embracing the conservative position of the Roman Catholic hierarchy and embracing the fundamentalist conservatism of neo-Pentecostalism. Some are additionally active in a campaign to achieve medical recognition of what they call "post-abortion syndrome," a fabricated psychiatric syndrome modeled very closely on the definition of "post-traumatic stress disorder" found in the American Psychiatric Association's Diagnostic and Statistical Manual. Such a disorder is, strictly speaking, a culture-bound disorder in the sense that it is relevant only within a Charismatic culture that defines the experience of abortion as *necessarily* traumatic. Leaving that point aside for the present, I will briefly describe the Catholic Charismatic movement and its system of ritual healing, and then go on to the specific healing technique in question.

THE CHARISMATIC RENEWAL AND CATHOLIC RITUAL HEALING

The Catholic Charismatic Renewal is a religious movement within the Roman Catholic Church. This renewal began in 1967 in the United States. It borrows Pentecostal ideas and practices such as baptism in the Holy Spirit, speaking in tongues, and faith healing. In 1976, the movement's directory reported the existence of 2,183 prayer groups of varying sizes in the United States, and, as early as 1977, movement sources reported a total of 1,600 prayer groups in 82 countries. By 1986, there were a reported 4,814 Catholic Charismatic groups in the United States; by 1988, it was reported that as many as 10 million people in the United States, and another 20 million internationally, had been exposed to movement activities such as public healing services. In 1992, the movement directory contained listings for 5,141 groups in the United States. At that time, though, it was admitted that overall participation had declined, and most groups appeared somewhat smaller in size.

Statements by the Catholic hierarchy, including the last three popes, about this predominantly lay, middle-class movement have been generally supportive, while at the same time cautioning against potential excesses and elitism (McDon-

nell, 1976). The overall stance of the movement appears to be theologically radical and politically conservative, and it is a viable hypothesis that the hierarchy's
embrace of the movement is predominantly a recognition that, despite its Pentecostal tendencies in theology and ritual practice, its social and political conservatism is a strategically valuable counter to movements such as liberation theology
and feminism. Catholic Charismatics, particularly in some of the tightly organized
covenant communities, tend to adhere to a patriarchal model of gender roles
in which women defer to male leadership. This deference is rationalized in part
on Biblical grounds, and in part on the pseudoempirical grounds that men are
"less emotional" and "hold up better under stress" (Csordas, in press; cf. Rose
1987).

In general, the movement as a whole can be described by the following four
characteristics:

1. *Communitarian.* The notion of community applied to Christianity as a
whole lends the movement its strongly ecumenical tone; applied to interpersonal
relations among participants it is realized as a strong emphasis on "brotherhood."
Most significant is the emergence within the movement of communitarian bodies
("covenant communities") which cultivate strict internal discipline and intense
intimacy in interpersonal affairs.

2. *Enthusiastic.* Catholic Pentecostalism exemplifies both what religious
scholars following Knox refer to as "enthusiasm" and what sociologists following
Durkheim refer to as religious "effervescence." Both communal and private rituals, while not as dramatic as those of other forms of Pentecostalism, tend to be
demonstrative rather than contemplative. Emphasis is on active, spontaneous,
divinely inspired participation in ritual.

3. *Healing-oriented.* Personal transformation and integration of individuals
into the community of believers is effected in part through ritual healing. Occasions for healing include the Baptism in the Holy Spirit, the Catholic sacrament
of Reconciliation (confession), special prayers for physical illness, psychothera-
peutic rituals for "deliverance" from the power of evil spirits and "inner healing"
of emotional disabilities acquired in past experience.

4. *Revitalistic.* Catholic Pentecostalism fits the broad descriptive type of "revitalization movement." The notion of "renewal" applies to individual spirituality, to
the Catholic Church as a whole, to Christianity as a whole, and ultimately to all
humankind. It is significant that the movement operates within the world's largest
single institutional structure, the Roman Catholic Church, in which it is potentially either a source of internal change or schism.

Emphasis on these themes varies within the movement: the communitarian
impulse is expressed in degrees ranging from highly committed, tightly structured
"covenant communities" to small, informal parish "prayer groups"; enthusiasm
may amount to as little as spontaneous prayer or as much as ritual states of dissociation ("resting in the Spirit"); ritual healing may be the primary focus of one
group's activities, while another may emphasize evangelization or communal
prayer; revitalization may be anticipated on a cosmic scale, or its scope may

extend only as far as renewed individual spirituality or intensification of small-group relations.

Healing practices among Catholic Charismatics show a remarkable uniformity across regions and locales, at least within North America. This is in part due to a highly developed distribution system for movement publications including books, magazines, and audiotapes, as well as the existence of a class of teachers and healers who travel to workshops, conferences, retreats, and "days of renewal" at which such practices and their rationales are disseminated. The three principal forms of healing are prayer for healing of physical or medical problems, deliverance or casting out of evil spirits, and inner healing or healing of memories.[1] The healing of memories is the ritual transformation of the consequences of emotional trauma or "woundedness" by means of prayer. This prayer often includes imaginal processes in the form of guided imagery initiated by the healer or the spontaneous enactment of a scenario by the patient. At times the memory identified as in need of transformation is that of having had an abortion. In Charismatic culture, undergoing an abortion is presumed traumatic to the pregnant woman, entailing the emotional consequences of guilt and the grief of bereavement, and is also presumed to produce a death trauma for the aborted fetus.[2]

Healing of memories for the mother and fetus is described in a book by the highly popular Charismatic Jesuit priests Dennis and Matthew Linn and their collaborator Sheila Fabricant (1985:105–39). Their chapter treats miscarriages, stillbirths, and abortions as a single class, beginning with a theological discussion emphasizing that while these unbaptized do not necessarily end up in the "limbo" of Catholic lore and can go to heaven, they are in need of healing. The authors go on to a psychological discussion of prenatal research, arguing for the emotional viability, and hence vulnerability, of these beings. Then follows a discussion of grief among mothers, which quickly turns to focus on abortion and argues for the commonality of grief and guilt among women who choose abortions.

The authors narrate two cases of praying for such women. The first was a woman who had had one abortion, and had attempted to abort her daughter who was then 18, and who had frequent violent outbursts against family members. During a Mass offered for the aborted fetus and for "any part of" the living daughter that had died during the abortion attempt, the adult woman collapsed on the floor and experienced all the pains and contractions of labor, following which the healers invited her symbolically "to give her baby to Jesus and Mary to be cared for." Subsequently the woman claimed that her chronic back pain improved, as did her daughter's violent outbursts, both changes interpreted by the healers as evidence of relief of "the trauma of the abortion." The second case was a woman for whom healing hurt and self-hatred from having an abortion nine years previously caused a variety of other hurts to emerge, including the perinatal effects of grief experienced by her own mother over the death of her father and anger at her relatives who refused to allow the pregnant woman a deathbed visit, as well as the effects of being born with her umbilical cord wrapped around her neck, and of having been physically and sexually abused during childhood.

These examples exhibit an ethnopsychology in which abortion (in a degree greater than miscarriage or stillbirth) is a powerful pathogenic agent, and in which ritual healing is a powerful and occasionally dramatic antidote. The rite often includes specific imaginal techniques. Linn, Linn, and Fabricant describe four steps: (1) the patient visualizes Jesus and Mary holding the child, and the patient holds it with them, asking forgiveness from the deity and the child for any way in which he or she hurt the child, and is instructed to imaginally "see what Jesus or the child says or does in response to you," and with them to forgive anyone else who may have hurt the child; (2) the patient chooses a name for the dead fetus and symbolically baptizes it, with the instruction to "feel the water cleansing and making all things anew," thus granting the fetus the cultural status of a person and, in effect, ritually "undoing" the abortion; (3) the patient prays that the fetus receive divine love, and is instructed to imaginally "place it in the arms of Jesus and Mary and see them do all the things you can't do," and to ask the fetus to become an intercessor for the patient and the patient's family; (4) the patient has a Mass offered for the child, and while receiving the Eucharist is instructed to "let Jesus' love and forgiving blood flow through you to the child and to all other deceased members of your family tree."

PERSON, GENDER, AND EFFICACY

The degree of multisensory vividness that can be attained in what we can call this embodied imaginal performance (cf. Csordas 1994) is evident in the following case narrated by a team of two Charismatic healers (G and H):

G: ... one lady that we had prayed over for an abortion [was so upset that] she turned purple at one point. ... Anyway, we asked the Lord if she could have the vision of her baby, aborted baby. And she physically cupped her hands, arms and hands, as if she was holding a baby. And if you saw her, if you saw any of us, [you'd] probably think we were all nuts. But if you saw her, it looked like she was holding a baby. I mean she was there like this. And talking to it. Of course there was nothing there that anyone could see. But we had just asked the Lord if He would allow her to hold the baby. And the next moment she was holding her baby.

TC: You asked aloud with her or you asked [God] silently whether she could ...

G: No, we asked her first, out loud. And she said she wanted to. Then she wouldn't give it up. So we were quite a while until she was able to let the baby go.

H: And we would just remain silent and just keep praying silently and with our hands on her. So that He [God] would go into her ...

G: Real physical manifestation ...

H: And you could just feel it all around, in the air, of the Lord just loving her.

TC: Did she have the physical experience of holding the baby?

G: Oh, yeah.

TC: And what did the purple in her face mean?

G: Well that was before [the imagery sequence]. I just think it was the guilt and the mourning over it.

H: See the thing is she didn't want to come to the acceptance that she had anything to do with the abortion. It was "all her husband's fault." And when she finally came to realize that she had to take a responsibility too . . .

G: She started screaming.

H: Then it was kind of scary, ya know. But [we] just loved her through that. And He was there with us. So it was a beautiful experience.

G: And something very interesting on that was, when we deal with the healing for an abortion, we always ask them if they have a sense of what gender the baby is, and if they have any sense of a name . . . if they even hear a name or see a name or the Lord places a name in their heart. And I forgot what the name was, but it was a girl. And both . . . we dealt with them separately. Husband and wife. Both had a sense it was a girl and both came up with the same name. And they did not consult with each other. Because we saw her first, and then we ushered her out of the room. There was no communication between the two. And both sensed that it was a girl, and both came up with the exact same name. And neither one had talked about this since the day that the abortion occurred. Never brought it up again. So I mean there was no possible way that they could have named it . . . that before the abortion they had even thought of it.

I will organize my analysis of this text around the four elements that in previous work (Csordas 1988, 1994) I have identified as essential to therapeutic process in ritual healing. Regarding *disposition,* it is evident that the supplicant must be culturally disposed not only to accept the possibility of divine healing, but also to regard having undergone an abortion as a problem in need of healing. The healer's presumption that the supplicant's "turning purple" indicated states of guilt and mourning are part of the taken-for-granted nature of the latter disposition, apparently never challenged by participants. The presence of both dispositions is suggested by the apparent fact that the healing was directed specifically toward the abortion experience, and that the woman's husband was included in a systematic way, separate from his wife. The disposition to maternal attachment enacted in the woman's refusal to relinquish her imaginal baby is consistent with a rejection of abortion as a cultural practice, and the disposition to engage readily in imaginal performance is likewise consistent with participation in the healing system.

Nevertheless it is necessary to recognize that the presumption of guilt as an emotion in the supplicant can, through performance, act as an induction of guilt. This is especially the case when guilt is regarded not only as an emotional but an objective state; i.e., a state of sin. Characteristically for Charismatics, there is no explicit discussion of sin and repentance, which remain implicit in the reference to "taking responsibility for" the action. In no way does this phrase mean that healing is constituted by "coming to terms with having made a responsible, though difficult, decision." Instead, it means that emotional healing requires "acknowledging that by consenting to your husband's demand you too are responsible for a sin," and accepting divine forgiveness.

Experience of the sacred is actualized by multisensory imagery in several cultural forms. Gendering and naming the fetus is achieved through revelatory imagery, and the conviction of divine empowerment is reinforced by the concurrence of husband's and wife's images in the absence of consultation. Divinely granted haptic, kinaesthetic, and visual imagery of an exceedingly vivid, eidetic quality is evident in the woman's holding the imaginal baby and talking to it. The experience of divine presence as a phenomenon of embodiment is attested by the healers' account that, for their own part, they could "feel it all around, in the air," and that the supplicant's imagery sequence was a "real physical manifestation" of divine power entering her. Finally, although not specifically recounted in this text, it is likely that the supplicant with her child was led through a complete imaginal performance of baptizing the baby and finally letting it go into the hands of Jesus.

While the imaginal form and eidetic quality of these experiences define them as sacred, their content achieves the third therapeutic function of *elaboration of alternatives*. Two such alternatives are implicit in this episode. First is that of actually having a baby, elaborated in the imaginal holding of the baby and its cultural thematic of maternal-child intimacy. Second is that of having the fetus die in a culturally appropriate way, that is, as a baby with definite gender, name, and Christian baptism.

It is the latter alternative that is taken up as part of the *actualization of change*, for part of the efficacy of ritual performance is precisely transforming the fetus into a person. A person in this sense is a cultural representation, or more precisely an objectification of indeterminate self processes (Csordas 1994:5, 14–5). While both a fetus and a baby are biological entities, whether, and at what point, they are objectified as "persons" varies across cultures. The current North American debate is based on whether the person begins at conception, at birth, or in one of the culturally established "trimesters" between the two. In cross-cultural perspective we see that the issue of personhood extends even beyond birth, however. Among the Northern Cheyenne, children are not participants in the moral community because they lack knowledge or responsibility for their actions, and are therefore considered only "potential" persons (Fogelson 1982; Strauss 1977). Among the Mande peoples of Africa, a newborn is not yet a member of the worldly family, remaining unnamed till eight days after birth. The shape of the placenta is examined to determine whether the newborn is in fact not a human person but a *saa* or spirit child (R. Whittemore, personal communication). Among the Dogon, a fetus is conceived as a kind of fish until it has received a series of names and has been circumcised or excised, at which time only it is recognized as truly a boy or girl (Dieterlin 1971:226). For the Tallensi, "it is not until an infant is weaned and has a following sibling (*nyeer*) that it can be said to be on the road to full personhood," a status that is in fact "only attained by degrees over the whole course of a life" (Fortes 1987:261). Among the poorest of Brazil, children are often neither baptized nor named till they are toddlers, and the infant that dies is considered neither a human child nor yet a blessed angel. Instead, "the infant's humanness, its personhood, and its claims on the mother's attention and affections grow over time, slowly, tentatively, and anxiously" (Scheper-Hughes 1990:560).

Such examples could be multiplied, and indeed a recent paper by Lynn Morgan (1989) does a masterful job of synthesizing the cross-cultural data on the personhood of neonate humans. However, in all of these examples, the contrast with the Charismatic practice could not be more striking: whereas in these instances an already-born infant is *not yet* a person, in Charismatic healing a never-to-be-born fetus is *still* a person. The difference is doubtless grounded in the circumstance that in the former cases, where infant mortality is high, no infant can necessarily be expected to survive, whereas in the middle-class North America of the Charismatics, no infant is ever expected to die. Nevertheless, in all the cases it is the ritual action of naming (and baptizing or its equivalent) that bestows the cultural status of person. Phenomenologically reinforced by imaginal performance, part of the actualization of change in the healing of abortion is creation of a person that can subsequently be prayed for and regarded as being "with Jesus."

This is not all, however, for in this instance actualization of change includes the dual movement of "accepting responsibility" and "letting go." In the healers' account the supplicant's screaming must be categorized as a kind of therapeutic breakthrough that was buffered as they "loved her through that" in collaboration with the divine presence. The rather peculiar juxtaposition of "scary" and "beautiful" to describe the situation carries a dual message related both to efficacy and to situational dynamics. To redefine a scary situation as a beautiful one is at once to say that what was potentially negative and dangerous was, in fact, highly successful—beauty is synonymous with efficacy. At the same time, it is an acknowledgment that the dynamics of the situation nearly got out of hand but didn't—and here, beauty is synonymous with control. Finally, the actualization of "letting go" is the epitome of the Charismatic surrender of control to the deity in exchange for emotional freedom. Here again is a dual meaning. On the one hand, the supplicant "lets go of" the guilt expressed in her cathartic scream, and on the other she "lets go of" her cherished maternal intimacy and the associated grief over its absence by relinquishing the imaginal baby.

In brief summary, in the Charismatic rite for healing abortions we see the rhetorical power of multisensory imaginal performance to create a proto-Gileadean cultural reality for women who participate in the ritual healing system of the Charismatic Renewal. A clear ideological choice is made not to make them feel alright about what they have done but to presume their guilt and absolve them of it through divine forgiveness; not to affirm the pre-personhood of the fetus but to create a person and bestow upon it an identity by naming/baptizing it and specifying its gender; not to emphasize the termination of the woman's pregnancy but the death trauma of the fetus and to resolve it by commending the unborn soul to the care of the deity.

In her important cultural analysis of the abortion debate in the contemporary United States, Ginsburg (1989) identifies a series of what she calls "interpretive battlegrounds" in the struggle between prochoice and prolife forces. The Charismatic ritual is not a public battleground, but an internal ideological exercise where what is at stake is to intensify the world view that binds the ranks of antiabortion warriors by ritually enacting that world view in a way that displays its doxic qualities. The spontaneous entrainment of multisensory imagery is a product of deeply inculcated dispositions of a patriarchal habitus, and by its spontaneity is a rhetorically powerful display of an ethnopsychological reality. In this capacity the healing ritual goes beyond addressing the issue of fetal personhood to play a powerful role in what Ginsburg calls the "renegotiation of pregnancy, childbirth, and nurturance . . . in the construction of female gender identity in American culture" (1989:110). Since the legalization of abortion, motherhood can no longer be presumed to be an ascribed status, the inevitable result of pregnancy conceived as an inevitable process in women's lives. Instead it becomes an achieved status, the result of a decision that "comes to signify an assertion of a particular construction of female identity," in the face of necessity for rhetorical strategies for reproducing the culture in the absence of its formerly taken-for-granted self-reproduction (1989:109). The ritual undoing of the abortion is just such a strategy, restoring through imaginal performance the inevitability of pregnancy, childbirth, and nurturance. Ginsburg argues that an essential aspect of prolife political action is "the refiguring of a gendered landscape through prayer, demonstration, and efforts to convert others, particularly women in the vulnerable and liminal position of carrying an unwanted pregnancy" (1989:110). The Charismatic healing of abortions extends this refiguring from women who choose to carry an unwanted pregnancy to women who once chose not to carry a pregnancy.

In the example recounted above, the patient was chastised for blaming her husband, an escape from responsibility by citing lack of accountability in the face of the patriarchal authority of the husband. On the one hand, the healers insistence that she take a share of responsibility for the decision to abort may seem to proffer a degree of empowerment, and the inclusion of the husband in the ritual carries the message that the woman is not abandoned to the emotional consequences of the abortion. On the other hand, insofar as the notions of sin and guilt are inevitably contained within this acceptance of responsibility, the patriarchal logic is enforced wherein the woman is obligated to bear children at all costs, even if her husband abdicates his procreative conscience.

Japanese *Mizuko Kuyo:* **Notes toward a Comparison**

In the above discussion of efficacy I situated the Charismatic ritual ethnologically by surveying definitions of the objectification, or coming into being, of persons across a variety of cultures. In this final section I want to return to the same theme with a more precise comparison in mind. Contemporary Japanese society is the site of a more public ritual practice of postabortion healing.[3] It is a ritual in which the spirits of aborted fetuses are propitiated through prayer and through representation by stylized statues or tablets. These rites are called *mizuko kuyo*, where *mizuko* refers to fetuses miscarried, stillborn, and aborted, as well as the already-born who succumb to infanticide (LaFleur 1992: 16) and *kuyo* is a type of ritual based on an offering of simple gifts in thanks to objects or beings that have been in some sense used up, ranging from domestic objects like sewing needles to deceased humans (LaFleur 1992:143–46). The *mizuko kuyo* rites appear to be essentially Buddhist in nature but originated in the social context of the Japanese New Religions since the 1970s (Blacker 1989), and are cited as evidence of the commercialization of contemporary Japanese religion since they are often highly profitable to the temples and organizations that perform them (Picone 1986). In what follows I will briefly discuss the Japanese Buddhist *mizuko kuyo* in relation to the North American Catholic Charismatic healing of abortions in order to begin to point to the place these overtly similar practices occupy in the cultural config-urations of their respective societies.[4]

First let us take care to contextualize the relative social space occupied by these two practices. The American practice is largely a private one that takes place within the membership of a discrete religious movement within Christianity, and is a specific instance of the healing system elaborated within that movement. The Japanese practice has a relatively public profile not limited to a particular social group, and is an instance of a type of ritual common to a variety of forms of Bud-dhism. Historically, the Charismatic Renewal and the *mizuko* cult are contempo-raneous, products of the post-1960s cultural ferment that spawned the New Age, Christian fundamentalism, and a renewed interest in Eastern spiritualities in the United States, and the various New Religions and a florescence of interest in spir-it possession in Japan. Just as the Charismatic Renewal and other forms of neo-Pentecostalism have been associated with the neoconservative Christian right in America, some of the Japanese *mizuko* have been observed to have right-wing fun-damentalist, naturalist, or Shinto connections.

In the United States, abortion was legalized for the first time in the early 1970s as a result of the Supreme Court decision in Roe v. Wade, while in Japan abortion has a deeper history. Both abortion and infanticide were common from the early 1700s to the mid-1800s, when an abortion debate ensued among Bud-dhist, neo-Shinto, and neo-Confucian positions in the context of a nationalism that demanded population growth and condemned such practices. Only follow-ing World War II in 1948 was abortion again legalized. Since that time, it has become the most popular form of birth control in Japan. Just as in the context of the American abortion debate the Charismatic prayer for healing tends to emphasize the aborted rather than the stillborn or miscarried fetus, in the con-text of the postwar commonality of abortion the aborted fetus has taken prece-dence as the primary referent of the Japanese term *mizuko*.

In both societies the affective issue addressed by the ritual is guilt, but whereas in the United States this is a guilt occurring under the sign of sin, in Japan it is guilt under the sign of necessity. For the Americans, abortion is an un-Christian act, and both perpetrator and victim must be ritually brought back into the Christian moral and emotional universe; for the Japanese both the acceptance of abortion as necessary and the acknowledgment of guilt are circumscribed within the Buddhist moral and emotional universe. Both rites are intended to heal the distress experienced by the woman, but the etiology of the illness is somewhat differently construed in the two cases. For Charismatics, any symptoms displayed by the woman are the result of the abortion as psychological trauma compounded by guilt, along with the more or less indirect effects of the restive fetal spirit "crying out" for love and comfort. In Japan such symptoms are attributed to vengeance and resentment on the part of the aborted fetal spirit that is the pained victim of an unnatural, albeit necessary, act.[5] Finally, not only the etiology but the emotional work accomplished by the two rituals is construed differently. As we have seen, for the Charismatics this is a work of forgiveness and of letting go. For the Japanese it is a work of thanks and apology to the fetus, where in cultural context gratitude and guilt are not sharply differentiated. Thus, "[t]here is no great need to determine precisely whether one is addressing a guilt-pre-supposing 'apology' to a *mizuko* or merely expressing 'thanks' to it for having vacated its place in the body of a woman and having moved on, leaving her—and her family—relatively free of its physical presence" (LaFleur 1992:147).

We can now compare the two postabortion healing practices with respect to what they assume and what they produce with regard to the ethno-ontology of the person. The American Charismatic ritual is largely an "imaginal performance" (cf. Csordas 1994) in which the woman may vividly experience holding the imaginal fetus/baby, while the Japanese ritual typically includes the concrete representation of the fetus/baby in the form of a statue. For the Americans, the fetus is a distinct little being that at a certain point is given over to Jesus who is its savior and protector. The Japanese statue (*mizuko jizo*), on the other hand, assimilates the infant and savior in the same representation, a bald and diminutive monklike entity with infantile features sometimes described as "the Bodhisattva who wears a bib." This contrast in the ontological status of the fetus is recapitulated in the respective cultural notions of the coming into being of persons. American Charismatics regard personhood to be definitive at the moment of conception, whereas for Japanese becoming a person is neither a matter of conception nor of birth, but a gradual ontological process wherein "in coming bit by bit into the social world of human beings there is a thickening or densification of being," the inverse of a thinning of being as a person ages into ancestorhood and Buddhahood (LaFleur 1992:33). Thus, for the Charismatics, abortion is the definitive termination of a human life, while in the Japanese view the aborted fetus can as easily be thought of as returning to a state of prebeing where it may be held till a later date as to a state comparable to that of deceased ancestors.

Given these differences, the intent of the Charismatic ritual is to move rhetorically the dead fetus ahead into a secure postlife union with the deity, whereas the intent of the Japanese ritual is to secure the fetus' good will either as it slips back into its prelife state or as it advances to the realm of the Buddhas. Charismatics tend to eschew the old Catholic folk notion of a limbo where unbaptized infants must remain separated from the deity (Linn, Linn, and Fabricant 1985), whereas Japanese may embrace a kind of limbo from whence the fetus may return at a later date. In this respect it is instructive to consider the difference in meaning of the ritual symbolism of water and of naming. In the Charismatic ritual imaginal water is used to baptize the fetus, an act that ensures the reunion of the fetus with Jesus. In the Japanese case, water is an essential element in the very definition of the fetus: the term *mizuko* means literally "children of the waters," which in a literal sense refers to the amniotic fluids, while in an ontological sense refers to the ambiguous status of the fetus we have been discussing. Whereas for Charismatics water baptism and return to Jesus is the cultural constitution of the fetus as person, the use of water symbolism in Japan highlights the fluidity of being that characterizes the ontological status of the fetus. Given that in Buddhism impermanence, suffering, and the absence of self are fundamental characteristics of all things, "the fetus as a *mizuko* in the process of sliding from its relative formedness as a human into a state of progressive liquidization is doing no other than following the most basic law of experience" (LaFleur 1992:28). A similar point can be made with respect to naming the aborted fetus. For the American Charismatics, naming is an aspect of baptism that contributes to the objectification of the fetus as person. For the Japanese, while the process of bestowing a posthumous ancestral name (*kaimyo*) is often a part of the ritual, it is more controversial, in part of a debate over whether it is more appropriate to allow an unnamed fetus to "slip back" into prebeing or to be named and thereby advanced into a state comparable to ancestorhood.

Contemporary civilization has advanced too far into the process of globalization to allow us to presume that the two rituals we have been discussing are necessarily isolated one from the other. Werblowsky (1991) critically refers to claims that there is a movement in the United States that is learning from Japan to fill the lacunae within Christianity, and sarcastically asks whether "in addition to their belief in souls they also believe (in good Japanese fashion) in family-trees of souls, in which the souls of even unborn children remain closely related to the ancestors" (1991:327, 328). In this Werblowsky appears to confuse the movement associated with the label of "Zen Catholicism" among progressive Catholic monks with the quite separate and markedly more conservative Catholic Charismatic Renewal. The former is doubtless connected in some degree with the Japan-based Catholic journal of religious studies in which Werblowsky's own article appears. In his own text, however, he implicitly refers to the Catholic Charismatic Renewal, even citing the work by Linn, Linn, and Fabricant. While in addition to Zen Catholicism there is some proselytizing with respect to *mizuko kuyo* on the part of Japanese Buddhists in the West (cf., LaFleur 1992:150, 172), if such an influence is present among Charismatics it is certainly less direct than Werblowsky presumes. Charismatic healers Linn, Linn, and Fabricant in passing acknowledge awareness of *mizuko kuyo*, citing another Charismatic author who in turn cites an article in *The Wall Street Journal*, of the practice of Japanese women "increasingly going to Buddhist temples where they pay $115 for a ritualized service to get rid of their guilt for the abortion, experienced in recurring bad dreams" (1985:128).

On the other hand, to answer Werblowsky's comment about family trees, in the 1980s many Charismatics adopted a form of healing called, variously, healing of ancestry or healing the family tree. Along with their more psychological inter-pretations of guilt and grief, Linn, Linn, and Fabricant (1985) favorably cite this notion, popularized by the British Charismatic psychiatrist Kenneth McAll (1982). They write that the fetus that has not been lovingly accepted by its family and committed to God "will cry out for love and prayer to a living family member," with subsequent psychological impact on parents, on parents' abilities to relate to older children or children yet to be born, and on such children themselves. What is noteworthy here is that McAll's practice was inspired by observing Chinese practices with regard to ancestors and ghosts, implicitly assimilating them to souls in purgatory or limbo, while living and practicing abroad. More significant than whether the Charismatic practice is an instance of either classic cultural diffusion or spurious cultural borrowing, what this suggests is that despite its overt funda-mentalist tendencies, the Catholic Charismatic Renewal and contemporary New Religion/Buddhism are mutually participant in the globally prevailing postmod-ern condition of culture.

CONCLUSION

For a society in the throes of moral debate about abortion, where claims are made in terms of moral absolutes, the limits of cultural relativism are tested with the mere observation that "ritual performance creates a cultural reality." In this chap-ter I have attempted to give an account of the creation of meaning and the nature of therapeutic efficacy in a ritual that rhetorically partakes in this serious cultural debate in contemporary American society, and to contrast it with a par-allel ritual in contemporary Japan. The account and the cross-cultural compari-son point beyond relativism to the observation that within the limits posed by their own configuration, cultures can create and define the very problems to which they then develop therapeutic solutions. In the end, to cultivate guilt in order to relieve it is doubtless a form of creativity, but this cannot be said with-out also acknowledging that one of the products of human creativity can be human oppression.

Acknowledgements. An earlier version of this paper was presented to the Invited Session on "Bridging the Discipline: Erika Bourguignon's Contributions to Anthropology," at the annual meeting of the American Anthropological Asso-ciation, 1993, in Washington, DC.

NOTES

1. For comprehensive treatments of Catholic Charismatic healing, see Csordas 1983, 1988, 1990, 1994 and McGuire 1982, 1983.
2. For a cultural analysis of the loss of wanted pregnancy that includes religious and sym-bolic responses see Layne (1992).

3. I am grateful to Susan Sered for drawing my attention to the Japanese case.

4. My discussion of *mizuko kuyo* and abortion in Japan relies heavily on the excellent account provided by LaFleur (1992).

5. Necessity is sometimes conceived under the metaphor of "culling of seedlings," which is performed in order to enhance the viability of those that survive (LaFleur 1992:99). The notion of *tatari*, that spirits of those who die untimely, unnatural, or unjust deaths may seek revenge on the living, is an old one in Japan, and is currently rather controversial with respect to the practice of *mizuko kuyo* (LaFleur 1992:55, 163–72).

REFERENCES

Atwood, Margaret
    1985   The Handmaid's Tale. Toronto: McClelland and Stewart.

Blacker, Carmen
    1989   The Seer as Healer in Japan. *In* The Seer in Celtic and Other Traditions. Hilda Ellis Davidson, ed. Pp. 116–123. Edinburgh: John Donald.

Csordas, Thomas J.
    1983   The Rhetoric of Transformation in Ritual Healing. Culture, Medicine, and Psychiatry 7:333–375.
    1988   Elements of Charismatic Persuasion and Healing. Medical Anthropology Quarterly 2:121–142.
    1990   Embodiment as a Paradigm for Anthropology. Ethos 18:5–47.
    1994   The Sacred Self: A Cultural Phenomenology of Charismatic Healing. Berkeley: University of California Press.
    In press Language, Creativity, and Charisma: The Ritual Life of a Religious Movement. Berkeley: University of California Press.

Dieterlin, Germaine
    1971   L'Image du Corps et les Compsantes de la Personne chez les Dogon. *In* La Notion de Personne en Afrique Noir. Germaine Dieterlin, ed. Pp. 205–229. Colloques Internationaux du C.N.R.S. no. 544.

Fogelson, Raymond D.
    1982   Person, Self and Identity: Some Anthropological Retrospects, Circumspects, and Prospects. *In* Psychosocial Theories of the Self. Benjamin Lee, ed. Pp. 67–109. New York: Plenum Press.

Fortes, Meyer
    1987   The Concept of the Person. *In* Religion, Morality, and the Person: Essays on Tallensi Religion. Meyer Fortes, ed. Pp. 247–286. Cambridge: Cambridge University Press.

Ginsburg, Faye
    1989   Contested Lives: The Abortion Debate in an American Community. Berkeley: University of California Press.

LaFleur, William R.
    1992   Liquid Life: Abortion and Buddhism in Japan. Princeton, NJ: Princeton University Press.

Layne, Linda
    1992   Of Fetuses and Angels: Fragmentation and Integration in Narratives of Pregnancy Loss. Knowledge and Society 9:29–58.

Linn, Matthew, Dennis Linn, and Sheila Fabricant
    1985   Healing the Greatest Hurt. New York: Paulist Press.

McDonnell, Kilian
    1976   Charismatic Renewal and the Churches. New York: Seabury Press.

McGuire, Meredith
    1982   Pentecostal Catholics: Power, Charisma, and Order in a Religious Movement. Philadelphia: Temple University Press.
    1983   Words of Power: Personal Empowerment and Healing. Culture, Medicine, and Psychiatry 7:221–240.

Morgan, Lynn
    1989   When Does Life Begin: A Cross-Cultural Perspective on the Personhood of Fetuses and Young Children. *In* Abortion Rights and Fetal "Personhood." Ed Doerr and James Prescott, eds. New York: Centerline Press and Americans for Religious Liberty.

Picone, Mary J.
    1986   Buddhist Popular Manuals and the Contemporary Commercialization of Religion in Japan. *In* Interpreting Japanese Society: Anthropological Approaches. Joy Hendry and Jonathan Webber, eds. Pp. 157–165. JASO Occasional Papers No. 5, Oxford: Oxford University Press.

Rose, Susan D.
    1987   Women Warriors: The Negotiation of Gender in a Charismatic Community. Social Analysis 48(3):245–258.

Scheper-Hughes, Nancy
    1990   Mother Love and Child Death in Northeast Brazil. *In* Cultural Psychology: Essays on Comparative Human Development. J. Stigler, R. Shweder, and G. Herdt, eds. Pp. 542–565. Cambridge: Cambridge University Press.

Straus, Ann S.
    1977   Northern Cheyenne Ethnopsychology. Ethos 5:326–357.

Werblowsky, R. J. Zwi
    1991   *Mizuko kuyo*: Notulae on the Most Important "New Religion" of Japan. Japanese Journal of Religious Studies 18(4): 295–354.

Political Economy, Gender, and the Social Production of Health and Illness

■ *Linda M. Whiteford*

INTRODUCTION

> In reality, if medicine is the science of the healthy as well as of the ill human being (which is what it ought to be), what other science is better suited to propose laws as the basis of the social structure, in order to make effective those which are inherent in man [sic] himself? Once medicine is established as anthropology, and once the interests of the privileged no longer determine the course of public events, the physiologists and the practitioner will be counted among the elder statesmen [sic] who support the social structures. Medicine is a social science in its very bone and marrow. . . .
>
> —Rudolf Virchow (quoted in Foster and Anderson 1978:3)

Writing in the late 1840s, the German pathologist Rudolf Virchow identified political-economic conditions as an underlying cause of the deaths of thousands during a typhus epidemic (Waitzkin 1981). According to Virchow, the crowded living conditions, lack of sanitation, widespread famine, unemployment, and political disenfranchisement of the poor made them more vulnerable to disease, while their social class and history made the government less than willing to protect them. Virchow was arguing, in essence, that the biological model of disease was not a sufficient explanation of why some people got sick and died while others did not. He suggested that health, like illness, was socially produced, and that to understand health or illness one must understand the social conditions in which health and illness are created, identified, defined, and continued. Virchow used his training as a pathologist to identify the biological causes of typhus, and his perception as a social critic to identify the social conditions that caused its spread and its disproportional deadly effect on the poor.

This chapter takes its lead from Virchow's innovative, insightful perception of 150 years ago, and describes how a political-economic analysis can advantageously be applied to understanding the social production of health today. Virchow argued that the poor were often in bad health not from their own negligence, but from social conditions that systematically deprived them of resources, and historical conditions that isolated them and kept them separate. Since the 1960s, authors have written similarly about the effect of gender barriers: that they artificially create social conditions that define women in terms of gender roles and systematically isolate them from access to resources. This chapter provides the reader with an introduction to anthropological analysis of political economy, paying particular attention to how the study of political economy, gender, and the social production of health can overlap and mutually enrich the resultant analysis. A considerable body of literature exists in anthropology reflecting the intersection between any two of the three focus areas: between political economy and gender, gender and the social production of health, and between political economy and the social production of health. However, more work needs to be conducted using the three conceptual tools of political economy, gender, and the social production of health. This chapter is not intended as an exhaustive review of the literature pertinent to these areas of discourse, but rather as a means to engage readers in this type of analysis through an overview of major conceptual orientations and the presentation of a case study. The case study is a political economic analysis of how the social production of health reflects social class, gender, and ethnic categories. The case study describes how African-American pregnant addicts are subjected to harsh treatment in the medical and law enforcement systems because of class, race, and gender prejudices. In sum, the chapter describes the gendering of political economy in anthropology and its contributions to our understanding of the processes underlying the social production of health.

ANTHROPOLOGICAL POLITICAL ECONOMY AND GENDER

Political economy begins far earlier than its introduction in anthropology. According to Clark (1991), classical political economic thought can be traced to developments in Europe between the 14th and 17th centuries. Adam Smith and Thomas Malthus in the late eighteenth century, and Marx and Engels in the nineteenth century focused on the production and reproduction of systemic relations of power. More recently, anthropologists have used a political economy perspective to integrate analysis of global processes with local and national histories grounded by ethnographic detail (Leacock 1981; DeWalt and Pelto 1985; Finkler 1986, 1994; Mintz 1985; Wolf 1982).

According to William Roseberry (1988), political economy in anthropology began to take form in the 1940s with the seminal work of Julian Steward, Eric Wolf, and Sidney Mintz in Puerto Rico. Wolf and Mintz, in particular, defined the aim of their work as creating an intersection of global political and economic interactions and local systems, communities, and actors (Roseberry 1988:163). To do this, Mintz and Wolf paid careful attention to five hundred years of history, focusing on local cultural, social, political, and economic processes. Peoples' actions, they argued, are the result of a complex mix of local and national forces, shaped by past histories and current conditions. By the 1950s and 1960s, June Nash and Eleanor Leacock added gender in political economy with their research on the impact of colonialism on third-world populations and the effect of state structures on nonstate societies. Both Nash and Leacock explored the evolution of inequality, and particularly its effect on women. Other feminist ethnographers used a political economy perspective to insert women into the ethnographic picture, peopling peasant studies with previously absent rural women farmers and factory workers (Anna Rubbo 1975; Susan Brown 1975). Rubbo and Brown employed what di Leonardo has referred to as "a transformed Marxist paradigm" (1991), while Karen Sacks (1974) and Eleanor Leacock (1972) revisited Engels' model of egalitarianism.

A major thrust of the feminist analysis of political economy was to investigate women's activities within and outside of the household, to explain those activities in terms of cultural and historical forces, and to locate them in the global economic system. The aim was not only to make the previously invisible contributions of women's work visible, but also to place that work within its historical and international context.

The research on gender in the area of political economy grew rapidly with the work of scholars such as Helen Safa (1980, 1983), Mona Etienne and Eleanor Leacock (1980), Jane Collier (1974), Elsa Chaney (1976), Elsa Chaney and Mary Castro (1989), Maria Patricia Fernandez-Kelly (1984), and Florence Babb (1989). Safa's work in Puerto Rico, the Dominican Republic, and Cuba, and Fernandez-Kelly's study of the *maquiladoras* on the U.S.-Mexico border situated women in a gendered understanding of their roles in political-economic analysis. Feminist analysis of the global political economy emerged simultaneously with the increased presence of feminist anthropological scholarship in other areas such as history and political science. Much of that literature finds expression in the field of "women and development" (WID) studies.[1]

One set of readings that powerfully integrates gender issues in anthropology and political economy is Micaela di Leonardo's work, *Gender at the Crossroads of Knowledge: Feminist Anthropology in the Postmodern Era* (1991). In her excellent introductory essay, di Leonardo frames the anthropological analyses of political economy and gender studies by situating the topic in its historical development, and by describing its resultant contribution: a new analysis of feminism, culture, and political economy. According to di Leonardo, this new framework employs the phrase "culture and political economy" "to denote, loosely, work in anthropology that attends both to economics and politics and to the ways in which they are culturally construed by differing social actors in history" (1991:28). Di Leonardo writes that this framework of feminism, culture, and political economy can be summarized in five points. Her five points are significant to reproduce here because they provide a way in which to frame the synthesis among anthropological analyses of political economy, gender, and the social production of health and illness.

A feminist (and gender-contextualized) analysis of "culture and political economy" rests on the following five assumptions:

1. *The abandonment of the concept of social evolutionism.* This means the rejection of the idea that some living human groups represent life and culture unchanged from years before. According to di Leonardo, no group represents "living history," unchanged from earlier times and mirroring what life was like hundreds of thousands of years ago. The rejection of social evolutionism supports the idea that all human populations have had enough time over the thousands of years of existence to modify their languages, values, beliefs, and behaviors. Crediting all cultures with the experience of change allows the researcher to "assess the range of possible human gender arrangements and their connections to human biology through comparative ethnography . . . consider the many histories, in all types of societies, of changing gendered social life and its political-economic correlates, and join with other feminist social scientists, historians, and literary critics to research the mutually influencing histories of changing gender arrangements and ideologies in Western states and their colonized territories over the past centuries" (di Leonardo 1991:28).

2. *Careful reevaluation and recognition of the cultural basis for well-established patterns of behavior.* This element is intimately tied to a paradigmatic respect for history because a critical evaluation of history allows the researcher to reevaluate conceptual categories previously accepted and, in some cases even considered innate in human behavior, which can now be seen as no more than products of their time and place. That is, categories can be recognized as the social labels they are. For example, di Leonardo explains how the historians of sexuality have now shown that the categories "heterosexual" and "homosexual" have not always existed, but rather emerged in Europe and the United States in the nineteenth century, with few common definition boundaries (1991:29). Likewise the categories of class, ethnicity, and race have each been shown to be culturally constructed labels used for different purposes for various people over time. One example of analyzing categories in their sociopolitical context is the work by Greg Pappas. Pappas, a physician and medical anthropologist, has carefully traced the distinctive cultural origins of the demographic statistics kept by various countries. In the United Kingdom, class is documented in national statistics. On the other hand, in the United States, where the "classless" image is carefully maintained, race, rather than class, is documented (Pappas 1993). In both cases, data is collected in artificially created categories that tell us little about the actual people they are used to describe, but tell us a great deal about the values present in the society.

3. *Gender is a categorical concept that by its very nature is embedded in its social construction, both as a set of ideologies and the social institutions of which it is a part.*

Conceptualizing gender as culturally embedded reminds us that gender does not exist outside of, but is rather the reflection and product of, social identities. Gender cannot be studied in isolation; it must be studied in terms of its appropriate categories of reference, be they class, ethnicity, age, nationality, or sexual preference. Therefore, women should be studied not only in relation to men, but also in relation to each other because embedded gender identities cross-cut other social boundaries. As di Leonardo writes: ". . . feminist scholars can investigate both women's and men's differing economic activities and cultural conceptions of gendered labor, both human sexual biology and varying and changing cultural constructions thereof" (1991:31).

4. *All forms of patterned inequality merit analysis, particularly those based on power and economic differentials.* Social differentiation is reflected in patterned constraints of access to resources or being targeted for intervention based on social characteristics such as race, ethnicity, or socioeconomic status. For instance, in some areas of the U.S., poor women delivering their babies at publicly funded hospitals are routinely screened for drug use. If the screens turn out positive, the women may have their babies taken away from them and the women may be sent to jail. Women delivering their babies in nonpublicly funded hospitals are not routinely screened for drugs and therefore are much less likely to lose their babies and be sent to jail (Whiteford and Vitucci 1993, 1994). In addition to investigating the conditions underlying such differential treatment, di Leonardo reminds us that part of the embeddedness of gender is that women's social roles (and men's as well) cannot be analyzed solely in reference to attributes of the actors, for instance being "female," "Southern," or "working class." Analysis needs to locate actors in the intersections of class, race, ethnicity, and gender that reflect the complexity of social life.

5. *Feminist anthropologists need to remember and investigate the conceptual lenses that shape our consciousness.* Di Leonardo reminds us that we must remain aware of how our own thinking is shaped by those very social and cultural forces that influenced previous paradigms. Researchers must keep themselves actively centered in a self-reflective and critical mode of analysis, and be aware that they are not immune to the social vagaries and vogues that shape the professions. Just as Donna Haraway's (1988) work uncovered and made public some of the gender and cultural biases behind Washburn's "Man-the Hunter" evolutionary model, the consciousness of contemporary influences on our thinking needs to be recognized and revealed as well.

To summarize, the combination of feminism, cultural analysis, and political economy seeks to situate both the researcher and the research within historically specific forms of social relations. It attempts to investigate male-female power relations as socially contextualized expressions, and to give individual actors a voice while locating them in the larger global system. If that were not complicated enough, to our discussion we will add one more conceptual dimension to the mix: health.

ANTHROPOLOGICAL POLITICAL ECONOMY AND HEALTH

Several trends in medical anthropology converged during the late 1970s and early 1980s that provided an impetus to the increased interest in the political economy of health. By 1987, research in political economy and medical anthropology was sufficiently underway to warrant the following definition of political economy of health:

> ... a macroanalytical, critical, and historical perspective for analyzing disease distribution and health services under a variety of economic systems, with particular emphasis on the effects of stratified social, political, and economic relations within the world economic system. (Morgan 1987:132)

This macroanalytical, critical, and historical perspective grew out of several trends in the discipline: 1) a resurgence of interest in Marxism as a reaction to the failures of modernization theories of development; 2) a self-conscious and self-critical analysis of biomedical systems as a reaction to a perceived uncritical acceptance of such systems; and 3) an application of a global world systems approach as a response to the perceived inadequacy of studying medical systems in isolation (Baer 1982; Morgan 1987; Morsy 1990; Singer 1989; Whiteford 1990). Out of these dissatisfactions with the existing analytic modes in medical anthropology came the political economy of medical anthropology (PEMA) (Morsy 1979), and its sibling, critical medical anthropology (CMA) (Baer et al. 1986; Singer 1986; Donahue 1986; Singer 1989).[2] Both Morsy (1990) and Singer (1989) have written excellent historical reviews of the developments of both the Political Economy of Medical Anthropology and Critical Medical Anthropology. I will not repeat those discussions here. Instead, I will highlight some of the concepts salient for this particular discussion of gender and the social production of health.

Vincente Navarro, whose writings have been central to the development of both PEMA and CMA, echoed Virchow's writings from 100 years earlier when he wrote about the social production of health and the class-based control of resources that result in differentially distributed access to basic necessities as well as to health care. According to Navarro, "... the major cause of death and disease in the poor parts of the world today in which the majority of the human race lives is not a scarcity of resources, nor the process of industrialization, nor even the much heralded population explosion but, rather, a pattern of control over the resources of those countries in which the majority of the population has no control over those resources" (1974:7). Navarro's writings are used by proponents of PEMA and CMA. Both perspectives acknowledge the social production of health by focusing attention not only on individuals, but on relations between social categories (like classes), and social institutions (like the state). In addition, the role of the individual as a member of a socially constituted group is viewed in the larger context of the state as part of an interconnected global system. An explicit aim of both PEMA and CMA is to use a wide-angle lens to capture the complexity of human behavior in its global interconnectedness. Therefore, in both PEMA and CMA the macrolevel focus is seen as an antidote to earlier medical ethnographers' penchant for ethnomedical detail. According to the political-economic view, human behavior is shaped both by individual and local-level constraints and abilities, but also by the larger social factors that may restrict or provide access to critical resources. Analysis of those larger social factors is, therefore, critical to understanding human responses and resultant behaviors.

Analysis of gender and political economy as applied to the social production of health focuses our attention on the variables di Leonardo discussed, but in the context of health and health care. Instead of simply asking how women are treated in various health-care systems (a valuable question in itself), a political economy orientation seeks to understand the history of the social relations that give rise to particular gender roles and to relations between groups and the state, and among social classes. The following case study shows how the political economic perspective allows the researcher to focus attention on patterned inequality, and male-female power differentials contextualized within specific beliefs about ethnicity and gender roles, while providing identity to the individual in a discussion of the social production of health or, as in this case, the social discrimination of health access.

CASE STUDY: DEIDRE

In 1990 we began interviewing women immediately postpartum in a large, publicly funded hospital in an urban center on the west coast of Florida (Whiteford and Vitucci 1990, 1993, 1994). We wanted women's opinions about a Florida statute that made it possible for the state to jail women and take their babies if the women were known to be drug users. In 1987 Florida was the first state to jail women who delivered babies with positive postpartum drug screens at public hospitals. Initially, we asked women what they thought of the law and how it affected their behavior. However, as the research continued, our focus became more directed toward the differential applications of the law and how the law reflected, maintained, and even extended sexist, racist, and classist attitudes about women. What began as a descriptive study of barriers to prenatal care evolved into a critical analysis of some of the cultural, political, and economic assumptions underlying the statute and its enforcement.

In Florida, pregnant women can be jailed, putatively to "protect the fetus from damage," if the mother can be proved to have used certain drugs during pregnancy. Women sent to jail were denied prenatal care and addiction treatment. Rarely does an incarceration facility provide prenatal or addiction treatment to its inmates. In addition to the lack of treatment, incarcerated women were separated from their existing children. The women we spoke to said that this would not make women give up their addictions, but that addicted pregnant women would avoid prenatal care and try to give birth at home rather than risk the prosecution that might result if they were to seek prenatal care or deliver their babies at public hospitals. Far from protecting the fetus, the effect of the law is to put both fetus and mother at greater risk.

"Pregnancy" and "addiction" are each value-laden terms weighted by their sociocultural and biological identities. Each reflects the social construction of its associated ideal behaviors. However, in reality, pregnancy rarely reflects the ideals promulgated through the public media. Few women have the luxuries of time and money to spend on extensive preparation for a baby; nor does the state facilitate that preparation with family-leave programs or effective job guarantees following a pregnancy-related leave of absence. Similarly, addiction is a value-laden term incorporating both biological and cultural connotations. Without doubt drug addiction is a costly problem in contemporary society, yet little concerted effort has been made to remove the underlying social conditions that provide such a powerful environment for addiction, nor are therapeutic interventions easily available to the people most in need. Our analysis (using a political economy perspective) concluded that laws that jail pregnant women for their addictions are less about protecting the unborn than they are about punishing women for being poor, pregnant, and addicted in a society that denigrates each of those conditions. Using the following case study, we attempt to show how a political economy perspective applied to the social construction of health extends and enriches the analysis.

In 1987, Florida expanded its child abuse statute to include drug dependent newborns and, shortly thereafter, a judge on the west coast of Florida began enforcing the statute by incarcerating pregnant addicts (Whiteford and Vitucci 1993). Since then women in Colorado, California, Illinois, Kentucky, and Florida have been charged with giving drugs to their newborns. Under the Florida statute a physically dependent newborn is defined as an infant under 28 days of age with documented evidence that the mother used drugs during pregnancy, including admission by the mother of drug use during pregnancy, a positive maternal drug screen during pregnancy or the early postpartum period, or a positive newborn drug screen (Connolly and Marshall 1989).

"[T]he war on drugs has degenerated into a war on women" (Alan Rapoport quoted by Jan Hoffman 1990:35). The Rapoport quote highlights that women have been unequally targeted for judicial intervention because of their sex (and concomitant gender roles). Women are not the only unstated target of the attempt to remove the external manifestation of a disenfranchised population; whole categories of people bear the brunt of the war on drugs—African Americans, the poor, peasants in developing nations, as well as women. A characteristic of each category is the members' relative powerlessness. In the case of the pregnant addicts statute in Florida, the population most at risk—poor, pregnant, minority women already in the public health care system—are most powerless and vulnerable to state intervention. That this statute unfairly targets one population based on its sex is clear. We argue that it also unfairly targets women based on ethnicity, class, and powerlessness.

"While actual drug use is not higher among pregnant minority women," says

Ira Chasnoff, "they are ten times more likely than white women to be reported to child abuse authorities. . . . In this country, our two-tiered health care system allows inconsistency in reporting drug abuse. In Pinellas County [Florida], black women were also ten times more likely to be reported for [drug] abuse than white women, although white women were more likely to have used [drugs] prior to their first physician visit" (Vitucci 1993:19; Chasnoff 1990).

One way in which class bias translates into artificially elevated incarceration rates is through the unequal enforcement of routine drug screens. In Florida, for instance, only women delivering their babies at publicly funded hospitals are routinely screened for drug use. Private patients who see physicians outside of public hospitals are not routinely screened for drugs. One private physician admitted that he did not screen his private clients. "If I tested my patients for drugs, I would lose these women from my practice, and you can't run a business like that" (Vitucci 1993:20). Therefore, a social class bias against poor women who cannot afford private physicians becomes translated through the unequal enforcement of state regulations into a process that not only denies women access to preventive or therapeutic care, but also penalizes women by separating them from their children.

Although the American Medical Association defines chemical addiction as a disease, the social construction of gender roles blames women for their addiction during pregnancy and labels them "bad mothers." By focusing on pregnant women who use drugs, policy makers and the public have found a convenient scapegoat to blame, and thus avoid tackling the larger issues such as the effects of racism, classism, and sexism on members of our society. Deidre's[3] case exemplifies the unique perspective to be gained by situating the actor in the larger context of Deidre's life and its lack of access to treatment programs, funding, transportation and child care, and power relations between men and women where men are more often the policymakers, law enforcement officers, and judges.

The historical context of the struggle for women's rights, civil rights, and the rights of African Americans in particular, provides critical background for the power struggle of various groups that plays out in the creation and enforcement of the Florida statute. As Susan Faludi wrote in her book, *Backlash: The Undeclared War Against American Women* (1991), the 1980s epitomized an insidious, all-encompassing attack on women's rights—their right to work, their right to break out of stereotypical gender roles, and their rights to their own bodies (Whiteford and Poland 1989). At the same time, hard-won civil-rights victories engendered a backlash among nonminority members who believed that opportunities were being unfairly denied them. Therefore, both women and minorities experienced an increase in assaults and abuses against their social identities during this time. During the same period, the restructuring of federal funds for community mental health programs restricted access to community-based drug rehabilitation programs. The backlash against women and minorities, and the loss of community-based drug programs, combined to create a politically dangerous situation for addicted, pregnant minority women—the very women most affected by the Florida statute.

As Morgan's definition of political economy suggests, it is a "macroanalytical, critical, and historical perspective" (1987:132), but as we will see in Deidre's case, it also tries to present the individual within those macrolevel constraints. When Deidre was first interviewed she was 19 years old, already the mother of three and soon to be the mother of her fourth child. Her first child tested positive for cocaine at birth and was removed from Deidre's custody. The child was given to Deidre's mother. Deidre became pregnant again, but could not afford an abortion. Knowing that crack cocaine might cause her to abort, she used crack cocaine. But instead of aborting the fetus she delivered a premature infant who tested positive for cocaine.

Deidre was reported to the state in the form of the Health and Rehabilitative Services (HRS) hotline. The judge ordered Deidre to comply with drug treatment or lose custody of her child. A local drug-treatment center evaluated Deidre and recommended a 24-month residential program; however, there were no openings available for Deidre. The first available opening was six months in the future. Deidre complied, waited six months, and entered the drug-treatment program. Her child went to foster care. Deidre left the treatment center after three months and her child went to three different foster homes in the subsequent three years because she was not able to get him back.

Deidre got pregnant again. Still using drugs and fearing that HRS would take away her next child, she did not come in for prenatal care. But by her sixth month of pregnancy, she found herself in jail for shoplifting. The judge ruled that to protect her unborn child, Deidre should finish her pregnancy in jail. In jail she received neither addiction counseling nor prenatal care. She was, however, able to secure cocaine by trading cigarettes. The judge made drug treatment a condition of her probation, so eventually Deidre began drug treatment in a day-treatment program. The day-treatment program, however, provided neither child care nor transportation and Deidre was unable to find people to look after her child, so she dropped out of the program. That was in violation of her parole and the judge ordered her jailed, and her son placed with his paternal grandmother.

Pregnant again, Deidre requested drug treatment. She was able to get into a 28-day residential treatment center; however, having lost custody of her child, she was no longer eligible for Medicaid and so could not pay for the drug-treatment program. Pregnant with her fourth child, addicted, and wanting drug treatment, Deidre had to leave the treatment program. All too often, case studies end here because the woman is lost to the researcher. But in Deidre's case, the unexpected happened. She found a halfway house for pregnant and mothering women, and was finally able to get the help she needed to become free of drugs.

Deidre's case illustrates how gender, economics, and the historical construction of relations based on class and race unequally target poor African-American women for incarceration, while simultaneously reducing their access to treatment and their access to their own children.

The clearest effect of the Florida pregnant women and drugs law is to keep women out of prenatal care. In our interviews, women repeatedly said that they thought that Florida's law would not stop pregnant women from using drugs, but it would keep them from getting involved in the public health system and prenatal care. "Women will just have their babies at home or on the street." "Women will be scared they'll get caught, and they won't come [for prenatal care]." "The law probably won't stop pregnant women from taking drugs because drugs are more important to them." Women we interviewed said that women's fear of discovery would force them to deliver their babies alone, outside of the hospitals and the reach of HRS, but it wouldn't stop addicted women from taking drugs. The one thing that jailing pregnant women teaches other women is to stay away from the public health care system. Seventy-eight percent of the women we interviewed believed the Florida drug law would keep women out of the public health care system.

A second effect of the law is to isolate poor women, particularly those dependent on public facilities, from other women, and to reify their second-class citizen status. Using a public health care system as a mechanism to ensnare poor women, coerce them into treatment, and remove their children from them is to create a Dickensian welfare system designed not to support the rights of individuals, but to maintain the power of the state.

Such a system not only separates women by socioeconomic class, but also separates women from their children. "Prosecutors maintain that they are simply protecting children. But defense attorneys retort that law-enforcement officials are forcing a wedge between mother and child, making the relationship adversarial—"fetal rights" versus "maternal rights." Their interests should instead be seen as joined" (Hoffman 1990:35).

Targeting drug users shows a racist and classist orientation. It is significant to note that alcohol, the drug of choice for many European-American middle-class women, is specifically excluded from the Florida bill, regardless of the indicting literature concerning fetal-alcohol syndrome.

The intervention of the state during pregnancy is seen by some to abrogate the constitutional right to privacy and "turns pregnant users into second-class citizens, deprived of equal protection" (Hoffman 1990:35). The question of sexual bias also cannot be ignored. Lynn Paltrow of the A.C.L.U. suggests that pregnant women should be arrested for possession or use just the same as a man should be arrested. However, Paltrow says that women are instead being prosecuted for the crime of becoming pregnant while they are addicted (Hoffman 1990:44).

But perhaps the most dangerous aspect of the Florida statute is that it diverts our attention from the social ills that make crack cocaine so appealing to some. Making criminals of pregnant women who are addicted effectively reframes who they are in society's view. They become, like the women in Anna Tsing's "monster stories" (Ginsburg and Tsing 1990), symbolic of behavior that is irrational and out of the ordinary. The real crime is that, for far too many women, addiction is part of ordinary, everyday life.

CONCLUSION

Analysis of Deidre's case using a political economy perspective reframes the issues by situating the actor in the social construction of gender, race, and class categories. It changes our perspective of power and powerlessness by placing the actions of individual actors in their larger context and by showing the differential and unequal application of the law.

Another excellent and much more extended example of this combination of political economy, gender, and health can be found in Soheir Morsy's book, *Gender, Sickness, and Healing in Rural Egypt* (1993). With great attention to detail, Morsy provides the national context from nineteenth-century Egypt to the present, situating not only the cultural contexts of gender roles, but also the power of history as a driving force constructing those cultural contexts. ". . . [M]edical knowledge, illness experience, social legitimation of sickness and healing are addressed as sociocultural mechanisms which inform the reproduction of power relations, notable gender-linked differentiation" (Morsy 1993:6). The investigation of fundamental power relations is central to any political economic perspective. In a provocative review written by Morsy in 1979, she argued that medical anthropologists were maintaining the artificial position of ethical neutrality by ignoring analysis of power relations by studying cognition and social roles as though they were ahistorical and apolitical social creations (1979:349–363). The political economy perspective attempts to overcome that myopia.

Gender is a particularly significant type of power relationship. Its significance draws in part from the fact that it cross-cuts all other categories of relationships. That is, gender relations exist in peasant and capitalist societies, in the East and the West, and in simple and complex societies. Gender relations are always constructed to reflect the cultural values of the society. An example of research utilizing the political-economic gaze in medical anthropology, which focuses on power relations between patients and practitioners, can be found in Ellen Lazarus' work (1988, 1990, 1994). Lazarus demonstrated a set of contradictions with her analysis of an OB-GYN clinic in the Midwest. The contradictions she found mirrored societal attitudes about women and the role gender played in determining social relations between patients and their physicians. She found that the power differential between physicians and the patients they saw echoed the gender, racial, and class hierarchies of the profession; that residents' training focused on biomedical explanations and not patient care; that clinic organization and division of labor reflected provider specialization and mitigated against the patient being seen as a whole person with interrelated, mutually effecting systems; and that pregnant women patients, especially those from lower socioeconomic status, felt deserted by the very practitioners they had come to see (1990).

But even with the Morsy and Lazarus work incorporating gender into the political economy of health in medical anthropology, gender has not been a primary focus for most of the work using a political-economic perspective, except in the area of reproduction. The greatest amount of work on gender in medical anthropology has been in the area of reproduction—where feminist analysis has produced seminal works, such as Emily Martin's *Woman in the Body* (1987); Faye Ginsburg and Anna Lowenhaupt Tsing's *Uncertain Terms: Negotiating Gender in American Culture* (1990); and Lewin and Oleson's *Women, Health and Healing: Toward a New Perspective* (1985). Since the 1970s, the thinking and research in the area of the cultural construction of reproduction has been exciting and provoca-tive, incorporating a wide variety of perspectives in innovative and often chal-lenging ways. Two other stimulating and provocative reviews to which the readers are referred are the chapter by Browner and Sargent in the Johnson and Sargent book, *Medical Anthropology: A Handbook of Theory and Method* (1990), and the review article written by Ginsburg and Rapp for the *Annual Reviews in Anthropol-ogy* (1991). In addition, Carole Browner successfully incorporated an analysis of gender, health, and social class in her article "Women, Household and Health in Latin America" (1989), and Brooke Schoepf explicitly draws on a political-eco-nomic analysis of health and gender in her work on AIDS in Central Africa (Schoepf 1991; Schoepf, Rukarangira, et al. 1988; Schoepf, Walu, et al. 1991).

Feminist scholars have approached the topic of reproduction from a variety of perspectives. From outside of anthropology, scholars such as Arditti et al. (1984), Corea (1985), Treichler (1990), and Fee (1983) have taken gender as a primary variable to be considered in understanding the provision of health care to women. Within anthropology, analysis of class and race come together in works by Karen Sacks (1989, 1974), gender and health in Patricia Whelan's work on women and international health (1988); class, gender, and health in Rayna Rapp's work on amniocentesis (1993); gender and the cultural construction of infertility in the work of Whiteford and Gonzalez (1994); and class, capitalism, and health in research by Ida Susser (1985). However, given the remarkable amount of scholarly activity occurring on any two of the three topics, there seems to be a relatively small amount of work devoted to the in-depth intellectual dis-cussion of the intersection between political economy, gender, and health.

Given the popularity and interest in the work written from both the critical medical anthropology (CMA) perspective, and that of political economy in med-ical anthropology (PEMA), the question that must be asked is why so little has been written using gender as a primary focus? Perhaps because both PEMA and CMA have been busy defining and legitimating their points of view, they have not more explicitly focused on gender. Equally likely, however, is the fact that class, not gender, is a primary organizing principle for many political economists/crit-ical medical anthropologists. In review articles by Singer (1993, 1990, 1989, 1986), Morsy (1979), and Morgan (1987) dealing with political economy in med-ical anthropology/critical medical anthropology, little appears about gender as an explicit conceptual principle. CMA has been defined by Singer as focusing on "health issues in light of the larger political and economic forces that pattern human relationships, shape social behavior, and condition collective experience, including forces of institutional, national, and global scale" (1986:128). When listing the major contributions of CMA, Singer lists the following areas: exami-nation of the social origins of disease and ill health in light of the world eco-nomic system; analysis of health policy, health resource allocation, and the role of the State in Third-World nations; reconceptualization of contemporary under-standings of medical pluralism; attention to the role of conflict in health and health care; reexamination of the microlevel of the individual, including illness behavior and illness experience, within the context of macrolevel structures, processes, and relations; and the investigation of health and health programs in capitalist-oriented countries (1989:1196). Nowhere is gender mentioned. That is not to suggest that anthropologists employing the CMA or PEMA orientation are blind to the effects of gender on the topics they research. They are not; it is simply a fact that gender is rarely conceptualized as being pivotal.

What we have then is an intriguing lacuna between medical anthropology, political economy, and gender, with a great deal of very fruitful research focusing on gender from a political and economic framework, but not in medical anthropology. Simultaneously, a rich body of work has been generated on the social production of health using gender as a major component, but not necessarily relying on a political-economic perspective. As our analysis of Deidre's case shows, gender and its associated social roles are critical to our understanding of the political and economic constraints of Deidre's life. Gender roles influenced Deidre's decision to get pregnant, just as the results of her pregnancies were both constraints on her ability to get into treatment and a prime motivation to successfully get treatment. To understand the Florida statute and its effect on women, the analysis must situate the players in their cultural, political, and economic history, must recognize the socially constructed as well as biological nature of pregnancy and addiction, and must incorporate an analysis of the effect of gender roles. In the future, perhaps more medical anthropologists using a political-economy perspective will focus on gender and its role in the social production of health and illness.

NOTES

1. See the next chapter of this volume, written by Carole H. Browner and Joanne Leslie, for a review of some of those studies.
2. Critical medical anthropology (CMA) and the political economy of anthropology (PEMA) are both based on a political and economic analysis of health and illness. There are significant similarities between the two perspectives. In this chapter, they will be referred to interchangeably.
3. All names are pseudonyms.

REFERENCES

Arditti, Rita, Renate Duelli Klein, and Shelly Minden, eds.
  1984   Test-Tube Women: What Future for Motherhood? Boston: Pandora Press.
Babb, Florence E.
  1989   Between Field and Cooking Pot: The Political Economy of Marketwomen in Peru. Austin: University of Texas Press.
Baer, Hans A.
  1982   On the Political Economy of Health. Medical Anthropology Newsletter 14(1):1–2, 13–17.

Baer, Hans A., Merrill Singer, and John H. Johnsen
  1986   Introduction: Toward a Critical Medical Anthropology. Social Science and Medicine 23(2):95–98.

Brown, Susan
  1975   Love Unites Them and Hunger Separates Them: Poor Women in the Dominican Republic. *In* Toward an Anthropology of Women. Rayna Reiter, ed. Pp. 322–332. New York: Monthly Review Press.

Browner, Carole H.
  1989   Women, Household and Health in Latin America. Social Science and Medicine 28(5):461–473.

Chaney, Elsa M.
  1976   Women at the "Marginal Pole" of Economy in Lima, Peru. Paper presented at the Conference on Women and Development, Wellesley College, June 4, 1976.

Chaney, Elsa M., and Mary Garcia Castro, eds.
  1989   Muchachas No More: Household Workers in Latin America and the Caribbean. Philadelphia: Temple University Press.

Chasnoff, Ira J.
  1990   The Prevalence of Illicit Drug or Alcohol Use During Pregnancy and Discrepancies in Mandatory Reporting in Pinellas County, Florida. The New England Journal of Medicine 322(17):1202–1207.

Clark, Barry
  1991   Political Economy: A Comparative Economy. Westport, CT: Praeger Publishers.

Collier, Jane
  1974   Women in Politics. *In* Women, Culture, and Society. Michelle Rosaldo and Louise Lamphere, eds. Pp. 89–96. Palo Alto, CA: Stanford University Press.

Connolly, W., and A. Marshall
  1989   Drug Addiction, Pregnancy, and Childbirth: Legal Issues for the Medical and Social Service Communities. Unpublished manuscript.

Corea, Gena
  1985   The Mother Machine. New York: Harper and Row.

DeWalt, Billie R., and Pertti J. Pelto
  1985   Micro and Macro Levels of Analysis in Anthropology. Boulder, CO: Westview Press.

di Leonardo, Micaela
  1991   Introduction: Gender, Culture, and Political Economy: Feminist Anthropology in Historical Perspective. *In* Gender at the Crossroads of Knowledge: Feminist Anthropology in the Postmodern Era. Micaela di Leonardo, ed. Pp. 1–48. Berkeley and Los Angeles: University of California Press.

Donahue, John M.
  1986   Planning for Primary Health Care in Nicaragua: A Study in Revolutionary Process. Social Science and Medicine 23(2):149–157.

Etienne, Mona, and Eleanor Leacock, eds.
  1980   Women and Colonization: Anthropological Perspectives. New York: Praeger Publishers.

Faludi, Susan
  1991   Backlash: The Undeclared War against American Women. New York: Crown Publishers.

Fee, Elizabeth, ed.
  1983   Women and Health: The Politics of Sex in Medicine. Farmingdale, NY: Baywood Publishing Company, Inc.

Fernandez-Kelly, Maria Patricia
1984   Maquiladoras: The View from the Inside. *In* My Troubles Are Going to Have Trouble with Me. Karen Sacks, ed. New Brunswick, NJ: Rutgers University Press.

Finkler, Kaja
1986   The Social Consequences of Wellness: A View of Healing Outcomes from Micro and Macro Perspectives. International Journal of Health Services 16(4):627–642.
1994   Women in Pain: Gender and Morbidity in Mexico. Philadelphia: University of Pennsylvania Press.

Foster, George, and Barbara Anderson
1978   Medical Anthropology. New York: John Wiley and Sons, Publishers.

Ginsburg, Faye, and Anna Lowenhaupt Tsing, eds.
1990   Uncertain Terms: Negotiating Gender in American Culture. Boston: Beacon Press.

Ginsburg, Faye, and Rayna Rapp
1991   The Politics of Reproduction. Annual Review of Anthropology 20:311–343.

Haraway, Donna
1988   Remodeling the Human Way of Life. *In* Bones, Bodies, Behavior: History of Anthropology, Volume I, G. W. Stocking, ed. Madison: University of Wisconsin Press.

Hoffman, Jan
1990   Pregnant, Addicted—and Guilty? New York Times Magazine, August 19:32.

Johnson, Thomas M., and Carolyn F. Sargent, eds.
1990   Medical Anthropology: A Handbook of Theory and Method. New York: Greenwood Press.

Lazarus, Ellen S.
1988   Theoretical Considerations for the Study of the Doctor-Patient Relationship: Implications of a Perinatal Study. Medical Anthropology 2:34–58.
1990   Falling through the Cracks: Contradictions and Barriers to Care in a Prenatal Clinic. Medical Anthropology 12:269–287.
1994   What Do Women Want?: Issues of Choice, Control, and Class in Pregnancy and Childbirth. Medical Anthropology Quarterly 8(1):25–46.

Leacock, Eleanor
1972   "Introduction." *In* The Origin of the Family, Private Property and the State, by Frederick Engels (1884). New York: International Publishers.
1981   Myths of Male Dominance: Collected Articles. New York: Monthly Review Press.

Lewin, Ellen, and Virginia Olesen, eds.
1985   Women, Health and Healing: Toward a New Perspective. New York: Tavistock Publications.

Martin, Emily
1987   The Woman in the Body. Boston: Beacon Press.

Mintz, Sidney
1985   Sweetness and Power: The Place of Sugar in Modern History. New York: Viking.

Morgan, Lynn
1987   Dependency Theory in the Political Economy of Health: An Anthropological Critique. Medical Anthropology Quarterly 1(2):131–153.

Morsy, Soheir
1979   The Missing Link in Medical Anthropology: The Political Economy of Health. Reviews in Anthropology 23:349–363.

1990   Political Economy in Medical Anthropology. *In* Medical Anthropology: Contemporary Theory and Method. Thomas M. Johnson and Carolyn F. Sargent, eds. Pp. 26–46. New York: Greenwood Press.

1993   Gender, Sickness, and Healing in Rural Egypt: Ethnography in Historical Context. Boulder, CO, San Francisco, and Oxford: Westview Press.

Navarro, Vincente
1974   Imperialism, Health and Medicine. Farmingdale, NY: Baywood Publishing Company, Inc.

Pappas, Greg
1993   Personal Communication.

Rapp, Rayna
1993   Accounting for Amniocentesis. *In* Knowledge, Power, and Practice. Shirley Lindenbaum and Margaret Lock, eds. Pp. 55–78. Berkeley, Los Angeles and London: University of California Press.

Roseberry, William
1988   Political Economy. Annual Reviews in Anthropology 17:161–185.

Rubbo, Anna
1975   The Spread of Capitalism in Rural Colombia: Effects on Poor Women. *In* Toward an Anthropology of Women. Rayna Reiter, ed. Pp. 333–357. New York: Monthly Review Press.

Sacks, Karen
1974   Engels Revisited: Women, the Organization of Production, and Private Property. *In* Women, Culture, and Society. Michelle Rosaldo and Louise Lamphere, eds. Pp. 207–222. Palo Alto, CA: Stanford University Press.

1989   Toward a Unified Theory of Class, Race and Gender. American Ethnologist 16(3):534–550.

Safa, Helen I.
1980   Class Consciousness among Working-Class Women in Latin America: Puerto Rico. *In* Caribbean and Latin Immigrants to the United States: The Female Experience. June Nash and Helen I. Safa, eds. New York: Bergin and Garvey.

1983   Women, Production and Reproduction in Industrial Capitalism: A Comparison of Brazilian and U.S. Factory Workers. *In* Woman, Men, and the International Division of Labor. June Nash and M. Patricia Fernandez-Kelly, eds. Albany: State University of New York Press.

Schoepf, B. G.
1991   Ethical, Methodological and Political Issues of AIDS Research in Central Africa. Social Science and Medicine 33: 749–763.

Schoepf, B. G., W. N. Rukarangira, C. Schoepf, N. Payanzo, and E. Walu
1988   AIDS and Society in Central Africa: A View from Zaire. *In* AIDS in Africa: Social and Policy Impact. N. Miller and R. Rockwell, eds. Pp. 211–235. Lewiston, NY: Mellon Press.

Schoepf, B. G., E. Walu, W. N. Rukarangira, N. Payanzo, and C. Schoepf
1991   Gender, Power and Risk of AIDS in Central Africa. *In* Women and Health in Africa. M. Turshen, ed. Trenton, NJ: African World Press.

Singer, Merrill
1986   Developing a Critical Perspective in Medical Anthropology. Medical Anthropology Quarterly 17(5):128–129.

1989   The Coming of Age of Critical Medical Anthropology. Social Science and Medicine 28(11):1193–1203.

1990   Reinventing Medical Anthropology: Toward a Critical Realignment. Social Science and Medicine 30(2):179–187.

1993   A Rejoinder to Wiley's Critique of Critical Medical Anthropology. Medical Anthropology Quarterly 7(2):185–191.

Susser, Ida
1985   Union Carbide and the Community Surrounding It: The Case of a Community in Puerto Rico. International Journal of Health Services 15(4):561–583.

Treichler, Paula A.
1990   Feminism, Medicine, and the Meaning of Childbirth. *In* Body/Politics: Women and the Discourse of Science. Mary Jacobus, Evelyn Fox Keller, and Sally Shuttleworth, eds. Pp. 113–138. New York: Routledge & Kegan Paul.

Vitucci, Judi
1993   Cocaine in the Cradle: Punitive Power and Profit in Drug Treatment. Unpublished paper.

Waitzkin, Howard
1981   The Social Origins of Illness: A Neglected History. International Journal of Health Services 11(1):77–103.

Whelan, Patricia
1988   Women and Health: Cross-Cultural Perspectives. South Hadley, MA: Bergin and Garvey.

Whiteford, Linda M.
1990   A Question of Adequacy: Primary Health Care in the Dominican Republic. Social Science and Medicine, 30(2):221–226.

Whiteford, Linda M., and Lois Gonzalez
Infertility and the Social Stigma of Involuntary Childlessness. Unpublished paper.

Whiteford, Linda M., and Marilyn L. Poland, eds.
1989   New Approaches to Human Reproduction: Social and Ethical Dimensions. Boulder, CO and London: Westview Press.

Whiteford, Linda M., and Judi Vitucci
1990   Handcuffs on the Delivery Table . . . Cocaine in the Cradle: Pregnancy, Addiction and Legal Implications. Unpublished paper.
1993   The Criminalization of Motherhood: Law, Policy and Addiction. Paper presented at the 1993 annual meeting of the American Anthropological Association, Washington, DC.
1994   Pregnancy and Addiction: Translating Research into Action. Presented as part of an invited session at the annual meeting of the American Anthropological Association, Atlanta, GA.

Wolf, E.
1982   Europe and the People Without History. Berkeley: University of California Press.

Women, Work, and Household Health in the Context of Development

■ *Carole H. Browner*
Joanne Leslie

Scholars and policymakers seeking to understand the health sector in the developing world generally look to macrolevel factors such as percent of total government expenditure on health, the availability of potable water, the number and distribution of health professionals and hospital beds, and the proportion of the population vaccinated against communicable diseases to explain differences in health status across countries and over time. The focus of such analyses, implicitly or explicitly, is on the role of government programs and public policy as primary determinants of a population's health status. Although the importance of private behavior (and of decisions made at the household and local level) are often acknowledged, they rarely receive the same detailed attention. (See, for example, the recent report from the World Bank, *World Development Report 1993: Investing in Health.*) This has led to a tendency to underestimate the crucial role of women in the production of health (Browner 1989; Leslie, Lycette & Buvinić 1988).

Because women play a major role in both market and nonmarket production, their capacity to participate successfully in development activities (both paid and unpaid) is increasingly being recognized as a necessary precondition for sustained social and economic development. Therefore, scholars and policymakers concerned with understanding and promoting health sector development in particular and economic and social development in general have come to understand that they must be concerned with the roles of women (Bennett 1992; MacCormack 1988).

In the following pages, we look closely at the effects of recent changes in women's activities in developing countries on their own and their children's health. We begin with a broad review of changing patterns of women's work and of linkages between women's work, fertility, and household health. We then present two case studies that illustrate the more general findings, and challenge some common assumptions about the effects of women's economic activities on health-related outcomes.

WOMEN'S CHANGING WORK PATTERNS

Throughout the Third World, workloads are becoming more arduous for many women. The fact that women work is not new; women have always worked. In many parts of the world, most notably in sub-Saharan Africa, woman have a major responsibility for producing the food their families eat. One study conducted by the United Nations reported that at least 50 percent of the world's food—and as much as 80 percent in some rural parts of Africa—is grown by women (Sivard 1985). More recent studies suggest that women may have become even more important participants in food production as a result of men's increased migration. (Again, this appears to be particularly true in Africa [Food and Agriculture Organization 1987 in United Nations 1991].)

At the same time, increasing proportions of women are engaged in income-generating employment. By the most conservative estimates, about 40 percent of women in developing countries are in the labor force, although there are important regional variations. The highest official female labor-force participation rates are reported in East Asia and sub-Saharan Africa (45 percent to 59 percent), while female labor force participation is reported to be 32 percent in Latin America and the Caribbean, and as low as 16 percent in North Africa (United Nations 1991). While this is due in some part to improving educational levels and changing societal mores, the more important cause is declining living standards. In addition, more women work now than ever before because they are increasingly responsible for their families' economic well-being. Women are the sole bread-winners in one-fourth to one-third of the world's families (United Nations 1991). Two-thirds of working women are employed in agricultural work, with industry and services providing the remainder of jobs, in roughly equal proportions.

Indeed, the majority of the world's women continue to have multiple work responsibilities, including child care and household maintenance, market work (which includes agricultural work, self-employment and wage employment), and community support. Recently, however, population growth, environmental degradation, and/or male out-migration have, in many places, made the circumstances in which women work even more difficult. A study in rural Kenya, for example, found that agricultural marginalization and environmental degradation was increasing the work burdens of women of reproductive age more than those of other members of the household, with measurable negative effects on women's nutritional status and on the prevalence of chronic disability (Ferguson 1986).

WOMEN, WORK, AND PERSONAL HEALTH

Women in developing countries tend to hold low-wage, low-status occupations because their educational attainment tends to be lower than men's and because cultural biases restrict their employment opportunities. Equally important, however, may be their attempts to balance household and market production responsibilities by holding jobs that, while not well paid, allow flexible hours or permit them to bring along their children (Birdsall and McGreevey 1983). As poor women's economic responsibilities increase, they generally work longer hours while continuing to engage in household production activities. They appear not to trade off one activity for another, but instead give up recreation and devote less time to sleep, rest, and relaxation (Leslie, Lycette, and Buvinić 1988).

Women's health and nutritional status influences, and is in turn influenced by, these multiple roles in a number of important ways. With regard to household production, a woman's health and nutritional status directly influence her ability to conceive, give birth, and breast-feed, as well as her infant's health at birth and nutritional status (Leslie 1991). With regard to market production, a woman's physical capacity to produce food and/or generate income is directly affected by her own health and nutritional status (Leslie 1991). Competing demands on a woman's time for household versus market production may constrain her ability to protect and promote her own and her family's health (Leslie 1989b). For some poor women, the demands of their multiple roles require more energy than their food intake provides, leading to further deteriorating health and malnutrition. (International Center for Research on Women 1989).

Household Maintenance and Production Activities

Women are vital to maintaining the household economy and their family's health. Throughout the developing world, women work longer hours than men, and the poorer the country, the more hours women work. Most spend from ten to sixteen hours a day preparing food, doing housework, and caring for children (Fagley 1976; Khander 1988; McSweeney 1979; Mueller 1984; Nag, White, and Peet 1978). Women's other household maintenance activities include preventive health care and nursing sick family members. (For instance, this may involve preparation of special foods and herbal remedies, as well as seeking out medical treatment.) In developing countries, women's household activities create specific hazards. The relentless physical demands associated with the provision of firewood and water make these tasks particularly strenuous, demanding, and exhausting. There are obvious short-term physical effects, such as fatigue and painful legs, hips, and shoulders. Medical reports also document that carrying heavy loads such as firewood or large containers of water can lead to a prolapsed uterus (Prabha 1983); may cause spinal or pelvic damage (Stinson 1986); and is associated with menstrual disorders, miscarriage, and stillbirth (National Commission on Self-Employed Women 1988).

Women's household activities can also expose them to waterborne diseases such as schistosomiasis, onchocerciasis, and malaria. There are, moreover, specific risks associated with the use of open stoves or cooking fires, including burns and smoke pollution (ICRW 1989). Women's work in subsistence agriculture creates other health risks. Many activities such as weeding, transplanting, threshing, and postharvest processing require long hours of effort in uncomfortable positions, which can lead to chronic back and leg problems.

Market Production Activities

In addition to their household maintenance and production activities, many women engage in market production. These market activities are associated with health risks of their own. For instance, the technologies associated with the production of high-value cash crops such as flowers, fruits, and vegetables for export involve exposure to toxic pesticides (WHO 1994), which can negatively affect women's health and also that of their fetuses or breast-fed infants.

Two significant areas of women's informal sector employment are domestic service and piecework in cottage industries. Both kinds of work require long, continuous hours and often involve much repetition and little variety, with extreme fatigue and stress a frequent result. In addition, in cottage industries, the pressure to produce a large enough output to ensure an adequate income may induce women to continue working after dark, even when lighting is inadequate, which can lead to visual impairments (Chatterjee 1987; Mies 1981; Tripattri, et al. 1986).

Although formal-sector employment is associated with better pay, benefits, and job security, several studies of women's employment in factories and processing plants have raised concern about workers' health and safety due to: long shifts; the fast pace and intensity of monotonous and repetitive work; and possible exposure to carcinogenic acids, solvents, and gasses (IRCW 1989; National Commission on Self-Employed Women 1988).

WOMEN'S WORK AND FERTILITY BEHAVIOR

Women's work patterns in developing countries have also come under scrutiny in an effort to understand worldwide fertility patterns and how changes in fertility might affect women's health. The central hypothesis, initially developed in industrialized countries and generalized to developing ones, postulated an inverse relationship between women's labor-force participation and their fertility behavior (Leslie and Buvinić 1989). This hypothesis was based on an assumed incompatibility between women's employment and their childbearing and childrearing activities.

Extensive empirical research revealed a far more complex picture (Doan and Popkin 1993; Okpala 1989). While the hypothesis has generally been supported in industrialized settings, the relationship is much more variable in developing countries, and often the opposite of the original prediction. One factor that could explain these unexpected results is the relative lack of conflict in developing countries between women's roles as workers and as mothers. Some, in fact, have argued that the idea that women's labor-force participation and their reproductive and child-care activities are incompatible was derived from an ethnocentric Western model that does not apply to traditional and/or rural-based economies where women's work and child-care activities have always been combined.

WOMEN'S WORK AND CHILD HEALTH

Many studies demonstrate a positive relationship between increases in household income and children's well being. A number of studies have shown that increases in income produced or controlled by women are particularly important in improving child health and nutrition status (Engle 1993; von Braun 1989). This is in part because women's income routinely covers children's medicines and because women's savings are critical for medical emergencies. It is also because women seem to have a greater propensity to purchase high-quality, nutritionally valuable foods such as eggs, fruits, and meat. The positive effect of women's employment on children's health and welfare is not offset by negative effects of reduced child-care time by working mothers or the substitution of older siblings in child care to nearly the extent that has been assumed. (See Leslie and Paolisso 1989 for several case studies illustrating these relationships.)

An extensive review of the literature on the relationship between women's work and infant-feeding practices and child nutritional status found that women's work did not negatively affect child nutrition in the majority of studies (Leslie 1989a). The only significant difference found between working and nonworking mothers was that mothers who worked away from home began mixed (i. e., bottle and breast) feeding sooner (Leslie 1989a). Two more recently published studies suggest some negative effects of maternal work on child nutritional status (Rabiee and Geissler 1992; Wandel and Holmboe-Ottesen 1992). In both cases, however, the differences in nutritional status were small, and were between women categorized as having light workloads and women categorized as having heavier workloads.

Concerns about the incompatibility between women's work and breastfeeding have tended to focus on modern income-generating activities. However it is interesting to note that a study of time use and child care among Humla mountain women in Nepal who were engaged in subsistence agriculture found a widespread pattern of early introduction of supplementary foods, particularly during the busy agricultural months (Levine 1988). Similar to the findings reported in the Jamaica case study below, early supplementation among the Humla did not lead to early weaning; children were often partially breastfed until the age of three or four. Hence, the requirements of breastfeeding and women's traditional economic activities are not necessarily as compatible as is usually assumed.

Two case studies, one from rural Mexico and the other from periurban Jamaica support the general findings reviewed above on the relationship between women's work and fertility and family health. Each case study focuses on low-income women who are faced with many competing demands on their time and difficult choices as they strive simultaneously to fulfill productive and reproductive roles. At the same time, they illustrate the diversity that is masked by generalizations. In both case studies, we encounter a particular constellation of social and economic factors that influence the relationship between women's work and household health in ways that could be quite different in a different place or at a different time.

CASE STUDY: WOMEN'S WORK AND FERTILITY BEHAVIOR

The nature of the relationship between women's economic activities and their reproductive behavior has interested policymakers, demographers, and social scientists since the close of World War II, when rapid population growth was first viewed as a social problem (Cochrane 1979). Those experts anticipated that industrializing, Third-World countries would follow the same patterns as Europe and America. Demographically, this meant that increased levels of female labor-force participation would be associated with female fertility declines. Yet the following case reveals that, in today's developing countries, the empirical picture can be far more complex. Here we find a group of women who see clear, concrete advantages to reducing their own fertility, yet find that social pressures make it impossible for them to do so.

In an effort to gain some insight into how women's economic activities might shape their reproductive behavior, field data were collected in San Francisco,[1] a community of 1,800 indigenous subsistence cultivators located in highland Oaxaca, Mexico. The data were collected during a 1980–81 year-long field study that combined participant observation with in-depth interviews with 180 women and 126 men. The sample was constructed to represent the age, as well as residential and linguistic backgrounds of San Francisco's adult population (see Browner 1986a, 1986b; Browner and Perdue 1988 for more detail).

As is the case with women elsewhere in indigenous Latin American communities (Bossen 1984; Dole 1974; Harris 1980; Maynard 1974), Franciscanas contribute importantly to their households' subsistence. Women and men expect to share responsibility for the economic maintenance of their households. "They both eat so they both should work," said one man, echoing what his mother had told him long ago.

Women's tasks involve rather strenuous physical activity, including the preparation, and sometimes sale, of tortillas or bread; planting and harvesting crops; agricultural labor for wages; fertilizing, picking, husking, and drying commercial coffee; caring for farm animals; and maintaining stores and/or eating establishments they own. They carry out these tasks in addition to their routine domestic activities such as caring for their children, preparing food, hauling water, doing laundry, and collecting firewood. At least one-third of the women in the San Francisco study also worked for cash, either regularly or sporadically;

another 40 percent had previously done so. Over 80 percent of the women also routinely worked their own fields.

Families rely particularly heavily on women's economic contributions during men's terms of unpaid community service (*cargos*). These terms may total up to six years over the course of a man's adult life. Women commonly initiate cash-producing activities at this time to keep their households out of debt; many are credited with single-handedly maintaining their families during these periods. Women are also accustomed to supervising the activities in their households and ranches for weeks or months at a time without their husbands' help, for couples are often separated due to the varying tasks of the agricultural cycle. Men who live in town must periodically work their distant highland ranches while women remain at home in the town center where their children are required to attend school. The demands of urban wage labor also take some men away from home, often for years at a time. Because the earnings men send back are ordinarily insufficient for their families' subsistence, their wives must contribute to their families' incomes as well.

Franciscanas derive significant gratification and an important sense of self-identity from their economic activities. When asked about the sources of satisfaction in their lives, they rarely mentioned their children although the vast majority were, of course, mothers. Most cited other aspects of their routine that they particularly enjoyed: working with coffee, harvesting crops, the search for firewood, and the like. Both sexes adhere to a strong work ethic. The ability to endure hard work is the most commonly cited criterion by which women in the community earn respect. A woman's laziness or refusal to work may be the most legitimate cause of marital dissolution.

Severe illness is the main thing that keeps Franciscanas from their work. Ordinarily women are active throughout pregnancy and soon after childbirth they resume normal activities. They believe that doing heavy work soon after a birth is likely to damage their health, but most have no help at home and their responsibilities won't wait. Franciscanos of both sexes typically work as usual even when ill, although very high fevers or other disabling symptoms force some to modify their routines. The normal concession to illness is to retire early or arise late. Sometimes herbs or other medicinal substances are ingested or externally applied.

Franciscanas fear illness not only because it makes work more difficult or impossible, but because their recoveries tend to be protracted or uncertain. Nearly one of every three women who suffered postpartum complications (28/96) were sick for six months or more. One in six (18/104) who reported *any* serious illness in their medical histories were still suffering at the time they were interviewed. A great variety of serious chronic disorders were described. These included hernias, menstrual hemorrhaging, breast tumors, liver problems, and seizures.

Their economic indispensability causes Franciscanas to fear any illness that could interfere with their work. Therefore, although most say they already have all the children they want, they adamantly refuse to take the contraceptives available in the town's two health centers. They believe that these remedies would damage their health by causing protracted, possibly incurable or fatal illness.

Franciscanas most often believed that contraceptives would cause excessive menstrual bleeding or hemorrhaging. These symptoms, perceived as dangerous in and of themselves, are also thought to cause weight loss and weakness, which would make it difficult, if not impossible, for women to fulfill their normal responsibilities. The form of contraceptive most widely known in San Francisco, birth control pills, were seen as particularly dangerous because they were very "hot" and therefore liable to upset the body's natural balance, leaving the user more susceptible to the environmental assaults that can bring on disease. Sickness, however, was not the only hazard of contraceptive use the women feared. Some believed the resultant illnesses would be incurable, or that they could not afford to buy the necessary medicines. The understanding in the community is that traditional remedies are ineffective in treating conditions caused by physicians or modern medicine. Costly therapies would be the only hope, they believed, and such therapies were out of the reach of these impoverished peasants.

Although health considerations were usually foremost in women's minds when they talked about work, reproduction, and health, Franciscanas' attitudes about birth control must be interpreted within a broader political context (Browner 1986a). Maintaining a population large enough to sustain the community is a constant source of concern, for San Francisco is chronically beset by out-migration, threats of border incursion, and disease. These factors combine to produce relentless social pressure on Franciscanas to be prolific; in our experience, any who openly sought to limit their fertility were subject to unceasing harsh criticism and ostracism.

It is in these contexts that Franciscanas make decisions about using contraceptives. They expect that illness will result from contraceptive use. They find this unacceptable because although illness handicaps their productivity, work they must, even when sick. Compounding the threat of illness are their own and their neighbors' negative or uncertain experiences with recovery. The difficulties, frustrations, and disappointments they encounter in their quests for cures make Franciscanas extremely reluctant to experiment with medicines they perceive to be dangerous, including contraceptives.

This combination of economic and political pressure has important negative consequences for Franciscanas' health. Of the 180 women interviewed, two-thirds reported at least one health problem following a birth. These ranged from disorders the women considered minor, such as facial swellings and backaches, to more serious problem including prolapsed uterus and uterine hemorrhaging. Emotional complications were reported as well. Women state that the demands of constant childbearing damage not only their reproductive systems but their overall health. Their feelings are objectively based. The data show that, controlling for age, women who had experienced four or more pregnancies were significantly more likely to report both serious illness and minor health conditions including headaches, backaches, breast problems and *coraje* (anger sickness) (Browner 1986a:716).

While some might argue that high fertility among Franciscanas is determined solely by its inherent compatibility with women's domestic responsibilities, we have tried to show that fertility dynamics are both more subtle and more complex. Franciscano fertility patterns are brought about through complex interactions between community dynamics and domestic group needs. The historical pattern favoring high fertility has been intensified as households grow ever more dependent on women's economic contributions with San Francisco's transition toward a market economy. Economic and political forces thus act in concert to prevent women from controlling their own fertility, overpowering many women's strong personal desires for fewer children (Browner 1986a). These data clearly show that accurate generalizations about fertility patterns in developing countries cannot be made without taking local contexts and cultures into account.

CASE STUDY: WOMEN'S WORK AND INFANT FEEDING IN JAMAICA

Policymakers have been concerned that changing maternal work patterns in developing countries may be having detrimental effects on child welfare. In particular, the role of women's employment as a cause of declining rates of breast-feeding has received considerable attention. The following study in Jamaica was undertaken to explore these relationships in a detailed way (for more detailed information on methodology and findings see Powell et al., 1988). The intent was to go beyond the simplistic assumption that where women's labor force participation has increased and breastfeeding has declined the former is necessarily the primary cause of the latter. In fact, this study and others suggest that breastfeeding is a reasonably robust behavior but one that women adapt to fit into other high-priority demands on their time (Winikoff 1986).

The Caribbean region is characterized by historically high fertility levels, a high rate of female labor-force participation, and a high proportion of female-headed households (Sargent & Harris 1992). Jamaica is typical of the region. In 1970 Jamaica had a TFR (total fertility rate) of 5.3, which had fallen to 2.7 by 1991 (World Bank 1993); 68 percent of women were economically active in 1990 (United Nations 1991); and 42 percent of all households were headed by women (Louat, Grosh & van der Gaag 1993). Jamaica is classified by the World Bank among lower-middle-income countries, and its economic growth has essentially been stagnant in recent years (World Bank 1993). Given previously high fertility levels and currently high levels of poverty, it seems safe to say that most women currently of reproductive age in Jamaica have had no choice but to undertake simultaneously the roles of mother and market worker. This is particularly true in the nearly half of Jamaican households that are headed by women.

A one-year longitudinal study of new mothers who were also household heads was carried out in two Jamaican parishes from July 1985 through July 1986. A sample of 150 postpartum women who met the study criteria were selected by continuous sampling from two large public hospitals.[2] The final sample on which analysis was done consisted of 109 mother-child pairs because some individuals had dropped out of the study. Most of the attrition occurred between the time of hospital recruitment and the first household visit because women had given incorrect home addresses in order to be eligible for admission to the hospital. The mothers and infants were visited in their homes five times over a twelve-month period, at which time anthropometric measures were made of the infants to assess their growth, and detailed information was obtained through interviews with the mother concerning infant feeding practices, child care, employment, main sources of economic support, and informal social support networks.

The women in this study were young (average age 26 years), 89 percent were urban residents, and over 80 percent had completed primary school. The most common income-generating activities were higgling (street vending) and domestic work. Other income-generating activities included factory work, farming, and service jobs such as hairdressing, waitressing, and street cleaning. Because of the sample selection criteria, all of the infants began the study in good health, but by the time they reached one year, 11 of 109 (10 percent) had become malnourished.

Because of their pregnancy work patterns and their definition of themselves as the economic head of household, these women were considered to be likely to resume income-generating work during the first year postpartum, and indeed this is what was observed. Twelve of the 109 women were working at six weeks postpartum, 49 at three months, 67 at six months, 61 at nine months and 67 at one year. The majority returned to the same jobs or type of jobs they had had during pregnancy—higgling and domestic work. The higher rate of labor force participation at six months than at nine months was probably attributable to the greater availability of work during the Christmas season.

Somewhat contrary to what might have been expected, given the fact that they had infants under one year of age, most employed women worked away from home and worked long hours. By the three-month visit, over 80 percent of the working women reported spending six hours per day or longer on their income-generating activities. Several women reported working two jobs, and these women worked up to sixteen hours a day. In spite of the long hours and the effort they made to find and keep work, the average income of these Jamaican female heads of household was very low. Approximately one-fourth of the women earned less than $50J per week, which was the minimum wage in 1985, and half earned between $50J and $100J per week.

At any one time during the study, the highest proportion of women working was 61 percent. However, a much higher proportion of the women, 79 percent, were working at some point during the year. Thirty of the 109 women entered and left the labor force at least once during the year and 19 changed occupations one or more times. Only 37 entered the work force and continued for the duration of the year at the same job. The women who showed an intermittent rather than stable work pattern had, on average, less education. They were also less likely to have a partner living with them. In addition, entering and leaving the labor force, or failing to enter at all during the first year postpartum was almost entirely attributable to a lack of job opportunities, rather than a choice to stay home and spend more time in mothering and homemaking activities.

Although all of the women considered themselves to be the economic head of household, during the course of the year about half the women, at any one point in time, had a male partner living with them. This proportion is roughly the same for working and nonworking women, suggesting that the presence of a partner per se is not a major determinant of women's participation in the labor force. However, about half the women cited their partners as being the main economic support of the infant, and in this case, more than twice as many nonworking as working women reported that their partner was the primary economic support of their infant. As may be inferred from the above, there was little correlation between the presence or absence of the partner in the household and the extent to which he was considered to provide the primary economic support for the infant. It is also worth noting that the extent to which partners were reported as the main economic support of the infant declined over the course of the year, as did the frequency with which the father of the baby (who was usually but not always the woman's current partner) was reported as someone to whom the woman could turn when specific needs arose. It is relatively clear that male partners are neither stable nor long-term sources of support in the lives of most of these women.

As is the case throughout urbanized parts of the developing world, the predominant pattern of infant feeding among the Jamaican women in this study was mixed feeding (breastfeeding plus a supplementary liquid and/or solid). All of the women initiated breast-feeding. By the six-week visit, all but two were still breast-feeding but only 21 of those 107 were exclusively breast-feeding. Eighty mothers were supplementing breast-feeding with a variety of liquids including canned formula and bush tea (an herb tea made from a variety of locally gathered plants), and six had already introduced porridge or some other semisolid food. Contrary to what might have been expected, however, given the relatively early age at which supplements were introduced, this did not lead to an overall short duration of breast-feeding. At one year, 55 percent of the women (60 of 109) were still breast-feeding, and the percentages were quite similar among employed and nonemployed mothers (52 percent versus 59 percent).

There were several reasons given by the women for introducing supplementary feeding, the principal one being that their infants had rejected the breast. Women also reported that they stopped breast-feeding because they had insufficient milk or because they were ill. Less than 10 percent of the women reported that they had weaned their infant because of separation due to the mother's work. Of particular interest is the fact that, during the six-week and three-month visit, when the mothers were asked if they were giving anything other than breast milk, those who were exclusively breast-feeding were frequently apologetic, explaining that they could not afford canned formula.

One of the most striking findings from this study was the overall similarity in infant feeding patterns among the women we observed, regardless of their work status. The similarity in infant feeding patterns between employed and nonemployed women was characteristic not only of the timing of the introduction of supplements, and weaning, but also of the type and amount of foods given at different ages. In general, there seemed to be a normative pattern of appropriate infant feeding during the first year of life that all women made a strong effort to follow regardless of their employment or income situation. One or two suggestive differences did emerge that seemed to be correlated with work status. At most of the home visits, working women were more likely than nonworking women to be giving milk (other than breast milk) and among working women, wage earners were more likely than self-employed women to be giving milk (other than breast milk).

Health workers were reported to be the greatest influence or source of information for the mother concerning infant feeding practices. Female relatives also played a role, but were a less important source of information than health workers. It was particularly interesting to note that almost half the women reported having received no explicit information from anyone concerning appropriate infant feeding. It appears that most of their knowledge of infant feeding practices is not the result of a conscious learning process, but rather part of the implicit cultural information that women grew up with.

In general, the women had access to, and made use of, a number of substitute child caretakers to help with the supervision and feeding of their infant. Usually, but not always, these were others members of the household or nearby female relatives. By three months of age, only about half of the infants had their food exclusively prepared by their mothers, and only about a third were exclusively fed by their mothers. Working mothers were noticeably more likely than nonworking mothers to share or entirely delegate infant food preparation or infant feeding.

Beyond assistance provided that was directly associated with infant feeding, it was clear that the majority of women (both those who worked for pay and those who did not) turned to other people to help care for their infant. Once again, assistance was received from other household members or relatives. The only notable difference between working and nonworking women was that the nonworking women never reported paying for childcare, whereas a small fraction of the working women did report paying for childcare. A particularly striking finding concerning childcare was that, at every visit, there were a number of working mothers who reported using no childcare, leading to the unavoidable conclusion that even quite young children in this sample sometimes had to be left on their own while their mothers worked.

As noted at the beginning of this case study, by the end of the first year, 10 percent of the children had become malnourished as evidenced by inadequate anthropometric indicators of growth.[3] Given that all infants were healthy and had adequate weight at birth, this deterioration is clear evidence of the stressed environment in which they were living.

There were two household characteristics that showed a strong correlation with infant nutritional status. First, and not surprisingly, the longer that infants were breastfed, the better their nutritional status was at the end of the first year, with the highest average weight-for-age found for infants who were still being breastfed at twelve months. Second, neither maternal work status nor maternal income status per se were associated with infant nutritional status. However, maternal work stability did seem to be a predictor of infant nutritional status. Infants of mothers who worked intermittently, i.e., entered and left the work force at least once during the year, grew less well than either infants of nonworking mothers or infants of mothers who exhibited a pattern of stable employment.

These Jamaican female heads of household were clearly in an economically precarious situation, struggling to cope with the dual responsibilities of mothering and generating income. The majority lacked steady employment. In addition, they had limited social and economic support networks. The 109 women in this study reported a large range of informal sources of support, but not much depth in their support networks. In response to questions concerning what they would do if specific typical problems arose (such as a need they were unable to meet with their own resources for food, medicine, transport, school supplies, clothes, or cash) most women reported having someone to turn to as a first resort, but the majority reported no second source of help to turn to.

A striking finding from this study, however, is the extent to which the majority of mothers were able to meet the dual challenge of earning income and nurturing their infant. Although 10 percent of infants experienced growth failure during the first year after their birth, 90 percent did not. Equally striking, and contrary to frequent assumptions about maternal employment and infant feeding, was the similarity of infant feeding practices between working and nonworking mothers. Particularly notable was the fact that about half of infants of both groups of mothers were still being breastfed at twelve months. Maternal employment, per se, did not appear to represent a risk for infant health and nutrition (see also Samms-Vaughan 1994). To the contrary, any negative effects of maternal employment were primarily associated with job insecurity. A growth in secure, adequately paid employment opportunities would probably be one of the best nutrition interventions for women and their children in Jamaica.

CONCLUSION

Economic development and social change are complex processes, and even the most optimistic scholars and policymakers recognize that change cannot occur without negative consequences to some people, some of the time. Given that women make up more than half the population of the developing world, they are bound to have experienced a broad range of both positive and negative consequences of development. More fruitful than attempting to conclude that, overall, development has been *good* or *bad* for women, is the effort to disaggregate women's experience of development.

In this chapter, our aim was to contribute to a richer, more nuanced understanding of the relationship between women's changing economic roles and household health. Both case studies show women balancing their economic and reproductive roles, and in the process sometimes arriving at unanticipated compromises or consequences. Some women in both settings had access to diverse forms of domestic and extradomestic social support, but the extent to which its presence influenced their fertility behavior and their children's health and nutritional status was quite variable. Although one group was essentially urban and the other rural, both shared the experience that their ability to engage in economically productive activities was compromised because of a lack of access to unpaid assistance.

We may draw two lessons from the Oaxaca material. Many Western social scientists have assumed that the fertility declines that accompanied Western industrialization were rooted in an inherent incompatibility between women's reproductive and productive roles, for as Western women began to move outside the domestic domain, they began to have fewer children. Franciscanas experience no incompatibility in simultaneously performing productive and reproductive activities. In fact, for them, economic activities are as fundamental to their views of themselves as mothers as are childcare and other routine domestic tasks. Throughout many other parts of the developing world, particularly in rural areas, women experience a similar situation. Therefore, social scientists' and demographers' earlier predictions that fertility rates would fall rapidly as Third-World counties shifted from subsistence to cash economies have proven overly simplistic. Yet this is not to say that Franciscanas would not have had smaller families were they free to choose. But as members of a community intensely concerned about its growth, they were prohibited from doing so. The second lesson we may draw from these data, then, is that birth-control programs directed solely at individual women will be doomed in communities where they are denied the right to make fertility decisions on their own behalf.

The case study from Jamaica also reflects the compromises that women make as they balance their productive and reproductive roles in a changing economic and social environment. A majority of the Jamaican women household heads we studied were able to support themselves and their children during the first year after the birth of a new baby only by returning relatively quickly to paid work. The duration of exclusive breast-feeding in this population was significantly shorter than the four-to-six months recommended by WHO. However, it was notable that over half the women (regardless of employment status) continued partial breast-feeding for the first twelve months, and breast-feeding at twelve months was positively associated with child nutritional status. At the same time, the positive effect of maternal employment was demonstrated by the finding that the infants of mothers who did not work for pay at all during the first year (usually because they were supported by the father of the baby) or those who were able to work continuously at the same job had better nutritional status than those whose mothers worked only intermittently. Although not ideal, the survival strategy of initiating mixed feeding early, continuing partial breast-feeding as long as possible, and seeking regular work within the first six months postpartum worked for these women.

Both the periurban Jamaican women and the rural Mexican women made what they believed to be the optimal work and health choices for their own and their families' survival in light of the information they had and the resources available to them. Undoubtedly, with a wider range of employment opportunities, more complete information concerning infant feeding or contraceptives, and better private and public support networks they could do more to protect and promote household health. It is to be hoped that scholars and policymakers can work together to make this possible.

Acknowledgements. The Mexico research was supported in part by grants from the National Science Foundation (BNS-8016431), the National Institute for Child Health Development (HD-04612), and the Wenner-Gren Foundation for Anthropological Research (3387). Some of the Mexican data appear in Browner, C. H., La producción, la reproducción, y la salud de la mujer: un estudio de caso de Oaxaca, México. Anales de Antropologia 26:319–329, 1989. The Jamaica research was funded by the Carnegie Corporation of New York, the Rockefeller Foundation, and the Pan American Health Organization. Melissa Pashigian provided expert research assistance.

NOTES

1. A pseudonym is used at the community's request.
2. Approximately 75 percent of all births occur in one of Jamaica's twenty-six hospitals. The percentage is even higher for urban women (Wedderburn & Moore 1990).
3. All children who were malnourished in terms of linear growth (below 90 percent of reference height-for-age) were also malnourished in terms of weight gain (below 80 percent of reference weight-for-age).

REFERENCES

Bennett, L.
  1992   Women, Poverty, and Productivity in India. An EDI Seminar Paper. No. 43. Washington, DC: The World Bank.
Birdsall, N., and W. P. McGreevey
  1983   Women, Poverty and Development. *In* Women and Poverty in the Third World. M. Buvinić, M. A. Lycette, and W. P. McGreevey, eds. Pp. 3–13. Baltimore: Johns Hopkins University Press.
Bossen, L.
  1984   The Redivision of Labor. Women and Economic Choice in Four Guatemalan Communities. Albany: SUNY Press.
Browner, C. H.
  1986a   The Politics of Reproduction in a Mexican Village. Signs: Journal of Women in Society and Culture 11:710–724.
  1986b   Gender Roles and Social Change: A Mexican Case Study. Ethnology 25:89–106.
  1989   Women, Household and Health in Latin America. Social Science and Medicine 28:461–473.
Browner, C. H., and S. T. Perdue
  1988   Women's Secrets: Knowledge of Plants for Reproduction in Oaxaca, Mexico. American Ethnologist 15:84–97.

Chatterjee, M.
   1987   Occupational Health Issues of Home-Based Piece Rate Workers. Ahmadabad, India: Self-Employed Women's Association.
Cochrane, S. H.
   1979   Fertility and Education: What Do We Really Know? Baltimore: Johns Hopkins University Press.
Doan, R. M., and B. M. Popkin
   1993   Women's Work and Infant Care in the Philippines. Social Science and Medicine. 36:297–304.
Dole, G. E.
   1974   The Marriages of Pacho: A Woman's Life among the Amahuaca. *In* Many Sisters: Women in Cross-Cultural Perspective. C. J. Matthiasson, ed. Pp. 3–35. New York: The Free Press.
Engle, P. L.
   1993   Influence of Mothers' and Fathers' Income on Children's Nutritional Status in Guatemala. Social Science and Medicine 37:1303–1312.
Fagley, R. M.
   1976   Easing the Burden of Women: A 16-Hour Work Day. Assignment Children 36:9–28.
Ferguson, A.
   1986   Women's Health in a Marginal Area of Kenya. Social Science and Medicine 23:17–29.
Harris, O.
   1980   The Power of Signs: Gender, Culture and the Wild in the Bolivian Andes. *In* Nature, Culture and Gender. C. MacCormack and M. Strathern, eds. Pp. 70–94. Cambridge: Cambridge University Press.
International Center for Research on Women (ICRW)
   1989   Strengthening Women: Health Research Priorities for Women in Developing Countries. Washington, DC: International Center for Research on Women.
Khander, S. R.
   1988   Determinants of Women's Time Allocation in Rural Bangladesh. Economic Development and Cultural Change. 37:111–126.
Leslie, J.
   1989a   Women's Work and Child Nutrition in the Third World. *In* Women, Work and Child Welfare in the Third World. J. Leslie and M. Paolisso, eds. Pp. 19–58. Boulder, CO: Westview Press.
   1989b   Women's Time: A Factor in the Use of Child Survival Technologies? Health Policy and Planning 4:1–16.
   1991   Women's Nutrition: The Key to Improving Family Health in Developing Countries? Health Policy and Planning 6:1–19.
Leslie, J., and M. Buvinić
   1989   Introduction. *In* Women, Work and Child Welfare in the Third World. J. Leslie and M. Paolisso, eds. Pp. 1–17. Boulder, CO: Westview Press.
Leslie, J., M. Lycette, and M. Buvinić
   1988   Weathering Economic Crises: The Crucial Role of Women in Health. *In* Health, Nutrition, and Economic Crises: Approaches to Policy in the Third World. D. E. Bell and M. R. Reich, eds. Pp. 307–348. Dover: Auburn House Publishing Co.
Leslie, J. and M. Paolisso, eds.
   1989   Women, Work and Child Welfare in the Third World. Boulder, CO: Westview Press.

Levine, Nancy E.
  1988   Women's Work and Infant Feeding: A Case from Rural Nepal. Ethnology
          27:231–251.
Louat, F., M. E. Grosh, and J. van der Gaag
  1993   Welfare Implications of Female Headship in Jamaican Households. Living
          Standards Measurement Study Paper Working Paper No. 96. Washington, DC:
          The World Bank.
MacCormack, C. P.
  1988   Health and the Social Power of Women. Social Science and Medicine
          26:677–683.
McSweeney, B. G.
  1979   Collection and Analysis of Data on Rural Women's Time Use. Studies in Fam-
          ily Planning 10:379–383.
Maynard, E.
  1974   Guatemalan Women: Life under Two Types of Patriarchy. *In* Many Sisters:
          Women in Cross-Cultural Perspective. C. J. Matthiasson, ed. Pp. 77–98. New
          York: The Free Press.
Mies, M.
  1981   Dynamics of Sexual Division of Labour and Capital Accumulation: Women
          Lace-Makers of Narsapur. Economic and Political Weekly 16:10–12.
Muller, E.
  1984   The Value and Allocation of Time in Rural Botswana. Journal of Development
          Economics 15:329–360.
Nag, M., B. N. F. White, and R. C. Peet
  1978   An Anthropological Approach to the Study of the Economic Value of Children
          in Java and Nepal. Current Anthropology 19:293–306.
National Commission of Self-Employed Women
  1988   Occupational Health Issues of Women in the Unorganized Sector. Report of
          the Task Force on Health. Bombay: National Commission on Self-Employed
          Women.
Okpala, A. O.
  1989   Child Care and Female Employment in Urban Nigeria. The Review of Black
          Political Economy. 17:87–99.
Powell, D., J. Leslie, J. Jackson, and K. Searle
  1988   Women's Work, Social Support Resources and Infant Feeding Practices in
          Jamaica. Washington, DC: ICRW.
Prabha, R.
  1983   Just One More Queue: Women and Water Shortage in Tamil Nadu. Manushi
          (June/July).
Rabiee, F., and C. Geissler
  1992   The Impact of Maternal Workload on Child Nutrition in Rural Iran. Food and
          Nutrition Bulletin 14:43–48.
Rubel, A. J.
  1990   Compulsory Medical Service and Primary Health Care: A Mexican Case Study.
          In Anthropology and Primary Health Care. J. Coreil and J. D. Mull, eds. Pp.
          137–153. Boulder, CO: Westview Press.
Samms-Vaughan, M.
  1994   Factors Predictive of Low Birthweight, Growth Retardation and Preterm Birth
          in Jamaica. A Report to the Carnegie Corporation. Bristol: University of Bris-
          tol Department of Child Health.

Sargent, C., and M. Harris
  1992   Gender Ideology, Childrearing, and Child Health in Jamaica. American Eth-
            nologist. 19:523–537.

Sivard, R.
  1985   Women: A World Survey. Washington, DC: World Priorities.

Stinson, W.
  1986   Women and Health: Information for Action Issue Paper. Washington, DC:
            APHA.

Tripattri, G. C., N. D. Vasudeo, R. D. Majundar, and P. G. Deotale
  1986   Study of Some Health Problems of Beedi Workers. Indian Journal of Occupa-
            tional Health 29, no. 4.

United Nations
  1991   The World Women 1970–1990: Trends and Statistics. New York: United
            Nations.

von Braun, J.
  1989   Effects of New Export Crops in Smallholder Agriculture on Division of Labor
            and Child Nutritional Status in Guatemala. *In* Women, Work, and Child Wel-
            fare in the Third World. J. Leslie and M. Paolisso, eds. Pp. 201–216. Boulder,
            CO: Westview Press.

Wandel, M., and G. Holmboe-Ottesen
  1992   Maternal Work, Child Feeding, and Nutrition in Rural Tanzania. Food and
            Nutrition Bulletin 14:49–58.

Wedderburn, M., and M. Moore
  1990   Qualitative Assessment of Attitudes Affecting Childbirth Choices of Jamaican
            Women. Working Paper No. 5. Arlington: MotherCare Project, John Snow, Inc.

Winikoff, B.
  1986   The Infant Feeding Study: Summary. New York: The Population Council.

World Bank
  1993   World Development Report 1993: Investing in Health. Washington, DC: The
            World Bank.

World Health Organization (WHO)
  1994   Women's Right to Health (video). Geneva: WHO.

The Impress of Extremity: Women's Experience of Trauma and Political Violence

■ *Janis H. Jenkins*

INTRODUCTION

This chapter concerns traumatic events associated with political violence and their consequences for women's emotional well-being. The gender-specific nature of and response to events and conditions of political violence are analyzed here through a case study of Salvadoran women refugees' experience of extremity[1] as manifest in emotion and illness experience. In light of the recent explosion in refugee populations worldwide (Hein 1993; USCR 1994),[2] the critical need to examine the health consequences of forced departure from natal countries is obvious. To date, several investigators have reported that refugee populations commonly suffer from depression and post-traumatic stress disorders (Kinzie et al. 1984; Mollica et al. 1987; Westermeyer 1988). Insofar as the meaning and experience of refugee status is likely to vary for women and men, it is important that we take into consideration the way in which the health consequences of emigration may occur in gender-specific ways.

Illness experience is examined here in both indigenous (as *nervios*) and psychiatric terms (as symptoms of depression and post-traumatic stress disorder). Do events and conditions of extremity invariably evoke a traumatic emotional response? How can the specificity of this response be characterized? How is it that some women experience and characterize events and conditions of political violence as "extreme" or "extraordinary" while others represent these same events as "mundane" or "routine?" Finally, while the women discussed here certainly experienced pain and suffering in ways that are consonant with examination of their experience within an illness framework, my most striking observation concerning this ethnographic case is that it can be analyzed as a powerful example of the women's considerable resilience and resistance in the face of extreme human circumstances. The sustained emotional integrity—as opposed to a fragmented (psycho)pathology—must equally compel our attention.

I begin by briefly reviewing depression, trauma, and the social conditions of women's lives. The relationship between the social conditions of women's lives and their mental health status is well-established for depression (Strickland 1992; Weissman et al. 1991). Women are twice as likely to become depressed as are men (Weissman et al. 1988). This epidemiological difference does not appear confined to North America and Europe, but rather to occur with regularity cross-culturally (Jenkins, Kleinman, and Good 1991). This epidemiological difference is not reducible to biological factors (e.g., endocrinological) or methodological artifact but can be traced instead to extrinsic features of the social milieu (Weissman and Klerman 1981) and inequities with respect to cultural domains of power and interest (Jenkins, Kleinman, and Good 1991).

In a study of working-class English women residing in the London area, Brown and Harris (1978) empirically identified a set of factors that are predictive of clinical depression. The specific factors are: premature loss of mother; poor-quality housing; unemployment; lack of socially supportive relationships; and the exclusive charge of three or more young children. In India, Ullrich (1987) argues that the traditional cultural standard for women virtually guarantees women will see the world and themselves in the negative terms that comprise Beck's (1967) very definition of depression. Among Southeast Asian women refugees who have survived rape and torture, symptoms of depression (and post-traumatic stress disorder) are reportedly commonplace (Kinzie et al. 1984; Mollica et al. 1987; Westermeyer 1988). In light of studies such as these, depression appears diagnostic more of women's *social situations* than of women as *persons* (Howell 1981). However, while this characterization of depression provides an important opening for political analysis, it should not be invoked to obscure the immediacy of personal suffering that accompanies depression as a way of life.

Psychological trauma, especially as it affects women, has long been of empirical and theoretical interest to psychiatry (Ellenberger 1970; Freud 1973). Over a century ago, Janet (1920) theorized a process whereby traumatic experience is transformed into illness. In the wake of overwhelming emotions such as fear or horror, dissociation often occurs that may be followed by disturbances of memory or identity. The presumptively maladaptive character of these strong emotions is their subsequent association with semiautomatic behavioral responses that fail to take into account novel information about one's behavioral environment. While these early ideas about the psychic organization of emotion, trauma, and illness processes have served as a productive starting point, three aspects of Janet's analysis are subject to feminist critique: (1) emotion is pathologized as an "inferior" and inherently problematic form of experience; (2) theorizing about trauma and emotion are confined to the intrapsychic level; and (3) the case study basis of theorizing stems from the methodology of the time, that is, the "grand rounds" display of "hysterical" young females in Victorian medical theatre as much for male entertainment as for "medical-scientific" purposes (Havens 1966).

Only recently have conceptualizations of trauma in intrapsychic and personality-based functioning begun to be supplanted by feminist formulations of the problem in terms of institutionalized and collective social features, such as father-daughter incest and other forms of violence against women (Herman 1992). The full epidemiological parameters of these problems are currently unknown. Empirical studies are required to systematically identify traumatic events specific to women across a variety of cultural contexts. In accord with the diagnostic criteria for post-traumatic stress disorder (PTSD), symptoms that comprise the syndrome are the result of trauma-related events "outside the range of usual human experience" that would be "markedly distressing to almost anyone" (American Psychiatric Association 1987:250). These events include serious threats to one's life or physical integrity, sudden destruction of one's home or community, or witnessing another person who has been injured or killed through accident or violence. Flight from events of political violence—a global problem that has recently escalated on an unprecedented scale—clearly constitutes one such set of extremely traumatic stressors (USCR 1994). Below we explore the emotional and mental health consequences for women who have fled political violence.

EMOTIONAL AND HEALTH CONSEQUENCES OF *LA SITUACION*

The events and conditions of political violence that constitute *la situacion*[3] of El Salvador have been documented elsewhere (Jenkins 1991). Events of political violence may be discreet or recur as part of the established conditions of these women's lives. An example of a discrete event is the witnessing of an assassination or actually undergoing torture and interrogation. Recurrent events may include violent nightmares of *la situacion.* Following immigration to the U.S., the women's lives continue to be dominated by *la situacion.* Nearly all have family, including young children, who still reside in El Salvador. In addition, the terror of *la situacion* in El Salvador comes to be overlain by new fears associated with life in the U.S., including dread of deportation by immigration authorities, discrimination, and economic exploitation by employers and landlords. The 1992 settlement between the government and guerrilla forces has been met with a mixture of skepticism and uneasiness, leaving unresolved the question for refugees of whether and how to repatriate.

The Salvadoran women's refugee study reported here was conducted from 1987–1990 through an out-patient psychiatric clinic at a university teaching hospital in the Boston metropolitan area.[4] This ethnographic study included research interviews and observations with twenty-two women in home, community, and clinical settings. All of the women reported suffering from a variety of problems related to *nervios*. The cultural category of *nervios* has wide currency throughout Latin America (Low 1985, 1994) and refers unitarily to distress of mind, body, and emotion. In the Salvadoran context, complaints of *nervios* are embedded within conditions of chronic poverty and unrelenting exposure to violence.

The clinical and research diagnostic data reveal that these women commonly report symptoms of affective disorder (primarily major depression) and anxiety disorders (including post-traumatic stress disorders or PTSD).[5] For depression, the women often suffered from sleep and eating disturbances, irritability, difficulty concentrating, loss of energy, sadness, and hopelessness. Nearly all of the women report symptoms in accord with research criteria for diagnosis of the syndrome of major depressive illness.

Although the women reported symptoms of PTSD, the majority would not make full diagnostic criteria for this syndrome as outlined in the Diagnostic and Statistical Manual III-R. The primary symptoms include sleep disturbance, intrusive memories and feelings associated with the traumatic event, and an avoidance of stimuli associated with the trauma. Autonomic features include increased arousal, irritability, outbursts of anger, and hypervigilant monitoring of the environment. The criterion of an extreme stressor—one that threatens one's life, the sudden destruction of one's home or community, or the witnessing of another person who has been injured or killed—was present in all cases. Highly disturbing memories and reexperiencing of traumatic events were commonly reported as nightmares about violent scenarios and generalized terror for the safety of one's family. Less observable among these women were attempts to avoid feelings and memories of trauma.

Problems of application of the PTSD diagnostic category to this population may be related to (1) difficulties inherent in observing some of these symptoms; or (2) restricted cultural and/or gender validity of the full syndrome as currently constituted and applied to this sample. If the latter hypothesis were true, it could mean that the parameters of the syndrome should be differentially constructed for this group or that the PTSD construct is simply of limited utility in characterizing the nature of the distress manifest among this group of refugee women. A separate analytic point, that care be taken not to improperly pathologize that which is arguably a normal human response to abnormal human conditions, is further discussed below (also see Jenkins, in press).

POLITICAL ETHOS AND REPRESENTATIONS OF EXTREMITY

In a previous essay, I sought to expand anthropological discourse on the emotions by examining the nexus among the state construction of what I termed a political ethos, the personal emotions of those who dwell in that ethos, and the mental health consequences for refugees (Jenkins 1991).[6] By political ethos, I referred to socioculturally constituted feeling and sentiment pertaining to social domains of power and interest. What I am concerned with here—events and conditions of political violence—can be categorized in the forms of (1) generalized warfare and terror; (2) poverty; (3) violence against women; (4) death of kin due to political violence, and (5) torture and detention. These must be understood not as independent factors but as coordinate dimensions of a single political ethos. Specifically, preliminary analysis of the data reveals that the women (N = 22) who participated in the study were in different proportions subjected to these dimensions of political violence that define *la situacion*: twenty had witnessed violent death or evidence of violent death; nineteen were living in poverty; eleven had been physically and/or sexually assaulted; ten had experienced the death or disappearance of kin; and one woman had undergone three separate instances of torture and imprisonment.

Note that these themes are coded for what were active narrative issues for the women.[7] The precise manner in which these dimensions of violence combine to constitute a political ethos must be left for a more elaborated discussion. In the space available here I can only briefly excerpt from narrative responses that address the two questions with which I began. How can we account for the fact that some Salvadoran women experience and represent these situations as "extreme" while others would appear either to deny or minimize the impress of extremity under conditions of political violence? And in what respect can these dimensions be characterized as evoking traumatic emotional responses regardless of whether they are represented as extreme or mundane?

TERROR AND DREAD: POLITICAL VIOLENCE AS EXTREME

1. *"Everything Trembles, It's So Horrible."* From Gladys Gonzalez,[8] the forty-year-old, married mother of five, who came to the clinic with severe problems of *nervios*:

> I have seen so many dead bodies. It fills me with a great terror and dread, when you leave to go out on the highway, you see them without heads. . . . everything (in my body) trembles, and it's so horrible. And at night I am not able to sleep thinking about it, because I live with so many ugly, horrible things. When I was pregnant with my second child I saw things so close to the house. I would see people with sacks over their heads (being taken away to be assassinated). . . .

> I feel the right side of my face all numb and my lips "go to sleep . . ."

Gladys decided to leave El Salvador to come to the U.S. (and join her husband) after the following event:

> It was New Year's Eve, and they came to the house of my brother-in-law. He is from a very humble family and hasn't been involved in anything and they came to his house, knocked on the door, and because it's the custom that on the 31st of December at midnight neighbors and all of your friends arrive to give you a hug for the New Year, he thought that when the knock on the door came it would be some friend or relative. He opened the door and someone fired a shot straight in his head and he died and they never knew who or why. He died and we never knew who or why and then my husband told me that with all this he felt ill. With the money that he already had from being in the U.S. he preferred that we come. . . .

I didn't want to come, but life was so difficult there, more than anything I had to think of my children, to avoid also having them drafted into the military or being taken by the guerrillas, to lose their lives. I had such strong fear that something would happen to them. I consulted with a lot of people, to get their advice, and they told me "you have to do something. . . . "

I came here (to the U.S.) not to be alone, because my husband was already here. And as I said, the children had suffered, the children were so nervous because of everything that had happened. In the nights they didn't sleep because of the shootings. Shootings, here and there. They would throw bombs and destroy houses. The father of my husband was the landlord of a lot of places, and they would extort a certain amount of money they had to give, and it was too much. It was the danger of the war. The children were so nervous. When they would go to sleep, they didn't want to be alone. They would cry when they would hear all these things—bombs, shootings—they would say "mommy, if we die here alone, without our father, what then?" It was the same problem for them (as for me), a serious problem of *nervios*.

2. *"My Terror Was that My Children Would Study Too."* From Elsa Hernandez, a 36-year-old married mother of two children, who had arrived alone in the U.S. just six months before the time of this interview:

(I have seen) many dead bodies. Many, for example there in (specific town), many dead bodies, we went walking looking for a cousin, they had made him "disappeared," and . . . we never found him dead or alive, in any place and his mother also went out looking for him and we never found him and there were many young people who were persecuted, the students, and that was my terror that my children would study too, if I could have taken them with me I would have, but I couldn't . . . seeing all the dead bodies has affected me terribly, from that I am sick too, especially one time when I saw a woman that they killed right in front of me, this made me sick, and I felt very ill, desperate really. . . . They shot her in the head with me in front of her, I saw her fall and everything, then I became, like paralyzed, like I couldn't move to see that, then at that time lots of persons were killing people, and one time when I saw them kill that woman it made me afraid to go outside, at night we were used to locking the door, and I was used to thinking that they would come and knock on the door because I had seen this woman killed, right? (I was) thinking that they would come and knock on the door to get me too, and this for me made me ill with *nervios* and I was afraid for my husband, for my brothers and sisters, because I have nine brothers and sisters. . . .

3. *"He Would Have Hit Me at That Moment."* From 35-year-old Lucrecia Canas, married mother of two children still residing in El Salvador with her mother. Lucrecia's experience of *la situacion* as extreme derived from her regular encounters with violence both within and outside the home. An example of *calor* (heat) and *susto* (fright) in response to *la situacion* prior to fleeing El Salvador:

In my country I had a *susto* (a fright) when a man was dying. Already the man couldn't speak (but) he made signs to me with his eyes. It was during the daytime, and I was going to get some chickens for a Baptism. He could barely move his eyes. He had been shot in the forehead. It was the time of the fair in November. When I came back he was already dead. I returned home with a fever, a great fever, and it wasn't something I'd ever experienced. Since it was carnival time, strangers came. They kill strangers.

Recurring events of violence were also part of her experience in her new home in Massachusetts.

> I dropped a casserole dish with dinner in it and then *nervios* came on because my husband was right in front of me. When I dropped the casserole dish it gave me a shiver throughout my body and I felt immediate pain and then, so my husband wouldn't see that I was afraid, I didn't say anything. . . . He had seen I dropped the dinner and since he is really angry, well, I, so he would see that I'm not afraid I said nothing to him. I had the heat attack in the moment I dropped the dinner. I felt an electrical charge was put inside my body. It was because of the fear I have of him, it's because he would have hit me at that moment, he would have beat me because I dropped the food.

> When he goes out drinking on Fridays, he comes back at three in the morning on Saturday, then I feel my face is on fire, really numb, the middle (of my face) only, and the agitation in my chest, I feel desperate, with an urge to leave (the apartment) running, and running, running to get far away. . . . I feel the desire to run away, but I don't actually do it (just as) there's the same pressure when he goes out drinking and returns irritable. Then I want to focus my attention and not be afraid of him, be strong, but I can't. . . .

4. *"It's the Kind of Injury that Remains on the Brain and Can Be Difficult to Heal."* This 33-year-old mother of three (whose husband was assassinated) was imprisoned and tortured three separate times for activities as a union organizer:

> I have suffered a lot because of the torture. It is the reason I have the *nervios*, all the difficult experiences I've had, it results in a kind of injury that remains on the brain and can be difficult to heal. All the trauma over the war, the bombings, the arrests, the mutilated bodies produce a constant tension that cannot be gotten rid of. Ninety percent of the people are traumatized and since it can begin at a very young age it is very difficult to erase.

> My baby was born at the height of the strikes and violence and he was born with *nervios*.

THE DAILY GRIND: POLITICAL VIOLENCE AS MUNDANE

1. *"But That Was Clear across the Street."* A first instance of representing the violence of *la situacion* as unremarkable comes from 57-year-old Luz Pena, a divorced mother of five who had been in the U.S. for three years. She explained that she enjoyed working in her own *tiendita* (little store) making cheese in El Salvador because it kept her busy. Further, "no misery or suffering" had befallen her. She maintained she had come to the U.S. to be with her sons (who had emigrated earlier), and that *la situacion* played no role in her decision to come. She then went on to claim that she really had not witnessed any violence in her country

and that no one in her family had been affected. Later, when she narrated an event of violence in which eighteen persons were killed, I gently reminded her that she had said earlier that she hadn't really seen any violence in her country. She responded by saying

> but that was across the street from my house . . . and I had only lived there for nineteen days. I didn't know them.

Five of those (eighteen) murdered were lined up in front of the house directly across the street from where she was living, and were shot dead.

2. *"I Liked My Job."* A second example of *la situacion* construed as mundane is the case of Diana Vega, a 36-year-old middle-class woman with no children. Educated at one of the principal Salvadoran universities, she received an advanced degree and worked as a public official in cases requiring identification of dead bodies. Her job involved cases of criminal action, often requiring her to collect evidence from medical investigators concerning the (often mutilated) bodies of victims. She reported feeling pressured by her supervisors, on the one hand, and the relatives of the victims, on the other hand. She received death threats, was often followed, and her home was ransacked on one occasion. Following these events, she arrived in Boston with complaints of depressive and anxious feelings which she articulated in terms of *nervios*. Noteworthy in her narrative presentation was how much she enjoyed her job in El Salvador, claiming the problem-solving dimensions of identifying dead bodies held great intellectual interest despite the fact that "the bodies are decomposing" and "there is a lot of putrefaction":

> (The type of work I did) had always attracted me, but then in El Salvador, the judicial system has problems. . . . Sometimes the corpses are lost, or there is not sufficient personnel or adequate instruments (for examinations), the paperwork is not carried out at the time when it should be done. . . . Many times they destroy the victims (bodies).

Thus she enjoyed her job despite the bothersome irregularities of missing dead bodies and missing paperwork but appeared not keenly interested in precisely why or how the bodies had disappeared. Although Diana appropriately represented the process of identifying mutilated bodies as but part of the professional duties she carried, she simultaneously showed signs of having been marked by the process, saying she was haunted by thoughts of the dead bodies requiring her scrutiny.

3. *"We Never Had Any Problems."* A final representation of *la situacion* as mundane— virtually as nonproblematic—comes from 49-year-old Antonia Serrano, a married mother of four. Despite the fact that she came to the U.S. in 1979, a time when political violence had escalated tremendously in El Salvador, she made the unusual claim that *la situacion* played no part in her decision to emigrate. Citing health and medical reasons primarily—she could see doctors for severe headaches—it

was her expectation that the standard of living in the U.S. would be better. At the time of the interviews, she regularly traveled back and forth to El Salvador to visit relatives. Her most recent (three-month visit) was made just weeks following one of the bloodiest of rebel offensives (November 1989), coinciding with the government-sponsored assassination of the Jesuit priests, their cook, and her daughter. Claiming it was easy to travel and live in the country, she stated:

> I have not lived tortures and I go to El Salvador, I come and go and I don't have problems. . . . You may perhaps have heard that we had the last war in El Salvador just lately—and during this time I would go out at 9:00 A.M. and supposedly this (trouble) began at 11:00 A.M., but I never saw anything. My husband was head of a government campaign against (a particular disease) and he never had any problems.

MODES OF TRAUMA

In these examples, we are presented with two modes of representing the experience of the various dimensions of *la situacion* as a political ethos. Despite their apparent difference, my argument is that both are representations of experience that can be defined as traumatic. That such experience is sometimes represented as mundane can be accounted for by a combination of political constraints on expression and the psychological suppression of response—more precisely, by the overdetermination of repression as both a political process and a psychological defense. This dual sense of repression goes hand in hand with terror and violence on the one hand, and dissociation and denial on the other. This formulation leads directly to our second question, the characterization of *la situacion* as evocative of traumatic emotional response.

Upon analysis of the narratives of the twenty-two women interviewed, it was determined that each of the women was exposed to discrete events of violence to themselves or others. But if some expressed their experiences as mundane, how can it be said that they experienced a pronounced emotional response of the kind described by the DSM for PTSD? Of interest again is that this definition of PTSD identifies an "active" and a "numbing" phase of the disorder. This suggests as a preliminary hypothesis that the extreme and the mundane may be different expressive modalities for the same severe emotional responses. On the one hand, forceful emotion is actively and explicitly acknowledged; on the other, emotion is "numbedly" and implicitly acknowledged through denial, minimization, and withdrawal.

Between these two modalities lie a variety of phenomenological shadings of experience and expression among the relevant emotions of fear, terror, dread, anxiety, and anger. I mention only one here, the experience of *el calor*, or intense heat that suddenly pervades one's whole body. The emotional dimension of *calor* is defined by fear, dread, and anger in the face of severe social and political realities. More precisely, *calor* is existentially isomorphic with anger and fear, and is grounded in personal encounters with violence: the "domestic" violence of male kin and the broader political violence of *la situacion*. Both forms of violence contribute to the political ethos of a culture of terror in which brute violation is regularized. In conformity with cultural proscriptions of outwardly directed verbalizations of anger and rage by women, the refugee narratives in our study revealed that the women's association of their experiences with either anger or fear often remained implicit.

Cultural variation in the elaboration or suppression of the existential modes in which violence is experientially engaged is a potentially valuable dimension for examining cross-cultural differences in experiential and communicative worlds of emotion. *Calor* may actively engage unjust worlds of violence through justifiable anger, but may also reactively engage these same worlds through fear and trembling (Jenkins and Valiente 1994). Personally and culturally unwelcome, anger, fear, and heat engage the intentional body. Yet this engagement is clearly problematic: on the one hand it is described under the metaphor of *nervios,* and on the other these Salvadoran women speak specifically of their perceived need to control themselves—to harness their anger and fear (see also Jenkins 1991; Jenkins and Valiente 1994). In this way, they are not unlike most other women worldwide who, feel they must suppress their anger (Lutz 1990).

CULTURAL AND CLINICAL CONSIDERATIONS

As noted above, the experience of *calor* must be contextualized within the broader indigenous framework of conditions associated with *nervios.* Thus, while the experience of *calor* is common among these Salvadoran women, their narratives of illness and suffering are articulated within a universe of cultural discourse on *nervios.* As we have seen, both *nervios* and *calor* are semantically ordered by emotions of anger and fear. While this fear is sometimes expressed with reference to the emotion of *susto* (fright), the experience appears phenomenologically and etiologically distinct from conditions of *susto* commonly reported by other ethnographers throughout Latin America (Tousigant 1979; Rubel et al. 1984). Symptoms of *susto* as illness include problems with sleeping, eating, and difficulties in the performance of work or social activities.

Presentation of complaints of *calor* in medical settings poses a challenge not only for anthropological analysis of women, culture, and society but also for clinical practice in biomedical settings. Misdiagnosis of *calor* can result in serious problems, as the following case example illustrates. One young Salvadoran woman who had come to hospital emergency services was overcome by *calor* while waiting for a physician to come into an examining room. To obtain relief, she removed her blouse and soaked it in cold water from the sink. When the doctor entered the examining room to find she was not only quite distressed but also half-nude, he concluded she was psychotic and immediately had her transported to a local state psychiatric hospital, where she stayed for some days without benefit of an interpreter or her family's knowledge of her whereabouts.

Other common misdiagnoses are to conceive of *calor* as a problem of menopause. The fact that men also experience *calor* and that it is reported by women in the twenties appears to negate such a possibility. Diagnosis of *calor* as hypertension can also be ruled out on the basis of the distinctive differences in the symptom profile for these two experiences. Finally, *calor* cannot be appropriately diagnosed as a symptom of post-traumatic stress disorder and, as noted above, the women cannot be said to fully meet diagnostic criteria for PTSD. The lack of clear application in ways comparable to American Viet Nam veterans (for whom the diagnosis was initially fashioned) may stem partly from contextual features such as culture, gender, and sociopolitical meaning. In sum, *calor* is not reducible to psychosis, menopause, hypertension, or PTSD and these observations are of clinical relevance to diagnosis and treatment.

While I have contrasted cases in which women construe conditions of political violence in ways that can be described as "extreme" and in ways that can be construed as "mundane," it is important to make a broader observation about this group of Salvadoran women as a whole. Given the common condition of enduring and surviving human circumstances of conditions of political violence that cross-cut civil and domestic contexts, the overall resilience and resistance of these women is striking. Survival of such circumstances—often with a palpable grace and dignity—raises fundamental questions regarding gendered adaptations in the face of extreme circumstances.

CONCLUSION

The questions we have been considering with regard to the emotional consequences of existing within a political ethos of violence can be reduced to the single question of whether, when the extreme is common, its very commonality defines it experientially as not extreme. Certainly from these Salvadoran women's points of view, things are considerably other than usual. On the other hand, the regularly recurring circumstance of political violence on a global scale and the regularization of life under such circumstances would seem to suggest that such experiences cannot adequately be characterized as "abnormal." The circumstance of extremity comes to be thought of simply as "the way things are."

From these women's standpoint, the extreme and mundane are not necessarily alternatives, but simultaneous states of affairs that are lived with as a persistent existential contradiction. When this contradiction cannot be sustained, either with respect to living within the political ethos or living with psychological trauma, the survival strategy is a dampening of awareness and expression. Such a strategy is the direct consequence of repression in both the political and psychological senses of the word. Finally, however, while refined understandings of the emotional distortion that occurs subsequent to traumatic experience are needed, it is also clear that accounts of the sustained emotional integrity and resilience of persons surviving extreme horrific human circumstances must equally compel our attention. This will require not only informed analyses of individual and social dynamics surrounding traumatic situations but also closer attention to emotional response in forms such as *el calor*, and to actions ranging from "fight or flight" to immobilized dread in traumatic situations that threaten one's physical integrity.

NOTES

1. Forche (1993) has recently explored the poetics of trauma and memory under the "impress of extremity," a phrase I have borrowed for the title of this essay.
2. There are currently over sixteen million refugees worldwide, up some ten million from only ten years ago (UCHCR 1994).
3. *La situacion* is the most common way of referring to the intolerable conditions within El Salvador, including civil warfare, psychological terror, and poverty.
4. The study was carried out by the author, in collaboration with clinical staff of the Latino Mental Health Team of the Cambridge Hospital, Department of Psychiatry, Harvard Medical School. The primary collaborator was the USCR. E. Valiente, a Salvadoran clinical psychologist, worked closely with the author in providing clinical consultation and referrals to the study (Jenkins and Valiente 1994). The women in the study were 20–62 years of age. The majority were Catholic, of peasant background, monolingual Spanish-speakers with little formal education.
5. Diagnostic data were collected from clinical records through use of DSM-III-R categories according to the SADS research interview schedule (Endicott and Spitzer 1978). The case for productive use of specific DSM diagnostic categories (as opposed to generalized distress) has been argued by Good (1992). Good notes that although DSM categories are clearly based on Western cultural assumptions, they are systematic enough to be used in cross-cultural research and should be the subject of critique in light of empirical work. Preliminary analyses of these data suggest that the parameters of distress as outlined in these symptom criteria do not neatly adhere as syndromes (Jenkins, in press).

    In addition, there is the question of whether DSM categories may serve inappropriately to pathologize normal human response to horrific human conditions. While the adequacy and cultural validity of DSM categories are therefore subject to empirical and conceptual critique, these questions do not form the focus of this chapter.
6. Mary-Jo DelVecchio Good and her colleagues have advanced the problem of state control of emotional discourse defined as "the role of the state and other political, religious, and economic institutions in legitimizing, organizing, and promoting particular discourses on emotions" (DelVecchio Good, B. Good, and Fischer 1988:4). The need for analyses of the "state construction of affect" have been put forth by Mary-Jo DelVecchio Good.
7. This is not a comprehensive list of events and conditions of political violence, but does constitute a narratively salient set of experiences for this group of Salvadoran women. The coding does not necessarily deal with the biographically distant past and is also affected by the fact that some of the women did not currently have "domestic violence" issues in their lives by virtue of not living with a man (as lesbians, widows, or divorcees). There also may be instances of underreporting.
8. Pseudonyms are used and identifying details preserve anonymity.

REFERENCES

American Psychiatric Association
    1987   Diagnostic and Statistical Manual of Mental Disorders. Third Edition. Revised. Washington, DC: American Psychiatric Association Press.
Beck, Aaron T.
    1967   Depression: Causes and Treatment. Philadelphia: University of Pennsylvania Press.

290 Janis H. Jenkins

Ellenberger, Henri F.
  1970   The Discovery of the Unconscious: The History and Evolution of Dynamic Psychiatry. New York: Basic Books.
Endicott, Jean, and Robert Spitzer
  1978   A Diagnostic Interview: The Schedule for Affective Disorders and Schizophrenia 35:837–844.
Forche, Carolyn, ed.
  1993   Against Forgetting: Twentieth Century Poetry of Witness. New York: W.W. Norton.
Freud, Sigmund
  1973   New Introductory Lectures on Psychoanalysis. New York: Penguin Books.
Good, Byron
  1992   Culture and Psychopathology: Directions for Psychiatric Anthropology. *In* New Directions for Psychological Anthropology. T. Schwartz, G. White, and C. Lutz, eds. Cambridge: Cambridge University Press.
Good, Mary-Jo DelVecchio, and Byron Good
  1988   Ritual, the State and the Transformation of Emotional Discourse in Iranian Society. Culture, Medicine and Psychiatry 12:43–63.
Havens, Leston
  1966   Pierre Janet. The Journal of Nervous and Mental Disorders 143(5):383–398.
Hein, Jeremy
  1993   Refugees, Immigrants, and the State. Annual Review of Sociology 19:43–59.
Herman, Judith Lewis
  1992   Trauma and Recovery. New York: Basic Books.
Howell, E.
  1981   The Influence of Gender on Diagnosis and Psychopathology. *In* E. Howell and M. Bayes, eds. Women and Mental Health. New York: Basic Books.
Janet, Pierre
  1920   The Major Symptoms of Hysteria. New York: MacMillan Company.
Jenkins, Janis H.
  1991   The State Construction of Affect: Political Ethos and Mental Health among Salvadoran Refugees. Culture, Medicine, and Psychiatry 15:139–165.
  In press Culture, Emotion and Post-Traumatic Stress Disorders. *In* A. Marsella and M. Friedman, eds. Ethnocultural Aspects of Post-Traumatic Stress Disorders. Washington, DC: American Psychological Association Press.
Jenkins, Janis H., A. Kleinman, and B. Good
  1991   Cross-cultural Studies of Depression. *In* Psychosocial Aspects of Depression. J. Becker and A. Kleinman, eds. Hillsdale, NJ: Lawrence Erlbaum Associates.
Jenkins, Janis H., and Martha E. Valiente
  1994   Bodily Transactions of the Passions: El Calor among Salvadoran Women Refugees. *In* Thomas J. Csordas, ed. Embodiment and Experience: The Existential Ground of Culture and Self. Pp. 163–182. Cambridge: Cambridge University Press.
Kinzie, J. David, R. Frederickson, Ben Rath, Jennelle Fleck, and William Karls
  1984   Posttraumatic Stress Disorder among Survivors of Cambodian Concentration Camps. American Journal of Psychiatry 141:645–650.
Low, Setha
  1985   Culturally Interpreted Symptoms or Culture-Bound Syndromes: A Cross-Cultural Review of Nerves. Social Science and Medicine 22(2):187–196.

1994   Embodied Metaphors: Nerves as Lived Experience. *In* Embodiment and Experience: The Existential Ground of Culture and Self. Thomas J. Csordas, ed. Pp. 139–162. Cambridge: Cambridge University Press.

Lutz, Catherine A.
1990   Engendered Emotion: Gender, Power, and the Rhetoric of Emotional Control in American Discourse. *In* Language and the Politics of Emotion. Catherine A. Lutz and Lila Abu-Lughod, eds. Cambridge: Cambridge University Press.

Mollica, Richard, G. Wyshack, and J. Lavelle
1987   The Psychosocial Impact of War Trauma and Torture on Southeast Asian Refugees. American Journal of Psychiatry 144(12):1567–1572.

Rubel, Arthur J., Carl O'Nell, and Rolando Collado-Ardon
1984   Susto: A Folk Illness. Berkeley and Los Angeles: University of California Press.

Strickland, Bonnie R.
1992   Women and Depression. Current Directions in Psychological Science 1(4):132–135.

Tousignant, Michel
1979   Espanto: A Dialogue with the Gods. Culture, Medicine and Psychiatry 3:347–361.

Ullrich, Helen
1987   A Study of Change and Depression among Havik Brahmin Women in a South Indian Village. Culture, Medicine, and Psychiatry 11(3), 261–287.

United States Committee on Refugees (USCR)
1994   World Refugee Survey. Washington, DC: American Council for Nationalities Service.

Weissman, Myrna M., P. J. Leaf, G. Tischler, D. G. Blazer, M. Karno, M. L. Bruce, and L. P. Florio
1988   Affective Disorders in Five United States Communities. Psychological Medicine 18:141–153.

Weissman, Myrna, Martha Livingston Bruce, P. J. Leaf, L. P. Florio, and C. Holzer, III
1991   Affective Disorders. *In* Psychiatric Disorders in America: The Epidemiological Catchment Area Study. Lee Robins and D. A. Regier, eds. New York: The Free Press.

Weissman, Myrna, and Gerald Klerman
1981   Sex Differences and the Epidemiology of Depression. *In* Women and Mental Health. E. Howell and M. Bayes, eds. New York: Basic Books.

Westermeyer, Joseph
1988   DSM-III Psychiatric Disorders among Hmong Refugees in the United States: A Point Prevalence Study. American Journal of Psychiatry 145(2):197–202.

Women and Health Policy: On the Inclusion of Females in Clinical Trials

◧   *Jean A. Hamilton, M.D.*

Historically, there has been a marked preference for use of males as subjects for health research (Hamilton 1985). This preference for males has been widespread, at least in Western culture. Rationales for the overrepresentation of males in health research have varied, but some explanations have tried to suggest that women benefit from these practices. For example, the exclusion of women from studies of medication has been justified by claiming that women (and potentially unborn children) are thereby given "extra protection." Males, it would appear, go first as "guinea pigs" in pharmacology research, risking exposure to toxic side-effects while females are protected.

Others, however, see the "men-first policy" as far from benign, and as much less advantageous to women. Claims about these practices, while often beneficent sounding, must be understood against the background of women's subordinate social role. Scientists and policymakers in a position to affect decisions have been predominantly male. The interconnections between those who create, define, and transmit knowledge and those who "benefit" are often transparent. Instead of benefiting females, I argue that the preference for males in research—both as the observers and the observed—has doubly disadvantaged women, creating a male norm in health care research and practice (Hamilton 1993a,b).

Gender biases in science (e.g., Fausto-Sterling 1985/92; Fox-Keller 1985; Martin 1987/92; Rosser 1992; Tuana 1989) and in health care (Harrison 1993; Johnson 1992; Showalter 1985/87) have been documented extensively elsewhere. Recognition of such biases forms the background for the present discussion. The purpose of this paper is to reexamine debate over the exclusion or underinclusion of women in clinical research. The critical questions are not just *whether* and *when* to include women; but also, *how* to structure and institutionalize changes. Developments in the United States (U.S.) over the past ten-to-twenty years have highlighted problems associated with the underrepresentation of women in research. Since most visits to physicians in the U.S. result in prescription(s) for medication (Moeller & Mathiowetz 1989), pharmacology research studies (also known as clinical "[treatment] trials") will serve as the particular example for discussion. While research and practice in the U.S. do not, of course, provide the only example, the U.S. has arguably the most rigorous and highly regulated drug testing procedure in the world. Many countries do not fund extensive clinical trials but instead look to the U.S. for information about drug safety and efficacy. For reasons such as these, U.S. health research policy has implications internationally.[1] Events in the U.S. are also of interest because of controversy surrounding recent attempts to rectify biases affecting the representation of women in clinical treatment trials.

In order to *advance* health policy, it will be critically important to understand the reasons that drug policy developed as it did and to address barriers to change. To date, proposed solutions have been overly simplistic, framing the problem as the mere exclusion of women from clinical trials. Thus framed, the solution appears to be obvious: Just add women. Differently framed, however, the problem is revealed to be multilayered and complex, as we shall see.

RECOGNITION OF BIASES IN THE SEX-COMPOSITION OF STUDY POPULATIONS

In 1985, the U.S. Public Health Service (PHS) issued its *Task Force Report on Women's Health Issues.* The report documented that women in the U.S. were disadvantaged in health care research and service delivery and it recommended ways to rectify these inequities. Among other problems that were recognized, it was observed that women had not always been appropriately included in clinical trials (Hamilton 1985, pp. 55–56).

Even after the 1985 report, there was little if any recognition among law makers in Washington, D.C. that a problem existed in the sex-composition of federally funded studies. In 1988, for example, when women's health was raised informally as an issue deserving Congressional attention, the idea was considered politically untenable; it was dismissed because "women live longer than men" and "utilize more health care dollars."[2] Yet women were grossly underrepresented in government-sponsored clinical trials.

Women Were Excluded Because of Federal Guidelines

In part, women were underrepresented because of federal policy and guidelines that called for the *blanket exclusion* of women of childbearing potential (CBP) from certain types of pharmacological research (e.g., Food and Drug Administration [FDA] 1977).[3] The concerns that ostensibly drove development of these guidelines were possible untoward effects of drug exposure on the fetus and, hence, financial liability. Discussions in the late 1960s and 1970s that led to the guideline's publication, and the ways in which the guidelines were interpreted, might thus be considered the "proximal cause(s)" underlying the dearth of women in certain clinical trials over the past two decades.

The criterion for defining CBP, as described in the guidelines, is this: A premenopausal woman *capable* of becoming pregnant. If the guidelines had stopped with this description, then women without a reasonable risk of pregnancy (e.g., those using reliable means of contraception) might still have been included. Unfortunately, however, the guidelines went on to say that among those targeted for exclusion were women using contraceptives (including long-acting injectable and mechanical types), women who were celibate, and women whose male partners were infertile (e.g., due to vasectomy or illness). Thus, *capability* was defined broadly, in a manner devoid of recognition for the *social context* of individual women's lives (e.g., ignoring whether or not they were sexually active and exposed to semen). While the criteria might have appeared founded on an idealized notion of "physiological" capability, "immaculate" and parthenogenic[4] conceptions (i.e., those occurring without insemination) are commonly known to be highly improbable, if not impossible, in humans. The strict letter of the guidelines was more likely based on the stereotype of (all) women as mothers, rather than on a reasonable standard of safety; thus stereotypic attitudes toward women could be considered "distal" (global) cause(s) of (or contributors to) the exclusion of women from clinical trials.[5]

Even so, there were sizeable numbers of women in groups that were not, per se, excluded. As examples, women posthysterectomy met the strict criteria for being *incapable of becoming pregnant*. Women who could *prove infertility for at least 5 years*, as verified by a fertility expert, would be considered if they agreed to certain birth control measures. Moreover, any reasonable, contextualized interpretation would have held that lesbians not seeking pregnancy or insemination and, arguably, other women not exposed to semen (e.g., members of cloistered religious orders), were likewise incapable.[6] Despite these apparent exceptions, it has been claimed that recruiting such women would have been burdensome, as though they were small in number and troublesome to locate. Instead, empirical evidence shows that substantial numbers of hysterectomized women were available for study. For example, as many as 30 percent of women in the U.S. reach menopause surgically (e.g., prior to the age of natural menopause, by removal of the ovaries and uterus or both; Krailo and Pike 1983). The rates of hysterectomy in the U.S. have been high for many years (e.g., as compared to rates in Europe; see Payer 1988). Using a more lenient interpretation of the guidelines, as many as 20 percent of all (presumably heterosexual) couples have been said to be infertile (Sparks and Hamilton 1991). Definitions of infertility typically refer to lack of conception with unprotected intercourse for a year, not five years.

Since women incapable of pregnancy and others at minimal risk might have been recruited, but were not, it is clear that more was operative than solely the guidelines. Indeed, the guidelines, at a minimum, would have freely allowed inclusion of *postmenopausal* women (who were thereby incapable of pregnancy; apparently, even their infertile status would also have had to be proven to be of at least five years duration). Yet we know that investigators were lax even in recruiting postmenopausal women; this was true even when postmenopausal women were to be among the prime users for medications that were tested (Gurwitz, Col, and Avorn 1992). Why didn't investigators include women when they might, and arguably should, have done so? It appears that some investigators and institutions were overly strict in interpreting and applying the FDA guidelines.[7] In actual practice, women with*out* a reasonable reproductive risk were excluded along with those who actually were at risk. Perhaps the habit of excluding women, once it took hold, was overgeneralized. But that "habit" must have taken hold against a cultural backdrop providing fertile ground for such attitudes and behaviors: e.g., gender biases and stereotypes about women.

The Government Is Prodded into Recognition of Problems

As of 1989, the federal government's 1985 recommendations for advancing women's health had been all but ignored. Members of Congress called for a study of practices affecting women at the federally funded National Institutes of Health (NIH). The General Accounting Office (GAO), an investigative arm of Congress, presented their findings before a House Subcommittee in June of 1990 (Nadel 1990). According to the Congressional Caucus for Women's Issues' press report (1990), the GAO strongly criticized NIH for neglecting the study of women and failing to implement PHS and NIH recommendations (see also Okie 1990; Kolata 1990; Hamilton 1994). For example, NIH failed to implement its own 1986 recommendation that women be included more often in clinical trials.

In response to the GAO report, legislators on the House Subcommittee, as well as others in Congress, decided to mandate changes. They were in a powerful position to do so because they voted on NIH appropriations. Even with attention from members of Congress, however, barriers to change were of such magnitude that they prevented prompt, meaningful action. As one example, an initial response to the GAO report at NIH was to increasingly publicize policy concerning the inclusion of women in clinical trials. Investigators applying to NIH as of 1991 were directed either to include women in studies, or else to explain why doing so was inappropriate or unnecessary. In practice, however, virtually any rationale for exclusion was acceptable, revealing a continued lack of seriousness on the part of administrators. For example, investigators proposing cardiovascular studies needed merely to point to "extra costs" or to the stereotype that cardiac illness was a "man's disease" in order to acceptably "justify" excluding women (this despite the fact that heart disease was the leading killer of females in the U.S.; see Hamilton 1992).[8] In order to further explore barriers to advancing health policy, institutional and individual responses to the exclusion or underinclusion of women in clinical trials are detailed below.

PROBLEMS WITH EXCLUDING WOMEN ARE DENIED OR RATIONALIZED

Despite the fact that several arms of the federal government itself (e.g., PHS, NIH) had found that women were disadvantaged in research by 1984–85, the feminist critique of existing policy and practice met with considerable opposition and resistance. The first line of defense was typically to assert that no problem existed because—contrary to critics' claims—women were appropriately represented in clinical trials.[9] This line of defense sufficed for many years, partly because records were not routinely kept at NIH/NIMH (Mental Health) as to the sex-composition of study populations. In the absence of such data, it was difficult to mount a compelling argument that problems existed. An absence of data can thus be used in a circular (and negative) manner, serving both to justify the *status quo* and to perpetuate, or "reproduce," ignorance and neglect of certain issues (I will refer to this later as the "negative circularity principle," a special type of self-fulfilling prophecy). Later, this argument gave way to claims that disparities in the sex-composition of samples might exist, but when they did, they were unimportant. And finally, it was argued that problems were, in any case, impractical and too costly to remediate.

Denial that a Problem Exists

For well over a decade, federal health officials had actively claimed that women needn't be systematically included in clinical studies, nor data analyzed by sex (Hamilton 1985). Despite profound physiological and psychosocial sex-related differences known to affect health, mostly male decision makers persisted in their preference for a "mostly male" norm. In the words of Representative Patricia Schroeder (D-CO), "[y]ou fund [and study] what you fear. When you have a male-dominated group of researchers, they are more worried about prostate cancer [and its treatments] than breast cancer" (quoted in Goodman 1990; here I do not mean to suggest that women necessarily study women's issues, but instead that women are less likely to have massive "blind-spots" when it comes to issues affecting women, a point that I return to in a later section).

I say *mostly* because officials were on occasion moved, *in a peculiarly desultory manner*, to *add-on* samples of women to ongoing studies.[10] Examples of this unaccountably haphazard approach to women's health research include early reports from the Framingham Heart Study (see review in Eaker 1989; Tofler 1987) and reports from approximately the first ten years of the Baltimore Study of Aging (see Hamilton 1994). With regard to heart disease, it is only recently that female-specific issues, such as effects of postmenopausal hormone "replacement" treatments on cardiac risk factors, have begun to be examined. In the Baltimore study, started in 1969, women were first included in 1976 (Older Women 1984). Even then, women comprised a smaller proportion of research subjects than men. This was true despite the fact that women live on average eight years longer than men, thus making the study of aging a prime women's health issue.

Even in recent years, examination of issues pertinent to aging in women (e.g., hormones and cognition) has been sparsely supported.

Denial that Disparities Are Important

As a backstop, it was claimed that even if sex-based disparities in sample composition exist, they are unimportant. This might have been true when and if, for example, data for males could be appropriately generalized and applied to females. There are some studies where this is the case. For example, antibiotics are typically effective in both sexes.[11]

Nonetheless, it is not always true that results from all male samples can be generalized to females (Bennett 1993; Cotton 1990; Hamilton 1985; see also Hamilton 1994). As examples, certain dietary changes recommended generically to (all) Americans for the prevention of cardiovascular illness and stroke were not only based mainly on studies of males, but are also more effective for males than females (Crouse 1989). Women were excluded from a large study of aspirin as a *primary* preventative for cardiovascular death in men (Steering Committee of the Physician's Health Study Group 1989), and data have subsequently shown that aspirin is effective for this indication in men but not women (Hamilton 1992; McAnally, Corn, and Hamilton 1992).[12] Usual pharmacotherapy for mild hypertension is known to be effective in males, though not necessarily in females (Anastos, Charney, Charon, et al. 1991); in fact, some evidence suggests that usual treatments may even be harmful to women (Schnall et al. 1984). Nonetheless, many physicians continue to prescribe in a manner that is blind to gender, needlessly exposing women to side effects without adequate cause for expectations of benefit (e.g., gastric bleeding, in the case of aspirin; and even death, in the case of certain antihypertensive regimens). These examples thus demonstrate what is wrong with excluding women from research participation that is deemed reasonable for men. Such practices are problematic because a.) research data serve as guides to clinical decision making and the delivery of health care, b.) the health care needs of women are sometimes different from those of men, and c.) this is true for women generally (e.g., for heart disease and hypertension), and not just for treatments that are specific to the female reproductive system.

Furthermore, policy discussions that acknowledged problems with generalizing from all-male samples to females are known to have occurred in the early to mid-1980s. Women were excluded from study of a cholesterol-lowering drug (cholestyramine) even though officials privately acknowledged that results for males could not readily be applied to females (see Hamilton 1985).

Claims that Problems Are Impractical and Too Costly to Remediate

Even when problems in the sex-composition of samples were acknowledged, they were held to be relatively unimportant in comparison to the *effort and cost of remediation*. If research were not a guide to clinical decision making, then the cost of health research would perhaps be too high for men as well as for women. Clinical research might then be an appropriate target for congressional budget cuts. Health officials, however, did not propose to scrap as too costly research thought to benefit (primarily) men's health.

Instead, officials claimed that data *were* worth the cost, but only for men (less than half the population) and not for women (who comprise the majority of the U.S. population, i.e., 51–52 percent). For example, data confirming that dietary changes prevent heart disease (due primarily to concerns about men's health) were considered worth the cost, but data on dietary change and the prevention of breast cancer in women were not.

The fate of a proposed study of the effects of reduced dietary fat on breast cancer prevention illustrates the role of cost (and the relative evaluation of benefits) in determining the fate of research on women's health (see Hamilton 1994). By the mid-1980s, Maureen Henderson, an eminent cancer researcher in Seattle, had summarized data on the role of dietary fat as a risk factor for breast cancer. On the basis of her review, she proposed a large-scale trial to demonstrate that lowering dietary fat would decrease rates of breast cancer, a leading killer of women. Her proposal was reviewed by a panel of experts for the NIH. These experts found her proposal to have considerable scientific merit. Instead of funding the entire study, however, the experts requested that NIH first fund a smaller demonstration project, known as a feasibility trial. That is, before undertaking a larger study, Henderson first had to show that women were willing and able to change the amount of fat in their diet, and that measurements of change were reliable and valid. When data from the demonstration project were examined, it became clear that the study was indeed feasible, but that a larger number of participants than originally planned would need to be studied. Since the cost of a study is related to the number of subjects, this meant that the cost of Henderson's study would be higher than originally anticipated. The higher price tag was thought to be *too* high, however, and in 1988, the project was discontinued (Hamilton 1992).[13]

Of course it is much more reasonable to conclude, as members of Congress eventually did, that if data were of practical importance for anyone, then they were potentially important to everyone, including members of subgroups that are comprised differently from that of decision makers, e.g., based on characteristics such as sex, age, class, and culture/race/ethnicity.

Menstrual Cycle Studies Require Time and Money. The menstrual cycle has been assumed to have effects on measurements used in health studies, including pharmacology. Instead of realizing that this, when true, means that menstrual effects *must* be studied, paradoxically it has been used as a rationale for excluding women from research. This rationale, while often framed as eliminating unwanted "noise" in research, often boils down to an argument about cost as well. Since the cost of research rises with the number of observations made, studying women twice (or more often) in the menstrual cycle will elevate the cost of studies, as well as the time to complete them (Hamilton 1991; in press).

Appropriate Efforts at Recruitment May Be Costly.   Although there were probably adequate numbers of women without CBP for studies (according to both strict and lenient interpretations), it is also true that there may have been real cost-based obstacles to recruiting and retaining women in research studies. As examples, the burden of caretaking (both child care and elder care) falls largely on women. Unless research budgets make provisions for alternative care, as well as transportation and other costs, many women will be unable to participate in research (Hamilton 1993a).[14] These obstacles, however, are not in theory irremediable. Instead, if the inclusion of women had been a research priority, investigators and policymakers would have budgeted for these costs.

In addition, several obstacles for the recruitment, enrollment, and retention of minorities, including special populations of women, have been summarized elsewhere (Allen 1994; El-Sadr and Capps 1992; Young and Dombrowski 1989). Examples include: limitations or biases in referral networks; suspicions among potential participants about medical research; inadequate explanations of research, homelessness, and poor nutrition; and location of studies at sites that differ from those used for usual care (El-Sadr and Capps 1992).

And finally, some women have been alienated by attitudes and practices of researchers, which may be seen as rigid and uncaring (Hamilton 1993b). Among African Americans (Warren 1993), levels of comfort and trust are believed to be heightened when research teams visibly include African Americans in positions of authority. Similarly, female volunteers will likely feel more comfortable participating in research when women are included in high-profile positions as members of research teams (Hamilton 1993a).

"Extra Protection" Rationales

As mentioned earlier, the linch-pin justification for exclusionary practices, which may on its face appear to be more reasonable, is based on the supposition that generic "women" are at risk for pregnancy. Women's participation in research may negatively affect a hypothetical unborn child (which virtually all women with a uterus always—at least in the minds of certain scientists and policymakers—seem to carry about with us). This concern was translated into policy that excluded women with CBP from research. Thus, it has been denied that women (and/or a potential child) are disadvantaged or harmed by biases in research; instead, *women have been seen as the recipients of "extra protection."*

Ironically, this rationale, offered under the guise of doing women (and/or a potential child) a favor, actually has the reverse effect: women's exposure to new treatments (e.g., drugs) is merely *delayed* (Kinney, Trautman, Gold, et al. 1982). Once a treatment is released and marketed, it will be offered to women in the general public (who may indeed be unknowingly pregnant), but with less knowledge of its use in females compared to males. With the exception of one early study (Ogilvie and Ruedy 1967), women have been shown to suffer more negative side-effects—including fatalities—from pharmacotherapy, than do men (Bottiger, Furhoff, and Holmberg 1979; Domecq, Naranjo, Ruiz, and Busto 1980;

Hurwitz 1969). These statistics almost certainly reflect our lack of knowledge about drug use in women (Hamilton and Parry 1983; Hamilton 1991; in press).

POLICY CHANGES

After the 1990 GAO report was released, legislators were both increasingly attentive to women's health as a political issue and angered by unresponsiveness to the issue on the part of NIH scientists and officials. Health policy in the U.S. has since shifted toward allowing, and in some cases requiring, investigators to be more inclusive of women. While FDA regulations apply to research funded by both the government and private industry, NIH policies apply only to government-funded studies. For this reason, policy changes for the NIH and the FDA are considered separately below.

The NIH

The argument long made by NIH officials that exclusionary practices were reasonable was, ironically, so extreme that even the cloak of scientific mystification and expertise was no longer able to silence common sense among legislators. At the GAO hearing in June of 1990, members of a House Subcommittee, including Pat Schroeder (D-CO), Olympia Snowe (R-ME), and Henry Waxman (D-CA) listened as NIH experts claimed that studies including over 22,000 to 350,000 men, but not a single woman, (Iso et al. 1989; and Steering Committee of the Physician's Health Study Group 1989, respectively) were scientifically sound.[15,16]

Lawmakers eventually became so frustrated with scientific sleight-of-hand and double-talk by NIH officials that they took scientific matters into their own hands, mandating by law that women be included in clinical trials sponsored by NIH. In the words of Rep. Pat Schroeder (D-CO) "[w]e trusted once before and got burned" (cited in Kaufman 1992, p. 13). This law (Section 131 of the NIH Revitalization Amendments) was passed in June of 1993. Furthermore, lawmakers were so cynical about the hostile attitudes and discriminatory practices of NIH scientists and policymakers that they legislated that *data also be analyzed by sex*. It is noteworthy that legislators felt it necessary to specify what might appear to be routine behavior: That data, once collected using mixed-sex samples, be analyzed by sex. This provision highlights legislators' awareness of the extent of institutionalized resistance to addressing women's health issues.[17] It is, however, highly unusual and controversial for members of Congress to legislate aspects of what is traditionally thought of as research design (see Wittes and Wittes 1993; these events are also described in Hamilton 1994).

The FDA

Despite increasing interest on the part of pharmaceutical companies in better representation of women in clinical trials (Edwards 1992, cited in Merton 1993),

FDA officials such as Robert Temple continued to maintain that there was no need, *scientifically,*[18] to include women in pharmacological research. However, a second GAO report, entitled *FDA Needs to Ensure More Study of Gender Differences in Prescription Drug Testing,* was issued in October of 1992. Finally, in March of 1993, the FDA announced in response to criticism that it would "end its ban on women's participation in most drug safety tests and require companies to carry out analysis by sex in virtually all applications for new drugs" (Hilts 1993). As Merton (1993) has observed, however, *lifting the FDA ban on the inclusion of women—* unlike the 1993 law pertaining to NIH—falls far short of imposing an affirmative obligation to include women in studies (p. 392).[19]

One remaining gap in policy concerns the need for animal reproductive-related teratology studies before women (but not men) can be included in certain phases of testing; previously there had been no need to include women, so the expensive multisystem teratology studies, including examination of reproductive and fetal effects, often were not done in females. Now, however, since women can (and probably more often will) be included, animal studies, likewise, will need to be done more often. Here, the *absence of data* (at least for females) is not merely condoned, which is the usual practice according to the negative circularity principle (see Table 1). Instead we see an exception to that "rule," as female animal teratology studies are affirmatively required for women to be included in trials. This might be considered "positive" circularity (see Table 2A): Women are assumed (in the absence of data, without proof) to show fetal abnormalities. But there is no such assumption and there are no strict provisions for preclinical animal reproductive-related teratology studies for males, a point to which we shall return.[20]

REVISIONIST JUSTIFICATIONS FOR CHANGES

In explaining the reasons for policy changes, federal officials have had to acknowledge that there were problems in the past. In doing so, officials expose

TABLE 1   Most (Non-Reproductive Related) Drugs: Sex-Biased "Circularity"

	If data are lacking (e.g., on sex differences), then do you include the group in research?	
Is there much data (by sex)?	*Yes (include)*	*No (exclude or under-include)*
Male: Yes (much data exist)	POSITIVE (gain more data and the male norm is perpetuated)	
Female: No		NEGATIVE (lack of knowledge about females is maintained)

TABLE 2   Fetal Effects and Reproductive Drugs: Sex-Biased "Circularity"

A. Fetal or Reproductive Effects		
	When there is a female-stereotype and when data in males are lacking (e.g., on fetal effects), then do you focus on the group in research?	
Is there much data (by sex)?	*Yes (include)*	*No (exclude or under-include)*
Male: No		NEGATIVE (minimize study of possible male-mediated fetal effects and maintain the dearth of data)
Female: Yes	POSITIVE (continue excess study of women as mothers, ignoring fathers)	

B. Reproductive-related, Hormonal Drugs (e.g., OCs, DES, Depo-Provera, Norplant)		
	When there is a female-stereotype and data in males are lacking (e.g., on contraception), then do you focus on the group in research?	
Is there much data (by sex)?	*Yes (include)*	*No (exclude or under-include)*
Male: No		NEGATIVE (there is a dearth of study of hormonal contraceptives in men and the status quo is maintained)
Female: Yes (much data exist)	POSITIVE (excess study of hormonal contraceptives in women is perpetuated)	

themselves to criticism for past practices. In order to frame past practices and recent changes in the best light, spoken explanations[21] for traditional practices have promulgated a set of oblique, *post hoc* justifications, which are oddly off-point in relation to the critical issues for women (see also, Hamilton 1994).

Speakers such as Ruth Merkatz (1993), Special Assistant to the Commissioner for Women's Health Issues, of the FDA routinely speak before women's health groups about recent drug policy changes. In a peculiar retelling, Merkatz used graphic slides to illustrate the twin tragedies of Black men in Tuskegee, who unknowingly participated in a study of untreated syphilis, and malformed babies, who had been exposed to thalidomide *in utero*. In doing so, Merkatz made only global references to these events, apparently in order to evoke a sympathetic emotional response and bolster claims that, in view of these tragedies, policymakers were (historically) right to have excluded women from research in the past. These claims are detailed below and are shown to be applied erroneously. Since it is critical to understand the reasons that the field developed as it did, these accounts are potentially problematic. If attention is directed to tragedies that function as "red herrings," then it is deflected from other potentially important issues; policies aimed at change might then be misdirected or even derailed.

Tuskegee

Tuskegee refers to a forty-year study sponsored by the U.S. Public Health Service. Beginning in 1932, investigators studied untreated syphilis among rural Black men in Alabama. Participants were not told that they had syphilis, nor were they offered appropriate treatment (thus potential female or male sexual partners also were left unprotected). Prior to the advent of penicillin, the men were inexplicably given only about half of the then-usual dose of medication.[22] By the early 1940s, when penicillin had become the treatment of choice for syphilis, the men were still denied effective treatment.

The central policy issue highlighted by Tuskegee is the affirmative need for *informed* consent procedures (Jones 1981). The risks of untreated syphilis, and later the benefits of penicillin, were simply not discussed with the men participating in the study. Thus Black men were clearly denied the specific information required to make an *informed* risk-benefit analysis, although they were *allowed to consent* to participate nonetheless. However, denial of information per se has little, if anything, to do with restrictive policies that instead *denied women* with presumed CBP *the right to consent*. Thus Tuskegee is being used erroneously and imprecisely in order to illustrate and justify the kind of concerns that led to the denial of women's right, not to information, but to consent to participate in research.

Thalidomide

Thalidomide,[23] a sedative widely available in Europe, was used by a relatively small number of women in the U.S. in the 1940s and 1950s. The drug was apparently used to prevent early miscarriage (Oberman 1994, p. 267); but it led to limb defects in children born to women who had taken the drug *during pregnancy*. Knowledge about this tragedy surely played a role when policies for informed consent and participation in research were studied in the U.S. in the late 1960s and early 1970s. To be precise, however, the central policy issue raised by experiences with thalidomide was whether women should be *allowed to consent to take any drugs specifically during pregnancy, including drugs given as part of a clinical trial or, perhaps even more broadly, when women might unknowingly be pregnant*. This is, however, a different issue from what it is being used to justify: Namely, a policy declaring that women with assumed (but unproven) CBP are ineligible to give *consent* for participation and the prohibition against consent applies even when studies are *not focused on pregnancy*.

If interpreted strictly and consistently and if construed broadly, the issue raised by thalidomide would have implications for use of *all drugs* by women with CBP, i.e., including those that are already *tested, approved, and widely marketed,* and not just drugs that are currently being tested (see Kinney et al. 1982).[24] Taken to an extreme, women might be obligated to prove they are *not pregnant* in order to obtain any prescription (or even over-the-counter [OTC]) medication(s). But this approach would be so restrictive that it would backfire, making women second-class patients.[25] Thus, an extreme interpretation reduces the message of thalidomide to the absurd. Currently, women are allowed to take many drugs associated with teratogenic effects (e.g., lithium), even though they might unknowingly be, or become, pregnant. Thus, vague references to thalidomide are being used erroneously, in imprecise and global ways, in an attempt to provide a benign rationale for past inequities. "Extra protection" rationales, illustrated by references to thalidomide and Tuskegee, serve as smoke-screens behind which policymakers have hidden. Both of these self-justifying accounts of drug policy history in the U.S. are based on the stereotype of all women being mothers, while ignoring fathers. And both accounts deflect attention from other issues that deserve scrutiny, as discussed in the next section.

INCONSISTENCIES IN DRUG POLICY

Drug policies in the U.S. have been notably inconsistent, particularly around female reproduction and hormonal drugs that affect it. These inconsistencies undermine claims that previous policies were benign or even beneficial to women, as suggested by oblique references to Tuskegee and thalidomide (see also, Hamilton 1994). Inconsistencies will be discussed separately for reproductive-related and fetal risk (RR) and for usual, nonreproductive risk (N-RR).

Reproductive-related Risk: Harm to the Fetus

With regard to reproduction, females obviously are not the only persons contributing to genetic or developmental defects in the fetus. Males taking medications, like those individuals who are exposed to lead or other toxic chemicals at work, may also expose potential offspring to adverse effects (Davis et al. 1992).[26] It could be argued that males were ignored, in part, due to pervasive and powerful stereotypes about women as mothers, so that fathers tended to be forgotten (Rieker 1990). But if "protectionism" was really the aim and origin of restrictive policies, then it is striking that issues in males were largely unaddressed. The effects discussed below relate to N-RR and RR drugs.

Reproductive/Fetal Effects with Usual (Nonreproductive) Drugs. The 1977 FDA Guidelines observed that if testicular or spermatogenic abnormalities were known to occur in male animals (something that might occur rarely and by chance, since reproductive and fetal testing in offspring of males was not required and went against stereotypes), then the inclusion of men in all phases of testing would depend on a constellation of factors, such as the nature of the abnormalities and the importance of the drug. Merton (1993, p. 392) points out that ". . . this textured, case-by-case, only-if-reason-for-concern-has-been-demonstrated approach . . . [differs markedly from] the categorical language of the rule about women of child-bearing potential." Even now, when investigators are encouraged to verify that women in drug studies are using contraceptives and are not pregnant (another example of positive-circularity, see Table 2), policymakers have shown no similar interest in verifying that men in studies are regularly using contraceptives (which, admittedly, would be more difficult to obtain).

Effects with Hormonal, Reproductive-related Drugs.   Inconsistencies are also revealed by practices with hormonal, RR drugs, including oral contraceptives (OCs, developed for females, not males) and DES (diethylstilbestrol, a synthetic estrogen).[27] For RR drugs, women, not men, come first and (nearly) last. By 1960, Enovid, the first OTC, was approved by the FDA. The drug was released based primarily on short-term (one-year) efficacy and safety data from a sample of only 132 Puerto Rican women (another 718 women took the pill for less than a year or were lost to follow-up; Corea 1977/78, pp. 15, 158, 324–25; Norsigian 1980; Seaman 1969/80; Seaman and Seaman 1977/78, pp. 82–83, 528–30; Vaughan 1970; Zimmerman et al. 1980). Further testing on the U.S. mainland was carried out, in part, on poor, Mexican American women who believed that they were receiving effective birth control and who were not told that they might be given an ineffective placebo (though they were asked to continue using other, less effective means of contraception; Goldzieher, Moses, Averkin, et al. 1971a,b). Thus other ethical abuses had occurred or were occurring around the time that informed consent policies were enacted (Cowan 1980; Veatch 1971; Rosser 1994).[28]

DES was approved by the FDA in the early 1940s (Oberman 1994, p. 269), again based on relatively little data on efficacy and safety. A popular (albeit unproven) indication was use in pregnancy for prevention of miscarriage. By 1953, however, it was shown that DES was ineffective for prevention of miscarriage. Yet the FDA failed to officially recognize these data. Eighteen years later, DES—which was still being used to prevent miscarriage—was linked to cancer in offspring. Finally, the FDA issued a warning against the use of DES during pregnancy (Corea 1980, p. 295; 1985, pp. 274–284, 291–294; Crowe 1976/84; Herbst, Ulfelder, and Poskanzer 1971; Ruzek 1979, pp. 38–42; Weiss 1983). Nonetheless, it was used in government-funded research protocols well into the 1970s for another unproven indication: that is, as a "morning-after" pill (Seaman and Seaman 1977). Yet ironically, this "indication" also involved carcinogenic exposure in a population *specifically believed to be pregnant or at risk for pregnancy.* Cowan (1980, p. 41) found that women on college campuses (e.g., University of Michigan, University of Pennsylvania, Yale) received DES without being told that it was an experimental drug (i.e., that it was not approved by the FDA for the indication it was being given). At the University of Michigan, a thousand women students were given DES between 1968–1974. Of these, Cowan interviewed 65, finding that less than half (43 percent) were aware that they were taking part in a contraceptive drug study (pp. 41–42). Furthermore, in the 1970s, investigators at the University of Chicago studied DES in women who were not even aware that they had been given the drug. Thus, DES illustrates inconsistency in actual practices at a time when beneficent policies were supposedly developed and enacted.[29] At a minimum, concerns about females and their offspring were ambivalently held and implemented (Hamilton, in press).

Nonreproductive Risk: Women May Be Harmed

Even apart from risk to a fetus, it is ironic that some authorities have held that drugs commonly available to women in daily life are potentially too dangerous to be studied in the laboratory (even in the usual dosages). Protocols for testing drugs are routinely evaluated by Institutional Review Boards (IRBs). Some drugs that are officially considered so safe as to be available OTC have been considered too risky—not to the fetus, but to the women themselves—to be approved for testing.

My colleagues and I had proposed to study phenylpropanolamine (PPA), an amphetamine-like drug that is the main ingredient in nonprescription diet pills. Drugs of this type have blood pressure-elevating effects and can be associated with stroke (they are called "sympathomimetics," referring to their stimulation of sympathetic arousal mechanisms). Prior to release and marketing, the FDA found that PPA was quite safe, but this assessment was based almost exclusively on data in young men. This might not have seemed remarkable except that it was well known that PPA and similar drugs have higher blood pressure-elevating effects in females and in animals with high levels of estrogen, also typically females. The sex ratio for use of PPA diet pills is 9:1 female. Clinical case reports of stroke in young women using PPA-containing diet pills have revealed a type of damage to cerebral blood vessels that is characteristic of PPA and similar drugs (i.e., areas of dilation alternating with vasoconstriction). The type of stroke associated with this pattern of damage involves multiple, small breaks in blood vessels. Termed "multiinfarct, hemorrhagic stroke," it occurs naturally mainly among the elderly and is highly unusual in young people. Thus the occurrence of this type of stroke in young women using PPA diet pills is of high interest. Yet when we proposed to study pharmacological effects of PPA in young women, we were (initially) told by an IRB that our protocol could not be approved for testing, not because our rationale was faulty, but instead, because it would be *too dangerous to examine effects of this OTC drug in women* (Hamilton 1989).

Our experience with PPA illustrates a paradox that is telling: We can allow women to use drugs in daily life without having tested them in females; yet women cannot be allowed to take the same drug in the lab in order to test its safety in women (this might be called the "safe to use, but dangerous to test" contradiction). The lack of data in females is thus used in a negatively circular way, perpetuating itself. As shown in Tables 1 and 2, the "circularity principle" is applied in an inconsistent, gender-biased manner. Sometimes it operates "negatively," as when we fail to study what is already under-studied and devalued (e.g., N-RR drugs in women, see Table 1) or what is stereotypically presumed to be unimportant (fetal effects in men, see Table 2A; or RR, hormonal contraceptives in men, Table 2B). And sometimes it operates "positively," as when we further study what we already know about and value (N-RR in men, see Table 1) or what we stereotypically presume to be important (fetal effects, Table 2A; or hormonal, RR contraceptives in women, Table 2B). (Eventually, as drug policy changed, an IRB did approve the study and results are pending.)

Oberman (1994) has observed that a peculiar trade-off occurred with regard to women's risks for untoward effects of drugs: The risks for harm to the fetus were considered so great that drug companies avoided the risk by agreeing to exclude women from studies; yet once the (under-studied) drug is released, companies found themselves "off-the-hook" in terms of liability as long as they warned against use during pregnancy. Thus individual women shouldered unstudied risks; whereas business interests, as the saying goes, seemed to have the "best of both worlds."

The Broader Historical Context in Which Drug Policy Developed

In addition to ignoring the foregoing examples, Merkatz fails to discuss the larger historic and cultural context in which U.S. drug policy enacted in the 1970s developed. By 1949, the Nuremberg Code required investigators to require *informed consent*, ensuring that subjects had the freedom to refuse participation. As a result of a variety of ethical abuses in research, including Tuskegee, Senate hearings on biomedical research with human subjects were held in the early 1970s. These hearings resulted in the creation of the "National Commission for the Protection of Human Subjects of Biomedical and Behavioral Research" (NCPHSBBR 1978; *Public Law* 93-348, 1974; see Oberman 1994, pp. 267–268). Findings were also published as the influential "Belmont Report" (1979).

Importantly, Merton (1993 p. 376) found that a 1978 report of the NCPHS-BBR states a "principle of *justice*" (emphasis added) or fairness: That is, investigators should not offer potentially beneficial research only to some patients (as happened even in the 1980s when, for example, experimental treatments for AIDS were offered to males but not females; see Ickovics and Epdel 1993; Ickovics and Rodin 1992; Rodin and Ickovics 1990); nor should they select only "undesirable" persons for risky research (which arguably continues to occur well into the 1990s, as when females are singled out for the bulk of contraceptive research and use).[30] If applied evenhandedly as of the late 1970s, a principle of fairness would have eliminated "male first, except for contraception" policies long before 1993.

Several authors have concluded that concerns about legal and financial liability for harm to the fetus were in fact the driving forces behind exclusionary practices aimed at women. Oberman (1994) found that exclusionary policies were "fear-based," fueled by litigation in the 1970s concerning DES, Enovid, and the Dalkon shield[31] (pp. 269–270). Merton (1993) also concludes that the . . . "real explanation . . . [for past discriminatory policy and practice is] tort phobia"

(p. 400). While I agree that cost, including potential liability, has been an important factor, it is clear that decision makers are not always motivated in logical,
rational, nor even in economically self-interested ways (e.g., sex-based employment discrimination may lead to dismissal of a company's most productive
employee). Instead, nonrational biases can influence decision making. Legal
scholars such as Merton (1993) have recently concluded that *failure to test drugs
in women carries liability at least as great as that due to harming a fetus.*[32] Since this
interpretation was available earlier, even in the 1970s, it appears that other, presumably nonrational factors tipped the balance as to how an ambiguous situation
was to be read. Inconsistencies in policy point to a deeper explanation, one that
I believe is deeply rooted in gender inequality.

WHAT PROMPTED CHANGES IN HEALTH POLICY?

Why did federal policy change in the early 1990s? Did changes result from new
scientific evidence, or from emerging knowledge that had finally come to the
right expert's attention? Having discovered an historic "blind-spot," did changes
come quickly, in a fair-minded effort by scientists and policymakers to right a
wrong? While explanations such as these might be reassuring, they are not, in
fact, the case.

Instead, a well-orchestrated effort wrought over several years brought about
begrudging and reluctant change. In August 1988, an unusual coalition of
women's health advocates—from scientists (including myself), to executive directors of women's public interest groups, to attorneys and lobbyists—met in Washington, D.C. to plan a response to the demise of Henderson's proposed study of
dietary fat and breast cancer prevention, known as the "Women's Health Trial"
(WHT).[33] Out of that meeting, which was sponsored by the Institute for Research
on Women's Health (IRWH), came a three-pronged action plan that went well
beyond the fate of the proposed WHT (Hamilton 1992).

The IRWH Task Force determined that we had to begin by changing perceptions of women's health. In order to do so, we needed to: a.) obtain an economic analysis of NIH spending on women's health research in order to demonstrate that, despite the 1985 U.S. Public Health Service report, there was still a
problem; b.) formulate a consensus research agenda on women's health research,
which the 1985 report had not accomplished, so that we could point to what we
wanted; and, c.) mount a media campaign to bring these issues to the attention
of lawmakers and the general public (Hamilton 1992).

Partly in response to congressional interest stimulated as a result of the plan,
an NIH committee found that only 13 percent (instead of, for example, 50 percent) of the annual NIH budget was spent on women's health (Squires 1989).
This economic disparity further galvanized congressional interest and led to the
1990 GAO report on NIH policies and practices. Also in 1990, a consensus development conference involving over one hundred experts nationwide was convened
privately in Washington, D.C. The conference resulted in a Women's Health

Research Agenda in four areas: breast cancer; cardiovascular disease; menopause and osteoporosis; and clinical pharmacology, with a focus on depression (Blumenthal, Barry, Hamilton, and Sherwin 1991). And finally, each of these events spontaneously received media attention, and journalistic interest has continued. Thus the events leading to change were neither accidental, nor were they the result of new scientific findings or ethical analyses. Instead, changes in perceptions of women's health were the result of a deliberate strategy and concerted effort to politicize the issue. This was a "top-down" strategy, not a "bottom-up," grassroots movement. It was effective only because women had been trained in law, and public education and lobbying, and held powerful enough positions in the media and politics. Ironically, women in science and the health professions, while critical to the effort, played only an auxiliary role in comparison.

FRAMING THE QUESTION IMPLIES THE SOLUTION

Dramatic and highly controversial changes in health policy have been mandated by members of Congress and barriers have been lifted by the FDA. The blanket exclusionary policy toward women has given way to a blanket inclusionary policy in U.S. government-funded clinical trials. *If excluding women had been the problem, then what would be the solution?* Framed in this way, blanket inclusion seems to follow. Just as women had previously been *generically excluded* (or underincluded), legislation passed in June of 1993 has called for the *blanket inclusion* of women along with men (and other subgroups) in clinical studies. While NIH has yet to develop full guidelines for implementation, the new law has been criticized by those both for and against women's rights. It has provoked controversy even among women's health advocates who had pushed for change.

I will argue that both past and present policy and practices are critically flawed, with the latter being an overreaction to problems with the former. In addition to concerns about Congress legislating research design, there is concern that sample sizes will be markedly increased, thereby increasing the cost of studies. With a static or diminishing budget, this will mean that far fewer studies will be initiated (Marshall 1994; Wittes and Wittes 1993). In addition, laws requiring the inclusion of both males and females will make it harder to redress past inequities, since the use of all females in such an instance would make the most sense.

The Institute of Medicine (IOM) is another advisory group to Congress and part of the prestigious National Academy of Sciences (NAS) in Washington, D.C. In February of 1994 the IOM released a report that supported the NIH in taking a *conservative* approach to developing guidelines for implementing the new law (see also note 19). For example, a conservative interpretation might hold that women and minorities don't really need to be included to the extent that the law, on its face, might suggest (the amendment, in fact, has several qualifiers, but these give administrators and investigators considerable discretion; see Merton 1993 for a more detailed discussion of problems resulting from allowing leeway for "interpretation" of guidelines). Unfortunately, reliable sources in a position to know have recently observed that NIH officials are again seeking to sabotage efforts aimed at gender equity. Apparently in an effort to undermine congressional efforts to more fairly include women and minorities in clinical trials, some powerful NIH Directors have issued extreme directives, requiring, for example, 50 percent minorities in some (or potentially all) clinical trials (this would be an impossibility in some major medical centers, e.g., in the Midwest). In effect, the directives reduce the intent of equity-based legislation to an absurdity in actual practice. In an effort to provoke backtracking on the issue among legislators, it can also reasonably be expected to generate letters of complaint to members of Congress. Before proposing an alternative method for structuring the inclusion of women and men in clinical trials, I will briefly examine two related issues: women in science and the international implications of U.S. policies.

RELATED ISSUES

Women and Clinical Trials: What about the Women in Science?

Using case examples of women scientists who had sought to study sex differences in pharmacology at NIMH in the 1980s, Jensvold and her colleagues (1994) have documented the ways in which "who does" the research directly impacts on women's health research. Their point is summarized in the paper's title: "Inclusion of women in clinical trials: *How about the woman scientists?*" (emphasis added). When women's careers in science are blocked by sex-based employment discrimination, for example, their studies are typically blocked or sabotaged as well. In an environment known to be hostile toward women in science (GAO 1986; Greenberger 1993; Solomon 1993), women studying women's issues at NIH have been doubly disadvantaged. Thus we must pay attention to women's involvement in clinical trials, as *observers* as well as the *observed.*

As suggested earlier, the link between who has power and who benefits is transparent (see earlier quote from Patricia Schroeder in Goodman 1990). This is not to suggest, of course, that all women scientists study women's health issues; but rather, that women on average are less likely to be gender-blind to women's issues than are men (e.g., see Tuana 1989, and previous caveat). But when women are marginalized in the health sciences, legislators have reason to suspect that gender-blindness will go uncorrected. Better representation of women (and men) who are concerned with and knowledgeable about women's issues in positions of scientific and policy-making authority will likely a.) reduce unblinking acceptance of gender inequities in health research, b.) help to recruit and maintain women's participation in research as volunteers, and c.) help to assuage the cynicism apparent among members of Congress, who will otherwise (continue to) overreact to past problems in a way that creates new ones.

International Implications and Cross-cultural Issues

Although what happens in the U.S. is far from the whole story, it is an important and influential piece. Payer (1988), in *Medicine and Culture*, examined varieties of treatment in the U.S., England, West Germany, and France. She portrays pharmacotherapy in the U.S. as much more aggressive than in other countries. This makes it doubly ironic that U.S. drug testing has not adequately studied women in some clinical trials of usual, N-RR drugs. In fact, there is reason to believe that dosages in the U.S.—which are *already high relative to dosages used in other Western countries*—are specifically *too high for females compared to males* (Hamilton, Grant, and Jensvold, in press; Hamilton and Yonkers, in press; Yonkers and Hamilton, in press); this problem doubtless contributes to the excess of adverse drug reactions in females. Testing of drugs among females has been characterized by ambivalence, at best. Justifications for undertesting N-RR drugs in females are contradicted by cavalier testing and release of drugs related to female reproduction (e.g., OCs, DES, and the long-acting, injectable Depo-Provera; Corea 1980; Cowan 1980; Levine 1980; Rakusen 1981; Seaman and Seaman 1977).

Even when women are included in studies, there is no guarantee that minorities are adequately represented. In general, testing among minorities has been far from adequate (see El-Sadr and Capps 1992).

Cross-culturally, another unfortunate policy and practice is for administrators and scientists in the U.S. to allow the export of drugs and devices for testing in Third-World countries (e.g., Depo-Provera, see Bell 1976/84, pp. 247–248; Bunkle 1993; Diskin 1976/84; also, Heller 1977; Silverman 1982). Levine (1980, p. 104) cites former FDA Commissioner Donald Kennedy as having supported the export of drugs that had not been approved for marketing in the U.S., leading to a "double-standard" (p. 101) in ethical practices. Corea (1980, p. 114) refers to the "Drug Regulation Reform Act" (which was pending in 1979), which would allow for export of unapproved drugs.

Recently, Norplant (a long-acting hormonal contraceptive placed under the skin, subdermally) was largely tested in other countries. As examples, the U.S. government (non-PHS, e.g., Agency for International Development, AID) helped to fund studies in locations such as these: Bangladesh (Akhter, Dunson, Amatya et al. 1993), Sri Lanka (Thapa, Lampe, and Abeykoon 1992), the Phillipines (Balogh, Klavon, Basnayake et al. 1989), the Dominican Republic (Faudes, Brache, Tejada et al. 1991), Chile (Diaz, Pavez, Cardenas, et al. 1987), and Nigeria (Fakeye and Balogh 1989.)[34] One problem with such testing is that women given Norplant have reported being abandoned by doctors and researchers (Garcia and Dacach 1991). (U.S. researchers have also been involved in testing a nonsurgical type of female sterilization technique—where a toxic substance produces inflammation and fibrosis in the fallopian tubes—in women in Chile (Kessel, Zipper, and Mumford 1985) and India (Bhatt and Waszak 1985).

A similar issue has recently been discussed for trials of an AIDS (HIV) vaccine. Ethicists have suggested that use of an experimental AIDS vaccine in high-risk populations in Third-World countries (e.g., prostitutes in Thailand) may be appropriate since a.) such populations have a near-certain risk of infection and death, and b.) other treatments such as AZT and pentamidine are not generally available due to their cost. Nonetheless, exportation of dangerous protocols may violate the "principle of justice" in human research that has been endorsed (but not consistently practiced) in the U.S.

The "Council of International Organizations of Medical Sciences" of the World Health Organization recently acknowledged problems with the exclusion of women from clinical trials worldwide. Yet the current draft of the *International Ethical Guidelines for Biomedical Research Involving Human Subjects* makes no provisions for changing policy (see Merton 1993, p. 396). Nonetheless, changes in the U.S. will affect and improve, if not policy worldwide, then at least the available knowledge base for using drugs in women.

One risk faced by concerned researchers in the U.S. is the catch-22 identified by Reinharz (1992, p. 122): Western feminists are criticized for *not* studying Third-World women due to "ethnocentrism"; and they are simultaneously criticized for *doing so* as outsiders to those cultures, which smacks of "colonialism." One course of action is a true collaboration between insiders and outsiders.[35]

REFRAMING THE QUESTION: PROPOSED FUTURE DIRECTIONS AND CONCLUSIONS

Both past and present policy and practices are flawed, with one being an overreaction to problems with the other. Blanket exclusion (or underrepresentation) of women is sex-biased and results, for example, in less knowledge about how to use drugs in women. On the other hand, blanket inclusion leads to inefficient use of resources and impedes research that may benefit both women and men. In addition, a law requiring mixed-sex samples mitigates against using all females in order to fill gaps in knowledge rapidly and economically. Given these dichotomous alternatives—exclusion or inclusion—the fundamental task for feminists is to reframe the question.

Proposed Future Directions: Toward a Contextualized Approach

Feminist theory suggests that we utilize more *contextualized* approaches to problem definition and the conduct of research (Hamilton 1993). I believe that a contextualized approach to the problem of sample composition will help avoid blanket, dichotomous, "across-the-board" prescriptions for research. As one example of this approach, I and my colleagues working in the field of clinical pharmacology research have described a method for targeting areas that require further sex-related, or gender-intensive study (Hamilton 1991). For example, those drugs used for serious illnesses, having severe or potentially fatal side effects, having a narrow margin of safety, showing effects of sex or sex steroid hormones in animals or humans, or being metabolized by pathways known to be sex-linked, may require intensive study in females as well as males. At the same time, we can also begin to profile drugs where there is little or no need to study effects of sex. Instead of requiring males and females in nearly all clinical trials, we could thus identify drugs requiring intensive study in one or both sexes.

While this approach risks negative circularity (wherein a lack of knowledge perpetuates itself, see Table 1), I (and others) believe that pharmacology is a field where sufficient evidence exists to make such an approach practicable. The other major stumbling block, however, is ill will, since the approach is clearly vulnerable to sabotage. Those entrusted to develop or direct such a program would need to have a.) *a preexisting commitment to women-centered research*, and b.) *sufficient resources, power, and autonomy to do the needed work.* With sufficient safeguards, however, the "targeting" strategy might prove to be a viable option.

But there is another alternative: In the absence of reasons to suspect important sex differences (or to play "catch-up"), why not just alternate between female and male samples, with women in one trial and men in the next? Again, there is the risk of circularity, but this approach would be less costly than (nearly) always including representative numbers of males and females (Hamilton, in press). By specifically calling for single-sex samples, "alternating" would also allow for all-female studies in order to rapidly fill gaps in knowledge about the use of drugs in women. Scientifically, we could even begin to assess possible effects of treatment by sex with such an approach. The magnitude of effects for males and females (known technically as "effects sizes," e.g., Cohen 1992; Rosenthal and Rubin 1982) could be compared and summarized statistically across studies (using an approach that is known as "meta-analysis," e.g., Wolf 1986; along with recent refinements, e.g., Becker 1992). The fact that we did *not* alternate, of course, considerably weakens claims that a "men first, except for contraceptives policy," even if problematic, merely represents benign neglect. Instead, males have been preferentially advantaged and females disadvantaged, as discussed earlier.

CONCLUSIONS

"Targeting" issues and "alternating" between subgroups for study are proposed strategies for restructuring the inclusion of women and men in clinical trials. These methods are aimed, in part, at using limited resources to the best advantage. But these methods also highlight the need to avoid blanket, decontextualized prescriptions for research. Women's health will be better served by a more contextualized approach to research. Such an approach will allow for discretionary judgements to be made, however, opening up opportunities to sabotage efforts aimed at gender equity. Contextualized approaches will be ill-fated, for example, if women are included only as subjects in clinical trials, but are effectively excluded from research teams. Thus we must pay attention to women's involvement in clinical trials, both as observers as well as the observed, as scientists as well as research subjects.

Inconsistent policies and practices in drug testing reveal highly ambivalent attitudes towards women. While men may appear to serve, chivalrously, as "guinea pigs" for most of the usual (N-RR) drugs, this practice ultimately advantages males and disadvantages females. Yet because of the excess focus on female reproduction and the stereotype of women as mothers, women have assumed virtually all of the risks for testing and chronic use of hormonal contraceptives (RR drugs). Similarly, women in developing countries have shouldered the burden of drug testing and drug usage that would not have been (officially) condoned after the early 1970s in this country (Diskin 1976/84). While it is meritorious for the U.S. to proclaim a principle of justice in clinical research, it would seem most fair and appropriate to apply this internationally as well.

Acknowledgment. An earlier version of parts of this work appears in a chapter in Brown, Kramer, Rieker, and Willie, eds., (1995) and in the *Women's Review of Books*, "Going to extremes," Special Issue, "In Sickness and in Health," Vol. XI (July), pp. 15–16, 1994. The author thanks Ellen Cantarow, Associate Editor, *WRB*, for helpful comments and suggestions.

NOTES

1. Connections between the U.S. drug industry and Third-World countries will be further discussed in later sections (see also Diskin 1976/84). At least 90 countries have procedures for drug approval (see Working Group on the Health Consequences of Contraceptive Use and Controlled Fertility 1989, p. 46). The United Kingdom has a Committee on the Safety of Medicines (see Rakusen 1981, p. 76). In addition to those in the U.S., large-scale trials are typically supported by Western European nations, such as the United Kingdom, France, Germany, the Netherlands, and Sweden.

2. In 1988, while serving as Director of the Institute for Research on Women's Health, I contacted a senate staffer about a plan to make women's health a political issue. Here I describe the response I received from a female staff member for a senator interested in health and in women's issues. It should be noted that politicians and health bureaucrats are known to respond with a knee-jerk reaction, seeking to find ways to discount, and thus to dispose of, issues.

3. Although FDA guidelines apply to government scientists studying drugs, changing regulations at the FDA would not necessarily mean that women would be included in government-funded studies. The policy issues are complex because health care agencies are fragmented. Lawmakers in the U.S. would have to address separately issues for, e.g., the NIH, FDA, Centers for Disease Control, the Veterans Affairs Administration, and so on.

4. Parthenogenesis refers to a form of conception that does not require insemination. Thus, genetic and cytoplasmic material in the mother's ovum is sufficient for pregnancy. This occurs, for example, in turkeys.

5. University of Wisconsin law professor and ethicist, Alto Charo (Institute of Medicine Planning Panel on the Inclusion of Women in Clinical Trials, Washington, D.C., February 1991), has observed that the appropriate standard for avoiding liability is use of reasonable precautions to minimize risk, not to aim for zero risk, which, of course, is impossible.

6. As one example, my male collaborator at the National Institute of Mental Health (NIMH) in the early 1980s refused to include a woman who sought entry into a study

of drug effects across the menstrual cycle. She emphatically stated that she was *not* at risk for pregnancy because she was a) in a monogamous marital relationship, and b) her husband was in Europe for six months, so that she would not c) be inseminated for that period of time. Although I believed her and would have accepted her consent for entry into the study, my colleague in this instance was not convinced. This difference in our evaluation of women's stories occurred time and again. It is unclear whether his skepticism was due to the general distrust that physicians have for what women patients report; or, more specifically, whether it was due to disbelief that women can be trusted to regulate their sexuality.

7. After the fact, Robert Temple, a high-ranking official in the FDA, has stated that the *Guidelines* should never have been interpreted as requiring exclusion of women. However, the agency did nothing to dissuade investigators from that interpretation. In a 1991 survey of pharmaceutical companies, the Pharmaceutical Manufacturers Association (Edwards 1992, unpublished) found that nearly 80 percent reported that FDA reviewers had required them to exclude women with CBP (cited in Merton 1993, p. 394).

8. For further discussion of how policy was interpreted, see Merton 1993. Ruth Kirschstein, who chaired the committee concerned with women's health issues at NIH and who later served as the first Acting Director of the Office of Research on Women's Health, was a seasoned bureaucrat. Some observed that Kirschstein was no "natural champion" of women's health. Instead, she was the highest-ranking female at NIH, and thereby deemed suitable for appointment. As one example, Kirschstein was reportedly furious that she was bothered by complaints about the U.S. government's role in supporting sexist psychiatric diagnoses in the late 1980s (J. Gentry, personal communication).

9. For example, FDA official Robert Temple made this claim at meetings (such as the IOM in 1991 and PMA in 1992) repeatedly in the early 1990s.

10. One problem with merely adding women to existing samples is that measures and procedures based on an implicit male norm remain unchallenged. In contrast, a woman-centered approach to research will be needed to challenge existing models and advance women's health.

11. Even here, however, there may be sex-related considerations due to interactions between oral contraceptives [OCs] and other drugs, e.g., certain antibiotics can interfere with OCs.

12. See work by McAnally & Corn (1992), who reported that low-dose aspirin is *not* recommended as *primary* prevention for cardiovascular death in women, although it is recommended for reducing further cardiovascular morbidity and mortality in women with known cardiovascular disease.

13. Later, Henderson's work was "resurrected," leading to the Women's Health *Initiative* (emphasis added), announced by then-NIH Director, Bernadine Healey, and sponsored by NIH. This is the largest follow-up study related to women's health in the U.S.

14. This issue was addressed in several meetings held by the IOM, e.g., in 1991 and 1993.

15. As a physician-scientist who had worked at the NIH Clinical Center, I watched as officials went through the same rhetoric that had worked so well for them, for so long, at NIH (see Hamilton 1994). Standing before members of Congress, who sat on a raised dais as if in judgement, Charles Lenfant, then acting Director of the Heart, Lung and Blood Institute at NIH, attempted to justify the complete absence of women in large-scale, government-funded cardiac trials. To paraphrase part of this exchange: Congress-person (C): "Isn't it true that women also die of heart disease?" NIH official (N):

"Well yes, but we don't need to study them . . ." C: "Why not?" N: ". . . [silence]." Thereafter, the acting NIH Director, William Raub—but not Lenfant—was downright contrite. At long last, another "emperor"—that of objective, value-free biomedical science—had been shown to have no clothes! Having previously witnessed the shameless, cavalier use of erroneous rationales by NIH officials, it was remarkable to witness their new-found (albeit short-lived) humility. All it took was for persons of clout (those voting on NIH appropriations) to make it clear that thinly reasoned, spurious arguments were unacceptable.

16. Partly in collaboration with U.S. scientists, investigators in the United Kingdom (U.K.) also published an all-male study of physicians, although findings were inconclusive (*Br Med J*, 296:313, 1988). At about the same time that the U.S. and U.K. were publishing results from all-male studies, investigators in other countries were publishing data on both sexes (e.g., the U.K., in *J Neurol Neurosurg Psychiatry*, 54:1044, 1991; Sweden in *Lancet*, 338:1345, 1991; the Dutch in *New Engl J Med*, 325:1261, 1991; European Stroke Prevention Study in *Acta Neurol Scand*, 84:286, 1991 and in *Neurology*, 41:1189, 1991). It is difficult to compare studies because of differing inclusion criteria, sample characteristics, clinical end-points, and duration of follow-up. Many of the European studies are secondary intervention/prevention studies, unlike the U.S. primary prevention Physician's Health Study. In the U.S. a large-scale, *randomized* trial of aspirin was completed for men (Physician's Health Study), while a similar study in nurses was turned down as too expensive. Hennekens was ultimately able to get U.S. funding for a *nonrandomized* (less expensive) study of over 87,000 nurses, published in *JAMA*, 266:521, 1991. But the findings were difficult to interpret and a randomized trial in women was still needed.

17. In its 1993 *Guidelines*, for example, the FDA acknowledged that new drug applications analyzed data by sex (when it was possible to do so) in only about 50 percent of cases (p. 7). This rate was observed even though 1988 FDA "Guidelines for the Format and Content of the Clinical and Statistical Sections of New Drug Applications" called for analyses of gender-related differences in response. If one could assume "good faith," however, then stipulating the inclusion of women would be enough, as one could reasonably assume that data, once collected, would be analyzed. The fact that this could not realistically be assumed reveals the extent of gender-bias among NIH/NIMH researchers and officials. According to Jensvold and colleagues (1994), for example, women scientists collected data pertinent to women's health at NIH but the data were in some cases sequestered, apparently as part of discriminatory efforts to block women's careers in science. In addition, we have seen that "good faith" efforts can easily be undermined. For example, legislators had already witnessed callous circumvention of the intent of the 1986 and 1991 NIH policies calling for inclusion of women. Such behavior was tolerated, if not condoned, by the NIH leadership and even by those seeming to have an interest in women's health (e.g., Ruth Kirschstein).

18. By "scientific," officials such as Temple mean to contrast objective, politically neutral rationales with those that are "political." It is as though science is a pure enterprise, unmarred by mere political ends and pressures.

19. Also, as this chapter goes to press, the Institute of Medicine (IOM) released two reports: A. C. Mastroianni, R. Faden, and D. Federman, eds., 1994. *Women and Health Research: Ethical and Legal Issues of Including Women in Clinical Studies, Volume I and II.* Washington, D.C.: National Academy Press.

20. Merton (1993) also points out that requirements for a "New Drug Application" leave room for interpretation as to whether effects on reproduction and the developing

fetus must be done, "depending on the nature of the drug and phase of the investigation" (pp. 394–96).

21. In contrast, written explanations have appeared more forthcoming. For example, a draft of the 1993 FDA Guidelines states that ". . . from the viewpoint of the 1990s, [the content of the 1977 guidelines] has appeared *rigid and paternalistic . . .*" (p. 4, emphasis added).

22. Even though the usual treatment for syphilis, prior to penicillin, was of dubious efficacy, one wonders whether Blacks were given half the generally recommended dose (e.g., of that used for Whites) because they were considered, in effect, about half as valuable. The lower dose probably functioned as a placebo.

23. Thalidomide is the generic, chemical name of the drug, so it is usually not capitalized. In some cases, capitals are used, however, not to indicate a brand name, but to recognize that it came to be emblematic of an issue.

24. Thalidomide was not approved in the U.S., but was brought to this country from European countries where it was widely available.

25. If the real concern had been zero risk of teratogenic effects, women of CBP also would have been entirely excluded from having abdominal x-rays, since these can adversely affect the fetus. Prior to recent policy changes for drugs, however, women were allowed to have abdominal x-rays if they reported where they were in their period and the timing was considered safe enough. No effort was made to verify such reports. But this practice—reasonable safeguard, which consisted in believing what women told us—was not considered sufficient when it came to participation in drug studies, where even a woman on OCs, and having an IUD, and not exposed to semen would have been excluded.

26. Merton (1993, pp. 400–402) provides a review of the role of the father in genetic defects. However, some of the examples she cites have to do with a narrow class of drugs, called alkylating agents, which specifically cause genetic alterations. There is a need for more studies of effects of other types of drugs on the genetic contribution of a male to a fetus. Most genetic mutations are believed to be tied to the father in most cases (J. F. Crow cited in Angier 1994). This is another example of the circular principle, where ignorance and neglect are self-reproducing.

27. The other prominent example is Depo-Provera (see Bunkle 1993).

28. In fact, the limited testing of OCs on women of color is perhaps more pertinent to the inclusion of women in clinical trials than is the example of Tuskegee. Allen (1994) also reminds us that J. Marion Sims performed 42 operative procedures on slave women in Montgomery, Alabama. These women were lent to Dr. Sims by their owners, obviously without the women's "consent." The procedures took place before modern anesthesia existed. Another example described by Allen is a study by Pereyra of a surgical procedure to correct stress incontinence (needle urethropexy) among 31 female prison inmates.

29. It could be argued that these are instances of the unethical behavior that policymakers were trying to correct. It might also be an example, metaphorically, of the right hand not knowing what the left hand is doing.

30. This had happened earlier with Black men for study of untreated syphilis. It also happened in the late 1960s or early 1970s involving poor, Mexican American women in the study of OCs; and it happened in the 1970s in the study of hormonal agents such as DES.

31. This refers to an intrauterine mechanical device that led to infections.

32. A number of legal scholars were commissioned by the Institute of Medicine to study the problem. A report was released in the spring of 1994.

33. The meeting was sponsored by the Institute for Research on Women's Health (IRWH). Other organizations represented included the National Women's Health Network and the Older Women's League (OWL). Important contributions to the plan were made by Joan Kuriansky (OWL) and Chai Feldblum, an attorney previously active in health policy "on the hill" (as an aid in the U.S. Congress), and then active with AIDS action groups. Renee Royak-Schaler, a health psychologist, also played an important role in mobilizing attention to the fate of Henderson's proposed study. In about 1989 the plan was given to the public policy/P.R. firm of Bass and Howes; the principals of this firm, Marie Bass and Joanne Howes, played a critical role in its implementation.

34. A MEDLINE search was done on July 11, 1994 using the search terms Norplant and human. Of the 100 study citations/abstracts evaluated, 52 did not specify where the study took place. Of the remaining 48, only 1 gave a specific location in the U.S. (thus about 2 percent are known to have occurred in the U.S., although it is possible that more may have been). A total of 84 did not indicate that any funding was received from the U.S. government; and while 16 were funded by the U.S., 15 of these were *not funded by the PHS, but by other government agencies and were carried out in other countries.*

35. Two important resources are S. Reinharz's 1992 work, *Feminist Methods in Social Research* and S. Harding's, ed., 1993 work, *The "Racial" Economy of Science: Toward a Democratic Future.*

REFERENCES

Akhter, H., T. R. Dunson, R. N. Amatya, K. Begum, T. Chowdhury, N. Dighe, S. L. Krueger, and S. Rahman
  1993   A five-year clinical evaluation of Norplant contraceptive subdermal implants in Bangladeshi acceptors. Contraception 47:569–582.

Allen, M.
  1994   The Dilemma for Women of Color in Clinical Trials. Journal of the American Medical Women's Association 49:105–109.

Anastos, K., P. Charney, R. A. Charon, E. Cohen, C. Y. Jones, C. Marte, D. M. Swiderski, M. E. Wheat, and S. Williams.
  1991   Hypertension in Women: What Is Really Known? Annals of Internal Medicine 115:287–293.

Angier, N.
  1994   Genetic Mutations Tied to Father in Most Cases. New York Times Science, May 17, p. B9.

Balogh, S. A., S. L. Klavon, S. Basnayake, N. Puertollano, R. M. Ramos, and G. S. Grubb
  1989   Bleeding Patterns and Acceptability among Norplant Users in Two Asian Countries. Contraception 39:541–553.

Becker, B. J.
  1992   Using Results from Replicated Studies to Estimate Linear Models. Journal of Educational Statistics 17:341–362.

Bell, S.
  1976/84 Birth Control. *In* The Boston Women's Health Collective's The New Our Bodies, Ourselves. Pp. 220–262. New York: Touchstone, Simon & Schuster.

Belmont Report
  1979   Ethical Principles and Guidelines for the Protection of Human Subjects of Research. April 18. U.S. Department of Health, Education, and Welfare, Washington, DC.

Bennett, J. C.
  1993   Inclusion of Women in Clinical Trials: Policies for Population Subgroups. New England Journal of Medicine 329:288–292.

Bhatt, R., and C. S. Waszak
  1985   Four-year Follow-up of Insertion of Quinacrine Hydrochloride Pellets as a Means of Nonsurgical Female Sterilization. Fertility and Sterility 44:303–306.

Blumenthal, S. J., P. Barry, J. Hamilton, and B. Sherwin, eds.
  1991   Forging a Women's Health Research Agenda. Washington, DC: National Women's Health Resource Center.

Bottiger, L. E., A. K. Furhoff, and L. Holmberg
  1979   Fatal Reactions to Drugs. Acta Medica Scandinavia 205:451–456.

Bunkle, P.
  1993   Calling the Shots? The International Politics of Depo-Provera. *In* The "Racial" Economy of Science: Toward a Democratic Future. S. Harding, ed. Pp. 287–302. Bloomington: Indiana University Press.

Cohen, J.
  1992   A Power Primer. Psychological Bulletin 112: 155–159.

Congressional Caucus on Women's Issues
  1990   News Release, June 18 (Leslie Primmer, contact person). Congresswomen Testify on Quality of Women's Health Research. Congress of the United States, Washington, DC.

Corea, G.
  1977/78 The Hidden Malpractice. New York: Jove, HBJ.
  1980   The Depo-Provera Weapon. *In* Birth Control and Controlled Birth: Women-centered Perspectives. H.B. Holmes, B. Hoskins, and M. Gross, eds. Pp. 107–116. Clifton, NJ: Humana.
  1985   The Hidden Malpractice. Revised edition. New York: Harper and Row.

Cotton, P.
  1990   Is There Still Too Much Extrapolation from Data on Middle-aged White Men? Journal of the American Medical Association 263: 1049–1050.

Cowan, B.
  1980   Ethical Problems in Government-funded Contraceptive Research. *In* Birth Control and Controlling Birth: Women-centered Perspectives. H. Holmes, B. Hoskins, and M. Gross, eds. Pp. 37–46. Clifton, NJ: Humana.

Crouse, J. R., III
  1989   Gender, Lipoproteins, Diet, and Cardiovascular Risk: Sauce for the Goose May Not Be Sauce for the Gander. Lancet, February 11, 318–320.

Crowe, M.
  1976/84 Some Common and Uncommon Health and Medical Problems. *In* The Boston Women's Health Collective's The New Our Bodies, Ourselves. Pp. 475–552. New York: Touchstone, Simon & Schuster.

Davis, D. et al.
  1992   Male-mediated Teratogenesis and Other Reproductive Effects: Biologic and Epidemiologic Findings and a Plea for Clinical Research. Reproductive Toxicology 6:289–292.

Diaz, S., M. Pavez, H. Cardenas, and H. B. Croxatto
  1987   Recovery of Fertility and Outcome of Planned Pregnancies after the Removal of Norplant Subdermal Implants or Copper-T IUDs. Contraception 35: 569–579.

Diskin, V.
  1976/84 Developing an International Awareness. *In* The Boston Women's Health Collective's The New Our Bodies, Ourselves. Pp. 611–625. New York: Touchstone, Simon & Schuster.

Domecq, C., C. A. Naranjo, I. Ruiz, and U. Busto
  1980   Sex-related Variations in the Frequency and Characteristics of Adverse Drug Reactions. Int J Clin Pharmacol Ther Toxicol 18:362–366.

Eaker, E.
  1989   Psychosocial Factors in the Epidemiology of Coronary Heart Disease in Women. Psychiatric Clinics of North America 12:167–173.

Edwards, L. D.
  1992   Design and Conduct of Research in Women: To Include or Exclude. A Pharmaceutical Industry Physician's Perspective. Pharmaceutical Manufacturers' Association Meeting, February (Washington, DC). Unpublished manuscript.

El-Sadr, W., and L. Capps
  1992   The Challenge of Minority Recruitment in Clinical Trials for AIDS. Journal of the American Medical Association 267:954–957.

Fakeye, O. and S. Balogh
  1989   Effect of Norplant Contraceptive Use on Hemoglobin, Packed Cell Volume, and Menstrual Bleeding Patterns. Contraception 39:265–274.

Faudes, A., V. Brache, A. S. Tejada, L. Cochon, and F. Alvarez-Sanchez
  1991   Ovulatory Dysfunction During Continuous Administration of Low-dose Levonorgesterol by Subdermal Implants. Fertility and Sterility 56:27–31.

Fausto-Sterling, A.
  1992   Myths of Gender. Biological Theories about Women and Men. 2nd ed. New York: Basic Books.

Food and Drug Administration (FDA)
  1977   General Considerations for the Clinical Evaluation of Drugs (Sept.). 5600 Fishers Lane, Rockville, MD 20857. HEW (FDA) 77-3040.

Garcia, G., and S. Dacach
  1991   Norplant—5 Years Later. *In* Women and Pharmaceuticals. B. Minkzes, ed. Pp. 29–33.

General Accounting Office (GAO)
  1986   Report on EEOC Compliance at NIH. U.S. Superintendent of Documents, GAO/HRD. Washington, DC.
  1992   Women's Health: FDA Needs to Ensure More Study of Gender Differences in Prescription Drug Testing. Report to Congressional Requesters. U.S. Superintendent of Documents, GAO/HRD-93-17. Washington, DC.

Goldzieher, J. W., L. Moses, E. Averkin, C. Scheel, and B. Taber
  1971a A Placebo-controlled Double-blind Crossover Investigation of the Side-effects Attributed to Oral Contraceptives. Fertility & Sterility 22:609–623.
  1971b Nervousness and Depression Attributed to Oral Contraceptives: A Double-blind, Placebo-controlled Study. American Journal of Obstetrics and Gynecology 22:1013–1020.

Goodman, E.
  1990   [Personal Column]. New York Newsday, June 23, p. 74.

Green, M.
  1994   Interview in G. Kolata, In Ancient Times Flowers and Fennel for Family Planning. New York Times Science, March 8, Pp. B5, B9.

Greenberger, S.
  1993   Science Fiction: The Struggle of Female Researchers at NIH. Washington Post, July 11, p. C3.

Gurwitz, J. H., N. F. Col, and J. Avorn
  1992   The Exclusion of the Elderly and Women from Clinical Trials in Acute Myocardial Infarction. Journal of the American Medical Association 268:1417–1422.

Hamilton, J. A.
   1985   Avoiding Methodological and Policy-making Biases in Gender-related Research. *In* Report of the Public Health Service Task Force on Women's Health Issues. Volume II. U.S. Superintendent of Documents. Washington, DC: U.S. Government Printing Office. Section IV. Pp. 54–64.
   1989   Reproductive Pharmacology: Perspectives on Gender as a Complex Variable in Clinical Research. Social Pharmacology 3: 181–200.
   1992   Biases in Women's Health Research. Women and Therapy 12:91–101.
   1993a   Feminist Theory and Health Psychology: Tools for an Egalitarian, Woman-centered Approach to Women's Health. Journal of Women's Health 2:49–54.
   1993b   Inclusion of Women in Clinical Trials. Testimony on Behalf of the American Medical Women's Association. National Institutes of Health, Bethesda, MD.
   1994   Going to Extremes. Special issue, In Sickness and in Health. Women's Review of Books, Volume XI. Pp. 15–16.
 In press Sex and Gender as Critical Variables in Psychotropic Drug Research. *In* Racism, Sexism and Mental Health. B. Brown, B. Kramer, P. Ricker, and C. Willie, eds. Pittsburgh, PA: University of Pittsburgh Press.

Hamilton, J. A., ed.
   1991   Clinical Pharmacology Panel Report. *In* Forging a Women's Health Research Agenda. S. J. Blumenthal, P. Barry, J. Hamilton, and B. Sherwin, eds., Pp. 1–27. Washington, DC: National Women's Health Resource Center.

Hamilton, J. A., M. Grant, and M. F. Jensvold
 In press Sex and Treatment of Depressions: When Does It Matter? Psychopharmacology of Women: Sex, Gender and Hormonal Considerations. *In* M. F. Jensvold, U. Halbreich, and J. A. Hamilton, eds. Washington, DC: American Psychiatric Press.

Hamilton, J. A., B. L. Parry, and S. J. Blumenthal
   1988   The Menstrual Cycle in Context, I: Affective Syndromes Associated with Reproductive Hormonal Changes. Journal of Clinical Psychiatry 49:474–480.

Hamilton, J. A., and K. Yonkers
 In press Sex Differences in Pharmacokinetics of Psychotropic Medications: Part I, Physiological Basis for Effects. *In* Psychopharmacology of Women: Sex, Gender and Hormonal Considerations. M. F. Jensvold, U. Halbreich, and J. A. Hamilton, eds. Washington, DC: American Psychiatric Press.

Harrison, M.
   1992   Women's Health as a Specialty: A Deceptive Solution. Journal of Women's Health 1:101–108.

Heller, T.
   1977   Poor Health, Rich Profits: Multinational Drug Countries and the Third World. Nottingham, England: Spokesman Books (Bertrand Russell Peace Foundation).

Herbst, A. L., H. Ulfelder, and D. C. Poskanzer
   1971   Adenocarcinoma of the Vagina: Association of Maternal Stilbestrol Therapy with Tumor Appearance in Young Women. New England Journal of Medicine 284:878–881.

Hilts, P. J.
   1993   F.D.A. Ends Ban on Women in Drug Testing. New York Times, March 25, section B, p. 8, col. 4.

Hurwitz, N.
   1969   Predisposing Factors in Adverse Reactions to Drugs. British Medical Journal 1:536–539.

Ickovics, J. R., and E. S. Epel
    1993   Women's Health Research: Policy and Practice. IRB: Review of Human Subjects Research, July–August, Pp. 1,3.

Ickovics, J. R., and Judith Rodin
    1992   Women and AIDS: Epidemiology, Natural History, and Mediating Circumstances. Health Psychology 11(1):1–16.

Institute of Medicine (IOM)
    1994   Report of the Committee on Ethical and Legal Issues Relating to the Inclusion of Women in Clinical Studies: Changes Needed to Encourage Researchers to Enroll More Women in Clinical Studies. Pp. 1–6, press release. February 24, Washington, DC: National Academy of Sciences.

Iso, H., D. R. Jacobs, D. Wentworth, J. D. Neaton, and J. D. Cohen
    1989   Serum Cholesterol Levels and Six-year Mortality from Stroke in 350,977 Men Screened for the Multiple Risk Factor Trial. New England Journal of Medicine 320:904–909.

Jensvold, M. F., J. A. Hamilton, and B. Mackey
    1994   Inclusion of Women in Clinical Trials: How about the Woman Scientists? Journal of the American Medical Women's Association, July, 49:110–112.

Johnson, K.
    1992   Women's Health: Developing a New Interdisciplinary Specialty. Journal of Women's Health 1:95–100

Jones, J. H.
    1981/82 Bad Blood: The Tuskegee Syphilis Experiment: A Tragedy of Race and Medicine. New York: The Free Press (Collier Macmillan).

Kaufman, L.
    1992   Closing the Gender Gap. Government Executive, July 10–13.

Keller, E. Fox
    1985   Reflections on Gender and Science. New Haven, CT: Yale University Press.

Kessel, E., J. Zipper, and S. D. Mumford
    1985   Quinacrine Nonsurgical Female Sterilization: A Reassessment of Safety and Efficacy. Fertility and Sterility 44:293–298.

Kinney, E. L., J. Trautman, J. A. Gold, E. S. Vessell, and R. Zelis
    1982   Underrepresentation of Women in New Drug Trials. Annals of Internal Medicine 95:495–499.

Kolata, G.
    1990   N.I.H. Neglects Women, Study Says. New York Times, June 19, section C, p. 6, col. 6.
    1994   In Ancient Times Flowers and Fennel for Family Planning. New York Times Science, March 8, pp. B5, B9.

Krailo, M. D., and M. C. Pike
    1983   Estimation of the Distribution of Age at Natural Menopause from Prevalence Data. American Journal of Epidemiology 117:356–361.

Lenfant, C.
    1990   Testimony before the Subcommittee on Health and the Environment, Committee on Energy and Commerce, House of Representatives, June 18, pp. 1–10. Director of the Heart, Lung and Blood Institute, Bethesda, MD: NIH.

Levine, C.
    1980   Depo-Provera. Some Ethical Questions about a Controversial Contraceptive. *In* Birth Control and Controlled Birth: Women-centered Perspectives. H. B. Holmes, B. B. Hoskins, and M. Gross, eds. Pp. 101–105. Clifton, NJ: Humana.

Marshall, E.
    1994   New Law Brings Affirmative Action to Clinical Research. Science 263:602.

Martin, E.
  1987/92 The Woman in the Body: A Cultural Analysis of Reproduction. Revised edition. Boston: Beacon Press.

McAnally, L. E., C. R. Corn, and S. F. Hamilton
  1992 Aspirin for the Prevention of Vascular Death in Women. Annals of Pharmacotherapy 26:1530–1534.

Merkatz, R.
  1993 Ethical Issues and Women as Subjects in Pharmacological Protocols. *Presented at* Toward a New Psychobioloy of Depression in Women: Treatment and Gender, November 4. Bethesda, MD: National Institutes of Mental Health.

Merton, V.
  1993 The Exclusion of Pregnant, Pregnable, and Once-Pregnable People (a.k.a. Women) from Biomedical Research. American Journal of Law & Medicine XIX:369–451.

Moeller, J. F., and N. A. Mathiowetz
  1989 Prescribed Medicines: A Summary of Use and Expenditures by Medicare Beneficiaries. *In* National Medical Expenditure Survey Research Findings 3. DHHS Publication Number (PHS) 89-3448. Washington, DC: National Center for Health Services Research and Health Technology Assessment.

Nadel, M. V.
  1990 National Institutes of Health: Problems in Implementing Policy on Women in Study Populations. Testimony before the Subcommittee on Health and the Environment, Committee on Energy and Commerce, House of Representatives, June 18. Pp. 1–14. Washington, DC: United States General Accounting Office.

National Commission for the Protection of Human Subjects of Biomedical and Behavioral Research (NCPHSBBR)
  1978 Department of Health, Education, and Welfare, Pub. No. 78-0012. U.S. Superintendent of Documents, Washington, DC. (See also Belmont Report for Ethical Principles and Guidelines.)

Norsigian, J.
  1980 Foreword. *In* B. Seaman, The Doctor's Case Against the Pill. New York: Dolphin (Doubleday).

Nuremberg Code, Rule 1
  1949

Oberman, M.
  1994 Real and Perceived Legal Barriers to the Inclusion of Women in Clinical Trials. *In* Reframing Women's Health. A. J. Dan, ed. Pp. 266–276. Thousand Oaks, CA: Sage.

Older Women
  1984 Older Women: Research Issues and Data Sources (April 8–10, Background Document). Institute of Gerontology, University of Michigan, p. 1.

Ogilvie, R. I., and J. Ruedy
  1967 Adverse Drug Reactions during Hospitalization. Canadian Medical Association Journal 97:1450–1457.

Okie, S.
  1990 Study: NIH Slow to Include Women in Disease Research. Washington Post, June 19, p. A10.

Olsson, S. E., V. Odlind, E. D. Johansson, and I. Sivin
  1988 Contraception with Norplant Implants and Norplant-2 Implants (Two Covered Rods). Results from a Comparative Clinical Study in Sweden. Contraception 37:61–73.

Payer, L.
1988   Medicine and Culture: Varieties of Treatment in the United States, England, West Germany, and France. New York: Penguin Books.

Rakusen, J.
1981   Depo-Provera: The Extent of the Problem: A Case Study in the Politics of Birth Control. *In* Women, Health and Reproduction. H. Roberts, ed. Pp. 75–108. London: Routledge & Kegan Paul.

Reinharz, S.
1992   Feminist Methods in Social Science. New York: Oxford University Press.

Rieker, P. P., E. M. Fitzgerald, and L. A. Kalish
1990   Adaptive Behavioral Responses to Potential Infertility among Survivors of Testis Cancer. Journal of Clinical Oncology 8:347–355.

Rodin, J., and J. R. Ickovics
1990   Women's Health: Review and Research Agendas as We Approach the 21st Century. American Psychologist 45:1018–1034.

Rosenthal, R., and D. B. Rubin
1982   A Simple, General Purpose Display of Magnitude of Experimental Effect. Journal of Educational Psychology 74:166–169.

Rosser, S. V.
1992   Biology and Feminism. New York: Twayne.
1994   Gender Bias in Clinical Research: The Differences It Makes. *In* Reframing Women's Health, A. J. Dan, ed. Pp. 253–265. Thousand Oaks, CA: Sage.

Ruzek, S. B.
1979   The Women's Health Movement. Feminist Alternatives to Medical Control. New York: Praeger.

Seaman, B.
1969/80 The Doctor's Case against the Pill. Revised edition. New York: Dolphin (Doubleday).

Seaman, B., and G. Seaman
1977/78 Women and the Crisis in Sex Hormones. New York: Bantam.

Schnall, P. L., M. H. Alderman, and R. Kern
1984   An Analysis of the HDFP Trial: Evidence of Adverse Effects of Antihypertensive Treatment on White Women with Moderate and Severe Hypertension. New York State Journal of Medicine 84:299–301.

Sewell, S. S.
1980   Sterilization Abuse and Hispanic Women. *In* Birth Control and Controlled Birth. Women-centered Perspectives. H. B. Holmes, B. B. Hoskins, and M. Gross, eds. Pp. 121–123.

Showalter, E.
1987/85 The Female Malady: Women, Madness, and English Culture 1830–1980. New York: Penguin Books.

Silverman, M. et al.
1982   Prescriptions for Death: Drugging the Third World. Berkeley: University of California Press.

Solomon, A.
1993   Snake Pit. Mirabella, April, pp. 140–144.

Sparks, C., and J. A. Hamilton
1991   Psychological Issues Related to Alternative Insemination. Professional Psychology 22:308–314.

Squires, S.
  1989   There Is Concern that Data from Studies of Males Will Not Apply to Females. Washington Post Health, December 12, p. E5.

Steering Committee of the Physician's Health Study Group
  1989   Final Report on the Aspirin Component of the Ongoing Physician's Health Study. New England Journal of Medicine 321:129–135.

Thapa, S., P. Lampe, and A. Abeykoon
  1992   Assessing Potential Demand for Norplant Implants in Sri Lanka. Advances in Contraception 8:115–128.

Tofler, G. H., P. H. Stone, J. E. Muller, et al.
  1987   Effects of Gender and Race on Prognosis after Myocardial Infarction: Adverse Prognosis for Women, Particularly Black Women. Journal of the American College of Cardiology 9:473–482.

Tuana, N., ed.
  1989   Feminism and Science. Bloomington: Indiana University Press.

Vaughan, P.
  1970   The Pill on Trial. New York: Coward-McCann.

Veatch, R. M.
  1971   Experimental Pregnancy. Hastings Center Report 1:2–3.

Warren, J.
  1993   Too Little, Too Late? A Look at the Notorious Tuskegee Study Focuses on One Repentant Doctor. Chicago Tribune, May 20, Tempo Section, p. 2.

Weiss, K.
  1983   Vaginal Cancer: An Iatrogenic Disease. In Women and Health: The Politics of Sex in Medicine. E. Fee, ed. pp. 59–75. Farmingdale, NY: Baywood.

Wittes, B., and J. Wittes
  1993   Research by Quota: Group Therapy. New Republic, April 5, pp. 15–16.

Wolf, F. M.
  1986   Meta-analysis. Quantitative Methods for Research Synthesis. Beverly Hills, CA: Sage.

Working Group on the Health Consequences of Contraceptive Use and Controlled Fertility
  1989   Contraception and Reproduction: Health Consequences for Women and Children in the Developing World. Washington, DC: National Academy Press.

Young, C. L., and A. Dombrowski
  1989   Psychosocial Influences on Research Subject Recruitment, Enrollment and Retention. Social Work in Health Care 14(2):43–57.

Zimmerman, B. et al.
  1980   People's Science. In Science and Liberation. R. Arditti, P. Brennan, and S. Cavrak, eds. Pp. 299–319. Boston: South End.

Zimmerman, M. K.
  1987   The Women's Health Movement: A Critique of Medical Enterprise and the Position of Women. In Analyzing Gender. A Handbook of Social Science Research. B. B. Hess and M. M. Ferree, eds. Pp. 442–471. Beverly Hills, CA: Sage.

Risk, Prevention, and International Health Policy

■ *Carol MacCormack*

INTRODUCTION

The Netherlands overseas aid agency recently made a film, "Isingiro Hospital" (Development Corporation 1993). This low-budget film about the everyday work of a rural hospital in Tanzania begins with a local staff member lighting kerosene lanterns to place about in the wards, giving some light through the night. Imported fuel to run a generator to make electricity is too much of a luxury for most rural hospitals in Africa. The film places us in Isingiro and we vicariously must deal with, for example, a woman who has been in labor for days. She is carried in on a litter by four men, over mountains, from a village far from any road. Although hospital staff do their best, she dies, and a further problem arises. Where can she be put to rest? Can even more money be found to carry her, a mere young woman, back to her village for proper mortuary ceremonies? Then there is a very gentle interview with a small, graceful, soft-eyed gazelle of a girl who has brought her baby in. She is 15, and the baby is failing to thrive. Yes, she has AIDS, infected by an elderly traditional healer who has left the area without making any provision for the girl or his baby. He may, in fact, be dead. There is a widespread belief in Africa that a man can get rid of a sexually transmitted disease by having sex with a virgin. And so, the film goes gently on, people giving kindness when there is little else to give.

This chapter considers gendered health risk, prevention, and policy in an international comparative framework. It looks at risk, prevention, and policy through two kinds of lenses: the concepts that are part of everyday discourse in

326

international health, and case studies that give the reader a feel for both risk "on the ground," as well as the dilemmas that must be faced when financial and other resources are severely constrained. Global primary health care policy, epidemiology, and economics must be balanced against careful local-level studies so we know about needs and perceived priorities in some detail. Those needs can then be related to social and other resources that may already be in place at the local level. We need to know what the sexual division of labor looks like and how risk arises out of daily activity. Risk might be thought of as direct and indirect. Women experience direct risk when their work causes them to stand in water where schistosomiasis transmission is intense. Indirect risks arise from the subtleties of low female status, early age of marriage, or family preference for making all kinds of social investments, including health care, in males over females. But especially with the primary health care approach, many countries are making good attempts to extend equitable primary health care across class and gender lines, so we need to know in some detail about women's actual and potential roles within a primary health care service. How might women be central to planning, evaluating, and sustaining appropriate health care?

RISK

For virtually all diseases and health conditions there is some gender difference in risk and effective control strategies. In Sierra Leone, for example, where a cultural consensus on the sexual division of labor has arisen over centuries, women spend more time than men in ponds, streams, and at the margins of lakes and rivers. They stand in swamps transplanting rice seedlings, and they go into rivers to collect drinking water, wash clothes, wash children, or fish with hand nets. Predictably, prevalence rates for schistosomiasis haematobium, a disease transmitted by free-swimming parasites that work their way through the skin of people standing in water, are higher for women than for men (White et al. 1982).

One of the symptoms of s. haematobium is bloody urine, which results when the spined-egg form of the parasite penetrates the bladder. It is then ready to be urinated back into water to complete the transmission cycle. The parasites' hit-or-miss path to a bladder may damage the reproductive system along the way. The parasite is gender blind, and blunders about in the bodies of both men and women. However, in women, consequent infertility may be far more socially damaging than for men in most societies. Seldom, especially in societies with an ideology of patrilineal descent, is infertility attributed to the husband. Infertile and neglected, abused or abandoned wives consequently carry many subtle, and not-so-subtle, health risks.

Although the schistosomiasis parasites cause blood loss from males and females alike, the cumulative effect in women may be far greater. Women also lose blood in menstruation or in episodic abortion, ectopic pregnancy, or childbirth. After about the 14th week of pregnancy, women lose their acquired immunity to malaria. As a result, plasmodium parasites may destroy large numbers of red blood cells. If women do not have cash for sandals or access to latrines they may have more of a risk than men of becoming infested with hookworm. The parasites enter the body through the feet and migrate to the gut, where they attach themselves to its wall and draw out blood. A situation of serious anemia builds up, with untreated bacterial infections also contributing to the condition. Finally, there may be gendered food taboos or unequal access to protein and iron-rich foods, and risk deepens (Schofield 1979; Chen 1981; Pelto 1984; Khan et al. 1985). About 65 percent of pregnant women in developing countries (excluding China) are anemic, compared with about 14 percent in industrial countries (Royston 1982).

The situation for a seriously anemic woman becomes dire in pregnancy and childbirth. In a healthy and well-nourished woman, reserves of iron are stored in her bone marrow. During periods of physical stress, such as pregnancy, when the growing fetus and changes in the uterus require more nutrients, the body can call on such reserves. But without adequate iron, folic acid, other vitamins and trace elements, hemoglobin will not form and will not be available to do its work of transporting oxygen to all parts of the body. Anemic women in labor, especially if there is much bleeding, soon tire as their muscles become starved for oxygen, and they may die of heart failure, or shock. If they survive birth they may die of infection that has taken advantage of their impaired resistance to disease.

Anemia, of course, is not the only risk of death in pregnancy and childbirth for women in poor countries. In rural areas, especially, a range of suitable contraceptives is not available. Abortion is illegal or scarcely available under sterile conditions in many countries and carries great risk. For example, a hospital survey in Lagos, Nigeria, reported that 51 percent of maternal deaths were due to abortion complications, especially sepsis from incomplete abortion (Rosenfeld 1989). Another risk is ectopic pregnancy that is not swiftly diagnosed and treated. Untreated sexually transmitted diseases, of course, predispose for that condition. Hemorrhage may occur in pregnancy, as with an ectopic pregnancy, or during birth or following birth. Eclampsia, where blood pressure soars and a pregnant woman goes into convulsions, is not well understood, but often lethal. Where hospital facilities for a cesarean section are not available, obstructed labor may directly result in death, or the immediate cause of death may be a ruptured uterus as desperate attempts are made to apply fundal pressure (MacCormack 1994). A woman's liver, impaired by malaria, hepatitis, or other blood diseases may also cause death in pregnancy and birth, and the risk is especially high for poor women living in a physical environment where drinking water and food may be contaminated with fecal matter, or where poverty allows them few work options and they may be exposed to other people's contaminated body fluids.

These are some of the direct causes of risk in pregnancy, but there are indirect causes as well. Women may work very hard with little rest and actually lose weight during pregnancy (Greenwood et al. 1987). In some rural areas there is a lack of health services where pre-eclampsia might be diagnosed or iron supplements given. Where services are available, women may experience economic and cultural barriers such as domestic seclusion, services with only male health workers, or humiliating treatment. Women may speak only a local language or have little education and therefore not be able to express themselves in an appropriate way to receive good services. Where women have little education, they tend to marry before their bodies have fully developed. For example, half of the women in Bangladesh are married before age 15 and half the women in the country are mothers of at least one child by age 19. In one microstudy in Bangladesh, girls aged 10 to 14 had a maternal mortality rate five times higher than women aged 20 to 24 (Royston and Armstrong 1989).

Within an international comparative framework, the range of risk between rich and poor countries is shocking. In developing countries, the average lifetime risk of dying of pregnancy-related causes is between one in 15 and one in 50. However, in industrial countries the risk is between one in 4,000 and one in 10,000. Maternal mortality is often expressed as a rate, and Western European countries report about 10 deaths per 100,000 live births. But rates go as high as 1,100 maternal deaths per 100,000 births in Somalia, where infibulation is only one contributing cause. Maternal mortality rates average about 640 per 100,000 in all of Africa. To put the matter another way, between one-quarter and one-half of all deaths of women in their reproductive years in developing countries can be attributed to causes associated with pregnancy and birth, and most of those deaths are preventable (Royston and Armstrong 1989:9, 32–37).

Within regions of the world, it is very difficult to generalize. For example, in the Asian region, a 1984–85 study in Andhra Pradesh, India, found a maternal mortality rate of 874 per 100,000 in rural areas and 545 per 100,000 in urban areas (Bhatia 1986). By contrast, China reported 59 per 100,000 in rural areas and 25 per 100,000 in urban areas. Japan averages about 15 per 100,000 (Royston and Armstrong 1989:33).

Historical information from Europe has guided international policy. Church records from 16th-to-18th century England suggest a maternal mortality rate of over 2000 per 100,000, and until 1935 the rate for England and Wales had been at about 400 per 100,000 for some time. The causes of those high rates were presumably similar to causes in poor countries today: inadequate nutrition, hard physical work, many pregnancies, close birth intervals, no knowledge of asepsis, and no means such as transfusion, antibiotics, or cesarean section for dealing with life-threatening complications (Loudon 1992).

PREVENTION

If we keep the focus on maternal mortality, there are two principal variables that result in high death rates: risk and fertility. Although both variables are ultimately about risk, it is useful for analytical purposes to keep them separate as we think about prevention. Risks might be thought of as direct and indirect. A direct risk, for example, is anemia exacerbated by postpartum hemorrhage. The indirect risk is poor nutrition in childhood and a lack of rural health services that control and treat the parasitic diseases that contribute to amemia. The other variable is fertility, which allows the possibility of being pregnant, and therefore of dying in childbirth. In Africa, for example, each pregnancy carries about a one in 140 chance of death. The risk is cumulative and, with many pregnancies, the lifetime risk increases to about one in 15 chances of death. Contraception is especially important for women aged 10 to 19, women with birth intervals shorter than two years, and women with high parity, since risk takes a u-shaped curve and rises again after several pregnancies. These are the fertility categories that carry highest risk and therefore where prevention in the form of good contraceptive choice is most important.

In a comparative framework, total fertility rates (the number of children an average woman would have in her lifetime) range from 6.3 in Africa to 2.0 in industrial countries (United Nations 1987). Royston and Armstrong looked at information from 38 developing countries and found a fertility rate of 3.9 among women with seven or more years of schooling and 6.9 among women with no schooling (p. 190). Therefore, an "up-stream" preventive strategy such as targeted functional education for girls is a very practical policy. Projects in Costa Rica, Bangladesh, Botswana, Jamaica, and other countries are now helping low-income women gain marketable skills, basic literacy and numeracy, and, often, business skills for running cooperatives as well. General health and contraceptive services become a logical part of skills and self-esteem enhancement.

The roots of some problems, such as cephalopelvic disproportion, in which a woman's pelvic area is too small to allow the baby to be born, or anemia, usually begin in the woman's childhood (Boerma 1987). Therefore, effective strategies go beyond medical interventions. They are fundamentally about social class, as well as ethnic and gender justice. Selective technical interventions such as immunization campaigns, while good in themselves, are insufficient preventive strategies and often represent the illusion of value-free science in solving problems. Even girl's education has become something of a technical fix without acknowledging that one society is very different from another in its propensity to make any kind of social investment in girls and women, and the correlation between more education and fewer deaths may reflect a deeper underlying cultural ethos.

For example, in regions such as South India with wet ecologies and very labor-intensive economies, where women's productive and reproductive roles are overtly valued, women tend to have greater social power. These are the kinds of societies where one sees equal numbers of dead girls and boys. In drier ecologies, with plow cultivation and draft animals owned by men, women have little direct role in the production of goods and services, and may be in domestic seclusion. They own few practical or prestige goods which they can give to other people and therefore put those people in their social debt. They have little with which to initiate such social reciprocities, and have few avenues for increasing their social power. In the ecological environment and gendered economies of North India, Pakistan, or the Horn of Africa, for example, we see far more dead girls than boys, an indication of families' reluctance to make social investments, including education and health care, in females (MacCormack 1988).

We might think of two related approaches to understanding women's health risks and therefore working out preventive strategies. One is to look at the sexual division of labor in a population to know in some detail what women are actually doing. Since "women" is not a homogeneous category, one must disaggregate by social class, caste, age, ethnicity, and other relevant categories. From this "on-the-ground" perspective, we clearly see those women in Sierra Leone standing in water, or the multiple risks that poor young women doing low-paid factory work in Mexico, Philippines, Thailand, and elsewhere incur. Hypotheses about risk derived from a study of the sexual division of labor can then be confirmed with health surveys that document schistosomiasis, injury, or heat stress. The other starting point is to begin with epidemiological patterns disaggregated by gender and other social categories. If there is more schistosomiasis in women, follow the trail back into their daily activities in order to know how to prevent the risk. China, for example, has used this kind of two-way research to design control strategies linked with effective community action. With schistosomiasis, for example, the number of infected people is now only one-tenth the number infected in China before this kind of effective control approach began, and they are mostly in high mountain regions where the population is sparse (WHO 1985:79–80; Bundy 1988).

PRIMARY HEALTH CARE STRATEGIES

Much of the debate about preventive strategies has revolved around the concept of primary health care. In 1978 the World Health Organization and UNICEF jointly put out a policy paper advocating a broad-based approach to improving health in all countries (WHO/UNICEF 1987). For example, intersectoral collaboration might link education, nutrition through better farming policy, and health together. The focus shifted from doctors and hospitals to a higher ratio of paramedical workers, dispersed health centers, and community health workers. Equitable distribution of services, linking family planning with maternal and child health care, and collaboration with traditional practitioners such as traditional midwives were directly advocated. Countries such as Tanzania took the idea of community involvement seriously and combined mass literacy campaigns with provision of wells and latrines at the village level. Communities selected their local health workers, and took other kinds of direct social action. In some countries where social and political reform was badly needed, health became the entry-point for marketing cooperatives, land reform, and other social transformations (Heggenhougen 1984).

These basic preventive measures have often been opposed by local elites, professionals, and some international agencies. Only a year after the WHO/UNICEF policy document, Walsh and Warren (1979) attempted to restore a "top-down," management-focused view that targeted specific cost-effective disease-control strategies. Their paper, which subsequently influenced policy in agencies such as UNICEF and U.S.AID, claimed to be a hard-headed scientific approach, based on the numbers of disease prevalence and intervention costs. They calculated that a life saved in an immunization campaign only cost one-half to one-third the amount per life saved compared to a life saved in a more comprehensive community approach. But, as we shall see, it is very difficult to put a dollar value on a community process, especially if one is looking not in the short term but at sustainability over the long term.

The WHO-UNICEF policy document emphasizes equity and empowerment of the community to become active on behalf of their own well-being. It invites a process of social transformation that would be of great benefit to women. By way of contrast, the disease-targeted approach has little power of social transformation. With little emphasis on broad-based local training, once the specific campaign or intervention has ended, little of lasting value is left behind (Rifkin and Walt 1986). From the point of view of this book, the most serious criticism is that the disease-focused approach is not interested in women's health problems unless they are related to targeted interventions in pregnancy and birth. All those subtle, up-stream causes of women's anemia, for example, do not come into view. When anemia is seen in the clinical moment it is to be overcome with a pill a day. The phenomenon of women coming together to protect their forest, to demand better factory conditions, or to oppose dowry deaths is not defined as health. Sensitive questions of how to provide care for women in domestic seclusion, or allow untouchable women access to a village well are not amenable to quantitative calculations of costs and benefits and therefore not part of narrowly defined scientific discourse.

Even presuming the benefits of technological approaches, we know that many technologies for better health have long been available but are underutilized by women who are poor and have little free time (MacCormack 1989). Much of the literature about women and primary health care has the unstated assumption that only mothers should be caregivers and they are leisured housewives. But women appear to be the only financial support for as many as one-third of the families in the world, and those tend to be poor families. As early as 1970 Esther Boserup identified what she called "female farming systems," in which women spent more labor time in agriculture than did men, and domestic work beyond that (1970).

The gendered politics of primary health care emerges in its true complexity when we realize that the majority of health objectives revolve around women in their mothering and nurturing roles, but in many societies women are not expected to speak in public meetings, control money, or have overt political power. Those who advocate a disease-intervention technological approach to primary health care deceive themselves into thinking they can ignore these complications since important decisions are taken at higher levels and imposed downward. But if we are serious about health priorities being set at the local level, health workers being the ones the community wants, and the sustainability of programs, we need to utilize anthropological methods. Even in societies where women are officially politically invisible, they are often well organized and active, exerting subtle rather than crude political force.

For example, Gambian village councils rarely include anyone but aristocratic elderly men, and village development councils, which were originally an attempt to overcome political nonrepresentation, tend to drift toward council look-alikes. People from other ethnic groups, commoners, former slaves, youth, and women are not usually included in those councils that receive information, funds, and other resources. However, when we looked more carefully at 33 villages, a 14 percent sample of all primary health care villages in the country, we found indigenous women's organizations already functioning in all the villages. They were far more representative of the village population, including all ages, ethnic groups, classes, and castes. All but one of those 33 women's organizations kept funds for potential investment. Alas, those organizations had seldom been formally included in primary health care planning and one of the consequences was almost universal selection of men as village health workers. At the time of our study, 21 percent of those male health workers had embezzled health funds, but in no village had money been embezzled within the women's organizations, although some of these groups had lost their money when they turned it over to male caretakers. In one case they turned it over to a mobile bank that failed (Cham et al. 1987).

Another aspect of gendered policies is illustrated by this Gambian case study. Following international guidelines, the country had been selecting only one traditional midwife in each village for further training. Villages had as many as nine midwives working in them. In some villages, we found that the midwife who had been selected and given primary health care training was, in actuality, seldom called upon. This situation existed for several reasons. First, since selection was a mark of village respect, the woman chosen was often the wife or sister of the village head. Thus she was quite likely to be old. Even if she had been a practicing midwife, which was not always the case, in old age, her young apprentice actually did most of the hands-on work in pregnancy, birth, and pediatrics. Secondly, all villages contained more than one ethnic group, and villages were further internally divided into neighborhood lineage segments, or *kabilos*. In this society, childbirth is viewed as a dangerous and vulnerable state. For this reason, the women we studied had a strong preference for receiving care from midwives they could trust—women from their own ethnic and kinship group. Therefore, when they went into labor, they and their kin often bypassed the single trained midwife in the village. When asked why in formal questioning, they usually said "the baby came too fast." But in informal chats, their quite reasonable preferences were explored in some detail. Furthermore, Gambian midwives tend to work in teams, giving each other and the laboring woman support as the time passes. Given these realities on the ground, the policy implication seems quite clear. All recognized traditional midwives in a village should be trained. After all, the resources spent on these brief training sessions are minimal compared with other Ministry of Health expenditures, and the potential health benefits are great. The ready-made policy had the effect of splitting the pool of village midwives into one superior, trained woman placed hierarchically against the others, which exacerbated the very tendencies toward village political factionalism that accounted for disrupted health services at the local level.

In this case study, control of basic pharmaceuticals at the village level was only in the hands of the male community health worker, but, of course traditional midwives were much more in touch with sick women and children. The embezzlement problem is especially telling as international ideologies work their way out in Third-World villages. Many IMF/World Bank structural adjustment packages require that national health services be at least somewhat commercialized (Kanji et al. 1991; The Lancet 1994). Some donor agencies, following the "Bamako Initiative," have been encouraging countries to shift primary health care funding from general national revenue to profits from selling pharmaceuticals at the local level. Therefore, the male village health worker is only to treat malaria if the sick child or pregnant woman has cash for the antimalarial drug. We did this study in The Gambia during the rainy season, when killing diseases such as malaria peak. That is the season when the granaries are empty, the last reserves going for seed. There is very little cash about at that stressful time of year. The situation is especially dire for low-status people: ethnic "strangers," children, and women. However, traditional midwives continued to work in a barter economy, accepting what people could give whenever they were able to give it.

We see the same pattern in Sierra Leone, now exacerbated by a meaningless civil war, fed by the arms trade, heaping misery upon misery. There the traditional midwives continue to give care when formal health services have broken down. They are embedded within a woman's religion, even more systematically organized in every village than was the Gambian case. The traditional midwives are skillful diagnosticians for a range of illnesses and conditions; they have long pooled their skills and resources. The German government has wisely funded studies to encourage further training of those respected women. They may keep essential drugs in their sacred house and dispense them within a commonwealth rather than cash-and-carry cultural milieu (Jambai and MacCormack, in press).

GENDER PLANNING

A literature is slowly building on gender planning (see for example Moser 1993; MacCormack 1992). Within the traditional sexual division of labor, women collect water, clean latrines, care for the sick, sweep, clean, wash, prepare food, educate children, and *produce* health in many other ways. They are a formidable health resource already on the job. They may already be organized into groups where they can facilitate preventive and curative public health activities. Especially in settled agricultural economies, traditional midwives are already giving a wide range of services. To ignore their knowledge, curiosity, and their social legitimacy to provide care is to squander a valuable human resource. Because their status is achieved, not ascribed, they tend to be very receptive to training programs that offer real skills, but they are quick to switch off in training programs that attempt to teach them dependency (Jordan 1989).

The participation of women in preprogram identification of needs, priorities, and available resources brings them into the mainstream of primary health care. That is the first step toward greater empowerment for the traditional producers of health. Women have too often been viewed from the top down as passive objects for interventions. Once women have helped identify needs, priorities, and resources they are in a position actually to plan primary health care initiatives. Local information gathered for planning should be integrated with evaluation indicators, and the men and women of the community who "own" this information might play their role in a type of participatory evaluation and replanning. This is the way to sustain primary health care so that there is something left after the immunization campaign has rolled on.

There are hopeful signs that women as women, not just mothers, are becoming visible in health research. In the United States, Canada, and most of Europe, for example, women's health has become a political issue. Women, too, have heart disease. Within the international health context, since 1990 Canada's International Development Research Centre has collaborated with the World Health Organization's Special Programme for Research and Training in Tropical Diseases (TDR) to sponsor a C\$5,000 award for the best paper on "Gender and Tropical Diseases." In 1993, TDR was reorganized. Its old disease-specific steering committees were replaced by a new structure "designed to bring expertise from many disciplines and areas of interest to bear on critical obstacles to disease control" (TDR 1993:3). Applied field studies research priorities explicitly name "Gender and Tropical Diseases" as a focus, including such specific problems as cultural obstacles to treatment facilities, as well as women's access to, and use of, these facilities (TDR 1993:6). Currently TDR is, among other topics, developing and testing a "healthy women's counselling guide" and investigating the nature and extent of genital complications of urinary schistosomiasis and lymphatic filariasis. This represents a sea-change in thinking from only a decade ago when the consensus on schistosomiasis field methods was to select a sample of (elite) school boys.

In March 1994, TDR sponsored an international workshop on using quantitative methods in social research, acknowledging the subtle aspects of risk and primary health care functioning. Since the prestigous TDR part of the World Health Organization is jointly funded by the World Bank and the United Nations Development Programme, they too are investing money, the symbolic good that really counts, in gender-awareness in health. Under donor pressure, change is coming to all the international agencies.

REFERENCES

Bhatia, J.C.
  1986   A Study of Maternal Mortality in Anantapur District, Andhra Pradesh, India. Bangalore: Indian Institute of Management.
Boerma, T.
  1987   The Magnitude of the Maternal Mortality Problem in Sub-Saharan Africa. Social Science and Medicine 24:551–558.

Boserup, E.
1970   Women's Role in Economic Development. Chicago: Aldine.

Bundy, D.
1988   Gender-dependent Patterns of Infection and Disease. Parasitology Today 4: 186–189.

Cham, K., C. MacCormack, A. Touray, and S. Baldeh
1987   Social Organization and Political Factionalism: Primary Health Care in The Gambia. Health Policy and Planning 2:214–226.

Chen, L. C. et al.
1981   Sex Bias in the Family Allocation of Food and Health Care in Rural Bangladesh. Population and Development Review 7:55–70.

Development Corporation
1993   Isingiro Hospital, a film made by the Information Department, Development Corporation, P. O. Box 20016, 2500 EB The Hague, The Netherlands.

Greenwood, A. et al.
1987   A Prospective Study of Pregnancy in a Rural Area of The Gambia, West Africa. Bulletin of the World Health Organization 65:635–644.

Heggenhougen, H. K.
1984   Will Primary Health Care Efforts Be Allowed to Succeed? Social Science and Medicine 19:217–224.

Jambai, A., and C. MacCormack
In press Maternal Health, War and Religious Tradition: Authoritative Knowledge in Pujehun District, Sierra Leone. Medical Anthropology Quarterly.

Jordan, B.
1989   Cosmopolitical Obstetrics: Some Insights from the Training of Traditional Midwives. Social Science and Medicine 28:924–944.

Kanji, N., N. Kanji, and F. Manji
1991   From Development to Sustained Crisis: Structural Adjustments, Equity and Health. Social Science and Medicine 33:985–995.

Khan, M. E. et al.
1985   Health Practices in Uttar Pradesh: A Study of Discrimination against Women. Baroda: Operations Research Group, Working Paper 45.

Lancet, The
1994   Structural Adjustments Too Painful? 344:1377–1378.

Loudon, I.
1992   Death in Childbirth: An International Study of Maternal Care and Maternal Mortality, 1800–1950. Oxford: Clarendon Press.

MacCormack, C. P.
1982   Health, Fertility and Birth in Moyamba District, Sierra Leone. *In* Ethnography of Fertility and Birth. 2d ed. C. MacCormack, ed. Pp. 105–130. Prospect Heights, IL: Waveland Press, 1994.
1988   Health and the Social Power of Women. Social Science and Medicine 26:677–683.
1989   Technology and Women's Health in Developing Countries. International Journal of Health Services 19:681–692.
1992   Planning and Evaluating Women's Participation in Primary Health Care. Social Science and Medicine 35:831–837.

Moser, C.
1993   Gender Planning and Development: Theory, Practice and Training. London: Routledge.

Pelto, G. H.
    1984   Intrahousehold Food Distribution Patterns. *In* Malnutrition: Determinants and Consequences. Western Hemisphere Nutrition Congress, ed. New York: Alan R. Liss.

Rifkin, S., and G. Walt
    1986   Why Health Improves: Defining the Issues Concerning Comprehensive Primary Health Care and Selective Primary Health Care. Social Science and Medicine 23:559–566.

Rosenfeld, A.
    1989   Maternal Mortality in Developing Countries. Journal of the American Medical Association 262:376–379.

Royston, E.
    1982   The Prevalence of Nutritional Anaemia in Women in Developing Countries. World Health Statistics Quarterly 35f:52–91.

Royston, E., and S. Armstrong
    1989   Preventing Maternal Deaths. Geneva: World Health Organization.

Schofield, S.
    1979   Development and the Problems of Village Nutrition. London: Croom Helm.

TDR News
    1993   TDR Undergoes Major Reorganization. TDR News 43:1–8.

Walsh, J. A., and K. S. Warren
    1979   Selective Primary Health Care: An Interim Strategy for Disease Control in Developing Countries. The New England Journal of Medicine 301:967–974.

White, P., M. Coleman, and B. Jupp.
    1982   Swamp Rice Development, Schistosomiasis and Onchocerciasis in Southeast Sierra Leone. American Journal of Tropical Medicine and Hygiene 3:490–498.

World Health Organization
    1985   The Control of Schistosomiasis. Technical Report Series no. 728. Geneva: WHO.

WHO/UNICEF
    1978   Primary Health Care. Geneva: World Health Organization.

United Nations
    1987   World Contraceptive Use, Data Sheet. New York: Population Division of the UN.

Gender Relations, Sexuality, and AIDS Risk among African American and Latina Women

◨ *Margaret R. Weeks*
Merrill Singer
Maryland Grier
Jean J. Schensul

INTRODUCTION

The AIDS epidemic has thrust sexuality and sexual practices into the spotlight as major public health issues. Limits to existing treatment and lack of a vaccine for this deadly disease mean that, over ten years since the first AIDS case was diagnosed, our primary means for saving lives remains the identification of strategies for promoting behavioral changes in highly charged, socially prescribed, personally profound, and intimate behaviors.

AIDS has brought enormous suffering to millions of people of all races, social classes, sexual orientations, nationalities, and genders. Yet, the effects of the epidemic have been disproportionate among homosexual men, people of color in developed nations, and whole populations in less developed countries. The predominance of the disease among people who are personally, socially, economically, and nationally oppressed has been suggested as the reason for the limited and slow response to the need for effective prevention, treatments, prophylactic vaccines, and a cure (Shilts 1987; Singer 1992; Singer et al. 1990a). The political and economic subordination, disenfranchisement, and stigmatization suffered by those hardest hit by the epidemic shapes the response of these groups to sudden social demands by mainstream institutions to modify behaviors that are closely interwoven with group definition.

In the U.S., the ability of highly impacted groups or communities to reduce the spread of infection has rested on their redefinition of socially constructed behaviors and relationships in the domains of sexuality and drug use. White gay men, whose identity and strength as a unified group grew out of the sexual revolution of the 1960s and 1970s, were able to use their own existing organizations, networks, and media to build AIDS risk reduction into standard sexual practices and to redefine sexual pleasure to include activities less likely to transmit HIV. A critical issue that had to be addressed in setting new standards for sexual practice was how to reduce risk without losing the sexual freedoms and power of identity that they only recently had realized (Bolton 1992; Crimp 1988; Shilts 1987).

Two lessons stem from this example. The first is that the degree to which those at particular risk for HIV infection identify themselves as a unified group affects their ability to coalesce around political or social action to address the common threat of this deadly epidemic. The second is that AIDS prevention within any such group is only as effective as that group's social capacity (including resources) and freedom to redefine accepted and acceptable practice without losing the strength of their group identity. It is important to recognize that macrostructural "power relations invade and shape all discourse" (Crimp 1988: 248), including the discourse of intimacy and contestation expressed in the realm of human sexuality and gender interaction. Such shaping has real and potentially painful consequences. Thus, external forces, including ideas and social relations, have a direct and potentially negative impact on a group's ability and commitment to redefine desired or acceptable sexual practice, even in response to a potential life threat.

We know now that the AIDS epidemic was spreading rapidly among injection drug users (IDUs) in urban areas of the Northeast and impacting heavily on urban communities of color during the period when epidemiological, governmental, and media attention were focused almost solely on the gay population (as well as on the safety of the blood supply). While the number of men thus infected was significantly larger than women in these communities, the latter were increasingly impacted both through their own drug use and that of their male sex partners. Institutional neglect of this arena of HIV transmission, combined with a significant lack of resources in impoverished communities, and the panoply of competing health and social problems faced by these communities, contributed to the rapid development of an inner city AIDS epidemic. A reluctance on the part of some minority community leaders to acknowledge and address the need for a unified response to stopping the disease also slowed recognition of the serious impact of AIDS in urban neighborhoods. This reluctance stemmed from their own negative attitudes toward homosexuality and drug use, behaviors associated with HIV transmission (Baker et al. 1989; Freudenberg, Lee, and Silver 1989; Friedman et al. 1987; Dalton 1989; Singer et al. 1990a). Additionally, political factors played into their hesitancy to focus attention on the growing evidence of AIDS, including a desire to avoid further stigmatization of their communities, resistance to warnings by the nation's power structures about HIV in their communities, and beliefs by some that AIDS was created as another tool of racial oppression and that condom promotion was aimed at genocide.

The contours of the epidemic are increasingly catastrophic. AIDS is now the leading cause of death among women and men between the ages of 25–44 in

African American and Latino communities in the U.S., where it is primarily transmitted through injection drug use or unprotected sex with an IDU (CDC 1993a, 1993b; Miller, Turner, and Moses 1990; Slutsker et al. 1992; Singer 1994). Rates of heterosexual transmission are increasing rapidly and disproportionately among women in these groups (Cochran 1989; Fullilove, Fullilove, Haynes, and Gross 1990; Holmes, Karon, and Kreiss 1990; Miller, Turner, and Moses 1990), as well as among their children (CDC 1993b).

As a result of the devastating toll of AIDS in minority communities, both national and grassroots community responses among African Americans, Latinos, and other nonwhite groups have developed in recent years (although some of these efforts date to early in the epidemic) (Freudenberg, Lee, and Silver 1989; Singer et al. 1990a; Singer 1995). These efforts have contributed to increasingly supportive attitudes towards those at highest risk or already infected in these communities. Political action, combined with targeted outreach and community-based intervention, have affected drug use practices, including the incorporation of safer needle use patterns among IDUs and reduction of drug use among those contacted by these programs (Brown and Beschner 1993). Nevertheless, these projects have primarily targeted men, and have had limited success in recruiting and adequately intervening with women (Weeks et al. 1995; Weissman 1991). Prevention among women of color has been limited by their lack of social power through group unity (whether around ethnicity, gender, or another mechanism) and consequent unified political activity to build common means of protection.

In addressing the issue of prevention for women, consideration of the nature of culturally prescribed gender relations and lived patterns of interaction is paramount. New terms have had to be developed to define sets of behaviors associated with prevention of sexually transmitted HIV. These terms include "negotiating" sexual practices, a phenomenon that takes place in a social environment assumed to afford greater power to men (Connell 1987), and which ultimately depends on the man's willingness to put on a condom or accept noncoital sexual activity or abstention, or a woman's ability to refuse the relationship. While some degree of male power in sexual relations with women is widely evident in American culture, specific sources of men's authority in heterosexual relationships and of women's ability to negotiate or control sexual activity vary among different ethnic groups and class strata (Cole 1986; Kline, Kline, and Oken 1992; Rosaldo and Lamphere 1974; Rubin 1976), and as such, differentially affect possibilities for establishing behaviors that reduce the spread of AIDS.

Change in sexual practices to reduce risk of HIV transmission among heterosexual partners has proved slow. Such change must overcome powerful cultural definitions of sex and sexuality, as well as the structure of gender relations and its impact on sexual decision making. Because one of the primary mechanisms of HIV risk reduction in this context (aside from abstinence) is increased condom use during penetrative sex, acceptance of condom use for purposes other than HIV prevention conditions the potential for such an approach to stop the spread of AIDS. Ethnic differences in attitudes toward, and use of, condoms have been noted (CDC 1992; Norris and Ford 1992; Nyamathi, Bennett, Leake, Lewis, and Flaskerund 1993; Valdiserri, Arena, Proctor, and Bonati 1989; Weeks, Singer, Schensul, Jia, and Grier 1993). Research on adolescents and adults has found Latinos are less inclined to use condoms than African Americans or Euro-Americans, though intraethnic differences by class are also apparent (CDC 1992; Norris and Ford 1992). For example, Euro-Americans that we surveyed in an urban working class neighborhood of Hartford reported using condoms more frequently than African Americans or Latinos, while in our study of out-of-treatment IDUs, whose economic status was clearly poorer, Euro-Americans reported less condom use than African Americans. Latinos (primarily Puerto Ricans) in both studies reported the least use of condoms (AIDS Community Research Group 1989; Weeks et al. 1993).

These differences raise questions about the nature of the social and cultural factors that affect HIV prevention for specific ethnic groups and economic classes. It is our contention that culturally defined and socially shaped gender roles and definitions of sexuality directly influence sexual decision making around condom use, male or female control of heterosexual sex, and related issues that impact HIV risk and prevention. Furthermore, gender and sexuality are created and continuously reshaped by political economic forces of the broader social structure that define, present, or render virtually inaccessible options for individual behaviors in intimate relationships.

GENDER ROLES, SEXUALITY, AND HIV AMONG AFRICAN AMERICANS AND LATINOS

Concepts that define women and men, gender roles, and sexuality reflect webs of meaning that are spun in relationships, both intimate and personal, and played out in significant social institutions, such as the family and the work place. Holland and colleagues (1990) define sexuality as the complex of values, concepts, and behaviors that includes sexual practices, a group's or an individual's understanding of what constitutes acceptable and desirable sexual activity, and sexual identity. Sexuality is influenced by culturally defined sex roles as well as by factors related to mating, reproduction, and parenthood (cf. Scott et al. 1988).

Gender definitions and relations embody multidimensional ideals and interactions among women and men, including those associated with sexual desires, preferences, and practices. They also express and embody relations of power and dominance, assign value to kinds of sexual behaviors and relationships, and impose codes for "traditional," acceptable, and forbidden roles and behaviors. Expectations of women and men regarding reproduction, such as socially prescribed contexts, timing, and partnerships for pregnancy, childbearing, and child rearing, as well as most aspects of family life, are embedded in gender role definitions, sexuality, and gender inequality.

As this discussion suggests, issues of sex, gender, and sexuality cannot be isolated as, nor limited to, intimate, private, and personal interactions between and among women and men in society. Cultural models of heterosexual or homosexual relationships and family structures are conditioned by political economic relations across class, ethnic, religious, and gender lines, as are options available to members of different social groups to acquire means of survival and fulfill culturally prescribed and meaningful roles inside and outside of the household.

Political, economic, and other social forces that shape individual identities and interpersonal relationships also condition the options for changing beliefs and practices, including patterns known to be risky for the transmission of HIV. AIDS prevention has been based on the premise that if sexual and drug-related behaviors could be changed to eliminate transmission risk practices in contexts in which HIV might be present, the incidence of HIV infection would decline significantly. Most AIDS prevention efforts focus on modifying the behavior of individuals. Since sexual practices must involve at least two people for HIV transmission to occur, effective intervention must address sexual roles, definitions, and preferences minimally at the level of the dyad. In addition, intervention strategies must consider the wider context of sexuality, reproduction, economic and political conditions, and other cultural and structural factors that shape the ability of individuals and social groups to change beliefs and practices related to sexual interaction.

The following discussion outlines issues of sex roles, sexuality, and gender relations and their implications for HIV risk behavior and risk reduction in the social and political context of inner-city African American and Latino communities. Our presentation of these issues draws on the social science and popular literature on these two groups broadly defined by class and ethnicity, as well as our own studies of African Americans and Latinos in Hartford, Connecticut. We focus here on heterosexual transmission, and particularly on those factors that define and shape interactions between women and men in intimate relationships within these groups, and in an environment characterized by urban poverty. It is important to note that the discourse on gender relations and sexuality among inner-city African Americans differs in many respects from that on Latinos similarly situated. The dominant issue shaping the literature regarding African Americans is the impact of racial and class oppression on sexual interaction, responses to this oppression, and the negative effects of ideological stereotypes. The focus of the discourse on Latino gender relations is the nature and impact of a set of cultural ideologies and behaviors referred to as "traditional." Despite this varying emphasis in the literature, Latino gender roles also are shaped by oppression by Anglo society; further, African American sexuality is conditioned by both African and American cultural traditions and is not solely a set of responses to racial oppression. For these two groups, relations between sexual partners demonstrate a broad spectrum of behaviors, only a small portion of which actualize socially dominant images defined by ethnicity or racial stereotyping in the American social context. This chapter includes analysis of the ways these dominant themes and images, as well as actual practice, are significant in developing appropriate responses to prevent heterosexually transmitted HIV.

AFRICAN AMERICANS

Social concepts and practices of gender relations, sexuality, and family formation among African Americans are rooted in precolonial African cultures, directly influenced by the history of slavery and Jim Crow laws, and shaped by mainstream American values as well as ongoing *de facto* segregation and discrimination. These factors affect all aspects of sexuality and reproduction among African Americans today. The degree to which precolonial African cultural traditions influence modern African American families and heterosexual relations is unclear, but may be reflected, for example, in the emphasis among African Americans on strong extended kin ties and matrifocal family relations (Stack 1975; Tanner 1974). The social ideals of conformity to Euro-American family structures, division of labor that ascribes power and importance to men, and male domination in heterosexual unions have been instilled in African Americans, as they have in Euro-Americans. Many African Americans accept and integrate these ideals into their personal and family relations, even if racial and class conditions make achieving these ideals impossible (Hooks 1981; McAdoo 1986; Staples and Mirandé 1986; Terrelonge 1984). Social conditions of racism are evident in reduced employment opportunities that limit economic options for blacks and invasive policies regarding family structure in the welfare state. These conditions create barriers, particularly for impoverished African Americans, to establishing idealized family structures by limiting the involvement of men in welfare-supported families, and by creating a need for parents to work multiple jobs, with limited access to socially valued and meaningful work. Racism also is manifest in pervasive ideologies that portray the lifestyles and choices available to African Americans in this context as negative, undesirable, or wrong, and that hold them responsible for their poverty and lack of opportunity (Baer and Singer 1992; Hooks 1981; Jones 1985; Stack 1975; Weinberg and Williams 1988).

Despite the ubiquitous nature of racism in American society that creates these circumstances, the experiences, social institutions, values, behaviors, and belief systems of African Americans are broad and varied. Differences in economic class, regional variations between north and south, and between inner-city, rural, and suburban, and other intra-ethnic differences result in an array of lived relationships, family organizations, and sexual interactions. Much discussion about African American families and heterosexual relationships focuses on the experiences of African Americans documented primarily through studies of impoverished urban black neighborhoods. Though it is thus limited in its source, it is often portrayed as characterizing all individuals defined by African descent in the U.S., regardless of economic status or geographic differences. Yet even urban African American families that similarly experience unemployment or are working poor have varied and diverse life experiences (Hannerz 1969; Stack 1975; Willie 1976). Furthermore, to the degree that they reflect the conditions of the city and the predominant economic class of blacks living there, urban "ghettoized" families differ significantly from those of the growing African American middle class, as well as from rural families. In many cases, these differences parallel those of Euro-American families of similar economic class and socio-geo-graphical situations (Staples and Mirandé 1986; Willie 1976; Heiss 1975). This variation in experiences, beliefs, and behavior patterns creates corresponding dif-ferences in potential for establishing practices in sexual relationships that protect against the spread of HIV where transmission is a possibility.

Social, political, economic, and cultural forces in the U.S. that shape rela-tions in the black family and between African American men and women in het-erosexual relationships also impact on common conceptualizations of these rela-tionships, and concepts of Black men and women themselves. Positive and negative social and cultural forces have generated a complex and contradictory discourse on gender relations and sexuality among African American men and women. This discourse unfolds in various arenas, including in the mass media, government policy settings, social science and other literature, and the day-to-day lives of African American men and women in interaction. Its contradictory nature is compounded with the introduction of AIDS and the consequent need to shape heterosexual interaction around preventing transmission of a deadly disease dur-ing sexual contact.

It is important in this context to differentiate between cultural values and beliefs, stereotyped images created out of oppression, and actual behaviors. Images and stereotypes ascribed to African Americans include both positive cul-tural ideals and negative attributions, and are variously held by all members of American society. These images impact on African Americans' self-concepts and beliefs about members of the opposite sex among their own ethnic group, and shape the comparison between Blacks and other ethnic and racial groups in America, particularly Whites (Bowser 1992; Cazenave and Smith 1990; Hannerz 1969; Hooks 1981; Joseph 1986; Liebow 1967; Stack 1975; Weinberg and Williams 1988). Yet they do not reflect the whole nor limit the actual behaviors and rela-tions of black women and men in their work, their families, and their intimate interactions. The following discussion reviews a number of ideologies defining black women and men and their heterosexual relationships, and the impact of these concepts on their self-described sexual relationships.

Contradictory images of "good" and "bad" role models shape the socializa-tion of young African American girls regarding sexuality and sex role definitions and can generate ambivalence in their aspirations. An example of the "good" model is the idealized image of the woman who carries out her socially approved mother role in the context of economic hardships, as heroine and martyr (Han-nerz 1969), the emotional pillar and source of strength for the family (Joseph 1986). In this image, the black woman is the wellspring of high morals in the fam-ily, is church-going and respectable, and passes her ennobling values on to suc-ceeding generations (Hannerz 1969; Jones 1985). Within this idealized model, having children is highly valued, considered a positive goal and a right, to be attempted within the confines of any economic conditions (Carovano 1991; Davis 1986; Stack 1975; Worth 1989). Thus, birth control, abortion, sterilization, and, of special importance in the context of AIDS, condom use take on particular sig-nificance (Davis 1986) and present a potential dilemma for women to protect themselves from HIV in the context of aspiring to attain this highly valued model. Additionally, striving to live an ideal that relies on women's self-sacrifice and self-denial (Hooks 1981) reduces their ability to pursue their own needs and desires with their male partners, including protecting themselves from AIDS. Yet African American women's strength within and for the family provides them a source of resiliency and power to protect themselves and family members from HIV risk.

Some studies of black communities document African American women as very independent and as strong and assertive in their relations with men (Pittman et al. 1992), primarily as a result of kin supports and economic independence that have evolved throughout the history of black experiences in America (Anderson 1990; Hooks 1981; Stack 1975). This independence and assertiveness in relationships with men emerges also in studies of African American women's sexuality. Positive images include both sexually restrained and sexually freer models of behavior. Many African American girls are socialized to emulate the "good girl" model of sexual restraint in terms of faithfulness to one partner at a time, even if in serial monogamous relationships, including premarital relations, and even if taking pleasure in sex (Fullilove, Fullilove, Haynes, and Gross 1990). Positive images of less restrained sexuality among black women are exemplified by traditionally female blues singers, and more recently by female comedians, who counter puritanical ideas of sex by reflecting it as a source of inner life and as humanizing and enjoyable (Joseph 1986). These images of African American women portray them as assertive in sexual decision making, including whether or not to have sex and what kind of sex to have (Kline, Kline, and Oken 1992). Such assertiveness offers them significant potential, should they desire it, to ensure incorporation of precautions against HIV transmission into their sexual activities with male partners.

The sexually assertive image of African American women is contradicted, however, in other studies that describe sexual and personal domination of black women by black men, even, in some cases, with violence (Anderson 1990:120; Jones 1985:103; Joseph 1986; Pittman et al. 1992:341; Shervington 1993; Worth 1989). Although independence and personal strength are taught as essential for African American women to survive the hardships of racism and economic struggle, many are socialized also to believe that their self-worth depends on their relationships with men, that they are validated only within those relationships, and as a result, that they are relatively powerless to change because they fear risking those relationships (Shervington 1993). For example, some of the African American women from various socioeconomic backgrounds interviewed in Shervington's (1993) focus group study equated "wellness" with being involved in a heterosexual relationship. These women said they consider female control of sexual activities difficult, if not inappropriate or impossible, because of the potential "risk" to the relationship and consequently to their well-being (cf. Joseph 1986; Worth 1989). Such an assessment necessitates a rank ordering of this risk with others, such as potential HIV infection, prompting differential response based on this hierarchy of perceived dangers.

Negative images and interpretations of African American women and their sexuality are commonplace in a social context of racial oppression against blacks, and male domination within all ethnic groups. For example, as Hooks (1981: 54–55) points out, though most African American men and women after slavery adopted the values and behaviors of mainstream Euro-American society regarding sexual morality and virtue, white images of black sexuality portrayed all blacks as sexually promiscuous and uncontrolled. One common negative image of African American women is manifest in the notion of the "bad girl" (Fullilove, Fullilove, Haynes, and Gross 1990), or the "sexually promiscuous" woman (Pittman et al. 1992:340). The "bad girl" takes pleasure in seeking men's company and having multiple sexual relationships, is open about sexual pleasures and casual about giving sex, or exchanges sex for money (Fullilove, Fullilove, Haynes, and Gross 1990; Hannerz 1969). This image evolved out of postslavery white ideologies portraying all newly freed black women as sexually loose and was adopted by some black men who interpreted the broader racist ideology in the context of a male-dominant social hierarchy among African Americans (Hooks 1981:60, 70). Concern that a woman's sexual behavior might be labeled in this way may make her reluctant to appear assertive about sexual activity, even for protection against HIV (such as encouraging noncoital sex or use of condoms).

A related version of this negative image connotes black women's intimate sexual relationships with black men as entrapment, for example, using sex to attract a partner, to get material support such as groceries or other goods, and possibly to get a commitment from the man for a long-term relationship. In two separate studies of urban African American "ghetto" communities, this concept was documented in the dialogue of men and boys describing their concerns about the intentions of women (presumably black women) in relationships with them (Anderson 1989 and 1990; Joseph 1986). One African American man interviewed in Anderson's (1990) ethnography of an urban ghetto described this feeling of entrapment by a woman:

> My wife done that to me. Before we got married, when we had our first baby, she thought, well, hey, if she had the baby, then she got me, you know. And that's the way she done me. [She] thought that's gon' trap me. That I'm all hers after she done have this baby. So, a lot of women, they think like that. . . . (quoted in Anderson 1990:121).

In another rendition of this negative image, some young men in Anderson's study indicated belief that a teenage girl will use boys to get pregnant, so she can use the baby to get on welfare and out on her own, and then be done with the boy, thereby asserting control over the situation for her own ends (Anderson 1990:126). While such ethnographic text should not be read as depicting all, or even "typical" heterosexual relationships in this setting, it shows how negative images and stereotypes permeate popular thinking and influence beliefs about the opposite sex. This negative imaging of black women degrades their attempts to initiate and control intimate sexual partnerships by portraying such behavior as manipulative and emasculating of their male partners.

Perhaps the most widespread image of black women that has obtained a negative connotation is their decision-making power in the family, especially as the single head of household. A significant body of social science literature, founded on Moynihan's (1965) study of the black family, analyzed this image of African American women's power in the home as a black "matriarchy." Black women, in this complex conceptualization, are described as having too much power and control in the home, and are identified as the source of an evolving pathology within and disintegration of the African American family and community (Moynihan 1965; for critical reviews of this concept, see Cazenave and Smith 1990:150; Hooks 1981:70ff; Jones 1985:312). Thus, characteristics considered strengths in the context of economic deprivation and racial discrimination are transformed by this image into causes of family disorganization and unhappy, disoriented youth (particularly boys, who are presumed to lack strong male role models in the home).

A related negative image is depicted in the belief that African American women socially "castrate" or emasculate black men, for example, by participating in keeping black men down economically and politically (Cazenave and Smith 1990). This conceptualization is bolstered by the experience that qualified black women are more in demand for opportunities in education and employment than black men. African American men have expressed resentment of what they perceive as better prospects for African American women that have been created, for example, by affirmative action practices (Cazenave and Smith 1990). Thus, both internal ethnic and external social images and economic and political forces contribute to the idea that black women succeed at the expense of black men. Such imaging has the dual effect of pitting African American men and women against each other for control of the relationship within the family, and of reducing women's legitimacy in demanding such control in the context of men's reduced social stature outside the home. This context exacerbates the difficulties African American women face in "negotiating" for protection against HIV with close male partners.

In sum, in a social and historical context defined by racist ideologies of African American subordination and inferiority, mirror imaging portrays black women's strength, tenacity, and independence as the source of African American social and familial disintegration. Likewise, positive images of black women's sexual assertiveness, allure, and "humanizing" sexual activity are cast as socially deviant, deceitful, and self-serving. Thus, political economic conditions of racial oppression actively shape gender ideologies and gender relations among African Americans, superimposing negative meaning on sources of strength and resiliency. This has created contradictory images, such as those described here, of African American women, both positive and negative aspects of which are internalized by black men and women alike, and most negative aspects of which reinforce racist stereotyping of African Americans. But while such contradictory concepts prevail for all African Americans, their paradox is most evident for the poor. Thus, those at greatest risk of HIV infection are most negatively affected by the personal and social impacts of these racially constructed gender models and of African American men's response to them.

Yet, despite the ambiguity of these gender constructs, African American women over the centuries have maintained their families economically, emotionally, and spiritually, built strong relationships with male partners, and contributed significantly to their communities and to American society. It is these strengths, positive images, and contributions that, when identified and emphasized, create a source of pride and a sense of self-worth in African American women. These, in turn, support efforts to implement changes in accepted practices and norms of sexual interaction to incorporate protection against heterosexually transmitted HIV.

As with African American women, contradictory images and stereotypes exist for African American men regarding their sexuality and sex roles in heterosexual relationships. The "good man" ideal image parallels that in dominant American culture; that is, he holds a steady job, provides for his family, and stays home and out of trouble (Hannerz 1969; Anderson 1989, 1990). In urban black neighborhoods, many African American men have serious intentions to achieve this goal, but few possibilities and little confidence in their ability to do so in the context of the inner-city and broader social forces that restrict their educational and employment options (Anderson 1989).

With the exception of this ideal image of the black man, positive images are limited and negative stereotypes and interpretations of African American men's behavior abound. Dominant racist ideology has defined black men as shiftless, lazy, and irresponsible, as well as sexually uncontrolled (for a critical discussion of these stereotypes and their effects, see Cazenave and Smith 1990:151; Jones 1985; Hannerz 1969:97; and Pittman et al. 1992:340). To the degree that dominant ideology affects all members of society, this stereotype has influenced African Americans' own assumptions about, and definitions of, black men. Several studies of African American communities describe black women's distrust of black men, and their assumption that most black men are "naturally" or inherently bad, sinful, and untrustworthy—particularly in their relationships with black women (Hannerz 1969:99; Joseph 1986:292; Stack 1975:111). One woman in Joseph's (1986) study described how she interprets men's sexual intentions:

> Sisters have been socialized to believe that involvement with males is a real true relationship—a sincere commitment. The brothers, on the other hand, believe that the "rap" is most important in order to get over [have sex] (quoted in Joseph 1986:295).

Black men's distrust of black women, and black women's, of black men, is associated with the likelihood of infidelity in contexts and through images such as the "rap" or "game," leading to the assumption that the result will be a broken marriage or dissolved intimate relationship (Hannerz 1969:101; Joseph 1986:292; Pittman et al. 1992:340; Shervington 1993:344). These negative images of African American men are shaped by a context in which the means to achieve positive models are elusive, and most men, if not all, are perceived or expected to fail. The power of negative stereotyping shapes the perception that pathological relationships between African American men and women predominate, and the resultant mutual distrust reinforces dynamics that can undermine their relationships. Introduction of mechanisms for protection from HIV complicate further the already contradictory images and expectations of the relationship.

Both positive and negative concepts of the black family and heterosexual relationships give meaning to interactions between African American men and women (Heiss 1975; Hill 1972; McAdoo 1978; Scanzoni 1971; Stack 1975; Willie 1976). The sexual division of labor in the African American family historically has differed from the Euro-American, middle-class ideal. Although African American men play a dominant role in many families, both men and women often by necessity earn income, possibly of different kinds and under different economic conditions (Hooks 1981; Jones 1985). Given this context, black heterosexual couples have fewer gender-based responsibilities than their white counterparts, including financial contribution to support the family. The influence that an African American woman can garner from her economic contributions can increase the balance in decision-making power and authority between her and her husband within the family (Pittman et al. 1992:340). These differences in African American family structure and marital relations from the Euro-American, middle-class ideal of the 19th and 20th centuries have often been maligned and used to "explain" social problems experienced by African Americans (cf. Jones 1985; Stack 1975).

Negative images of African American marriages and family structures can be traced to white critiques of late 19th-century black families. In this appraisal, the black family was described as a partnership between an irresponsible black man and his hardworking wife, which resulted in a dominant black woman breadwinner and decision-maker in the family (thus the basis for the concept of the "matriarchy"). This critique changed in the mid-20th century to incorporate the concept of irresponsible, "absent" fathers, with the development of the welfare state to support single women with children (Jones 1985:104), a condition that paradoxically was created in part by the structure and procedures of the welfare system itself, rather than the impoverished and unemployed men (of all races) who were forced to absent themselves from their families to ensure continued financial income for their partners and their children.

The contradictory images of African American heterosexual relations described above portray African American male/female partnerships as both matriarchal and patriarchal, and of black women's independence in the family as an indication of both heroic personal strength in the face of hardship and as domineering and emasculating of black men. "Minority" status and a subordinate position of power in American society have lent a negative hue to concepts and actions that can be defined as inherently either good or bad. Significantly, research by Cazenave and Smith (1990) has shown that African Americans who hold more negative stereotypes and images of the opposite sex also appear to experience more conflict in their heterosexual relationships. This presumably carries over into the domain of "negotiations" for sexual behavior that can prevent transmission of HIV.

African American men and women do not necessarily agree with the ideologies, stereotypes, and definitions of black men and black women and their heterosexual relationships outlined here. As noted above, intracultural diversity is evident in the wide variety of values and behaviors within the context of racism, class structure, and ethnic culture, which are not singly determined by any one of these factors (cf. Joseph 1986:286). Joseph's (1989) and other studies (e.g., Holmbeck, Waters, and Brookman 1990; Johnson et al. 1992; Weinberg and Williams 1988) suggest that no monolithic standards define African American sexuality, gender roles, heterosexual relationships, and family structures. Historical racist ideologies have a widespread impact, but limited relationship to lived experiences and values of African American men and women. Recognition of this diversity of experience and the impacts of this panoply of positive and negative forces on, and images of, African Americans must be directly identified and addressed in HIV prevention efforts in order to place HIV and its associated effects within a social context and to build on potential sources of unity and support for reduction of HIV transmission.

LATINOS

Relationships between women and men in Latin American communities in the U.S. are based in economic and political processes similar to that of African Americans. These processes include the destruction of indigenous populations and the introduction of Catholicism and later, fundamentalist Protestantism, which define and place parameters around the roles and responsibilities of men and women and their relationships, including their sexual relationships with one another. The undermining of traditional economies following the Spanish colonial period led to the slow disintegration of the economic role of the male in the household. A consequence important for the changing structure of the family was the resulting migration from rural to urban areas, and from Latin American countries to the urban U.S. Among migrating households, poverty resulting from the shift in economy from industry to services, which displaced male and eventually female industrial workers, and led both to welfare-based income and the growth over time of single-parent, female-headed households. These conditions of migration also disrupted, to some degree, traditional cultural institutions and social structures that protected women against early pregnancy, substance use and abuse, and sexually transmitted diseases, and created environments, especially for poor women, conducive to both physical and sexual abuse.

In examining the special issues facing Latina women and girls, we will consider both the traditional and contemporary images defining and prescribing female and male roles and sexual relationships, and what we know so far about the responses, which reflect considerable class, cultural, and generational diversity of beliefs diversity of beliefs and behaviors. Latino populations in the U.S. are varied and include several important subgroups based on country of origin, such as Mexican Americans, Puerto Ricans, Cubans, other Caribbeans, South Americans, and Central Americans. We focus this discussion on Mexican Americans and Puerto Ricans, the two Latino subgroups with the lowest education and income levels and the highest HIV infection rates in the U.S. While there are important differences between those two groups, many of the cultural values and social conditions that contribute to AIDS risk are similar between them.

Specific studies of gender relations, AIDS risk, and AIDS prevention among the different Latina women in the U.S. are limited (Amaro 1988; Arguelles and Rivero 1989; Flaskerund and Nyamathi 1990; Kline, Kline, and Oken 1992; Mays and Cochran 1988; Singer et al. 1993; Worth and Rodriguez 1987), especially among women who are poor (Rogler and Cooney 1984; Zambrana 1982). Studies of Latina women outside of the U.S. also are few, though increasing in number (Fox et al. 1993; Gil 1992; Robles et al. 1990). However, a theme common to much of the existing literature is that Latino gender roles restrict the ability of women even to broach issues of sexual practice or condom use. Even within enduring intimate relationships, women are viewed as lacking sufficient power to effect change. Additionally, because condoms, by design, interfere with reproduction, they are seen as violating significant cultural ideals of virility and womanhood (Turner et al. 1989).

Prior to Spanish rule, gender relationships appear to have varied as greatly as the economies and cultural practices of the tribes and nations throughout what is now called Latin America and the Caribbean. The notion of female subordination is commonly linked in the literature to the Latino gender concepts of *machismo* and *marianismo*, concepts introduced by the Spanish, which along with Catholicism, limited and prescribed women's rights, roles, and expectations in relation both to men and reproduction in many Latino cultures. Based on his research among Mexican Americans in south Texas, Madsen (1964:48) notes the basic features of the *machista* complex: "While the Mexican-American male may be a second-class citizen in an Anglo-dominated world, he can be a king in his own home. He is entitled to unquestioning obedience from his wife and children. He is above criticism due to his 'superior' male strength and intelligence." This relationship of male dominance and female subordination is said to be based on "an indubitable, biological, and natural superiority of the male" (Diaz-Guerrero 1955:41).

Descriptions of other Latino populations parallel Madsen's account of the masculine role. Writing about Puerto Rico, Torres-Matrullo (1976:710) notes the dominance in Puerto Rican island culture of the family institution and the strict sex role differentiation within it, in which the man "traditionally occupies a position of strong authority, governed by the norms of *hombre de respecto* and *machismo*. . . ." Torres-Matrullo maintains that this type of family structure and rigid sex roles are prevalent throughout Puerto Rico, regardless of class or education.

Commonly coupled with *machismo* in the literature is the female role ideology known as *marianismo*. Rubel (1964:67), based on his work in a Mexican American community in a lower Rio Grande Valley Texas city, reports that "the consistently idealized portrait one receives of Mexican-American mothers is that of suffering (*padeciendo*) women." Similarly, in his south Texas study, Madsen (1964) found that women are expected to provide comfort and pleasure to their husbands. A woman must acknowledge male authority and superiority and place a man's needs before her own. Further, a woman is supposed to accept physical abuse, her husband's extramarital affairs, and large amounts of his time spent away from the home without complaint. As wives and mothers, women are frequently compared with the Virgin of Guadalupe, who embodies the most prized cultural values of womanhood: purity, sanctity, tolerance, love, and sympathy. The social institutions that have reinforced traditional relationships between men and women have included mandatory virginity of the woman prior to marriage, reinforced and sustained by chaperonage of parents, siblings, and extended family members and community gossip; the nonmarriageability of the woman who has lost her virginity; the "*casa chica*," or the socially sanctioned secondary households of a married man; and the inability of women in marriage and in other arrangements with men to work outside the home for income, resulting in economic dependency and sexual and social disempowerment.

The *machismo/marianismo* gender concept implies that household as well as public decision making is dominated by men and that women have little or no power to refuse or negotiate their differences, including those in the domain of sexual practice. This pattern has significant AIDS implications. For example, men whose relationships with multiple sex partners are sanctioned, and who define condoms as a threat to masculinity, may be exposed repeatedly to the risk of STD infections, which they may transmit to their unsuspecting partners. Various researchers have asserted that a Latina woman who suggests that her partner use a condom or questions his refusal to do so may be placing herself at risk for rejection or possible abuse (Marin 1992; Worth and Rodriguez 1987).

However, an increasing literature has begun to illustrate the very significant influence that Latina women have over household decisions and the variations that occur in this domain as a consequence of migration, economic status, acculturation, and ethnic/racial identity. This evidence of efficacy in relation to men has important implications for AIDS prevention and risk reduction. Cromwell and Ruiz (1979), for example, review the literature on household decision making among Mexicans and Mexican-Americans and conclude that it is a myth to assume that males dominate this activity, noting that despite traditional cultural ideals, Mexican American women do indeed have a significant role in household decision making. Madsen (1964:48) suggests that this is a relatively recent development adopted from the surrounding Anglo society. He presents the case of one family that is described as undergoing this type of acculturative gender role change. According to the father of this family:

> My home is not my own. Now my uncle is a man I admire. He consults no one and his wife is humble and obedient. My woman! Lord but she gets me down. She questions my word and is always demanding this thing or that. I have no peace and my kids laugh at us when we fight. Sometimes, I belt the woman and she shuts up for awhile, but not for long. I don't know whether men are getting weaker or women are getting stronger (quoted in Madsen 1964:50).

He goes on, however, to acknowledge that even Latina women who appear to conform to traditional *marianista* submissiveness find ways to achieve their own goals through skilled manipulation of the *machista* notion that a man must be a good provider and protector of the well being and public image of his family.

A closer reading of the literature reinforces the notion that Latin American women have found ways to negotiate or manipulate to meet their personal and household needs. In a study of women's attitudes about men in Puerto Rico, Lopez Garriga (1980) found that of the sixteen adjectives that women most commonly use to describe men, only four were positive. Indeed, she found that women commonly describe men as "irresponsible," "immature," "egotist," and "not very understanding." As Koss-Chioino (1992:5), based on her research among women in Puerto Rico, comments, "Women often view men as immature and demanding by nature and assert that they must be treated with care and manipulated—much as one tries to control a wayward child who is too big and powerful to spank. . . ." Similarly, in her observations of Mexican families, Diaz, while noting that the ideal marriage is between "a virile, aggressive male, and [a] *mujer abnegada*, the self-sacrificing, dutiful woman" (1970:78), nonetheless found that in day-to-day life "women are maneuvering busily" (1970:88) to achieve their own ends. While men acted as the formal decision makers in the households Diaz studied, she observed that women functioned as informal decision makers. Thus she concludes, because a woman "can manipulate [a] situation in such a way that she decides whether a piece of property should be sold or what occupation the son should go into, [this] means that there are possible modes of action whereby she becomes the *de facto* instrumental leader" (Diaz 1970:80).

These studies suggest that while Latino men may emphasize male superiority and an inherent right to make decisions, women have a different view and have developed their own strategies for achieving their self-defined goals. It is likely that these patterns are not recent developments nor merely responses to exposure to external influences. Indeed, the view of female assertiveness as a product of dominant Euro-American U.S. influence is rejected by Puerto Rican feminists such as Edna Acosta-Belen (1986:24), who refers to such statements as "simply a manifestation of disguised *machismo* and a subtle way of attempting to perpetuate the inferior status of women." Safa (1980:78), however, reminds us that the manner in which women manipulate men to obtain what they want is "similar to that employed by both men and women toward all persons in higher authority" and stems from the colonial tradition of patron-client relationships.

Latina women appear historically to have long had a strong voice in household decision making, which in any individual household may or may not extend to decisions about sexual practices. As Espín (1986:278) notes, while a woman traditionally was expected to stay with one man her whole life and tolerate his extramarital liaisons, she also was expected to exercise her right "to decide whether or not a man is going to live with her, and [to] choose to put him out if he drinks too much or is not a good provider." The degree to which this expectation might be met is subject to the resources available to the woman for survival without a male householder.

With migration to the U.S. and significant changes in the social environment and living conditions experienced by Latinos, fairly explicit cases of female

assertiveness and household decision making have been described in the literature. Presenting the case of Lydia, a 29-year-old Puerto Rican woman in Hartford,
Singer and colleagues (1990b:99), in their discussion of AIDS risk among Latina
women, stress that she "has taken control of her and her children's situation,
including forcing her husband to leave the house because of his drug habit, press-
ing legal charges against him, and during the occasional times they have sex,
insisting that he use a condom." A more extensive case study of a Puerto Rican
woman named Marta also casts doubt on the contemporary veracity of conventional portrayals of Latino gender relations. During life history interviewing,
Marta commented on her marital experience and her changing views on gender
relations in the following words:

> I had always thought that the lady of the house should stay at home and be respect-
> ful and the man could go out and come back when he felt like it. That's the way my
> mother taught us. But it was a big mistake. One day, I remember, I had twenty dol-
> lars and it was close to Father's Day. [My husband] asked me for money and I told
> him I didn't have any. But then I went out with the lady next door and bought him
> a pair of sandals and some T-shirts for Father's Day. He met me on the street and
> asked me where I'd been and started arguing with me. We got into a big fight, a fist
> fight. I took the kids and ran upstairs and he ran after me. That day I wound up with
> two black eyes and everything was broken in the house. After that things started
> changing. Before that I had to do everything in the house, even though I was work-
> ing. And if he brought men home to drink, I had to get up and cook for them. He
> would accuse me of a lot of things, having affairs. . . . My husband accused me of
> being with [another man], but I denied it. He didn't hit me then because I got a
> gun. I threatened him with it. The next day I left for Puerto Rico (quoted in Singer
> and Garcia 1989:166–167).

It is of interest to note that, in discussing her marital conflict, Marta makes reference to her employment outside the home. This pattern is not unique to Puerto Ricans. While various writers indicate that traditionally having "a working wife
[was] considered an embarrassment by most Mexican American men" (Moore
1970:117), the actual source of distress for men may lie with the woman's resulting ability to get along without the man, and thereby force him to leave if he does
not respect her interests (cf. Rubel 1964:68). Thus, women's employment in the
public sphere changes the nature of the dependency relationship between men
and women, contributing to shifts in other arenas of male/female social relationship in the Latino community.

The migration of Latinos to the U.S. in significant numbers began during
World War II. Thus, many families have lived in the U.S. for up to four generations. Rogler and Cooney (1984), in a study of intergenerational differences in
role relationships between two generations of Puerto Rican married couples, the
first born and raised in Puerto Rico and the second born and raised in New York
City, demonstrate significant variation in first *and* second generation couples, with
an increasing trend toward overlapping or sharing of domestic and income-producing responsibilities. "In comparison to the parent generation, the husbands
and wives in the child generation have a substantially stronger bicultural ethnic

identity and less role segregation or more sharing in marital functions . . . the migration experiences sharply separate the two generations in the cultural settings of their early socialization . . ." (Rogler and Cooney 1984:121). In their conclusion, Rogler and Cooney make the interesting observation that social change through migration, urbanization, and education "consistently and decisively favored the acquisition by women of competency in areas of performance customarily associated with the male role or representing an extension of it" (Rogler and Cooney 1984:206), and that while the reverse happened, especially with regard to male assumption of some household tasks, it was not without stigma. These changes contribute to a diversity of lifestyles among Latinos and help create a range of attitudes and behaviors relative to AIDS risk and prevention.

Also, it is important to emphasize that many Latina women in the U.S. are heads of household, whether they are or are not in relationships with men. Rodriguez (1987:61), for example, found in his study in the Fordham-Tremont area of New York, "43 percent of Latino households, 29 percent of black households, and 5 percent of white households . . . are headed by women." Research by Pelto and coworkers (1982) in three Puerto Rican neighborhoods in Hartford found the following distribution of household configurations: man or woman alone—9 percent, man and woman together (with or without children)—43 percent, woman with children—48 percent. A restudy of household composition with a random community sample of 241 households (that included at least one adult woman) drawn from two Puerto Rican neighborhoods in Hartford by Davison (1995) found that the most common pattern (56 percent) was a woman living alone with her children. The second most frequent household type was partnered households with children (23 percent), followed by unpartnered women living with their extended family (16 percent). The remaining households included couples living without children, partnered households with extended family, and women living alone.

There are several factors that contribute to single-parent, female-headed households. Various studies have emphasized the loss of stature and self-esteem experienced by many Latino men as they have encountered discrimination in the labor market. Unemployment created a situation in which men feel that they are not living up to the Latino cultural value to be a good provider for the family, an important element of traditional *machismo*. Additionally, as described above with regard to African Americans, the welfare system, which is the only means of support for many Latino families in the U.S., has allowed women to receive benefits only if they are not living with a man. Furthermore, women have been favored when hiring entry-level workers, especially in the garment industry, while Latino men, by contrast, find themselves barred from a labor market that requires higher education and technological skills (Rosario 1982).

Resulting depression and hopelessness have pushed many Latino men to escape into alcoholism or drug addiction (Singer et al. 1990b; Singer and Jia 1993). Thus, in his study of Puerto Rican drug users in Chicago, Glick (1983:286) found that they explained their drug involvement in terms of the desire to elude "existing life problems, feelings of failure and depression." In the words of one

Puerto Rican addict, heroin "anesthetizes the whole damn ugly world. All your troubles become forgotten memories . . ." (Rettig, Torres, and Garrett 1977:13). However, the risks of addiction and street life take a heavy toll on Latino men. Among Puerto Ricans in New York City, there are approximately 54 women for every 46 men. While similar numbers of males and females are born in this population, by the time they reach puberty, females begin to outnumber males. By the age of 30, there are only four Puerto Rican men for every five Puerto Rican women (Rodriguez 1989).

Rubel's account of Mexican-Americans also reveals the degree to which actual behavior tends to diverge from stated cultural ideals concerning gender roles. In observations in the homes of Mexican-Americans, he noted fathers exhibiting warmth and affection toward their young sons and daughters under ten years of age. On other occasions, he observed fathers feeding children from bottles while holding them in their arms (Rubel 1964:66). Ideal images of a strict division of labor within the household is not supported by observations like these of men in their daily experiences within their families.

Latino men and women in the U.S. have been influenced to varying degrees by their interactions with Euro-Americans and African Americans, as well as by their encounter with diverse elements of North American culture. The concept of *acculturation* has been developed in the literature to illuminate the considerable degree of cultural diversity now found among Latinos of the same nationality (Padilla 1979). Acculturation refers to the adoption of mainstream frames of reference, values, ideas, modes of relations, role expectations, and related beliefs and practices, while nonetheless maintaining some cultural patterns from their own traditions. Individuals who tend to speak Spanish in their day-to-day interactions in the home as well as in the public sphere and who tend to have Latino friends are the most likely to retain more of their traditional values (Marin and Marin 1989). Work by the Marins in California has found that lower levels of acculturation are strongly associated with possessing less accurate knowledge about AIDS and its transmission among Latinos (Marin and Marin 1989, 1990; Marin 1989, 1990).

Education level is another factor that influences gender relations and attitudes. Rosario's (1982) study of the self-perception of Puerto Rican women, for example, found that women's education was associated with more liberal attitudes toward women's role. The more education a woman has, "the more egalitarian are her attitudes toward women" (Rosario 1982:15). Latina female assertiveness, whatever its sources, has important implications for AIDS risk. To take one example, in a study of injection drug users, Friedman and colleagues (1993:204) note that "Puerto Rican women say they used condoms a greater proportion of the time (39 percent) than black women"; indeed, data from this study indicate that Puerto Rican women's reported rates of condom use are also somewhat higher than for Euro-American women.

Finally, it is not possible to gain a comprehensive understanding of Latinas without considering the unique position of black Latinas both in the U.S. and in

Latin America and the Caribbean. The origins of black Latinas lie in the introduction of slavery to Latin America by the Spanish, Portuguese, and English. The influence of people of African origin is apparent in spiritual traditions and practices such as santeria and vodun and through linguistic, genetic, and cultural elements that permeate Latin American societies. While racism in Latin America is covert, often overshadowed by social class differences and colonial status, in the U.S., racism is overt and experienced in different ways by black Latinas of different generations and appearance. Angela Jorge (1986) writes of the poignant situation confronted by black Puerto Rican women who are caught in the contradiction between the racist concept of "whitening" or *adelentar la raza* (furthering the race), and the "racially integrated character of the Puerto Rican community." Seda-Bonilla (1970) noted that black Puerto Ricans tend to adapt and assimilate into American society as blacks. Jorge believes that black Puerto Rican women are socialized to believe that their features are unattractive, find that outside the community they are seen by others as neither blacks nor Puerto Ricans, and feel uncomfortable establishing relationships with white, black, and Puerto Rican men for different reasons rooted in the inherent racism of American society. She comments that "these observations on the black Puerto Rican woman in contemporary American society have no . . . solutions . . . until such time that the Puerto Rican community is able to recognize overtly its racism and deal with it within the context of the search for a meaningful Puerto Rican identity . . . [in light of] the wider social questions of injustice, inequality and prejudice which are the heart of racism in the society at large" (Jorge 1986:186).

Taken together, the studies and issues reviewed above suggest the need to move beyond simple culturally determinant understandings of AIDS risk among Latina women to the development of a nuanced awareness of the multiplicity of factors that contribute to increasing or reducing that risk. While it is critical to learn the cultural ideals in any setting, it is equally important to assess the degree to which lived behavior adheres to the stated ideal. As Baca Zinn (1979:65) stresses, the literature on Latino families often fails to capture fully "contradictions between conceptual frameworks and empirical findings." Most common in this regard is a "disparity between the patriarch ideal and women's [actual] power in the family" (Baca Zinn 1979:65).

Moreover, this same author notes that despite the frequent observation of women's level of independence in Latino families, this topic was long neglected in the development of social scientific understanding of Latino gender roles. Consequently, there is need, especially in AIDS research, to move beyond conventional stereotypic accounts toward an empirically grounded understanding of gender roles and associated behavior among Latino groups (Alvirez and Bean 1976; Andrade 1982; Singer et al. 1990b). Critical to this work is an appreciation of the heterogeneity of Latino populations as well as a recognition of the impact of social and political economic forces, such as access to employment or adequate housing, in shaping the development and expression of cultural ideals. Moreover, it is important to remember that gender roles in Latino households in the U.S.

and elsewhere are in flux and that traditional ideals are under challenge, a change that also reflects broader political economic developments.

An example of the significant changes going on in Puerto Rican gender roles—as well as the AIDS risk inherent in some of these changes—is seen in the case of Rosa, a Puerto Rican woman enrolled in the Hispanic Health Council's *Cuidate Mujer* drug treatment program in Hartford. Rosa was born in Arecibo, Puerto Rico. At the time she was born, her biological father was in jail. She was raised by her mother and stepfather, both of whom she describes as alcoholics. Since she was a child, Rosa remembers being abused by her parents and witnessing her mother being beaten by her stepfather. She reports, "I remember when the blood of my mother was all over me, because he cut her with a knife, and I tried to hold him by his legs so that he stopped beating her up." Only eight at the time, she desperately wanted to leave home. Three years later, her family moved to New York. Her mother and stepfather commonly would go out to parties and leave her and her brother locked in the apartment. On one of these occasions, at age eleven, her brother raped her. She recalls, "I wanted to go back to Puerto Rico. I was so depressed because I knew that if I told my stepfather he would kill my brother. My stepfather [also] always molested me. He got up at night and touched me all over; I was afraid of saying anything." The witnessing of domestic conflict and violence continued: "Every day at four [o'clock] when I got home, my stepfather used to start fighting with my mother. I would hide under the bed, because I knew that if he got me, he was going to beat me up. One day he chased me with a knife."

During her teen years, Rosa was placed in a special high school for children with problems. With some friends who were involved in drug use, she ran away from the school. She eventually got a job working in a bar, where she met a man and began to live with him. The relationship lasted for nine years, during which time Rosa reports that she was regularly subjected to angry beatings. His physical mistreatment of her resulted in five spontaneous abortions. After her fifth miscarriage, she left her partner and initiated a lesbian relationship. However, she reports, "I didn't want to live that life; I felt insecure. I didn't want to leave her because I was afraid to be back on the streets homeless again." She started working in a bar again, where she met her third partner, a male. She went to live with him and over the next several years had two sons. He too abused her physically. After the birth of her second child, she went back to her mother's house, but the problems there continued. Her older child was taken by her mother and she decided to get back together with her first partner. Again, she was physically abused and left him.

At this point, Rosa found another bar job and began to support herself. During this period, she became involved with another woman. During this relationship, she began smoking marijuana and using cocaine. Later, she began injecting drugs intravenously. After her partner suffered a drug overdose, Rosa decided to end the relationship. Rosa moved back to Puerto Rico, where she became involved with a married man. In this relationship, she became pregnant. At this point, she moved where she met her current partner. At the time she entered the

Cuidate Mujer program, Rosa's partner was in jail for selling drugs and Rosa and her second son were living in a homeless shelter. Her youngest child is living with her former lesbian partner.

Rosa's case highlights how greatly individual lives can deviate from traditional social images and how culturally constituted gender roles can be reshaped by harsh social circumstances. While the details of Rosa's life are unique, the broad patterns are not. For many lower-income, inner-city Latina women, relationships are fragile, drug use is ubiquitous and alluring, routines of daily life are overcome by crises, and opportunities for HIV infection are multiple.

POLICY IMPLICATIONS FOR AIDS PREVENTION

The complex of images, sexual practices, and interpersonal relationships of African Americans and Latinos, as affected by ethnicity and economic class, impact differently on, and create multiple contexts for, heterosexually transmitted HIV and its prevention. A study by Kline and colleagues (1992) identified ways some African American and Latina women assess their risk with specific partners to determine how they want to behave sexually, including refusing intercourse or any sexual activity if a condom is not used. For these women, sexual assertiveness and a general sense of independence provide them sufficient power in their relationships with male partners to carry out protective measures against HIV transmission. However, other women in similar studies of comparable ethnic and class backgrounds expressed concern about their limited ability to get male partners to wear condoms, particularly if these women felt dependent on their partners for social and economic support, or if they perceived themselves to have lesser sexual decision-making power than their men (De La Cancela 1989; Kane 1990; Shervington 1993; Worth 1989). Multiple and mixed messages about sexuality and gender relations, as well as potentially conflicting obligations to partners, family, and community, create dilemmas that women must resolve within their relationships, and result in a diversity of responses they consider desirable, acceptable, or necessary.

The context and ideologies of sexuality and gender relations for African Americans and Latinos differ in some respects. The historical creation by a dominant white society of ideologies of difference based on race contributed to the development of paired contradictory images regarding blacks. Concepts of African American women as strong and weak, independent and dependent, respectable and unrespectable, highly moral and immoral, assertive and passive, manipulative and manipulated, deceitful and deceived, shed little light on the specific situations and relationships of which black women are a part, or the means available to assure their ability to "negotiate for," or guarantee protection against, heterosexually transmitted HIV. Contradictory models and stereotypes of African American women and men differentially promote or obstruct black women's power in sexual negotiation to avoid heterosexual HIV transmission. For example, images of self-sacrifice, and the subordination of African American women's needs and desires to support the family, as well as defining their self-worth only if within a relationship with a man, can potentially reduce some black women's ability to assert their own interests in their heterosexual relations and in sexual practice. By contrast, many images that have obtained negative connotation, such as African American women's power in the family (the so-called "matriarchy"), their economic independence (assumed to emasculate black men), and their sexual assertiveness (labelled "promiscuous"), are also potential sources of self-esteem, autonomy, and effectiveness in controlling sexual activity and a relationship with a male partner. To use these concepts positively for AIDS prevention, however, requires removing the stigma attached to them, and recognizing their negative forms as stemming from social relations of racial, class, and sexual oppression.

Ideologies of racism also affect Latinos, particularly those who are both Latino and black. Nevertheless, the process of colonialization in Puerto Rico and other Latin American countries, and subsequent developments of capitalism affecting the relationship between the colonized nations and mainland U.S., created a somewhat different set of contradictions for Latinas. This dynamic has evolved through sex role and gender relationships defined by a traditional ideology of male domination combined with a more ambiguous set of gender beliefs and practices that reflect Latina women's increasing power relative to men's. The contradiction between the pervasive *machismo/marianismo* image of Latino heterosexual relationships and the indications of women's power within family and couple interactions suggests opportunities to build on men's and women's gender role expectations and interactions to support protection of each other and those close to the couple from such threats as HIV infection and AIDS.

Cultural ideals, social-historical contexts, and gender role concepts and practices create a complex of contradictory images regarding sexuality and heterosexual relationships among African Americans and Latinos additionally confounded by the dynamics of poverty in the inner city. Individuals may hold conflicting beliefs that impact on their choices and behaviors in relationships with members of the opposite sex. Lacking in much of the literature is analysis of the ways women in this context interpret these contradictory images in their relationships and daily lives, and the meanings they give these conflicting ideals and the broader social forces that impact on and generate them. A necessary step in AIDS prevention for African American and Latina women at risk of heterosexually transmitted HIV is to assess their understandings of gender role and sexual images, learn the ways they find to resolve the ideological contradictions and conflicting messages regarding their roles and expected behavior, and assess how their understanding translates into practice in their relationships with male partners.

Because many of these concepts are attached to socially constructed categorizations of people based on race (i.e., color) or ethnicity, they are commonly depicted in the literature as representative of the entire or multiple ethnic or racial groups, and as created internally by and within those groups rather than as the result of a particular historical context. Certain dynamics under the political conditions of racial hierarchy and colonialization affect equally all members of a subordinated group, but class, gender, and other social conditions mediate the effects of these political conditions on individuals. For African American women, racism generates negative self-images that influence black women both directly and through the impact of negative stereotypes on black men. In the case of Puerto Ricans, Mexican Americans, and other Latino groups, political and economic conditions appear to be undercutting "traditional" gender oppression, and are potentially thus liberating for women, while possibly threatening to men. In all three cases, gender relations and gender ideologies have been generated and continually reshaped as political and economic conditions necessitated, with resulting potentially deadly consequence with the appearance of AIDS.

The discussion here suggests several gaps in the literature and issue areas for further research on gender, sexuality, and sociopolitical context as these affect AIDS risk and prevention for African American and Latina women. First, studies of intraethnic variations and transformations in gender roles and relationships are needed, as well as investigation of the ways in which images and contradictions affect women's views of themselves, their sexuality, and their vulnerability to sexually transmitted HIV. Second, research on perceptions and assessments of "risks" and power, and on actual negotiation behaviors in circumstances in which HIV can be transmitted need further inquiry. Third, analysis of comparative interventions designed for African American and Latina women must increase to test the efficacy of different interventions for these groups. Finally, the special circumstances of black Latinos, and others who cross multiple ethnic, racial, or other group identities need elucidation and analysis in the context of AIDS and its prevention.

Content and methods of AIDS prevention for African American and Latina women must be designed through understanding of the ways social and political factors shape gender meanings, relationships, and individual behavior choices. The complexity of macroeconomic historical and current conditions, as they generate and influence gender relations and ideologies of gender and sexuality, as well as local contextual factors, must be incorporated into prevention strategies if such approaches are to be effective. Prevention of heterosexually transmitted HIV for impoverished African American and Latina women must address: a) guilt and anger they may feel about not living up to culturally constructed ideals, b) anger about life experiences, and possibly resentment toward men, c) contradictory images they hold of themselves and of men, and d) resulting choices based on their ideals and their needs to feel like good women who have good and trustworthy men (cf. Sobo 1993). AIDS prevention also must stress that women are not powerless, despite the barriers and difficulties they face in enforcing their wishes within a heterosexual relationship.

Preventive methods must build upon sources of cultural, ethnic, or personal strength and positive relationships, and must work to change concepts that create potential for HIV-risky behaviors or that reduce an individual's sense of personal power to control these interactions (Schensul 1985; Singer et al. 1993; Weeks et al. 1995). Clearly, some of the images, models, and stereotypes used to define African American and Latino women and men, and to characterize their heterosexual relationships, when translated into behavior, indicate significant potential for sexual risk-taking or engagement in behaviors that could result in transmission of HIV. It is positive aspects of sexuality and heterosexual interaction within these groups that require special focus in developing AIDS prevention, to build appropriately on strengths of women's and men's individual power and that of their relationships in order to support norms for HIV risk reduction (Weeks et al. 1995). These must be contrasted with the negative behaviors and images likely to result in a woman's powerlessness in the face of a domineering male partner, or low self-esteem in both members of the dyad, which can lead to risk-taking behavior.

Also critical to AIDS prevention for women in general, including African Americans and Latinas, is to build means to organize women around AIDS/HIV research and prevention. Identifiable groups of women in communities of color created and unified to address issues of AIDS prevention are rare, and few prevention programs are designed to organize women for this purpose. Lack of trust and separation of women from one another with little group or class consciousness or venues for organizing themselves obstruct their ability to coalesce around this and other health and social issues. The women's movement has had little influence among lower-income and impoverished African Americans and Latinas. Among African Americans, while women have always played a critical role in the community and family, the emphasis is on strengthening relationships between men and women first, rather than on creating empowerment that might separate men and women of the same ethnicity from one another. Among Latinas, women have been organizers, but poor women often are bound by dependence either on their men or on welfare. These limitations have implications for women's efficacy to impact sexual relationships, and to build organizations to effect deliberate change in sexual norms and practices.

Policy must allow for the creation and operation of community-based and community-run prevention by trained indigenous female educators and organizers who understand these contradictory issues, can help to train other women to understand them as well and their risk potential, and can direct research questions to build greater understanding of the meanings of social and gender context within which women make decisions or attempt to influence their partners. Through resource provision, these local female community educators can empower women who identify with them by ethnicity, class, or other organizing characteristic, to work together and protect themselves. An important new direction in resource provision is the female condom. Field research among women by Gil (1994:83) found the female condom "to be significantly acceptable, cognitively, to a majority of Puerto Rican and other Latinas." Introduced as part of a gender-sensitive, indigenously run, community-based prevention program, the female condom holds considerable potential as an AIDS prevention approach.

Similar programs for men to build greater understanding of the dynamics of gender relationships within the broader socioeconomic context, as these conditions affect their female partners, and to generate support for incorporation of AIDS preventive measures (including the female condom) into sexual practice, also are essential to ensure effectiveness of HIV risk-reduction programs. Significantly, there is growing evidence to suggest that AIDS prevention serves both immediate and longer-term goals. Not only does effective prevention protect the participants in any given potentially risky encounter, but slowing rates of infection also appear to contribute to a lowering of virulence in the virus itself (Cowley 1993). Broad-based prevention programs that seek to address gender relations and concepts within the social and political context of the women and men who may be at risk of HIV transmission can potentially reduce the "risk" of the community as a whole.

REFERENCES

Acosta-Belen, E., ed.
　1986　The Puerto Rican Woman: Perspectives on Culture, History and Society. New York: Praeger.

AIDS Community Research Group
　1989　AIDS Knowledge, Attitudes and Behavior in Hartford's Neighborhoods: A Report to the Connecticut State Department of Health Services. Hartford, CT: Institute for Community Research.

Alvirez, D., and F. Bean
　1976　The Mexican American Family. *In* Ethnic Families in America. C. Mindel and R. Habenstein, eds. New York: Elsevier.

Amaro, H.
　1988　Considerations for Prevention of HIV Infection among Hispanic Women. Psychology of Women Quarterly 12:429–443.

Anderson, E.
　1989　Sex Codes and Family Life Among Poor Inner-city Youths. ANNALS, AAPSS 501:59–78.
　1990　Race, Class, and Change: Street Wise in an Urban Community. Chicago: University of Chicago Press.

Andrade, S.
　1982　Family Roles of Hispanic Women: Stereotypes, Empirical Findings, and Implications for Research. *In* Work Family and Health: Latina Women in Transition. New York: Hispanic Research Center.

Argulles, L., and A. Rivero
　1989　HIV Infection/AIDS and Latinas in Los Angeles County: Considerations for Prevention, Treatment, and Research Practice. California Sociologist 11:68–89.

Baca Zinn, M.
　1979　Chicano Family Research: Conceptual Distortions and Alternative Directions. The Journal of Ethnic Studies 7:59–71.

Baer, H., and M. Singer
　1992　African-American Religion in the 20th Century: Varieties of Protest and Accommodation. Knoxville: University of Tennessee Press.

Baker, J. N., R. Elam, V. E. Smith, L. Wright, V. Quade, and N. Abbott
　1989　Joining the AIDS Fight. Newsweek, April 17:26–27.

Bolton, R.
　1992　AIDS and Promiscuity: Muddles in the Models of HIV Prevention. Philadelphia: Gordon and Breach Science Publishers.

Bowser, B. P.
  1992   African-American Culture and AIDS Prevention: From Barrier to Ally. *In* Cross-cultural Medicine: A Decade Later [Special Issue]. Western Journal of Medicine 157:286–289.

Brown, S. V.
  1985   Premarital Sexual Permissiveness among Black Adolescent Females. Social Psychology Quarterly 48:381–387.

Brown, B. S., and G. M. Beschner, eds.
  1993   Handbook on Risk of AIDS: Injection Drug Users and Sexual Partners. B. S. Brown and G. M. Beschner, with the National AIDS Research Consortium, eds. Westport, CT: Greenwood Press.

Carovano, K.
  1991   More than Mothers and Whores: Redefining the AIDS Prevention Needs of Women. International Journal of Health Services 21:131–142.

Cazenave, N. A., and R. Smith
  1990   Gender Differences in the Perception of Black Male-female Relationships and Stereotypes. *In* Black Families: Interdisciplinary Perspectives. H. E. Cheatham and J. B. Stewart, eds. Pp. 149–170. New Brunswick, NJ: Transaction Publishers.

Centers for Disease Control
  1992   Sexual Behavior among High School Students—United States, 1990. MMWR 40:885–888.

Centers for Disease Control and Prevention
  1993a   Update: Mortality Attributable to HIV Infection/AIDS among Persons Aged 25–44 Years—United States, 1990 and 1991. MMWR 42:481–485.
  1993b   Update: Acquired Immunodeficiency Syndrome: United States, 1992. MMWR 42:547–557.

Cochran, S. D.
  1989   Women and HIV Infection: Issues in Prevention and Behavior Change. *In* Primary Prevention of AIDS: Psychological Approaches. V. M. Mays, G. W. Albee, and S. F. Schneider, eds. Pp. 309–329. Newbury Park, CA: Sage.

Cole, J. B., ed.
  1986   All American Women: Lines That Divide, Ties That Bind. NY: The Free Press.

Connell, R. W.
  1987   Gender and Power: Society, the Person and Sexual Politics. Stanford, CA: Stanford University Press.

Cowley, G.
           The Future of AIDS. Newsweek, March 22, pp. 47–52.

Crimp, D.
  1988   How to Have Promiscuity in an Epidemic. *In* AIDS: Cultural Analysis, Cultural Activism. D. Crimp, ed. Cambridge, MA: The MIT Press.

Cromwell, R., and R. Ruiz
  1979   The Myth of Macho Dominance in Decision Making with Mexican and Chicano Families. Hispanic Journal of Behavioral Sciences 1:355–373.

Dalton, H.
  1989   AIDS in Blackface. Daedalus 118:205–227.

Davis, A. Y.
  1986   Racism, Birth Control, and Reproductive Rights. *In* All American Women: Lines That Divide, Ties That Bind. J. B. Cole, ed. Pp. 239–255. New York: The Free Press.

Davison, L.
1995   "Las Cosas Que Las Mujeres No Hablan": The Social Construction of Reproductive Illness in a Puerto Rican Community. Doctoral dissertation, University
of Connecticut.

De La Cancela, V.
1989   Minority AIDS Prevention: Moving Beyond Cultural Perspectives Towards
Sociopolitical Empowerment. AIDS Education and Prevention 1:141–153.

Diaz, M.
1970   Tonalá: Conservatism, Responsibility, and Authority in a Mexican Town. Berkeley: University of California Press.

Diaz-Guerrero, R.
1955   Neurosis and the Mexican Family Structure. American Journal of Psychiatry
112:411–417.

Espín, O. M.
1986   Cultural and Historical Influences on Sexuality in Hispanic/Latin Women. *In*
All American Women: Lines That Divide, Ties That Bind. J. B. Cole, ed. Pp.
272–284. New York: Free Press.

Flaskerund, J., and A. Nyamathi
1990   Effects of an AIDS Education Program on the Knowledge, Attitudes, and Practices of Low Income Black and Latina Women. Journal of Community Health
15:343–355.

Fox, L., P. Baily, M. Clark, C. Kazu, O. Mauricio, and F. Barahona
1993   Condom Use Among High-risk Women in Honduras: Evaluation of an AIDS
Prevention Program. AIDS Education and Prevention 5:1–11.

Freudenberg, N., J. Lee, and D. Silver
1989   How Black and Latino Community Organizations Respond to the AIDS Epidemic: A Case Study in One New York City Neighborhood. AIDS Education
and Prevention 1:12–21.

Friedman, S., J. Sotheran, A. Abdul-Quader, B. Primm, D. Des Jarlais, P. Kleinman,
C. Mauge, D. Goldsmith, W. El-Sadr, and R. Maslansky
1987   The AIDS Epidemic Among Blacks and Hispanics. The Milbank Quarterly 65:
455–499.

Friedman, S., P. Young, F. Snyder, V. Shorty, A. Jones, A. Estrada, and the NADR Consortium
1993   Racial Differences in Sexual Behaviors Related to AIDS in a Nineteen-City
Sample of Street-Recruited Drug Injectors. AIDS Education and Prevention
5:196–211.

Fullilove, M. T., R. E. Fullilove, K. Haynes, and S. Gross
1990   Black Women and AIDS Prevention: A View Towards Understanding the Gender Rules. The Journal of Sex Research 27:47–64.

Gil, V.
1992   Sources of HIV/AIDS Information and the Negotiation of Sexual Risk by Low-
income Puerto Rican Women. Final Research Report to the American Foundation for AIDS Research, Grant 001588-12-RC.
1994   Attitudes Toward the New Female Condom Among Puerto Rican Low Income
Women at Risk for HIV/AIDS. Final Research Report to the American Foundation for AIDS Research, Grant 001875-14-RGR.

Glick, R.
1983   Demoralization and Addiction: Heroin in the Chicago Puerto Rican Community. Journal of Psychoactive Drugs 15:281–292.

Hannerz, U.
   1969   Soulside: Inquiries into Ghetto Culture and Community. New York: Columbia University Press.

Heiss, J.
   1975   The Case of the Black Family: A Sociological Inquiry. New York: Columbia University Press.

Hill, R.
   1972   The Strengths of Black Families. New York: Emerson-Hall Publishers.

Holland, J., C. Ramazanoglu, S. Scott, S. Sharpe, and R. Thomson
   1990   Sex, Gender, and Power: Young Women's Sexuality in the Shadow of AIDS. Sociology of Health and Illness 12:336–350.

Holmbeck, G. N., K. A. Waters, and R. R. Brookman
   1990   Psychosocial Correlates of Sexually Transmitted Diseases and Sexual Activity in Black Adolescent Females. Journal of Adolescent Research 5:431–448.

Holmes, K. K., J. M. Karon, and J. Kreiss
   1990   The Increasing Frequency of Heterosexually Acquired AIDS in the United States, 1983–88. American Journal of Public Health 80:858–863.

Hooks, B.
   1981   Ain't I a Woman: Black Women and Feminism. Boston: South End Press.

Johnson, E. H., L. Gant, Y. A. Hinkle, D. Gilbert, C. Willis, and T. Hoopwood
   1992   Do African-American Men and Women Differ in Their Knowledge About AIDS, Attitudes About Condoms, and Sexual Behaviors? Journal of the National Medical Association 84:49–64.

Jones, J.
   1985   Labor of Love, Labor of Sorrow: Black Women, Work, and the Family from Slavery to the Present. New York: Basic Books, Inc.

Jorge, A.
   1986   The Black Puerto Rican Woman in Contemporary American Society. In Acosta-Belen Edna, ed. The Puerto Rican Woman: Perspectives on Culture, History and Society. New York: Praeger.

Joseph, G. I.
   1986   Styling, Profiling, and Pretending: The Games Before the Fall. In All American Women: Lines That Divide, Ties That Bind. J. B. Cole, ed. Pp. 285–301. New York: The Free Press.

Kane, S.
   1990   AIDS, Addiction, and Condom Use: Sources of Sexual Risk for Heterosexual Women. The Journal of Sex Research 27:427–444.

Kline, A., E. Kline, and E. Oken
   1992   Minority Women and Sexual Choice in the Age of AIDS. Social Science and Medicine 34:447–457.

Koss-Chioino, J.
   1992   Women as Healers, Women as Patients: Mental Health Care and Traditional Healing in Puerto Rico. Boulder, Co: Westview Press.

Lewis, O.
   1965   La Vida: A Puerto Rican Family in the Culture of Poverty—San Juan and New York. New York: Vintage Books.

Liebow, E.
   1967   Tally's Corner: A Study of Negro Street Corner Men. Boston: Little, Brown.

Lopez Garriga, M.
    1980   Estrategias de Auto-afirmacion en Mujeres Puertorriqueñas. *In* La Mujer en la
                Sociedad Puertorriqueñas. E. Acosta-Belen, ed. Pp. 42–59. Rio Piedras, PR:
                Ediciones Huracan.

Madsen, W.
    1964   The Mexican Americans of South Texas. New York: Holt, Rinehart, and Win-
                ston.

Marin, B.
    1989   Hispanic Culture: Implications for AIDS Prevention. *In* Sexuality and Disease:
                Metaphors, Perceptions and Behavior in the AIDS Era. New York: Oxford Uni-
                versity Press.
    1990   Drug Abuse Treatment for Hispanics: A Culturally Appropriate Community-
                oriented Approach. *In* Prevention and Treatment of Drug and Alcohol Abuse.
                R. Watson, ed. Clifton, NJ: Humana Press.
    1992   Hispanic Culture: Implications for AIDS Prevention. *In* Sexuality and Disease:
                Metaphors, Perceptions and Behavior in the AIDS Era. J. Boswell, R. Hexter,
                and J. Reinisch, eds. Pp. 27–36. New York: Oxford University Press.

Marin, B., and G. Marin
    1989   Information About Human Immunodeficiency Virus in Hispanics in San Fran-
                cisco. San Francisco: University of California, Center for AIDS Prevention
                Studies.
    1990   Effects of Acculturation on Knowledge of AIDS and HIV Among Hispanics.
                Hispanic Journal of Behavioral Sciences 12:110–121.

Mays, V., and S. Cochran
    1988   Issues in the Perception of AIDS Risk and Risk Reduction Activities by Black
                and Hispanic/Latina Women. American Psychologist 43:949–957.

McAdoo, H. P.
    1978   Factors Related to Stability in Upwardly Mobile Black Families. Journal of Mar-
                riage and the Family 40:762–778.
    1986   Societal Stress: The Black Family. *In* All American Women: Lines That Divide,
                Ties That Bind. J. B. Cole, ed. Pp. 187–197. New York: The Free Press.

Miller, H., C. Turner, and L. Moses
    1990   AIDS: The Second Decade. Washington, DC: National Academy Press.

Moore, J.
    1970   Colonialism: The Case of Mexican-Americans. Social Problems 17:463–472.

Moynihan, D. P.
    1965   The Negro Family: The Case for National Action. Washington, DC: Office of
                Policy Planning and Research, U.S. Dept. of Labor.

Norris A. E., and K. Ford
    1992   Beliefs About Condoms and Accessibility of Condom Intentions in Hispanic
                and African American Youth. Hispanic Journal of Behavioral Sciences 14:
                373–382.

Nyamathi, A., C. Bennett, B. Leake, C. Lewis, and J. Flaskerund
    1993   AIDS-related Knowledge, Perceptions, and Behaviors Among Impoverished
                Minority Women. American Journal of Public Health 83:65–71.

Padilla, A.
    1979   Acculturation: Theory, Models and Some Findings. Boulder, CO: Westview Press.

Pelto, P., M. Roman, and N. Liriano
    1982   Family Structures in an Urban Puerto Rican Community. Urban Anthropolo-
                gy 11:39–58.

Pittman, K. J., P. M. Wilson, S. Adams-Taylor, and S. Randolph
 1992   Making Sexuality Education and Prevention Programs Relevant for African-American Youth. Journal of School Health 62:339–344.

Rettig, R., M. Torres, and G. Garrett
 1977   Many a Criminal-addict's Story. Atlanta: Houghton Mifflin Co.

Robles, R., M. Colon, A. Gonzales, and T. Mateos
 1990   Social Relations and Empowerment of Sexual Partners of IV Drug Users. Puerto Rican Health Studies Journal 9:99–104.

Rodriguez, C.
 1989   Puerto Ricans Born in the U.S.A. Boston: Unwin Hyman.

Rodriguez, O.
 1987   Hispanics and Human Services: Help-seeking in the Inner City. New York: Hispanic Research Center, Fordham University.

Rogler L. H., and R. S. Cooney
 1984   Puerto Rican Families in New York City: Intergenerational Processes. New York: Hispanic Research Center, Fordham University.

Rosaldo, M. Z., and L. Lamphere
 1974   Women, Culture & Society. Stanford, CA: Stanford University Press.

Rosario, L.
 1982   The Self-perception of Puerto Rican Women Toward their Societal Roles. *In* Work, Family and Health: Latina Women in Transition. R. Zamrana, ed. Pp. 11–16. New York: Hispanic Research Center, Fordham University.

Rubel, A.
 1964   Across the Tracks: Mexican-Americans in a Texas City. Austin: University of Texas Press.

Rubin, L.
 1976   Worlds of Pain. New York: Basic Books.

Safa, H. I.
 1980   Class Consciousness Among Working Class Women in Latin America: Puerto Rico. *In* J. Nash and H. I. Safa, eds. Sex and Class in Latin America: Women's Perspectives on Politics, Economics and the Family in the Third World. Pp. 69–85. South Hadley, MA: Bergin and Garvey.

Scanzoni, J.
 1971   The Black Family in Modern Society. Boston: Allyn and Bacon.

Schensul, J.
 1985   Cultural Transmission and Cultural Transformation Among Puerto Rican Women. Paper presented at an invited session on Cultural Transformation, American Anthropological Association Conference.

Scott, C. S., L. Shifman, L. Orr, R. G. Owen, and N. Fawcett
 1988   Hispanic and Black American Adolescents' Beliefs Related to Sexuality and Contraception. Adolescence 23:667–688.

Seda-Bonilla, E.
 1970   Requiem por una cultura. Rio Piedras, PR: Editorial Edil.

Shervington, D. O.
 1993   The Acceptability of the Female Condom Among Low-income African-American Women. Journal of the National Medical Association 85:341–347.

Shilts, R.
 1987   And the Band Played On. New York: St. Martin's Press.

Singer, M.
  1992   AIDS and U.S. Ethnic Minorities: The Crisis and Alternative Anthropological
          Responses. Human Organization 51:89–95.
  1994   AIDS and the Health Crisis of the U.S. Urban Poor: The Perspective of Criti-
          cal Medical Anthropology. Social Science and Medicine 39:931–948.
  1995   The Evolution of AIDS Work in a Puerto Rican Community Organization.
          Human Organization 54 (in press).
Singer, M., C. Flores, L. Davison, G. Burke, and Z. Castillo
  1990a   Owning AIDS: Latino Organizations and the AIDS Epidemic. Hispanic Journal
          of the Behavioral Sciences 12:196–212.
Singer, M., C. Flores, L. Davison, G. Burke, Z. Castillo, K. Scanlon, and M. Rivera
  1990b   SIDA: The Economic, Social, and Cultural Context of AIDS among Latinos.
          Medical Anthropology Quarterly 4:72–114.
Singer, M., C. Flores, L. Davison, and W. Gonzales
  1993   Reaching Minority Women: AIDS Prevention for Latinas. Practicing Anthro-
          pology 15:21–24.
Singer, M., and R. Garcia
  1989   Becoming a Puerto Rican Espiritista: Life History of a Female Healer. *In*
          Women as Healers. C. Shephard McClain, ed. Pp. 157–185. New Brunswick,
          NJ: Rutgers University Press.
Singer M., and Z. Jia
  1993   AIDS and Puerto Rican Injection Drug Users in the U.S. *In* Handbook on Risk
          of AIDS: Injection Drug Users and Their Sexual Partners. B. Brown and
          G. Beschner, eds. Pp. 227–255. Westport, CT: Greenwood Press.
Slutsker, L., J. Bruent, J. Karon, and J. Curren
  1992   Trends in the United States and Europe. *In* AIDS in the World. J. Mann,
          D. Tarantola, and T. Netter, eds. Pp. 605–616. Cambridge, MA: Harvard Uni-
          versity Press.
Sobo, E. J.
  1993   Meaning and Its Usefulness for Inner-City HIV/AIDS Interventions. Practicing
          Anthropology 15:56–58.
Stack, C.
  1975   All Our Kin: Strategies for Survival in a Black Community. New York: Harper
          and Row, Publishers.
Staples, R., and A. Mirandé
  1986   Racial and Cultural Variations Among American Families: A Decennial Review
          of the Literature on Minority Families. *In* Family in Transition: Rethinking
          Marriage, Sexuality, Child Rearing, and Family Organization. A. S. Skolnick
          and J. H. Skolnick, eds. Pp. 474–497. Boston: Little, Brown and Company.
Tanner, N.
  1974   Matrifocality in Indonesia and Africa and Among Black Americans. *In* Women,
          Culture and Society. M. Z. Rosaldo and L. Lamphere, eds. Pp. 129–156. Stan-
          ford, CA: Stanford University Press.
Terrelonge, P.
  1984   Feminist Consciousness and Black Women. *In* Women: A Feminist Perspec-
          tive. J. Freeman, ed. Pp. 557–567. Palo Alto, CA: Mayfield Publishing Com-
          pany.
Torres-Matrullo, C.
  1976   Acculturation and Psychopathology Among Puerto Rican Women in Mainland
          United States. American Journal of Orthopsychiatry 46:710–719.

Turner, C., H. Miller, and L. Moses
 1989   AIDS: Sexual Behavior and Intravenous Drug Use. Washington, DC: National
         Academy Press.

Valdiserri, R., V. Arena, D. Proctor, and F. Bonati
 1989   The Relationship Between Women's Attitudes About Condoms and Their Use:
         Implications for Condom Promotion Programs. American Journal of Public
         Health 79:499–501.

Weeks, M. R., J. J. Schensul, S. S. Williams, M. Singer, and M. Grier
 1995   AIDS Prevention for African American and Latina Women: Building Cultural-
         ly and Gender Appropriate Intervention. AIDS Education and Prevention,
         7(3) (in press).

Weeks, M. R., M. Singer, J. J. Schensul, Z. Jia, and M. Grier
 1993   Project COPE: Preventing AIDS Among Injection Drug Users and Their Sex
         Partners: Preliminary Data Report. (Unpublished report).

Weinberg, M. S., and C. J. Williams
 1988   Black Sexuality: A Test of Two Theories. The Journal of Sex Research 25:
         197–218.

Weissman, G., B. Brown, and the National AIDS Research Consortium
 1991   Drug Use and Sexual Behavior Among Sex Partners of Injection-Drug Users—
         United States, 1980–1990. MMWR 40:855–860.

Willie, C. V.
 1976   A New Look at Black Families. Bayside, NY: General Hall.

Worth, D.
 1989   Sexual Decision-making and AIDS: Why Condom Promotion Among Vulnera-
         ble Women is Likely to Fail. Studies in Family Planning 20:297–307.

Worth, D., and R. Rodriguez
 1987   Latina Women and AIDS. Siecus Report, January–February, 63–67.

Zambrana, R. E., ed.
 1982   Women, Family and Health: Latina Women in Transition. Monograph #7, His-
         panic Research Center. New York: Fordham University.